UN Voices

United Nations Intellectual History Project

Ahead of the Curve? UN Ideas and Global Challenges
Louis Emmerij, Richard Jolly, and Thomas G. Weiss

Unity and Diversity in Development Ideas: Perspectives from the
UN Regional Commissions
Edited by Yves Berthelot

Quantifying the World: UN Ideas and Statistics
Michael Ward

The UN and Global Political Economy: Trade, Finance, and Development
John Toye and Richard Toye

UN Contributions to Development Thinking and Practice
Richard Jolly, Louis Emmerij, Dharam Ghai, and Frédéric Lapeyre

UN Voices

The Struggle for Development and Social Justice

Thomas G. Weiss, Tatiana Carayannis,
Louis Emmerij, and Richard Jolly

Indiana University Press

Bloomington and Indianapolis

This book is a publication of

Indiana University Press
601 North Morton Street
Bloomington, Indiana 47404-3797 USA

http://iupress.indiana.edu

Telephone orders   800-842-6796
Fax orders   812-855-7931
Orders by e-mail   iuporder@indiana.edu

© 2005 by United Nations Intellectual History Project

The paper used in this publication meets the minimum requirements
of American National Standard for Information Sciences—Permanence
of Paper for Printed Library Materials, ANSI Z39.48-1984.

Manufactured in the United States of America

Library of Congress Cataloging-in-Publication Data
UN voices : the struggle for development and social justice /
Thomas G. Weiss ... [et al.].
    p. cm. — (United Nations intellectual history project)
  Includes index.
  ISBN 0-253-34642-8 (cloth : alk. paper) — ISBN 0-253-21788-1 (pbk. : alk. paper)
  1. United Nations—History. 2. United Nations—Interviews. I. Weiss, Thomas George.
II. Series.
  JZ4984.5.U532 2005
  341.23'09—dc22   2005000230

1 2 3 4 5 10 09 08 07 06 05

On résiste à l'invasion des armées; on ne résiste pas à l'invasion des idées.

—Victor Hugo, *Histoire d'un Crime*, 1851–1852

Contents

Part One. Individuals Make a Difference

Part Two. Hope, Creativity, and Frustration

Part Three. The World Organization, Ideas, and Twenty-First-Century Challenges

Foreword

The United Nations, and the individuals of whom it has consisted, is the great unexplored subject of contemporary history. The UN has been the location for many of the most dramatic political events of the late twentieth century. It has been intimately involved, as *UN Voices: The Struggle for Development and Social Justice* shows, in the evolution of economic, social, and environmental policies; it has been the site for the exchange of ideas across vast distances of culture, language, nationality, and politics.

There are extraordinary resources available for this new history: in the forty-one archives within the UN itself and the other international organizations (see www.unesco.org/archives/guide); in virtually all national archives; in the correspondence and oral histories of individuals who have been engaged with or worked for the UN (from the tape recordings of soldiers who participated in international peacekeeping missions, preserved by the Nigerian Legion in Enugu, to the diaries of English officials working on public health in Cambodia in the 1950s, in the Bodleian Library in Oxford); in the records and memoirs of UN staff associations; in the cyclostyled records of committees and conferences, somewhat dispiritingly called "grey literature"; in the art and architecture of the great UN sites themselves, the Palais des Nations in Geneva, and the UN headquarters on the East River in New York City.

But this treasury of resources has been very little used by historians. The UN itself has had very little of the historical memory—the public records which have so often been at the heart of political continuity—that is taken for granted in national institutions. One of the "troubles with the UN," as Brian Urquhart says in his interview in the present volume, "is the fact that it never had a historical section." The outstanding archivists within the UN system have had to contend, on many occasions, with shortages of resources, policies, and guidelines; there are locations where archives of importance to UN history are in immediate risk of physical deterioration; the papers, especially of the earliest generation of UN officials, are often uncollected and unpreserved. History is dependent on the "supply" of archival and other primary materials and on the "demand" of historians for these materials. The UN, at its sixtieth anniversary, is only beginning to capture the imagination of historians, as of scholars in other disciplines.

UN Voices can inspire this sort of imagination. The authors have cajoled, intrigued, or reassured their seventy-three "voices" into telling a fascinating story of the UN and its institutions, which is also a story of seventy-three individual lives; of women and men who are no longer simply voices but individuals with their own complicated histories of emigration and education, family relationships and professional choices, hopes and successes. They come to life, listening to stories in Nahuatl in a Swiss-Mexican family in Argentina (Lourdes Arizpe) or playing the piano in Woolworth's in Syracuse, New York (Margaret Snyder), or reading Livy in Sierra Leone (James Jonah). They have ideas, and they reflect on the place of ideas in public life.

Thomas G. Weiss, Tatiana Carayannis, Louis Emmerij, and Richard Jolly are distinguished practitioners and social scientists. Historians who read the volume, and I hope there will be many, will always want more; more of the transcripts and recordings (which will be available, as the authors explain in their introduction, on CD-ROM from the UN Intellectual History Project), and more interviews, especially with the uncelebrated women and men, the nurses and soldiers and technicians and statisticians who also constituted the UN's world of ideas. Historians who use oral histories are expected to avoid the "celebratory and the ahistorical," and the volume is from time to time distinctively celebratory and conscious of present circumstances. But it is intended, as the editors say, to encourage future work; it is a contribution, very long overdue, to the "institutional memory" of development and of the ideas by which it is shaped.

The UN is at the moment undercelebrated. One of the individuals interviewed in the volume, Paul Berthoud, says of UNCTAD, the UN Conference on Trade and Development, that it is "a coffin full of remarkable ideas." This is a good kind of coffin, in some respects; for ideas, unlike almost everything else, are very difficult to destroy. But the UN system is not at all like a coffin, as this volume also shows. UN institutions are in jeopardy, on occasion, and one of the most compelling common themes of the lives recounted here is the memory of the League of Nations, as it was observed in Slovenia and Egypt and Peru. Another even more compelling theme is the influence of the mothers of these women and men, especially in relation to their education.

But the UN is vastly more important to worldwide public life than the League of Nations, or any earlier international organization, had ever been. "The legitimacy conveyed by the authority of the United Nations," as Secretary-General Kofi Annan said in March 2003, has never been more prized. This is the outcome of an institutional history, and a history of ideas and sentiments, including economic ideas, which ought to be remembered and studied and even, from time to time, celebrated.

Professor Emma Rothschild
King's College, University of Cambridge
November 2004

Acknowledgments

One of the most pleasant tasks in writing a book is thanking the people who helped along the way. Since 1999, when the United Nations Intellectual History Project (UNIHP) began, we have incurred many debts. For this volume and the effort to create an oral history archive of individuals who have contributed to economic and social development efforts by the United Nations, we owe above all our deepest appreciation to those seventy-three individuals who agreed to be interviewed and shared their memories and insights with remarkable candor and good humor. They appear in the pages of this book, some with greater frequency than others, and all have taught us much. We are extremely grateful for their contributions.

This effort also reflects the support of donors and the hard work of the staff who aided us. To state the obvious, an oral history project of this scope requires considerable financial resources. Preparing for interviews, traveling to them, and transcribing and indexing them are necessary and costly. Hence, we are extremely appreciative for the generosity of the governments of the Netherlands, the United Kingdom, Sweden, Canada, Norway, Switzerland, and the Republic and Canton of Geneva as well as of the Ford and Rockefeller Foundations, the Carnegie Corporation of New York, and the Dag Hammarskjöld and UN Foundations. Without their support, this book and this project would have remained where it had been for too many years—on the drawing boards.

In acknowledging individuals, it is hard to know where to begin or end. Although we have taken great care to insist upon the independence of the United Nations Intellectual History Project from the UN, we start nonetheless by thanking Secretary-General Kofi Annan for his unfailing support and encouragement and his participation, along with the other living former secretaries-general, in the oral history itself.

Ambassador Robert Fowler of Canada, who was one of the early supporters of the project, deserves mention for having suggested the need for a book with a readable selection from the oral histories.

We also thank numerous friends and colleagues within the UN family for their interest and support, especially those in the libraries and archives in New York and Geneva. Any professional historian will testify to the vital importance of good information and sources. Indeed, we hope that a spillover from the project will be a renewed interest—by individuals, governments, and the UN system itself—in safeguarding and cataloguing UN archival information that has been long underresourced.

The project has benefited from the guidance of an International Advisory Council, composed of eleven distinguished individuals—five of whom were also interviewed for this book. A warm thanks is thus extended to Galal Amin, Margaret Joan Anstee, Lourdes Arizpe, Eveline Herfkens, Enrique Iglesias, András Inotai, Thandike Mkandawire, Gert Rosenthal, John Ruggie, Makoto Taniguchi, and Ramesh Thakur.

We began this effort with only the vaguest of understandings about how to organize and create an oral history archive. Fortunately for us, we had Mary Marshall Clark and Ronald Grele, the current and retired directors of the Columbia University Oral History Research Office, to introduce us to this field of inquiry. Through a series of discussions, training sessions, and critiques of our first efforts, they patiently instructed us in the techniques and methods of their trade.

Our friend and colleague Yves Berthelot directs the project's liaison office in Geneva and edited and contributed to the second volume in our book series, *Unity and Diversity in Development Ideas: Perspectives from the Regional Commissions*. His contributions and friendship are greatly appreciated.

It is no exaggeration to state that we could not have done this book without the able assistance of many graduate students at the Ralph Bunche Institute for International Studies of The Graduate Center of The City University of New York (CUNY), where our project is located. Sophie Theven de Gueleran and Diana Cassells did a lot of the background research necessary for the conduct of fruitful interviews. Ron Nerio transcribed and indexed the bulk of the interviews and contributed to designing the protocols for the transcripts. Elisa Athonvarangkul assembled the biographical summaries for the interviewees and patiently and with good humor entered the many corrections to the manuscript. Danielle Zach cleaned up and checked and rechecked the final manuscript. Max Bernstein and Priscilla Read translated Spanish and French quotes into readable passages. The sharp eye of our copyeditor, Kate Babbitt, helped make this a better book. Nancy Okada, who oversees the finances and personnel of the Bunche Institute, made sure that the inevitable administrative headaches of such an immense undertaking were minimal. We are truly grateful to them all.

A final thanks goes to our families for their support and feedback along the way. To all who participated with such dedication and exceptional skill, "thanks" is but a pale reflection of the gratitude that we feel.

T. G. W., T. C., L. E., and R. J.
United Nations Intellectual History Project
The CUNY Graduate Center, New York
November 2004

Abbreviations

AFL-CIO	American Federation of Labor-Congress of Industrial Organizations
AIDS	acquired immune deficiency syndrome
CDP	Committee for Development Planning
CEPAL	Comisión Económica para América Latina y el Caribe
CHR	Commission on Human Rights
CIA	Central Intelligence Agency
CIEC	Conference on International Economic Cooperation
DAWN	Development Alternatives with Women for a New Era
DD1	First Development Decade
ECA	Economic Commission for Africa
ECAFE	Economic Commission for Asia and the Far East
ECE	Economic Commission for Europe
ECLA	Economic Commission for Latin America
ECLAC	Economic Commission for Latin America and the Caribbean
ECOSOC	Economic and Social Council
ESCAP	Economic and Social Commission for Asia and the Pacific
ESCWA	Economic and Social Commission for Western Asia
FAO	Food and Agriculture Organization
FBI	Federal Bureau of Investigation
G-7	Group of 7
G-8	Group of 8

G-15	Group of 15
G-20	Group of 20
G-77	Group of 77
GA	General Assembly
GATT	General Agreement on Tariffs and Trade
GNP	gross national product
GDP	gross domestic product
HDI	Human Development Index
HIV	human immunodeficiency virus
IBRD	International Bank for Reconstruction and Development
ICRC	International Committee for the Red Cross
IDA	International Development Association
IDB	Inter-American Development Bank
IDEP	Institut de developpement économique et de planification
IDS	Institute of Development Studies
IFAD	International Fund for Agricultural Development
ILO	International Labour Organization
IMF	International Monetary Fund
INSTRAW	International Research and Training Institute for the Advancement of Women
IPRA	International Peace Research Association
ITO	International Trade Organization
JIU	Joint Inspection Unit
LPA	Lagos Plan of Action
LDC	least developed country
LSE	London School of Economics
MDG	Millennium Development Goal
MIT	Massachusetts Institute for Technology
NATO	North Atlantic Treaty Organization
NAM	Non-Aligned Movement

NGO	nongovernmental organization
NIEO	New International Economic Order
ODA	Overseas Development Assistance
OECD	Organisation for Economic Co-operation and Development
OEEC	Organisation for European Economic Co-operation
OPEC	Organization of Petroleum Exporting Countries
SAP	structural adjustment program
SARS	severe acute respiratory syndrome
SUNFED	Special United Nations Fund for Economic Development
TNC	transnational corporation
UNCTAD	United Nations Conference on Trade and Development
UNCTC	United Nations Centre on Transnational Corporations
UNDP	United Nations Development Programme
UNEP	United Nations Environment Programme
UNESCO	United Nations Educational, Scientific, and Cultural Organization
UNFPA	United Nations Population Fund (originally the United Nations Fund for Population Activities)
UNHCR	United Nations High Commissioner for Refugees
UNICEF	United Nations Children's Fund
UNIDO	United Nations Industrial Development Organization
UNIFEM	United Nations Development Fund for Women
UNIHP	United Nations Intellectual History Project
UNOG	United Nations Office in Geneva
UNITAR	United Nations Institute for Training and Research
UNRISD	United Nations Research Institute for Social Development
UNRRA	United Nations Relief and Rehabilitation Administration
UNU	United Nations University
USAID	United States Agency for International Development

USSR	Union of Soviet Socialist Republics
WEP	World Employment Programme
WFC	World Food Conference
WFP	World Food Programme
WHO	World Health Organization
WIDER	World Institute for Development Economics Research
WTO	World Trade Organization

UN Voices

Introduction

The **United Nations Intellectual History Project** was born because after nearly sixty years, it was high time to trace the economic and social ideas that have been launched or nurtured by the UN system. Many of the individuals who have struggled for the cause of multilateral cooperation have had largely undocumented careers and experiences that are essential for the historical record of the twentieth century. And perhaps just as important for the future of multilateralism, our intention is to introduce the world to the organization's human dimension by making more accessible the people who animate the United Nations.

Outsiders—and especially the next generation of students and scholars—rarely experience the UN firsthand; they usually do so only through newsclips and op-eds, Web sites and textbooks. The world organization thus seems more a collection of boring bureaucrats than a creative center of gravity for international problem-solving.

The book presents a different view. It gives the stories of seventy-three individuals, all of whom have spent a substantial part of their professional lives in UN affairs and who have helped shape the organization's thinking about development and social justice over the last six decades. Their human stories, qualities, and commitments reveal a picture—not of tired bureaucrats but rather of a focused and highly experienced group of professionals with an extraordinary range of past and present involvements in national and international life. There are secretaries-general and presidents, ministers and professors, social workers and field workers as well as diplomats and executive heads of UN agencies—men and women from countries all over the world.

The voices resonating here are inevitably a small and very incomplete sample of those found in the United Nations—and even among the seventy-three included, we have space only for a small selection of their experiences. We can do little more than remind readers that there are thousands of others who contribute and have contributed to the international struggle for a better world but whose voices are unheard.

We have employed the oral narrative to do what it does best, namely to give life, color, and imagination to the experiences of individuals and to extract the meanings that each attaches to them. Our voices reflect the expectations, events, and efforts of the second half of the twentieth century that contributed to the economic and social record of the UN's life and activities. Whether it was the idealism of the early years of the UN, the anguish of the Cold War, or the initial euphoria and then the uncertainties of the post–Cold War era, our participants recall how their perceptions of events evolved over time, how tumultuous experiences forced themselves into public consciousness, and how they themselves changed perspectives through knowledge, exposure, experience, and the passage of time.

Who are the persons whose memories form the heart of this volume? A little over half of them served directly in the international civil service. They come from thirty-five countries, covering all of the world's regions and most of the UN's major language groups. A third of those interviewed spent part or all of their careers in academia and a quarter or so in government service in their own countries. A fifth are women, in part a reflection of the paucity of women in positions of influence in and around the UN until recently. Most have advanced degrees, and about half studied economics, undoubtedly reflecting our focus on issues of economic and social development.

A little over half trace their family origins from the industrialized "North," and nearly half from developing countries (Africa, Asia, the Middle East, and Latin America) in the "Global South." Ten percent come from the former "Eastern bloc," and forty percent from the "West." Nearly one-quarter of them experienced the dislocation that comes with growing up a refugee of war or in political exile. Many share strong recollections of their families' experiences during the Great Depression and World War II. And virtually all of them express powerfully the importance of international cooperation in improving the lot of the have-nots. Brief biographies are found in Appendix 1. Most of the interviews were conducted in English, although a handful were not (six were in French and one was in Spanish); English translations of the extracted interviews appear here and the appendix indicates the language in which the interview took place.

Our choice of persons to interview was inevitably subjective. We chose persons in senior positions who were able to reflect on several decades of experience, but this meant missing younger persons of the next generation. We concentrated on economic and social development and thus omitted many whose experiences were primarily in peacekeeping and humanitarian action. And we focused on the development and promotion of ideas, underplaying the contribution of many doers, not because they have not often generated important ideas but because their contributions are less frequently written down and accessible.

We have maintained throughout the project the distinction between the "two UNs"—the forum in which states make decisions and the international civil service. For the former, over the last six decades the decision-making arena for states has become more and more pluralistic. States are still the dominant actors in the UN and national interests have not receded as the basis for making decisions, but nongovernmental organizations (NGOs), the private sector, and other non-state actors are playing larger roles. The success or failure of this UN depends upon governments' perception of their vital interests (or raisons d'état) and the accompanying political will or lack thereof to move ahead.

We are especially interested in the oft-ignored "second UN" of semi-independent secretariats and outside experts and consultants whose job descriptions include research, policy analysis, and idea-mongering. This second UN is capable, under certain circumstances, of leadership and influence which alters international outcomes. We have consistently maintained that individuals and leadership matter—for international secretariats as for all human endeavors. Success or failure in implementing ideas is, of course, not totally independent of governments, resources, or political support. Yet there is more room for maneuver and autonomy, particularly in the intellectual and advocacy realms, than is often supposed.

The outset of the new millennium is a remarkable vantage point from which to look back over sixty years of experience in international cooperation. The woes of our world are obvious—raging wars, glaring poverty, and life-threatening disease in many parts of the world, human rights abuses aplenty. Tragic events are part of the record, but there are successes as well. And they are more numerous and crucial than many cynics realize and certainly more than even many idealists had hoped for when the San Francisco Conference on International Organization was convened in April 1945. Since that time, there has been no world war. Decolonization is virtually complete. Economic and social development has been impressive in many instances so that life expectancies are now higher, child mortality lower, literacy higher, and malnutrition lower. In some cases, the march of democracy has led to greater political participation. Human rights norms and conventions characterize international diplomacy to an extent unimaginable even a few decades ago.

The United Nations, of course, is only part of the story—but certainly an essential chapter of contemporary history. There have been shortcomings, to be sure, and many will be sketched in these pages. At the same time, the world organization and its specialized bodies and agencies have played a central role in bringing ideas and issues into the limelight on the world stage and helping in the concrete realization of new policies. By the standards of previous historical periods, international achievements have been striking since the signing of the UN Charter in June 1945 and the opening of the first General Assembly in London in January 1946.

But what precisely do we mean by "ideas?" We define them as normative or causal beliefs held by individuals that influence their attitudes and actions; in this case, toward economic and social development. The two types, normative and causal, are worth distinguishing at the outset. Normative ideas are broad, general beliefs about what the world should look like. That there should be a more equitable allocation of world resources is an example. On the other hand, causal ideas are more operational notions about what strategy will have a desired result or what tactics will achieve a particular strategy. At the UN, causal ideas often take an operational form—for instance, the target of 0.7 percent of national income as overseas development assistance (ODA). Causal ideas are, therefore, more specific, but they usually are much less than full-blown theories.[1] For example, if we were to begin with the sweeping ethical proposition that the world should be more just, then the idea of a more equitable allocation of resources can be both a normative idea and one way to improve international justice.

The recent research about the role of ideas that informs this project can be grouped into three broad categories. The first, institutionalism—such as Judith Goldstein and Robert O. Keohane's analyses of foreign policy[2] and Kathryn Sikkink's analysis of developmentalism in Latin America[3]—is concerned with how organizations shape the policy preferences of their members. Ideas can be particularly important to the policymaking process during periods of upheaval. Ideas about the end of World War II, of the Cold War, or of the post–September 11th challenges, for instance, provide a conceptual road map that can be used to understand changing preferences and definitions of vital interests of state and non-state actors alike. This approach helps us to situate the dynamics at work among ideas, multilateral institutions, and national policies. It also enables us to begin thinking about how the UN influences elite and popular images, as well as how opinion-makers affect the world organization.

The second category consists of expert-group approaches, which incorporate Peter Haas's theory of epistemic communities,[4] Peter Hall's work on analyzing the impact of Keynesian economists,[5] and Ernst B. Haas's work on knowledge and power[6] as well as more recent work by Sikkink on transnational networks of activists.[7] These approaches examine the role of intellectuals in creating ideas, of technical experts in diffusing them and making them more concrete and scientifically grounded, and of all sorts of people in influencing the positions adopted by a wide range of actors, including and especially governments. Networks of knowledgeable experts influence a broad spectrum of international politics through their ability to interact with policymakers irrespective of location and national boundaries. Researchers working on HIV/AIDS or climate change can have an impact on policy by clarifying an issue from which decision-makers may deduce what is in the interests of their administrations. Researchers also can help to frame the debate on a particular issue, thus narrowing the acceptable range of bargaining in international negotiations. They can introduce standards for action. These networks can help provide justifications for alternatives and often build national or international coalitions to support chosen policies and to advocate for change. In many ways this approach borrows from Thomas Kuhn's often-cited work on the nature of scientific revolutions.[8]

The third category that informs our work consists of constructivists such as Alexander Wendt[9] and John G. Ruggie.[10] These analysts seek to determine the potential for individuals, their governments, and international institutions themselves to be active agents for change rather than mere robots whose behavior reflects the status quo. The critical approaches of those more influenced by the Italian school of Marxism, such as Robert Cox and his followers,[11] are also pertinent. These view the work of all organizations and their ideologies, including the United Nations, as heavily determined by material conditions. The UN system has spawned or nurtured a large number of ideas that have both called into question the conventional wisdom and reinforced it. Indeed, the very definition of what passes for "conventional" at a particular point in time in certain parts of the world is part of the puzzle that we have only begun to address.

Our oral history interviews were designed to capture important perspectives before they are lost, to preserve the memories of what it was like to be a pioneer in international cooperation. The UNIHP has an archive of those personal testimonies and recorded life narratives. The complete transcripts of the oral histories have already informed various specialized books produced by the project and will do so for the other volumes to be published in the series by Indiana University Press. The complete transcripts will be made available upon completion of the project so that researchers worldwide can have full access to the material. We hope that these interviews will provide an essential element in solving a key puzzle in contemporary affairs, namely which ideas eventually become part of international discourse, policy, and action and how.

In these pages, our main objective is to let the "voices" of our interlocutors speak for themselves. They are poignant and amusing, insightful and forward looking. Some are selfless, some self-serving. These personal accounts reflect despair and hope, tragedy and triumph, blindness and insight. International cooperation is so necessary yet so distant. Readers discover our interviewees at both their heroic and less exalted moments. Professional training, national origins, religious upbringing, class backgrounds, and ethnic and gender identities shaped attitudes and efforts. Many of our interviewees disagree among themselves, and we have not shied away from highlighting such differences. Views are often unvarnished and refreshing. Moreover, we do not always agree with the interviewees, and where memories attempt revisionism, we have pointed out different interpretations for historical accuracy.

Those interested in a more detailed discussion of this project's oral history component are referred to Appendix 2, "A Methodological Note: Making This Oral History." Nonetheless, a word is in order here about oral history. It is a method of research for preserving and creating knowledge of historical events as recounted by participants. Personal testimony comes from an in-depth interview conducted by an observer knowledgeable about the individual being interviewed and the subject matter under investigation.

Although storytelling has been used worldwide by cultures to preserve—and by ethnographers to study—family and social traditions, the use of recorded oral history as a method of social science research emerged only with the advent of the portable tape recorder after World War II. Since then, oral history has become a method of data collection that cuts across the social sciences. Oral historians locate the individual in a social context with a central research question in mind and explore constraints on the individual's life story as well as the perceived impact of his or her decisions and actions.

While it is a method of research, oral history is also a tangible *product*. As a result of the interviewer's questioning, new evidence is created which, in turn, can be analyzed much like other historical documents. The value of oral history as a method of investigation is that it is qualitatively different from other written documentary sources such as reports, correspondence, and diaries. The interviewer asks for clarification and fuller explanations of matters; personal memory, recollection, and interpretation are key. Oral history allows for more nuance and passion than antiseptic administrative or scholarly prose. Future researchers can hear the dynamic quality of personal accounts.

One of the intentions of oral history is to ensure that the voice of the interviewee rather than of the interviewer dominates. The former determines how her or his story will be told. Nonetheless, at the end of the day we wanted to be able to compare and contrast perspectives across conversations, so our interviews were conducted following a loose thematic structure within a biographical chronology. We wished to go beyond the more traditional mode of lengthy extracts from individuals that has characterized the more popular oral histories of Studs Terkel or those emanating from the academy.[12]

We imposed our own narrative structure on the text so that readers are able to hear the voices but also understand the main themes of international cooperation debated within the UN system. A similar technique was used effectively in an effort to recount the early years of the AIDS pandemic.[13] As an aid to future research, citations are used to indicate books or important primary documents that enter into conversations.

The importance of this archival collection reflects two realities. First, there is precious little institutional memory at the UN. Second, only a few people write their memoirs after they leave or retire from the organization. Our experience with this project leaves us ever more convinced of the importance of the UN's archives and those of its specialized agencies to UN history and the lessons of sixty years of global governance.

The Cast of Characters and Their Stories

Part One, "Individuals Make a Difference," contains three chapters that introduce the cast of characters through their biographical material. This first part permits us to explore an individual's family, educational, and professional background and career choices as well as her or his ideas regarding social and economic issues. The formative years and social backgrounds of these individuals were also critical in determining subsequent views. Childhood, family, and religion play essential roles, as does education, particularly at the university level. Initial encounters with foreign languages, cultures, and international careers are other crucial factors. Rich and intriguing sets of experiences help dispel facile stereotypes. Backgrounds of poverty or silver spoons, for instance, are represented in our pool, but a commitment to justice and a better world emanates distinctly from the voices regardless of backgrounds. However committed they are to nationalism and patriotism, those we interviewed display a palpable passion for international cooperation. Nonetheless, differences abound. Indeed, any earlier thoughts about simple generalizations have vanished in compiling this collection.

Part Two, "Hope, Creativity, and Frustration," consists of Chapters 4 to 8. They move chronologically from the pre–World War II years of uncertainty, the turmoil of the war, and the hopeful founding of the next generation of universal organizations to the tumult following the end of the Cold War in the globalizing world at the dawn of the twenty-first century. In between, decolonization and the broadening of development aspirations led to an expansion of the UN's influence on ideas and action, followed by a period of frustration and defensiveness in the 1980s. Decades are an arbitrary way of dividing history, but the familiar ten-year chunks of time proved useful organizational devices.

We have grouped material that spans a longer time period in the decade when an idea first appears on the UN's agenda—for instance, human rights in the 1940s because of the adoption of the Universal Declaration in 1948 and the environment in the 1970s because of the UN Conference on the Human Environment (UNCHE) held in Stockholm in 1972.

In each chapter in Part Two, we have grouped our narratives and the voices under specific historical events or UN activities. Our typology maps some of the economic and social ideas promoted by the world organization since 1945 and probes the intersection of power, politics, and institutions and the acceptance or rejection of significant ideas. Ultimately, our own generalizations about the value and impact of the world organization and its ideas take a back seat to the UN's apparent impact in a particular decade according to the voices.

These five chapters explore various individuals' evaluations as to whether and how particular global occurrences have had an impact on new thinking. Such major events as the UN's founding, decolonization, the rise and fall of the Berlin Wall, and September 11, 2001, enter into our conversations as voices evaluate the influence of major events and shocks on the creation, utilization, and transmission of ideas with particular reference to economic and social development. Stories and anecdotes, insightful or amusing, enliven the text and embroider the story.

Part Three is "The World Organization, Ideas, and Twenty-First-Century Challenges." The four chapters in this section break out of the preceding chronological presentation in order to highlight what our voices said about the nexus of ideas, international public policy, and enhanced multilateral cooperation. Chapter 9, "A Revolutionary Idea: The International Civil Service," and Chapter 10, "The Power of Ideas and People inside the UN," are two parts of a detailed examination of individuals and processes in international secretariats.

Chapter 11, "Blending Outside Intellectual Energies," explores sources of ideas from "outside" the world organization—mainly from universities, independent commissions, and NGOs. Also found here are the global ad hoc conferences where outsiders and insiders mix. There can be no real division between this chapter and the previous two because many of the individuals interviewed are difficult to categorize. Their voices are from what may be considered inside-outsiders or outside-insiders. But we believe that the presentation of material in this way helps illuminate our main themes.

Voices provide personal perspectives on how well or poorly various UN organizations have adapted to global events. What ideas emerged in response to particular problems or crises? What ideas were discarded as a result of specific world events? More specifically, these voices reflect views about what happened to critical ideas within the UN system and what factors may have affected their lifespan, trajectories, and ultimate impact. Specifically, opinions are set forth about the importance within the UN of leadership, the staff, the dynamics of global conferences and eminent commissions, support or opposition of particular governments and regional groups, and the influence of North-South relations. The impact of group negotiations and of NGOs also looms large. Chapters 9, 10, and 11 contain insights about behind-the-scenes processes that are crucial to understanding international discussions but are rarely visible to those not part of them.

Chapter 12, "The Legacy and Future Intellectual Challenges," concludes this book. The project's first book, *Ahead of the Curve? UN Ideas and Global Challenges,* ended with two brief declarative sentences: "People matter. Ideas matter."[14] What clearly emerges from the chapters in this volume is how seventy-three individuals mattered for the UN, for better or for worse. Too frequently, there is a tendency to think that efforts by individuals are fruitless. The present text is an antidote to such cheap nihilism.

This final chapter also sheds light on the second key assumption behind the United Nations Intellectual History Project—namely, that ideas matter. *The Economist* recently aptly noted: "You can record the 20th century as a story of astonishing technical progress. You can tell it as a rise and fall of powers, or as a painful recovery from modern society's relapses into barbarism. But if you leave out ideas, you leave out what people were ready to live and die for."[15]

Our voices help substantiate four propositions about ideas that figure in recent academic literature about the role of ideas in international relations. We highlight them here so that readers can keep them in mind while enjoying the insights, anecdotes, and wisdom in the voices echoing from the pages of this volume.

The first is that ideas can change the nature of international public policy discourse. For example, ideas about dependency and the concept of center-periphery, which were developed within the UN Economic Commission for Latin America (ECLA) in the 1950s, fundamentally altered, at least for a while, the discourse on modernization. Other instances are the appearance of such "new" issue areas as the environment and gender. These are illustrations of crucial changes in discourse and the reframing of possible solutions to international challenges.

The second proposition is that ideas can help states as well as individuals to define and redefine their identities and interests. Our special concern is to let the voices illustrate the impact of ideas over time on the willingness of governmental and international bureaucracies to embrace, or at least consider, the perspective of common interests rather than narrower self-interests. This kind of impact includes the ability of new ideas to provide a tactical guide to policy and action when older and existing norms conflict or when sequencing or priorities are disputed. The need to broaden the narrow orthodoxy of neoliberalism by putting a "human face" on structural adjustment is one such example. Another was the recognition of the need to override state sovereignty with military force in cases of genocide and mass murder and displacement.

The third proposition is that ideas can alter prospects for forming new coalitions of political or institutional forces. For example, the call by the UN Conference on Trade and Development to take seriously the declining terms of trade for economies in the South and pleas by developing countries and their allies to establish a different way to distribute the benefits of growth, a New International Economic Order (NIEO), became the glue of solidarity in the South, at least for a while. The "common heritage of humankind," a notion to use as-yet-unexplored seabed resources as the property of the planet, provided a way to form unusual partnerships among states and NGOs. The Integrated Programme for Commodities (IPC), a comprehensive design to stabilize prices for raw materials, provided the framework for producers and consumers, and subgroups within them, to come together in new ways. In some issue areas, gender and sustainability provide the way for many private groups across the North and the South to form coalitions.

The fourth possible influence is that ideas become embedded in institutions and not only challenge the founding principles of those institutions but also help in setting future agendas. The establishment of new agencies—the UN Environment Programme (UNEP) or the International Fund for Agricultural Development (IFAD), for example—is one manifestation, as is the mainstreaming of such issues as rights and the creation of new units within governments and established organizations. Institutional manifestations of ideas can readily be observed and charted over time.

We anticipate at least three generic criticisms of our use of voices. First, foggy or even self-serving and selective memories can pose problems for accurate history. This difficulty is commonly associated with using memoirs as sources. However, we have tried to attenuate such shortcomings by conducting background and archival research before and after interviews and by checking facts when an event or an interpretation appeared to be controversial or disputed.

Second, we recognize the problems arising from elite interviews, as we pragmatically decided to interview older and prominent participants who have generally been opinion leaders and who have set agendas. However, they all began their careers as junior officials or academics before joining policy or academic elites, and many overcame substantial personal challenges along the way. We would be the first to admit that it would be desirable to broaden the interview base. But given limited resources, this is the first, not the final, word in building an institutional memory about economic and social development discourse and practice.

Third, we are not unaware of the inherent dangers in an eclecticism that draws upon existing theories and a small number of interviews, however interesting. Our approach may seem a way to avoid or finesse tough epistemological and methodological choices. However, we proceeded with what already is an ambitious enough effort at intellectual history. Surely, in the coming years, other analysts will build on our fledgling efforts.

Finally, we should be straightforward about our normative agenda. A better understanding of the sources, evolution, and impact of ideas could improve the world organization's future contribution to economic and social development. More specifically, a better comprehension of the United Nations as an intellectual actor and of the processes in the multilateral marketplace of ideas could lead to improved strategies and different tactics in the twenty-first century. In moving toward the future, the voices of our interviewees provide essential guideposts. As William Faulkner noted, "The past is not dead. It is not even past yet."[16]

The following account is not hagiography. Our aim has been to present neither romanticized depictions nor cheap caricatures but to help understand complex problems and the responses to them by those who dealt with global challenges within the UN system. Our voices capture an enduring dimension of the never-ending human endeavor to invent ideas and better organize ourselves in order, as the Preamble to the UN Charter reminds us, "to save succeeding generations from the scourge of war ... and to promote social progress and better standards of life in larger freedom."

Part One.
Individuals Make a Difference

We launched this oral history to establish missing information and insights about the world of ideas within the United Nations itself. But soon we became fascinated with the individuals who were sitting across from us. Part One revolves around early experiences, permitting us to probe influences of these individuals' social backgrounds, educational and professional interests, and career choices.

Kofi Annan, Secretary-General of the United Nations, spoke about the influence of growing up in Ghana and witnessing the end of colonialism on his own beliefs in the possibilities for political change: "My father worked . . . for a company called the United African Company, which was part of Unilever . . . and one of the trading companies in Africa. We moved a lot. We lived in almost every part of Ghana when I was growing up, because he was a district manager and he moved from district to district. Sometimes he'd go there for a couple of years, and we'd go to school there. And then of course, when he became director, we moved back to Accra. But in the process of moving around in a country that had many different tribes, speaking different languages, and sometimes people looking at themselves in terms of their tribe, rather than in national terms as Ghanaians, it was very interesting for me to grow up dealing with and getting to know so many different groups in Ghana. It gave you a sense of being able to relate to everybody and different groups at a young age. It was also during the period of independence—the struggle for independence. To see the changes taking place, to see the British hand over to the Ghanaians, and have a Ghanaian prime minister, which was Kwame Nkrumah—he was the leader of government business, they called him, and he eventually became president. You grew up with a sense that change is possible, all is possible."

Kofi Annan's school experiences—and some of his activism to improve school meals—also prepared him for life on the UN's 38th floor. "The headmaster of my school, Mr. Bartels, who eventually ended up working in Paris with UNESCO [UN Educational, Scientific, and Cultural Organization] . . . thought I was a troublemaker or a ringleader—there was a measure of justification in those suspicions, I have to admit. . . . I organized a strike at the age of fifteen about the food, which was bad at the boarding school. We kept telling them and they wouldn't do anything, so we arranged it in such a way—about 600 or 700 of us—that on a Sunday nobody ate. Having arranged to make sure they had something to eat first, when we went to the dining room we all refused to eat. The housemaster tried to calm the situation down, but he couldn't. But of course, I, who had organized it and knew the headmaster would call for me, went to the dining room late. And when I got there, the place was in pandemonium. The next morning, when he called me, he said, 'Young Annan'—he called me young Annan because he knew my father—'I understand you had something to do with all this strike nonsense. If you have an issue to discuss, come to me and we'll discuss it man to man. You are reasonably intelligent. Given the chance, you may become a useful member of society.'"

It is not only the Secretary-General who has a colorful past. The childhood and formative experiences of all our "voices" are fascinating. They raise questions for us, as for them, about how their social backgrounds, early years, education, and opportunities affected their later work at the United Nations.

We decided from our interviews that the most salient stories could be grouped under three chapters: The first is about the impact of childhood, family background, and religion; the second recounts the influence of education and mentors; and the third highlights the importance of cultures, languages, and first job opportunities. The following extracts not only introduce the cast of UN characters who appear throughout the book, they also provide fascinating and inspirational portraits that stand on their own.

1

Growing Up

- **The Great Depression and the Demise of the League of Nations**
- **World War II**
- **Faith and Family Matters**

The earliest experiences of childhood, family, background, and religion are often crucial in the formation of an individual. For our voices, these formative early experiences were salient in nurturing an interest in international cooperation and in launching the pursuit of active and often intellectually rewarding international careers. "The world, then, in which I was born, was affected by two major events," said Adebayo Adedeji, who was born in 1930 in colonial Nigeria and who would one day head the UN's regional arm for a liberated continent, the Economic Commission for Africa (ECA). "The Great Depression . . . affected, in a way, the fortunes of the family. And then I myself grew up in the World War II years. I knew a little more about the economics of export commodities because that was what my parents specialized in . . . mainly cocoa and kola nuts. I also knew about how wrong Hitler was in World War II. We were not taught what Hitler did. We were taught to believe that he was the devil incarnate, and we had all sorts of school songs and plays that demonized Hitler. Don't forget that Nigeria was then a British colony."

Those whom we interviewed often spoke about their parents, in many cases their mothers, as critical influences in their lives. Many grew up as what today some would call "third culture children"[1] as they had early experiences with cultures other than their own, including a large number whose own families or neighborhoods were multicultural. Others noted that they had been influenced by international conflicts and leaders or had family members involved in international or foreign services. Some interviewees grew up in privileged families, others were raised with more modest means, and yet others came from families that were shaken by the Great Depression, World War II, or forced migration. Surprisingly for that generation, a number were the only child in the family. We have, in fact, two overlapping generations: those who grew up during the Great Depression and were schooled during World War II and those who grew up during the war years and were schooled during the wave of decolonization and the Vietnam War.

The Great Depression and the Demise of the League of Nations

The first generation of universal international institutions, the League of Nations and the International Labour Organization (ILO), emerged from what had been prematurely described as "the war to end all wars," World War I. The League was established in 1920 in Geneva following a suggestion two years earlier by U.S. president Woodrow Wilson in his proposed Fourteen Points for ending the armed conflict that had raged across the continent since the assassination of Archduke Francis Ferdinand in August 1914. The legacy of the League is dominated by dramatic failures in the political arena—an inability to react to Japan's annexation of Manchuria in 1931, Italy's invasion of Abyssinia (Ethiopia) in 1935–1936, and Germany's attacks on its neighbors. It was also unable to attract and maintain the major powers—the United States never joined, while the Soviet Union, Germany, and Japan withdrew when it was convenient.

The League was also active in economic and social analysis, making some pioneering contributions, as in nutrition, although this aspect of its work is less emphasized. But in spite of much useful research, the efforts by the League and the ILO during the 1930s made little headway against the Great Depression, which had desperate worldwide consequences for economic activity and unemployment and ended only with World War II.

The Wall Street crash of October 29, 1929, wiped millions of dollars of value from stocks in hours. Serious repercussions occurred in Europe and in the colonies, leading to steep declines in international trade. "Beggar thy neighbor" became the flavor of the year and then of the decade. Many of those interviewed reflected on the worldwide economic downturn, in particular its impact on their families.

As for many of our interviewees, prominent peace activist Elise Boulding's memories of the Depression were vivid. She was born in Norway but moved to the United States at age three: "I remember vividly when my father lost his job. I went into our pantry and around the house writing down everything we had to see what we could sell to buy food, worrying how we were going to manage to keep going."

Julia Henderson, who would later be in charge of social affairs at the UN, remembered living through the Depression as a university student in the

United States: "The unemployment rate, of course, was very, very high. So many times students had to drop out because even though the tuition at the university was very low, they just couldn't make it. . . . The whole community was in such sad shape."

Robert Cox, who after twenty-five years in the ILO went on to have a distinguished university career, recalled the Depression as something felt on and off by his family but not openly discussed. His family's strained circumstances caused him to withdraw from Lower Canada College where, even with a scholarship, they could no longer send him. "So I had that experience of the Depression which was not one of serious deprivation, but nevertheless something you were aware of as being there and as having affected you. But I think in the long run what it did is to inculcate a certain sense of self-discipline and living without too many of the unnecessary accoutrements of life."

Across the Atlantic, Paul Berthoud, who later worked in Geneva for UNCTAD and elsewhere for a host of other UN agencies, recalled that "Switzerland had bad times, too, during the Depression. . . . I have alluded to those three years of a 'red government' in Geneva. In fact, the first measure . . . that socialist government, when it took power in 1933, did was to cut by 10 percent the salary of all the officials working for the government. That affected my father. I remember my mother and father recounting the budget of the family because it pinched very much. I was studying cello at the time, and they had to extend the down payment on the cello which they had bought for me because the plan had to be reviewed."

Stéphane Hessel, who ended up in the UN almost by chance and went on to serve France as an ambassador with multilateral portfolios, recalled the Great Depression as "a great shock." He said, "Of course, unemployment in France, in Europe, was a terrible challenge. I began immediately to have great admiration for Roosevelt. And what we heard about the New Deal, for instance, was felt as really a much better answer to our problems than any other statesman had ever done. I am now, and have always been, convinced that we never would have had a United Nations organization if it had not been for the commitment and conviction of Franklin Roosevelt."

Janez Stanovnik, who would become the executive secretary of the UN Economic Commission for Europe (ECE) before assuming the presidency of independent Slovenia, noted that the Great Depression did not spare the Balkans: "Suddenly, everything had broken down." He knew the purse was tight, "when for Christmas, the Christmas tree in my family was suddenly decorated by the cakes that mama prepared herself and not by the decorations which usually were bought." He recalled, as a ten-year-old, having the "feeling that now our family is broke. This was not quite accurate because my father had savings he had invested into the land property, so he managed over the crisis. But I would remember, you see, after every meal, there were two or three people ringing on the door, asking if something was left after lunch. . . . There was real starvation."

The adverse effects of the Depression were not limited to the North, however. "The Depression affected me directly because my father's business collapsed," recalled Alister McIntyre, later to become deputy secretary-general of UNCTAD, in referring to his childhood in Grenada. "He was one of the casualties of the Depression, and he was, at the time, running a very substantial pharmaceuticals business. When he said that his business was failing, it was because people couldn't afford drugs. That struck me. I said, 'My God, I never thought about the possibility that people could not afford drugs.'" The impact on the family was direct and immediate: "Our own circle began cutting corners and trying to get rid of the less essential items of expenditure. My father, after some bumps, ended up doing something similar, but not identical, which involved our moving from one part of the island to another. Of course, he was not then his own boss and that was a bit of a humiliation for him. . . . How did this Depression come about? Oddly enough, nobody in Grenada, at the time, [had] even heard of the name Lord Keynes. This was something that came to my attention when I went to the university. But on the island, people just thought it was one of those acts of nature. How could the prices for our nutmeg and cocoa just plummet downwards? No one could understand it."

When we interviewed Enrique Iglesias, he had long served as president of the Inter-American Development Bank (IDB); he would subsequently be elected to an exceptional fourth term. His relatives were from a very poor farming family in northern Spain who moved in an effort to avoid the effects of the Depression. Many Spaniards at the time headed to Cuba, but the devastation of that island's economy by the Depression meant that Iglesias's father headed to Uruguay. The calculations of the future minister of foreign affairs of Uruguay began in the family store: "We lived in a colorful neighborhood in Montevideo. My father owned a small grocery store . . . where I learned, while keeping my parents company, the duties involved in running the shop, especially those tasks in which they struggled, such as adding up the customers' notebooks. These were black notebooks where we recorded the daily expenses. At the end of the month we had to add them up in order to charge our customers the bill. That was my first intellectual task. . . . My father was a very simple, humble person with only a modest education. My mother, on the other hand, had more of an inclination to read, which gave her a significant advantage in cultural matters. . . . But my father had the conviction, as many

Spaniards did who came to America, that he had to give his children the education which he had been denied."

While initially effective in promoting international cooperation during the more prosperous and peaceful 1920s, the League of Nations could not withstand the pressures of the Depression. The worldwide poverty and unemployment heightened international tensions, making multilateral problem-solving ever more difficult. Whereas in some parts of the world economic dislocation facilitated the rise of fascist governments (Germany and Italy), in others, it encouraged empire-building (Japan). By the first calls of war in the late 1930s, the League had been effectively sidelined.

Oscar Schachter taught about UN issues and human rights at Columbia University's Law School until his death at eighty-nine, shortly after we interviewed him. Earlier, he had been the UN's chief legal advisor and afterward director of research at the UN Institute for Training and Research (UNITAR). He remembered his childhood and education in Brooklyn: "As far back as high school—1928 to 1932—I was interested in politics, both domestic and international. On the domestic side, the Great Depression affected our personal lives. My father's business collapsed, we required government aid to meet mortgage debts, some of our close relatives were unemployed, and after-school jobs were scarce. When I was fifteen, I had a summer job in a fur factory at $12 a week, which required me to be at work around 6 A.M. and to leave about 7 P.M. Some considered me lucky to have the job. Early in high school, in Brooklyn, I took an active role in student government. We had a student arbitration court for disciplinary cases. I served as the president judge. I was also the president of the general organization, the highest student position. My only international link occurred when one of my history teachers required his classes to take part in an annual national examination on the League of Nations, sponsored by the NGO supporting the League. I had the highest score and received the prize, but I cannot remember the amount. Still, the League was nonetheless remote and I never thought of it in career terms."

Despite its ultimate demise, for some, studying the institution influenced their own thinking about politics and their course of research. Victor Urquidi died in 2004 as we were going to press. He worked at the Economic Commission for Latin America before becoming the president of the Colegio de México and credits the early period of the League with sparking his interest in international affairs at a young age, "I was brought up believing in the League of Nations, because one of the things I did as a matter of my studies was to read the League of Nations *World Economic Reports*. I was familiar with them and I kept reading the stuff until they ceased publication." He also looked back to his country's entrance in the organization: "When Mexico was finally admitted to the League of Nations in the 1930s, the man who was appointed by Cárdenas as ambassador to the League of Nations, was . . . a close friend of my father's. When my father died in 1938, and I informed [him] of it by telegram, he invited me to go and spend Christmas with him and his wife and family in Geneva. I went there, and it was a great consolation to be with him. He showed me the League of Nations buildings. We talked about his activities there."

Bernard Chidzero, who would serve as UNCTAD's deputy secretary-general and minister in Zimbabwe, recalled studying the League of Nations while at the University of Ottawa. "We had to go through the various treaties," he reports. "And I got more and more interested in how the conquered native countries were treated in these international organizations. Hence, the question of the Mandates System came up. Various countries were allocated to important countries to be protected in their own interests, or to be preserved for the interests of the conquerors, by administrative authority. This is an entirely new subject because, as you know, I drifted fairly soon to concentrating on the Mandates System of the League of Nations which compares with the Trusteeship System of the UN."

Stéphane Hessel credited his wife's father for teaching him about the League: "My father-in-law was Russian-born and became a French jurist and a constitutionalist. For him, the League of Nations was the outcome of a long history of international cooperation. He was also a great specialist of the French Revolution and, therefore, of the French Declaration of the Rights of Man. Speaking with him, and having quite close relations with him in the years 1937, 1938, and so on, I did realize that the League of Nations was important."

One of our interviewees, Jacques Polak, served in the League's secretariat, initially as a research assistant to the distinguished Dutch economist Jan Tinbergen in the economics section. He remarked on the intellectual vibrancy of the organization in its heyday: "In the late thirties when the League was in desperate shape, the economic secretariat was considered to be first-rate. For example, the Rockefeller Foundation put its money there. This business cycle stuff was financed not by the League but by the Rockefeller Foundation. Everybody who was anybody in economics came through Geneva. The way they would now go through Chicago maybe, or Washington. I met a lot of these people." However, the onset of war would put an end to that. Polak recollected that "in the summer of 1940 it became very clear that people in Geneva were horribly isolated, so to say, except from the German world. The Germans were all the way around Switzerland, a few kilometers away at the Route de Ferney. . . . Of course there was always the risk that Switzerland would be invaded. This gave the Americans, who were not members of the League, the idea that it would be a pity if the economic section would collapse or become irrelevant because of its isolation in Switzerland. They didn't care for the rest of the League. The United States government organized an invitation for part of the economic section to move to the United States, got them visas, which was of course the most wanted thing at that time. I'd been trying to get one, but the ordinary person couldn't get that. And they gave them a place to work, which was the Institute for Advanced Studies in Princeton." In fact, a few of the staff in the economics section of the League, including Polak, were soon transferred to the United States and others were transferred to Canada. Polak noted, "The League never died. The League was transferred into the UN when the UN was established in 1946. . . . And all of the people in Geneva were transferred. . . . Some of the people who were still in Princeton (I wasn't there anymore by that time) moved over."

Elise Boulding's husband, distinguished economist Kenneth Boulding, was at Princeton University at the time. She recalled: "The economic and social secretariat [of the League] was housed at the Princeton Institute for Advanced Studies. I remember attending the social gatherings. The other participants, of course, were all Europeans. There were very distinguished economists in the group. I particularly remember Ragnar Nurkse. There were no Americans in that group. They would be talking about current events. Every once in a while, one of them would turn and say to me, very patronizingly, 'You wouldn't understand these things, you're an American.' And I would be very indignant, because I was Norwegian and I understood them very well."

Janez Stanovnik recalled the hope and subsequent disappointment in that first generation of international organization: "I cannot find the names and the words to describe to you what kind of almost worship for the League of Nations there was. Partially it is due to my educators. . . . I would remember, in school we had, for the League of Nations Day, a kind of competition where we had been writing essays about the League of Nations. You see all these big names of Briant, Titulescu, Benes, and so forth. Those were all very familiar to us. . . . We have been here as a small nation, but oppressed or in danger by fascist Italy. Our sympathies were very much with Ethiopia and on Haile Salassie's side. . . . The abandonment of Hitler's Germany and breakdown of the League of Nations was, for my generation, particularly painful."

Mostafa Tolba, later to become executive director of the UN Environment Programme, was more disillusioned: "The issue of the League of Nations was very heavily debated at the time when I was just entering the university, 1939, after the beginning of the war. . . . The general feeling among the young intellectuals in Egypt was that the League of Nations proved itself to be completely useless and very weak. . . . Nobody ever believed that the weakness was because the secretariat was weak or the offices were weak, like what sometimes happens now. The general feeling was that the countries of the world had become very weak, that they were not raising any finger against any wrong-doings. . . . We were relieved that the League of Nations was gone and this [the UN] was a new organization based on the optimism of stopping the aggres-sion of Hitler."

The League, the first great experiment in universal international organiza-tion, has virtually disappeared in living memory.

World War II

The upheaval of the Great Depression occurred only a decade after the end of World War I. Although that "war to end all wars" finished in 1918, another took place from 1939 to 1945. An estimated 55 million people lost their lives during World War II. The use of nuclear weapons for the first time in August 1945 in Hiroshima and Nagasaki fundamentally altered the nature of geopolitics.

The globe's trauma was mirrored in the lives of many of our interviewees. For some, the war was a distant but fascinating news item. For most, it was a powerful and often traumatic learning experience. Among those interviewed were a number who endured dramatic family upheavals as a result of the war.

Margaret Joan Anstee, who was to become the first woman resident repre-sentative of the UN Development Programme (UNDP) and later the first fe-male UN under-secretary-general, recalled that her school days in rural England were heavily colored by the war and fear of violence: "At the begin-ning of the war, for a whole term, we only had school once a week because there weren't any air raid shelters ready for us. We were in a bombed area, a defense area. So I used to wander the countryside. I became very bookish and very keen on country things. . . . I was very self-reliant, which made it easier to go and live in remote places afterwards. At Chelmsford High School, I had met someone who had a great influence on my life. . . . One of the families in the village had adopted, or taken as a foster child, a German/Jewish girl, who became my very bosom friend. I went with her through all of the problems—her parents disappearing and, after the war, hoping that they were going to be found. They died in a concentration camp." She further recounts the impact of World War I on her family: "My father had been in the war. He had lost a brother. My mother lost her favorite brother in the war. All of my uncles had been, in one way or another, involved in the war. So their conversation was all about growing tensions and the threat of another war. . . . I will never forget the 3rd of September 1939, when the war broke out. . . . I remember being absolutely terrified, because this whole shadow of war had hung over all my childhood."

Likewise, Robert Cox recounted the impact of both these wars on his Canadian-immigrant family and on his own development as a critical theorist: "My mother's family had been decimated in World War I. She had quite a number of brothers, and two of them were killed in World War I. There was not, I would say, a kind of revulsion against war as a result of that, but [against] a kind of glorification of heroism, if you like. That was the spirit I grew up with, and I suppose I began again with this kind of sense of criticism, perhaps unwisely, but nevertheless became rather alienated by that overpowering sense of commitment to something that ought to be more questioned."

Mihaly Simai is a prominent Hungarian economist who was one of the first Eastern Europeans to work in the EEC. Later, he was part of numerous expert groups and participated as both a government official and NGO representative in many UN conferences. His father was a reasonably well-off farmer and trader of agricultural goods in prewar Hungary who had separated from his mother, an English teacher and political activist. He recalled "pretty much following the world as a child" through his mother's involvement with the Hungarian Social Democratic Party. "She was a kind of a 'black sheep' in the family, with which she had no ties. So, then the war came, and at the time Hungary became involved on the side of the Axis powers. . . . She was involved in some illegal organization activities in the Social Democratic movement." He recalled the painful moment on November 15, 1944, ironically in the final moments of occupation, when as a fourteen-year-old he was obliged to watch Nazi soldiers execute his mother and four other people who took part in a clandestine meeting of the Social Democratic Party. "I was in the next door in the apartment and everybody had to watch the execution including myself. So I remained alone and was helped by some families and particularly by a Roman Catholic group in Hungary which was called the Gray Missionaries. These were Hungarian Christian Socialist missionaries who were close to the Social Democrats."

Sotiris Mousouris would later hold a number of positions in UN agencies revolving around development and transnational corporations (TNCs). Born in Komotini, the capital of western Thrace in the north of Greece, his first and most powerful memory was being a refugee: "We fled to Athens a few days before the Bulgarians invaded Greece along with Germans. . . . Well, being from a well-to-do family and then losing everything as a refugee, and losing my father in an air crash, I got the belief in my life that two things matter: friendships and education. Nobody can take away these two assets in your life. I was never interested in making money; but having memories of the war, the occupation and the civil strife that followed the liberation, I felt that I wanted to do something to improve conditions for my compatriots. I recall people dying of hunger. I saw men being hung from trees by the Nazis. So this affected me. I was politicized very early in my life."

Gerald "Gerry" Helleiner was born in Vienna and escaped just as World War II began. He would eventually become Canada's leading development economist, especially on issues of trade and development, and would lead countless international efforts to lessen North-South disparities. "Well, I was only three years old when I left Vienna as a refugee. . . . My mother's father was a Jewish social-democratic leader. He was actually a minister of state in one of the governments in the 1920s in Austria and subsequently a leader of the Schutzbund, the socialist underground army that came afoul of the Dollfuss regime in 1934. And after the Anschluss [Germany's annexation of Austria in 1938], the combination of my mother's Jewish half and our one-quarter Jewish origins; the political background of the time; and an explicit warning to my father, after he had already lost his job for having married a Jew and refused to divorce her, that he was going to be arrested led him to leave quickly for the UK. My two older brothers also soon left on refugee trains. . . . My mother and I left on the last plane to leave Vienna before the outbreak of war. So there is concern in my background for social-democratic values and human rights and so forth." After fleeing to the UK, they emigrated to Canada, where his father, an academic, worked as a butler until he learned English. "Our family was brought out by a trust of some kind . . . and some people at the University of Toronto, one of whom knew my father personally, and others who were very interested in the rescue of European intellectuals."

His recollection of the university then was that "at that time, this was a very conservative, Oxbridge-dominated institution. So when my father did come here, he was very much a curiosity and stood out, because people assumed he was Jewish, which he was not. His wife was. He had a thick accent at the time. He was an historian, though he was in the Department of Political Economy, because there were no vacancies in the history department. He converted himself into an economic historian for the purpose of the job. For all sorts of reasons he was peculiar, and students remembered him and the university regarded him as part of a vanguard, and a little bit in advance of what became a major shift in the composition both of the faculty and the student body after the war." Helleiner recalled that his family was "warmly welcomed by those in the university who had brought them. . . . We arrived with nothing. . . . And we were provided with furniture for our flat. People were extraordinarily kind. On the other hand, it was wartime, so I was instructed never to speak German. . . . I remember being chased home, and my brothers were chased down the street and had rocks thrown at us . . . with the kids shouting 'bloody foreigner' at us, and 'why don't you go home' and that kind of thing."

John Gerard Ruggie, also born in Austria, complemented his distinguished academic career in multilateralism (at Berkeley, Columbia, UC-San Diego, and Harvard) with a half-decade stint as advisor to Secretary-General Kofi Annan, including preparations for the Millennium Assembly in September 2000. He recalled: "I was born in Graz, Austria in the fall of 1944, during the war, in fact, according to my mother, during a British bombing attack on our city, which prevented the doctor from showing up for my birth. . . . I come from a poor, working-class family. My parents were divorced when I was four. I think one of the strongest impressions of my childhood was being able to get out of our one-room flat, with no running water, and out of the city during the summer, which was made possible by the fact that I qualified for a summer camp subsidized by the labor unions. My family was a strong union family. I do remember a couple of times being required to march on May 1. There were different factions of the left-of-center movement in Austria, and once I made the wrong turn on the way home and ran into the wrong faction, who could tell to which one I belonged by the emblem on my shirt and who chased me down the street. So the cost of factionalism, even among people who pursue roughly similar goals, was certainly impressed on me at an early age."

In reflecting back on his subsequent interest in transnational issues, he recalled the different approaches of the United States and Soviet Union to the Allied occupation of postwar Austria: "I must have been eight or nine, I went by train to visit some family relatives in Vienna, which was still under Soviet control. When the train got to the Semmering Pass, which was where the Soviet occupation zone began, it was like crossing an international frontier. I was by myself. The Russian soldiers, looking very intimidating wearing their bear hats and with their rifles slung over their shoulders, came on the train and started barking orders to see documents. I guess I got a little frightened because for the next fifteen or twenty years, whenever I approached an international frontier my palms got moist. . . . Not long thereafter, there was a knock on the door of our flat, and we received a CARE package which had written on it, 'From the people of the United States of America.' We opened it up and found Hershey bars, flour, and sugar, and some yellow powdery stuff that we couldn't identify, so we threw it out. I learned many years later, in the Army, that it was powdered eggs. That was a very different way to encounter the two superpowers. One frightened me, and the other, in a sense, provided positive incentives and help."

Paul Streeten would make his mark as one of the West's best-known development economists, also serving as a key consultant for a host of UN institutions. He founded and edited *World Development,* a leading multidisciplinary journal on the topic. He recalled the impact of the interwar years in the 1920s and 1930s on his thinking: "In interwar Vienna, it wasn't very difficult to be concerned with the poor. It was a terribly mismanaged situation, as we all know. I have felt, since my primary school days, quite strongly that great inequality and great poverty should be eradicated. They are not tolerable. I joined, at the age of perhaps ten, eleven, or twelve, a socialist youth movement. There again, we discussed and talked about national and global issues of poverty, inequality, and policies of how to remove or reduce them. . . . But my own interests turned, perhaps at the age of fifteen or sixteen, towards thinking about these issues, as well as doing things about them. It started with action and then eventually got onto thinking."

He remembered the main intellectual stimulation: "My main influences were partly my uncle, by whom I was brought up, and partly a socialist sociologist who was very idealistic—he wanted to combine Karl Marx with Immanuel Kant—called Max Adler. Even when I was still in school, I attended some of his lectures at the university—also some of the lectures given by Moritz Schlick, for instance. He was a philosopher, not a sociologist. He was anti-Kantian. He didn't think that the main purpose in life was to fulfill our duties, but to achieve happiness. That again is easily related, on a national and global scale, to a social concern for all human beings. It is what we would nowadays call human development."

The mixture of allies created some problems: "When I was a student we had much closer links with communists. There were meetings at which we were told we had to shed all moral inhibitions if we wanted to further the good cause. The Blue Pilgrims only came on the scene later when I left Austria for England. But my sympathy had changed by that time. I was, in a sense, prepared for them, because at one stage, I began to see quite clearly, I think at the age of sixteen or seventeen, that the ends do not always justify the means, which was the creed of the more revolutionary colleagues of our group. I turned more towards individual values and the view that the means should not be sacrificed to the ends. That was a preparation for a group that was also connected with the Quakers. They were the people who, when the time came to leave Austria, when the Nazis had marched in, in March 1938, influenced my thinking and my actions very much. It was in a more conservative direction, or away from the violent revolutionary attitude that we had adopted in our extreme youth."

Cornelio Sommaruga, later to become the president of the International Committee of the Red Cross (ICRC) in Geneva, recalled that his family was spending the summer in Switzerland, where they had a home, when the war broke out. Unable to return to Italy, "my mother stayed with the children during two years in Lugano. I went to school there and this was important because I then created a network of friends in Switzerland . . . in the middle of all of these refugees who had come from Italy, from all kinds of families, also a lot of Jews. And my father had taken in our apartment in Rome a number of Jews because the children were no longer there and he had room. And this was very badly seen by the Nazis at the time, because he was known to protect them. But in principle, legally, they couldn't do anything to him because he had diplomatic immunity." In thinking about how the war influenced him, he said, "Certainly I had discovered a lot of things in my youth, first of all the disasters of the war. Even if I was not involved directly, I heard, I saw, I felt the problems of the war. Secondly, I had heard a lot about what diplomats were trying to do around me. Also, the old problem of these connections between refugees and their families that my mother tried to realize; the work of my mother in the Swiss Red Cross in the two years when she was in Lugano."

Hans Singer was a refugee from Hitler's Germany who worked for over two decades in a host of UN agencies and then became a distinguished scholar and pioneer of development economics. He was one of the first representatives of the "dismal science" recruited by the UN in New York in the late 1940s. He returned eventually to a career as a teacher and researcher at the University of Sussex's Institute for Development Studies (IDS). He describes himself growing up as "a member of a minority within a minority within a minority, because I was a member of the Jewish community which was a small minority in a Protestant town which was itself a minority in the Catholic Rhineland, which was itself a minority in Protestant Germany. . . . When I lived and went to school in this town, until 1929, I never had the feeling of being a suppressed minority. I had a fairly normal life, my family was very strongly assimilated. My father was a German patriot, serving in a nonfighting capacity in the Medical Corps as a doctor with the German army in the First World War. Up to 1929 I, myself, never felt any type of anti-Semitism or anything like that because I was a member of a small minority within a minority within a minority."

Johan Kaufmann died shortly after our interview in The Hague in 1999. He played an important role in early UN debates, including those about the Special UN Fund for Economic Development (SUNFED), the precursor to the World Bank's International Development Association (IDA). His Dutch diplomatic career meant many postings linked to multilateral negotiations, experiences that inspired him to write about the processes of UN decision making.[2] As a Jewish refugee he had to interrupt his university studies and flee to France when Holland was invaded. "Well, the strange thing is that in Vichy France, I wasn't arrested or anything. They permitted us to go ahead and do whatever it was we wanted to do. And there was no effort to push one in a particular direction." He worked illegally as a bookkeeper. He noted that in some ways being in Vichy France was a "liberating feeling" after Nazi-occupied Holland. Having also lived through the Great Depression caused him "to believe that something has to be done and you cannot sit back and do nothing."

Jan Pronk, a Dutchman of a later generation, once set records as the youngest member of Parliament and the minister whose commitment to development issues and frankness earned him a reputation as the *enfant terrible* in the Netherlands and internationally. "I do not remember much from the Second World War. But the last winter period, I was about four to five years old, does contain a number of events which I really was conscious of: the hunger; the Germans in the streets also chasing people; the liberation; the planes flying over The Hague, which is the city in which I was born, in the Netherlands; bringing food to the people; the liberation with Canadians in the streets; the flags being waved."

"I was born in 1940 when the Second World War had just hit Malta," recalled Michael Zammit Cutajar, but "I have no recollection of it as an ongoing event. My parents and my family lived through it, so I heard about it from them and feel that it was part of my life, which has somehow colored my view of the world and of what is right and what is wrong. I feel part of that generation. It isn't history to me; it was part of my life. I grew up to see the physical damage caused by that war to Malta and lived my youth in a time when Malta was recovering and then trying to find its own feet in a world in which it quickly lost its strategic importance." He reflected on the impact of the war on his own intellectual development that served him well in a number of jobs within the UN system and in NGOs. "What it has affected, I guess, is my sense of what is right and what is wrong. Of justice and of the need to work for justice. That has played a very important part in my choice of career. It isn't an accident, I guess, that I went to a developing country for my first job. I was interested in that. I was interested in the issue of poverty as against wealth and how to overcome imbalances, injustices in society. This didn't come from any family influence that I know of, because my family was either apolitical or center right, in today's terms. There was no socialist influence in my family, but I grew up as somebody who would instinctively vote left."

Stéphane Hessel served as a junior official in the UN Secretariat in the late 1940s and then went on to a distinguished diplomatic career in France, much of which was directly linked to UN economic negotiations. His family's background as artists fleeing Germany was part of the explanation: "Obviously the fact of being born German and then becoming a young Frenchman, and then being sent to London when I was fifteen and learning English, and becoming acquainted with Great Britain—all of this was a great preparation for someone who already did not believe in nationalism in any narrow sense. Also perhaps, part of it was the half-Jewish origin. People who come from my father's family came to Germany at a time when the Jews were very much welcomed in Germany and then when they began to be pushed out, all of this was preparation for multiculturalism." His family was "very cosmopolitan. They were firm in their German culture until Hitler came to power. They were definitely anchored in German culture. They were interested in Greek culture. My father was a translator of Homer. My family was purely German and yet they chose, in 1924, to come and settle in Paris and forget about Germany."[3]

Maurice Bertrand, another Frenchman who went on to lead the UN's Joint Inspection Unit (JIU), an internal watchdog and evaluation group, and who has written extensively on reform in the world organization,[4] recalled his childhood in prewar France: "I'm from a family of modest means, and I have a secondary school education. I entered [the equivalent of] the 6th grade in 1933. That was the first year secondary education became free. I had taken the competitive exams for scholarships, but I never benefited since as of that year everyone received free education. I studied at the lycée in Nimes. It was excellent. I had some absolutely remarkable teachers, and I still have fond memories. I observed what was going on. I was interested in political issues. I followed them closely. In my family before the war, I was surrounded by pessimists who thought that we were headed straight for war. In fact, they were right. I lived in this atmosphere of pessimism, of preparation for war, but I wasn't struck by either Edouard Daladier or Albert Sarraut. . . . No French or foreign political figure particularly impressed me except, to a certain extent, Léon Blum."

Donald "Don" Mills, later to become chairman of the Group of 77 (G-77), said of his experience in Jamaica during World War II, "You could hardly avoid [the war]. A Jamaican had given his small radio station to the government because there was a war coming, so you got some news. It was rather British, this little radio station. It was only operating a few hours a day, a lot of loyalty to the cause, of course. Jamaicans started a fund to buy warplanes for Britain, and people subscribed. Then quite a lot of Jamaicans went off to Britain, to the war, at different levels. First of all, a number of people who were in school, friends of mine. Some of them died. Many went into the air force. Then a number of young women went into the Auxiliary Territories Services. Then they were running short of labor, so they recruited a lot of young men to work as ground crew for the air force. They started recruiting people to work in British factories. So across Jamaican society, quite a number of people had members of their families who had gone off."

Alister McIntyre recalled the impact of the war on neighboring Grenada: "They began voluntary recruitment of a supplementary security force. We never had any soldiers at all. And anybody who was anybody joined up. My father was a member and all of his friends. . . . On one occasion, I remember a lot of excitement, because a submarine had been sighted. . . . I became interested in the war. Every night, I sat with my parents listening to the wireless, to the BBC, and listening to Churchill's speeches and so on. I became very much involved in the unfolding of events, and Montgomery's famous victory at El Alamein, and then the Normandy landing, and then, of course, V-E Day, as it was called and V-J Day that followed. . . . On the first occasion that wheat flour was once again imported into the island, we had bread for the first time in some years. I remember the remarkable crush on the bakeries and how my brother and I scaled the wall to get a front place in the lines."

Bernard Chidzero recalled his exposure in colonial Rhodesia: "I wouldn't say I knew of the outbreak of the war in an informed manner, such as who were the players or the antagonists and why it started, what sort of war. But we used to sing songs which, even now, remind me that we had some good knowledge that there was a war. . . . I recall that we used to sing a song which, translated into English, went like this, 'We shall suffer, we shall suffer. German women can handle guns, and move and direct their guns in a manner which was surprising to people. . . . German women shoot like men and they dance like doves.' . . . We heard about people being recruited to go overseas. . . . But we did not know exactly why the war was being fought and where exactly."

James O. C. Jonah, who would serve as UN under-secretary-general and then as minister in Sierra Leone, looked back to the end of the war, when he was eleven: "One thing stuck in my head. It is very hard to explain why. But there was a parade made by the British troops in Freetown. There were lots of sailors, a lot, because Freetown was a major port and all the major vessels of the Allies were in Freetown . . . it was a transit point. Even the American cargo flights were coming from Brazil, because we were the shortest point across the Atlantic, from Brazil to Freetown. So there was a hive of activity—prisoners of war from Burma. They were all stationed in Sierra Leone. . . . But I remember this distinctly, at the end of the war. At this parade, there were British papers which said, 'Hitler is dead. Victory is ours.' . . . So yes, I was conscious. But I was not aware of the disputes that went on between the Allies and the Axis powers."

Rubens Ricupero, a minister in his native Brazil and later the secretary-general of UNCTAD, recalled the end of the war when he was only six or seven: "I clearly remember that I followed all the advance of the Red Army into Germany. I followed all the articles about the Nuremberg trials. I remember the names of the generals of the last phase of the war. One of my oldest memories is the liberation of Paris. At the time, Brazil was very close to

France, as in the past it had always been. All the students, the pupils of the public schools, had to participate in a sort of contest making a drawing of the liberation of Paris. I remember our teacher explaining to us what that meant. That was in 1944. . . . My strong interest for international affairs dates back to that time."

Celso Furtado, another Brazilian but from the previous generation—he was a soldier prior to becoming a development economist—told us: "The distinctive thing about my memoirs[5] is that they begin with the war when I was an officer in a Brazilian infantry division that was incorporated into the 5th Division of the American Army. That experience led me to write a book of fiction and some short stories."

Javier Pérez de Cuéllar, the UN's fifth Secretary-General, recalled putting his then-fledgling language skills to work in the 1930s: "I could listen to Germany because we had a Telefunken radio. I remember having listened to the speeches by Hitler, because I used to listen to foreign stations—Spanish, English, French. Then I remember having listened to him without understanding a single word. I could recognize the word 'Hitler.' I hated him, of course, as it was normal for a young man who was fourteen or fifteen years old who used to read the newspapers. . . . I don't remember whether I was that interested in the League of Nations until Peru had a problem with Colombia and this problem went to the League of Nations. . . . The Spanish Civil War was from 1936 to 1939. That I remember very well because I was at a Catholic school where the teachers were all Spanish priests. And that's why I followed the war more or less. As you can imagine, they were all against the republican regime. . . . And then in 1939, the Second World War broke out, and my country was rooting for the Allies. Something important happened for me in 1944 before the end of the war. I came to Paris when France was still occupied in the north, more or less on the border with Belgium."

Ignacy Sachs would have a long and distinguished career as a development economist whose work intersected with the United Nations on numerous occasions, beginning with preparations for the 1972 Stockholm Conference on Environment and Development. He worked and studied in Poland, France, Brazil, and India before becoming a naturalized French citizen in 1968, a tumultuous year when he quit Poland for Paris. He worked a lot in and on Brazil, which he discovered early in life: "I tend more and more to think that I discovered Brazil in the mirror of the Poland that I knew as a child. That was quite a shock, quite a shock in several respects. Firstly, the visual beauty. Entering the Bay of Guanabara by boat after a year of war was really something. Secondly, surprise at the extent of modernity in a city like Rio compared with the only other large city that I really knew, which was Warsaw. And then everything that follows from it: racial mixing, the tropics, et cetera. I continue to think today at the end of the road, or at least a good deal further along, that comparison is an essential element in the epistemology of development and that such comparison is meaningful because of the reflection that it creates. So from this point of view, the passage from Poland across France and the French collapse and through other not very happy episodes obviously had an enormous effect on my life."

Guido de Marco was a professor turned politician who, beginning in 1999, served a term as president of Malta, a small country that has played an unusually large role in UN negotiations, especially between Europe and the Muslim world but also with respect to the Law of the Sea: "The events leading up to the Second World War were very important in my childhood formation. I followed the events of the war of Abyssinia and those of the Civil War in Spain. . . . I remember being with my maternal grandfather and he met a friend of his . . . and this gentleman whom he met told him '*Hanno sfrondato la linea Maginot*' [the Maginot Line has been pierced].[6] And I saw that my grandfather's face went white. . . . Malta formed part of Great Britain as a colonial possession, and therefore, this would affect us very directly. . . . My parent's house in Valletta was severely damaged. Our house was close to the Law Courts; we used to go to the shelter under the Law Court Building. The building was almost completely demolished as a result of a cluster of mines exploding. This was early 1941. The Luftwaffe staged one of its many heavy air raids. Only one of the exits remained available. Were it not for this we would have been buried alive. When we left the shelter we went home [and] my father opened the door only to discover that the house was from the inside almost complete rubble. . . . As a young man, then, I started following the United Nations and what it really meant for us all." He also recalled following the Nuremberg trials and found that "the absence of an international criminal court can be substituted by *ad hoc* tribunals with a considerable credibility deficit. In the Nuremberg trials the victors were trying the vanquished. War crimes may be committed not only by the vanquished; they may be committed also by the victors. So these issues created in me a more vivid interest in international law and international relations."

Faith and Family Matters

Some of our voices began their lives with the advantages of a wealthy or solid middle-class background, but others struggled with the challenges of poverty. The absence or presence of silver spoons ultimately seemed less important than family values and religious ethics in the decisions our interviewees made to devote a career to the struggle for social change. This generalization applies across geographic origins—whether from the Global South (Africa, Asia, the Middle East, and Latin America) or the industrialized North.

James Jonah's life revolved around politics—as a student, as a career UN official who attained the rank of under-secretary-general, and as minister in his own war-troubled country of Sierra Leone in the 1990s. However, he confided that "I wanted to be a priest. So I went into classics. My first degree was in the classics, and I enormously enjoyed it. I think I got a tinge of interest in state politics, or city politics, through the Latin scholars like Levy and Cicero. . . . I read about wars and politics but it didn't make an impact on me. I still wanted to go into the ministry."

However, 1956 was a crucial year for him and for the United Nations: "That was when things turned around, during the Suez Crisis, which came to me like a bolt from the blue. My father was always interested in international politics. He would always be discussing with his friends. They would come to the house for exchange of views on global developments. We had what was then a radio system in Sierra Leone; not everybody could have it in the house. It is not like today's radio, but was piped in from a central place. . . . By means of that, you had all the BBC programs throughout the world. My father was an avid listener and reader. So I listened to most of the developments regarding Suez. But what struck me most about the Suez Crisis was that as I was listening, I heard Anthony Eden use a phrase which I will never forget: 'An act of plunder will never be allowed to succeed.' Mainly because of my religious leaning, I thought, 'What does he mean—a head of state, Nasser? What could he have stolen?' . . . I can say, frankly, from that day, I have never stopped my daily obsession with international politics."

He recalled that after listening to the voice of Dag Hammarskjöld on the wireless, he "wanted to learn more about him. Luckily for me, there was the British Council. . . . So I started going there to find things, developments in Europe. Right there, in the library, the English lady who was the chief librarian came to me and observed that I was a frequent visitor. I told her of my interests. She brought me a book of Trollope. Of course, I was coming to the library mainly for newspapers and books on politics. . . . So gradually I said, 'Okay, let me see. Politics is where I want to be.' So I had to change my focus from the ministry. Then a friend of mine, Dr. Edward Blyden, suggested, 'If you want to change, then you will eventually have to study political science.' It was he who then recommended for me to come to the United States."

Shridath "Sonny" Ramphal had many interactions with the UN as secretary-general of the Commonwealth for fifteen years from the mid-1980s and as a member of numerous international commissions and expert groups. He emphasized his Indian roots because his great-grandmother immigrated to Guyana in the 1870s with a young son who became his grandfather: "All that came out of the indentured labor system, which was a cousin to slavery. My grandfather, though basically a farmer, rose through the lay side of the Canadian Presbyterian Church to a role in the church, where he became what they called in those days a 'catechist,' which was a lay preacher. And my father was then rising in the Canadian Presbyterian mission schools to the status of a teacher, and then himself became a pioneer in secondary education in Guyana. So I grew up as the grandson of a farmer and preacher and the son of a quite serious schoolmaster."

He attended his father's school in Georgetown, but he recalled more than his classroom: "The great movement of struggle on the West Indian plantations and of the evangelical movement in Britain that fought the sugar planter at Westminster. The combination of those forces led to the ending of slavery but led also to the evolution of indenture, and Indian indenture in particular, in which lies my own roots. So my own history is much involved with this process of imperial domination through slavery and indenture, and of course through sugar, which was the lure of it all. . . . Women were outside the mainstream of education. One of my father's missions in life was to bring on the education of girls in Guyana. . . . My mother kept the family together and did a very essential job in that respect. She helped to make the role as a schoolmaster possible in economic terms by running a dormitory for out-of-town boys, which had the dual effect of bringing in some money for the family and also of facilitating the education of boys from the country, many of whom went on to do great things in education and the professions in Guyana."

His father stopped being a schoolmaster to pursue politics and he became the first Guyanese commissioner of labour. Ramphal recalled his own awareness of problems on the sugar estates: "Political parties didn't exist, but trade unions came into being. And the trade unions, in their turn, produced the political parties. My father, involved in industrial relations, was at the heart of those trade union developments."

Sartaj Aziz became an assistant director-general of the Food and Agricultural Organization (FAO) and deputy director of IFAD and then returned to his native Pakistan as minister of finance and later of foreign affairs. As for many of our interlocutors, his family's religion was influential. His grandfather was a civil servant but "he resigned after twelve years to concentrate on the study of religion and to visit holy places. He felt that his purpose in life should be to collect as much knowledge as he could and leave it for posterity. So after fifteen years, in 1914 he published a book called *Flay-ul-Qalb*, or *Treatment of the Heart*. He said it is not a religious book but a moral and spiritual treatise which will help everyone to discover his inner self and to overcome things that damage one's spirit—greed, selfishness, anger, bitterness, and above all ignorance. My father used to read to me passages from this book when I was very young. Later, he also used to read to me passages from an Indian mystic called Swami Ram Tirath."

"So this early education added a spiritual dimension to my being which guided me throughout and helped to create what I would call faith," Aziz continued. "I am not talking about faith in a narrow, religious sense only, but faith in whatever you are doing. Human beings have limits to their capacity. No matter how powerful or strong, they have their limits. Like a child needs the love of the mother to clean him and feed him and put him to sleep, we all need some kind of a lap at the end. And if you have faith, then in the end you fall back on it the moment you reach your limits. So that way you get a motivation which is superior, which is not material. . . . Because of this early disposition toward nonmaterial satisfaction, I developed what I would call a capacity for selfless work, which means not wondering how it would help me or what it would do for me."

Mostafa Tolba, the second head of the UN Environment Programme (1976–1992), recalled his childhood as the son of a teacher in Zifta in Upper Egypt: "I do not know if it was different from other villages at that time. But when I was five or six years old, when I started noticing things, I remember that the village was something like 6,000 or 7,000 people. Now it is over 35,000. These 6,000 people or so, out of them something like 6 percent or 7 percent were Christians Copts and the rest were Muslims. Between all the Muslims there were intermarriages. So everybody in the village was either my uncle, my aunt, my nephew, my niece, whatever it is. Even if the relation goes back to the grandfather number six or seven, all of them consider one another first uncle, first cousin and so on. That sort of knitted relation between the family members left a very big impact on my way of life."

Tolba remembered one defining characteristic: "I am the fifth child of my father, the first four died. I am the only one left and in spite of that I had not been a spoiled child. Both father and mother were kind but were extremely firm because they were coming from village culture and traditions and they wanted a strong man coming in the family." Having become the rent collector for the family's holdings, he recalled: "My father, in spite of the fact that he is a graduate of the theological university, he has never been involved in religious groups or Muslim brotherhoods or anything of that sort. He was himself a very respected person in the family, in the village, and they wanted his advice on religious matters when he went home during the summer holiday but he was not part of any political thinking." Tolba left Egypt for the Imperial College in

London and a Ph.D. He looked back at the Arab student cohort after World War II: "Collectively, we were sitting together, addressing the issue of where the Arab world would sit after the 1945 war and how far our issues and situations were going to be reflected in the new structure that is being designed."

Jack I. Stone's career has been spent analyzing development—moving from the Marshall Plan and the Organisation for Economic Co-operation and Development (OECD) to the director of research in UNCTAD. His parents were both immigrants from Lithuania but actually met in Minneapolis. "My interest in international affairs really developed as part of my education. . . . [I was] stimulated to an intellectual career of some sort by the whole environment of Jewish second-generation immigrants, many of whose parents put an extremely high emphasis on academic excellence. The dramatic events in the 1930s in Europe were a constant reminder of the importance of international affairs. My parents placed academic achievement as the highest aspiration for their children—and in my father's case, well ahead of the pursuit of wealth, or sports, or social prominence. My father, an intermittently unsuccessful merchant in the 1920s, was religiously very devoted and pursued Talmudic studies throughout his life in preference to hustling for worldly success. . . . My mother was a strong driving force for academic effort by her children and was very proud of our achievements. She herself came from a line tracing back to some famous rabbinical scholars in seventeenth- and eighteenth-century Lithuania. My older brother, Walter, got a Ph.D. in English at Harvard and went on to teach at Vassar and was beginning to enjoy considerable success as a short story writer, essayist, and poet, when he met an untimely death at forty-two. He was a major influence, inspiration, and stimulus on my own intellectual development."

Stone examined his first memories of politics: "In 1932, at the age of twelve, I supported Herbert Hoover and believed those two-page graphic ads which said, 'Don't change horses in the middle of the stream.' My parents, of course, were rabid supporters of Franklin D. Roosevelt. I quickly became an ardent Democrat. In senior high school I founded the Forum, a group which regularly discussed questions of economic and social policy and international relations. . . . I looked to the New Deal solutions to most economic problems."

Nafis Sadik, a Pakistani physician, headed the United Nations Population Fund (UNFPA) from 1987 to 2000. Her family came from Jaunpur, India— the United Provinces at that time, now Uttar Pradesh, about forty miles from Benares or Varanasi. Her beloved grandfather moved there from the village and "was obviously someone who made something of his life in a professional way. He was a lawyer . . . and was very keen on education and insisted that all his sons be well educated. Story has it that my father was so brilliant that his age was reduced [*sic*; increased] by a couple of years to enable him to matriculate. . . . It took him a long time to get his right age recorded, because generally parents registered their children's ages lower than they actually were, not higher. . . . At that time, bright people joined the civil service. It was called the ICS at that time—the British civil service, but the Indian version of it. My father didn't get into the civil service, again because my grandmother says because she prayed so hard that he wouldn't because if he did that would mean that he would have to go away to England for a year or two."

Sadik, who would become an outspoken proponent of women's rights, looked back: "So, contrary to the norm in Asia at that time, for me personally I was a very much wanted child. . . . My grandfather used to wait for me to come back from school whenever he was visiting us in Calcutta and wait on the porch with his arms out and I would run into them. . . . I grew up as a child very much of the view that boys and girls were not different. . . . My father was a great, great believer in equality of opportunity for his children. Indeed, he started that with my mother."

Clearly her father's devotion to educational opportunity and equality went beyond the usual: "My father would say, 'If any girl comes to this house during the school year, she is going to school with my daughters.' And you know, my mother had some young cousins who were our age—a few years older. I remember this aunt of mine was enrolled in school with me for three months. The nuns used to go along with it—'Well, you know, father is coming to enroll another girl.' He would just put them into school. He said, 'Everyone has to be educated. . . . Without education no country can prosper, and no individual can prosper. . . . It's an investment in people.'" Sadik recalled the most important room in her house: "We had all these family members always visiting, so . . . my brothers and sister and myself, we never had our room. We slept like in a dorm, and we used to complain like anything. . . . My father said the only room that can never be given to anybody was the children's room, the library. The library, he said belonged to the children."

The value accorded education did not mean that playing parents against each other was not a sport: "I remember when we were a bit older, eighteen or nineteen, we wanted to go to parties and my mother would say no. We would sulk and try to ask our father to intercede. . . . He said, 'Come here and we'll all sit down. Let's have a cup of tea. Why all these glum faces? Why is everyone angry?' I said, 'I am upset because I want to go and all my friends are going.' He said, 'But that's not the way to get your way. You have to negotiate. You must convince us why you must be allowed. Convince your mother. Convince me. Once you convince us, and we are convinced—but if you can't win the argument, then that's that.'"

Sadik's renowned negotiating skills in international forums were thus honed at an early age, as was her independent spirit. She recalled a meeting in Calcutta at which Mohammed Ali Jinnah came to speak: "It became evening prayer time, and so everyone said they had to go and say their prayers. But Mr. Jinnah said, 'Well, let everyone go to say their prayers. I will sit here and smoke a cigarette.' I thought that was so cool. . . . My mother said, 'You shouldn't go around saying that.' I said, 'But look at him. He doesn't care what people think about him. He is just honest and straightforward.'"

Alister McIntyre, who would become vice-chancellor of the University of the West Indies after his UNCTAD career, reminded us of the very different expectations for boys and girls: "I grew up in a fairly sheltered middle-class family where one was expected to do all of the right things—go to school through secondary school. If you were a boy, you were expected to get to a university. Girls had a different track. In fact, my father quite opposed the idea of my eldest sister going to university, which she has greatly regretted."

Devaki Jain, a prominent feminist development economist and founder of Development Alternatives with Women for a New Era, better known by its acronym of DAWN, has participated in numerous UN conferences, expert groups, and gatherings. She looked back and explained why she moved beyond the typical pattern for Indian girls: "My father was a civil servant in a princely state in India, Mysore, which was different from a British province. . . . The princely states were more autonomous during the colonial times. They had their own army and their own administrative service. They were not as colonized in the sense that there were no white officials running the administration, as they were doing in some of the other states of India, called presidencies. Therefore, my father was a young civil servant under the Maharaja. . . . My mother and father were married when my mother was eleven, so she had not studied beyond the second primary or elementary class. So when she was confronted with the British ladies who came with what was called the resident, who was the British representative in a princely state, she felt terribly humiliated because she could not speak the language and she looked very 'native.' So in some sense, I think it drove her to send all her daughters to English schools so that they wouldn't suffer the humiliation that she did because she couldn't speak English. And I know she fought a great deal with my father, who was very firm about nationalistic, indigenous aspects of our education, saying, 'Don't send them to Christian schools. It's bad for them.' But she said, 'No, the Christian schools are the only ones who teach in English.'"

While Jain and her sisters attended English-speaking schools, her four brothers went to schools in Kannada, where the local language was used for instruction. "So forever my brothers have always had the handicap that they were not so smart in English as the girls were. I think this was my mother's way of overcoming the humiliation of what was considered the British presence." Reflecting on her own penchant for rebellion, she recalled "the first time I protested when I was about twelve or thirteen. There were only two of us Hindus in a majority class of Christians, and they asked us to sing songs celebrating the British Empire and the English language and the flag. We both said we wouldn't sing, and therefore we were both turned out of class."

Her father eventually became the prime minister of Gwalior. "So we used to see Nehru having dinner with my father. . . . So politics of that kind was very much part of the home. We could never be liberated from it because my father would be on the phone to Nehru and other leaders at midnight. Gandhi's assassination—he had sort of feared it because the assassin actually came from Gwalior, from the Hindu Mahasabha, which was the extreme Hindu fundamentalist movement at that time—was another traumatic event. My father had been with Gandhi the previous evening and was totally shocked and bereft when he heard the news."

I. G. Patel recalled his own Indian upbringing en route to the UN and a career as a prominent development economist: "As far as my influences are concerned, like in everybody else's case, my parents, a few teachers, and I think this city itself had a certain culture of education. It was an Indian state, not a part of British India. But the ruler in Baroda at that time was a very enlightened person, and he had, long before this became fashionable or popular, had a primary school in all his villages. He had a library in all of his villages. Even in the city of Baroda, we had a children's library and a major general library. You also knew that there were scholarships to take you to England."

Another compatriot and Indian developmentalist, Surendra Patel, was born in southern Gujarat, the eldest of five children. He described his parents: "My mother, Divali Ben, was the very first girl to be educated in the district. Her father was very respected in the area. . . . He was the one to insist on my mother's education, even if in the early part of twentieth-century India, girls' education was very rare, almost unheard of, especially amongst common people. She made a career as a teacher until she became a school inspectress and received several awards. . . . My father, Jivarajbhai, was also an exceptional man. He was a teacher as well but soon decided to change his profession and became a farmer. He established a modern farm experimenting with the scientific growth of a particular fruit in India, which is known as bher (commonly called the poor man's apple). In his own right, my father gained recognition and received the prestigious President of India's Award for his contribution to scientific farming."

The struggle for independence was very much a family affair: "My father became very involved in the politics of decolonization. My mother not only supported him but she was also very active. For instance, my father organized the very first students' and teachers' strike against the British. As a punishment, my parents and their colleagues were posted far away from their hometowns."

Patel himself took a similar path, being inspired, like many on the subcontinent, by Mohatmas Gandhi: "Gandhiji had organized the Salt March in 1930 and its impact had been so strong that in less than five years the whole atmosphere had changed in India. . . . All over the country we would hear the slogans of 'long live the country,' 'long live the motherland,' and so on. I did not really understand the meaning of these slogans, but even then I joined in the general mobilization. . . . For one month the Congress Convention was held in Gujarat in 1937. . . . In his struggle for freedom, Gandhiji powerfully upheld the values of equality. Gandhiji refused to have any bodyguards or any fancy type of surrounding. He had asked the organizers to form three groups of young boys from twelve to fourteen years old. Each group would guard Gandhiji's tent for three to four hours, in turn. At night, he would not have anyone there. . . . I was privileged to be one of those selected for the task of guarding Gandhiji's tent. . . . Every day coming in or coming out of his tent, Gandhiji would address each of us personally, asking a few questions. . . . He would take deep interest in us in the most simple and touching manner. . . . Soon after I turned fourteen years old, two of our great national leaders, Mrudula Ben and Prabu Das, took me and my sister, Niru Ben, with them to tour Gujarat. On the 26th of January 1937, for the first time, I addressed a large crowd of people in our area. My sister had a beautiful voice. She was singing nationalist songs. From then on, we became very involved in the national movement for independence. . . . In 1942, Gandhiji had launched the 'Quit India Movement' and was jailed. In protest, the students of Ahmedabad and most of Gujarat forcefully got the schools and universities closed for a whole year. I had been nominated as an executive member of the All India Students Federation. For one year, with other boys of my age, we traveled through the whole country. We were touring cities and villages, talking to the people, mobilizing them and organizing the local units. We would raise the national flag everywhere we could."

Under the circumstances, this was heroic, and soon thereafter Patel and some friends took a more dramatic step: "We wanted to blow a bridge at a place called Nilka Nadi. We had no experience whatsoever in handling explosives so we blew up the bridge but very little damage was caused. Nonetheless as freedom fighters, we felt very proud. I was arrested along with my sister. . . .

The police reassured my family that I would be released very soon. That is indeed what happened, but I was not deterred from carrying on the struggle." Eventually he had to go underground because a price was put on his head. With a scholarship in hand, Patel was taken by his mother to Calcutta where he took a steamer to Philadelphia.

Lourdes Arizpe's lifelong interest in education and culture blossomed in universities and as assistant director-general for culture of UNESCO, where she was initially a member of the World Commission on Culture and Development, chaired by former UN Secretary-General Javier Pérez de Cuéllar after his retirement. After joining the UNESCO secretariat she launched the *World Culture Report.*[7] She recalled her own multicultural heritage—a Mexican father who met her Swiss mother, who spoke five languages, through his international business. She looked back to growing up in Buenos Aires, then Latin America's cultural capital: "We had Argentinean magazines arriving at the house, a household which was half-Swiss, half-Mexican in food, discipline and decoration and books of world literature in English. My mother spoke several languages with her parents who lived with us. . . . My father spoke English fluently, and took us to the United States on visits. . . . And there were women and men who worked at our house as domestics, or as chauffeurs. I had a very close relationship to some of the women employees, one of whom happened to be a Nahuatl-speaking Indian from San Martín Texmelucan. She used to tell me stories without end, which fascinated and terrorized me, stories of spirits and the Devil, of trees that spoke and animals that flew. She interspersed words in Nahuatl. I loved to listen to the cadence of the way she told stories, to the sounds of the Nahuatl language but more especially a universe grew inside me, vast and dark, full of mysterious powers and beings. . . . I attended an American primary school, and I was put in the class with American children. So most of what I had read as a child and as an adolescent were the typical books about Merlin and the Knights of the Round Table, about mysteries solved by Nancy Drew and the Hardy Brothers. At the same time, the whole social environment was Mexican with this great emphasis on family relationships, on ritual kinship, on the life in the *barrio,* and on knowing and visiting rural communities."

Arizpe was a student radical at the Colegio de México when its president was Victor Urquidi, whose first international experiences were at the Bretton Woods Conference in 1944. His father was in the Mexican foreign service and his grandfather was a political figure in Mexico. He was born in Paris and then moved to London with his family. "I learned English before Spanish," he said, "and when I returned to Mexico at the age of three, I had to learn Spanish quickly, and everybody made fun of me." His mother was a trained nurse who was "born in Melbourne, Australia, and was brought up by her British parents in Managua."

He recalled a time that his family was summering in Spain just as the civil war broke out in 1936. They all got out except for his mother, who missed the last train out of Madrid. "She stayed behind just that fateful day, and the next day there were no more trains. The uprising of Franco had started. . . . She had already given up, for the duration of the summer, the apartment that we rented in Madrid, so she stayed temporarily at the embassy residence. . . . She was a registered nurse from Mount Sinai and thought, 'I am a nurse, I have a duty to go and help.'" He recounted how she went to the International Committee of the Red Cross to help and they turned her away. "They just thought that she was a stuffy diplomat's wife who wanted to help there but did not know anything. So she did something very risky. She went to the International Red Aid, the Socorro Rojo Internacional. This was the Comintern's Red Cross."

Enrique Iglesias also spoke of the influence of his mother: "In the Spanish family of the time, as is probably the case in many other places, the woman is at the center of everything. Women are real slaves to family life. In our case she had to look after the house, work in the store, care for her children. And all of this fundamentally instilled in us, as I say, a strong work ethic, and no doubt a religious ethic. She gave great support to our personal growth, both my brother's and my own. I had a very intense relationship with my mother, more so than with my father. She was a very important figure in my life."

The practical orientation of the family meant that, in addition to basic education, Iglesias sought money-making skills, including shorthand and especially languages. "I learned French in school. . . . It was a primary school where the priests—they weren't actually priests, but 'brothers'—spoke French and taught French and English. I learned French very early on. Our life was very limited. It was a life, as I used to say, that was very frugal, yet very rich in human contact. I have a number of memories from back then. First, the social integration of the Uruguayan. The way the immigrant became quickly integrated into social life. The grocer was a very important person in his neighborhood, someone who lived closely with others. He knew their problems, their hopes and fears."

Like many immigrants everywhere, Iglesias was passionate about his new country: "I would say those were challenging times in the history of Uruguay, in which I really became a Uruguayan. I arrived at age three and came to love the country from a young age. . . . My father was a man who would tell us, every morning, to kiss the land that had adopted us. Because there was a great difference in what life was like between one country and the other, between what Spain was back then, the impoverished Spain, the depressed Spain, and a country that was young, that had some problems but also a lot of promise. My father conveyed to us an affection we would learn to feel for our country."

Margaret Joan Anstee, who eventually would be knighted by Queen Elizabeth for her service to the United Nations, described her simple childhood, which was quite removed from the corridors where she rose through the ranks to walk as the first woman to attain the UN's second-highest position at the time, under-secretary-general: "Well, I was a country child. I was born in what was then a small village in rural Essex, called Writtle, into a rural, working-class family. . . . My mother went to an elementary village school . . . but she had to leave school at the age of twelve to look after her father. When he died, she was put into domestic service. She earned ten pounds a year.[8] . . . My mother told me, when she was old, that she hadn't wanted to have any children. She had had to sacrifice so much to the younger children in her family. The older ones had to earn money. And when my parents married, they had to take on the youngest sister of my mother. My mother launched two women (my aunt and myself) on their own careers, something that circumstances hadn't allowed her to have herself, though she was equally able. . . . My parents were very sold on education, which had been denied to them. . . . But they were determined that they were only going to have one child because they were both determined that the child should be educated."

Anstee reflected on how her upbringing affected her later life: "Both sides of the family were country people. I think that made it very easy for me to live in developing countries. I never really liked living in big cities." She remembered "the importance of education and social justice because there was a terrible amount of discrimination, especially regarding women's rights. I have to say, I was very much a tomboy and I do remember when I was a child, I thought it would be much nicer to be a boy than a girl. I got over that and decided that I would, after all, accept the inevitable and try to make the most of being a woman. My mother had a wonderful phrase, which is the title of my autobiography, which was *Never Say Your Mother Had a Jibber*.[9] No one ever knows what this means, but a jibber is a horse that jibs at a fence, that is, refuses to jump over it. So, she used to say, take your fences and I spent the rest of my life jumping them headlong."

Don Mills, a career diplomat who played major roles in North-South negotiations until retirement, was born in a small town in central Jamaica to a father who was in the police force and a mother who was a teacher. "As I say, my father died when I was fourteen, so my mother had to look after the three children of the family on a schoolteacher's salary. Talk about financial experts! Especially women, you know, who performed miracles, bringing up their families on very limited means. . . . One of the remarkable things about my life is that my mother was a teacher and my father had a brother who was also a teacher. . . . And really, I count at least ten persons who have been teachers in my family."

Jan Pronk described his family as "members of the Dutch Reformed Church. . . . It was the regular, bigger Protestant church in the Netherlands. My father was a schoolteacher, my mother was a schoolteacher as well. As a matter of fact, the whole family does consist of schoolteachers—my brother and sister. I am the only exception. From my father's family—his father, for instance—I have a relation with the, well, fisheries industry, because I was born in The Hague, but in particular, in Scheveningen, which is a part of The Hague, a seaside resort at present. But it mainly was known as a fishing harbor. And my grandfather was a skipper. My grandmother never had regular Dutch clothes, she was always wearing a traditional costume. My mother has a background, her family in Rotterdam, and that was a background of civil servants."

Adebayo Adedeji, who would lead the Economic Commission for Africa for over a decade and a half (1975–1991) during which he challenged the orthodoxy of the World Bank's structural adjustment programs (SAPs), recalled the strict discipline of his upbringing: "Not only was I the only child, my mother was the only child. Therefore, for my grandmother, I was like a second child, as it were. She was very loving and at the same time very stern. She didn't want anything of me other than shining scholastic work. So even as a little kid, I would go to school from 8:00 to 2:00 and then after go for special coaching sessions. I would eat my lunch in the place for coaching. The result was that I had only four years of primary education before I went to secondary school. . . . I developed the habit of spending more time reading as a kind of sport. It was hard work. But in terms of the outside work, she always insisted that it was a very competitive and unfair world. Therefore, one had to be the best. . . . At the end of the war in 1945, already in secondary school, we were exposed to postwar development, particularly to the nascent nationalist struggle for independence for Nigeria. That coincided with a really very exciting period in the history of the country, when the founders of new Nigeria, like Dr. Nnamdi Azikiwe and Chief Obafemi Awolowo, were demanding and agitating for 'self-government now.' We used to subscribe, with our little pocket money, to all the newspapers which were, of course, banned by the principal of our school, who thought that the newspapers were too nationalistic and politically left wing. But we would buy the newspapers and read them, nevertheless."

In 1974, Francis Blanchard began the first of three five-year terms as the director-general of the International Labour Organization. He recalled the differences between the two sides of his family. "My grandmother, small, always dressed in black, her hair covered by a little bonnet, spoke the dialect of the Pyrenees. She expressed herself with difficulty in French. She had been widowed relatively young. Having limited means, she lived very simply. She had never visited the capital." Taking a risk, she went to New York and became an au pair for a rich family. Returning to France, she met her husband on the eve of World War I: "This contrast between the poor Ariège and the wealthy Bourgogne always struck me. . . . The large tribe that I belonged to had a humble, even poor and thus reserved branch and a well-off branch that had made its wealth in commerce through the entrepreneurial spirit of my great uncle, brother of my grandmother, a legendary figure in the family. Among other things, he had been in the war in Mexico [the French-Mexican war of the 1860s]. My paternal grandfather was a baker, as was the father of Albert Thomas, first director of the ILO from 1919–1932, the year of his death. I became his sixth successor in 1974."

The family of Fernando Henrique Cardoso, a Brazilian who stepped down as president of his country in 2003, had a military background, an irony in view of his subsequent exile after the 1964 military coup. He defined his early life: "At the time of my father and the time of my grandfather, the military played a very strong role in Brazilian politics. My great-grandfather was close to those who created the Brazilian republic, and my grandfather was in favor of the abolishment of slavery and in favor of the republic and so on and so forth. My grandfather, at the end of his life, was a field marshal, at the top of his career. But at the time, the military were involved in politics, and . . . they were authoritarians . . . but trying to solve poor people's problems. . . . Also, they had some intellectual aspirations. My father wrote articles for newspapers and was a man who read literature, French literature, and was highly influenced by the thinkers of the beginning of the century, and even of the nineteenth century—evolutionism, and positivism, of course. So this is my background. To me, political life and intellectual life were not something outside of my life experience."

Javier Pérez de Cuéllar was born in Lima in January 1920 to a family of Spanish and Italian stock. He recalled his early interest in foreign countries and languages that would serve him well in Peruvian and UN diplomatic circles: "I was the only one in the family interested in foreign news. I always liked stamps. Stamps are really very important if you want to learn about geography and about foreign countries. I still have many from different countries, and of course from the United Nations. I like coins and medals and I still treasure them. I think that it was for me a kind of introduction to this idea of 'abroad.'" He continued about his language studies: "I started learning English with a Polish teacher, which was not ideal for learning good English.

Later on, because I was the only child, I was living with my cousins and one of them had a French teacher. She was not very interested, but I myself, was eager to learn when I was thirteen or fourteen. . . . Everything foreign was attractive to me . . . I think that my family was rather foreign-minded, in a way—not very local. Even the food in my house was not exactly Peruvian cuisine."

The UN's fifth Secretary-General remembered a subsequent payoff from his hobby of stamp collecting. Pérez de Cuéllar told us about the scene when he was received by Emperor Hirohito at his summer residence: "The man in charge of protocol told me, 'Please do not speak to his majesty about politics.'" He struggled to think of something with which to make conversation with the Emperor. Finally, "I told him . . . 'Ever since I was a child I knew about Japan from stamps.' And he was very interested in my hobby."

His successor in the UN's highest post was Boutros Boutros-Ghali, secretary-general from 1992 to 1996. He pointed proudly to his background as part of the Coptic land-owning elite in Egypt: "I belong to the Egyptian upper bourgeoisie, and my family has always been in public service. My great-great-grandfather took care of the finances of Mehemet Ali. My great grandfather was the one who managed the fortune of the brother of the khédive, or king of Egypt, who at that time owned a good part of the territory of Egypt. My grandfather was the prime minister of Egypt and several of my uncles were ministers. The king's first minister of foreign affairs was my paternal uncle, Wassaf Boutros-Ghali." This background led him to think about a career in politics: "When I was a child and someone asked me, as people often do of children, 'What do you want to become?' I responded, 'A politician.' Then they always asked, 'Do you know what it means to be a politician?' I answered, 'yes,' rather vaguely. I didn't know what it meant, but I added, 'Like my uncles, like my grandfather.' When I was eighteen in 1940, I was involved in the campaign of my cousin who wanted to be elected deputy from the district of El-Fagalah. . . . At that age, everything was pushing me toward politics, and I had political ambitions."

Dharam Ghai reflected on his childhood as a link to his distinguished career as a development specialist inside and outside of the world organization, retiring as the head of the UN Research Institute on Social Development (UNRISD). He is widely recognized as one of the originators of the basic needs strategy, which gives priority in development to meeting the requirements of all of a country's population for adequate food, basic education, ordinary health care, and other essentials. "I was born in Kenya. My parents migrated from India. So Africa has had a lot of influence on my thinking and my work plans. At the same time, I was a member of a minority group and I think, in various ways, that has affected my outlook on life and also my work plans. I grew up in a colony. . . . It affected me in several ways. First of all, it is pertinent to recall that Kenya at that time was a 'semi-apartheid' society. It wasn't, of course, like South Africa. There was not the kind of oppression and apartheid legislation as there was in South Africa. But at the same time, there was compartmentalization of different races in terms of residence, schools, hospitals, community facilities, clubs, and so on. So you really moved in your own community for the most part. There was little interaction and communication between different racial groups. . . . And the second important influence was that . . . I was a member of a minority—the Asian community. And, while the community became quite prosperous over a period of time, for the most part it started off relatively poor."

Ghai continued: "Therefore, in that sense, like minorities everywhere, one lived under various kinds of discriminatory regimes. Maybe it affects other people differently, but the way it affected me is that it reinforced my belief and commitment to equality, to the rights of people as individuals—of course, as communities as well. . . . Because the Africans were discriminated against in a much more significant way than the Asian community throughout the colonial period, I came to believe in affirmative policies. I felt that it was appropriate that those who had been deprived and kept down through various kinds of discriminatory policies should be given special opportunities to move up. . . . So I fully supported Kenyanization, and Africanization, throughout East African countries." Ghai's family was perplexed. "My father used to tell me, 'Now, look, you can't on the one hand condemn discrimination and on the other hand favor new kinds of discrimination. You are employing double standards.' I had to explain, 'No, there is a difference. There are some communities that were left behind, that were systematically discriminated against. It is only right and proper that they should get some preferential treatment so that we have more balanced representation of different racial groups in the economy, politics, and societies in our region.'"

Many of our voices came from the South Asia of Ghai's grandparents. For example, Ponna Wignaraja went on to become secretary-general of an international NGO, the Society for International Development, which was an arena for many critical debates about economic and social development. He came "from an elite Western-oriented Sri Lankan background, but with a mother who had her roots deeply in the village, its value and culture, I instinctively felt the contradictions between the values that came from the urban industrial consumer society and those of traditional rural life." He recalled that during vacations he was always sent back to live in his mother's village 250 miles away from Colombo and spent time "in a simple cottage made of local materials and a thatched roof. The floor was mud. . . . Looking back, one may be romanticizing this, but this contact with village life was one of the major influences in my later perspectives on development and life itself."

Like so many of our interviewees, Wignaraja pointed to the example of his mother, who "at seventeen was the first girl from the village to pass the Senior Cambridge examination and quite attractive. When the time came for my father, who was a medical doctor, to marry, my grandfather, who also had migrated from the village, went back to the village to find him a bride. My grandfather didn't want my father to go to England without being married. . . . My father came from a banking family and that was where the wealth came from, because my grandfather was the local link of the Hong Kong and Shanghai Bank at that early colonial period. . . . Marriage as such was not his immediate priority, but my grandfather was rather insistent. At that time, a number of young people from elite Sri Lankan families had gone to England. The only social life they had—and I'm thinking of the 1920s—was with the landlady's daughters or with the barmaids. Several had actually married them and brought them back. My grandfather was not going to allow this. Maybe it was the old man's arrogance and his own values. He literally dragged my father back to the village. My mother was a real beauty. My father looked at my mother, fell in love with her, and married her."

Values were a dominant theme in the conversation with Wignaraja: "The Hindu values and way of life were very important in giving her that inner confidence and adaptability. First, Hinduism is a holistic philosophy. It is pantheistic. It has no rigid dogma. It incorporates a vast knowledge system."

As he was transferring from high school to the University of Ceylon, Wignaraja remembered the ferment in neighboring India and its impact on what would become Sri Lanka: "The independence movement in India was building momentum, and we were focusing on Gandhi and the nonviolent movement. We were focusing on what would happen in Sri Lanka. How would decolonization take place? Don't forget that at the time, Sri Lanka had a limited form of democracy. We got adult franchise in 1933. . . . Of course, there were also the Marxist influences then. I personally, being a Hindu, and in that sense being more holistic, did not become a Marxist, per se, though many of my friends naturally thought that this was the new way to move after independence. Sri Lanka was a multiethnic and multireligious country. As a member of the minority community, we were focused on the issue of fundamental human rights. . . . The Gandhian influences were beginning to penetrate our thinking. What he had done in South Africa, through nonviolence, for example, influenced the Indian independence movement. Civil society mobilized around the values implicit in the nonviolent struggle against colonial rule. Of course, Gandhi also spoke of greater political self-reliance. . . . To us the British handed over independence on a platter."

Gamani Corea held senior banking and finance positions in Sri Lanka before heading UNCTAD for a decade beginning in the mid-1970s. The board of the South Centre, which he chaired for many years afterward, summarized him as "among those few towering personalities and intellects which have ably led the South and provided it with its own identity in the global arena."[10] Corea looked back to Ceylon before independence: "I was born in 1925, a little more than two decades before independence, and I was brought up in a family circle, many of whom were involved in public life, both on my father's side and my mother's side. . . . I grew up a single child without brothers and sisters. My parents both lived with my grandmother in a big house, in which I still live. It was built in 1875 in Colombo. My grandmother was a very active person who traveled frequently abroad and had a lot of social life. She had lots of friends in all communities, including the British people, the civil servants. She used to invite the governor for lunch in our hillside home in the mountains once a year. The family was reasonably affluent on my mother's side. So nobody prodded me to look for a professional career, although some of my relatives had qualified as barristers in England. . . . Nor was I pushed to study very much. I think the idea was that one would grow up and somehow involve oneself in looking after the family properties and estates. . . . They also thought I was too quiet, somewhat retired and shy, to get into the tumble of politics. . . . But on my own, I began to take a deep interest in public affairs, national affairs in Ceylon. But even more than that I was very much inspired by the Indian National Movement, the work of the Indian Congress, figures such as Gandhi and Nehru, but particularly Nehru, of whose writings I read everything I could get my hands on. This gave me a kind of intellectual or even a subjective passionate interest in national politics, but without taking me to the point of wanting to participate actively."

Virendra (Viru) Dayal was a veteran of several UN postings, including a final one as *chef de cabinet* for Secretaries-General Pérez de Cuéllar and Boutros Boutros-Ghali. He recalled growing up at the time of India's independence: "I was influenced by Gandhi and Nehru, as my entire generation was. We were instinctively in search of our place in the world and of ideas that contributed to a world that made sense to us as we came to independence. There was something about my generation that felt the need to be linked to the rest of the world, because our country was emerging, as it were, into a new world itself. So it was perfectly natural that all through my school and college days, I was keenly interested in what was happening outside, especially in the United Nations."

Indeed, he recalled his first trip to New York to visit his father's younger brother, Rajeshwar Dayal, who eventually wrote a memoir on his experience in the Congo, *A Mission for Hammarskjöld*. Dayal recalled the juxtaposition of his idyllic setting of childhood and the foreshadowing of violence: "That small town—I am reminded of e.e. cummings's poem, 'anyone live in a little how town, with up so many floating bells down' because it had a lake cradled in the mountains at about 6,500 feet. On the banks of the lake, there was the Hindu temple with its bells. There was a church. There was a mosque. There was a Gurdwara for the Sikhs. And all of us lived in perfect harmony. The school in which I studied was an Anglican school. But there was never any strain or competitiveness or violence between the religious communities when I was a child. That's why, at the time of independence—fortunately—there was very little violence where I was a child, but still I saw two homes being set afire. It was something very painful."

Amartya Sen, winner of the Nobel Prize in Economic Sciences in 1998, recounted his early years. "My family is from Dhaka, which was the second city of pre-partition Bengal, later the capital of East Pakistan, and now the capital of Bangladesh (since its independence in 1971). We lived in the old, historic part of the city of Dhaka (modern Dhaka extends very far beyond that), but like many urban Bengalis, I too saw my 'home' as the village from which the family had moved to the city, in my case, two generations earlier. My home village is a tiny one called Matto, in an area called Manikganj, not far from Dhaka, but it used to take a long time to get there, mostly on boats through a network of rivers. These days you can drive there on good roads in a few hours. We used go there once a year or so, just for a few days, but such was the power of the theory of an ancestral 'home' that on those rare occasions I would firmly think, as a child, that I was 'back at home.'

"My father, Ashotosh Sen, was a professor of chemistry at Dhaka University, and his father, who was a lawyer, was also closely associated with the University. I wasn't born in Dhaka though—that happened in my mother's family home in Santiniketan, in what is now West Bengal in India. My maternal grandfather, Kshiti Mohan Sen, taught Sanskrit and Indian philosophy in Santiniketan, in the higher education part of what was mainly a school started by Rabindranath Tagore, the poet. I was born in the campus where my mother's family lived.

"One the big influences on my understanding of the world has certainly been Tagore. I must say that initially I did not recognize that it was a major influence, since it came so implicitly and in so many different ways. Also, politically, I was often tempted to think of Tagore as too tolerant of economic inequality. He certainly wasn't moved by the need for economic equity in the way that many of us instinctively were. He was keen that everyone should have the opportunity of leading a worthwhile life, but he did not grumble much about economic asymmetry in general. It was not so much that he was unmoved by very big asymmetries, and he did raise his voice in protest against them in some of his writings, but he did not devote as much of his energy to it as he did to combating other social problems.

"Tagore concentrated much more in arguing against political inequalities and social divisions rather than inequality of income or wealth distribution. He was particularly occupied in disputing the narrowness of mind in various forms that he saw around him—from unreasoned traditionalism and dogmatic conservatism to belligerent sectarian attitudes, reflected in religious communalism and intense nationalistic fervor, not to mention the racism that was implicit in imperialist theories (including the theories behind the British Raj in India).

"What was, for me, particularly influential in the long run was Tagore's insistence on the priority of reason. He was very well versed in the richness of the inherited traditions of India as well as of many other countries, but he refused to accept any tradition or convention without rational scrutiny. He was also uncompromisingly universalist and totally rejected the insularity and narrowness of parochial thinking in India—or anywhere else. He could admire what he found reasonable about Indian values and admirable about its past while being very critical of other parts of the established value system. I was greatly impressed by Tagore's insistence that you have to be open to cultural influences from the whole world, that this need not in any way diminish your appreciation of your own cultural background, and that—as he once put it—anything from anywhere that you come to admire 'instantly becomes yours.' These ideas had a profound impact on me, even though at that time I did not actually realize that there was anything especially unusual about these universalist beliefs.

"I was also helped by my parents' propensity to take a broad and open perspective on Indian culture—not treating it as a fragile object that would split to bits if it came in contact with influences coming from elsewhere. I think my younger sister, Supurna, and I took these understandings to be absolutely natural, whether they came from Tagore's theorization or our parents' practice.

"When I was a little over three, we went to Mandalay—my father taught at the agricultural college there. That gave me an exposure to another country when I was very young. In fact, some of my earliest memories are of Burma. It was wonderful to go to another country with a different culture—and such an interesting culture too, in this case. We were in Burma for three years."

Juan Somavía was elected director-general of the ILO in 1998 after a career in Chilean diplomacy as well as an earlier one in human rights with NGOs that protested the policies of the government that had sent him into exile. He recalled his international meanderings: "I was born in Britain in the middle of the Blitz and then moved to Chile, the Dominican Republic, Belgium, the Netherlands, the United States, and then Ecuador. . . . So my schooling is both my formal schooling and the fact that I moved around the world. My upbringing gave me a natural linkage with the world. . . . Probably the most important benefit of that upbringing is that you get to know there are differences. You can't just look at the world through your own eyes. There are other people looking at the same thing with other eyes. . . . That, of course, leads later on to a much greater understanding of multiculturalism and, further on, as you reflect on these things, to the need for respect for the other. . . . You have no option but dialogue. You don't find solutions that are imposed by force."

In thinking about a variety of experiences, Somavía recalled a particular painful one in the Deep South of the United States: "One single thing that shocked me relates to the time when my dad was counsel in New Orleans and I went to school there. We are talking about the period from 1953 to 1956 when they were beginning to move away from segregation but it was still a segregated society. I remember that I took a streetcar to go home. The streetcar would stop right in front of the high school. I remember the anguish—the streetcar separated white people from black people. They were separated by a little thing that sort of moved forward and backwards. So from here onward it was white, and from here backward it was black people. . . . And there were a couple of old black ladies sitting, and I got in with a twelve- or thirteen-year-old kid, who picked up the thing and put it in back of them and asked them to stand up. These women actually did. . . . I remember running off the streetcar. That was something that shook me. I didn't put any cultural interpretation on it; it was more just a human reaction. How could people be treated this way? That was probably one of the strongest feelings of injustice—yes, you have to listen to the other, respect the other, understand the other, but there are limits. There are limits that have to do with certain basic values that you hold, and which ought to be universal."

As a voice for women's rights in the Philippines and internationally, including as chair of the 1985 Nairobi conference on women, Leticia Shahani was a proud product of the Philippines. In particular, she pointed to her father's influence over her eventual interest in international cooperation: "Narciso Ramos was one of the pioneers of the Philippine Foreign Service. He served as the first foreign secretary of President Marcos. So I knew the diplomatic world quite well. The UN was not really a stranger to me."

Michael Doyle, who later became a widely published political scientist and advisor to Kofi Annan in the new millennium, also grew up in a foreign service family: "My father and, for a while, my mother were both U.S. civil servants. They were in counterespionage operations during World War II. Then my father went into the FBI and Justice Department for a career serving in U.S. embassies in France, Germany, Italy, and Switzerland. He was a hardworking civil servant, but he was also an inspiring person. He was someone of real commitment to both U.S. civil rights and national security; a genuine patriot. He inspired in me an appreciation for government service—that would be the most important connection. Then, living overseas undoubtedly played a role in some degree of awareness of the world. So throughout my career, I've leaned toward public service and academia and never really being able to sort out one or the other and in fact enjoying a combination of the two. So that is one connection that brings me to the world of the UN."

"My family was made up of two strands," recalled Malta's Michael Zammit Cutajar, a "lifer" in the development business, both inside the UN system and in NGOs, including as secretary-general of the UN Framework Convention on Climate Change (UNFCCC). "My mother's side were basically lawyers with a couple of doctors thrown in, typical professionals in a country in which the professionals, the *notables*, were rather important socially and politically. My father's father, my grandfather, was a businessman, so I was at an early age exposed to the wonders of the family business as an institution! Worked in it, did vacation jobs, that sort of thing, and was destined by the tradition of primogeniture to be the chief executive but decided at a certain point to go my own way. I think this was basically out of a spirit of rebellion, which has continued to characterize some of my life decisions since then."

Paulo Sergio Pinheiro was an activist lawyer and human rights proponent in his native Brazil before becoming the UN's special rapporteur for human rights in Burundi and then in Burma. He joked that he failed the diplomatic exam and "escaped the navy . . . because I have flat feet." He traced his roots: "My mother's parents—my maternal great-grandfather was Brazilian. The first of my great-grandfathers had arrived in Brazil in the seventeenth century. . . . My maternal great-grandmother was German, from a family of merchants who came to Brazil before the First World War. And the other side of my father, they are very humble Portuguese migrants. My grandfather was a taxi driver, and before he was a shoemaker manufacturer. But my father was very much involved in employees' labor unions. I think that my connection with social labor law was also through my father."

As with many families whose offspring choose different paths, Pinheiro mentioned his grandmother's consternation with his career choice: "Why

Paulo, we spend so much money for education. We went to France. And now you return to Brazil to visit prisons. We don't have anything to do with this kind of people." For Pinheiro, the answer to his grandmother was clear: "I began to be attracted to all the debate of social justice. It was a very convenient moment, because we had a good pope, John XXIII. I read a lot of his biographies and his memoirs and all the social encyclicals, *Pacem in Terra, Mater Magister,* and the Second Vatican Council. And I participated in many activities with other Catholic professors, progressive people in university, particularly a very renowned Catholic thinker, a Jesuit sociologist, Father Fernando Bastas de Avila. . . . My indignation—I was in the window of my apartment and I saw some people, part of the police, putting a man inside the trunk of a car. I was very shocked about that. . . . I was compelled to address these human rights issues because of my Catholic formation."

Firsthand encounters with painful images were striking in the memories of many of our voices. Amartya Sen, for example, remembered this: "In the difficult days of riots, what sticks in my mind most strongly is the sight of violence. The first murder I saw was that of a Muslim laborer outside my home in what was, I think, 1941. I was actually playing in the garden. I was eight then. I was playing in a little shed in the garden, inside our house compound, when I heard a scream. There was a thin man, profusely bleeding, who had been knifed in the stomach. He sought refuge in our garden. He was asking for water, I got him some, while I was also shouting for help. My father was somewhere else but was soon fetched, and he rushed the person—his name was Kader Mia—to the hospital. And there this guy died.

"I had a few minutes of conversation with him while help was coming. I had not only a profound sense of sadness and of helplessness but also one of bewilderment. Why would someone—the assailant was clearly one of the local Hindu thugs—have knifed a person he did not know? It seemed incredible at eight. But also, he kept on saying that he was aware that as a Muslim laborer, he was taking a risk in coming to a mainly Hindu area for a daily laborer's job. It would give him some income, and he did need the income because there was nothing to eat at home. He had to come and take the risk. As I tried to understand why he did something so risky, it told me something about the extensive reach and overpowering consequences of economic penury—the 'unfreedom' it generates.

"Aside from going over the brutality and the overwhelming sadness of seeing a person bleed to death, I felt I had to understand things of which I had no understanding earlier. One lesson was that people who fostered and fomented the belligerence of 'identities' will kill another without having anything against the person other than just the identity of his being of another community.

"An amazing and incredible thought. But secondly, I also learned something about the nature of economic un-freedom—the fact that Kader Mia had to go out to work and in a sense was compelled to go to the only place where work was offered to him, which was in a Hindu area, which was dangerous. And he said his wife told him not to go. But he had to go in order to get something for the family to eat. So the idea that economic un-freedom can generate other kinds of un-freedom, including not having the freedom to live, was again a very shocking recognition. In a sense, these were dimly perceived ideas, but they made me think a lot already then and that line of thinking gripped me more clearly over the years." Sen's book *Development as Freedom* was published in 1999.[11]

Rubens Ricupero recalled growing up in a ghetto of Italian immigrants in São Paulo. The most important influence was his religious education, but the clashing ideologies of immediate family members influenced him as well: "A less powerful influence on me, but also significant, was the influence of one of my uncles on my mother's side who was a communist. He had been the secretary-general of the Communist Party in the city of São Paulo in the years of the 1930s, when, as you know, Stalinism was the norm. He was very much a Stalinist in his thought, but not in his heart. He was a very generous man. And on my mother's side, my family had a communist tradition. They were communists and trade union leaders. . . . The influence from that side was not so much intellectual, because I have never been attracted by communism. Even in the times when a good proportion of the Catholic youth movement was under this influence, I must say that I never felt much sympathy with the ideology. For me, the question of the freedom to spread the gospel was more important than social organization. But what impressed me about the examples, particularly of my uncle and my cousin, was their capacity to devote their own lives to a noble cause. That example was almost similar to the Christians of the first times of the Church—this complete dedication to an ideal, above all, the ideal of social change in a country very strongly marked by an abnormal degree of inequality in income and wealth distribution."

Gert Rosenthal, the former executive secretary of the UN Economic Commission for Latin America and the Caribbean (ECLAC) from 1988 to 1997 and later permanent representative of Guatemala to the United Nations in New York, explained "why somebody with the name of Rosenthal is from Guatemala. . . . I was brought up in a tricultural home. . . . My grandfather on my mother's side is the one who immigrated to Guatemala. I was told he got there in 1891. . . . It seems he liked the place . . . and then at some point he went back to the old country to get married. So he came back to Guatemala with his newfound bride in the early part of the last century, I guess in 1901 or so.

And my mother was born in Guatemala in 1903." His mother was sent to high school in New York, "so she must have been a pretty worldly figure for somebody living in the backwoods of Guatemala in her time. And she went back to the old country in the 1920s, where she got married to my father. And I guess if Hitler had not intervened, I would have been born in Germany. . . . My father was a lawyer—actually, he was a judge—and he was barred from being a judge in 1933. So my mother, who was not used to the type of anti-Semitism that she saw in Germany, insisted that they go back to Guatemala, at least to sit things out while it blew over. First they went to Amsterdam, where I was born. And when things got worse, they went to Guatemala. . . . My father settled in there, in the family business of my grandfather. I think he was probably a little unhappy in the early years, because he had come from a very sophisticated city—Frankfurt am Main—in Germany. And he went to this little backwater which was Guatemala City in the 1930s, into a business he knew nothing about—a hardware store. . . . They spent the whole war years in Guatemala."

Samir Amin, one of the more visible and radical development economists, recalled the importance of his multicultural family in prerevolutionary Egypt: "I was born in Egypt in 1931 to an Egyptian father, a physician, and a French mother, also a physician. My family milieu, bourgeois, was not a reactionary milieu. On my mother's side, they were convinced Jacobins, and on my father's, leftist members of the Wafd, so middle-class democrats of nationalist but modernist convictions, and not anti-European in the cultural sense of the term."

Margaret "Peg" Snyder would later become a senior U.S. government and UN official, but she began her life in Syracuse, New York. The belching black smoke from the second-largest railroad yard in the United States at the time provided the scene for her father's practice as a country doctor with paying and welfare patients. She remembered that part of her formation "came from sitting with my father at night when he'd come home, and he'd talk about his welfare patients and ponder: How do you effect change? How can people come out of their situation, and have jobs as everyone else has, and pull themselves out of being on the dole, so to speak—being on welfare?" Snyder struggled with those ideas in the evenings while her mother prepared to teach her Latin and German classes. She also played the piano in the silent movies and recalled that "the fellow who played on opposite nights was getting seventy-five cents a night playing the same movies as she was playing, and she was getting fifty cents. That experience introduced me to the need for equal opportunities for women in employment." After leaving the silent movies, she went to work at Woolworth's playing the piano, where "if you wanted to buy a piece of sheet music, there would be someone to play it for you." She took these jobs to earn enough money to take the streetcar to the university and buy her lunch.

Her two older brothers became a medical doctor and an aeronautical engineer. "As the third child, I was permitted to be more adventuresome and was also in the shadow of two very bright brothers who received all kinds of honors. So I had to live up to that and try to be a good student. I became valedictorian of my class. . . . I lived what you'd call an American childhood . . . [with] parents whose grandparents had come from the old country and who were themselves first-generation achievers. In that atmosphere, we had to do more than they did."

Margaret "Molly" Bruce worked on human rights and women's issues during her three decades in the United Nations. She recalled growing up in industrial Yorkshire and the role of her father who "came from a poor background, but . . . was, in his own way, quite brilliant. He went to work in a textile mill at the age of eleven and educated himself at home and in technical colleges. That led him to want to help the underprivileged get a good basic education." She remembered the Fisher Act that was passed after World War I in Britain that required employers to release their young workers one day a week to attend school until they reached the age of sixteen or eighteen. "My father went to Rugby to head the Day Continuation School there and apparently kept the scheme alive in Rugby long after it died everywhere else. . . . It is called a public school in England but was in fact an elite private school—originally for male students only. Rugby football was born there. So it's interesting how my father kept the concept of the day continuation school alive and gradually built it into a technical college where radar research was done during World War II."

Sadako Ogata was the UN High Commissioner for Refugees (UNHCR) from 1991 to 2001. This position marked an ironic turn in light of her family's participation in one of the dramatic events that scuttled the League of Nations. "I come from a family who were involved in public affairs. I am part of the third generation who has served in the foreign ministry and represented Japan in the League of Nations and the United Nations. So the involvement in international affairs has come more naturally from what I heard as a child, followed as a family that was very much involved in World War II and in peacetime afterwards. And also all the books on the shelves had been very much history and public affairs. . . . My grandfather was the Japanese representative to the League at the time of the Manchurian incident. I think my family all came from the liberal—and they were the liberal nationalists, not the liberal socialists—streak of the political tradition. My great-grandfather, who was a politician, then serving as prime minister, was assassinated by the military in the May 15th incident of 1932."[12]

Cornelio Sommaruga became the president of the ICRC (1987–1999) after spending most of his life in national government service. He described himself as "a Swiss citizen from abroad, *un Suisse de l'etranger*." His mother was from Rome, where he himself was born; his father was born in Switzerland but moved to Italy to take care of a widowed aunt and in 1939 was appointed to the Swiss Legation in Rome. Sommaruga's uncle had not only been a successful businessman in Italy but also was vice president of the Italian Red Cross. "From the family of my aunt," he explained, "I was, in a certain sense, introduced in a certain circle of Italian public life. . . . My grandfather from my mother's side was a professor of pediatrics at the University of Rome. He was then a *senatore del regno*; these were the members of the Senate appointed by the king. . . . He was the private doctor of the royal family of Italy. . . . This gave another circle of people around our family."

Paul Berthoud, a career international civil servant with experience in a host of UN organizations at both headquarters and the field, came from a "mixed" (German- and French-speaking) Swiss family and was born in Geneva. He recalled: "Later on in my career, this very often provoked raised eyebrows on the part of people who had been working there for a long time but had never met a real Genevese." Berthoud's childhood took place alongside the first experiment in a universal international organization. "The League of Nations and I grew together. My father was very interested in politics and international politics. Maybe I should add that there was a special international angle in my family. My father had a cousin who had married a Chinese, Chan Choung Sing, who was one of the close collaborators of Albert Thomas in the ILO. Therefore, the idea of cultural diversity, of that other world that existed outside of our little world in Geneva, was very much alive in my own family. . . . I should add that we had two daily newspapers at home. We had *Le journal de Genève*, which was a very good solid conservative paper, and *Le Travail*, which was the newspaper of the Socialist Party. . . . My father, since I started to read, told me, 'You always have to read both because you cannot rely on only one view of the world. It is much too complicated.'"

Berthoud remembered that when the Japanese occupied Manchuria in 1931: "We were playing League of Nations during recess. We had a cardboard, on which we put a CD [Corps Diplomatique] license plate. We tucked that to our belt, and we were driving to the Assembly Hall during recess in a corner of the courtyard, and started to argue the Chinese-Japanese War. . . . My next very clear recollection is of the day I skipped school, three years later, in 1935 . . . to go to the railway station in Geneva to applaud Haile Selassie when he came to the League of Nations to defend his case after Mussolini had invaded Ethiopia. . . . A bunch of Italian journalists in the public tribune of the League of Nations interfered when Haile Selassie took the floor and created chaos in the Assembly Hall. This was during the only three years in which Geneva had a socialist government—1933 to 1936. And the government of Geneva proceeded to arrest those journalists. There was immediately a federal intervention, which gave an injunction to the Geneva government to set them free. There was a conflict between the vision which the Geneva government had of this role and the very benevolent-toward-fascism atmosphere which reigned in the Federal government in Bern."

The past of the fourth UN Secretary-General, Kurt Waldheim, has been the subject of much scrutiny and negative publicity, but he remembered his family's harassment at the hands of the Nazis: "It was always my desire—my wish—to see other countries, to get out of the confines of my own narrow country. I was interested to live with other people, to learn to know their way of life. . . . My father wanted me to become a medical doctor because he himself had wanted to become one. However, the money for his studies was not available. He came from a poor family, so he was put up in a Catholic school on the outskirts of Vienna. He became a successful teacher and later, district school inspector. . . . When the Nazis came, they dismissed him immediately and put him in the local prison in Tulln. Fortunately, he was not sent to a concentration camp. He was set free after a few days. They searched repeatedly our house to find some material which the Nazis could use against him. He was a member of the Christian Social Party and participated in political rallies. That was the reason why they immediately dismissed him and put him in prison. When he was freed, my parents left Tulln and moved to Baden, south of Vienna."

Robert Cox's career was divided between twenty-five years in the international civil service of the ILO in Geneva and the remainder as a teacher and researcher at Columbia and York Universities. His father was an accountant in an English-speaking section of Montreal, and he recalled that "Montreal, in those days, was very much a segmented community. First, there was the linguistic division between French and English. And there was a religious division between Catholic and Protestant. So you had, in a sense, the three communities that were virtually self-contained—the Anglo-Protestant and the Irish-Catholic, both Anglophone; and the French-Catholic. . . . Now, as you can imagine, that could be a really claustrophobic type of environment growing up. And I think as I was into high school and certainly moving towards the university years, I became very conscious of this sort of exclusionary situation." He took particular interest "in the French-Canadian nationalist movement, which was right on the other side of town. I used to take the streetcar down to the east end of Montreal and go to political meetings. . . . It was regarded as very strange behavior."

Julia Henderson played a central role in setting up the UN's system of technical assistance and helping to recruit personnel. She fondly recalled growing up in Du Quoin, Illinois: "The town I grew up in was a town of about 7,000; it had 10,000 at its peak. Its economic base was coal mining. My father was a carpenter at the mines and my grandparents were all involved working at the coal mines—some on top, as they say, and some down in the mines. . . . We always had a very good support for good schools. . . . But I learned after I went to the University of Illinois in Champaign that I had had a better education than a great number of the students there. . . . That stood me in good stead for the rest of my career."

Elise Boulding, a lifelong educator and peace activist who served on numerous advisory groups, including the UN University (UNU) in Tokyo, recalled her childhood: "My people were seafaring people, and we have burials and houses going back to the 1400s on the coast of Norway. And when grandfather died and the days of the clipper ship were over, grandmother sold the shipping business and bought the farm. I have family on that farm today. . . . Father and mother were actually cousins, so that history really applies to both of them. Father was one of the group of engineers who were having trouble in Norway in the 1920s finding jobs. So a lot of Norwegian engineers immigrated to the U.S. I was three-years-old when we came here. . . . We never spoke English at home or in social occasions with other Norwegians. So I have a very strong understanding of ethnic identity. . . . Mother said Americans are materialistic and that I should not be like that. She was homesick until the day she died. So Norway was built up in my mind as the place where people really know how to live right on the planet." Her world was apolitical and revolved around music until Hitler invaded Norway. "Then I really began listening to what was happening in the world. I went to hear Norman Thomas speak on campus and was deeply impressed—thinking perhaps I should become a socialist."

Lawrence Klein reflected on moving beyond his background as a basis for becoming a Nobel Prize–winning economist in 1980. "I was raised in American middle-class society and background values in that period and was mainly influenced by education in the public schools of Omaha. One significant experience was the particular high school [Omaha Central High School]. . . . Many very intelligent people who have made significant contributions to American life have come out of that school. . . . That was a very isolationist part of the United States. I think our exposure, in general, to world events and to what was going on in the world at large, particularly the build-up to the Second World War, was not really adequately put before me in that setting. Eventually I went to university in California, and then my horizons expanded a great deal."

Virginia Housholder concentrated for years on the intricacies of the UN's administration as a senior U.S. government official. Fortunately, she maintained a sense of humor: "I was born in Salem, Missouri, which is where the sinkholes in Missouri are. I may have been born in a sinkhole. We moved to Illinois when I was very young and settled in Peoria when I was five. . . . My oldest brother was five years older than I. I was born on his fifth birthday and his story is that he would rather have had a puppy."

Just Faaland spent his career in development economics, much of which was linked to the UN through a lifetime of professional participation in and leadership of UN expert groups and field missions: "I was born into a family which I think one would classify as a middle-income family. My father was a teacher in high school, teaching classical languages. At the time, in his first job, he was up in northern Norway, in Tromsø where I was born. But by the time I was two and a half, we moved on to near Oslo, where I really grew up. . . . I can remember from the time of my schooling, even in primary school, which started at the end of the 1920s, being a happy boy. I was fortunate in terms of health and got along well in school. . . . In retrospect, I sometimes reflect a bit on how little we did to really include those who were from poorer homes, and sometimes very much poorer homes. . . . It bothers me—not for me but for mankind—that I wasn't more aware of it than I actually was. I was probably more than average bright, and it scares me even more that even someone with a good home like me, that we didn't really concern ourselves more than we did with the ills of society. And there were plenty in the 1930s."

In contrast with those whose family backgrounds led them toward internationalism, Richard Gardner's schooling was what most opened his eyes to the world. His career in U.S. government service (including following UN affairs within the Kennedy administration and later as ambassador under Presidents Jimmy Carter and Bill Clinton) led to assignments on expert panels. As a prominent practicing international lawyer, he also continued to teach a popular course at Columbia University on the United Nations. "My father was a single practitioner lawyer in New York. My mother was a housewife. I was an only child. I think that the things that influenced my worldview were not so much my parents, who didn't have that great an interest in international affairs, but my education."

After the collapse of the Berlin Wall in November 1989, many observers looked at countries that had been members of the Socialist bloc and considered them to be closer to levels of technological and economic development in the Global South than to their erstwhile adversaries, the countries of the OECD. Yet for much of the UN's history, the Eastern bloc played a special role. So voices from there have a different resonance. Janez Stanovnik came from a large family with seven children and could hardly imagine becoming the head of a UN agency (the Economic Commission for Europe, 1967–1983), let alone the president of Slovenia (1988–1990) after the breakup of the country in which he had grown up, the former Yugoslavia: "It looks as if politics was somehow in the blood of the family, as my grandfather was deputy already in Vienna, in the Austro-Hungarian Parliament. . . . My father was a lawyer. . . . But he was also active in politics, particularly in local politics. He was vice mayor of Ljubljana immediately after the First World War and again after the Second."

Vladimir Petrovsky was under-secretary-general and director-general of the UN Office in Geneva (UNOG) from 1993 to 2002. He was the most senior Soviet official within the UN system when the Union of Soviet Socialist Republics (USSR) imploded in December 1991—at which point he became the most senior Russian. Earlier, he had risen through the governmental ranks as a Soviet official. He recalled his first encounter with a foreign culture: "I was born in 1933 in the city which was called at that time Stalingrad—now Volgograd. My father was a railway engineer, my mother was a doctor of medicine, a hygienist. Then my father became a military man, and during the war, in 1943, when he was wounded, he was moved to Novosibirsk. . . . For us, there was no question whether we would go to the public or to other sectors, because all the sectors were public at that time. But being born in the province, living in a multicultural community, I was very much interested in relations between nations and states, and the outside world looked very much attractive. But it so happens that during the Second World War, Novosibirsk was one of the major stopovers when the American delegations came to Moscow, because the route was very difficult during the war. They traveled from New York through San Francisco and often made stopovers in Novosibirsk. . . . And once, when Vice President Wallace of the United States came to Novosibirsk, the local authorities had decided to organize a meeting with him and the schoolchildren. At that time, we had a pioneer organization, a kind of boy scout organization. And I, as representative of the pioneer organization, welcomed Vice President Wallace. . . . Anyhow, that was my first international experience."

Bernard Chidzero, who died in 2002 shortly after our interview with him in Harare, where he had retired after serving as minister during the first fifteen years of Zimbabwe's independence, had earlier spent some two decades as an international civil servant (his last position was UNCTAD deputy secretary-general, but he also was a candidate for the UN's top job in 1991). He worked as a child with his father in tobacco fields on an estate in Southern Rhodesia. "My first instruction was at the age of twelve when Chirimuta [a family acquaintance] started a school across the river, the Nyatsime, and we were writing on sand. We all enjoyed that. It opened our eyes. Then we would have a break, after which we would go to the garden to do some gardening. Each of us had a small bed of vegetables, onions, cabbage, et cetera. In a sense, it was a form of education with production at that early level." He began an amazing journey from illiterate preteenager to a Ph.D. in Canada, but his real break came when he was selected to attend a missionary school run by Jesuits, where he met "others who later played an important role in Zimbabwe, like the president of Zimbabwe, Robert Mugabe." Before going off to secondary school, he worked as a tailoring assistant on the same farm and proudly announced, "So you may wish to know that I know a bit of tailoring!" He enrolled in secondary school in Natal Province because Rhodesian schools at the time were totally segregated, whereas preapartheid ones in South Africa were not.

Noeleen Heyzer had a fascinating journey from Singapore to become the third head of the UN Development Fund for Women (UNIFEM). She traced what drives her today to her multicultural background and poverty as a child: "The moving force in my life has been the coming together of two lineages. My father had a middle-class Dutch burgher background, from Holland, Sri Lanka, and Calcutta.[13] He came down to Singapore with the British army during the colonial period. The Dutch burghers had a lot more power in Sri Lanka in the colonial era than they did after independence. My mother's lineage came out of the Straits Chinese population as well as the famine of southern China. . . . This history did shape my life because of the way these forces intertwined and created family structures, relationships, processes of change in the context of Singapore as a colony. I was affected by the struggle against colonialism and what colonialism did to people as well as their livelihoods. I was born in 1948, just after the world war, when Singapore was still under colonial rule. From very early on, I experienced how a middle-class household fell into poverty. . . . My father came to Singapore from Calcutta with the British army. He was brought in because he knew homeopathic medicine and traditional massage. During the war, he was used by the army medical unit to provide alternative healing for stress and traumas. But after that period, his skills were considered illegitimate because he did not have a degree. He could not find a livelihood. So we lost a male income earner. And the society was not ready for women to play a very strong role in the economy. . . . My father was destroyed by his war experience and the devaluation of his knowledge; my mother's life ended when she was twenty-six."

Following her mother's death, Heyzer landed in one of the poorest slum areas for migrants, which also had the highest concentration of anticolonial resisters: "Here was where the main leaders at that time from China, from India, would visit to mobilize the migrant workforce. It was a highly creative, bubbling kind of community with its mutual-aid societies, clans, markets, street operas and temples. From there, I saw the creativity of human resistance. I saw the capacity of people to recreate new worlds. And I also experienced the way in which networks were being built by people to support one another. A sense of solidarity was there. But whilst I was in that space, I was also sent to a very elite Catholic school in Singapore [through the intervention of the archbishop of Singapore]. People would create policies, would define what the world was. Their conversations did not capture the reality that I was experiencing or the kind of admiration I had for people in the community I was living in. And yet there was a sense of power and righteousness. So I knew about power relationships, about who had the right to define whose reality. These very complex forces captured my imagination as a child. By the time I was in my teens, the independence struggle in Singapore had already begun. So I knew about resistance. I knew that people could create new worlds. I also experienced the processes of nation-building, of developing social institutions for stability. . . . Development was not just a theoretical issue for me; it came from having lived it very deeply."

2

Formal Education

- **Education at Home**
- **Studying Abroad**

Virtually all of our voices, from the North and South alike, have advanced university degrees, many from elite institutions. Those who entered universities during World War II often saw their studies interrupted by the war or were forced to abandon their original plans because of it. By contrast, those who came of university age in the 1950s and 1960s found themselves on college campuses lit with debates about African nationalism and decolonization or civil rights challenges to American Jim Crow laws. University life often was a radicalizing experience for both generations and a time in which early childhood impressions of inequality and injustice were given a direction and a context, although many would later find themselves surprised at the career path they followed.

For many, it was a first encounter with new cultures and the beginning of lifelong friendships and professional solidarities. For example, Dharam Ghai pointed to how much his university years in England changed his worldview, which was originally developed in Britain's East African colonial schools. "Going to Oxford was a great experience for me. It opened up a world I had not even dreamed of before. . . . I developed an interest in problems of poor countries. This became my lifetime preoccupation. But also, it was at Oxford that I first made my true friends among Africans from other African countries as well as from Kenya. You won't believe it, but the first really good African friendships that I had were made at Oxford. Also there . . . I met people from other developing countries, and particularly Commonwealth countries. . . . It was at that time that I think I first became conscious of the Third World. I had never before thought in those terms. I had never thought in terms of developing countries versus the rest of the world and that they had things in common and that they should cooperate on certain issues."

Then, as now, a mentor was often the most crucial variable in determining a course of study or a professional orientation. For instance, Jan Pronk's commitment to social change was obvious in his selection of a field of study: "I was extremely lucky to have as a teacher Jan Tinbergen, who was the most well-known Dutch economist, world famous. I wanted to study with him irrespective, more or less, of what he was teaching, because I thought to be very close to such a renowned scholar could not be missed. You should not avoid such an opportunity. And he was the teacher who really helped me to establish a link between my discipline, macroeconomics, and politics, the thinking of political order, a social order, peace, development. . . . I was developing a rather logical interest in questions of development, world order systems. Without the two important events, the Second World War and having Jan Tinbergen as a teacher, it would perhaps have been different."

Stirred by the devastation of war and the dislocation of the Great Depression, young students were introduced to the new intellectual currents taking hold in this period of great social and intellectual turmoil. President Franklin D. Roosevelt's New Deal was held up as a model for a more just world, and the Universal Declaration of Human Rights, pioneered by Eleanor Roosevelt, gave hope that this could be achieved. Many of our voices were also influenced by existential philosophers and radical social thought that flourished in Western universities during the 1950s and 1960s. Keynesian economics that prescribed state action to stabilize economies and to fight unemployment dominated university courses. For instance, leaving Guatemala for California was crucial for Gert Rosenthal, who remarked, "There are moments in history where humanity craves for some kind of paradigm, maybe after a very traumatic experience, like the Great Depression. Lord Keynes came and made a major contribution, offered a major paradigm, in the wake of the events of the interwar period."

Education at Home

While the chance to study abroad opened many eyes, others pursued university education at home. We begin by listening to experiences with eye-opening encounters closer to home. Janez Stanovnik explained a path not taken in his itinerary from prison to president: "In my youth, I expected to become a priest. But life's destiny turned my dices differently. So after puberty, at fourteen or fifteen years, I had made a rather basic turnover, partially, I would say, because of psychological and physical maturity, and partially because of the developments in Europe." Instead, in 1940, he went to study law at the University of Ljubljana. "And I just finished the first year of legal studies when the late Yugoslav government signed a tripartite agreement with Hitler. This, for my generation, was so outrageous that here on the streets of Ljubljana I was beaten by the police on 27 March 1941 when we went to a demonstration against the pact."

His political activism as a student continued during the war. "I went with all my youthful energy and enthusiasm immediately into the resistance . . . a kind of tripartite coalition: Liberals, Christian Socialists, and communists. Our group, the Christian Socialists, was the largest in numbers. . . . We were students. . . . Probably few of the European universities have a record like Ljubljana's university. . . . The university lost about 25 percent of its students in partisan warfare." He recalled that when the Italians occupied Slovenia and Dalmatia, they "did not close the university immediately, because they had a kind of paternalistic attitude at the beginning toward us. . . . Some considered, even under wartime, [that] our actions should be 'cultural silence' and therefore the university should be closed. We did not take this attitude. We had taken only the attitude that the diplomas which would be obtained for the price of being members of the so-called GUF [Gioventú Universitaria Fascista], which was a fascist organization in the university, would not be recognized after the war." The Italians arrested him for his resistance activities, and he spent four months in prison.

Paul Berthoud eventually pursued the study of international relations that he had fantasized about with his make-believe diplomatic license plates as a child in the schoolyard. After classical studies, he pursued his interest in international law, particularly international organization, at the Graduate Institute of International Studies in Geneva: "I studied the work of the League of Nations on minorities; the control of the implementation of mandates, which was my first direct contact with the question of Palestine, which was one of the mandates which gave rise to the hottest debates in the League of Nations; the control of the narcotics conventions—there were a number of them, which were providing for some mechanisms control; then the work on disarmament. There had been a conference on disarmament running parallel to the assembly of the League since 1932. I made a study in depth of whatever discussions had taken place on the mechanism."

Maurice Bertrand recalled what for him was a predictable path from his baccalaureate to the study of law but then to a less-predictable first job in occupied France: "In 1944 I had to undergo that typically Pétainist stint in the Youth Work Brigades because one had to get military obligations out of the way in order to take competitive exams. As I wasn't well off and needed to make a living, I aimed to go into public service. The next competition on the horizon was for administrator at the Ministry of Finance because at that time there existed a distinction between the administrators at the ministry and the finance inspectors. I took the written exam in Vichy, then the oral in Paris, where I placed well. But I was not able to take up my duties. My 'class,' the one of 1942, was mobilized, no exceptions permitted, for forced labor in Germany.

I refused to go. I joined the Resistance and left in June 1943 for the movement in the Alpes-de-Haute-Provence, where I had family, which made things easier for me."

Jacques Polak began his professional life as a junior staffer for the League of Nations and retired half a century later as the director of research at the International Monetary Fund (IMF). After five years as executive director, he retired again. Polak recounted thinking about what to study in university: "I wanted to study economics, with the idea of joining my father in his accountancy firm. That subject was taught as a postgraduate study to economics in both Rotterdam and Amsterdam. My parents thought that studying away from home was a good thing, so I went to Amsterdam." What changed his mind was Jan Tinbergen, who would later win the first Nobel Prize in Economic Sciences in 1969 but at the time was teaching at the University of Amsterdam. Polak was in university during the period "when the fight between the Rotterdam school and the Amsterdam school was fundamentally about whether the guilder should be devalued or not. I did my final exams a few days after the devaluation in September 1936. My teacher, Frijda, had always been against it. The people of Rotterdam had been in favor of it. The impression was made not so much by the University but by the surroundings in Amsterdam, which was a city with lots of unemployed and some degree of revolutionary feeling against the whole establishment. . . . Of course, that is what made economics far more interesting than accountancy."

Margaret Anstee decided to study modern languages. Had she studied English, a teaching career would have been her only option. "The problem was we didn't have a second language at the school; we only had French. Oxford wrote back and said, 'Sorry. You can do mixed classics and modern languages. Latin and French.' Newnham College, Cambridge, on the other hand, wrote back in August 1943—the exam was in November—and said, 'If you can pass our entrance exam not only in French but also in either Spanish or Italian, we will take you on for a modern languages degree.'"

So Anstee did a three-month crash course and passed the exam. "Cambridge transformed my life. French was my major language still, but there was the most wonderful Spanish professor there, J. B. Trend. It was a very small faculty. I became secretary of the University Spanish Society. . . . When I went to Cambridge, the Spanish Civil War was a very lively topic in the Spanish faculty. My professor had known all the best writers of the generation of 1898 in Spain. He had been a personal friend of Lorca. He was the British expert on Manuel de Falla and he had been a *comendador de la republica*. So he was very much a supporter of the Republican side. And I suppose he was a very pink professor. Generally, my sentiments in politics were always on the left. . . . We had a complete split in the Spanish faculty. One lecturer was totally Franquista. And two parts of the Spanish faculty were not talking to one another. So this brought home to me very much the problems of war, conflict, and social justice."

The tumultuous 1930s figured in many conversations. Molly Bruce remembered a formative experience. Like Anstee, she was among the first women at Cambridge and liked foreign languages: "I studied French and German and the European history that goes with it. And I spent my school vacations with different families in both France and Nazi Germany." During her first visit to Frankfurt, she stayed with a family who had a daughter her age. She recalled: "I loved the father, who had been a general in the Kaiser's army during World War I. His wife was half Jewish. They came to stay with us in Rugby, and then I traveled back with the daughter and spent a month with them. But my German was really not very good and I was very homesick. . . . My parents were upset over my return journey. The mother and daughter put me on the steamer sailing down the Rhine to Cologne, where the father met me. I was amused with all the 'Heil Hitlering' that went on among the passengers. . . . The mother and daughter had given me some jewels and some incriminating letters to take with me to Jewish relatives in England, refugees. Well of course, when my father saw what I had on me and that they might have incriminated me, he was very upset. . . . I was blonde and Aryan-looking in those days, and that is perhaps why they took a chance. I don't know. I think if I had realized the danger I probably would have done it anyway. I would do it today but I wouldn't do it as well."

Robert Cox recalled having "never taken a course in political science, though I have been a professor of political science these last years. But . . . the main feature in my life in those days was that sense of the existence of a nation that was living alongside us but that most people I mixed with did not really know about. I was interested in trying to find out more about them, but I was certainly not integrated with them in any way. I was not part of any movement or organization; I was strictly a lone figure in that interest." When he graduated from McGill University with a B.A., he spent a year researching a master's thesis. "I did a thesis on the Québec General Election of 1886, which was the first time in which a real nationalist movement emerged in Québec. . . . So my interest in that thesis was to really explore the ideological and sociological roots of nationalism."

Stéphane Hessel studied philosophy at a French university after his parents had made the decision to flee Germany. But he then decided to focus on more practical matters. "The idea of becoming a diplomat arose very early in my life. And then I gave it up as something for which one had to be better prepared than I was and engaged, rather, in the study of philosophy. But after all, philosophy is not so very far away from culture and diplomacy. So it was not an altogether surprise to my friends and my family when just after the war I turned towards multilateral cooperation." Watching his father struggle to write, he realized that "the family had produced a sufficient number of writers and it was time for something else to come into the family."

Another refugee who attended university in his new home was Paul Streeten, who recalled university life in Aberdeen, UK: "I wanted to study sociology because I wanted to improve the society in which we live. But there was no sociology department at Aberdeen. There was only an economics department— one professor, one lecturer, and one economic historian. It was very small. The classes were very small. But again, I happened to fall into the right hands, because Lindley Fraser, the professor of economics, was a kind of social democrat. He was a very lively and interesting man who later on worked for the BBC. Again, I found an echo to my ideas, and my approach to things in his approach. We understood each other, and I did quite well, up to the point when I was arrested by the police as an enemy alien[1] and put into an internment camp in 1940. . . . My Aberdeen psychology professor, a colorful man called Rex Knight, wrote to me saying that though he regretted my misfortune, he agreed with the government's decision." His next stop was Oxford, which "in those days was a very odd place. . . . After the war was over, there was a great influx of ex-warriors who weren't disabled. But before the end of the war, there was an interesting mixture of people, as I said—those who were unfit to be in the army and those who were no longer fit."

Gerry Helleiner attended the University of Toronto, which was free for him as the son of a faculty member, even one who had arrived as a refugee. In deciding on his course of study, he recalled that "I was advised by a guidance counselor in high school that I would be an excellent candidate, according to aptitude tests, for a course called commerce and finance, which is basically a business course but in this university had a high theoretical economics content. And my father was happy because he knew it was mainly economics. But I hated it the first year. I hated the accounting and the mathematics, which I had no trouble with. I got 100 in calculus and 90-something in accounting, but I was so bored in the actuarial science course I took that I nearly flunked because I could not keep my eyes open. . . . I wanted something more social, more political, a little broader."

Elise Boulding's route to social science was less direct and was influenced by the chance encounter with her future husband: "I could date my peace activism to my reaction to the invasion of Norway. Up until then, I had mostly been playing the cello, and languages, literature and music were my world. I never took a course in social science in college. . . . So I went up to Syracuse, where my family then was, and entered graduate school. I was planning to write a master's thesis on the influence of the Viking invasions on English literature. Instead, I met Kenneth Boulding at a Quaker meeting. We were engaged eighteen days after we met and were married at the end of the summer. . . . But being with Kenneth, who was already an internationally known economist and disarmament researcher, suddenly I was plunged into the world of the social sciences and learned to think about issues of world peace in social science terms. . . . Quakerism was a new phase in my life . . . the turmoil of the war situation did lead me back into religion." Recalling her fateful meeting for worship with her soon-to-be spouse, she said: "We were practically sitting knee to knee, because he was already a Quaker elder and sitting in the facing bench. He rose and said, 'I hate moonlight. Moonlight is half-light and romance, and romance is evil.' Then added, parenthetically, 'It is all right to love wife and child.' I thought, 'Gosh, he must be married.' What he was talking about was the moonlight bombing in England. You see, here he was, safe in the U.S., and it was very traumatic that all of his family and friends and his country were all being subjected to these bombings and he was safe."

Julia Henderson was the first in her family to attend university, a common thread among many of our interviewees. "If you were a graduate of the University of Illinois, you were looked up to in the community. It was also one of the cheapest places to study. It was a public institution, and it had a very good reputation."

Enrique Iglesias spoke fondly of his secondary school preparation as a sound foundation for his subsequent university training: "School was really another very interesting experience. Back then the school system in Uruguay was extraordinary. First of all, there were only a few students in the entire country and the teachers were very educated people, steeped in a very rich humanist tradition . . . with an excellent knowledge of national and world history, as I later realized from personal experience."

Iglesias charted his own path in university, much to the objection of his father, who wanted him to study medicine: "Perhaps the only profession in which I had no interest was medicine. My father wanted me to study pharmaceutical chemistry. For him, pharmaceutical chemistry would give me independence in my profession. He valued independence highly, perhaps as a result of his years as a worker in Spain. And after that he spent the rest of his life working in the grocery store, providing for the modest economic base on which we lived for so many years. . . . I chose to major in Economics and Management, which was mainly management with economics on the side. . . . I believe that I chose this out of uncertainty. I was scared. It was a very difficult decision, because in our higher education system our studies are very compartmentalized. . . . Well, I believe I chose this profession because I thought it was what I would least regret if it later turned out to have been a mistake. At the time my father didn't want me to study Economics and Management, because he felt I would have to report to a superior, a company manager."

His father's concerns notwithstanding, Iglesias forged ahead: "I chose this profession and the truth is, I am very glad that I did, because communication and the elements of political action, which are perhaps the areas in which I feel most at ease and I enjoy the most, play a big part in this career. . . . Maybe this is why I felt so comfortable at the United Nations, because I very much like and have always liked the task of interacting, of mediating, of convincing." In thinking back to his university years, one of his fondest memories was encountering new ideas: "In the second year of my studies I took a much more dynamic course, with a great professor, Luis Faroppa. . . . He also tended to follow the steps of the neoclassical schools, and he taught us of course everything having to do with some of the really difficult texts such as *Value and Capital,* by Hicks, and others on the theory of economic cycles. . . . Now this course was given in the year 1950. Around the middle of the year the report by [Raúl] Prebisch for ECLA came out. . . . Faroppa was profoundly impressed by this text. He called off all our studies of the great classical and neoclassical texts and we devoted ourselves to analyzing ECLA's report. . . . The ECLA meeting of 1950 took place, which I boldly attended as I was still a student. And from a distance, on the podium I could see Prebisch. Pierre Mendes-France presided over the meeting. Philippe de Seynes was there as Mendes-France's assistant. . . . And I was in the back, in the last row of that large hall. This experience made a strong impression on me and I became really interested in this new type of economic vision for Latin America. We were all seduced by it."

Iglesias continued working at the family's store in the barrio during his years at the university: "I had all my books on the counter. . . . I studied on the counter. And people would come to shop but would see me studying and would tell me: I'll come by later. Which didn't really please my father. When he would come to see what we had sold, we had sold nothing."

Unlike Iglesias, Cornelio Sommaruga followed his father's directive: "You are going to study law because you want to become a diplomat, and I think you will be a bad diplomat. You will not be enthusiastic at all [about] the classical diplomatic career. If you wish to serve your country in this kind of work, you should go directly to economic diplomacy, *à la Division du commerce.*" At the time Sommaruga did not know what it was, but two decades later, he became the head of the Ministry of Trade in Switzerland. "My father died during my studies. But I never forgot that."

Vladimir Petrovsky recalled that in 1951 when he began at the Institute of International Relations, "my dream was to become an academic and to write. I wanted to study diplomacy and, first of all, different national styles. And when I was a student, I prepared what was called a thesis . . . on the reform of British foreign service in 1943."

Lawrence Klein remembered what tickled his intellectual curiosity: "the technical study of economics, and the use of mathematics and statistics in that subject. . . . During my first two years, I was at City College of Los Angeles followed by the last two years at the University of California at Berkeley. I learned a lot of technical material in the Los Angeles experience, but I got a much broader view at Berkeley from people who were immigrants, in some cases forced immigrants because of what was happening in Europe. . . . I had had an accident as a child that injured a leg, and I was not accepted for military service. I finished my degree, and I had a scholarship to go to MIT [Massachusetts Institute of Technology] at the time of the second year in which they were providing advanced teaching in economics for the Ph.D. program. I was the first doctoral recipient in that program. Paul Samuelson was my supervisor. That provided a continuation of the kinds of ideas I had been forming at Berkeley."

Former Secretary-General Kurt Waldheim recalled an educational experience with a Jewish friend. "When I expressed the wish to study at the Consular Academy, I noticed that my father was quite surprised and said: 'How do we get the money? It is very expensive school.' . . . In 1938 the ordeal began. In March, the Nazis came and occupied Austria. I wasn't sure whether they would close the Consular Academy or whether I would have a chance to finish the second year of studies. Finally, it was possible to finish the second year and to get the diploma in 1939." The former Secretary-General recalled his friendship with George Weidenfeld, who later became a well-known publisher in London after he had emigrated following the Anschluss in 1938.[2] "In his memoirs, which came out two years ago in London, he describes very kindly the help I had given him in order to finish school. Being Jewish, the Nazis did not permit him to continue his studies. The strange situation was—and it was George himself who told me this story—that the Nazi authorities permitted him to make the final exams but not to attend the courses. But, as he said to me, 'How could I pass the final exams without having a chance to attend the courses?' So it was at that time that I could help by giving him my notes; and in this way he could prepare himself for the final exams, which he passed very well and got the final degree of the Consular Academy."

Richard Gardner remembered his first schooling as an important backdrop to the kinds of career choices that he made: "I went to the Ethical Cultural

School in New York and to the Fieldston School. . . . There was great concern with ethical values in the sense of social justice at home, but also—and with Franklin Roosevelt and Eleanor Roosevelt in the White House, and they were sort of our role models—how to do good things in the world. Then I went to Harvard College, and I majored in economics. I was very fortunate in having as professors people like Alvin Hansen and Seymour Harris, who were very interested in international monetary and trade issues. Then I had a wonderful professor, Payson Wilde, who taught courses in international law. He also had a profound effect on me. By this time, I was pretty well convinced I wanted to do something in my life that had to do with peace and security, economic development, and human rights. At Yale Law School, I fell under the influence of two great professors—Myres McDougal and Harold Lasswell. They were very much interested in a modern approach to international law— one that used law as an instrument of social policy. At Yale Law School, I co-authored an article in the *Yale Law Journal* with McDougal called 'The Veto and the Charter: An Interpretation for Survival,' in which Professor McDougal and I laid out the international law basis for the action of the UN Security Council in 1950 in coming to the aid of South Korea. . . . I applied for and received a Rhodes Scholarship and went to Oxford. I decided to do a Ph.D. in economics. . . . It was quite inspirational to me to see the kind of constructive internationalism that had come out of the Roosevelt and Truman administrations in these areas."

While at Oxford, Gardner attended the Sixth UN General Assembly in Paris. "When Warren Austin, who was the chief American delegate, became ill, Eleanor Roosevelt became the pro tempore head of our delegation. During the long winter vacation from Oxford, I followed Eleanor Roosevelt around the Palais de Chaillot, which was where this meeting was held, and wrote an article about her, about her role, and sent it to the *New York Times Magazine*. . . . And to my surprise, they used it. She was so pleased with the article that . . . I spent a weekend at Hyde Park in the summer of 1952 in which she would walk me around the grounds and tell me about her life with the president. I learned an awful lot from her."

Just Faaland looked back to an experience at the gymnasium (the top secondary school in countries such as Norway, Germany, and the Netherlands), which he finished in 1940. "I can remember one teacher who was quite good when I was ten or twelve years, who I thought was very clear and pointed. As it turned out, a few years later he became a Nazi. So I have thought of that. I have to be careful with my judgments. . . . At the end of November 1943, all students at the university were rounded up by the Germans and the Nazis. . . . We were put into a camp in Norway first, and everyone was interrogated and so on. It so happened that my father had been in prison for about six months for the same sort of activities, and my uncle. So they had my name from various other things. I think it was more that than my own doing that I was not among the half of us who were released. I was sent to Germany to Buchenwald for a year and a half, until the end of the war, together with 700 other Norwegian male students."

After the war, he was anxious to make up for lost time and crammed his remaining economics studies into one semester. "I went through these studies. I married. We had a child in May 1946. So it was a pretty active year, including going to Oxford. . . . Donald MacDougall was very influential in interesting me in the international world. . . . I got a feel for what was going on in these international organizations and what sort of people were there. . . . That's where I became an economist."

Guido de Marco recalled committing himself to politics from 1948, when he began attending university in Malta. "I started my first interventions in political life by doing what was then forbidden: forming a committee for nationalist students. At that time, it was forbidden in university to have any kind of political activity. All student activities used to end by the playing of the British national anthem. . . . I, in protest, used to walk out. My wife, then my girlfriend, used to feel very embarrassed seeing this boyfriend of hers performing this unholy rite of moving out whenever the British national anthem was being played. . . . I was never anti-British but I never felt happy at being a British subject."

He recalled the impact Franklin Delano Roosevelt had on him when he was in secondary school. "I started reading what Roosevelt was proposing, his freedoms—freedom from fear, freedom from want—these concepts were so much in keeping with my thinking as a young secondary school student. And when Roosevelt died in 1945, I was then thirteen years old, I remember I wore a black tie. I went to school with a black tie, as a sign of mourning." Later, he "was very much influenced by Keynes. I always found Marxism to be unacceptable for human dignity. . . . Whilst negating Marxism because I found that, in actual fact, it means a leveling down of people, I believe that a social market economy that has a social conscience, I think can be the solution to many of the ailments."

Jack Stone was at a junior college in Kansas City when he took a scholarship exam to go to the University of Chicago in the height of the era that put the university on the map under the presidency of the famous educator Robert Maynard Hutchins (1929–1951): "I eventually took a degree in political science at Chicago, but I was strongly interested in economics when I discovered that all political policy questions were grounded in economics. . . . As an undergraduate at Chicago I had heard all about Keynes. And Chicago was very much in flux then. There was an occasion, perhaps in 1939, when a man named Friedrich Hayek showed up and gave a lecture at the University of Chicago in which he purported to torpedo Keynes, you see, with numerical examples. . . . Of course, everyone around was very skeptical and pro-Keynes at that time. But Hayek later achieved a vast reputation at Chicago—and a Nobel Prize."

Stone returned to the United States after eight years in Germany and after working on the Marshall Plan, just in time for the McCarthy hearings, "which were something that kept one glued to one's television." He went to Harvard as a mid-career fellow: "I'm still all-but-dissertation, and I may in effect still do it. . . . When I left Harvard in 1959 and I went down to Puerto Rico, I had hoped to write a dissertation using material down there. But I'm afraid I was in the position of commuting too often to the United States because I was pursuing Jane, my wife."

Peg Snyder attended the College of New Rochelle, a Catholic women's college then. "My two brothers went to Notre Dame University. Our parents liked the idea of a Catholic school—and that was part, I think, of my formation in terms of social justice and economic justice." Influenced by the ideas of the Young Christian Students (YCS) that fused religion and student life, she remembered: "You had to live a whole life, and you had to be committed to other people. I suppose the influence was coming from my classes as well, and the example of our teachers. And then trying to understand the thought processes in the world through philosophy and relating them to everyday life. . . . YCS taught a thought process—observe, and judge, and act—that I use to this day. You look at what the situation is. You judge it in accordance with what you would hope it would be. . . . And then you plot your strategies and actions. Those three steps have stayed with me all my life." Going to graduate school at Catholic University in Washington and living in the South was traumatic: "My 'little sister' at New Rochelle [was] an African-American. She lived in Washington, so when I went down there I said, 'Oh, let's meet, Janie. Let's get together.' I proposed meeting her in a drugstore, and she said, 'We can't.' I tried to find a place where we could even sit at a counter and have a meal together. I became angry and speechless. I hadn't experienced what she had lived with all her life. Racial inequality and injustice really hit me in the face." Snyder then began working with the Catholic worker movement in New York and still receives the *Catholic Worker,* which still costs one cent, the price when Dorothy Day began publishing it. "And if you think you can get off their mailing list, you can't. . . . I had to do a master's thesis. . . . I did it on the Equal Rights Amendment for women."

In spite of his family's modest means, Francis Blanchard attended the prestigious Lycée Louis le Grand and studied law at the Sorbonne. He recalled: "The studies that I was pursuing were very expensive at that time. I was aware of this and uncomfortable about it. My father had only his salary as a staff member at the Compagnie Internationale des Grands Express Européens, where he was assistant head of personnel." He initially steered clear of politics: "I did not join a political party or a political association except for the France/Poland group with which I got involved out of a sense of commitment to Polish friends. In fact, my political knowledge consisted only in anxiously following events: the dramatic ones of 1934 in front of the Chamber of Deputies,[3] which the crowd in which I was swept up tried to approach; the Popular Front of 1936; and the rise of Nazism accompanied by a growing fear of war. Added to that was my reading of newspapers and more particularly the information that I followed on an ad hoc basis with an enormous thirst to learn but without the advice of a tutor or guide, for my father was uninterested in my studies, though my mother followed their evolution with worried tenderness. My relations with my father, whom I judged severely because of moments in which his anger was directed against my mother, made me speed up the completion of my studies in law as well as in political science."

Ignacy Sachs, who would distinguish himself as a comparative development economist, began his area of specialization "by accident." He remembered: "I began working very young and had to go to night classes. I had a choice between economics and law and bookkeeping. Well, faced with that choice, I opted for economics, especially since I was pretty much involved in politics and thus these studies lent themselves well to my interest in the world in which I was living."

Rubens Ricupero moved from studying law to economics, in part stimulated by his work organized by a Catholic organization of social assistance in a favela in São Paulo. "It was inspired by Dom Hélder Câmara, who was then the auxiliary bishop of Rio de Janeiro, where he had started this work. So the combination of the Catholic Action and the intellectual influence of Catholic authors were very important in giving me my basic values. . . . It was in the years immediately after the Second World War, when there were mainly three influences disputing the minds of young people. One was Marxism-Leninism and communism in general. The second one was existentialism, philosophical existentialism. The third one was what could be called center-left liberal—in the American sense—Catholicism. The major influence was Jacques Maritain, in philosophy, through the intermediary of some Brazilian thinkers, like Alceu Amoroso Lima—also known by his literary pseudonym of Tristão de Athayde—who was the greatest Catholic leader in Brazil at the time."

He drew sustenance from Catholic French writers such as Charles Peguy, Paul Claudel, Georges Bernanos, and François Mauriac in addition to the famous Jesuit theologian, Teilhard de Chardin.

Although he does not wear it on his sleeve, Jan Pronk's religion was directly linked to his choice of an academic path: "I was always, each Sunday, going to church, and I was also in my student days a Sunday school teacher, because I liked, though I was not a schoolteacher officially, I liked to teach. And I was very much interested in questions on the relation between religion, church, and society. Where I was going to church in Scheveningen, there was a traditional interest in preaching on those specific issues—ethics and religion, but in particular not only microethics but macroethics. You may say that, for instance, religious philosophers, such as Karl Barth, Dietrich Bonhoeffer, German scholars were often quoted and were seen as guiding teachers, a link perhaps also with what was known in Germany as *Die Bekennende Kirche,* the church which makes a choice. I also was influenced by Dutch religious teachers, such as Kraemer and Verkuyl, who on the basis of Christian mission in developing countries had become politically progressive, tried to do away with traditional missionary activities, bringing in humanitarian activities as well as political activities, to the extent that they were asking for understanding for wishes of people in developing countries who wanted to become independent. . . . The quest for liberation and independence was linked with the necessity to change the societies of the richer countries themselves. In Uppsala, for instance, a very important agenda item was how to combat racism within northern countries. And the question how to give shape to missionary activities in developing countries, the traditional mandate of the churches, was formulated upside down: do missions at home. You have to change your own societies rather than going out of your own societies to Third World countries to preach the gospel. Don't preach the gospel overseas, but translate the gospel at home into such a change in domestic policies that people in other countries really are able themselves to find a good place in God's creation."

The impact of Pronk's economic studies and ethical commitment were mutually reinforcing: "Politically, I had chosen in favor of democratic socialism in the 1960s. It was a rational choice, on the one hand—the result from my study in economics. It was also a political, ethical choice, following discussions on church and society. In the 1960s in the Netherlands, a New Left movement renewal took place, whereby young people took a political stance already very early in their student days and didn't allow themselves time to reflect. Twenty years later, in the 1980s, this resulted in many of these people shifting to the right. I did not. I had made my political choice less emotionally and not as a teenager."

Michael Doyle recalled being taught "by Jesuits only for two years, or actually three years—my education was so erratic and there were always different schools, so it amounted to three years. I was inspired by the intellectual quality. The Jesuits have an impressive track record in attracting high-quality secondary school teachers. I was also attracted by their attitude towards the world—my freshman history class started out with *The Guns of August*. The inspired agenda of Mr. Torres, who was teaching this class, was that there was a real danger of the world stumbling into wars. This was the early 1960s, the era of the Cuban Missile Crisis, so there was genuine connection. . . . The analytic worldview came through without the religious doctrine—I was never very religious. Nor did they teach us casuistry, other than through osmosis. But the overall orientation towards public service—that you had to make a difference in the world—was real to them. I don't think they inspired a single person in my entire school, at least in my class, to become a priest, but a lot of people became lawyers and doctors and officials and military officers."

Those growing up under colonial occupation pointed to striking educational experiences in primary or secondary school as influencing their views and orientations. In Noeleen Heyzer's case, the Jesuits came to the rescue, but she recalled the bitter poverty that had temporarily prevented her education: "My grandmother was shocked that by the time I was eight I was still not in school. So she went to see the archbishop. I don't know how she did that, not knowing English, yet she managed to communicate with him. Through strength of personality, she got him to visit the family. When he saw me he thought I was intelligent and decided that the best place to put me was this elite Catholic school." The fees were paid by the grandmother and relatives.

Heyzer moved beyond an initial feeling of ambivalence and came to value the Christian priests who opened her eyes: "Yet much later—and this shaped me in not thinking in black and white or coming to quick stereotypical conclusions, because I saw the complexities of things—I realized that the people who were really instrumental in shaping my mental strength, and even my power of analysis, were the Jesuit priests. It was the priests who somehow noticed me. There were at least five priests in my life, and each one of them gave me a different gift. One basically taught me what it meant to be a leader. He stressed that real leadership was service and doing the ordinary things extraordinarily well. Another taught me a new way of thinking about the world and myself so that we could get out of how society defines us. Singapore was still an identity-based society, so you had to fit into ethnic groups. You were either Chinese, Indian, or other. But he literally shifted my thinking out of the social construct of identity into another more universal and spiritual frame. The whole idea of transcendence, that you can actually transcend and recreate from that position of transcendence was very powerful and has always remained with me. Another priest taught me social analysis. I was very much influenced by the theology of liberation at that time, and definitely by the issue of social justice. So for me, this relationship—if it did anything to me, it developed a sense of moral commitment, of moral outrage about social injustice, as well as an understanding that development must have an ethical base. . . . There were many things that I disliked about the Church. I found it very autocratic, unable to take in other peoples' experiences. I found so many things wrong with it, especially since I was living in a community that practiced Buddhism, Taoism and Chinese religion. But at the same time, there were still things in it that strengthened me."

Her initial training was in mathematics and the sciences, but she came to realize that "it didn't give me enough. There was so much in me that I needed to understand. I knew there was a world with human complexities, and I was fascinated by the interfacing of everyday human life with the context in which people lived and with the strong historical forces that were being played out. . . . So sociology fascinated me, anthropology too, and political science. I was very lucky because I was too poor to be sent abroad, but at that time Singapore made some wise decisions. Among them, the decision to bring the best minds and the best teachers from different universities to the country so that more people could be exposed to them."

After being elected secretary of the Democratic Socialist Club, Heyzer went on a sponsored trip "to the Scandinavian countries at the age of about twenty or twenty-one to learn what they called the 'third way.' And this was about how could the market economy be used for socialist purposes, for social needs? . . . That trip to Europe was very special because I went to the Nordic countries and had discussions with the youth, internationally as well, while looking at what else people were doing with labor unions and other democratic institutions. There I met Gunnar Myrdal, who discussed and gave me his book *Asian Drama*. It was very interesting for me to get a much larger perspective not just on Singapore but also on the whole region and what people thought about our experience."

Returning home, she completed a master's degree after a first work experience: "I went to work in a British bank because my family wanted me to work after the first degree. But within six months, I knew it was not for me." She then won a fellowship to the UK: "Cambridge, in a way, made me who I am today. . . . Actually, it was the library of Cambridge. I never had time nor space to be alone because of the closeness of the family structure. I never had my own room until the last year of university. I never had a place where I could actually think through things properly. Many things still didn't crystallize for me. I was still trying to read and trying to understand. Cambridge gave me space. It gave me time. And it gave me the chance to be alone. That was the best part, because it was in that solitude that I found my own voice."

Unlike her well-behaved siblings, Nafis Sadik admitted somewhat sheepishly that "I was sent to school because I was so naughty that I needed school discipline." As a Muslim, her family was creative about the options, and like other voices, she too was a beneficiary of Catholic schools: "I went to a convent and the nuns were always trying, now in retrospect I think, to convert me. Some girls did convert. Most of the girls in the school, Loretto House, were not Catholics. Most were Hindus and a few Muslims. I wanted to go to college. I wasn't sure what I wanted to do, whether engineering or medicine. Anyway, I decided that I would do physics and chemistry and biology and thus decide on my profession. . . . There was none of that in the college attached to . . . Loretto House. The nuns then got some teachers especially for me so that I would stay in the college. Can you believe that? And they even gave me a scholarship of some very small amount. But still, it was a scholarship to keep me in the college. And they told my father, 'You know, she must stay here. She is brilliant.' . . . Then they told my father that they were giving me this fellowship and this would help to pay the fees, because the fees would have to be increased to pay for the professor. He said, 'Oh, that's good for you. That will be your pocket money.' And the nuns were so shocked. So he said to them, 'But she earned it, not me. I am responsible for her education.' So the money was mine. It was the first money I earned."

Sadik fondly recalled those days: "They didn't teach us catechism, but we knew a lot about the scriptures. We knew a lot about Christianity as such. They didn't denigrate other religions and just said that the Catholic approach was so good. But I remember having many arguments with them. And yet, I really adored my teachers because they were really very, very good, and they were very interesting. There were many Irish nuns. They played basketball with us. I was on the basketball team, on the badminton team. So it was good fun." The Loretto Convent had its 200th anniversary several years ago, when Sadik's work on family planning was well known: "Of course, I never got an invitation because I think they found out what I was doing."

Her choice of medicine was anything but straightforward: "I decided myself that engineering was not a profession that I could really ask to go into because everyone would laugh. It was not a profession that women went into. I was excellent at math and physics. . . . I decided I wanted to do medicine, I told my uncle that I wanted to do medicine. So my uncle said, 'It's no problem, I'm sure. Your father is so fanatical about education.' I said, 'But I'm not sure, because everyone is trying to arrange for me to get married. I certainly don't want to be married to anyone. I don't even know who these people are that are asking.' So he talked to my father. My father was most upset: 'How could you go to your uncle to ask this?' To show that he really cared about education, he took me to all interviews for getting into medical school himself. . . . I got into medical school—Calcutta Medical College. . . . In Calcutta, there were very few girls, especially Muslim girls. There were just two of us."

The impact of French academics in São Paulo was influential for former Brazilian president Fernando Henrique Cardoso, who recalled: "The social science branch was organized by the French—so Levi-Strauss, and Braudel, and Bastide, et cetera. I entered the university in 1948 or 1949. Levi-Strauss was no longer there. I met Levi-Strauss many, many years after that, in Paris. My wife's master's degree was under the guidance of Levi-Strauss in France. But, at one point in time, I guess in 1950, practically all my professors at the university were French, and they gave us class in French. At the time, the influence was enormous. Then some years later, another generation of French came, like Alain Touraine—who since then is a friend of mine—as well as several others. In practice, we were kind of a subsidiary of the French university. I mean this group at the University of São Paulo—the influence was enormous, of course, and Jean-Paul Sartre—even Sartre personally. Recently, I found a small message Sartre sent me in the late-1950s. I was organizing my old files when I found it. Sartre handed me a written permission authorizing me to publish any of his books or articles or anything from *Les Temps Modernes* in Portuguese."

As his studies progressed, a rivalry grew that helped him confront the conventional wisdom in the capital, Rio de Janeiro. "What they were saying was kind of rubbish—ideology. So we were against the ideological approach to the analysis of social phenomena. . . . We started this group on Marxism. I don't remember exactly, but it was probably at the end of the second half of the 1950s." But he was careful to indicate that they were "reading Marx in the sense of a philosopher. So this group was composed by different people—historians, economists, sociologists, anthropologists, people close to the literature. The idea was, let's take the text and to make a phenomenological analysis of the text. So we wasted hours and hours discussing details. We were very pedantic people. So one was with a book in German, another in Italian, another in Spanish, and Portuguese—to compare. So I read the whole critical history of surplus value—books and books and books about it—and economic theory, and then *Das Kapital,* page by page. I still have my books with handwritten remarks. It was difficult to understand how it was possible to be so isolated from real life. So this was the so-called 'Marx seminar.'" Colleagues were not uniformly impressed with the content: "Florestan Fernandes later became a deputy for the Workers' Party, a fellow deputy, at the end of his life. Now he is a big totem of Brazilian Marxism. At the time, he once called me and he said, 'What are you debating, reading this kind of poetry?' It was Lukács, because we were discussing Lukács. For him, he was trying to alert me to the risks of wasting time reading this kind of people instead of doing research and a concrete analysis of social processes. . . . He said, 'We have three or four big masters—Durkheim, Weber, Marx, and also Parsons and Merton. It depends on the subject. It depends on what kind of question you are dealing with. If you are dealing with long historical processes, maybe you can use Marx. If you prefer to discuss contemporaneous processes, well then it is better to aspire to Durkheim, or the functionalist approach.'"

Returning to his original interest in philosophy and Jean-Paul Sartre, he said: "So the bridge between our training and our research and Marxism was Sartre. Why? Because Marxism at the time was very, very rigid. It was all determinism. Sartre had a quite free interpretation of Marx in his essays on methodology. I don't remember the name of it. He has a big book, and in some papers Sartre wrote about how to deal with issues of method. So we took from Sartre the possibility to revise a little bit Marxism in order to reinterpret more flexibly. So my first important book was *Capitalism and Slavery in Southern Brasil*."

Mostafa Tolba looked back to his late teen years, when "the Muslim Brotherhood had already become extremely, extremely active in Egypt. There was nothing whatsoever at that time related to terrorism or usurping power or anything of that sort. . . . I was already a member of the Muslim Brotherhood, and I helped my friends establish a little mosque in the faculty of science." Among the evening sessions were efforts to understand alternatives: "We were staying in the faculty all night. We had *Das Kapital* by Karl Marx with us, and each one of us studied a chapter and gave a synopsis of what was in this chapter, an analysis of how we felt this was relating to our feudalist system at that time, the emerging capitalist system in the country and the Islamic system, which is more towards social equity than the capitalist system. . . . So when the revolution came in 1952, there was a clear direction towards social justice and the application of socialist economy rather than the feudal system, thus jumping over the capitalist system directly into a social system." His mother was keen that her only surviving child pursue an education. "At that time I was like all the young people in Egypt, extremely fascinated by the uniforms of the students in the military schools. They had beautiful red tapes and things.

At the age of sixteen and for all of us, it was very attractive to the girls. Egypt was a closed society, so [it was] something to show off."

Changing his focus later was as a result of a clerical error because he was too young to apply to the military college but was accepted. A friend commented: "I am the sixty-seventh, and I applied to the faculty of medicine and you are seventeenth and going into this rat hole. You are going with me to the faculty of medicine." The errors continued and Tolba filled in a form for the faculty of science instead of medicine.

Oscar Schachter recalled the intellectual cauldron for talented students of modest or no means that was The City College of New York in the 1930s. "The great majority of students were leftists—communist, socialist, Trotskyist, even anarchist. The civil war in Spain had a powerful effect on many students. It also brought out the strong differences among the anti-Franco leftist groups. Later, collective security emerged as a controversial issue focused on aid to Britain. The great debate between the 'America First' supporters and the collective security adherents split student opinion from 1936 until the early years of World War II." He recalled sorting out his views toward the coming world war: "I can now recall moving from one pole to another on the issues during 1934 to 1939. American progressives, such as Senators LaFollette and Wheeler Nye, whom I tended to support on domestic issues, were strongly critical of 'intervention' into the European war. I moved to a collective security position in the late 1930s because of Nazi aggression during my last two years of law school, 1938 to 1939. I recall that many of the international law professors leaned toward the 'America First' position and favored American neutrality rather than intervention on the Allied side. Although I was deeply moved by the threats of fascism—Franco in Spain, and of course the Nazis—it never occurred to me that my career would have an international aspect."

Michael Doyle, probably our youngest voice, traced his experience with another war, Vietnam. While he initially joined the U.S. Air Force Academy out of a desire for public service, he transferred to Harvard University: "The Air Force, like the priesthood, like a prison, is a total institution. For a few months after leaving the Academy I experienced an immense sense of liberation. I had been there for two straight years, with two weeks off total, during the whole time. So I had been totally in their grip, intellectually and psychologically. On leaving, one of the very first things I did was to walk to a grocery store and walk through the aisles to see all this consumer choice in front of me. There was an immense sense of liberation when I went to Cambridge, both personally—I felt so free it was extraordinary—and second of all, intellectually, in that I could take this whole smorgasbord of a course catalog that was 400 pages long. I felt the excitement in scholarship—scholarship and the freedom of it. Those were the two things that were most extraordinary. . . . I walked into a politically and socially radical environment; to me it was another planet. What were these people about? It took a long time to figure out that they were engaged in issues that I should be interested in. The whole first year I spent every waking moment in class or in the library working, just soaking up an intellectual feast available to me. In my senior year, I got more involved in politics, as we all did."

Doyle went on to describe his involvement in avoiding the war and fulfilling the obligations that he had assumed by attending the Air Force Academy: "At that point, I was very much opposed to the Vietnam War. So it was either go to Canada or find some easy way out. Like so many people in my generation, I took an easy way out, which was to go into the U.S. Air National Guard for the next four years as a weekend warrior, like George Bush and Dan Quayle. . . . I showed up every weekend. Unlike what we read about the president, I had a perfect attendance record. I was there playing blackjack every weekend for the next four years. That's how I did my military service. The ironic thing was that the National Guard unit was in Wellesley, Massachusetts, so we kidded ourselves that the only danger we ever faced was the Veterans' Day Parade every year. They marched our unit right downtown through Wellesley. And the Wellesley College Students were out there shouting and throwing things at us. That was the only 'combat danger' to which I was exposed in the Vietnam War: the Wellesley women."

Adebayo Adedeji looked back at his fiery differences with his father over early schooling and fondly recalled his grandmother's warm support: "My primary school teacher, Mr. Olatunji Dosunmu, because of the way I had been brought up, thought that it would be a waste of my talents to keep me in primary school for six years or more. He therefore persuaded the school headmaster to allow me to sit the entrance examination to Ijebu-Ode Grammar School in 1943 when I was only twelve years old. . . . My grandmother was very hesitant with my primary school decision that I should sit the entrance exam because my father had always wanted me to go to King's College. . . . Grandma relented and paid the examination fee. So without the knowledge of my father . . . I took the exam in July 1943. . . . I had become an instant hero in the school, because of all the thirty boys who went for the exam from my school—all in standards 6 and 5, only three of us had succeeded. Now how could I go back? So I told this to my mother . . . 'I am not going to my primary school again.' To make my point, I went on a hunger strike. Of course, that nearly killed my grandmother when she was told."

He set aside an earlier interest in medicine and gynecology after a family financial crisis: "My father joined others in establishing the Farmers Bank. Of course, he didn't have anything to do with the management of it. But those who were appointed to manage it did it so very badly, and the bank went bankrupt. It was clear after that that whatever his ambition had been for me in terms of medicine would have to wait for two or three years at least.... The job that was first offered to me through my uncle I refused to take. It was in the Customs Department, and customs officers were generally perceived by the public to be very corrupt.... So I went home and convinced my uncle's wife to give me transport money to go to Ibadan from Lagos.... Fortunately, the Colonial Government had just established WAISER [West African Institute for Social and Economic Research] and attached it to the University College, Ibadan.... The authorities were looking for research assistants to help a Professor W. B. Schwab of Pennsylvania State University, who was coming to do a socioeconomic survey of a medium-sized town in southern Nigeria. So I signed up for that job and was one of a team of ten research assistants."

The experience led Adedeji to obtain a first degree in economics from London University in June 1958. After a brief year in the civil service, he pursued a master's degree at Harvard through a Ford Foundation grant. He recalled: "In Britain, you were more concerned with the world, including Britain. In America, you were more concerned with the United States and then the world. ... There were a lot of expectations in terms of the development capabilities of the Third World. But, increasingly, even before I left Harvard, there was a kind of revisionism in terms of the prospects of Asia for development. And at that time, it was felt that Africa, being a *tabula rasa,* was likely to achieve more rapid progress. Gunnar Myrdal had just done his seminal study.... At Harvard there was more knowledge about Asia than about Africa.... There was a lot of extrapolation . . . that the development problems of India were the same as those of Africa, except that, because the Indians are not Christians, they don't have protestant ethics, they don't have the spirit of capitalism."

Samir Amin recalled his education in Cairo at a French lycée, the preferred training for the elite of that time: "Contrary to fashionable gossip, it was of a very high cultural level and quite progressive in content. I learned more and better about Egyptian history at the lycée than Egyptians learned in Egyptian schools. When I compare, for example, the lycée with what Edward Said, a friend who came from English schools, says of Victoria College! That College was terrible, its teaching and staff racist, colonialist, in the most violent sense of the terms. The lycée wasn't that at all; quite the contrary. At that time the students, at least the Egyptian students, who were a large minority, were extremely politicized by the time they reached secondary school. We were divided into two groups, communists and nationalists. Those were the labels that we gave ourselves. The nationalists were anti-British, not necessarily pro-

Germany and certainly not pro-Nazis because they didn't really have any idea what that meant. They were fundamentally anti-British and nothing more. Those who called themselves communists assigned more importance to the social dimension of the problem and linked the question of imperialism and colonialism to that of the social class structure in Egyptian society, as we put it then. Of course, I belonged to the group that proclaimed itself communist."

He went on to complete a doctorate and recalled: "I arrived in Paris and didn't want to be a political emigrant because I saw around me the degradation that affects political emigrants who live with the illusion that they are continuing to be active in their country. Having been a student in France from 1947 to 1957, I was active in the UNEF [Union des Étudiants de France/ Union of French Students] in the Communist Party and also in organizations of anti-colonialist students, both those of Arab, including Egyptian, students and those of Asians and Africans, who were numerous in Paris at that time, the most active being the Vietnamese, of course, but also Algerians, North Africans, and black Africans. That's where I met a good number of those who were to become the political class of French-speaking black Africa as well as young people from the Middle East who were also numerous at that time, Egyptians, Syrians, Iraqis."

For Virendra Dayal, reading history was an important preparation for his career: "Anyone who read modern history, and the history of the interwar period, knew about the League and its catastrophes and knew why the UN was needed and why it had to be careful to avoid the same mistakes. I think all of that was in our bones." Recalling his experience at St. Stephen's, "the best college in the country," led to the following observation: "So it was a curious institution because it was Anglican, associated with Cambridge University, had plenty of Englishmen on the staff, and the finest of them were sympathetic to India's independence. And there were Indian principals to head it, many decades before independence."

The ironies continued when Dayal won a Rhodes scholarship; he "had a sense of guilt about it for many years after. . . . For many years, I hid the fact that I had been the beneficiary of Cecil Rhodes's will because of his rather strange role in imperial history. But the truth came out and no one held it against me." At the same time, he nostalgically admitted that "the auspices under which I went to Oxford were quite charmed. . . . I used to always stay with a wonderful lady who was a member of Parliament, Dame Joan Vickers, who was later a member of the House of Lords. She used to live in Thackeray's house." Yet the magical experience of Oxford was mitigated by remnants of empire: "There was a certain tension there between, should I say, the *ancien regime* of Britain and those of us who came from what used to be British colonies or other parts of the world. I remember once meeting someone at Rhodes House who talked about friends of his who had served in the Indian civil service. He said, 'How unfortunate India's independence is—all those brilliant careers were aborted!'" Dayal was anxious to return to India for several reasons: "But for all of that, I was very homesick. And I was very keen on getting on with my life, partly because the woman I loved was in India and I was alone in Oxford. Partly, I just needed to get on with doing things. . . . I wanted to work in development."

This fluidity between overseas education and at home was present in many stories. Amartya Sen recalled: "We came back in 1939, in late 1939. When the Japanese army advanced into Burma and just an inch or two into the extreme east of India, I was going to school in Dhaka—a liberal missionary school, St. Gregory's, in old Dhaka, not far from my home. And then my father, who was back from Burma and teaching again at Dhaka university, got suddenly persuaded then that Dhaka and Calcutta would be both bombed by the Japanese. So I was dispatched to Santiniketan, to my mother's town, where my maternal grandfather was still teaching. I went there as a primary school student and absolutely loved it.

"St. Gregory's was academically very distinguished—I expect more than Santiniketan was in terms of hard-nosed education—but I liked the more relaxed and less academic priorities in Santiniketan and the magnificent combination of focusing on India's own traditions with much opportunity to learn about other countries and their cultures. Santiniketan was a very different kind of school from St. Gregory's, and it was sometimes even described as being a nationalist school.

"Yes, in an odd way it was, despite Tagore's intense suspicion of nationalism. It was a Bengali medium school, and we studied a lot about ancient India, medieval India, and Indian culture generally. But Santiniketan was also very open to the world, not just India. Nor did we assume that the world outside India consisted primarily of Britain—an implicit priority that was standard in much of India then. I mean, in those days of the Raj—in fact its very last days—being "international" often meant being thoroughly focused on Britain, really. In contrast, we were involved both with Indian and with world history, rather than only British history. We were aware—more than in most of India—of not only the French, the Italian, the German, the Russians, and so on, but also seized of the huge presence of China in world history, along with the rest of Asia and Africa. Santiniketan had, I think, the first institute of Chinese studies in all of India, the distinguished 'China Bhavan' (as it was then called), the Institute of Chinese Studies, directed by the great scholar Dr. Tan Yun-Shan. Then there was a lot about Japan, a lot about Korea, a lot about

Indonesia, Thailand, Korea, Malaysia, Indochina and so on, and quite a bit about the Middle East, and of course the huge excitement in learning about Africa."

It was during this period that Sen got interested in politics through his extended family: "Well, my maternal uncle and a number of my cousins in the generation ahead of me (they are often generically called 'uncles' and 'aunts' in India) were in prison. They were in prison under what was called 'preventive detention'—not that they had done anything dreadful, but the Raj's theory was that they could possibly do something dreadful for the Raj, and the Raj would incarcerate them to prevent future actions, since they had written or said things against the British dominance of India.

"My mother's only brother, who belonged to the socialist wing of the Congress Party, was in prison under preventive detention for many years. I liked him a lot and as a young boy went to see him often in prison. I was quite amazed that he was in prison. I kept asking him what had he done. He explained he hadn't done anything much yet other than writing, except the British rulers did think that he might do something damaging to them if he had been let free.

"These imprisonments lasted quite a few years. One of the cousins of my father actually died in prison of tuberculosis—or more accurately, shortly after being released and placed in home confinement. This was in the 1930s. There were quite a lot of prisoners at that time. They were involved in different political parties. Among that generation of so-called uncles—that is, both my real uncle as well as cousins of my father and mother—there were people who were in the mainstream Congress Party, the Congress Socialist Party, and in the Communist Party. None, I should add, in the right-wing Hindu party, the so-called Hindu Mahasabha—which was the predecessor of Jan Sangh, which in turn was the predecessor of today's BJP [Bharatiya Janata Party], which leads the coalition that runs the central government as we speak. But on the secular left or secular center, there was quite a lot of versatility within the family. I quite enjoyed chatting with them on politics. It was very exciting and rather instructive for me."

Studying Abroad

The postwar period witnessed the emergence of new fellowship opportunities for study in universities in the North—from the emergence of Ford Foundation Area Studies grants and Fulbright fellowships for study in the United States to state scholarships to study in the Eastern bloc. For many of our interlocutors, the opportunity to study in another country was a life- and career-altering experience.

While attending a student meeting in Freetown in neighboring Sierra Leone, Kofi Annan was informed about a Ford Foundation program for foreign student leaders by a gentleman who said, "I think you are the type of person who would do well in this program, and I'm going to put your name forward. They will send you an application, and fill it out." And so the future secretary-general left Ghana and attended Macalester College in Minnesota. He remembered his first winter: "You had read about snow, you felt you are familiar with it until you finally confront it. . . . As somebody from the tropics, I didn't like putting on layers and layers of clothing to keep warm. . . . One thing I swore never to wear was earmuffs, until one day I had gone out to get something to eat and almost lost my ears. I went and bought the biggest pair of earmuffs I could find. When I went back to Macalester a few years ago, I told them this story. I said, 'The lesson I walked away with was don't go to a place and pretend you know better than the natives. Listen to them and do what they do.'"

A West African visitor was unusual in the Minnesotan capital that was a center for large-scale Scandinavian immigration to the United States. "There weren't many Africans, and for that matter, that many black Americans in the college," Annan told us. "But it was interesting there. For somebody who had gone through the independence movement, to come to the States and see the rumblings of Black Power and the civil rights movement is something that resonated, and I could relate to, and I could understand. But there were also moments when you realized that there was a gulf—a gulf between Africans and the black Americans. . . . At that time, there was quite a lot of turmoil. It wasn't just the black movement in the U.S. There was also support for the struggle for independence in Africa." He remembered "a convergence in the black struggle here and the African struggle for independence. You had students quoting Frantz Fanon, *The Wretched of the Earth, War and Peace, Cry the Beloved Country,* the American Constitution and the UN Charter, and, not surprisingly, the speeches of Abraham Lincoln."

Bernard Chidzero obtained a B.A. in psychology from Pius XII University College in Basutoland (now Lesotho), which was part of the University of South Africa. He had first left Rhodesia to be schooled in what he and his family considered a less racist country—preapartheid South Africa. He recalled that his education was financed "partly from my father and partly from my mother's brewing beer and selling it on weekends." His international interest "was the result mainly of being exposed to people who came from various parts of the world: the Irish, the Canadians, the English and fellow Africans from Kenya, Uganda, and so on. Partly from the subjects I took: history and, of all things, Latin. I spent five years studying Latin. It was for me a great stimulation of the imagination. Can you imagine Caesar declaring: *Veni, vidi, vici* [I came, I saw, I conquered]? We repeated the words and acted like Romans. . . . For young people in Africa, to study Roman history and the wars between the Carthagenians and the Romans called for imagination and when Scipio says, *Delenda est Carthage* (Carthage must be destroyed) you want to know where is Carthage."

Basically illiterate until about age twelve, he quickly made up for lost time and earned his Ph.D. in government and international relations at McGill University in Montreal and then spent two years doing research at Oxford's Nuffield College. He recalled that when he arrived in Mattawa, Ontario, Canada, in the 1950s, there were "only two black people." The other was a Haitian medical doctor. Like many North American students during the summer holidays, he found a summer job. He "worked as a sleeping car porter, riding Canadian Pacific Railways from Montreal to Detroit and from Montreal to New York, making passenger beds."

Victor Urquidi studied economics at the London School of Economics (LSE) in the late 1930s. "My knowledge of statistics came from keeping scores of jai alai games, working out percentages," he recalls. "I was at the hub of a school dedicated to international studies, to international politics, to international economics. . . . I was better trained than most young entrants into the university. And I also had the advantage of knowing Spanish and French."

Don Mills studied mathematics and chemistry at Jamaica College in the 1930s and "wondered whether it would have been more appropriate . . . to have studied, say, history and literature at an advanced level and at university." After graduating, he wound up working in the island's Treasury Department, which turned out to be fortunate for North-South negotiations because "by reason of working in the development area and with these older persons, I ended up getting a scholarship to go to LSE to study economics." After the war, he noted, "A large number of young persons from the colonies, myself among them, went . . . to universities in Britain, France, and other European countries, having in most cases no universities of their own at the time. So England in the war and postwar years had a significant number of what they called colonial students. I ended up living in a hostel, which was full of Africans, Asians, and Caribbean people. That was a marvelous experience. That was my introduction, if you like, to what we call the Third World. Also, it was the place where the West Indian connection was nurtured. As students, we formed a West Indian Students Union, which was very active, and we got to know each other—you better believe it."

Alister McIntyre also went to LSE as an undergraduate: "Then my eyes were further opened by a number of things. But I was particularly disappointed, in a way, that there was no teaching in development economics *per se,* except for a set of graduate courses taught by Peter Bauer, who was very controversial and not then thought to be a sympathetic exponent of the subject from the point of view of developing countries."

During those years, the first important gathering to promote cooperation among African and Asian countries occurred in Indonesia, at Bandung.[4] McIntyre recalled: "At LSE, a Bandung Society was formed. After the initial discussion of the major political issues of the day, the Bandung Society got into development questions. It invited a number of prominent speakers, persons in Britain from the political or academic communities or from the media. They were invited to come for a luncheon discussion or something equivalent. Actually, in the three years that I spent as an undergraduate at the London School of Economics, I spent a lot of time reading about development issues, discussing development with my peers, and listening to views. I remember being particularly influenced by Andrew Shonfield, who himself was influenced by Lewis. Shonfield was a kind of middle-of-the-road liberal, but on development questions I think that he was much more inclined towards liberal in the U.S. version, that is, somewhat left of center."

McIntyre's mentor was James Meade, who pushed the young Grenadan. McIntyre recalled the question: "Look, you must change institutions. Why don't you try to get into Cambridge and work with Joan Robinson?" McIntyre continued: "Well, I had read some of Joan Robinson's work, and I did not think that small open economies were a major interest of hers. So I told him that I wasn't too keen. He was rather surprised, because at that time she was writing on China, and she was really quite an exceptional scholar. I had met her twice as an undergraduate. . . . So then he reviewed other options, and said, 'Why don't you try to get into Nuffield? Donald MacDougal is there. He has done some work on the Caribbean, and you might find him interesting.' Ian Little was also there. He was then working on India. So I applied and went to Nuffield. . . . Because of MacDougal's influence, I had begun reading Prebisch when I was a student at Nuffield. He was very skeptical about the Prebisch-Singer hypothesis, and so we had some quite lively discussions in his rooms. But nonetheless, he brought the literature to me. I became particularly interested in Prebisch's advocacy of a Latin American Common Market partly to see what insights could be gained for the Caribbean."

Indeed, in tracing his path to graduate work, McIntyre interrupted the chronology and pointed back to a memorable experience in secondary school: "I came across the books of Arthur Lewis. He had donated copies of his books to the leading politician on the island prior to Gairy, T. A. Marryshow, who is often called the father of Caribbean Federation. Marryshow in turn donated them to the school library. . . . [I] was very proud to find that this young man from St. Lucia was now among the leading economists in Britain. That sparked my interest in economics so much so that when I came to take the equivalent of A-levels, I told my headmaster that I wanted to do economics. He said, 'How can you? We don't teach this here.' I insisted. I said I would teach myself, and I think I am still suffering from the scars of that."

One of the benefits of studying overseas is, of course, a comparative perspective. McIntyre recalled his impressions as a Fulbright scholar in the turbulent 1960s in the United States: "I didn't meet too many blacks at Princeton at the time. In fact, I went into the library once to put some books on the reserve list, and the lady told me, 'I'm sorry. You can't touch those. They have been reserved by Professor McIntyre.' . . . The degree of activism that I found at Columbia on the racial issue was much higher at the time than it was at Princeton. I remember on one occasion I was given a carrel and some students came to see me, mainly Puerto Ricans. They said, 'Why are you not in a big office?' . . . They were really quite upset. So I went and said to the office manager, who was a very pleasant woman, 'I don't know what is involved, but a number of people feel that my office is inappropriate. They are suggesting that I should appeal to the Congress on Racial Equality.' She nearly had a heart attack. The next thing I knew, I was moved to a very palatial office, which remained quite out of proportion to my comparatively humble status as a Fulbright scholar."

Surendra Patel, like many of our interlocutors, recalled that "what gave me the incentive to study was the constant encouragement and support of my parents. I had good marks at school. I was therefore privileged to obtain scholarships, which permitted me first to join the Commerce College at Ahmedabad. Thereafter, I received a fellowship to go to Wharton School at the University of Pennsylvania in Philadelphia." After meeting Nobel laureate Simon S. Kuznets, Patel completed his doctoral thesis under Professor Daniel Thorner in July 1949 on income development and distribution. "My thesis, [published as] *Agricultural Labourers in Modern India and Pakistan,* traced back the social evolution of India and Pakistan's agricultural society from pre-nineteenth century onwards. It was my first published book in English. . . . Before that I had written a number of articles, both in Gujarati and in English. One of the main pieces I wrote was as a tribute to Keynes. He had just died. It occurred to me that Keynes's and Marx's contributions to modern economics were immense. I decided to write a piece titled 'Marxism and Recent Economic Thought.' I submitted the article to Kuznets. He liked it and distributed it in the class. Kuznets also advised me to send it to *Science and Society.* . . . My article was published in the winter 1947 edition. . . . This article argued that after the Great Depression, a re-evaluation of the earlier capitalist thinking was inevitable. While Marx had been ignored, rejected, or mocked in the past decades, the Keynesian concept of the income stream was divided into the channels of consumption and investment, which strikingly resembled Marx's reflection on the dangers of 'dis-equilibrium.' The Great Depression had definitely shaken the arrogant posture of overconfident capitalism, and Keynes had no doubt redefined the rules of the game in a structure that appeared to me as very close to Marx's own thinking."

Michael Zammit Cutajar remembered that he studied economics because "I thought, mistakenly, that it might be helpful in carrying the family business forward and also thought that it might appeal to my father as something relevant and therefore fundable. The latter worked, the former didn't, and I stayed out of the family business after having done my first degree, which is my only degree, at the University of London. . . . I didn't really integrate well and therefore didn't get much into discussion about the big issues of the day. . . . But [I] felt myself somehow naturally drawn to the side of the reformists, the Labour Party in the UK."

Gert Rosenthal, having been sent to the United States to finish high school, "ended up at the University of California at Berkeley. And I felt some sort of commitment to development in general, and to Guatemala in particular, trying to make sense of my life. So I went into development economics. . . . I had that idea even before I went into college."

Echoing Rosenthal, John Ruggie explained his choice of study as an undergraduate at McMaster University in Canada. "What led me into history, politics, and political economy was, quite frankly, to try to make sense out of my own life: why the situation in which I found myself as a young boy existed; how it got to be that way; what the prospects were for overcoming those kinds of social, economic, and political constraints; if [there were] other instances in history that were like this; and what happened. So I think it was part of a personal odyssey."

Next was graduate school. "There wasn't any place to go other than Berkeley in the summer of 1967." After marrying, he drove a series of cars across the country and finally arrived to what was an initially frightening encounter: "The first person I met was from Yale, and Yale University Press had published his B.A. thesis. The next three or four people were from Princeton and Harvard. One had published an article with his professor in one of the main political science journals. I thought, 'Oh, my God. What am I doing here?'" But dropping out never occurred to him "because the one thing I learned growing up the way I did was that you wanted to go on in school absolutely as far as you could so that you wouldn't have to struggle in life the way my par-

ents did. . . . The first professor I encountered, and the mentor I remain closest to even to this day, was Ernie Haas. He, as you know, was a student of
multilateralism, of international transformation, and of the relationship between multilateralism and change in the world system. While I never bought
into his specific formulations, the kinds of questions he asked—how did the
system of nation-states get here? Where is it going? And what is driving that?—
I found those questions fascinating, then and now. . . . At Berkeley almost
everybody was on my left. . . . I never bought into the underlying historical
materialism of the work, but the questions always interested me and were
very complementary to questions I was asking."

Sadako Ogata remembered fondly a variety of educational institutions she
had attended prior to becoming a university teacher and administrator herself: "I was in the Academy of the Sacred Heart, a private girls' school . . .
playing tennis much more than studying in those days. . . . I had just finished
high school at the time of the end of the war. . . . We all went to study abroad—
a lot of scholars of my generation. And I think we had a common interest in
trying to understand one thing: Why did Japan start that war? So it was really
part of our generation—the first postwar generation of scholars all studied
our own diplomatic and political history. My own dissertation, that I presented later to the University of California, came out in a book called *Defiance
in Manchuria*. But it was really trying to link the domestic political situation
and Japan's own advancement or aggression to the continent. I think this is
something that I know. I know war. I know peace."

Between her time at Georgetown as an undergraduate and at Berkeley as a
graduate student, Ogata returned home for a Japanese diploma in political
history. "After having come to the United States and seeing Japan from the
outside—I became seriously interested in the political and diplomatic context of Japanese history. From a normal, ordinary, young, fun-loving student,
I think I turned into an inquiring, dedicated student. . . . That's why I went
back to do much more serious study. And I concentrated on the political and
diplomatic history of Japan." She received her Ph.D. in 1963 after beginning
a family. "In those days, you didn't travel so easily with foreign exchange
control. . . . I had to get the orals done, so I went to Berkeley with a baby in
1962. But anyway, I managed."

Hans Singer recalled that his father "had a great desire I should study medicine and follow him. . . . He discouraged me from studying economics. . . . But
he said 'If you want to be an economist, okay, but then you require practical
business knowledge,' and he wanted to put me into the local bank. . . . But I
wanted to study economics. So I went off to Bonn, half intending to study
medicine. At least my father understood that I was going up to Bonn to study

medicine, and actually I did attend some medical lectures first. I think that is probably how I met Ilse, my wife."

But then, as did many of our interviewees, Singer found a mentor. A friend told him that Joseph Schumpeter, the distinguished economist, was "a brilliant lecturer and very stimulating. So I went to hear Schumpeter and smuggled myself in as a member of the audience. I had not registered with the economic faculty there. And well, from that moment, I knew I wanted to study economics. He was a decisive influence." However, as a Jew he had to flee the Third Reich, and in 1933 Singer went to Turkey, where he contemplated opening a bookstore if he could not make contact with a university there. "But I had only been a very short time in Istanbul when I got a letter from Richard Kahn, [saying] that Schumpeter had written to Keynes and had mentioned my name as a candidate for this scholarship which King's College had established. Richard Kahn wrote that he thought if I presented myself for interview I would stand a very good chance. Would I care to present myself for interview? Well, I cared very strongly to present myself for interview. It was heaven-sent."

Gamani Corea joked that his family's connections had determined not only where he would attend university but how he would physically get there: "Like my relatives, most of whom . . . had been to Cambridge, it was taken for granted that I, too, would go to England, to Cambridge. But the war was on." At the end of the war, "I applied for a passage to England, which I was given. In those days, ships went in convoys and you were given a bunk with other students. But I didn't have to take that. In 1945, in the month of July—I was due to sail in September—my grandmother came and told me that Mr. D. S. Senanayake, the leader of the House, was going to England. He had been invited to discuss the Soulbury reforms and the move towards Dominion Status. The RAF [Royal Air Force] had put a plane at his disposal. He was taking some other people with him, including his doctor, his official senior secretary, his personal attendant, and the son of another person who was working closely with him. He said you can come because the plane was empty. . . . That was a memorable trip, because in Ceylon's history, Mr. Senanayake's visit to London was one of the key steps in the move towards independence."

Once there, economics became his passion: "I didn't merely want to pass the exam, I wanted to absorb the science of economics, the methodology of economics. And I did both parts of the economics tripos in Cambridge, after which I wanted to follow the family practice of becoming a lawyer. . . . But I didn't do my law exams. Instead, Nuffield College at Oxford, my tutor told me, had advertised for studentships, and he suggested I apply. . . . If you had a Cambridge degree, as I did, you could incorporate into Oxford and obtain the same equivalent Oxford degree, that is, the B.A. And after a while you get the M.A. both from Cambridge and Oxford. So with one exam, I got four degrees: B.A. Cambridge, B.A. Oxford, M.A. Cambridge and M.A. Oxford."

He recalled becoming "a little more conservative in my thinking. When I came to Cambridge I had a lot of influence from the Left Book Club,[5] from socialist thinking, and so on. In Cambridge, I became more interested, as a technocrat, in economics; that made me focus on and take more of an interest in the workings of the market system—all of the things that form part of classical economics, together with the Keynesian supplement of full-employment theory. So at that time I was drifting away intellectually from a kind of socialist set of ideas to a more what you would call liberal techno-cratic set of ideas. I kept up with that frame of mind until UNCTAD was set up in 1964, when I began to move away from the rigidity of orthodox formal economics into looking at all these other dimensions."

Ponna Wignaraja's academic and analytical career was shaped by his doc-toral experience in New Haven, Connecticut. He pointed out that moving out of the expected colonial pattern for higher education as well as a first degree at home had been crucial for him: "I went to Yale in 1948 and continued my work in economics. The decision to go to Yale and not Oxford-Cambridge, which would have been the normal process for someone of my background in Sri Lanka, was a major point of departure in my intellectual development and career. My father had insisted I do my undergraduate work in Sri Lanka and not go abroad. That was a good decision. It strengthened my roots. . . . Now that again was his instinct, born of his own experience, whereas people like Gamani Corea and Lal Jayawardena all went straight to Britain for under-graduate studies. They were all from the same sort of elite, and by going abroad so young they missed some of the debates, albeit incomplete, that were taking place internally. They were also not deeply rooted in the cultural or the Sri Lankan reality. Similarly, there were others who went abroad early and formed Marxist 'cells'—what they saw as the alternative. They were also equally igno-rant of the reality."

The decision to branch out was based on advice from a family friend, Sir Ivor Jennings, the vice chancellor of the university in Colombo, who contrib-uted to the shaping of the Sri Lankan constitution from dominion status to independence: "Although he was an Englishman, he said, 'If you are inter-ested in development, I would not advise you to go to a traditional university in Britain, where you will tend to get more of the same.' This was 1948, mind you. Of course, LSE was supposed to be progressive but not necessarily inter-disciplinary. 'Why don't you go to a university in the United States,' he said, 'because they are tending to rethink development. There is certainly a new sound in the air, and you will get the benefit.' . . . Sir Ivor Jennings gave a strong recommendation and Yale accepted me. This was the first time I was going out into the big wide world. . . . A remarkable thing happened when I went to Yale. You see, there I came under the influence of Henry Wallich, Klauss Knorr, Arnold Wolfers, Gabriel Almond, and others, who were all part of that Chicago School that came to Yale. They were into policy analysis, not just development. They were interested in social change. And then from Yale they got thrown out because they were too interdisciplinary when Yale went big on quantitative analysis and economics, and the group went into Princeton. . . . But I happened to have had the benefit of it while they were at Yale. Then at Yale, there were a number of very bright people who were in graduate school with me who went into the Kennedy administration later—Roger Hilsman and several others, who came out of that school of thought. . . . Each was located in programs that needed to be interdisciplinary. I stuck fairly close to the economics but did all the interdisciplinary courses related to development as well. You are permitted to do this in an American university. In British universities at that time you go to a narrower discipline-oriented field. Of course, universities like Sussex, which came later, were different. This interdisciplinary team saved me from a narrow orientation of development as 'economic' development. I didn't go into this quantitative analysis."

In contrast, Mahbub ul Haq was enthusiastic about the new quantitative methodology at Yale. Although he is most well known for his intellectual work on human development, ul Haq cautioned Wignaraja to keep his focus on science. Wignaraja recalled a conversation: "One day at Yale in the mid-1950s, Mahbub cornered me and said, 'If you keep talking of this humanism and culture in your Ph.D. thesis, you will not be considered a good economist.'"

Dharam Ghai pointed out the eye-opening experience of reading philosophy, politics, and economics (PPE) at Oxford, "I was influenced by classical economists, like Smith, Mill, and Marx. But in my second degree at Oxford, my interest shifted towards development economics. There, I was influenced by people like Sir Arthur Lewis, Gunnar Myrdal, and Albert Hirschman. And of course much, much later, Amartya Sen. When I studied at Oxford, Keynesian economics was the thing to do. . . . But we understood that Keynesian economics was primarily relevant to industrial economies and not so much to poor countries. . . . I never acquired a deep passion for very technical economics. I have always been interested in societies and human beings, their welfare, and their progress. I am more interested in a broader outlook on society and development."

Although he could have begun an academic career in East Africa with his first two degrees, Ghai felt the need to go deeper into economics on the other side of the Atlantic: "The U.S. was a natural choice because, firstly, I had already studied in the UK and I thought it would be nice to diversify my experience, expose myself to a very different culture and a different country. . . . If I did not have a fellowship, it would have been difficult for my parents to finance my education. They financed my studies at Oxford. My father did not want me to apply for a scholarship in Kenya, because he thought that there were other poorer families who deserved it. He felt he could afford to finance my studies at Oxford. . . . We were not really that affluent, but my father felt people from more modest backgrounds should have an opportunity."

After saving money working in a canning factory and as a clerk, Ghai was delighted when "Yale was the first to come out with an offer of admission. . . . When it came to technical economics, it was way ahead of Oxford. . . . I guess I became an economist at Yale, rather than at Oxford. . . . I did my coursework, and then I spent six or seven months on my work for a dissertation. . . . I discovered the United Nations. For my dissertation, I wanted to work on the dualistic model of development in East Africa. At that time, the UN library was one of the best, from the point of view of documents on colonies."

When Sonny Ramphal was seventeen, he completed A levels—then called the London Higher Certificate—in Guyana and went to London to read law at King's College, where he stayed on to pursue his LL.M. "I wasn't a terribly serious student as a youngster. I didn't have any burning ambition to be anything. In my final year of high school, I co-produced and performed in *A Midsummer Night's Dream,* edited the college magazine, and played some cricket. So I didn't come to university with a burning desire to be a lawyer."

His formative years coincided with "the years when the UN was trying to find its role and its place, going through some terrible problems. In fact, I think my first big awareness of the UN was Suez. Suez played an important part in my own life. It was the event that switched me on politically. Until then, a lot of international issues were in my awareness, but they were academic. . . . But I really did become passionate about internationalism over the Suez crisis. I was doing a dissertation on federalism in the Commonwealth. . . . I became very angry about the British and French action in Egypt and the Suez and very excited by the role that Eisenhower played as an American president in saying to the British and the French and the Israelis, 'Take it to the UN. Military intervention is not on. The place where this must be settled is in the Security Council.' What a wonderful contribution, I thought, by the major Western power, which the United States already was. I wish it was a mood that had lingered in Washington. It certainly fired me with a lot of enthusiasm."

At the same time, the Caribbean was becoming politically conscious against the background of the trade union movement. "I did not live in one of the hostels in London, so I missed the opportunity to meet people like Seretse Khama and Kwame Nkrumah. . . . But I did associate with those in the West Indian student body in Britain. . . . Not surprisingly, that student body became a seedbed of federalism in the West Indies. . . . So Britain was, in fact, the nursery of that whole generation of West Indian politicians who went on to become federal politicians."

James Jonah recalled a striking fact for an African thinking about university pecking orders in the United States in the early 1950s: "The only university worth going to was Lincoln. . . . All of our African leaders went to Lincoln, nothing else. They didn't want to hear about Harvard. . . . Azikwe, Nkrumah, all of our earlier leaders went to Lincoln." He recalled an encounter with another West African, Edward Blyden III, who had finished at Harvard and returned home. "I was very much anti-Nasser. . . . So he began to tell me a lot about imperialism, about colonialism. He put me in touch with both Nkrumah and George Padmore. . . . So Nkrumah came to Sierra Leone, and George Padmore came, and they spoke to me. They said, 'You must go to the United States and go to Lincoln.' . . . My parents wanted me to go to Oxford, because for them English education was the only thing that matters."

His parents were from an elite family called the Kreolos who had not experienced discrimination and were wary of the notorious American brand of prejudice. Arriving seasick, he was welcomed by a Baltimore couple who accepted him as family, and this helped change the stereotype: "We had this idea of America being cowboys. It [racial tolerance] was not supposed to happen in America. That was a big shock to me. I stayed with these people for two months in Baltimore, this white couple. They became like my parents. They were my first experience, in a sense, in America. So that was my big shock. I gathered that that was not what it was supposed to be. It was supposed to be rejection and all of this other thing."

Upon arriving in Lincoln, Jonah was struck by "the low motivation of the black students. I couldn't understand. It was very difficult, because coming from an elite family where education was such a high priority, and you know you are going to make it. You are highly motivated. And these boys were sitting down playing cards. I used to go and talk to them. I couldn't understand their lack of motivation. And they would tell me, 'It doesn't matter if we study hard and obtain academic degrees.' That was a big shock to me, that they were not motivated to achieve."

Having finished his B.A. at Lincoln, he wanted to study under Rupert Emerson at Harvard but was reticent about studying for a Ph.D. and so enrolled in an M.A. program at Boston University. However, he took all of Emerson's courses across town, "which were on colonialism, imperialism—

all the 'isms.' . . . By that time, my mind was changing about Africa, because my first lecture under Rupert Emerson was a course he gave on imperialism. . . . I had only studied imperialism from the Leninist point of view. And here he was talking about Schumpeter's theory of imperialism. . . . I realized that I had a narrow approach to the subject matter. That was a big change in my life. So I began to question a lot of things which Africans would say."

At that time, his interest in Germany coincided with the availability of funding, so he went to Germany as a Friedrich Ebert fellow: "At times, I was sitting there, the only black man. People were frightened that I had come to chop off their heads." After a trip to the Middle East on a study tour, he stopped in Geneva before returning to Germany, where he encountered a "problem which I have had throughout my professional life. The African students were meeting in Geneva and I went there. I made the only defense of Hammarskjöld after the death of Lumumba. I didn't have much information, but just my feeling about Dag Hammarskjöld, since 1956. But I did not know then some of the information which I now know as related in books, like in the *Congo Cables*. But I felt that Hammarskjöld had nothing to do with the death of Lumumba, that there was no conspiracy, which was the argument which was made against him by most Africans. . . . I was totally a minority among all the African students, and in fact they used to attack me. They called me all kinds of names." Jonah returned and completed his Ph.D. with Karl Deutsch at MIT.

In looking back over her education, Lourdes Arizpe thought that her multicultural environment "made everyday life very problematic because I had to juggle different values and usually ended up either not understanding enough or understanding too much. The need to understand cultures drove me towards anthropology, although it took me a long time to find my vocation. I always say that anthropology is my vocation, yet literature is my passion. Having begun reading English books for adolescents, my sister then gave me European books to read. So I was reading *War and Peace* and *Anna Karenina* at thirteen. I also became familiar with the French literature, because when I was nine years old, my sister took me to learn French with a highly cultured French lady who played French parlor games with me at first. Then she opened up this marvelous window into the world through French literature. One of the most influential writers for me was Victor Hugo. So I think that my whole intellectual outlook was formed through French literature and European literature generally. . . . The first experience with university I had was the University of the Pacific in Stockton, California. Surprisingly, when I arrived, since I had taken the SAT [Scholastic Aptitude Test], I was assigned to the Honors English class! Nobody could believe a Mexican was in that class. In fact, after reading so voraciously, I liked to write and had written my first mini-novel when I was twelve. At the University of the Pacific I was on the Dean's List but I left after a year. I didn't like it because of the sororities and the racial undertones of this private university."

Not having a clear idea of what to do next, Arizpe went to Geneva, to the School of Interpreters: "I listened with total awe to these interpreters who could translate not only the words but also the meanings through the many semantic and inflective tones that could be used. If the delegate coughed, the interpreter coughed. . . . After Geneva I went back to Mexico. I began to work as an interpreter but then decided I needed many more subjects to fill the spaces of the multicultural universe in my mind."

Next came the traumatic events of May 1968. "I arrived just at the time when student demonstrations were exploding everywhere. But the amiable conversations with six-foot bobbies accompanying the marches in London was very different from the brutal treatment we were getting in Mexico in marches and meetings. A frightened macho president, Diaz Ordaz, ordered the brutal massacre of more than 300 students and innocent bystanders on October the 2nd, when students that I knew were not only murdered, but they simply disappeared. The worst thing was the silence after the 2nd of October. There was not a word in the newspapers about the massacre. Why? Because the Olympics were beginning a few days later, and the Olympics had priority over the lives of young people in Mexico. You can imagine how devastatingly indignant that made me and all my fellow students and how much it politicized and radicalized me."

Radical student activities were an avocation but anthropology came first, including fieldwork in a mountain village in the Sierra Madre Occidental of Puebla, where a monolingual people speaking only Nahuatl were the subjects. She recalled being at Oxford and attending a lecture that Claude Levi-Strauss gave at the ancient Bodleian Library early in the 1970s: "I remember it was very difficult for me to understand what he was saying because I had just arrived in London, and I found that I could understand the words he was using but not the meaning he was conveying. So I spent the first three months with a new intellectual space in my mind in which all the words I was reading floated freely and chaotically until finally, little by little, I was able to build the cognitive structure needed to connect circuits of words into ideas. I must say that taught me very much to about the dynamics of culture. And about the difficulties of intercultural dialogue. You cannot translate cognition."

Devaki Jain's educational story and itinerary strike a remarkable chord: "My oldest sister got married pre-puberty, and I was next on the platform. . . . So going to college was a revolutionary event and I did a B.A. in Mathematics in 1953. At that time, i.e., 1954, I met—curiously enough, through a Quaker seminar (because that was the only thing my parents would allow me to go to as a girl)—some young Gandhians—a British and an Indian boy—both aged nineteen years. I was about seventeen, and they transformed me. They showed me the value of simplicity, of working with the poor, as Gandhi used to do. There were no gender feelings, they said, in the ashrams (the Gandhian collectives) at all. Boys and girls were all, in one sense, sexless—performing roles with total equality. And I think that interest in Gandhi's method of transforming an unequal society into a just society and economy stayed with me for most of the rest of my life."

Surreptitiously avoiding her authoritarian father, she managed "many things without his knowing. And it was the usual difference, I am sure other women have told you, between father and mother, that my mother was in some sense an accomplice to all of our desires, whether it was the boys or the girls. Anything mischievous she would allow. My father was a disciplinarian who would say, 'no' to going to a movie and 'no' to my brothers for anything they wanted to do which was outside the strict frame."

Her punishment for categorically refusing to go on the marriage block was draconian: "I was stopped at home, not allowed to do postgraduate study, as they were looking for bridegrooms for me. One of the bridegrooms happened to be a man who was studying in Paris. My father at that time was on the Air India board and was always traveling on Air India to London and New York. So he invited me and said, 'I'll take you to Paris if you'll agree to meet this man.' So we went to Paris and I met him. Of course, he proposed to me and all that, but then I cheated my father. When we went to London, I said, 'Can I stay for a week in a boarding house and join you later?' He said, 'Sure, here's your ticket.' And I didn't go back. I just stayed there. I worked in London for half a year as a dishwasher and a maid to pay for boarding and lodging and then got admission to Oxford to an unknown college called Ruskin College. The college was run by the trade unions and the Worker Educational Council. . . . It was a series of coincidences, accidents that took me there."

A chance tourist trip to Oxford led to a new option: "I talked my way into the college even though I was only twenty and I had never been in a trade union. I was so charged with the desire for education that the principal admitted me, gave me a room, and the college completely supported my boarding, lodging, and fees. The principal was a die-hard socialist, and I was this apolitical creature. I lived for a year with working-class men in the hostel. There were only three girls and about 120 men in one building, and it was a great experience. All my holidays were spent in miners' homes, in cockney homes. I was drinking every Saturday with them in what they called 'pub crawling.' I was smoking a pipe. I was eating everything that was available to eat because there was no money to be choosy and vegetarian. So there was no problem with beef or bacon, you name it. Tom Mboya, who later became the first prime minister of Kenya, was my regular Saturday evening dancing partner, and through the conversations with him I got my first lessons in racism, in the struggles for liberation from colonization in countries other than India, knowledge about Africa too."

Jain spent six months at Harvard, returned to India, and worked as a junior researcher for Gunnar Myrdal's team working on *The Asian Drama*. Returning to Oxford with Myrdal, she was attached to Balliol College and worked with Paul Streeten, Thomas Ballogh, and Nicholas Kaldor before doing a second degree, from 1959 to 1962, at the all-women's college of St. Anne: "And mind you, I was not a feminist. I didn't know what feminism was all about. I was just a fighting female trying to get educated. I couldn't care less about anything on women's rights. . . . But there was joy in meeting women academics and other women as students. . . . I was pampered by Iris Murdoch and got some of the best tutors in Oxford because she and I fell in love with each other—not as a lesbian, which she was at the time, but we just liked each other's ideology."

After a few years, it was time to return home. "Since I had been completely away from India for four years from 1958–62, and missed all my brothers' marriages and everything I decided to go home for a bit but planned to come back. . . . I got a teaching job almost immediately in Delhi University." In 1956 at work she met a man rejected by her family: "Much as I could have just married him and said 'that's it,' I had some kind of a terror that my mother would have a heart attack and down the line die of shame because I wanted to marry a man who was two castes lower than mine. But the fact that I was wanting to marry somebody and didn't marry him for eight years, from 1958–1966 the subterfuge, the negotiating attempts, while also teaching for thirty hours a week, became such a preoccupation that I couldn't do my Ph.D. at all. It was constant tension of meeting my parents, talking to them, being told that 'You're going to kill us. We'd rather you committed suicide.' You know, you talk of honor killings now—those were the days when they would have rather had me die than shame them by marrying this person. . . . Finally, of course, I did what I wanted to. I married him, and my parents survived."

Juan Somavía shook his head and laughed when we asked about his study of law: "It wasn't the result of any particular thing. I reacted instinctively, not so much rationally. . . . Given the options of studying economics or law—the sort of liberal profession that you have to choose in the context of my own upbringing—law seemed to be the one that interested me most." Reflecting on his interests in social justice, he stated: "It is the university period that gives you the identity, I think. I acquired this sort of world experience, if you want, by traveling with my parents. At the same time, I sort of nationalized myself by studying law in Chile and then working afterwards for some time in Chile. . . . That is the moment which defined me—I am very Latin American, very strongly so."

His Chilean and Latin American identity "was complemented later on by a strong developing country identity that came through the period I studied in Paris. I sort of met the Third World there and realized the differences we had but also how much we had in common with countries that were so far away, and up to then not in my line of vision. . . . I was living in the Cité Universitaire, and there you have—at that time it was about 5,000 students—half of them were French, half of them were foreigners. . . . I was living in France, which had gone through the Vietnam experience in Dien Bien Phu and then through the Algerian experience. So these societal issues were also very much present in the place where I was studying. . . . We tended to see that we had similar problems, that we came from countries that were inserted in a world in which the rules of the game were stacked in favor of some and not others. . . . We had more common causes coming from developing countries than might have been the case with people coming from developed countries." Building on the European experience, he worked on a thesis with Celso Furtado. "He had come from a situation which I myself would eventually live years later. He had to leave Brazil because of the coup d'état and became a professor in Paris."

Nafis Sadik recalled one fortuitous development for her and for international public health; namely, her father's posting to Washington at the World Bank as an executive director for Pakistan and six Middle Eastern countries: "I had just graduated from medical school. Normally I would have gone to England, but because he was going to the States, my mother didn't want me to go away. So I got the internship at Baltimore City Hospitals under something called the Point Four Program. . . . President Truman's program."

Boutros Boutros-Ghali looked back at his graduate studies in France and the United States as critical in his intellectual development: "I did my four years of legal studies at the Faculty of Law in Cairo. I was not at all well-disciplined. I ended up not among the best but rather among the poorest in my class." Having received two French and two Egyptian secondary school diplomas, he thought that he might study humanities, law, and political science in France, but he quickly changed his mind: "It was in Paris that I began to write in Arabic articles about political events that appeared in a daily called *Masr*. In point of fact, my first article appeared in a weekly when I made my first trip to the Sudan with a group of students in 1945. Sudan interested me particularly because it was my grandfather who in 1899 signed the treaty with

Great Britain that created the Anglo-Egyptian Condominium of the Sudan. I made my first trip to Sudan in order to get to know that country because when I was a child, people said to me, 'Your grandfather sold Sudan to the English.'" An uncle who had formerly been foreign minister offered a piece of advice: "You can't allow yourself to criticize France because you are a guest in France; if you wish to continue writing anti-French or anti-colonialist articles, then go study in Switzerland or Belgium, but do not stay in France."

However, he maintained his anticolonialist fervor with a tinge of pan-Arabism: "I had dreams of Arab federalism. Professor George Scelle, who used to teach international law, was an advocate of world federalism. It was he who at that juncture got me interested in international law. I must add that at the same time I was studying political science. After finishing my two diplomas, one in public law and the other in political economy, I chose Charles Rousseau as my professor and "Les ententes régionales" ["Regional Agreements"] as my thesis topic. The Arab League was the first regional agreement recognized by the UN."

He helped set up the Institute for Political Science in Cairo, which was intended to train military officers supporting the revolution, and an unexpected opportunity developed: "In 1954 I was offered a research fellowship as a Fulbright Professor in the United States and spent a year during 1954–55 in New York. It was one of the most enriching periods of my personal development. Indeed, having taught for four years from 1949 to 1954 as a young professor, I took the American shock without suffering unduly. It forced me to master English; to give lectures in that language, I had to prepare them carefully. At the same time, I was in New York at Columbia University, encountering for the first time a teaching method totally different from the European or Egyptian approach that I had known."

I. G. Patel graduated from Baroda College in 1944, but he was keen to receive more formal training in economics than what was available in India at the time. An early mentor, Professor D. Ghosh, encouraged him to explore overseas options: "It was from him that I first learned words like 'Cambridge,' 'King's College,' and 'Keynes.' And he said you must go there when you finish." The war intruded initially to prevent his taking up a fellowship at King's College, so Patel went to Bombay School of Economics until an unexpected turn of events: "As luck would have it, [King's College] called me a few days later and said, 'Can you leave within a week? There is a ship coming from Hong Kong which has been converted to civilian use to evacuate the families of British missionaries in China. They are coming to Calcutta and Bombay also, and if you can go within a week, you can go.' So I did."

The list of his mentors reads like an index from a textbook of that time, including Joan Robinson, Maurice Dobb, A. C. Pigou, Gerald Shove, Nicky Kaldor, and Harold Laski. For research on his dissertation, the other side of the Atlantic beckoned and a scholarship from Harvard University permitted his research on Japan and Argentina: "Harvard has a wonderful library. You get access to almost anything you want. But there was not much literature on economic development at that time. There was not even that much literature on the extension of Keynesian economics to the international sphere. And the international economics was more of a traditional kind. And on development there was hardly anything."

Klaus Sahlgren, who would become the director of the UN Centre for Transnational Corporations (UNCTC) and later the executive secretary of the ECE, went to Åbo Academy in Turku, Finland. This is the only Swedish-speaking university outside of Sweden, a linguistic heritage from the conquering Swedes of the twelfth century who remained the colonial power until the Russians took over in 1809. "It is a small university; in those days it was very small indeed. I chose as my major subject economics. . . . It so happened that I did not study English at school at all. I read French and German, but my English was very sketchy. Therefore, my mother, who thought that English would be important, started to teach me English. Then at university, I practiced my English by reading UN publications, especially those by the ECE. The professor actually required that the students should read everything that came from the Economic Commission for Europe. . . . I still feel familiar with all that stuff because of those academic years. So I met, in a sense, and at a distance, the United Nations early."

Sartaj Aziz finished high school in 1944, three years before the bloody partition of India and Pakistan that interrupted his studies. He left Peshawar to join a sister in Lahore, a stopover en route to a stay in the United States: "That was a kind of turning point, because Lahore was the center of political activity just before Pakistan was created. . . . In those two years, Quaid-e-Azam Mohammed Ali Jinnah came three times to the college and I had firsthand interaction. That created in me a tremendous enthusiasm for a separate homeland for Muslims. . . . The Hindu-Muslim riots started one year before partition, i.e., in 1946, and the refugees started pouring in from June 1947, when the partition plan was announced. In all, six million Muslims migrated from India to Pakistan in very desperate conditions. I worked for several months in refugee camps in Lahore. . . . So I matured prematurely by getting involved with suffering and commitment to devote my life to building the country we had secured after so many sacrifices. . . . Earning a lot of money never became my objective. In fact, I shunned opportunities where I could go to positions where I would exert a lot of influence and have power. Service to humanity remained my motto."

Aziz recognized his privileged status, and in reading history he discovered what happened to local resources as a result of an unfair trade regime: "So when I started studying economics from 1946 to 1949, these issues hit me like a rock. At that time, one out of every five inhabitants of the world was in India and 95 percent were very poor. And this is where I turned to development." He recalled a radio broadcast during which a Hindu professor defined education as knowing "something about everything and everything about one thing." However his intellectual curiosity made him ask "What is that one thing about which I should know everything? . . . I decided that it has to be development, because this subject has a political dimension, a social dimension, and a human dimension. . . . So this became my passion."

An overseas opportunity beckoned when Harvard University set up in the Littauer School of Public Administration (now the Kennedy School of Government), a special program of fellowships for about twenty middle-level officials from developing countries leading to a master's degree. "In 1962, one year after I joined the Planning Commission, I was selected for this course. Since my education was interrupted from 1946 to 1949 because of the partition disruption, Harvard gave me a very good opportunity to catch up. It also was a remarkable period because development as a subject was becoming very topical at that time. Kennedy's program linking aid to policies was increasing demand for development specialists. So it was the heyday of mixed planning systems."

Paulo Sergio Pinheiro has spent much of his career (when he was not working on human rights in Brazil) in universities overseas, beginning with a scholarship in Paris at the Institut d' Études Politiques, where he received his doctorate. One of the more formative of his experiences was in May 1968: "I went to all the meetings, and I was in the Comité Paritaire at the Institut d'Études Politiques. For me, it was the seismic event in my life—the critique of the university and the possibility of revolt and of active involvement in political life. I was also reading Herbert Marcuse and all the radical critique of power, of political science. . . . I became more connected with these issues because of the May Revolution. And in a certain way—I was not a leader, but I participated when I could. I was the only foreigner in that *comité*. You had students and professors in equal numbers."

During the military regime in Brazil, many Brazilians went to France, including Fernando Henrique Cardoso—this is not unlike the University-in-Exile at the New School, which attracted Jewish intellectuals from Europe during World War II and had prominent theorists like John Dewey and Hannah

Arendt on the faculty. Pinheiro put forward one irony: "I discovered the University of São Paulo in Paris, because everybody was there. The first time that I met Cardoso, as I said, was in 1967, and all of his colleagues—very important people like the sociologists, the anthropologists expelled by the military from the University of São Paulo. They were all teaching or they came to Paris to visit. . . . These seminars were very much worried about fascism, about the Third International, about popular democracies. I don't remember taking any seminar on international law or international institutions. . . . It was not fashionable. The UN was something old fashioned."

Although exchange programs are frequently the victims of parliamentary budget axes, Pinheiro recalled the importance to him of another overseas experience financed by just such a program: "In the 1960s, an American woman was a friend to the Kennedys. She established a foundation to invite Brazilians to come to the United States. We spent fifteen days in a summer course in Harvard, one week in Washington visiting people like Robert Kennedy, and ten days with a family. . . . I was one of those fellows. Who are those guys now? In the Cardoso government, the vice president of the Republic of Brazil, the minister of development, the former leftist governor of Brasilia, a leftist minister in the military supreme court, the former minister of justice. . . . We were leftists, but we were not anti-America."

3

Serendipity and International Careers

- **Mentors Opening Doors**
- **Advanced Studies as a Gateway**
- **Post-University Homecomings**
- **Starting Out in Teaching and Research**
- **Beginning in National Public Service**
- **Juggling Family and Professional Life**

The pursuit of a career in and around the United Nations was rarely a natural outgrowth of academic interests. Exposure to foreign languages and cultures provided one possible entrance, but pure happenstance was more typically the case. One such case was described by Brian Urquhart in his autobiography, *A Life in Peace and War*. His career in Britain's 1st Airborne Brigade ended somewhat prematurely in August 1942 when his parachute "opened like a budding tulip instead of a mushroom."[1] After convalescing, he attended the Staff College at Camberly and joined the staff of General F. A. M. Browning en route to a posting as an analyst in Arnold Toynbee's Foreign Office Research Department. Gladwyn Jebb, who headed the Preparatory Commission of the United Nations, was a friend of Toynbee's. Urquhart worked on the commission and then began at the UN as assistant to Trygve Lie, the first UN Secretary-General. He would go on to become under-secretary-general for special political questions, taking over the peacekeeping helm in 1971 from Nobel Prize–winner Ralph Bunche upon his death.

One of Urquhart's colleagues in those early years was Stéphane Hessel, whose recruitment resulted from a fortuitous stopover for a meal with his in-laws in New York en route to China for his first posting with the Quai d'Orsay (France's Ministry of Foreign Affairs) after World War II: "I wanted my wife to be able to see her parents and so we decided to go to New York. There was my father-in-law who was a great friend of Henri Laugier [UN assistant secretary-general at the time],[2] and Laugier said, 'Why don't you stay?' And I did. So it was not something like a strategic plan."

Other interviewees had less abrupt landings than Urquhart, but very few consciously pursued a career in the foreign or international civil services. Indeed, the vast majority are like many of us: They did not plan careers or their lives, for that matter. For instance, Enrique Iglesias quipped: "I never had long-term plans. Events in my life happened spontaneously. I have always had a lot of confidence in God. . . . In life, chance is a very important factor." Some studied international relations or economics or languages, which made a career linked to development possible, but many essentially stumbled into international careers. In any event, almost everyone experienced a chance event that resulted in an exposure to an unexpected international career option. And the rest, as they say, is history.

Mentors Opening Doors

Our interlocutors' earlier stories about educational experiences often highlighted the crucial influence of teachers in instilling values and ethics, but here several voices also indicate how mentors also helped launch careers. Jacques Polak recalled his first job at the League of Nations in Geneva in 1936. Like many a student before and since, he had concentrated on the desired subject matter listed in a job vacancy, but it was Jan Tinbergen who opened the door: "The job market in Holland for economists was pretty miserable at that time, as the job market for everybody was. I was thinking of trying to get a job teaching economics in a secondary school or something of that sort. Then out of the blue I got a letter from Tinbergen, offering me a job as his research assistant."

As we learned earlier, the first Nobel laureate in economics was also inspirational for Jan Pronk, who pursued his vision of internationalism and changing the rules of the international economic game, beginning shortly after his M.A.: "I was offered a choice between two options. I was selected for the diplomatic service or I could join the team of scientific collaborators of Jan Tinbergen in Rotterdam in order to do research, to assist in teaching at the university. I wanted to go abroad, but I thought it would be better to further educate myself by continuing research . . . on development questions as well as on another field of work of Jan Tinbergen, which was the theory of optimum regime: What is the best economic order for a society? It is a kind of sequel to his thinking on what is the best economic policy in a country, being followed by his research on development planning or on economic planning."

In looking back to the inspiring role of his humble mentor, Pronk recalled: "He was, with Ragnar Frisch from Norway, the first Nobel Prize winner in economics. I remember how he received the prize. He was very pleased with it, but he also did say, which was characteristic, that he would have wished to have received the Nobel Prize for peace. For him, it was always more important to translate his theoretical thinking into concrete development and peace and reconstruction activity. . . . He was a very good teacher. He was able to make even the most complicated questions transparent. I became fascinated by his way of thinking: orderly, systematic, and focused on the purpose of finding solutions for priority problems. He was extremely modest also as a person. He had the smallest room possible you could think of in the university, about one-quarter of the size of the room in which we have this interview. He always took with him just handmade sandwiches by his wife to the office and nothing else—no official lunches, never. Everybody loved him." Pronk commented on his simplicity: "He loved tramways. When he got the Nobel Prize, we organized a festivity for him in Rotterdam, and we were driving with an old-fashioned tramway through the city, and he enjoyed it very much. He died in 1991 [*sic*; 1994]. . . . Until the last week of his life, he was still writing articles, sometimes giving an interview, writing letters, also to me—which he had done since I had become a minister in the early 1970s—sometimes giving me advice on his own initiative. So he never stopped thinking, writing, working."

Based on that example, Pronk described his own career, including a stint beginning in the mid-1980s as UNCTAD's deputy secretary-general: "I gradually became the person who in particular did the popularizing, the addressing of other groups in the Netherlands on issues such as development aid, international trade, and UNCTAD questions." His abandoned his academic research in favor of an informed venture into politics: "I was working on a Ph.D. thesis on the optimum economic regime, but gradually I became more interested in development questions themselves, which took most of my time. And then we had elections in the Netherlands in 1971. As a matter of fact, the spokesperson for my party, the Labor Party, on development cooperation died. I was at the time, in the Netherlands, well known as a spokesperson for development issues. I was active in my party, so I was asked to run as a candidate. I just made it in 1971 and became a member of Parliament. I had to relinquish my ties with the university because being a member of Parliament is a full-time profession in the Netherlands. So I became the spokesman of the opposition for development issues right away. I was pleased, as a matter of fact, to leave academics, because I like studying and analyzing, but I really missed a link with action or with politics." In 2003, however, Pronk returned to academia as a professor at the Institute of Social Studies in The Hague.

Robert Cox's road to the UN followed a different but not atypical pattern. His starting position in the UN "was sort of an accident of history." When he completed his master's thesis, he "was called into the office of the president of McGill University, an Englishman whose name was Cyril James, who was particularly interested in economic history. He said that he had been contacted by the ILO, which was recruiting, and would I like to go for an interview. So, with his sponsorship, I went and interviewed with the ILO and they hired me. And I went in at the lowest professional level, as a research assistant. They were based in Montreal during the war years."

In 1949, Surendra Patel was among the first Asian economists recruited by the UN's Department of Economic Affairs in New York. Professor Michal Kalecki, a well-known Polish economist, was in charge of the department's often cited publication. "It was on the recommendation of Professor Kuznets, under whom I had studied, that Kalecki took me straightaway. . . . I was to be part of the team that had to prepare the first major *World Economic Survey* of the United Nations. In this famous team . . . I was to start working right away on the *World Economic Survey* without any previous experience and hardly any briefing. . . . Kalecki must have seen some of the confusion in my mind. . . . 'How are you?' he asked. 'What are you doing?' I replied, 'Sir, I am not very sure about what I am doing.' Kalecki literally burst at me. He was well known for his high temper. . . . I think he appreciated my sincerity. From then on, we established a very good collaboration and we even became very close friends."

Enrique Iglesias recalled his first job as an economist in Uruguay: "Professor Dominguez Nocetti, who was also the department chair, and Professor Faroppa agreed in 1952 to create an institute for economic research. Faroppa was the institute's first director. And they both invited me to be a research assistant while I was still a student. . . . That was my first formal, everyday job ever, with a monthly salary starting on January 1st of 1952. I will never forget that experience. That was where my professional career started."

James Jonah applied and was selected for a junior UN post—many years later, in 1991, he was a candidate for Secretary-General. He was attracted to the international civil service even before his two Harvard advisors (Professors Louis B. Sohn and Rupert Emerson) encouraged him. He recalled that his research experience overseas, in European and not Third World affairs, made him the most competitive candidate: "Germans were supposed to be highly nationalistic, very, very nationalistic. I was very lucky that I came in contact with some of the theoreticians of the Socialist Party in Germany. . . . I observed that they were aiming to transcend German nationalism. People like Willy Brandt and others were saying, 'Look, our history is because of our supernationalism. We must look wider.' . . . And I said, 'Well, if these people have come to realize that nationalism is not the end of everything, why are we Africans talking about nationalism? Where will it take us? Are we going to repeat the European history of wars?' They said that nationalism is what caused all of their problems. Also at the same time, I was becoming concerned with the African leaders. Corruption was beginning to surface. Dictatorship was

beginning to surface. So all of my heroes, except one—Nyerere—were becoming terrible people. So I just felt the only way to do it was to be an internationalist." The combination of his internationalist orientation and his
knowledge of Germany made him an ideal candidate for his first UN post: "I
was brought in because of the German problem, which was very acute in the
1960s—the Berlin Wall had been established. I remember that the very first
thing they asked me to write about was Kennedy's speech at American University on 10 June 1963. They said, 'Look, explain this speech to us along with
that of Mr. Gromyko before the General Assembly on 19 September, 1963.' . . .
So this paper impressed the Secretariat. . . . That is how I got to meet many
people on the 38th floor."

Amartya Sen's links to the UN would come mainly as an advisor in a number of capacities over the years. He recalled the role of his mentors in steering
him toward the academy and away from the international civil service: "The
first job that was ever offered to me was offered by the UN. Sidney Dell offered me a job, which I eventually decided not to take. I had barely got my
Ph.D., I think. But I was flattered that I was offered that job.

"Actually, when he offered me the job, I hadn't met him. I think he had
written to Nicky Kaldor and Joan Robinson, and they suggested my name.
But Joan Robinson told me that while she had to mention my name in answer
to Sidney's question, she also thought that she must tell me not to go there.

"Joan thought that I should do more academic work before I [thought]
about anything like the UN. But I must also say that she did not really think
that the work being done at the United Nations at that time would be sufficiently interesting or exciting for a theoretically minded young economist.
She was tough about what she took to be her kind of excellence which she
wanted her students to emulate. Nicky [Kaldor] did too, I think. They had a
view of what good economics consisted of, and no matter how worthy the
UN work might be, it wasn't a great home for those whom Joan or Nicky
expected to work on what they saw as the frontier issues of economics. It was
a very different view from the way the comparison would look to me later on,
when I got very closely involved in working at the UN on the foundations of
project evaluation for UNIDO or on human development for UNDP (they
were to me very much the frontier issues of economics). But Joan Robinson
or Richard Kahn or Nicky Kaldor would not have been very excited by these
works either."

When asked about his master plan for an international career, Just Faaland
replied: "No there wasn't [any] really. . . . In the early years after Oxford . . . I
was interested in international affairs indeed, but it was only at the end of the
1950s that I got interested, workwise, in the wider world. So I was sort of pushed

and pulled into this international life. In 1948 when I came back from Oxford, I went to the Oslo University Economic Institute to work with Ragnar Frisch. . . . He had all sorts of ideas he tried out in the Economic and Social Council. I worked on a paper as his assistant then. I happened to disagree with the way he was doing it. But it was a very good learning experience for me, and it had to do with the international system and trade issues. . . . So then out of the blue for me, at the end of 1948, the invitation came to come to OEEC.[3] I was, without knowing it, pretty well ready for it." Faaland's thesis supervisor, Donald MacDougall, became an economic advisor to the Organisation for European Economic Co-operation (OEEC) in late 1948 and did what most officials do: "He came to a place where there weren't many economists. He had to build up a staff, so he contacted his friends."

When Alister McIntyre returned to the University of the West Indies (UWI) from England, he found an unexpected situation: "I discovered, to my shock, that a lot of the ideas that I had been playing with, discussing, and so forth, were very quickly dismissed by my colleagues. Actually, at the time, I had few colleagues in economics, because economics was just a subject in a general studies degree. We were still then a college of the University of London, and London had advised that UWI develop arts and sciences before going to a full-fledged program in social sciences. But there was an Institute of Social and Economic Research, and in that institute were some extremely bright sociologists and anthropologists. So I was almost contemptuously shoved aside as belonging to a discipline that was only peripherally relevant to development. They seemed to have all of the answers."

A few years later, McIntyre met Albert Hirschman at a conference in Rio de Janeiro in 1963 and felt emboldened to say, "I am the only person working on international trade in Jamaica and I feel quite isolated sometimes." Hirschman said, "Why don't you come and spend a year with me at Columbia?" And so McIntyre applied for a Fulbright Fellowship and went to Columbia and worked with Hirschman: "I read all of his material. It was very good being associated with him. Although he was a very busy man, he found time for me. . . . While I was at Columbia, Arthur Lewis, who had then become vice chancellor of the University of the West Indies, said to me that Jose-Antonio Mayobre, who was then executive secretary of ECLAC, wanted somebody to start some work on the Caribbean. . . . So after leaving Columbia, I did, in fact, go to ECLAC for about seven months to work on that topic which resulted in a long essay on "Aspects of Trade and Development in the Commonwealth Caribbean." The period in [the ECLA office in] Mexico gave me a much more direct link to the CEPAL thinking.[4] It also gave me the opportunity of trying to sort out in my own mind how much of it was relevant to small island states, as against

the larger type of Latin American economies, where import substitution industrialization was something that was more feasible than it would be in small
islands with very limited markets and a narrow resource base."

Hans Singer recalled that while teaching at the University of Glasgow in
1940, his mentor opened two doors, one to a visa and the other to employment. "I suddenly got a letter at that time from a man I had never heard of
before, Alvin Johnson. He was a well-known American, not only a scholar but
also a great friend of Roosevelt. He had a singular part in the New Deal. . . .
The letter said that he was the president of the University-in-Exile [the present-
day New School University in New York] . . . and Professor Schumpeter had
mentioned my name to him and it had occurred to him that if Hitler invaded
England, prospects for people like me might not be good. . . . And if I presented the enclosure to the letter to the U.S. Embassy in Dublin . . . I would . . .
be able to get a visa to come to the U.S. And the enclosure was an appointment to the Faculty of the University in Exile." Singer declined and arrived in
New York after the war in 1947 to become one of the first young professional
economists recruited by the UN Secretariat. He would soon publish his
pathbreaking work on terms of trade,[5] and he taught evening courses at the
University-in-Exile.

Advanced Studies as a Gateway

The great majority of our voices earned advanced degrees which in turn
influenced career paths. Gerry Helleiner recalled that his career orientation
grew organically from his undergraduate studies: "I had become persuaded
that of the social sciences, economics was the one that was most significant
for public policy formation—rightly or wrongly. I had by then developed a
certain social awareness and consciousness, and I wanted to work in public
policy matters. The critical decisions were made in the summer job I held in
Ottawa at the Department of Labor, Economics and Research Branch, between the third and fourth year of my undergraduate studies. The first two
summers I had spent in the navy. These were all devices to earn money, basically, which I needed to get through. My first *real* job . . . was with the Department of Labor, and it was with very able people. My boss was a guy called
Doug Hartle. . . . He was subsequently a very well-known economist in this
country. . . . And he had a profound effect on me and persuaded me that I
really needed to go to graduate school in economics."

So Helleiner went to Yale University, where he began his lifelong interest in
international development. "There was a group in the department there at
that time," he recalled, "that was passionately interested in what was going on

in the developing countries. It was the time of independence in Africa for a whole range of countries. There was a lot of excitement about that. It was the time immediately prior to the Kennedy election and the Peace Corps and all of that." After being hooded, he joined the faculty and the newly established Yale Economic Growth Center. "It was intended to be *the* repository of development statistics in the country and it was to be the leading, cutting edge of research in the U.S. on development. . . . They had a so-called country study program. . . . They hired people right out of Ph.D. programs, by and large. I was the first. And Lloyd Reynolds I remember offered me the job and said, 'You are the first and the world is yours. Anywhere you want to go, we will pay for you.' . . . I chose Nigeria to go to simply because they spoke English and it was the biggest country in Africa."

Lawrence Klein would win the Nobel Prize for Economic Sciences in 1980, and his dissertation, later published as *The Keynesian Revolution,* was supervised by another future Nobel laureate, Paul Samuelson, who won the prize in 1970. "When I gave the summary paper at a meeting of the Econometric Society, the first since their postponement during the war, Jacob Marschak approached me and said, 'What this country needs,' meaning the United States, 'is a new Tinbergen model to help in postwar recovery and planning.' I said, 'That is just the job I really want.' I disregarded all other possibilities and went to Chicago to join his team."

Richard Gardner recalled his excitement when his dissertation was published,[6] "but the biggest thrill of all was the people I met in the course of writing it—to be able to interview some of the people who had had a hand in the creation of the Bretton Woods organizations and GATT [General Agreement on Tariffs and Trade]. I was truly inspired by what I guess I too melodramatically then called the 'thin blue line' of internationalists on both sides of the Atlantic who devoted themselves to creating these postwar institutions, combining idealism and pragmatism. I didn't get to interview Keynes, who had passed away, but I had access to his private papers. I didn't get to interview Harry White who, by then, was discredited in the McCarthy period and also no longer living. I had access to Harry White's papers at the Firestone Library at Princeton. I interviewed a lot of the people who were involved and just learned a lot about life from them. Of course, they disagreed on some things. They had different perspectives. But I began to understand what creating international institutions really meant and decided I would like to do a little of that myself at some point." He was able to build on these encounters and this ambition when he became assistant secretary of state in the Kennedy administration responsible for international organizations in his early thirties.

In 1951, after completing his M.A., Ponna Wignaraja was picked up by the IMF: "I really didn't know what kind of a Ph.D. thesis I wanted to write. . . . Quantitative analysis was so unreal." Fortunately, he was asked to chair a meeting attended by one of the IMF's executive directors: "I chaired the session with a certain Wignaraja style. Even at that time, I was not a consensual chairman. I expressed our hope in the Bretton Woods institutions and provoked a debate. After the meeting a few of us went to dinner with this executive director and continued a lively discussion. Next morning he called. He said, 'Look, I was very impressed with your handling of the discussions at the meeting and I am looking for a young person from one of our group to be my technical assistant with English language skills. It is my personal choice. Will you come to Washington? I want to talk to you.' So of course this was very heady and exciting. This would give me some experience and time to further sort out my confusion of what development was about—global, national, Northern and Southern, development for whose benefit."

Juan Somavía captured what is true for many of our interlocutors whose professional paths were rewarding but perhaps existentially absurd: "My whole career has happened to me. Nothing has been planned." An opening came when he decided to write a thesis under Celso Furtado on the general scheme of preferences that had been proposed by Raúl Prebisch at the first UNCTAD: "So I came to Geneva—there wasn't much in Paris. . . . Somebody said, 'Look, why don't you go to the GATT? They have been dealing with the UK imperial preferences, and *la zone franche française* [the French free trade zone]. . . . At the end of the week, the person who had sort of organized this, who was the hiring person, offered me a job. . . . I went back to Furtado and I said, 'I am really tempted by this, but I want to finish my thesis. What would you advise me?' And the advice was quite extraordinary, I must say. He said, 'You are a person of action. You want to make things happen. It's so evident. So my suggestion is to take it. . . . You are in your formative stage and you are going to learn a lot.'" Somavía's experience with trade among developing countries was helpful, and he took the job while telling his mentor: "'Look, after the Kennedy round is over, I will write a thesis on the Kennedy round just like that.' He said, 'I don't think so. I think that you will never write your thesis, but you will never need a thesis.' Those were his exact words, and they were very prescient. In fact, I never wrote the thesis and I never needed it as a presentation card."

Post-University Homecomings

Many of our voices who were born in developing countries pursued university education in prestigious Western universities. Often, but not always, they then returned home to begin careers. Those who did not were usually committed to going home but instead an opportunity arose that postponed the eventual homecoming. Gamani Corea returned to Sri Lanka in the midst of his doctoral studies. "Partly because I had been away long, I wanted to come back home, but partly because I wanted also to collect some material for the thesis. During that period in 1950, the Central Bank was set up. I had no thoughts of a career anywhere at that time, but some of my friends, including my tutor . . . had joined the official founding group for the Central Bank. They said, 'Why don't you join the Central Bank?' I said, 'Okay, but I have to finish my thesis and I'll have to go back to Oxford on a kind of no-pay leave.'" He sent in an application and was interviewed and selected. "I spent a month at the bank and remember taking a distinguished Swedish economist around. But I didn't really work with the bank until I came back with my doctorate. No sooner had I come to Ceylon, the prime minister then, Dudley Senanayake . . . said: 'We're going to set up a planning mechanism and we want you to come.'"

After Cambridge and upon returning from an internship in Europe, Noeleen Heyzer immediately became involved with the labor movement. "Singapore was undergoing industrialization, trying to define how to build a strong enough economic structure to shift itself from an entrepôt economy to a more industrialized base, whereby it could integrate more with the international economy. . . . I was very interested in how all of these industries were being set up, who comprised the labor force, and what was happening to the emerging economy. I literally stumbled into the economic zones that were being set up and found that at the center were not your skilled male workers but a very young female workforce in the factories. And I felt that the labor movement, which I had known very well and respect so much, did not take into account the issues affecting these young female workers. I met my husband, or the person who was going to be my husband, on my trip in Europe. He is a Malaysian. He used to go to Jurong to visit the Malaysian migrant workers, some of whom came from his constituency. He was the youngest and most outspoken member of Parliament in Malaysia and represented the interests of the poor, including a constituency of Malaysian Chinese migrant workers in Singapore, most of whom worked in the shipyards. I would go there with him and just hang out, as you say, in the coffee shops and listen to the conversation. Those conversations were about the working conditions. . . . Because I was in that kind of an environment I also noticed all these young girls in the coffee shops. So whilst the guys were talking, I slipped over and started my own conversation. Then I realized there was a whole world there that had been overlooked. After that, I took up a job as a factory worker, to know and understand an entirely new experience."

This real-world encounter at home was supplemented by another overseas stint at the Institute of Development Studies at the University of Sussex, a powerhouse of independent thinking at the time. Heyzer recalled her first publications at the ILO: "It was at the World Employment Programme [WEP] that I got some of my articles published first. They were at the forefront of looking at the informal economy, going beyond the normal way of looking at economics. . . . A group of women came together and found that no systematic analysis had been done on many of these topics. So we created a network of women scholars and activists. Diane Elson was there. There were so many other people who were supportive. Lourdes Beneria was there. Zubi Ahmed was there. Dharam Ghai was there. It was important to have that kind of a space in the UN, to do that, to have partnership with people from the Institute of Development Studies. It basically pulled in a group of women academics with some UN policy advisors."

After completing his doctorate in France, Paulo Sergio Pinheiro returned to Brazil to teach in São Paulo: "In the first ten years, I was doing research on social history—for example, the Third International and large American and European socialist and communist parties, the anarcho-syndicalists, anarchists. Then I had some connections with the international scene, through the working class. . . . Then I became rather involved with human rights . . . [and] established the Center for the Study of Violence." A quarter of a century later, the minister of foreign affairs proposed Pinheiro as special rapporteur on Cuba, but that did not materialize. However, "in April 1995 he suggested to the chairman of CHR [the Commission on Human Rights]—I think he was from Bangladesh or Malaysia—my name to be the special rapporteur on Burundi. I think why I was selected was because I was not European, American, or African and I was fluent in French. . . . If I look backwards, it is not a complete accident, but I never had any plans to be involved with the UN. My daughter, Marina, when I was beginning to have several UN appointments, she said, 'Another UN-paid job?'" (Special rapporteurs receive no compensation.)

Dharam Ghai decided to temporarily set aside his dissertation at Yale and return to East Africa. "In fact, they wanted people to finish their Ph.D.s there before they went away, because they knew that once people go away, they either do not finish their Ph.D.s or they take a long time over it. But I felt that I had been away too long from East Africa. . . . I thought it was time that I went back and made my contribution to nation-building. This was the time when the East African countries were on the verge of becoming independent, and there was a desperate shortage of educated people who had been to universities. . . . In those days, if you wanted an academic career in East Africa or Eastern Central Africa, the place to go to was Makerere." He wrote his dissertation while doing full-time lecturing at the historic Makerere University in Uganda. During that time, the challenge of translating textbook knowledge to the reality in East Africa arose: "In my studies in the UK, I focused on the British economy. And in the States, the emphasis was more on economic theory and applied economics, and it was mostly linked to the experience of industrialized countries. . . . So when I went back, I did not know too much about the East African economies. I had to learn about them as I was teaching."

Victor Urquidi explained how his fluency in English put him in a position to be present at the creation of the postwar economic machinery. "In 1940, I arrived in Mexico hoping to start my career as an economist with a job at the Bank of Mexico, the central bank then run by another man who had been in exile with my father. . . . So I went to see him and he appointed me in the research department. . . . He needed somebody who knew English well. . . . And as an official in the Bank of Mexico, I was immediately drawn into the study of postwar proposals in monetary and financial matters that led to the Bretton Woods Conference in 1944."

The excitement of having been able to wander around the grounds at the elegant New Hampshire resort was palpable as Urquidi recalled an earlier preparatory session in Washington. "At the final banquet at the Mayflower Hotel the night the conference finished in Washington, they sat me next to Harry D. White. I had never talked with him. . . . There was a rather good-looking woman on the other side, but I had hardly paid attention to her. I found Harry White very persuasive. . . . And he said, 'Why don't you come to my office tomorrow. I think I can let you have an interesting document for you to read and mention to your boss.'" The following day an excited young Urquidi went to the U.S. Treasury, where White pulled out of a drawer a document of some 180 pages that was marked 'Strictly Confidential.'" Urquidi noted: "And when I started reading it back at the hotel, I found it was the first proposal to create the IMF."

I. G. Patel is another person who worked with the Bretton Woods institutions in their early years. He recalled moving from theory to practice, from Cambridge and Baroda to the International Monetary Fund, in 1950: "Those four years, I think, were very important from the point of view of my economic training. That is where I first learned to handle facts, to look at balance of payments, budgets, balance sheets, and at practical problems as they arose from day to day and to deal with the country as a whole or the problem as a whole."

After finishing his Harvard M.B.A. and Ph.D., Sotiris Mousouris visited New York but was intent on making money and returning to Greece to get involved in politics when a chance opened up: "I happened to be in New York for a function for Salvador Dali, and there some people suggested—and they were right—that I owed it to myself to live one year in New York, because New York was a fantastic city. For me, it was the forbidden fruit. . . . I was going to New York as a student with little money and I was always frustrated because there are so many things in New York to do and to see and to enjoy— the theater, the museums, art, music, the night life! New York is probably the center of the earth. I was introduced to Kostis Stavropoulos, who was under-secretary-general on legal affairs, who offered me to work in the legal office. But when he heard that I wanted to work as an economist and only for a year, he more or less sent me away. I made an application, and eventually a Chinese economist at the UN, Dr. N. T. Wang, read my thesis, interviewed me, and offered me a nine-month contract. That was October 1966, and my idea was to work in the UN for one year and then return to Greece. But then we had the dictatorship, the coup d'état of the junta of colonels in Greece in April 1967. I would have never lived under that regime. So I remained at the UN and in the evenings I was involved in various activities against the dictatorship."

Throughout his university training, Bernard Chidzero was consistent in his desire to go back to Zimbabwe and contribute to the nationalist move-ment. Having moved in a decade from being unschooled to being Dr. Chidzero, he was grateful: "I wasn't going to be distracted by anything else. I was going back home to join the nationalist movement. Colleagues had been writing to me—Chitepo, Chikerema, Shamuyarira, Mushonga—'Come now, come now,' they pressed on me. I said, 'No, I am preparing myself for a different phase of the struggle.' . . . I had been prepared when I was in Canada, through the contacts we had made with the Ford Foundation and the Canada Council, to go to Oxford, spend two years there, recast my Ph.D. into a book, which I did, and concentrate my study on what was happening in the Federation of Rhode-sia and Nyasaland. A new chair in government was going to be established at the University College of Rhodesia and Nyasaland. I would be the first to hold that chair. Therefore, I was going to join in the struggle at a level where I could make a contribution in the realm of ideas. As it is, fate decided otherwise."

That fate was his love and marriage to a white Québecois: "My God, the thing blew up in Rhodesia. . . . I got correspondence from the college's head, Sir Walter Adams, regretting the cancellation of the post for three reasons. It was difficult enough, Sir Walter stated, to establish a chair on a subject which we cannot really quantify (government and political science). And the first occupant would be black in a country that was still not liberated. And, thirdly, 'we would lose our financial support.' The university would lose local white support to finance not only the chair but the university as a whole. . . . And, of course, 'we don't know where you would live with your wife,' he added to good measure." After looking at other possibilities for supporting his young family, Chidzero remembered the visit to Oxford of the executive secretary of the ECA, Mekki Abbas. A Sudanese who had been a student at Nuffield College, Abbas listened to Marjorie Perham, who had been his tutor as well as Chidzero's. She pressed Mekki: "He has applied for a job at the UN. Why can't you take him at ECA where you are?" Chidzero laughed when he recalled: "And that's how the decision was taken, and I went to Ethiopia. I joined at P-2 level, as a social affairs officer."

Secretary-General Kofi Annan packed his Minnesota earmuffs for Switzerland and went straight from Macalester College to the Graduate Institute for International Studies in Geneva with a grant from the Carnegie Endowment for International Peace: "Prior to that, I had worked with Pillsbury. . . . I did a summer internship with them. They really wanted me to stay with them. They had a project to build a flour mill in Ghana and they had hoped I would join them. So I said, 'Let me go to Geneva and do my studies at the Institute, and then I will join you from there.' Whilst I was in Geneva, their deal with the Ghana government fell through because Nkrumah had become very socialistic and felt that he would much rather have the Bulgarian government build the mill. . . . So after my studies in Geneva—at that summer, in 1962, I was working in Paris, when a friend brought to my attention an advertisement that WHO [World Health Organization] was looking for young administrators. So I applied for the job, and I got it. My intention was to stay for two years maximum and go home. And here we are."

Adebayo Adedeji also confessed that he had made no plans for an international career, but he pursued a distinguished one nonetheless: "I never gave it a thought. . . . I left school and went to the only tertiary institution then in existence, University College, Ibadan—it was then a college of London University—and from there I proceeded to Britain on government scholarship to read for a degree in economics. . . . At that same time, the government wanted to attract young men and women like myself to the civil service. Of course, as I had gone on scholarship, I felt morally bound to work for the civil service for some time." In September 1960, Adedeji was admitted to the Littauer Center, now the John F. Kennedy School of Government at Harvard University, which opened new opportunities: "While at Harvard, I paid several visits to the UN at its headquarters in New York and in one of my graduate courses—Economic Development, taught by Professor Kenneth Galbraith—I became familiar with different ideas on development postulated by UN and its senior officials. But it was not until 1966 that I had my first direct encounter with the organization. The UN had become engulfed in a serious financial crisis because of the Congo War. The General Assembly decided to set up a committee of fourteen experts drawn from the different parts of the globe to look into the finances of the UN. Our then permanent representative to the UN used to be my boss, Chief S. O. Adebo, [who] must have submitted my name."

Sonny Ramphal returned to Guyana from his studies in Britain in 1953 as crown counsel—the first rung of the ladder in the legal department. He told us that he "was the only lawyer in the Caribbean who knew anything professionally about federalism, not because I was specially bright, but because I had had this wonderful opportunity of studying federalism at close range and studying it in this West Indian context." Ramphal was drawn into a series of regional conferences: "It was for me the beginnings of a love affair with the Caribbean as a region; I grew out of just being a Guyanese into being a West Indian from Guyana. And I have remained so all my life. . . . Eventually the federation was established. I became the assistant attorney-general in it. Sadly, ultimately, it foundered on political rocks, really because, I think, small-minded politicians in Jamaica took a stand against Manley. . . . I think he was unwise enough to submit it to a referendum. It lost, and with it went the federation. And with it went a lot of my own dreams. I didn't want to see a lot of West Indian politicians for a long time."

In 1962 he got a Guggenheim Fellowship and went to Harvard for "a wonderful year," after which he opened a private practice for only a year: "Towards the end of that year, Guyana had an election. It really was the election that would move the country to independence. . . . The election was won by Burnham, and I got a telephone call. I didn't know him terribly well. I knew him as a lawyer in practice. It was a call that said, 'I would very much like you to come back and be the attorney-general, draft the Independence Constitution, and help us to become independent.' It was the kind of request you couldn't refuse. . . . I gave up private practice, gave up our home in Jamaica, went back to Guyana, on those terms. . . . My preoccupation was, first of all, independence, and the Independence Constitution, which I drafted. . . . Along the way, I became Guyana's first foreign minister."

Starting Out in Teaching and Research

Mihaly Simai's first job was teaching courses on the UN at the Karl Marx University (now the Budapest School of Economics) right after finishing his first degree, but the repressive atmosphere was hardly what we usually associate with the academy: "All western literature was considered 'confidential,'" he recalled. "It was impossible, for example, to get the Charter of the UN. It was impossible to get documents such as the Universal Declaration of Human Rights, absolutely impossible. I think much, much later, when I became the president of the Hungarian United Nations Association, we were the first to publish this document in Hungarian, but it was already in the 1970s." Simai recounted how he got his first UN job: "The head of the department came one day—it was at the end of 1958, I think—and told me that the head of the Department of International Organizations in the Ministry for Foreign Affairs asked him whether he knew somebody who could go for a short period of time, for one year, to Geneva to the Economic Commission for Europe and work in a kind of a special category, which is called 'service-in-training.' The person would work on special projects [and] at the same time . . . would be trained as a future staff member of the United Nations." Simai was told, "'You are the only person in this university who knows anything about the UN.'"

John Ruggie recalled that his first job offer came from the University of California, Berkeley, but something was missing in the rarified atmosphere of the library stacks: "I think for somebody who does what I do, either as an academic or a practitioner, it is extremely important to get some sense of how people elsewhere view the thing that you are looking at. Here at the UN, that has become second nature. But it wasn't second nature for a young academic in California. You literally had to remove yourself and go somewhere else to realize how differently the Chinese viewed U.S.-Soviet relations from the way in which Americans viewed them, for instance."

Boutros Boutros-Ghali was intent on teaching law, but there was little demand in his native Egypt in the 1950s. Each of his brothers was able to keep part of the family's land even though over half of the family's large holdings was confiscated by the new revolutionary government of Gamal Abdel Nasser. Having left Egypt to study, he returned shortly before a major geopolitical crisis: "I hurried back to Egypt in 1955. It was at that moment [June 1956] that the Suez Canal was nationalized. . . . This was a difficult period for me to the extent that my political ambitions were checked because I come from what Nasser's regime used to call the 'feudal families.' Since the feudal families had no right to participate in political life, my ambitions to become a young deputy and then a young minister, et cetera, were curbed. So I focused my political ambitions on writing. I published a number of books and articles in Arabic." In spite of a new wave of expropriations and repression following the collapse of the United Arab Republic (the fusion of Egypt and Syria) in 1961, Boutros-Ghali was sheltered: "I benefited from what might be called a certain immunity to the extent that Mohamed Haykal, the new chief editor of *Al-Ahram*, was one of Nasser's close advisors. Secondly, the daughter of Gamal Abdel Nasser, Hoda, was my student in the new Faculty of Economics and Political Science. So my views, my political positions, my analyses had direct access to the sovereign, who was Gamal Abdel Nasser, by way of my articles and my publications, but especially through his daughter, who presented new ways of looking at things, new theories, new kinds of explanations. The president was very interested in what his daughter said and asked where these ideas came from: from Mr. So-and-So. Thus I benefited, shall we say, from a certain immunity-safety during this period that was very difficult for the class to which I belonged, a period in which it experienced confiscation, house arrest, and imprisonment."

Fernando Henrique Cardoso's plan of following an academic career began propitiously with the publication of *Brazilian Industrial Entrepreneurs and Economic Development* in 1963,[7] but this was just before the military coup that would drive him into exile the following year: "The idea of the left in Brazil was, 'We need to organize an alliance between the workers and the national bourgeoisie against imperialism and the agrarian class.' . . . There were two blocs—the progressive bloc, proposed by industrialists plus other middle class [and] students and workers, against the so-called *latifundiários* linked with imperialism. This was the normal approach, that development in Brazil depends on a revolution, a kind of liberal bourgeois revolution. Most of the Brazilian thinking—not only Brazilian, but Latin American thinking—was an attempt to repeat the European history. Indeed, my book [on] the entrepreneurs is a criticism of that. I did research, because of my training, to go to see people, to analyze, to do research, and in practice, the industrialists in Brazil were tied to the agrarian situation, too, also farmers, also traders. No such distinction [between] the industrial bourgeoisie . . . [and] the old-fashioned, more feudal people. No, this never existed here. So in practice, what I did was a criticism of this old-fashioned approach based on vulgar Marxism. This was when I went to Chile, in 1964. These were the ideas in Chile, too." During his stay (in exile) at the Economic Commission for Latin America, Cardoso wrote his well-known book on *Dependency and Development in Latin America* (with Enzo Faletto).[8] Santiago was a most conducive environment for the exiled Cardoso because earlier work there by Raúl Prebisch on center-periphery and import substitution had catapulted the commission into prominence.

Paul Streeten's academic path led to a focus on issues of justice in international economic relations. He recalled his first mentor, who would later become Lord Balogh: "Tommy Balogh, who was first my tutor and teacher and then my colleague and friend, and then we worked together on a number of things—he, in many ways, was quite sympathetic to what is called 'Austro-Marxism,' which . . . as propounded by Otto Bauer, and to some extent Karl Kautsky, is a very much more moderate and more accommodating form of Marxism than the revolutionary Marxism of Lenin or Stalin. Therefore, modern Keynesianism, as indeed Joan Robinson saw, was more compatible with that kind of background. But we didn't, of course, teach this. We taught conventional, ordinary economic theory and applied economics. The field was divided between Tommy and myself. He did the applied, and I did the theoretical side in those days. . . . My concern with development and the United Nations, I think, would date probably from the late 1950s—around 1958—when I began to write and think about development issues. Now UNCTAD was founded in 1964. I remember that very distinctly. Raúl Prebisch appeared on the cover of *The Economist.* It may have been the first picture on the cover. By that time, I was already quite deeply into development and UN issues. But the initial stimulus came partly from having worked with Gunnar Myrdal on translating and writing a postscript to *The Political Element in the Development of Economic Theory*[9] and partly from Thomas Balogh, who was also very interested in the underdeveloped countries, having come from Hungary. . . . I got to know Gunnar Myrdal, who was one of the great early brains of the United Nations, like Hans Singer, Arthur Lewis, and Sidney Dell. These were the great minds that had contributed to the early days of the UN ideas."

Lourdes Arizpe had decided to pursue research on rural-urban migration and returned to Mexico to look for work. "I was stopped in the hallway of the National Institute of Anthropology and History by a director calling out 'President Echeverría wants to know where all these Marías are coming from.' So I did the specific study that President Echeverría wanted, because he sincerely wanted to help these migrant Mazahua Indian women—and he did—dressed in their traditional dress, something very unusual at the time, who were invading the sidewalks of Mexico City to sell fruit. . . . The Marías were this very visible, 'folkloric' segment of the informal sector. When I did further research, I found that they actually belonged to an army of informal street sellers, most of whom were—again—not perceived in the urban culture, because there was nothing exceptional about them. But these Indian women, the Marías, were perceived because they were dressed in their colorful dress, active and, in fact, defiant. I was able to show, in fact, that their street selling was the most rational and profitable activity in the context of widespread urban unemployment."

Arizpe then went back to the LSE and proposed the rural-urban Mazahua migration to Mexico City as her dissertation topic. "By the time I finished my dissertation, in 1975, I could predict that rural outmigration would be one of the most important phenomena for the future of Mexican development after the 1970s. . . . At the same time, when I started the study of the Marías, I was accepted by Rodolfo Stavenhagen in the new sociology department he was starting at the Colegio de México. Stavenhagen was very involved in

advancing the theory and practice of rural development and Indian identities. So he led a group of us anthropologists in a movement of advocacy for
Indian cultures." Stavenhagen currently serves as the Secretary-General's special rapporteur on indigenous peoples.

Peg Snyder, who later at ECA chronicled women's contributions to development in Africa, took a first job as dean of women at a Jesuit liberal arts
institution, Le Moyne College. She explained how she got the job at the age of
twenty-four, when she was younger than many of the veterans who were students at the time: "What had happened was that the approving association,
called Middle States . . . had come along to approve Le Moyne, and they said,
'Look, you say you're coeducational, but there's not one woman on the faculty and there are 100 men—not one woman. So you must do something
quickly and at least get a dean of women.' So that's how the job opened up. . . . I
was certainly a pioneer because this was the first of the Jesuit colleges . . . to be
coeducational." One part of the challenge was the lack of facilities. "Men had
a beautiful dormitory on campus, but women couldn't live on campus. So we
had to buy a house. . . . There were men on the faculty who didn't want to hear
anything about this. And of course, I brought as role models people like Dorothy Day to come and speak to the students and to give them a spectrum of
the possibilities of their lives and futures. That brought plenty of controversy
down on my head."

At the end of the seven years, she decided that a change was in order: "That's
when I took a year's leave that turned out to be a lifetime." During a visit with
the Berrigan brothers, Jesuits who led the Catholic anti-Vietnam movement,
she met the president of the Kenya National Union of Teachers, Stephen Kioni,
who in turn introduced Ray Smyke, who was from the International Union of
Teachers. Her interest in Africa grew, and when it was possible to take a year
off, she said, "Well, why don't I go to Africa and see where the roots of all this
are and see if I can better understand the American situation." With modest
contributions from the five members of the LeMoyne College Board of Re-
gents and from her alma mater, the College of New Rochelle, she was able to
finance her first year. She recalled that as she traveled to Kenya by plane, "I
wore all my clothes. If you read that story about the Congo, *The Poisonwood
Bible*, how in those days—it was about the time I was going—you only had
very little weight allowance that you could carry on the plane. So you wore
everything, and that's just what I did. I really smiled when I read that book. I
sewed my sneakers into the sleeves of my jacket and got there."

Samir Amin had not thought of being an academic, but when he returned
to Egypt in 1957 he found a country in tumult. His own clandestine affiliation
with the Communist Party was hardly a useful background for a career in the

national bureaucracy. He remembered: "Thus, back in Paris, I said to myself that I was going to try to reintegrate in a country where I could continue to be involved in interesting work, politically useful, by choosing a system in which it was conceivable to do things that wouldn't be at variance with one's deep convictions. I chose Mali, because Mali had just taken, in September 1960, a leftist direction. That's how I became an expert—that is, 'expert' in quotation marks—at the Malian Planning Bureau. I said to myself that it was better, given that I felt more of a foreigner in Mali than I did in Egypt, that I take off before I was asked to leave!"

And so, by default, a university career suddenly seemed a better option for Amin: "For a brief interlude, not very significant, I was a professor at IDEP [Institut de développement économique et de planification, or Institute for Development Economics and Planning]. I resigned from IDEP because I recognized that it was phony, poorly conceived. . . . It was a United Nations project. . . . It had been conceived as an institute for teaching planning techniques, a bit on the cheap, whereas what struck me as necessary in Africa as elsewhere was a center for reflecting on the nature of all aspects of development challenges. On the contrary, the Institute was just *transplanting* policy instruments without giving any thought to the problems proper to Africa that they had to resolve. I resigned by sending a letter to U Thant, without much hope, telling him simply 'I am leaving IDEP because I think that this project is badly conceived for reasons, one, two, three, et cetera.' This resulted in the United Nations—three years later, after an evaluation mission that concluded pretty much what I had written in my letter to U Thant—inviting me to New York in order to offer me the position of director. . . . It was all due to Philippe de Seynes, an extraordinarily nice and intelligent man . . . to whom my letter to U Thant had been passed along." And so Samir Amin became director of the UN-related IDEP for ten long years.

Ignacy Sachs admitted to "having done very poorly in economics in Rio," a humble admission for a prominent economist. His mentor in Poland, the celebrated Oscar Lange, suggested statistics, and Sachs dutifully followed the advice. However, he closely followed the politics and economics of Brazil and returned to Warsaw in 1954 with boxes full of primary-source documents. "I was hired by the Institute of International Affairs in Warsaw, where I was told that there was no question of my focusing on a single country such as Brazil. Poland was too poor to fund a researcher specializing in Brazilian affairs; and that's how I became, if I can put it this way, the first Mister World in Poland because they assigned me Latin America, Asia, and Africa, with one colleague to share this universe. I returned to Poland in 1954. Kalecki came back [from the United Nations] in March 1955. I first had dealings with him in 1956 when

I wrote an article for the journal *Economista,* which was the journal of the association of Polish economists. It was about a savings equation for under-developed countries. I was not terribly sure about my argument, and I asked that they send the article to Kalecki for his opinion. At that time I was already teaching as a part-time lecturer at Warsaw University and at the School of Planning. One day my phone rang and it was Kalecki calling to say that it wasn't worth using mathematics to say what one could say more simply with-out mathematics. At my question as to whether I should withdraw my article, he said to me, 'You would be well advised.' I thus concluded that I was on the wrong track. 'I didn't tell you that,' Kalecki said to me. 'I told you that that article wasn't worth publishing. You just need to keep thinking. Perhaps in ten or fifteen years something will come of it.'"

Mostafa Tolba ruminated about his lack of vision: "I planned or thought I was planning my life in a completely different way and I got the exact oppo-site of what I was planning. . . . The only time that I applied for anything, and it was just as a joke, it was advertised in the University of Cairo that the Uni-versity of Iraq wanted two professors of botany in 1954. I was sitting in my room with one of my colleagues who was a little more junior than myself, and we just applied. He was assistant professor and I was lecturer, so I thought there was no point in them having a lecturer to become professor. In spite of that, three or four weeks later, we both got the offer to go as professors to Baghdad."

Beginning in National Public Service

Paul Berthoud maintained an intellectual interest in the United Nations as the organization was taking shape, but he also had to earn a living, so he took a job in Bern in the Ministry of Economics to investigate the parallel war economy. "So I ran, for about eighteen months, professionally after peasants who had slaughtered cows illegally. . . . My interest in the UN was so sharp then that I asked for and obtained permission from the government in Bern and registered at the University of Neuchâtel to give a course on the United Nations. . . . So for two and a half years, I was going to Neuchâtel half a day every week, giving a two-hour course, one hour on the United Nations, and an hour seminar which I focused on the question of Palestine. . . . So this is what brought me close to the UN intellectually, but of course, not into the organization. Here, I had a major problem. The Swiss had not been in San Francisco, and they were not joining the UN. . . . Nationality was an absolute obstacle. . . . So really it was just fate that decided otherwise. . . . In 1948, at some point, I became aware of the existence of an international bureau in

Bern, which was called the International Penal and Penitentiary Commission [IPPC]. . . . I applied. I must confess it was not at all because of the substance of the work, but I was interested in a mechanism of multilateral cooperation." Soon thereafter a negotiation began to determine whether the IPPC should be part of the United Nations. "By a stroke of luck, it was negotiated that in order to ensure the continuity of the activities in this field of prevention of crime and treatment of offenders, two staff members of the commission would be taken over by the UN Secretariat. I happened to be one of the two."

Another hélvétique, Cornelio Sommaruga, knew that he wanted to be involved in public service, partly motivated by his having lived abroad. "I had a very idealistic view of Switzerland, and I wanted to do something for Switzerland. . . . I thought this was a sector where I may be successful in helping my country, knowing languages, knowing a little bit of the whole atmosphere. . . . But there was a rule in Swiss diplomacy at that time that one couldn't enter diplomacy directly from university studies; candidates should have had two years of practical professional life. . . . I made the choice of banking only because my father, before dying, had asked me: 'Try to be at least a little bit aware of economics and financial problems. Go to a bank.' And I did."

Vladimir Petrovsky was unable to pursue higher studies immediately because the Soviet Union required three years of public service first: "So all of us postgraduate students were sent to the Foreign Ministry. But at that time, another reform was the changing attitude towards the United Nations, the increasing interest to use it not only for public relations but also for practical deeds. That's why all . . . postgraduate students who studied Britain, the United States, or other countries were sent to the Department of International Organizations."

In 1957, he was posted to the Permanent Mission to the United Nations in New York. Quickly, Petrovsky moved from more general to far more specific duties: "There was the period when the national liberation movements had started. I was assigned to work in the first and special political committees as an expert dealing with the problems of Algeria, apartheid in South Africa, and other colonial issues. . . . And it so happened that at that time, Khrushchev arrived for his official visit to the United Nations. It was another, I would say, unexpected development in my diplomatic career. His chief protocol had fallen ill and the ambassador had received the instruction to recommend somebody from his office as the chief of protocol of Mr. Khrushchev during his stay at the General Assembly. So I became a chief of protocol of the prime minister of the USSR, though I had not much experience in these matters. . . . So this experience as a chief of protocol brought me to the attention of the foreign minister, Andrei Gromyko."

Jack Stone described the indirect path from his first research assignment in Chicago to a job in postwar Europe: "I was around Chicago for a year or so after I got my bachelor's degree. I [had] a reading course with Hans Morgenthau. . . . I actually took the Foreign Service exam in 1945 at the U.S. main post office in Chicago. . . . I went overseas as a civilian in military government early in 1946, and I took the oral exams for the Foreign Service in Germany. I remember [that] the crucial question that they asked me, and which I perhaps naively answered, was, 'What would you like to do with your career?' I told them, 'I would like to get a doctorate in economics eventually, but I wouldn't mind serving in the Foreign Service for a time first.'"

Don Mills went into government service as a junior bookkeeper before being given a scholarship and going abroad to pursue university studies. His first job was in the radio station run by the War Information Office set up by the British government in Jamaica during World War II, which "helped to lay the foundations of my interest in international affairs."

Francis Blanchard, newly married in 1940 in occupied France, was desperate for work. His is another illustration that the road to a UN career has many bends with unexpected vistas. A cousin had contacts with the Ministry of Foreign Affairs in the Vichy government: "I contacted him in the fall of 1940, and he suggested to me a position with the Résidence Générale de France in Tunisia. This proposal was the more attractive since the date of our wedding was approaching. . . . He was proposing a modest position in the Résidence Générale de France, the Contrôle Civil in Morocco and in Tunisia. I had been enticed by this field. Moreover, I was very interested in the Arab World. . . . I accepted. The day after our wedding in November 1940 my wife and I embarked at Marseilles for Tunis."

Viru Dayal was among the few who had a clear vision of an international career and followed it to the United Nations: "I belonged to a community called the *kayasths*. And the *kayasths* have always been associated with government and with the professions, particularly the law, and with administration. . . . At that time, of course, the private sector in India was not very developed. The private companies that were there—like Shell and Imperial Tobacco and Caltex and ICI and so on—just didn't interest me. They seemed to have nothing to do with my life, and nothing to do with my vision or my future of India. I must say that some of my close friends and my family went into these companies, but I always viewed them as—we used to call them 'box-wallahs,' people who went around with boxes selling their wares. It didn't seem quite the right thing to do at my age. It wasn't intrinsic enough to the future of the country."

The transition from the national to the international civil service was un-expected but productive: "Then I came to the UN, fortuitously, because one of the things that I did was that at the ripe old age of twenty-four or twenty-five, I settled tens of thousands of refugees from what used to be East Pakistan, that came to be known as Bangladesh. They were being settled in what we call the Terai, in the foothills of the Himalayas in the district where I was stationed. We opened virgin land and, sadly as I see now, had to cut down forests to make a place for them. But we had to do it because they needed to be provided for. . . . So when, circa 1965, the UNHCR asked for somebody from India—because they had nobody from Asia at that time at all in the office in the organization, nobody—they wrote to the government of India and asked for names, and mine was one of three or four names that were sent to them. . . . So I always have the Bengali refugees to thank for my life in the UN—something which I have never forgotten."

Virginia Housholder's first encounter with the UN also involved refugees. She remembered an interview she had, while she was in graduate school at the University of Wyoming, with the National Institute of Public Affairs, where she became an intern in July 1942. "Julia Henderson was an intern about three years before I was. . . . There were two of us interns who went to work for the budget bureau—both female. The bureau maintained that it had no prejudice against women, but they'd had one woman budget examiner several years before and I think they lost her under a desk or something. In early 1945, I got a call from the National Institute wanting to know was I happy in my work and I said 'yes' and they said, 'Well, how would you like to go to Germany to work for UNRRA [UN Relief and Rehabilitation Administration]?' . . . I said, 'Who wants to go to Germany? There's a war going on.' And they said, 'Yes, but the war's about to end.' So I had had no previous particular interest in international organizations, but at the end of about six weeks, I was on a boat headed for first London and then France and then finally Germany. . . . We all got worried whether the displaced persons would all be gone by the time we got to Germany."

Housholder was relieved to find clients but reflected on her inexperience: "I was a good ripe twenty-seven and I had not had any dealings with people of other nationalities. But we wound up with this team of fifteen people and ten nationalities and no common language. . . . I used an interpreter and I wasn't very happy with it because I had no sense of communication with the people. So the next time I had to make a speech, I apologized for my bad German and went ahead and talked in German. Well, at that time we had Poles, and they spoke the same kind of ungrammatical German that I did. So we got along very well."

Javier Pérez de Cuéllar looked back over his long diplomatic career in his government and in the UN and pointed to "*encadenamiento,* a kind of a chain of events that led me to diplomacy. I decided to enter the Foreign Ministry as a clerk in 1940 and made the necessary studies in order to become a diplomat. I had my first appointment in 1944. As I was already fluent in French, I was sent here to Paris in December 1944. . . . I was totally—I would not say igno-rant, because that wouldn't be right—but I was not interested in interna-tional organizations until 1972. Actually, I had to make a tremendous effort in order to prepare myself to produce good work."

Maurice Bertrand recalled how chance and the end of World War II helped launch his career as an analyst and then a government official: "It was the last competitive exam for the senior civil service before the creation of the ENA, and so I was called upon to be a lecturer at the Ecole Nationale d'Administra-tion the same year that it was created, because it was a tradition: one prepared for the entrance exams for the State Council, for the Court, and for the In-spectorship in what were called 'stables,' . . . [which] were run by those who had taken the preceding exams. So they continued this tradition at the ENA by appointing as lecturers the people who had just taken part in the preceding competitions. I served in this position for six or seven years, teaching the young generations, among whom were many who have become very important to-day. After that, I pursued a career in the Court without being particularly interested—except that I found the work fairly dull. It was in 1968 that I read one day while in the hallway of the Court a job announcement for the United Nations. The Quai d'Orsay was proposing to magistrates of the Court and members of the Inspectorship of Finance that they become members of the Joint Inspection Unit of the United Nations. I applied and was selected, prob-ably because of my age. I was forty-five at that time, which, I believe, corre-sponded pretty much to what was needed for the job."

Max Finger obtained a B.S. at Ohio University and wanted to be professor of American history, but he graduated in 1935 in the midst of the Great De-pression and was unable to find a job in his chosen field. Later, he served in the U.S. Army French Liaison Unit during World War II. Following the war, he joined the U.S. Foreign Service and was stationed in Laos, where he could use his newly acquired French. "And that was helpful in my later assignments," he stated, "because I really knew what an underdeveloped country was like, and what its problems were." These assignments included almost two decades in New York at the U.S. Permanent Mission to the United Nations.

Our voices included many who were on the ground floor when the world organization was getting started. Molly Bruce was one of the first people hired in November 1945 in London and continued after the Secretariat first moved to Hunter College in the Bronx. She recalled her circuitous path to an international career. "I really wanted to join one of the armed forces, but because my brother was actually at Dunkirk receiving the Allied troops being evacuated, my parents persuaded me to look for something a little less dangerous. . . . It was the Cambridge University Appointments Board that encouraged me to apply to the Royal Institute of International Affairs. . . . We had access to newspapers from occupied Europe and from neutral countries. So you got a different slant on the news and a chance to read it and study it." Following the San Francisco conference, the UN moved to London for meetings of the Preparatory Commission to make interim arrangements for the first formal meetings of the General Assembly and the Security Council in February 1946. Bruce recalled: "The Foreign Office—the Royal Institute of International Affairs had become the Foreign Office Research Department—was looking for staff to service the UN meetings in London. . . . I wanted to contribute to peace. I had seen enough of war. . . . I'm not sure we even fully knew what was going on regarding the UN until we met as part of the UN staff in Church House, close to Westminster Abbey. Our offices were around a bomb crater."

The British Foreign Office's Gladwyn Jebb was in control of the UN's administration, a kind of "first" secretary-general whose personal assistant was Brian Urquhart. Bruce was one of those selected to be sent to the United States. "I flew over—it was my first flight ever—with one of the first teams and landed in New York after twenty-four hours. I did not like New York. I thought people were rude and pushy." Her first night was in the Hotel New Yorker, "which later became the headquarters of the Reverend Moon but was then a commercial hotel. I couldn't understand what people were saying. . . . And the person at the desk got very impatient and said, 'I'll send you an interpreter.' So I had an interpreter for my English my first night in New York."

Mary Smieton, another woman pioneer recruited for the Secretariat to work on personnel, described how she first came to the UN from service in the British government: "I was in the Ministry of Labor, working on manpower problems. But I had a regular sort of straightforward civil service training in the Personnel Department and so on. I was dealing with employment questions in 1946. I had two years off during the war, when I had helped Lady Reading start up the Women's Voluntary Services for Air Raid Precautions. And that was quite interesting. Indeed, that's the only bit of experience that was directly related to what I had to do in the UN, i.e., starting up something from scratch. . . . Eric Biddle had been sent on a trawl around European countries to find suitable staff. . . . He approached the Treasury in England. And the Treasury, in its turn, approached departments and said that there were these jobs going. Was anybody interested? I expressed interest. They weren't quite sure what job I was going to be offered."

Julia Henderson reminisced about her reaction to a totally unexpected telephone call: "I remember I was working for the Social Security Board, and Eric Biddle, who was at the Budget Bureau, called me one day and said, 'Julia, how would you like to help organize the United Nations?' Since I had a strong interest in international affairs, I was just thrilled with that and said, 'When do we start?'"

Janez Stanovnik's international career began when he was released from prison by the occupying Italians in 1942. "I then went immediately to the forests. I was then a partisan over the war time, from 1942 to 1945, in various parts of Slovenia." Even before the war was over and because he was a member of the underground political leadership, he was appointed "*chef de cabinet* of the man number two in Yugoslavia at that time. . . . At that time, he was minister for the constitution. Later on, he became minister of foreign affairs." This job exposed him to the UN and international relations more generally, as he accompanied the minister everywhere. Stanovnik notes that his interest in economic affairs resulted from those trips, during which he attended sessions of the General Assembly's Second Committee in New York. "This interest of mine for economic matters was so intense that . . . I came then, from 1952 to 1956, as economic counselor to the permanent mission in New York."

Conor Cruise O'Brien has had perhaps the most varied set of experiences among the group—literary figure and gadfly, government official, member of Parliament, journalist, and UN staff member. Interestingly enough, the title of the collection of essays in his honor mirrors one of the central themes of this volume: *Ideas Matter*.[10] He recalled that Ireland's long-awaited entrance in the world organization—which was delayed by disagreements between Moscow and Washington in the Security Council over membership—suddenly opened an unexpected path: "I had graduated in Dublin. I went in for the Irish civil service, which was at that time a very limited opportunity for intellectuals and the like. It was one of the few places where you could go and earn a living. So I went into that. When Ireland was admitted to the UN . . . there was a United Nations section set up at headquarters, and I was put in charge of that. I went to the General Assembly several years running." O'Brien's disillusionment with the UN starting in the mid-1950s through the Congo debacle of the 1960s is spelled out in a searing illustrated book, *The United Nations: Sacred Drama*.[11]

After finishing college in 1949, Sartaj Aziz realized that the opportunities for banking and finance were limited in Pakistan: "So I took the central superior services examination, through which officers are recruited for different service groups. I opted for the accounts group in order to move on to economic policymaking." When asked why he did not offer police services as one of his choices, he said, "Temperamentally, I can handle ideas better than people. So I cannot become a successful police officer. So it was a good choice to go into the field of economic and financial management." The opportunity to return to his first love, macroeconomics, came about nine years later when he became a member of the Planning Commission in Pakistan.

Klaus Sahlgren at first thought about a university career but then he moved toward government service. A first interview almost marked a catastrophic end to that career possibility: "I almost blew it. First, I paid my respects to the then minister of communications, Onni Peltonen. He was a Social Democrat and a well-known teetotaler. He asked me, in Finnish of course, do I drink? I answered in the wrong way: 'Yes, thank you sir, what can you offer?'" Despite the interview, he began as a trainee in the administrative department, which he remembers as dull, but another faux pas livened things up: "As a sign of our position we had a set of lead pencils, to be sharpened from time to time by an usher. One day, I took my pencils and I went out to the corridor and I saw a person whom I presumed was the usher. I said, 'Could you please sharpen these pencils for me?' He answered, 'Young man, I am the foreign minister, you had better sharpen the pencils yourself.'" Sahlgren nonetheless won a Rockefeller Foundation scholarship to work in the Economic Commission for Europe. He had found a home. "I then decided—I even told Myrdal—that one day I would return here as a boss, which I did."

Oscar Schachter's shift from domestic to international law was a surprise: "I never envisaged working on international problems until I found myself in the government from 1940 to 1944. I had not taken a course in international law, but I had some exposure to international law through my work as editor-in-chief of the *Columbia Law Review*. In my last year in law school, I had decided on government rather than private practice and I looked to the New Deal agencies—e.g., the Department of Labor and the Securities and Exchange Commission—as potential employers. I had worked a few months for a New York law firm in 1939 when, out of the blue, Philip Graham, later the publisher of the *Washington Post*, called to urge me to take a job under Joe Rauh in the Wage and Hours Division of the Department of Labor. In addition to my work in that division, Joe Rauh asked me to write some papers on current controversies, which he passed on to President Roosevelt's advisors, Ben Cohen and Tom Corcoran. This brought me, sort of, to the fringes of the New Deal intellectual community."

After only six months in the Labor Department, he moved to the Federal Communications Commission (FCC) Law Department and "some problems

related to international issues, such as legal questions involving foreign interests in international telecommunications facilities. In my second year at the
FCC, much of my work was as secretary of the Legal Committee of the Defense (later War) Communications Board. It was the kind of legal work I liked,
calling for quick reactions to policy questions with both legal and political aspects." Schachter went on to become the UN's legal advisor shortly after the end
of the war and then director of research at UNITAR before spending the end of
his career at Columbia University's Law School.

Juggling Family and Professional Life

Given the historical period when our voices entered the job market, it is
hardly surprising that many of those who speak most eloquently about the
difficulties of juggling families and professional lives are women. Elise Boulding
recalled moving into political activism as her children became older and her
family responsibilities changed: "I was very much a peace activist in the years
our children were growing up. When Kenneth and his colleagues set up the
Center for Conflict Resolution, they had a part-time administrative secretary
but were completely overwhelmed by mail. Letters were coming from all over
the world, people saying, 'This is what we are doing about peace and disarmament. What are you doing?' These letters were getting tossed into the wastebasket because there wasn't anybody who had time to answer them. I came
over as a volunteer and rescued the letters from the wastebasket. So I always
say that the *International Peace Research Newsletter,* and subsequently the International Peace Research Association [IPRA], grew out the wastebaskets at
the Center for Conflict Resolution in Michigan. . . . At the Michigan center,
they were kind of embarrassed at my slipshod rounding up of correspondence and sending out news. They didn't want to put the academic name of
the center and of the university on that newsletter. That is how it happens
that the first issue . . . was issued by the International Consultative Committee
on Peace Research, Women's International League for Peace and Freedom.
For the first two years, that is how the masthead of the newsletter read. . . . Of
course, I turned to UNESCO immediately. They started funding the newsletter even before IPRA was founded."

Devaki Jain's interest in the UN and women's issues also grew when juggling both her family responsibilities and a career became impossible: "I resigned from my permanent tenured position as a lecturer in the University
College for women and settled down to full-time mothering of my two sons,
born 1967 and 1969. Post resignation, too, I was unhappy—unhappy that I
had to leave the workplace, unhappy that my husband went to work while I

stayed home. The rewards were reaped later in life, when my sons turned out as wholesome young people admired by many for their composure and self-confidence. . . . But the resignation led me to doing a book at home, the official Indian volume for the Mexico conference for the UN World Conference for the International Women's Year, which in turn brought me to the women's question, which then has become the central interest in my life."

Jain recalled her application to the Indian Council for Social Science Research. "I made applications to them to do my famous time-use study, which Joann Vanek said was a 'trailblazer.'" Jain's grant permitted her to analyze self-employed poor women in a trade union: "I went to Ahmedabad, and I saw this amazing thing which has now become a world icon, called SEWA, the Self-Employed Women's Association. . . . What I saw there were street vendors, vegetable vendors, like you see in Africa and other parts—who are the poorest of the poor. . . . They had been made into a trade union. And what were they doing there as a trade union? They were going to collectively negotiate for better prices for either the rags they were picking or the soiled paper that they were collecting. Or the vegetable vendors wanted to sit on the pavement and they were being attacked by the police, so they formed a collective. . . . So I saw that and started writing analytically about them. I was perhaps one of the first to write how when women organize, it actually changes gender relations in the home."

When Sadako Ogata went to the General Assembly as a member of the Japanese delegation in 1968, it was her first and quite unexpected exposure to the UN. "Most of the things happening in my life have come by chance. But you see, when Japan was admitted to the United Nations, it was 1956. At that time, there were women leaders. One of them, Ms. Fusae Ichikawa, was quite well known. She was in the House of Councilors—a very outstanding person. She led the suffrage movement. They presented a request to the Japanese government, the foreign minister, to include a woman on the UN delegation. Since 1957, a woman has served on the delegation. However, I was very removed from all those kinds of public developments. One year—about ten years later—suddenly they ran out of people to send with the delegation. . . . They heard from somewhere that I had studied these things—international politics, international organization. I had good English. Somehow some research went around, and then Ms. Ichikawa appeared at my house one summer and asked me. So there was a big family consultation because I had two children. . . . They all got together and let me go. The next year, my family said, 'Well, you've had enough.' So I didn't go. I had good working relations with the Foreign Ministry, so I became rather active on UN fronts. Then I came again in 1970, because the Foreign Ministry asked me to . . . and then again in

1975. Then after that I joined the Foreign Ministry and was stationed as minister here at the Japanese permanent mission."

Nafis Sadik was married in Washington in 1954 while doing her medical internship while her father was posted with the World Bank: "Nixon came to our wedding. . . . My husband was in the [Pakistani] army, so I decided that I would get a job with the army, but in an army hospital, since they were the best hospitals—but not as a military person, because then I would have to be posted wherever they posted me, but as a civilian. It was always temporary. I didn't have any permanence in the job, and I could leave whenever I wanted. And I could get myself transferred whenever my husband got transferred. So in a sense, I was quite independent. But it was still like my husband's career was more important than mine at that time."

After several years of following her husband around and working in army and naval hospitals, she became disgruntled about how routine her days had become: "It was the same army hospital and the same poor people. . . . There was a tuberculosis ward for women in this hospital, and . . . I used to say, 'You can't get pregnant.' It was the same story again. . . . I started to think to myself, 'All my life I am not going to do this, tell people what should be done and not really making a difference. . . . And I hate this job. I don't like obstetrics. Why I ever went into it, I don't know.'" Her husband suggested a two-month break. "Of course, after two weeks of it everyone in the house was fed up with me— all the servants. I didn't know what to do with myself. . . . How many coffee parties can you attend, with the bridge and all that? . . . Then I decided that I would look for another job where I could make a difference. The Planning Commission I saw was advertising. . . . But I didn't have a public health background as such. So I asked USAID [United States Agency for International Development] if they would send me on a fellowship to do health planning, because I was getting a job as—which I wasn't, but I had applied for it. They gave me this fellowship, so I did this health planning course at Hopkins University, which had just started."

Leticia Shahani's marriage and her husband's first posting overseas provided her with an unexpected opportunity to work on UN issues: "After I finished my Ph.D. at the Sorbonne, my fiancé and I decided to get married, and so we came to New York. One of the first job offers I had was to assist the Philippine mission to the UN, helping in its campaign for the Philippines to have a seat in the Security Council." Like other interviewees, her language abilities helped launch her international career. "I spoke French," Shahani said, "a language not spoken commonly by Filipinos. I was asked to help in the campaign among the French-speaking delegates. . . . So I guess the combination of wanting to settle in an international community because I had married a foreigner and [wanting] to begin my career in the area of international cooperation greatly attracted me."

Margaret Anstee also married a diplomat, and a UN vacancy opened even if the circumstances were considerably less pleasant. She herself was employed by the British Foreign Office, but "if you were a woman in the Foreign Office and you got married, you had to resign immediately. So, that's what happened." She described how difficult this period was for her. "It turned out that my husband was an alcoholic, which I did not know, and the expatriate community in Manila was the worst possible environment for someone with those tendencies. He was an extremely nice man when he was sober but when drunk he was violent and insulted me in public about my working-class background. . . . I was distraught. I remember walking up and down the beach and thinking, 'What will I do?' . . . I hadn't enough money to go home." So she took a job as administrative assistant at the new UN Technical Assistance Office in Manila, the lowest rung among expatriates. She joked, "I think I am the only local staff member who has become an under-secretary-general!"

Part Two.
Hope, Creativity, and Frustration

Many of our voices recount—some at high- and some at low-decibel levels—how well various UN organizations have adapted to changes in international politics. They also reflect upon ideas that emerged in response to particular problems or crises and upon ideas that were discarded. Throughout these chapters, we have grouped comments around the first "explosion" of a particular idea or concept even if comments refer to subsequent decades. For instance, human rights material appears mainly in the next chapter because of the adoption of the Universal Declaration of Human Rights in 1948, although they retain a contemporary pertinence, as does a discussion of the Non-Aligned Movement (NAM) that emerged after the Bandung conference in 1955.

Ideas and concepts have been a driving force of human progress. They are arguably the UN's most important legacy. However, there is almost no analysis of the origins and evolution of ideas cultivated within the ambit of the world organization—hence, this book.

The lack of attention to the UN's role in generating or nurturing ideas is perplexing. As Oxford University political economist Ngaire Woods observed: "Ideas, whether economic or not, have been left out of analyses of international relations."[1] Many political scientists, especially analysts of international political economy and economic historians are discovering the role of ideas in international policymaking. The study of ideas, although relatively new in contemporary analyses of international politics and organizations, is common bill of fare for historians, philosophers, students of literature, and economists.

This part of the book explores how particular global events and shocks have had an impact on new thinking or on eliminating outmoded perspectives. A longstanding debate among intellectual historians is whether an idea should be analyzed in light of the historical and social context within which it emerged and evolved or whether it should be understood on its own. For us, the former appears infinitely more commonsensical because economic and social ideas at the UN cannot be divorced from their historical contexts. Key appointments, the tenor of multilateral negotiations, and the timing of agenda-setting within the world organization invariably reflect events and are contingent upon the geopolitics of a particular historical moment and the prevailing conditions in the world economy. As Dharam Ghai stated during our interview: "No one person can claim authorship of any idea. In a few cases a major work appears. Like on the environment, Rachel Carson's *Silent*

Spring. But even a work such as this is preceded by a lot of other work. Lots of people come to similar kinds of conclusions."

Kofi Annan illustrated the fine mosaic of ideas and historical backdrop with his perspective on the shock of independence and the right approach to economic development: "I think for Ghana, in a way, the struggle was very brief. It started in 1919 by a group of intellectuals. Then it lay fallow for a while until 1948, when a group of ex-servicemen demonstrated in Accra and energized the movement. That was the first real movement that was sustained. . . . Everybody was very aware—at least kids at my age and those who were at school with me and I played with. At home it was a constant discussion."

The seventh Secretary-General went on to comment on the paradoxes of this period: "The struggle for independence leads to the formation of national movements, not necessarily political parties. Independence is something that everybody wants, so sometimes you have one big movement, the national movement, that struggles for independence. And at the end of the struggle, people who may be very good at confronting the colonialists and fighting for independence and may have no idea about governance become leaders. They forget that the talents you need to fight for independence may be quite different from the talents you need to rule and to govern. . . . So we had some wrong people in leadership positions in terms of governance. And on the economic issue, they reduced the development issue to whether you do it through agriculture or industrialization."

Annan provided some specifics about the context in which the idea of decolonization was played out: "Nkrumah, for example, wanted to industrialize Ghana very quickly, and overlooked our natural advantage of agriculture. Here's a country that was producing more than half the production of world cocoa. . . . But instead of that, they wanted to get into industry and came up with the Ministry for Heavy and Light Industry—which was the Russian model—and other things. And in fact, when I look back, I see that Ghana and Malaysia got independence at the same time. They had roughly the same amount of reserves, and yet look at the two economies and where they are. . . . And at that point in time, the debate was over which model was more effective—the Soviet socialist model or the capitalist model. In fact, you had two countries, the Ivory Coast and Ghana, sitting side by side—Felix Houphouet-Boigny going the capitalistic and Western approach, and Nkrumah going the other way. And in fact, Houphouet took a bet with him. He said, 'You go your way, I'll go my way, and in ten years' time we will decide who has done more for his country.' Nkrumah died before they could look at the scorecard, but in my judgment Ivory Coast did much better."

4

From 1945 through the 1950s: Hope Held High

- **Establishment of the United Nations**
- **The Universal Declaration of Human Rights**
- **The Marshall Plan**
- **The Cold War**
- **McCarthyism**
- **Decolonization and the Non-Aligned Movement**
- **The UN Regional Commissions**

The San Francisco Conference on International Organization culminated on June 22, 1945, with the signing of the UN Charter by fifty-one participating states. This historic moment occurred after the end of the war in Europe but prior to the end of the armed conflict in Asia. Preparations for the United Nations were already advanced by the early phases of World War II, stirred by deep revulsion over the horrors that were engulfing so much of the planet. The political failure of the League of Nations and the Treaty of Versailles that underlay its creation highlighted for everyone except the most myopic a sharp awareness of the risks of failing again. The Great Depression and the mass unemployment and poverty amid affluence in the 1930s had generated radically new ideas and approaches to economic and social policy. These were readily available to the postwar world.

One of the extraordinary features of the UN's creation, indeed, is how much of its foundations were laid during the early phases of World War II, some before the United States had even formally entered the war. In August 1941, American president Franklin D. Roosevelt and British prime minister Winston Churchill agreed on common principles for their postwar policies as part of the Atlantic Charter and referred to "the establishment of a wider and permanent system of general security." Five months later, in January 1942, twenty-six governments—including China, Poland, Czechoslovakia, and a

number of Latin American states—signed a "Declaration of the United Nations," elaborating further these basic principles.

By October 1943, the need to establish "a general international organization based on the sovereign principle of the equality of all peace-loving states"
had been signed by the United States, the United Kingdom, and the Soviet
Union as part of the Declaration of Moscow. They were joined shortly afterward by China. The declaration emphasized action "at the earliest practicable
date." The experience of the Peace Treaty of Versailles had shown the risks
and dangers of waiting until after a war was over, when postwar ambitions
and alliances might form and prevent or water down agreement about international cooperation.

Planning then began in earnest. The most significant meeting was at
Dumbarton Oaks, then near (and now in) Washington, D.C., from August to
October 1944, where the fundamental principles of the UN itself were ham-
mered out in two parts (by the United States, the United Kingdom, and the
USSR and then again by the United States, the United Kingdom, and China).
The resulting proposals were put to the nations that assembled in San Fran-
cisco the following April.[1]

Meanwhile, a parallel process was under way to define postwar economic
and financial institutions. Beginning in December 1940, British economist
John Maynard Keynes, arguably the most important economist of the twentieth century, put forward initial sketches for postwar currency arrangements
in his usually poignant manner: "The authors of the Peace Treaty of Versailles
made the mistake of neglecting the economic reconstruction of Europe in
their preoccupation with political frontiers and safeguards. Much misfortune
to all of us has followed from this neglect."[2] His proposals became the subject
of intense discussion among a small circle of economists and government
officials in London and Washington. By late 1943, both the United States and
the United Kingdom had draft proposals, each covering postwar international
financial arrangements and a capital fund. This activity culminated in a major international gathering in Bretton Woods, New Hampshire, in July and
August 1944. Forty-four governments met to discuss ideas for an International Monetary Fund, an International Bank for Reconstruction and Development (IBRD, or the World Bank), and an International Trade Organization
(ITO). There were other preparatory conferences for specialized institutions,
part of a pattern of steady growth of specialized institutions since the middle
of the nineteenth century.[3]

The United States, whose late president Roosevelt was the principal architect of the new postwar order, was perhaps the most active supporter of the
new world organization. The United States was engaged in the world and
crafted a new rights-based order out of the horrors of World War II. This

vision reflected great optimism in the United States and elsewhere about the possibilities for multilateral cooperation. This all-too-brief moment would soon be overtaken by the onset of the Cold War, which quickly applied the brakes to this momentum of cooperation and which marked the beginning of a decades-long assault on the organization and its staff by the major powers. But we are getting ahead of ourselves.

The Establishment of the United Nations

Janez Stanovnik captured what drove the postwar generation: "I must tell you," he told us, "that the United Nations in my time and before 1952 when I was in New York and later on, but in this early period the UN was a true family of sincere believers, which it is not anymore. Everybody in the UN Secretariat at that time had a wartime story of his own. Therefore, whoever wrote the Charter and wrote this first paragraph . . . were mindful of the scourges of war and have been committed to never having war anymore, never again. We were lucky to survive, but we had a moral duty to honor the victims." Enrique Iglesias concurred: "As an adolescent I lived through the horrors of the war as well as the hopes for peace. The United Nations emerged in that time as the New World's institution." Ignacy Sachs joined the passionate chorus who described that first UN generation as "extremely motivated, politically involved, and shared a certain number of strong convictions: full employment, planning, priority for social issues, anticolonialism."

Oscar Schachter was equally emphatic in remembering the atmosphere in those early years: "There were certainly a lot of dedicated people, and there were also some kooks and time-servers. All sorts of people turned up in the secretariats. Some came through the military, some League of Nations staff, and UNRRA was a large source. For all, there was a problem of adjustment to a strange but stimulating environment. . . . The organization was small in 1946 and 1947. The legal department, for example, had five legal officers in 1946. There are over 100 now. In 1946, I shared an office with Abe Feller when at the Hunter College campus, which was two doors away from the Secretary-General, Trygve Lie, who came popping into our room, often several times a day. . . . At that time, most foreigners were happy to be in the Bronx. They even liked the subway. They loved the delicatessens and the bakeries. When we moved to Lake Success [on Long Island, outside New York City], many grumbled. . . . They were happy to have jobs and they were proud to be in an important organization. I remember that my secretary objected because I didn't let her attend the Security Council meetings. She felt they also had a right to attend Security Council meetings. After all, it was their organization."

In 1951 the UN headquarters moved into its permanent home on First Avenue bordering the East River in Manhattan.

Celso Furtado spoke passionately about his impressions of then and now: "In the beginning the United Nations had a crucial role, and now the UN is more or less out of the picture. . . . The first time that I participated in a United Nations mission, some fifty years ago, I had the sense that we were involved in something important that would have meaningful consequences. The world would not be exactly the same afterwards."

Jacques Polak recalled the mood at the Bretton Woods meetings in July 1944, having observed them firsthand: "It lasted three weeks. It was extended. It was not supposed to last more than eighteen days. It lasted twenty-one or something like that. Everybody who came there knew what they were there for, namely, to create an international monetary system that would not have the faults and not produce the failure and the mess that had prevailed during the twenty years preceding." Those institutions are still very much with us, joined since 1995 by the World Trade Organization (WTO).

Adebayo Adedeji remembered his child's-eye evaluation of at least one direct benefit from the world body's establishment: "We were given the day off. That was almost always welcome to schoolchildren. . . . We were convinced that the organization would accelerate the decolonization process. There was however fear that the UN might go the way of the League of Nations and sacrifice the interests of Africa as the League sacrificed the interest of Ethiopia. This was all part of what we were taught in school."

In thinking back to 1945 and his undergraduate days at Harvard College, Richard Gardner remembered: "I was very interested in the creation of the UN. I'm not sure that the students generally were as much interested as I was. I read carefully every dispatch that Scotty Reston wrote in the *New York Times* about the Dumbarton Oaks and San Francisco conferences. . . . There was a very dramatic visit to the Harvard campus by Cord Meyer, the founder of the World Federalists who then went on to become a CIA operative. I got into a big argument with him because he said, in speaking to students, that the UN was all wrong and that we had to form a world government right away. . . . Even I, at that early age, had done enough reading to say, 'That sounds great, but how would it work? And who's going to be willing to yield that degree of sovereignty? The UN is the best we can do at this moment. Don't badmouth it.'"

In lamenting the success of the United States in preventing the creation of the third pillar of the postwar international financial system, Gardner noted: "The ITO had the bad luck to come up in the period of 1948 to 1950. . . . It's one of those accidents of history. If the Bretton Woods stuff hadn't been done during the war, it would never have happened. These institutions were miracles—political miracles. They were only done because we were in the midst of a war. They were carried forward by wartime idealism."[4]

Juan Somavía believed that "one of the major mistakes of the immediate postwar period" was the separation of the Washington-based institutions and the world organization: "So you create the United Nations and you are weakening it at the same time.... So the Economic and Social Council is there on paper, but we want this to be controlled." He thought that by separating them, the major powers were basically saying to the UN, "You are about politics, and humanitarian and social issues."

Switzerland finally joined the UN in 2002, but Cornelio Sommaruga contemplated an interesting "What if?" during our conversation: "One has never to forget what happened in 1945 and 1946 when Switzerland did consider joining the United Nations. And then it was [John] Foster Dulles, the secretary of state of the United States, who made a very strong statement saying there is no place for those who did not participate in the victory, and we wish not to have neutrals in our circles. And this was confirmed in Switzerland. We stay outside the United Nations because we have a role to play outside under a foreign policy of neutrality, solidarity, universality, and availability."

The Universal Declaration of Human Rights

Many voices argued that the boldest ideas of all in the UN Charter are its statements about human rights. The compelling normative claim that all individuals have inalienable human rights has since spread far and wide. This initiative also sprang from a genuine U.S. enthusiasm for an international order based on rules and law. In a speech at the United Nations just after the adoption of the Universal Declaration in December 1948, Eleanor Roosevelt predicted that "a curious grapevine" would spread the ideas contained in the Declaration far and wide.[5]

As a personality, Mrs. Roosevelt was a towering figure who inspired many. Peg Snyder recalled that she broke many molds: "In America, Eleanor was thought by many not to behave the way a president's wife should behave. A president's wife should be a president's wife and look nice and be a hostess." In any case, Eleanor Roosevelt's aspiration has proved prophetic; the ideas embodied in the Universal Declaration have helped the powerless mobilize against the powerful in a quest to secure the most fundamental human rights. Molly Bruce worked closely with Eleanor Roosevelt, whose role "was quite interesting, because she knew that the U.S. Senate was highly unlikely to ratify any convention, even then. So she was pressing for a declaration. She carried the [Human Rights] Commission with her. She was quite formidable in the way she did things, because she never lost her temper. But she could be tough. She herself worked extremely hard and expected the staff to follow her example." Bruce also recalled that personal style: "To me, it was impressive, because she had actually been First Lady of the land and yet she herself was very humble. She often took her lunch in the staff cafeteria and always insisted in keeping her place in line whenever a staff member offered her his or her place."

Although no "bill of rights" was agreed to in San Francisco, a drafting commission was established within months after the UN began operations to define human rights, and the Universal Declaration containing thirty detailed articles was agreed to in 1948. The Charter and the Universal Declaration broke new ground and sowed the seeds in the 1940s for the recent development of intrusions into what formerly had been considered the exclusively domestic jurisdiction of states.[6]

These two documents are "absolutely the pillars of the temple," according to Virendra Dayal: "I think that if there are two things that sort of got drilled into my own head and consciousness in nearly thirty years at the UN—and that is not a great number of things, just two—one was the basic premise of the Charter, that you really can't have peace unless the rights of nations great and small are equally respected. The other is the basic premise of the Declaration of Human Rights, that you can't have peace within a country or a society unless the rights of all, great or small, are equally respected. I think these are the two key ideas that have come from these two great instruments. I think there is a complementarity there."

For Stéphane Hessel, and undoubtedly others, the UN was critical to this movement. "What makes the United Nations an exceptional moment in history is human rights." He recounted the tenor of discussions that he felt during the drafting of the declaration. "You see, when we worked on this strange text with all these strange articles, we were quite conscious of the fact that if this had to have any new meaning it would have to be de-connected from a purely intergovernmental treaty.... Members of the commission ... defended that point of view, and René Cassin was one of them—he happened to be a friend of my father-in-law ... so his influence certainly was there. He was so convinced that this declaration must be a declaration going beyond a purely intergovernmental agreement that he convinced me of that. That therefore the word 'universal' meant something else than intergovernmental or international." Hessel explained the ultimate choice between a narrower yet binding declaration versus a broader nonbinding one: "Therefore, the balance between making a declaration that would be very ambitious but have no legal constraining power or to make it less ambitious and give it more power—I was convinced that the first was the better attitude but that it had to be then continued with the pact and measures of implementation."

Molly Bruce remembered that when ECOSOC had set up the Commission on Human Rights, its first task in 1947 was to draft an international bill of rights. "Should it be a declaration or a legally binding convention? . . . The Commission on Human Rights decided that the international bill of human rights should be in three parts: a declaration, which the Americans wanted; a convention or conventions, which the British wanted at that time; and some kind of enforcement measures, which the Australians wanted. The Australians in fact wanted an International Court of Human Rights in 1947. The commission decided that all three—declaration; convention or conventions, to be called covenants; and measures of implementation—would together constitute the international bill of human rights."

But Bruce also noted that the UN as an intergovernmental body was hamstrung by its members: "When they were adopting a positive approach on the international bill of rights, they adopted rather a miserable procedure for dealing with alleged violations of human rights. We had received many letters from individuals all over the world complaining that their rights were being violated. I remember Charles Malik of Lebanon saying the Commission on Human Rights should consider complaints from the 'last lunatic in the last lunatic asylum.' But the procedure established for handling these communications sought primarily to protect the governments complained against. And of course, the colonial powers still had colonies and they didn't want complaints about their territories made public." Bruce recalled sadly that ECOSOC endorsed the CHR's proposals for handling these communications, which opened with the phrase: "The Commission recognizes that it has no power to take any action in regard to any complaints concerning human rights."

According to Oscar Schachter, the decision to adopt a nonbinding declaration had a deleterious effect for the public interest: "Many international lawyers and other observers shared the views of Hersch Lauterpacht—later a justice—that adopting a nonbinding declaration amounted to a deception rather than a commitment. But others saw the declaration as a first step to a binding agreement as foreseen—the two covenants were adopted in 1966. . . . Not many foresaw that the declaration would not only have rhetorical value but that it would be given effect in legal decisions and [be] included in several national constitutions. I must also add that in 1946–1947, the general public and governments were much more concerned over Soviet threats and the atomic bomb. . . . At this time, human rights clearly took a back place in comparison to the efforts to control or eliminate atomic weapons and other weapons of mass destruction."

Schachter recalled the irony about the controversy surrounding the so-called second-generation rights—the economic and social rights that supposedly were distinct from the first generation's individual and political rights: "It is sometimes forgotten that in the 1940s and earlier the U.S. government and NGOs favored economic and social rights. The New Deal legislation in the U.S. on Social Security, employment, and health was a factor. Even relatively conservative NGOs, such as the American Bar Association, included obligatory social and economic rights in its 1944 proposed bill of rights. This favorable attitude of the early 1940s changed in 1948 and 1949."

One of the "hot issues" was immigration, according to Schachter, who recalled that the "apparent threat of immigration from wartorn Europe was also used, by labor as well as by bigots, to cite the dangers of human rights." He wrote a 1951 article on "The Charter and the Constitution," in the *Vanderbilt Law Journal*, which was attacked by Senator Bricker in the *Congressional Record* and in several editorials: "As I look back today, it seems strange that the attacks on the California decision and on my article were not picked up in the UN human rights or legal committees. The idea that the Charter could be invoked to invalidate a national law that discriminated against people on racial grounds was still too novel for governments to accept. . . . The issue is still avoided in UN debates."

Schachter avoided such problems later in a famous article in the *American Journal of International Law* on "Legal Aspects of the United Nations Actions in the Congo," which he wrote under a pseudonym to avoid mounting attacks from the Soviet Union, which was seeking to replace the Secretary-General with a tripartite committee.[7]

Cornelio Sommaruga reminds us that "there has been a growing awareness of human rights being not simply an idealistic and philosophical aspect of life but a very clear legal constraint." But from the vantage point of the twenty-first century, it is important to recall that human rights were not always as unquestioned as they are today. What could be more subversive than the notion that every individual in every country throughout the world shared an equal claim not only to such individual civil and political rights as life, liberty, and the pursuit of happiness but also to a core of more collective economic and social freedoms? Was the world organization not founded on the principle of state sovereignty and the corollary of nonintervention in domestic affairs? Notwithstanding doubts and mixed motives, the record shows that the lofty vision has had more impact than either the cynics or realists expected. The conclusion resulting from a multicountry set of case studies is to the point: "Transnational human rights pressures and policies, including the activities of advocacy networks, have made a very significant difference in bringing about improvement in human rights practices in diverse countries around the world."[8]

In retrospect, we can see how the Charter's language led to a different approach to the equilibrium between state sovereignty and the respect for human rights. The attempt to finesse the obvious tensions between them did not succeed, but the basis for sometimes weighing rights more heavily than sovereignty was established and has made a difference. The basic conflict was built in and has arisen many times. It has often resulted in substantial intrusions on traditional state prerogatives, including a host of humanitarian interventions in the 1990s,[9] a subject to which we return in Chapter 8.

Our voices emphasized how important it was to insert the idea of human rights into the Charter even if the details were lacking and implementation slow. Action was slow at first, as was to be expected, because the Universal Declaration, in Stéphane Hessel's judgment, "could be only a first step in a long effort to make human rights a reality." But as Brian Urquhart asserted: "The so-called realists almost always get it wrong. Partly due to the development of NGOs, human rights has become a world-class movement, a movement that is not going to stop. It is very imperfect at the moment and all sorts of terrible things happen, but it is nothing like the kind of dead silence about human rights there was in my youth." He recalled that earlier, "the attitude ... in many countries was, 'Okay, you know the Americans and Mrs. Roosevelt want to talk about human rights. It isn't really important. But if it pleases Mrs. Roosevelt, okay, fine. It really doesn't have any practical meaning.' ... I think they still felt that human rights was a kind of nice-old-ladies' game which didn't really matter very much."

The Cold War had serious repercussions for rights because work to turn the Universal Declaration of Human Rights into a single covenant that countries could ratify was delayed and debates became intensely polarized. Political and civil rights (of the "first generation" emphasized by the West) became separated from economic, social, and cultural ones (of the "second generation" emphasized by the East). The West challenged the Communist bloc for failures to respect political and civil rights, and the communist countries pointed fingers at the West's failures to address poverty amid affluence and to ensure basic human needs. Juan Somavía, whose father-in-law (Hernan Santa Cruz) was a drafter of the Universal Declaration, spoke about that period: "The Cold War made the Western world forget about human rights, not to give a damn about human rights. ... If you were supported on the Cold War front, there were no questions asked on the human rights front and the democracy front."

Less emphasized was a more fundamental failure—human rights were separated from development. To a large extent within the UN until the 1980s, human rights were an ideological football, kicked back and forth in an international game between East and West. Western players wore the colors of political and civil rights, Eastern players those of economic and social rights. Depending on their political affiliations, Southern players actively joined one team or the other in the scrum or cheered from the sidelines for whoever seemed to be in the lead. The international game was mainly a shouting match with lots of attack and denunciation but little attention to the practical problems and issues that were often high on the domestic agendas at the time and could have benefited by sharing lessons and new approaches. Only as the Cold War was beginning to thaw and groups concerned with the rights of women and children entered the stadium did the game and the playing field change.[10] In looking back, Kurt Waldheim reflected on the sea change in human rights: "If you see what happens today in this field, we can say that progress was made. . . . Now, no government would dare to make proposals in the political, economic, and social field without referring to human rights."

Progress in human rights has been nothing short of extraordinary. The original idea has made substantial inroads into policy and legislation. Beginning in the 1980s, a surge of ratifications of human rights conventions occurred along with increasing implementation of many measures and outrage over abuses. Almost a hundred countries, over half the UN member states, have now ratified all six major human rights instruments, and about three-quarters have ratified the Covenants on Civil and Political Rights and on Economic, Social and Cultural Rights. Over 80 percent of countries have ratified the conventions on the elimination of all forms of racial discrimination and all forms of discrimination against women. According to UNICEF, only the United States and Somalia have not ratified the Convention on the Rights of the Child, largely because of an unwillingness to renounce capital punishment or the recruitment of soldiers under eighteen years of age.[11]

An initial review of the Universal Declaration took place in Teheran in 1968, but the 1993 Vienna Conference, which occurred forty-five years after the adoption of the declaration, was more controversial. The main dispute in Vienna centered on whether human rights were actually universally applicable—as had been agreed in 1948—or were subject to local, religious, and cultural interpretations. Female genital mutilation in Sudan, suppression of girls' education in Afghanistan under the Taliban, repression of dissidents in Singapore, or the use of the death penalty in the United States are illustrations. In spite of the ongoing rhetoric about how relative or how universal rights are, the 1993 World Conference on Human Rights reaffirmed their indivisibility and universality.[12]

Robert Cox addressed the debate between universality and cultural relativism: "There are certain things that could be recognized as common neces-
sities for the continued coexistence, in a peaceful manner, in this world of
differences. And they might be reduced to a fairly simple list of things. I think
the notion of human rights would arise within that concept. There would be
some sort of general recognition of basic human rights, but they would not
go into all of the details that might be reflected in the diversity of civilizations. My view about human rights is that they are not so much something
which on the global level can be enforced by the proclamation of a legal norm
but that they are something that arises out of conflicts within particular societies that establish for themselves their own sense of rights." Cox offered a
compromise between universalists and cultural relativists: "The solution . . . is
not the imposition by the West upon them of values but the encouragement
of the struggles within those civilizations to achieve their own success in terms
of the establishment of a set of human rights."

After retiring as Boutros Boutros-Ghali's *chef de cabinet,* Viru Dayal returned
to India to head up the National Human Rights Commission. Expressing his
impatience with relativistic interpretations of human rights, he asserted that
people who take a relativist stance often "want to perpetuate something which
is perhaps less than entirely pleasant or indeed Asian. It's a semantic technique
of protecting your turf or a wrong way of behavior. . . . Does it mean that if I am
an Asian parent I can offer my child to a torture chamber? . . . Does 'Asian
values' mean that you should discriminate against your daughter and not send
her to school? Does it mean that, in the name of 'Asian values' you can beat up
someone and be free to do so if he is not a Hindu, or a Christian, or a Muslim,
or a Shiite, or a Sunni, or whatever? It makes no sense to me."

Many comments addressed the relative weight given to universality or cultural relativism. A particular emphasis emerged regarding the tension between
individual versus communal rights. Bernard Chidzero, referring to these tensions in human rights debates, said "This is something of a double-edged
sword. You cannot have democracy which is not underpinned by human rights,
the right of individuals to speak, to move and to associate freely, to be protected, to be active in society without fear. Yet at the same time, you need to
organize yourself in . . . political parties which require discipline. And you
need to impose certain restrictions in order to buttress your independence. . . .
You have to recognize that in society there will always be individuals who
want to work for the opposition or to destroy the structures. So imposing
limitations or instilling responsibility becomes necessary. Those limitations
may impact negatively on human rights. The question uppermost in my mind
is, 'Who is for whom, or for what?' Man for human rights or human rights for

man? . . . Rights, like institutions, are to serve society and to serve human beings and not the reverse. . . . But freedom must also recognize certain obligations, limitations, duties. . . . If you become destructive, then I think society has a right to moderate your rights, to clip your wings for the purpose of maintaining unity of purpose or to avoid self-destruction."

Unlike most of our interlocutors, Chidzero was less than enthusiastic about human rights NGOs: "The NGOs promote human rights. This is fine. But I think the rights of the individual should be seen or promoted jointly with the rights of the state. The state has rights and duties as well, within which those of the individual are promoted and protected."

Janez Stanovnik advised the West to use caution in its worldwide advocacy for a universal application of political and civil rights: "I am all for this 'second basket' of human rights [the language of the Helsinki Declaration], for emphasizing human rights and so on. But as in all matters, I believe that one should have the sense of proportion. This I say in connection with China. I ask here, 'What kind of human rights did we have here in Europe before the French Revolution? What kind of human rights did you have in the United States before your revolution, which occurred before the French?' You say one has to accept that a China, with a completely different cultural background, may also need some more time to develop cultural values and political and societal values which will more correspond to the present day than they did in the past. But as our past is not only glorious, so the Chinese past might also not be only glorious. We Slovenes settled here in the sixth century. Don't ask me what we did with the settlers who were before here. There must have been a massacre, I guess. Similarly, I think everybody would have to be a little bit more modest when he thinks about his own past—including Americans!"

"The Soviet Union treated human rights very narrowly," Russia's Vladimir Petrovsky told us. "Because of the real interest in arms regulation, the Soviet Union agreed to deal with human rights but emphasized only social and economic dimensions. . . . But still it was a big compromise." The slippery slope of human rights led Moscow to agree to the Helsinki Final Act, which "provided this principle on inviolability of borders and the change of borders only by peaceful means. In exchange, the Soviet Union and its allies have accepted the broad concept of the protection of human rights, which included not only economic and social rights but also civil rights. But when *perestroika* started . . . we moved from words to practical deeds."

Sadako Ogata had her own dose of reality about Japan's attitude toward the right to development: "I don't think that was taken very seriously. Nobody took that very seriously, in those days anyway." Viru Dayal argued that civil and political rights are extremely important but in many ways "easier to talk about, and in a sense cheaper to talk about. . . . The fact of the matter is that with economic and social rights you have got to put your money where your mouth is. . . . Someone has to make sure that somewhere a school is constructed. Or if you talk about the rights of the child, it means that some-where, someone has got to get that child out of a carpet-weaving factory or a football-making factory and have that kid benefiting from free compul-sory education. In other words, there are costs to the purse when you talk about economic and social rights. . . . We are basically talking about issues of equity and justice in the economic and social area. And we are talking about what Amartya Sen has so beautifully and vividly described as devel-opment as freedom."

Noeleen Heyzer spoke emphatically about shortcomings in these earlier steps: "The universal standards of human rights are often denied full opera-tion when it comes to women and girls." This document was made truly uni-versal with the input of women, according to Heyzer: "Women changed the human rights agenda. Up to then, it was about political liberties. It was about political prisoners. It didn't take into account the divide between the public and the private. Women insisted on the discussion of violence against women within the household, violence in traditional practices, the issue of sexual violence, and made it into a big issue. The whole human rights dialogue changed. It had a major consequence and was immediately picked up. One major change was how rape was regarded in situations of conflict. In the Rwanda case, and even in the Bosnia case when rape was used as a weapon of war, there was a decision that rape was a war crime. It took ideas, discussion, and strategies by women to show that it was possible to change women's lives. It took a lot of courage to open up spaces and discuss painful silent issues and get policies and practices changed."

Paulo Sergio Pinheiro, a prominent Brazilian human rights activist and later junior minister, stated: "Until the 1970s the United Nations was not do-ing very much about human rights in terms of monitoring. They were just defining standards, writing conventions. I think that the real change was when the first special rapporteur or the other special procedures—resolution 1503 and the struggle against apartheid—were activated. At the same time, I con-sider it an extraordinary miracle that sovereign states are supposed to abide to some norms and some treaties." Having himself acted as rapporteur in two countries (Burundi and Burma), Pinheiro remained optimistic: "I think there are some very positive signs. Of course there was an enormous evolution in terms of the specificity of several rights. Today more than ever, more groups have norms, have rights to be protected and promoted. That is an extraordi-nary development. On the other hand, I think that despite all the efforts by

Kofi Annan and also by Boutros-Boutros Ghali, who was responsible for all the world conferences, I think that the United Nations as a whole continues to be dominated by political considerations and not by human rights."

"Perhaps you know that I proposed years ago, when I was Secretary-General, to include the Declaration of Human Rights, with some improvements, in the Charter of the United Nations, in order to make it compulsory," Javier Pérez de Cuéllar told us. "Speaking about that, another idea was to amend Article 2.7 of the Charter of the United Nations, which refers to nonintervention. I thought that it was high time to include an exception with reference to crimes against humanity."

As we go to press and with Saddam Hussein's prosecution up in the air and grisly photos of Abu Ghraib the daily bill of fare in the media, the notion of universal rather than double standards makes Guido de Marco's comments prescient: "I am always afraid of the politicization of human rights. There is a line of demarcation which is very flimsy. Those who believe in human rights, and genuinely believe in human rights, want to give their observance a structure. Those who politicize human rights find it very convenient to bring human rights as a political issue." In explaining why he was against ad hoc criminal tribunals and for the International Criminal Court, de Marco remarked: "Take, for example, Admiral Doenitz, who was found guilty because he gave orders to shoot the crew of a torpedoed vessel. But a similar order was also given by Admiral Nimitz of the U.S. Navy in the Pacific. Now, I don't like what Doenitz did, but I equally don't like what Nimitz did. . . . This is why I believe in an international criminal court. And this is why I hope the United States approves this International Criminal Court. . . . We want to have a structure in which we are all equal, all responsible, and all accountable."

Regardless of one's evaluation of human rights debates, most agreed with Brian Urquhart's sentiment: "It is hard now to remember that there was a time when human rights was the preoccupation of a very limited number of people."

The Marshall Plan

As perhaps the most generous manifestation on record of enlightened self-interest, the United States began a substantial economic aid program for European reconstruction after World War II that would serve as the first experiment in foreign aid. Commonly called the Marshall Plan after Secretary of State George Marshall because of his commencement speech at Harvard University in June 1947, the European Recovery Program invited European countries themselves to outline their requirements for recovery so that material and financial aid could be used effectively. The Soviet Union and its Eastern European allies refused to participate. Some $13.5 billion (or about 2 percent of the U.S. national income between 1948 and 1952) was distributed by the Organisation for European Economic Co-operation, which was specifically set up to administer the plan.[13] These efforts both got Western Europe back on its collective feet and facilitated a rapid expansion of trade.

This essentially U.S. idea has been adapted into UN practice and thinking. Hans Singer noted, for instance, that the Marshall Plan offered a "very important precedent" for food aid. It showed that under the right circumstances it could serve "as a tremendous instrument for reconstruction and development." Indeed, calls for a massive infusion of aid anywhere have often been accompanied by references to the European model—for instance, "a Marshall Plan for sub-Saharan Africa" or "a Marshall Plan in the war against terrorism." In thinking about its applicability elsewhere, Richard Gardner was skeptical: "What worries me about people who say, 'let's have a Marshall Plan for Africa.' I certainly favor a great increase in development assistance for Africa, but the Marshall Plan is a poor analogy because the Africans don't start with anything like the trained manpower, the entrepreneurial culture, and the drive for economic development that you had in Europe. So if we use the term Marshall Plan for the developing world we have to understand that we are using it as a metaphor, but it is a very different sort of challenge."

Hans Singer pointed out that despite the success of the central planning experience of the Marshall Plan in Europe, the Cold War led the United States and much of the West to view central planning with greater suspicion. He noted that agencies had to take great pains to emphasize that advocacy of import substitution and diversification of exports did not reflect Stalinist-designed central planning. "But this distinction," recalls Singer, "was sometimes very difficult to maintain in the minds of critics." Later dismissed as a "communist device" during the Cold War's ideological battles, the U.S. effort in Europe originally required a process of planning as a prerequisite for receiving assistance. Gamani Corea participated in his first planning mission in Ceylon for the World Bank "during the late 1940s, maybe early 1950s. It was not a pejorative word; people did not see it as linked to socialism and so on. It was to get the state organized in spearheading the development drive because the state was the only major actor in many developing countries."

The massive infusion of U.S. funds and credits for Western Europe was a concrete demonstration of Washington's capacity to frame its national interest in an imaginative and forward-looking fashion. Max Finger, who was based in Europe from 1944 to 1955, recalled: "I don't think the United Nations was taken very seriously at that time. The Marshall Plan was. And it was an enormous success. You had to be there to know how much devastation had occurred. How low public morale was. I had a feeling that the Russians could have walked in, if they so decided. There was just general despair. And the Marshall Plan actually lifted Europe out of that despair. . . . We did it mainly to have strength against the Soviet Union. But the effect was enormously beneficial to the Europeans."

Jan Pronk echoed this thought but noted its limited application: "In the 1950s, I became aware that it also was quite sophisticated. There was an economic interest for the United States in helping Europe, not only a political one. Moreover, it meant demand stimulation, which is important for world stability. And thirdly, it was sophisticated in terms of decision making. Countries taught themselves good economic governance. OECD countries were allowed to decide themselves how to spend the aid according to their own priority but taking into account some boundary conditions. The United States were not going to tell Europe which investment projects ought to be financed out of Marshall assistance. This was a sophisticated, modern approach. . . . At the same time, I soon became aware that the Marshall assistance could not be seen as the model for development assistance, because it was a capital injection into a structure which was basically healthy in terms of knowledge and social and political systems. It was reconstruction assistance. The bottleneck was capital. Everything else was more or less in place, which is not the case in a developmental process."

At the outset of his career as an applied economist, Just Faaland worked on country studies in the OEEC secretariat and recalled the unusual undertaking: "As you know, it was the Americans who took the initiative to invite countries that would be members of the Marshall Plan. They included even Russia. But Russia, understandably, declined. . . . I don't think anyone ever really questioned that or thought that it ought to be different. . . . What was odd was the generosity of the Americans and the willingness to let the Europeans go a long way in deciding how to divide the cake. It really was impressive. It is impressive to this day. It is exactly the opposite of what we see between donors and recipients these days. And the Americans are in front on both occasions."

The relevance of the approach was brought to the attention of one young development economist at the time. Ponna Wignaraja's two dissertation advisors at Yale asked him, "Why did you come to the U.S. to study development? You ought to go to Germany." He contextualized the impact of the Marshall Plan and what became known as the "German miracle" in the following way: "Here were the people saying it's not only the Marshall Plan, it's not capital alone that wrought the 'miracle.' Capital and aid helps. If your foundations have not been bombed out, you can quickly automate and re-build. But go and look at the real human and cultural dimensions, the holistic approach. . . . I learned it was not merely the Marshall Plan, it was not the narrow economic reconstruction that built the new Germany. The whole cultural dimension, the thrift, the savings that came out of traumatized people's wanting to be safe, their capacity for hard work, the 'Protestant ethic' that Max Weber had talked about, were contributory factors to the reconstruction and development."

His six months in Germany allowed Wignaraja to think through the development conundrum in India: "German recovery was not just an economic process fueled by Marshall Plan aid alone. . . . I saw a new pattern of development . . . a three-sector growth model. This is also a little bit of what Gandhianism was about. But Gandhi didn't put it in strong economic terms or in strong enough political terms. . . . He was talking of self-reliance, not a capital fetish. . . . Gandhi died too early before he could develop some of his ideas to meet the new post-independence challenge. The Gandhians that followed took it either in a romantic way or as ideology for the political struggle. Some Gandhians took this latter emphasis and started experimenting in a much more radical way at the grassroots. . . . I began to understand that German reconstruction was not just money-led, nor was it a purely economic response. It was a cultural response, a social movement by the German people, based on their reality."

While Washington was eager to have Europe open to Western investment and interests then, Moscow was wary of being encircled and menaced by its former allies and looked upon Eastern Europe as its sphere of influence. As early as his 1946 speech in Fulton, Missouri, Winston Churchill had noted that "an iron curtain" had fallen across the continent. As the USSR expanded its control over the countries of Eastern Europe on its periphery, the United States pursued a policy of containment. The Berlin Blockade and the formation of the North Atlantic Treaty Organization (NATO) in 1949 and the Warsaw Pact set the divisions in concrete. The nuclear rivalry—exacerbated by continuous covert activities, propaganda, and sanctions—led to a worldwide competition for countries to side with the West or the East.

The Cold War

Robert Cox recalled how the early euphoria about the UN was cut short by growing East-West tensions: "We were going to rebuild the world. . . . There was a tremendous sense of something new and something good that was going to happen and a great deal of optimism." It was, however, "a spirit that didn't last very long." The partnership among great powers all too soon landed in the historical dustbin. The mistrust between the Soviet Union and the West actually had begun with the Bolshevik Revolution in 1917 and was but temporarily suspended during World War II as part of the solidarity to defeat fascism. The high hopes for the United Nations and the postwar world were based on a continuation of such solidarity, which was quickly replaced by a return of ideological, political, and economic tensions. Guido de Marco employed religious imagery, "The United Nations was born with an original sin, the sin of the Cold War."

The impact of the Cold War on U.S. engagement with multilateral cooperation and on UN efforts to maintain international peace and security was immediate; the UN Security Council was unable to function as planned because of the need for unanimity among the five permanent members. This phenomenon has been the focus of substantial scholarly and policy analysis, but no less obvious was the impact of East-West tensions on the organization's economic and social activities.

Brian Urquhart recalled how the Congo conflict in the 1960s consumed the still-adolescent world body: "So we had the Cold War actually at its hottest possible form in a country where we were doing an enormous development exercise. None of us, I think, had understood any of this until we actually got there—I got to the Congo practically the first day, and I didn't even know which side of Africa it was on. For some unknown reason I thought it was on the Indian Ocean, and I was much surprised to discover it was on the Atlantic. That's the degree of ignorance that we had of the whole thing."

Urquhart noted that another casualty of tensions between East and West was the ability to openly analyze and catalogue the lessons of UN efforts: "One of the troubles with the UN, which you are now rather belatedly remedying, is the fact that it never had a historical section. I spent years and years, from the time when I was the personal assistant to Trygve Lie, trying to get them to establish a historical section so that people in all parts of the UN would actually record at the time what they were doing instead of doing it fifty years later with a sort of *esprit d'escalier*. The objection to it was that it would cost money, but worse than that, the Russians did not believe in history being impartial and objective. Even worse than that, in order to give the Russians important posts in the Secretariat, they made a Russian the head of the library and the archives, which is putting the fox in charge of the hen coop. So that you couldn't actually get responsible, objective people for a historical section, which would be part of the archives. You would have had to have established an independent unit, and that would have caused a huge row with the Soviets."

Urquhart concluded that the failure to create a historical section hampered the UN's ability to communicate to the world the intellectual contributions that have occurred in the system over the past fifty years: "So we never had a historical section. As a result nobody knows very much about the kind of serious intellectual work which went on. We all know about peacekeeping and all that because it got in the newspapers, but there is very little about the economic and the social side."

In recounting one of the positive outcomes of the Cold War, Leticia Shahani remembered that "when it came to women's rights, in theory, you know, the Soviets saw no reason why they shouldn't fight for women's rights at the United Nations. The Soviet constitution is the first constitution in the world to declare equal rights between men and women. Of course, it was only in the law that such rights existed. So the Soviet representatives at the UN would always come fully endorsing all of the legal rights of women. They wanted to show to the world that they were in the forefront of women's rights. But that advocacy role, lacking in credibility and substance as it may have been, helped to increase at the UN awareness of the importance of women's rights." Peg Snyder agreed and noted the stark differences between the Socialist bloc's rhetoric and its performance: "Even though the East Europeans talked a lot about their massive women's organizations, the women weren't able to do anything to persuade their governments to give even symbolic contributions to women's activities through the UN. . . . Seldom did you see women from the Soviet bloc."

Vladimir Petrovsky was head of UNOG when he was interviewed, but he recalled the flavor of the times during his first posting as a junior Soviet diplomat to the permanent mission in New York in the mid-1950s: "You were always told when you went into another country that you should be very much suspicious. . . . The first days we felt a little bit uneasy. But little by little, it changed. . . . The major problem, as I remember—and that's what shocked me and I took it very strongly—was that though I always looked at the United Nations as a kind of center for meeting between different countries and finding some solutions, I found that the UN was too often used as a rostrum for propagandistic purposes."

Others recalled the impact of the Cold War on their intellectual development. Bernard Chidzero explained: "We had experienced, as developing countries, the impact of colonial rule, which was basically capitalist in its approach to economics and which treated people, human beings, as tools, particularly workers. And that goes back to my own childhood, working on the farm. We were tools, instruments to be used. We were not human beings, really. . . . And after reading about the Bolshevik Revolution . . . and the concept of a classless society in which the people sort of control the economy, the concept and role of the state intrigued me. Yet, in fact, this was not so when you read what happened in the USSR—Stalin, in particular. Many thousands of people died. So, ideologically, this became a problem for me."

Where one stands depends on where one sits, according to the old adage. Hence, it is perhaps not surprising that Chidzero was not as obsessed by the Cold War. Africa's most pressing preoccupations were state-building and completing the process of decolonization: "The Third World, or the people of the world generally, could not avoid the struggle that raged between the East and the West. . . . And I must confess that at that time, because I was preoccupied with the problem of the Federation of Rhodesia and Nyasaland and the racial partnership system, when I was preparing to come [back] to Zimbabwe in 1958, the East-West struggle did not take uppermost position in my mind."

Rubens Ricupero asserted: "For me, if I had any sympathy for communism— which was not the case—it would have disappeared with the crushing of the Hungarian insurrection [in 1956], which I followed closely. . . . Then perhaps the most important event that had an impact on everyone in Latin America was the Cuban Revolution. The Cuban Revolution was first welcomed as a sort of a new era in the continent. But soon it became evident that it was going in the direction of a new kind of undemocratic government. I must say, for me, even at that stage, I never had any doubt that democracy should be a more important value."

Sonny Ramphal noted: "I don't think the Cuban model ever attracted any support at a significant level. . . . What the Caribbean sought to do was to get the benefit of the revolution without paying that price. So Cuban doctors proliferated in the region. West Indian students were trained at Cuban universities in very large numbers. But the political model didn't fly."

Ignacy Sachs spoke about the impact of the 1956 Soviet invasion of Hungary on his homeland, Poland: "It was a period that was extremely painful, turbulent, and yet, at the same time, rich with hope. And so we experienced the invasion of Hungary as though it were happening to us, and we were perfectly aware that if Poland had escaped the same fate, it was because of its geographical position, since the country was certainly in a mouse trap."

Vladimir Petrovsky took care to specify that he could "not agree with the first intervention of the Soviet Union—but for us the major shock was not Hungary. The real shock was Czechoslovakia, because Czechoslovakia had a strong reformist movement that wanted to give a human face to society."

In this climate, the ILO would come under fire because of a decision to hire a Soviet deputy for the organization. Francis Blanchard was its head when the United States withdrew in 1976 because of the lobbying by George Meany, the president of the AFL-CIO [American Federation of Labor-Congress of Industrial Organizations]. Blanchard recalled a telling comment from Meany: "Nonsense! Absolute nonsense! You don't know the meaning of the word détente. The right meaning is to pull the trigger.' And he added: 'This is what you should do with the communists.'"

For Dharam Ghai, "the Cold War affected ILO more than perhaps most other UN agencies. The reason for this goes back to the creation of ILO. When ILO was created in 1919 one of the main motivations was to stem the tide of Bolshevik-type revolutions. It was felt that there should be a global organization which should work to improve the working and living conditions of the workers of the world. So if you like, it was a capitalist response to the communist onslaught." Among other impacts, Ghai noted how it circumscribed ILO research: "It proved very difficult to do research which would compare the experiences of the Socialist bloc and the capitalist countries from the point of view of economic growth, employment generation, income distribution, and things like this. So that kind of comparative work was practically nonexistent in ILO."

Explaining the impact of superpower rivalry closer to home in the Eastern bloc, Janez Stanovnik recalled that it began much earlier than most people realize: "In 1948, as you know, a split occurred between Tito and Stalin. If you ask me about the Cold War, then I would speak from 1948 on, even though the Cold War started earlier. In my view, it started around Berlin. But it was felt already at the peace conference in 1946. The Yugoslav delegation at the peace conference felt a lack of support from the USSR for its claims. . . . After the split [with the Soviet Union], Yugoslavia, and more particularly, I am speaking for myself, felt suddenly free. Subconsciously we were auto-censoring, not only our words but also our intimate thoughts. Now the curtain was up. . . . The discussion was tremendous."

Klaus Sahlgren recalled how his country, Finland, created space between East and West: "I think that our membership in the UN had a very positive impact; it forced us to learn more and to train ourselves in multilateral diplomacy. . . . Soon a Finnish diplomacy at the UN developed which marked our neutrality, allowing us to establish a certain distance from the Soviet Union. The Soviets from time to time . . . exerted pressure on us on UN matters, but nevertheless, in the UN we could profile ourselves as a Western nation and as a neutral country. And we could also associate ourselves to a certain extent with the other neutrals and with the Nordics. That was a most welcome development. . . . Most people agree that the Swedish card kept the Soviets at bay. If the USSR would have done something drastic in Finland, Sweden would have turned West, abolishing its neutrality." Sahlgren went on to comment that Central European countries had considerably less room to maneuver. He recalled a conversation with Ambassador Janos Nyergues from Hungary about why Prague had been invaded in 1968. Reflecting back on Hungary's crushed revolution, Nyergues replied: "Everybody makes pee-pee in the swimming pool in the satellite countries, but the mistake of the Czechs was that they did it from the trampoline."

McCarthyism

Because the United Nations was located in the territory of the West's most powerful state, the ferocious and visceral American anticommunism of the day did not leave the international Secretariat unscathed. The campaign launched in the early 1950s by the Republican senator from Wisconsin, Joseph McCarthy, to discover plots against the U.S. government at the highest levels brought the United Nations under scrutiny. Although there had been no serious argument that the League of Nations was a Bolshevik plot, the notion that the new world organization would provide a breeding ground for the infiltration of communist values within the United States somehow seemed more plausible.

In 1953, as the chairman of the Senate's Permanent Subcommittee on Investigations, McCarthy conducted a series of televised hearings during which his vicious questioning and unsubstantiated accusations destroyed the reputations of many of his accused victims. Eventually his methods were denounced by President Dwight D. Eisenhower and McCarthy was censured by his Senate colleagues. Many American citizens objected to the "witch hunt" that targeted communists, perceived sympathizers, and homosexuals. Families and careers were devastated, and objections were neither widespread nor loud enough. The McCarthy period powerfully demoralized the Secretariat, which continues to this day to feel the long shadow of McCarthyism and its impact on silencing UN staff. Secretary of State Dean Acheson subsequently wrote that "the result was a highly unfavorable opinion of the United Nations in the United States and of the United States in the United Nations."[14]

Many voices still echo the angst of those times, which should stimulate readers to probe history for lessons relevant to contemporary versions of state-sanctioned hysteria and discrimination. Virginia Housholder remembered this painful period: "With McCarthy, there was an executive order that Truman issued saying that U.S. candidates for international organization jobs had to go through a vetting process. Unfortunately, my office was the one that had to administer this and we saw some of the FBI reports that they made on candidates for the UN. Some of it was the biggest bunch of garbage you have ever seen. We had to enforce the executive order and send whatever information we had to send to the UN, but it was something that we did with a great deal of distaste. McCarthy did an enormous amount of damage both to the international organizations, to the State Department, and to the U.S. government in general. And it was too bad that nobody had the guts to take him on until it was almost too late."

Kurt Waldheim recalled the McCarthy phenomenon from the perspective of a young Austrian diplomat: "It was a very bad experience. I was shocked to see how this development influenced the United Nations. There was great unease, and people became very uneasy by the attitude of McCarthy and his entourage. . . . Many in the United Nations were, in their eyes, secret agents of the communists trying to subvert the international organization. And there were human tragedies. I remember there was a suicide by one official who was accused of being an agent [Abe Feller]." Mihaly Simai put forward his unvarnished view from Budapest: "We had our own witch-hunters, hunting against the other side. And there was a kind of resemblance between them."

Oscar Schachter, who was an official in the UN's Legal Office at the time, reinforced this portrait of the poisonous impact on the Secretariat: "My recollection is that about six or seven of the American economists were called before a Senate committee and also targeted by McCarthy's counsel, Roy Cohn. Several had worked in the U.S. government under David Weintraub, director of the main division and a former assistant director-general of UNRRA. He and a few others refused to testify at the Senate committee, citing Fifth Amendment rights. The Secretary-General, supported by an outside legal committee he appointed, decided that refusal to testify reflected on the staff member's fitness, a position later reversed by the UN Administrative Tribunal. In some cases, U.S. staff members also refused to respond to the 'loyalty' investigation instituted by President Truman. While leftist views were at the center of the changes, accusations also often rested on associations of one kind or another by the staff member with suspected persons. For example, I was called for FBI interviews about my connection with Alger Hiss, whom I knew only slightly from the State Department and after he was the president of the Carnegie Endowment. The U.S. Loyalty Board and the related FBI investigations extended to all sorts of connections. One director was asked about his acquaintance with Albert Einstein, [who was] referred to in somewhat derogatory terms. Several feared they would be dismissed because of support for 'leftist' causes, such as Spanish loyalists. . . . There were also nonpolitical aspects— reports of staff members who were suspected homosexuals or were linked to 'character defects.'"

Schachter went on to recall complicity, even at the highest levels within the world organization: "Trygve Lie did not resist and even made critical comments about the staff members who were suspected of leftist associations. Hammarskjöld, faced with pressures from the U.S., set up a 'jurists committee,' which concluded that refusal to testify—i.e., based on the Fifth Amendment—reflected negatively on the staff member's character and violated the standards of impartiality and honesty. . . . An especially tragic aspect was that Abe Feller, who was never charged with leftist leanings, was so deeply affected by the pressures that he suddenly committed suicide, a tragedy that brought headlines around the world. At his funeral, attended by hundreds, the secretary of state, Dean Acheson, in an eloquent speech, praised Feller for his many achievements and for his character. I was deeply affected by Feller's suicide. . . . This was a terribly sad period, from 1950 to 1953, not only for me but for many staff members who felt threatened and fearful of charges that might destroy their lives."

Molly Bruce agreed that the Secretary-General "was threatened by the Americans or scared of the Americans." She also recalled the poisonous fear and suspicion of those times: "It was mostly the non-American citizens who were speaking up. The Americans were quite frankly afraid. It was the 1950s, because I had only recently been married and . . . we had just moved into a house in Mamaroneck in Westchester County, New York. The FBI came to all the neighbors inquiring about my husband. One of the neighbors never spoke to me again."

Hans Singer lived through this painful period: "I was known to be friendly with David Weintraub, who was the deputy director of the Economics Department and an American New Dealer and as such one of the main targets of the McCarthyites in the UN. . . . But the main reason was that I was the secretary of the SUNFED Committee. . . . McCarthy said it was part of a communist world conspiracy to take money out of the pockets of American taxpayers and use it for the benefit of left-leaning characters in the Third World."

Lawrence Klein recalled how deep the McCarthy frenzy penetrated American life with his career story: "At the University of Michigan, I was investigated by the House Un-American Activities Committee [HUAC] for having taught some classes in Boston and Chicago in the mid-1940s. The Boston class effort was . . . [at] the Samuel Adams School, and I taught macroeconomics there along the lines of my thesis work on Keynes, supplemented by Samuelson's growing involvement in an undergraduate textbook. The Samuel Adams School was investigated by the HUAC and other agencies for being a communist front organization, but I knew little about the administration of the school. When I moved from MIT to the University of Chicago as a fresh

Ph.D., I was contacted by a similar school, the Abraham Lincoln School, to teach seminar adult evening classes. . . . During this period, I briefly joined the Communist Party in Chicago but had little activity in it and dropped out within a year or less. In particular, I had formulated a theoretical correspondence between Marxian and Keynesian macroeconomic models and formalized the former for comparison with the latter. When I found that Communist Party members had no interest [in] or ability to think in this direction, I dropped out. . . . A few years later, in the mid-1950s, congressional investigators visited many academic institutions, and in Ann Arbor, at the University of Michigan, they investigated me. . . . The University of Michigan refused to give me a tenured professorship which had been proposed by the economics department, so I moved to Oxford to do the same things in research and teaching."

Surendra Patel also felt a direct impact. He had been in the UN Secretariat for two years when his first son was born in 1951. He took his young family on home leave to Bombay. The McCarthy residue appeared on his doorstep when he applied for a visa to the U.S. consulate and his passport was returned blank: "I wrote to Kalecki about the refusal of the United States to grant me a visa to return to my job at the United Nations. He was absolutely shocked that a regular staff member of the United Nations could be denied a visa. Thereafter, for a long period, Kalecki as well as I corresponded with the U.S.A. administration without success. The matter became public knowledge in India. The press caught hold of the story and extensively reported on my case. Krishna Menon was India's Foreign Minister at the time . . . [and] placed the matter before the Parliament. Meanwhile, I continued to stay in India for about nine months. . . . I was finally given a visa . . . but with strict restrictions on my movements within the country. Moreover, my name had been added by the American administration to the long list of 'undesirable people,' amongst whom were some great artists, writers, actors, and researchers—for example Paul Robeson, Charlie Chaplin, Gabriel García Márquez, and many others. . . . The U.S. visa restriction continued even after I retired from the UN in 1984. . . . [I was] not a communist but I had been to the left. I really believed in activism. The people have to struggle to get their due. I always stood by the people. This is at the center of my entire life and career."

The entire period was, for a green recruit like Paul Berthoud, "a very traumatic experience. . . . I had hardly taken foot in the UN when I was called to attend protest meetings of the staff council. This or that colleague whom I had just met was being called by the House Un-American Activities Committee of McCarthy." Brian Urquhart recalled the direct challenge to the staff: "The UN was a big focus center of the witch hunt, and the Americans in the Secretariat were going to the wall right and left. Even Ralph Bunche was challenged.

... Hammarskjöld [after being appointed Secretary-General in 1953] was tough. He put an end to that. He threw out the FBI, who were fingerprinting American members of the Secretariat in the basement of the UN building." The remedy, he continued, was as harmful as the illness and dealt another blow to the international civil service: "Truman's executive order . . . was in fact a devastating blow to the Charter principles governing the Secretariat, because what it really meant was that the appointments were ultimately made by governments and not by the Secretary-General and that the people ultimately were accountable to their own governments."

Sitting in the U.S. Mission to the UN on the other side of First Avenue, Max Finger disagreed about the extent to which McCarthyism mattered to him: "My own personal experience with it, strangely, was when I was at Harvard and I was up for a promotion in the foreign service. So they sent a security man to do a checkup. And I was in a house where there were two other tenants. And they were questioned. . . . They were shocked by this, being, you know, innocent academics. . . . I expected this kind of thing to happen. And I guess in the atmosphere of those days, the only damaging thing would be if I had brought home men who stayed the night."

Decolonization and the Non-Aligned Movement

A central idea present at the creation of the United Nations was that peoples in all countries had the inherent right to be politically independent and sovereign and make whatever national and international agreements their citizens might choose. The end of colonization and the achievement of sovereign independence came within the UN's first two decades and for almost all other countries by 1980. Instead of the fifty-one original signatories of the Charter in 1945, there are flags from over 190 countries currently flying in front of UN headquarters along New York's First Avenue.

Samir Amin recalled the intellectual climate of that decade: "Beginning in 1950 and particularly with the Bandung conference in 1955, I was among those who saw in this period a turning point in history that would lead not only to independence for the countries that had not yet achieved it . . . but equally to a major opportunity for development, for an affirmation of a will to develop. Of course, the term was very general, very vague—and thus inevitably took on varying connotations depending upon the internal political considerations of each national liberation movement." Amin continued with his view of politics and history, for which the terms "success" or "failure" had limited utility. "As far as scientific analysis is concerned, I prefer the term historical limits. If you look at contemporary Africa as compared with the Africa of 1960, it's amazing! . . . How many students are there in the Congo today? Those who have done advanced degree work, good or bad, can be counted in the hundreds of thousands. It would be fair to say that the worst African regimes have had more effect in thirty years than Belgian colonization had in a hundred. . . . On the other hand, one can argue . . . that their historical limits were reached very quickly, in one, two, or three decades at most, and then there was a dead end."

One of the six main UN organs was the Trusteeship Council, which was established in 1945, initially with eleven trust territories placed under its supervision. In the same year, a further seventy-two territories were identified as "non-self-governing." By 1959, eight of them had become independent. Many countries argued that the Charter principles were being applied too slowly. In 1960, the General Assembly passed a "Declaration on the Granting of Independence to Colonial Countries and Peoples." This called for immediate steps to transfer all powers to the peoples of non-self-governing territories without any conditions or reservations. In the years following this declaration, sixty more former colonial territories, with a total population exceeding 800 million people, attained independence and joined the United Nations.[15] The power of this notion is striking—it changed rapidly what had been dominant state practice for centuries.

A helpful historical perspective comes from Brian Urquhart's comment about the pace at which the age of colonialism ended: "The avalanche started with the Indian subcontinent in 1947. And once that had happened, and with people like Ralph Bunche really pushing, by the mid-1950s it was clear that this was going to be a very rapid process." This was a change from what he and most of his contemporaries had imagined: "The original idea had been that all colonies would go through a period of trusteeship. This was the American idea in 1945. All colonies would go through a period of UN trusteeship to prepare them so that they could manage their independence. But of course, it never happened, except with enemy colonies like Somalia and places like that, very few."

One of our voices, Oscar Schachter, laughed when we probed his recollection of this early period, and he directed us toward another conversation that he had for the membership American Society of International Law. When asked what had been his main mistakes, he pointed to an answer he had given in 1948 to the architects planning the future UN headquarters about the number of seats for a future General Assembly. "An international lawyer would be expected to know how many sovereign states existed and were potential members. I confidently answered the architects (after checking some textbooks) that they could safely add twenty seats to the fifty-one."[16]

Mostafa Tolba's immediate cohort in graduate school in London mainly had students from the UK itself or a British colony. He recalled that when the partition took place, "the decolonization of India was a real trauma.... Whether the independence of India was considered as the beginning of an iceberg of decolonization, I do not think so. I do not think at that time it was obvious to anyone of us that there is going to be a rolling effect of all this. And in fact, it did not. It started after the Bandung meeting, after the Non-Aligned Movement, and the fact that three of the leaders were very charismatic at that time and very respected globally.... I think the idea of a nonaligned group helped in a series of independence movements, including, I would say, liberating some of the countries from the very old backwards regimes that were on top of them, like Yemen for example."

Asked whether he had thought decolonization would proceed as rapidly as it did, Bernard Chidzero responded, "No. I did not think so at that time. Partly because I was, not fully but considerably, influenced by the thinking at Nuffield College, reflected in the work of Marjorie Perham. The Perham sisters had lived in Kenya; they were spinsters and they wrote a lot about Africa. Talking about Marjorie Perham, I have just come across a letter she wrote to me in 1962, when I had joined ECA: 'Independence in the Federation of Rhodesia and Nyasaland will take anything up to fifteen years or more, because of the investment made by the whites in that part of the world.' Unlike in West Africa, where there was not so much investment. Well, true enough, when she was writing, Ghana had become independent in 1957, Nigeria in 1961, and she was writing to me in 1962. I had written and was thinking about Tanganyika; I was then writing about the Federation of Rhodesia and Nyasaland, and she was trying to show me that it was going to take longer for nationalism to succeed in that part of the world. Well, as it is, the Federation broke up in 1963, followed by independence in Malawi and Zambia."

The dominant sentiment was more affirmative in Nigeria, according to Adebayo Adedeji's schoolyard memory: "We attended political rallies, in spite of the severity of the punishment should we be caught. Don't forget, the principal of my school, Reverend S. R. S. Nicholas, was half-British, and half-Ghanaian. So he was very pro-British. He didn't want us to get involved in politics. In fact, I remember when there was the case of an attempted assassination of the then-nationalist leader, Dr. Nnamdi Azikiwe, he told us that in an assassination story there are two asses. And of course, if you put two asses together, and then add n-a-t-i-o-n, you get the word 'assassination.' But he was not teaching us how to spell the word but was simply ridiculing the great nationalist and political leader.... But the environment was so exciting that any boy of our generation had no alternative but to inform himself about the struggle for independence." Adedeji went to England to study in 1955, on the eve of Ghana's independence in 1957: "Nkrumah was everybody's hero. He was then my hero, because he was pushing the African agenda of independence and pan-Africanism."

The appearance of over a hundred newly independent countries mostly from Africa and Asia—along with those countries in Latin America and the handful of other countries in Africa and Asia that had been independent since the early nineteenth century—changed the character and the dynamics within the United Nations. Between the UN's establishment in 1945 and the end of the first wave of decolonization in 1963, the actual number of member states swelled from 51 to 114. Only six countries from Africa and Asia were among the founders, but two decades later more than half of the UN's member states were from these two developing continents.

The UN Charter's daring main objective "to save succeeding generations from the scourge of war" became less prominent as an organizational objective because the Cold War effectively paralyzed the Security Council. Moreover, as an organizational matter, the first new colonies could not even become members of the UN because in a quixotic and shortsighted bit of tit-for-tat Cold War politics, Moscow and Washington attempted to regulate "whose" newly independent countries would have a vote in the General Assembly. Max Finger reflected on how decolonization affected competition between the United States and the Soviet Union, each of which struggled to keep allies of the other side from becoming members of the United Nations. His comment about instrumental calculations captures well the tenor of those times: "To [Ambassador Henry Cabot] Lodge, his primary job was to score points against the Soviet Union. So in his mind you didn't have to justify wanting to exclude a country that was a friend of the Soviet Union's. Then as you know, trades were made, so that a couple of their allies got in, and many of ours did."

Conor Cruise O'Brien looked back on the period in his characteristically pointed fashion: "When Eisenhower was president, he said he would be guided on African affairs by those who knew the continent. By this he meant not any Africans at all, but simply the British, French, Belgians, and Portuguese. And that was the prevailing doctrine until John Kennedy became president. Kennedy, of course, had enraged the French by writing a book in which he supported the Algerian claim for independence. In general, his idea was to push the former colonies in the direction of independence and to see off the British and French, and then that the newly independent countries would look to America for support for their development and would become, if you like, a part of an unofficial and unavowed American empire. This was certainly very much how it looked to the British and the French, and there were very strained relations there, as of course emerged particularly at Suez."

Richard Gardner recalled the immediate impact of the influx of newly independent countries: "I'll never forget the first time that Nigeria took its seat in the UN. Adlai [Stevenson, the U.S. permanent representative to the UN at the time] very idealistically said something about welcoming Nigeria and said, 'Our administration is committed to helping African countries, developing countries.' . . . And the Nigerian ambassador, instead of being gracious about it, came back with a really nasty speech to the effect that, 'Well, the West will have to pay for its decades of colonialism, and we are not here with our hand out asking for your charity, Ambassador Stevenson. We want a whole new world economic order based on justice. We want higher prices for our exports and different terms of trade. We want control over multinational corporations.' . . . We were all shell-shocked. Welcome to the new United Nations, with a large developing country majority."

In the popular imagination, the sun finally set on the British Empire and colonialism in 1997 when London handed over Hong Kong to China. In reality, colonial rule had been delegitimized by the UN Charter, and it had virtually ended at least two decades earlier when Portugal's empire collapsed. Some would argue that the real end was when the Soviet empire collapsed along with the Berlin Wall in 1989. But in any case, no new colonies were formed in the last quarter of the twentieth century. And in the few instances when military action was tried, there was immediate outrage (as in the case of Indonesia's annexation of East Timor in 1975, which was reversed in 1999 under UN-supervised elections). Today there are few colonies left, mostly tiny islands.[17] The idea of decolonization has meant, in the words of the late Tanzanian president Julius Nyerere, "that colonialism in the traditional and political sense is now almost a thing of the past."[18]

Decolonization was not only a powerful and important idea in and of itself, but it also led to a number of salutary personal feelings among our interviewees. It was "a change almost unparalleled in the world," enthusiastically asserted Don Mills, a former Jamaican ambassador to the United Nations and longtime observer of multilateral organizations. "To go to the UN in 1962, for Jamaica to stand before the world and claim the right to participate and for other countries to do so, this was extraordinary." He spoke of the connections that were being made among students from colonial states attending schools in Europe prior to independence and of the foundation such networks laid. "West Indians and other colonized students from Africa and Asia, meeting for the first time in such numbers—and in England, the very center of that empire, meeting the people of England in their numbers and in their territory. Add to that the fact that West Indians are in the main the descendents of Africans and Asians who were brought to the West in varying circumstances, so to speak! Altogether a historical event of enormous significance."

Nearby, in Guyana, Sonny Ramphal was thinking about the importance of the movement: "I was opposed by the leftists on civil liberties, and I was opposed by the rightists—which really was the West—on economic and social issues. . . . Now nonalignment came to mean many different things later on, but for young countries starting out in the world in the 1960s, nonalignment—this was at the height of the Cold War—was absolutely essential."

In revisiting the Bandung conference of 1955 and trying to recall his view from Colombo, Gamani Corea tried to place the conference in context: "Much of the inspiration for a bigger grouping came from Nehru's ideas of getting the poor countries together. At that time, there was also Chinese support. The Indo-Chinese rift had not come. And so it was seen not necessarily for setting up an organization or a mechanism for the coordination of policies and so on but as a demonstration of the Third World's arrival on the scene and of their ability, for the first time, to make contact with each other, to exchange views. . . . Nobody saw it as the first step toward Third World unity, political unity, and so on. But it was a meeting of the former colonies, and they were looking at their common experiences and the common goals they had in a context in which planning was accepted and the main idea was mutual support, cooperation, and so on."

While the Charter mentioned development, it was seen by the West mainly as a means to attenuate armed conflict. For the newly independent countries of Africa and Asia, development was of the highest priority in and of itself. And thus the agenda and negotiating processes within the UN were fundamentally changed. In particular, economic and social ideas and the importance of accelerated development became *the* work of the world organization.

One of the first visible manifestations was the momentous political gathering at Bandung, Indonesia, in April 1955, which has already been referred to by several voices: "It was the kind of meeting that no anthropologist, no sociologist, no political scientist would ever have dreamed of staging," wrote African-American novelist Richard Wright; it cut "through the outer layers of disparate social and political and cultural facts down to the bare brute residues of human existence: races and religions and continents."[19] The key figures at the conference were the great leaders of that first generation: Indonesia's president and host, Sukarno; Indian prime minister Jawaharlal Nehru; Egyptian president Gamal Abdel Nasser. Also present were Ho Chi Minh, leader of the Democratic Republic of Vietnam; Kwame Nkrumah, the future prime minister of Ghana; and Zhou Enlai, foreign minister and then prime minister of the People's Republic of China.

The original motivation was to find a way to steer between the Soviet Union and the United States within the confines of the United Nations, which had become enmeshed in the rivalry between the two giants. Specifically, many newly independent countries were fed up with the logjam resulting from their inability to secure UN membership. By 1954, no new members had been admitted since Indonesia in January 1950.

Eventually, the conference would lead to the formation of the Non-Aligned Movement in the 1960s. Following the 1955 conference, the African-Asian Peoples' Solidarity Organization (AAPSO) was founded at a meeting in Cairo, and then a more moderate group formed in Belgrade in September 1961, the First Conference of the Heads of State or Government of Non-Aligned Countries. Despite rhetoric, "most nationalist movements and Third World regimes had diplomatic, economic, and military relations with one or both of the superpowers."[20]

Not surprisingly, our interviewees had a great deal to say about the birth of Third World solidarity. Bernard Chidzero recalled, "What I was thinking of was Jawaharlal Nehru in India. And Nehru was concerned about the independence of India and how he could get the support of neighboring countries to cooperate to protect India's independence, but also to enjoy regional cooperation as well as South-South cooperation. . . . Of course, Nehru was preceded by the great mystic Mahatma Gandhi and the role he had played in South Africa in passive resistance. We looked to India for leadership. Therefore, I was impressed by Nehru's ideas, which really were adumbrated in this concept of nonalignment at Bandung."

Viru Dayal, who was a youngster at the time the session was taking place on his continent, recalled: "All of us, all of Asia, were talking about the five principles of Panch Shila and the five principles of peaceful coexistence.[21] Bandung meant a very great deal." But on the upper floors in the Secretariat in New York, Brian Urquhart had a different recollection: "I knew about the Bandung conference only because it was in the middle of a negotiation for getting the seventeen American prisoners out of China. The CIA had the brilliant idea of shooting down Zhou Enlai's plane on the way to Bandung. . . . I don't remember that we were thinking about the Third World or the Non-Aligned Movement just then. It was something that was happening, like so many other things that didn't seem to be more or less significant than anything else. Most historical events, at the time, don't seem like historical events."

Unlike Sir Brian and other voices, a sixteen-year-old Jan Pronk had quite distinctly different memories of the gathering in Indonesia, perhaps because of its location in a former Dutch colony: "It was heralded as a very important event in the newspapers. . . . As a matter of fact, I remember Sukarno, Nasser, Nehru as being portrayed as leaders, as heroes, not as villains." Conor Cruise O'Brien attended the conference, but his memories were more like Urquhart's than Pronk's: "Bandung really looked like a kind of propaganda circus without much reality behind it. It was also the sort of time when people were talking about a United Africa, a united African continent, which became Kwame Nkrumah's obsession at a later time and never had any reality in it at all."

"Bandung was important," according to Paul Berthoud, "but what it would mean for the United Nations, I think, became very clear only when the General Assembly started to vote the 'wrong' way from the Western point of view. Then, of course, you realized that you had a political force which had developed and would take its momentum."

Max Finger remembered Ambassador Lodge's reaction to the NAM: "Certainly as far as Lodge was concerned, they were simply a damn nuisance, and he couldn't see why anybody didn't perceive that we were on the right side and the Soviets were wrong. Therefore, nonalignment, in his mind, was just simply wrong. And he asked me one time about India and their taking aid from the Soviet Union. And I said, 'Well, they are so desperate for help they will take it any way they can get it.' He said, 'Well, isn't that kind of a whorish attitude?' I said, 'Not from their standpoint.'" At the same time, Finger noted the impact on the competition between East and West: "If the developing countries had not made a big issue of it, if Lodge, for example, had not worried about our having, as he put it, the monkey on our back and having to show something else, I don't think people in Washington would have responded with IDA and the Special Fund."

Mihaly Simai, from the other side of the Iron Curtain, noted that the conference "facilitated the clearer understanding of the global changes that it was not only East and West in the world, but that there was something in between. And the principles of peaceful coexistence which were formulated in Bandung found their way also to Hungary. For example, I immediately introduced this into the curricula in the university and I think the significance was not only intellectual. After Bandung, in Hungary, we had many, many more visitors from the Third World."

"I think it was inevitable sympathy for decolonization, as we had been a colony, although the historical differences were enormous," recalled Javier Pérez de Cuéllar. "My Spanish ancestors were colonizers, in a constructive way. I had a natural solidarity with them. But, at the same time, some of them were fighting for our independence." The fifth Secretary-General recalled that "the

Bandung conference, for some Latin American countries, including my own, was suspicious because of the participation of communist China. It was something that created a kind of mistrust in some Latin American countries that thought it was a mechanism that would serve mainly the interests of the international 'left,' if I can use this expression, which I do not now quite like because now I do not know where the left is and where the right is. But in those times, it was very clear before the end of the Cold War."

Lourdes Arizpe emphasized cultural dimensions—a topic that concerned her professionally, including her work with Pérez de Cuéllar on the World Cultural Commission—through a literary tour d'horizon: "In the 1960s, with the writings of Frantz Fanon, and other authors, including Albert Camus, decolonization began to be seen also as reinvigorating cultures repressed during the colonial experience. The idea was that any endogenous development had to be based on local or national cultures. . . . As part of the advocacy for decolonization, some leaders of Third World countries, such as Amilcar Cabral, also spoke of the need to decolonize the mind. This converged with the movement of the *négritude,* led by Leopold Senghor and Aimé Césaire in the Caribbean and, broadly, with the Non-Aligned Movement and the Bandung conference. . . . So as part of the ideology of the Third World, the idea was put forth that culture had to be one of the important factors in the models that were being proposed for decolonized countries. . . . In Latin America, this view developed through dependency theory and through what was then called the historical-structural perspective in the social sciences. At the end of the 1970s, Edward Said brought out his very famous book, called *Orientalism,* which further showed the need to dismantle the colonial intellectual structures that had been developed in the West to look at other cultures. Anthropology was central in this discussion. It had been accused of being the mother of colonialism but I always argued that it was also the aunt of national liberation struggles."

"Decolonization was, of course, the burning issue right through," noted Alister McIntyre. "It impacted on the prospects and the thinking of practically every student from a Third World country. This is why the idea of decolonization took strong root on the occasion of the Bandung conference. Here were Nasser and Nkrumah and other names that were very familiar to people gathering together to discuss a third way, neither aligned to the West nor to the East. So that was very interesting, and we followed it very eagerly. I remember Bandanaraike coming to the LSE to address us. Nkrumah also came. . . . Most of the major figures at the time showed up in one form or another while we were there. It was a very lively thing."

The UN Regional Commissions

Differences of perspectives and priorities emanating from each of the major geographical regions was an institutional reality in the United Nations almost from the outset.[22] The views of the three regions composed of countries that had been politically independent for the longest time found institutional expression early on. In 1947, both the Economic Commission for Europe and the Economic Commission for Asia and the Far East (ECAFE, later ESCAP for Economic and Social Commission for Asia and the Pacific) were created and located in Geneva and Bangkok, respectively. Latin Americans were a strong and united voice before and during the San Francisco conference, and in 1948 the Economic Commission for Latin America (ECLA, later ECLAC for Economic Commission for Latin America and the Caribbean) was created with headquarters in Santiago.

The debate about forming commissions in the regions with many newly independent states was far more controversial and slower to materialize. It was not until 1963 that the Economic Commission for Africa was created and located in Addis Ababa. And finally, after a debate that had raged for some time, in 1973 the Economic Commission for West Asia (ECWA, later ESCWA for Economic and Social Commission for Western Asia) was created with headquarters first in Beirut, then, but because of war and instability, in Amman, Beirut, Baghdad, and back to new headquarters in Beirut in 2002.

In reflecting upon his experience as a diplomat from a neutral country, Austria, situated on the border between East and West, Kurt Waldheim stated that "the Economic Commission for Europe, was, before the 1989 collapse of the Soviet empire, a very important economic and social institution. Members were not only the West European countries but also Eastern bloc nations. This offered the opportunity to discuss and negotiate issues which concerned the whole of Europe. After the end of the Cold War, it lost its importance. . . . Now the OSCE [Organization for Security and Co-operation in Europe] has taken over as the leading organization in the economic field."

When he arrived in Geneva from Budapest to take a position in the ECE, Mihaly Simai faced a steep learning curve: "I had to realize that there was a huge intellectual gap between my knowledge of economics and theirs. . . . It was the Keynesian economics which dominated the way of thinking in the commission, and I had an extremely vulgar knowledge of Keynes because his books were not available in Hungary."

Surendra Patel recalled his move to Geneva and the role of another intellectual giant: "After Gunnar Myrdal had become the executive director of the Economic Commission for Europe, he had come to New York in 1955. He invited me to join the ECE in Geneva. . . . I really enjoyed working in the ECE on new ideas, particularly on the patterns of consumption and expenditure in the European countries. And yet in the corridors of the ECE, as different European faces saw my presence, they wondered why I, a non-European, had been invited to the ECE. . . . One of my colleagues casually stopped me and said, 'What are you doing here? Don't you think you should be in the Economic Commission for Asia and the Far East?' I thought he was arrogant and nonchalantly replied, 'Considering the number of years, in fact centuries, that you Europeans have been in the Asian and other countries, my presence here is almost irrelevant.' No such incident ever occurred after that."

Patel put forward his judgment on the quality of research in the Geneva secretariat: "The ECE had done remarkable work. There were many separate studies. Some were on transport in Europe, others on trade, on currency, on the banking systems. . . . In the early days, there was very little expertise or evaluation on Eastern Europe and the Soviet Union. When Michael Kaser from Oxford University joined the ECE, he made a major contribution to the understanding of the Soviet bloc. . . . Without overemphasizing it, I also think that we made a very unique contribution to the European economic thinking when we undertook these studies on center-peripheral Europe. . . . The ECE no longer considered only the Western and Eastern countries but also the 'developing' countries of the South of Europe. These issues were taken up right at the beginning of our work at the ECE in the 1950s."

Ignacy Sachs recalled Michal Kalecki, one of his mentors and a towering figure in Geneva and in New York in the UN's early years: "He was a very independent thinker who never belonged to a political party but had very firm leftist convictions. . . . Keynes considered him something of a disciple. According to one argument, Kalecki actually was ahead of Keynes with an article published in German. The controversy, still unresolved today, revolves around whether Keynes had read the article. In any case, Kalecki himself has never personally insisted upon having reached these ideas first, except perhaps in a text written during the last year of his life." Sachs continued with his recollection of Gunnar Myrdal, who disliked Kalecki and commented that he was "the most eminent economist with the most barking voice." Sachs chortled and continued: "To which Hans Singer used to add that each time he got lost in the hallways of the offices at Lake Success, he tried to figure out where Kalecki's voice was coming from because that helped guide him back to his own office. Kalecki threw the ball back into Myrdal's court by recounting that Myrdal is supposed to have said that 'All the things important in economics were invented by people whose names start with *m*, first Marx, then Marshall, and now me.'"

Noeleen Heyzer was unequivocal about her unhappy encounter with Asia's regional body in Bangkok, where "certain people literally used it to store second-rate civil servants—it was a dumping ground." She resigned her permanent contract: "I was so saddened by what I found. I wouldn't say this of the whole organization, but of the space in which I was employed. It was a very corrupt space. I was shocked that it condoned and engaged in prostitution. Child prostitution was very prevalent in Bangkok at that time, and what I thought was a space that had standards just broke down. I was too young and angry at that time to differentiate between individual behaviors and the whole organization. I was shocked by how much the organization knew. When I was sure that the organization knew and did not act, I couldn't stay there."

Paul Berthoud looked at the record of several regional commissions, including the ones in which he worked in Latin America and the Middle East: "Malinowski was sort of an agent for the commissions, trying to obtain greater recognition at the headquarters of the work that was being done not only in Santiago but also in Addis and Bangkok. Whereas there was an orthodoxy at headquarters which I think was not very permeable to those ideas as they came. So the distance was there. And I don't think that the transfer of ideas was very easy at all. The New York Department of Economic Affairs remained a sort of self-contained ideological setup, which was not very susceptible to being influenced from those peripheral movements."

Berthoud pondered leadership style across continents: "The approach of a U Nyun to ECAFE, as it was known at the time, had little to do with the approach of Prebisch, or later Enrique Iglesias, to the work of CEPAL. I think also that the sense of Latin America having a commonality of interests dynamized the work of the commission more than would have been possible in Asia, where the presence of very large nations did not allow for developing the same sense of cohesion as was the case in Latin America. ECA was another problem, because Africa had just emerged and [its countries] emerged in a rather volatile and disorganized way. Mekki Abbas and Robert Gardiner were strong executive secretaries also, but the dough they were working with did not lead to cooking the same pie. I think it is a combination of a strong personality and also the circumstances of the continent, which caused the clicking of that intellectual burst which we had in Latin America."

Among the prominent development economists who were in on the ground floor in Santiago, Celso Furtado remembered that "all the young people who came to ECLA and made up my initial team at the end of the 1940s had been educated in the United States. I was the only one not trained there. . . . I came from Sciences Po in Paris, where the debate was much broader. . . . Keynes had explained to us that the world is ruled by ideas, and often outdated ideas.

From the beginning I recognized that ECLA was a phenomenon without equal because Raúl Prebisch had managed to disseminate his ideas without first having them vetted at UN headquarters in New York. That was a huge victory. At that time at headquarters there was a kind of censorship. . . . So imagine this little group of people in Latin America who aren't ordered about from outside and operate with total freedom to think." Furtado continued his recollections by speaking about his boss: "Prebisch was a guy who had ideas at a time that needed them because ordinary liberal thinking was completely inadequate then. The International Monetary Fund at that juncture accepted the notion of exchange controls because it was obvious that in order to manage a poor country of the Third World you had to manage exchange rates. One can be in a market economy without allowing market rules to take over. With his ideas, Prebisch created a school of thought that became the only influential one in the Third World. And all those who were Marxist sided with him. Cooptation occurred."

Samir Amin recalled the changing of the guard in Santiago: "The dependency theorists set themselves up to counter ECLA. ECLA's credo at that time was developmentalism (in Spanish, *desarollismo*); in other words, the idea of catching up by accelerating growth. . . . [Dependency theorists] had organized a revolt . . . saying: 'Catching up is impossible; capitalism doesn't allow it.'"

Fernando Henrique Cardoso, president of Brazil until 2003, noted ECLA's impact on the peculiar cultural views of Brazil: "We had no concept of being part of Latin America. This was too vague. . . . The Brazilian elite, at least, always preferred to see itself as part of Europe—France basically, and also to some extent the UK, and more recently the United States. Even the knowledge was very limited about what was happening in neighboring countries. . . . Cuba was maybe the landmark for the discovery of Latin America. Cuba had a tremendous impact on the social life and political life in all of Latin America. Much more than the rest, much more than the G-77, Cuba was really something concrete and very influential. The idea that a revolution is possible, a better way of life, good for people—this has been always very important as an influence. So ECLA and Cuba could be the basis for the rediscovery of Latin America."

Enrique Iglesias, who was executive secretary of ECLA from 1964 to 1967, recalled that from the vantage point of the commission he saw the political clouds gathering in the region, which would lead to the storm over the killing of the first socialist president of Chile, where ECLA was based: "During his whole government, I was in permanent contact with Allende until his death. In fact, I think I was the last person to have an official visit with him. We had dinner together on Friday, the night before that ominous September 11th. . . . The other one, September 11th of 1973. . . . I was confronted with that other front of difficulties already beginning to rise over the horizon. By this I mean the political front outside of Chile, constituted by the dictatorships that were beginning to predominate in Latin America. A dictatorship arose in Uruguay. Brazil already had one. In Argentina it started in 1976. In other words, it was a politically complicated time that came with a return to economic orthodoxy in its different variants. This created an atmosphere that was not congenial to the thought of the ECLA. On the contrary, we were accused of being the cause of the looming economic crisis."

On that fateful September 11th, twenty-eight years before the now equally infamous one, another of our voices was acting as the rapporteur of the Group of Eminent Persons on Multinational Enterprises that had, ironically, been created as a result of the initiative of the government of Chile. Juan Somavía told the story: "Suddenly you see your country disintegrate into something that is totally unknown, that you can't truly relate to. It takes some time to grasp the enormous implications of your country being controlled by the military. . . . Your first thoughts are . . . very concrete. Where were my wife and the children? So I took a plane that same night back to Chile. It was an Eastern Airlines flight, and the Chilean skies had been shut off. So we wound up in Buenos Aires. It took me about five or six days. . . . Still the airspace was shut, and there were no commercial airlines. But there was a UN flight that went into Santiago to take UN people out. And I got onto that flight into Chile. . . . From Buenos Aires I had resigned my functions right away. . . . Rather early on my wife and I concluded that it would be better for us to leave."

Because he had to return to his assignment as rapporteur of the eminent persons group, he headed to "the airport where I had gone in and out a thousand times, so I knew everybody there. I got on the plane, and then somebody from the police system of the airport comes and says, "*Don Juan, tiene un problema* [Juan, you have a problem]. . . . I was detained when I was going out. This lasted for about forty-eight hours. . . . In the end, some Chilean security people contacted me later on and said, 'We don't want to go into the details of what is going on in this country. You are taking the right decision. Leave and don't come back.'"

It is often difficult to disentangle judgments about substance and leadership. Adebayo Adedeji spoke frankly about his predecessor, Robert Gardiner: "The so-called progressive countries became disenchanted with economic analysis and strategy that advocate the persistence of a monocultural economic system in Africa. They saw ECA associating itself with an economic dependency paradigm rather than self-reliance. Robert Gardiner was a conservative economist who didn't see anything wrong with the extant development paradigm.... He lost the confidence of many African governments who came to regard ECA as a neocolonial institution.... In fact, when my appointment was announced, I got a message from the ambassador of Guinea in Lagos that his president was sending a message to me through a cabinet minister. That was unusual since heads of state only deal directly with their counterparts.... The president urged me not to take the ECA appointment.... If Nigeria did not want me any longer, he had a post for me in his cabinet!" In continuing his personal thoughts about his role as ECA's head, Adedeji continued: "One striking feature of the first post-independence decade in West Africa was the perpetuation of the divide between Francophone and Anglophone West Africa—thus perpetuating the colonial legacy and accentuating the dependence of these countries on their former colonial masters. Several attempts to break the barrier ended in failure."

On May 28, 1975, the treaty establishing ECOWAS (Economic Community of West African States) was signed in Lagos by the heads of state and government, and a few days later Adedeji took over the helm of the ECA in Addis. "When I went to ECA, I went with the idea that . . . I would try to establish similar regional cooperation entities for Eastern and Southern Africa, and for Central Africa." The problem, he said, "has not been lack of ideas from Africa or ECA but lack of positive interest in the rest of the world about ideas emanating from Africa. The only occasions when ideas on Africa receive serious attention in Europe and North America is when they have been generated from outside the continent, particularly by international financial and development institutions. It seems that in spite of independence and all that, the prevalent attitude is still that of 'Can any good thing come out of Africa?'"

Adedeji lamented, for example, that in 1980, after the African heads of state adopted the Lagos Plan of Action (LPA) that had been prepared over a three-year period by ECA with the support of the Organization of African Unity (OAU) and African Development Bank, "The rest of the world paid little attention and within a few weeks after the Lagos Summit, the World Bank had come out with its own alternative [the so-called Berg report] which is the very antithesis of the LPA. In 1989, when the ECA came out with the African Alternative to the World Bank Structural Adjustment Program, the document had to be released first in London to ensure that it caught the attention of the West.... So I don't think it is lack of ideas. In the world in which we live the acceptability of ideas does not rest entirely with their quality but also does depend on the source. The playing field is still far from being level!"

Peg Snyder remembered the importance of women on the ECA's agenda from the very outset: "In 1960/1961, they had 'Role of Women in Community

Development,' and 'Role of Women in Urban Development.' In 1964/1965, they spoke of the need for a study of population growth and the role of women in development. This was much before anybody was talking about women in development. . . . Helvi Sipila of Finland later said ECA had the lead in all of the regions toward the achievement of equal rights for men and women as set forth in the UN Charter. . . . No other region did anything for women at that stage. . . . What was making ECA a leader in this was that the concepts were very different from any at the UN or any others at the time, because we were talking about women as part of the active labor force."

In this regard, she had a different view of the second executive secretary, Robert Gardiner, who had created the women's center in 1975, his last official act before retirement and Adedeji's arrival: "We had a celebration at my place, and he said, 'I want to tell all of you my story. . . . My father died when I was a little tiny guy. My mother first started a bakery. Then she got into cars. And she told how once she took one of her cars to a mechanic and asked him about the carburetor. He said, "Madam, how do you know anything about carburetors?"' He said, 'She is the reason I went to Cambridge University. . . . Do you think I am afraid of women taking over? I wouldn't be here if some women didn't take over.'"

5

The 1960s: Widening Development Avenues

- **The First Development Decade**
- **UNCTAD and the Group of 77**
- **Technical Cooperation: The Road to the UNDP**
- **Influence of the Major Powers**

The explosion of dozens of newly independent countries on the world scene and the escalation of the Cold War between Moscow and Washington and their respective allies and clients led to growing and different demands for development by the Third World. It also resulted in a different kind of U.S. engagement with the world organization—one that was far more skeptical and far less supportive than at the world organization's founding. The need to accommodate the particular social and economic concerns of these newly emerging states coupled with fierce competition among the superpowers for backing from these countries created new coalitions and new UN institutions to advocate for or challenge orthodoxy. Increasingly, what is now known as the Global South relied on UN secretariats for ideas and approaches to their own development trajectories. Preparations for the UN Conference on Trade and Development began in 1962 and its secretariat was institutionalized in 1964. For the next decade, it acted as an essential hub for the UN's intellectual activity on economic and social issues.

The climate had changed. When the United Nations first turned to issues of economic and social development in the late 1940s, the term chosen to describe the objects of inquiry was at first "undeveloped," then "underdeveloped" countries. In fact, both were misnomers. The so-called underdeveloped countries had rich and complex histories and cultures, economies, and societies. They were economically poor rather than underdeveloped. Nor was development economics as undeveloped or underdeveloped as it appeared at the time. Adam Smith had published his *Inquiry into the Nature and Cause of the Wealth of Nations* some 170 years earlier,[1] and the nineteenth century was full of pioneering works on the early experience of development and industrialization in Europe. Robert Malthus, David Ricardo, John Stuart Mill, and Karl Marx were among the greatest theorizers, but there were many others.[2]

How did the 1940s and 1950s set the stage for the tumultuous 1960s? Brian Urquhart remembered how development first arose in discussion on the 38th floor: "That really started in 1948 with Truman's 'Point Four' speech . . . considered at that time to be an original idea. Truman's idea was that the only way to keep the world reasonably stable was to have a vast development program run by the UN, coordinating its own specialized agencies in what was then called 'underdeveloped countries.' Soon that phrase was considered rude, so they became 'developing countries.'"

Economics as taught in the 1940s, however, was not about development, economic or any other sort. Microeconomics was the standard bill of fare for theory and policy, with Keynesian macroanalyses of unemployment the exciting frontier.[3] Paul Samuelson's *Economics,* the classic textbook of choice, was then in the first of its now eighteen editions. It devoted just three sentences to developing countries.[4] When Hans Singer was recruited in 1947 by the UN to fill one of the first vacant posts for an economist to work on the problems of developing countries, he recalled that his mentor, Harvard's highly distinguished Joseph Schumpeter, retorted: "But I thought you were an economist!" Singer also recounted that his earlier experience in town planning got him a job in the UN in the field of economic planning and development.

Nevertheless, Singer was delighted to be in the Secretariat in those days, a hothouse for ideas: "I had the feeling of being at the center of things, very privileged to be there. After all, the UN was the home of mankind. It was then at the center of international organizations; the Bank and the Fund were very much on the periphery in those days." Article 55 of the UN Charter specified the importance of promoting conditions of economic and social progress and development and the commitment to full employment. Indeed, this call framed the UN's early work. The unusual character of this early work can even now be seen in three major UN publications: *National and International Measures for Full Employment* (1949); *Measures for the Economic Development of Under-Developed Countries* (1951); and *Measures for International Economic Stability* (1951).[5]

Rubens Ricupero recalled the intellectual climate of the tumultuous 1960s, which contributed to the idealism of the First Development Decade: "The youth rebellion in Paris and all around the world—the big campus manifestations in the U.S. and in many other countries; the radicalization that led to the terrorist movements in Germany and Italy; the Red Brigades. . . . It was in those years that Pope Paul VI said that development is the new name of peace. For me, this is a landmark—the idea of equating development with peace—a new moment in the history of humankind. It is also the moment of the new cultural revolutions, of the rock revolution, which is a sort of revolution in style but also in lifestyle. It is the moment of the sexual revolution, of the emancipation of women. So it was a moment when everything seemed possible."

The First Development Decade

Economic development was an element of the UN's business from the outset, but in the 1960s its prominence along with the assertiveness of claims from Latin America and the newly independent countries of Africa, Asia, and the Middle East became so quantitatively different as to constitute a qualitative shift. Broadening the avenues to development had by then become a preoccupation as the world organization approached truly universal membership. By the early 1960s, development in what was then called the Third World and would soon become known as the South was gathering steam through the NAM and the Group of 77. Sartaj Aziz was unequivocal: "The growth of the G-77, of course, has been a major development in the UN. . . . On the face of it, it is an advocacy group for all developing countries, but in practice it is divided up within the Group of 77, with different interest groups claiming different priorities. The developed countries, of course, tried to defuse the G-77 unity by offering crumbs to one subgroup or the other."

Decolonization had moved from controversy and conflict to practical arrangements for handover and independence, at least for more than a score of countries in Africa—with virtually all others to follow in short order. After a compromise between Moscow and Washington about membership for newly independent states, UN membership grew dramatically.[6] The Korean War seemed long past, as was the Suez invasion and the suppression of the Hungarian uprising—although the 1961 Bay of Pigs invasion of Cuba and the missile crisis of October 1962 meant that East-West relations remained extremely tense.

Economic and social development was high on the international agenda because it was *the* priority for the leaders of many countries coming to independence. In their examination of the politics of eight UN organizations over the decade in a pathbreaking book, one of our interviewees, Robert Cox, and the late Harold K. Jacobson of the University of Michigan noted "a shift in the dominant ideology . . . to developmentalism."[7] Newly elected U.S. president John F. Kennedy proposed a "development decade" when speaking at the General Assembly in September 1961. Richard Gardner recalled how the Kennedy initiative saw the light of day within the administration as the result of collaboration with his boss, Assistant Secretary of State Harlan Cleveland: "One of the things that I also learned in those days was the way that you get new policy initiatives in Washington is to put them into the president's speech. So Kennedy's speech to the UN General Assembly in September 1961 . . . was our opportunity—Harlan's and mine—to load into his speech as many policy initiatives as we could think up. We had one initiative that had to do with peacekeeping—and then there was outer space, which was one of the things I worked on. But in the economic field, we wanted a big economic idea. At that time there was a wonderful man in USAID named Frank Coffin . . . and Coffin sent a memo to Harlan saying, 'Why don't we have an international development year?' . . . So Harlan calls me into his office and says, 'Well, let's see. Maybe we can use something like this in the Kennedy speech.' But Harlan then said something very wise: 'But Dick, let's not call it an international development year. You don't do international development in a year. Let's call it something else.' Then we joked. We said, 'Should we call it the eon of development? No, that's a little too long.' So we came up with the idea of a decade of development, and figured maybe we would have a First Development Decade and a Second Development Decade and so on."

The main economic objective of the development decade was to accelerate economic growth in developing countries and more specifically "to create conditions in which the national incomes of the developing countries [would] be increasing by 5 percent yearly by 1970 [and would] also continue to expand at this annual rate thereafter."[8] With population growing at an estimated rate of 2 to 2.5 percent per annum, the economic goal was reckoned to be sufficient to double living standards in 25 to 30 years—though it was recognized that if population growth accelerated to 3 to 3.5 percent, doubling would take 35 to 50 years.

With hindsight, one can see that the "golden age" of development was well under way. But at the time progress seemed, in the words of an official UN report, "painfully slow."[9] The number of persons "living in distress and unacceptable poverty" was thought almost certainly to have increased rather than diminished over the 1950s. In spite of efforts to stamp out illiteracy, the number of illiterate persons was thought to have increased, in part because of the relentless growth of population.[10]

Against this background, the UN Secretariat and its member states responded positively to Kennedy's proposal. According to General Assembly resolution 1710 (XVI) of December 1961, member states and their peoples would "intensify their efforts to mobilize and to sustain support for the measures required on the part of both developed and developing countries to accelerate progress towards self-sustaining growth of the economy of the individual nations and their social advancement." In his address before the General Assembly, the young American president declared that if the United States could commit itself to put a man on the moon before the decade was over, it would certainly support the idea of improving the living standards of people in the poorest countries over the same period. Max Finger recalled that one of the "motivations was to highlight Washington's leadership in ODA at the time." Since then, Washington has unceremoniously tumbled from the top to the bottom of the aid ladder—today in terms of its GDP, the United States contributes less than 0.1 percent to ODA, the least among countries of the OECD.

"The aid people in the Kennedy and early Johnson administrations were very much aid motivated, as against the security motivation," Jack Stone remembered from his work at the time in the U.S. government. "You have to recall that the U.S. was still a leader among donor countries when the OECD established its Development Assistance Committee in the early 1960s, with the U.S. providing the largest amount of aid. . . . There was a great *esprit de corps* about all this."

The First Development Decade's (DD1) broad goal of accelerated economic growth was backed up by more specific goals for education in the document, which included the "mobilization of human resources, including particular attention to the needs of children and young people, which was explicitly recognized as a matter of their basic human rights."[11] There were quantitative targets for agriculture and industry and broad goals for the reduction of hunger and malnutrition; for natural, water, and mineral resources and energy resources; for large- and small-scale industrial development; for health and housing; for transport and communications.

Janez Stanovnik, who later became the ECE's executive secretary but at that time was an official in the Foreign Ministry of Yugoslavia, recalled the impact of Kennedy's proposal before the General Assembly. "He simply had taken us breathless," Stanovnik told us, when he declared that economic development without political advancement "is a farce." Stanovnik continued: "Now of course, that had given tremendous impulse to anticolonialism, to pressure for economic development. And also there were signs in the American administration that they had been much more broad-minded on matters of economic development of the South. You know that at that time, the idea of the partnership with Latin America developed. The first steps toward Africa were taken and much effort to establish good relations with India were undertaken." Stanovnik also recalled how, from his vantage point in Ljubljana, Kennedy's administration differed substantially from previous U.S. administrations: "So generally, it was not any more this kind of rigid attitude which America has had. I remember in the Second Committee [the Economic and Financial Committee] Henry Ford was representing the USA. Then we had another tycoon from California. . . . This period was, let me say, the 'period of meager cows' for us. But the incoming of Kennedy was a big push, which also contributes to understanding why suddenly the industrialized countries which did not permit earlier even discussion over trade had suddenly accepted not only discussion over trade but were willing to cooperate in constructive projects and ideas about international economy."

With reference to the development decades, Hungary's Mihaly Simai recalled the work of Jan Tinbergen as chair of the UN's Committee for Development Planning (CDP)—an independent group of experts who met regularly to address technical and policy issues: "He wanted a global plan, a framework for global development. The ideas of the First Development Decade were coming from within the organization and outside the organization and the interaction really helped a lot. . . . Tinbergen was, I think, very much open-minded but he pushed very firmly his ideas. . . . It was very difficult for him to change his mind. I had only one or two opportunities to have some arguments with him, but it was basically impossible to convince him. . . . His greatest contribution in the field of the planning experience was probably the fact that he understood very well the constraints." In thinking about the impact on policy of the first and subsequent decades, Simai continued: "[It] forced governments to think in terms of their own development problems and specific responsibilities. It helped also the evaluation of policies in international aid programs. How the external sources of development could be adjusted to the needs. . . . It was also important to understand what type of growth could or would be necessary to achieve certain goals, to relate the actual economic growth to development targets, so it gave a comprehensive framework to development thinking."

Part of these early efforts were devoted to finding numbers to describe what was going on, or should be going on, in the form of targets. In thinking about measurement, Nobel laureate Amartya Sen looked back: "As far as measurement is concerned, it's quite different, isn't it, because the UN had been at the center of it all. It was at the center of refining the measurement and standardization of the GNP. Richard Stone and James Meade were both involved in that. The UN was later on at the center of criticizing and challenging the ongoing reliance on the GNP. The critique came mainly through the *Human Development Reports* in particular and trying to replace the GNP by the Human Development Index, led by Mahbub ul Haq. There were also other voices of criticism for which the UN made room. For example, Keith Griffin and John Knight outlined an influential case for relying on human capabilities rather than on economic affluence only, and the UNICEF of course had been much involved in focusing on 'the state of the world's children,' rather than on any measure of GNP or GDP. This was all in the UN. There was also major work going on at WIDER [World Institute for Development Economics Research, a part of the UN University] in Helsinki. So in measurement-related policy, the UN had an enormous lead."

Hans Singer added: "The CDP helped to prepare the First Development Decade. . . . The target of 5 percent growth or the 0.7 percent aid target was largely due to the preparatory work under Tinbergen."

One of the elements of all of the development decades was the need to think comprehensively and look to the future. "Planning was introduced to colonial Africa by the British government which established the Colonial Development and Welfare Fund [CDWF] immediately after World War II, in 1945, and made the availability of three- to five-year development plans conditions for accessing the resources of the CDWF," remembered Adebayo Adedeji. "With a Labour Government in power in Britain, it was not surprising that planning was encouraged in African countries. A country needed an approved development plan to have access to CDWF. So each colony was required to prepare a ten-year development plan. In fact, the story was told of the then Nigerian governor who was on leave in London when a letter was sent to Lagos asking him to write Nigeria's ten-year development plan. When he was informed of this during his courtesy visit to the colonial office in London, he said 'That is no problem. Give me a piece of paper.' . . . The planning effort was further strengthened by the Kennedy administration in 1961. When Kennedy came to power, the administration announced an $80 million allocation to Nigeria, provided the country had an acceptable development plan. A large team of Americans, led by Professor Stolper of the University of Michigan, came to Nigeria to join us in preparing the first post-independence national development plan, 1962 to 1968. Stolper later wrote a book entitled *Planning without Facts*[12] on the basis of his Nigerian experience."

Adedeji went back to the theme of the Marshall Plan. He noted with irony that the necessity to plan would later become associated with the Socialist bloc and anathema for many Western donors but was required by international agencies: "The World Bank has also insisted on and assisted in writing development plans. . . . So the planning culture was not imported from the communists!" On the importance of planning even without all the facts, Adedeji quoted Professor Sayre Schatz, a professor of economics at Temple University, who told a seminar in Ibadan in the 1960s, "It is better to be vaguely right than to be precisely wrong."

Peg Snyder recalled a crucial idea that emerged at the end of DD1 just as preparations began for the next decade: "It's Gloria Scott who put in the phrase 'integration of women in development'; it was the first time that appeared globally. She says she rues the day because it—the 'integration' part—became a phrase nobody wanted to hear anymore. Now they call it 'mainstreaming' and it's the same thing. Perhaps it's a nicer word."

Always trying to put the role of ideas into a larger historical perspective, Samir Amin evaluated the importance of the efforts begun with that first decade: "Before the Development Decades—I don't think that the term itself ['development'] had ever been used—one spoke of exploiting colonies or exploiting a country's wealth. . . . With the independence of African and Asian countries and the switch in Latin America from 'developmentalism' to 'dependency theory,' there arose a new concept of development, for all that a rather ambiguous one. Development remained essentially synonymous with 'catching up,' the acceleration of economic growth, with more or less emphasis on the social question. The Development Decades were decades based on this ideology, which corresponded both to the socialist ideology actually existing at that time and to nationalist-populist ideologies."

A more direct expression of skepticism comes from Francis Blanchard: "I found the exercise of programming development decades to be surrealistic. . . . I had the sense that we were launching a process pregnant with serious misunderstandings between rich and poor. That's exactly what happened. I'm probably being too harsh."

Gamani Corea, who served as the chair for the final decade, reflected on how the idea evolved over thirty years: "Well, at the time of the Fourth Development Decade . . . there were the signs of weakening of will to push ahead with some of the old commitments and concepts; aid flow was one of them. . . . My contribution was to try to underscore the continued relevance of important elements of the old strategy. . . . Globalization-liberalization had not yet become a household world. But there was the feeling that with the changes that had taken place in the East-West relationship, a new scenario was unfolding. . . . We were trying to say that the global economic environment was not sufficiently supportive of the development efforts of countries."

UNCTAD and the Group of 77

A significant moment in development thinking took place beginning in 1962 during the two years of preparations for the first UN Conference on Trade and Development.[13] Ignacy Sachs told us that the creation of UNCTAD was "an extremely important date in the history of the United Nations, perhaps the point at which the influence of the South was at its maximum, especially if I compare the establishment of UNCTAD with the failure in 1975 of the New International Economic Order. Had it been left to me, I would have reversed the terms—'International Conference on Development and Trade' rather than 'Conference on Trade and Development'—because the crux of the idea is development."

What Alfred Sauvy had first characterized as the *tiers monde* (Third World) at the outset of the 1950s became the Group of 77.[14] The G-77 was named after the original number of members in a working caucus of developing countries— which also included while New Zealand for a short while. The numbers grew almost immediately and New Zealand was dropped, and although they now number over 130, the title stuck.[15] The crystallization of developing countries into a single bloc for the purpose of international economic negotiations represented a direct challenge to industrialized countries.[16] In parallel with the Non-Aligned Movement, which focused initially more on security issues, the Third World's "solidarity," or at least cohesion for purposes of international debates, meant that developing countries were in a better position to champion policies that aimed to change the distribution of benefits from growth and trade.[17]

Richard Gardner was part of the American delegation in Geneva for the 1964 founding conference and recalled the activism of the new bloc: "It was the first time that the so-called Group of 77 organized themselves politically. That was very unpleasant for us, because every day the [G-]77 would introduce another unacceptable resolution. . . . So suddenly I said to myself: 'Here I am, a believer in the UN, and I don't think I agree with anything that's going on here.'" Gardner then recalled a clever G-77 tactic to get around Western opposition: "This is not going to be a new UN specialized agency. At least if it had been, we could have refused to join. But it's going to be a subsidiary body of the General Assembly under Article XXII of the Charter, so we're going to have to pay for it as part of the UN. It's going to be one-nation, one-vote, and we're going to have a permanent organization voting resolutions on 'sovereignty over natural resources,' which was a euphemism for the right of developing countries to nationalize without compensation and to have commodity agreements to raise prices. We can't live with that."

Gardner went to Paris to seek support for the U.S. position that UNCTAD should become a specialized agency rather than remaining part of the UN Secretariat: "I sat with the head of the Quai d'Orsay's international organization directorate, who personified French cynicism in the extreme. He said, 'Monsieur Gardner, we don't want any special voting. We would prefer they vote anything they want in the normal way and then we can ignore it. If we follow your recommendation, you'll give legitimacy to these things. And then we'll have pressure on us to do something. Leave everything as it is.' . . . So UNCTAD was very tough. We stayed up night after night negotiating in Raúl

Prebisch's apartment. This went on for a week. I thought my wife would divorce me."

As an intellectual mover and shaker, no one's name came up more frequently in our interviews than Raúl Prebisch, who spearheaded preparations and then became UNCTAD's first secretary-general. Enrique Iglesias recalled some unsolicited advice from Don Raúl: "Don't read so much. Think. Reflect." Rubens Ricupero commented that Prebisch "deeply believed, almost with religious fervor, in interdependence, although at the time the word was not in common usage. The basis for the faith of Prebisch, who as much as I know was not a religious man—his is a sort of a lay religion—was that it made sense, it was rational, to help the developing countries with reforms in the trade system, because if those countries managed to export more and more valuable products, they would be better able to import the technology and the machinery from the industrial countries and pay for them without piling debt upon debt. And the industrial countries would gain by this process. He never believed that in the confrontation that took place in UNCTAD with the group system that he was trying to harm the industrial countries. He thought it was the interest of industrial countries to help the developing countries to be able to import."

Paul Berthoud had the satisfaction of serving in numerous UN organizations under the leadership of many mentors, but one stood out: "Prebisch was a very impressive man, a very kind and a very gentle man." He remembered three anecdotes about Prebisch's extraordinary intellectual ability and capacity to concentrate: "I have more than once quoted my experience with those absolutely boring general debates in the UNCTAD conference. Governments came and made their prepared statements, which were partly for the public opinion back home. Prebisch would be capable of sitting for three hours in the morning, three hours in the afternoon, and listening with attention to each and every word which was being pronounced. And how do I know that? The next morning, in the staff meeting, he would say, 'You remember the French delegate. About two-thirds into his speech, he said, 'dot, dot, dot, dot.' Why don't you go and ask him what he meant. Is that linked with that or this?' He had registered each and every point which had been made."

He gave another illustration: "In the early years of UNCTAD, Prebisch's speeches were an event in town, people would come to the public gallery just to listen to him. One day, he was telling us, 'I cannot do it in less than an hour and a half.' We impressed upon him, 'You cannot speak an hour and a half, even you.' He asked, 'So how much do you give me?' We said, 'Let's say an hour and a quarter is about as much as you can use.' The next morning, he entered in the room, he had his hands in his pockets—no paper, nothing. And he spoke for one hour and fourteen minutes!"

Finally, Berthoud recalled that once Prebisch had two little pieces of paper in front of him, but did not look down at them once: "Then at the fifty-fifth minute of the speech, he would take the paper and read a quote and put it back. It was all prepared, all set up in advance in his mind. In other words, Prebisch had a truly extraordinary intellectual capacity. I don't know whether it is comparable to that of a musical conductor or a chess champion. . . . Prebisch, in his way, was that kind of person. He has been in my whole career the person for whom I developed the greatest admiration, limitless admiration. He was very humane too, very open. . . . He had a reputation as a bon vivant, and he was."

Berthoud concluded: "It was not all Prebisch just shooting ideas at others. I think people of the caliber of Urquidi and Furtado and others—people like Balboa, like Vuscovic, Bardeci—they were all very bright chaps, full of ideas. And, of course, Prebisch was creating an atmosphere which was stimulating that boiling of ideas. . . . It needed a Prebisch to orchestrate it, but it would be wrong to attribute the whole of the movement to him. It was obviously his ability to take the best out of a very bright group of people which allowed for CEPAL to be what it was, what it became. . . . I think that Prebisch was, of course, not an economist but, in a sense, a prophet."

Just Faaland examined the Prebisch legacy: "He was very committed to his own idea about the way Latin America was underdeveloped and why Latin America remained underdeveloped. He was quite good about explaining but not totally convincing. . . . He tended, in a way, to come back to the bottom line in his conclusion as kind of a final counterargument when you put up something against it or in addition to it. But I did like the man. . . . I think his ideas provided a very important new dimension to the development debate. But like any important dimension, if you make it the sole, or practically the sole, determinant, it gets to be wrong. In fact, that is one of my feelings about a lot of writing. People come up with good ideas, but they oversell it totally." In contrast, Jack Stone remembered Prebisch's openness to new thoughts that was in evidence at a cocktail party at a colleague's home in Washington twenty years after Don Raúl's retirement: "He made it clear that it was time, the old ideas having been tried, to go on to other things. He was open-minded in that respect and recognized that a new cycle of ideas was in order."

Alister McIntyre, a longtime observer and then senior official in the UNCTAD secretariat, built on this image of Prebisch and reflected on subsequent UNCTAD heads: "I think that his essential message was a message of hope: that the gap between North and South could be closed and that institutions could be developed to support the process. . . . Prebisch was a great interpreter and polemicist, in the best sense of the term. And in a sense, his messages could cross continents with much more power than anyone else, largely because of his stature."

While in exile after the 1964 military coup in Brazil, Fernando Henrique Cardoso worked in the ECLA secretariat in Santiago under Raúl Prebisch, whom he considered a role model. He also linked his former boss to another towering figure, Hans Singer: "Prebisch himself was a very special kind of person, able to put people around the table and to motivate people to discuss and able to integrate different perspectives and to propose in a simple way what has been discussed around. . . . Prebisch was well acquainted with Keynes' ideas and became the founder of the so-called Latin American economic development theory. How? Because of Hans Singer from the UN. . . . Hans Singer was a man who was very competent in statistics and able to deal with different data. These were the main, basic pillars of what happened with the United Nations. In practice, the United Nations started this kind of uniformization of information—good statistical criteria to make analyses. So Singer made his contributions on what happens with prices—the so-called deterioration of terms of trade—and [Prebisch] perhaps took the idea and transformed the idea into a theory: center-periphery."

Indeed, the self-effacing Singer inspired many of our other voices. Sonny Ramphal, for one, admitted how strongly he was influenced by Singer's great personal commitment to and sense of responsibility for improving development prospects. As the secretary-general of the Commonwealth secretariat, an intergovernmental organization composed of the UK and its former colonies, Ramphal was based in London and able to call easily upon Singer nearby at the University of Sussex: "There was deep dedication, wonderful clarity. . . . He was unafraid to speak out. And of course through his letters to the media, bringing the quality of his professionalism to the causes of development, Hans played an important part in the work I did. Many a time, at the secretariat, when I wanted confirmation that I was on the right track, I would chat with Hans." In thinking about those intellectual leaders who had broken new ground before his arrival at UNCTAD, Gamani Corea of course acknowledged the contribution of Raúl Prebisch, a predecessor at the helm. But like Cardoso and Ramphal, he heaped praise on "Hans Singer [who] is a giant from whom I benefited really in my later years . . . [and] a source of continuous encouragement and support."

In fact, Corea was asked to come to New York as a consultant to help write the report for the 1964 conference. He was told by a colleague that Prebisch had a habit of writing his reports himself: "If you look at my draft now, it has all the main themes of the Prebisch report. I would like to say this started with me, but it was the other way around; all the ideas started with Prebisch. He wrote his own thing in Spanish. . . . After UNCTAD I, when I became the permanent secretary and the aid group was set up, my IMF friend Dr. Savkar found my talk more Third World–oriented, more interventionist in international policy, and asked, 'What has happened to you?' He saw me as a very good classical economist. So UNCTAD I had a big influence on me. My early period was the Left Book Club/India national movement period, followed by the technocratic phase. Then, with UNCTAD I, I began to think politically about North-South issues and the external environment for development. It all started with my working for Prebisch."

One strongly dissenting voice about Prebisch came from Jacques Polak, longtime staff economist at the IMF: "Prebisch in our view was completely wrong and in fact a very bad influence on these [Latin American] countries from the very beginning." Klaus Sahlgren also was not enthusiastic about Prebisch's "baby," the Geneva secretariat: "I did not get a very positive impression of UNCTAD. I saw it as an inefficient way of dealing with important problems—I had been dealing with GATT and that was more to my liking than UNCTAD. So my heart has never been very warm to the UNCTAD approach."

Jan Pronk reflected personally on his work as Corea's deputy in UNCTAD and in general: "I was organizing and facilitating negotiations. And I was participating and sharing in analyses on the process of international economic development and trade. I learned a lot during those six years. I was able to refresh myself." In examining the legacy, Pronk asked himself, "Was UNCTAD radical?" He responded: "It was highly ambitious, a little ideological, and a little confrontational and analytical. The original analytical base had been the center-periphery analysis. Northern countries despised this way of thinking. Whether right or wrong, in 1979 it became clear that in order to render negotiations successful, it would be necessary to choose a different analytical base. That is what Gamani Corea did: 'Let's define a mutual interest in change. After all, we are all interdependent, dependent on each other—some more than others, but no one is not dependent. Let's define the grades of interdependence and define possible bargains, sometimes in sectors, in an integrated whole.' As a matter of fact, this had been the message of the Brandt report [*North-South: A Programme for Survival*]."

Pronk also thought out loud about the "good life" alongside the cozy Lake Geneva and its impact on negotiations and thinking: "We were negotiating on an island. Geneva was an island. But on that island, you could study, reflect, come up with new ideas. . . . Also, coming from the younger generation of less traditional economists in Europe and the United States, UNCTAD was able to come forward with a number of new ideas—for instance, on non-tariff barriers, and also international trade in services."

Rubens Ricupero, UNCTAD's secretary-general from 1995 to the present, said: "It is no secret that UNCTAD was, by and large, a sort of outgrowth of ECLAC.... It was basically the thought of Raúl Prebisch and the group around Raúl Prebisch that set the ground for the creation of UNCTAD. Those people reached the point where they felt that Latin America was too narrow for their ideas. They needed to apply it on a global scale, and this is what was behind the resolution of the UN General Assembly.... The fact that Prebisch left [UNCTAD] immediately after accepting a second term, just a few months later, is a good indication that he finally became disappointed with the possibilities of realizing this dream. But the successors of Prebisch continued in this path, although it was becoming increasingly visible that this would not lead anywhere.... When I came, this was no longer possible. Any notion that things should continue to go on as in the past had by then completely dissipated."

In 1964, James Jonah was a junior staff member in New York and recalled why the new voice of the Third World was created inside the UN and not in Washington: "That is why the Americans never accepted UNCTAD and others, because they think that in contrast to the IMF and the World Bank, you don't have a weighted voting.... Whereas the Third World was saying, 'Yes, we need equal voting.'"

How sensible was, or is, the grouping for economic discussions of developing countries? Answers varied. "I do not think that we can club all the developing countries together," Surendra Patel, who served in the UNCTAD secretariat, told us: "In the early days, until the 1986 Uruguay Round, UNCTAD had complete access and high-level cooperation with the developing countries and the G-77. UNCTAD was officially invited to their meetings and we would reciprocate. The G-77 was even in favor of making UNCTAD a permanent UN agency. But, there was strong resistance against it and it never came through. UNCTAD is still called the UN *Conference* on Trade and Development."

"I had been at one time the chairman of the Group of 77," recalled Javier Pérez de Cuéllar in harking back to his time as Peru's permanent representative in New York: "How can you trust a Group of 77 that included, at the same time, Bangladesh and Saudi Arabia? How could coordination be possible? Impossible, you know. I think UNCTAD is more or less the same. UNCTAD was a disappointment. For instance, the Group of 77—does it exist? I don't know, but if it does it is really, totally useless. And the nonaligned group does not exist any longer.... Nonaligned against what? ... Everything has changed in a radical way.... I had been in touch with UNCTAD when I was Secretary-General, and even before. But it never worked properly. They had some good ideas. But I used to say to myself that ... we could paper all the United Nations walls with United Nations resolutions that have not been implemented." His successor, Boutros Boutros-Ghali, was more poetic in describing the impact: "It was a kind of international drumbeat ... noisy! It can mobilize public opinion, but more often without producing concrete results."

Gamani Corea agreed and disagreed with his former bosses by observing that developing countries had never been a homogeneous group: "You have the NICs [newly industrializing countries], the least developed countries [LDCs], and the landlocked countries. But again I feel that this does not negate the logic of the developing countries coming together. There is one important reason, and that is that in multilateral negotiations, despite their differences, the only strength they have comes from the strength of their numbers. ... Despite the allusions to the differences among developing countries, which come a lot from the North, the North itself does not recognize that much differentiation when they talk of the developing countries."

Alister McIntyre spent a decade of his career as UNCTAD's deputy secretary-general and later as officer-in-charge: "When I went to UNCTAD, I was rather impressed by the confidence with which many of the directors there felt that in their particular sector they could make progress. Gerry Arsenis in money and finance and Surendra Patel in the transfer of technology are two examples that come to mind. On the other hand, I found in UNCTAD a kind of attitude that once one had thought through the problem, in a sense, it had been solved. I had the greatest respect and admiration for our leader at the time, Gamani Corea, who believed in the power of ideas and was himself a very powerful intellect. But he did not do as well in marketing his and the organization's ideas, taking them beyond the meeting rooms downstairs out into the hinterlands, into the capitals where the decisions were being taken, and which one had to influence. To be fair, there were resource constraints to pursuing such a strategy, but the absence of it limited the impact of the institution. This was particularly important in Africa, where only a handful of countries had missions in Geneva."

Paul Berthoud looked back nostalgically to the period: "There is no question that in the 1960s, the spirit which motivated the group that worked at that attempt at changing the world was a sense of devotion which was very enhancing of the quality of relationships and the quality of the work itself.... In UNCTAD, you had a collective sense of mission which I found more articulate there than I have at any other place in all of my career." Berthoud lamented the death of that idealism in UNCTAD, but noted that "it is a coffin full of remarkable ideas which at some point might have to be dug back from oblivion. I always say that I am waiting for my grandchildren to hear someday that there is a center and a periphery in the world and develop an economic theory which would be based on that basic fact of life. The contribution of UNCTAD has been an absolutely remarkable, brilliant, alternative approach to the management of . . . economic relations among countries."

In thinking back to a common criticism of bias that was directed at the secretariat in Geneva from its earliest days, Berthoud recalled: "Once Prebisch was asked by a nasty Western journalist in a press conference, 'Mr. Prebisch, isn't it so that many of the papers you produce are reflecting positions which favor the developing countries? And isn't it so that really, in a sense, you are not neutral in that game? You are assisting them?' Prebisch remained very calm, but obviously he was somewhat tense. He said, 'Look, I received a mandate from the world community, and that mandate is to find accommodations to the world economy which will give a better participation to the developing countries. By definition of my mandate, I am looking for arrangements which will favor the position of the developing countries. This is what the mandate of UNCTAD is about. Now, I have to be impartial towards all parties in the United Nations community, and we are striving to be impartial at all times. But as for neutrality, we are not more neutral to development than WHO is neutral to malaria.'" Prebisch's view reminds us of Dag Hammarskjöld's statement "I am not a neutral as regards the Charter; I am not neutral as regards facts."[18]

Technical Cooperation: The Road to the UNDP

The location of funding to widen the avenues for development and the UN's comparative advantage in this arena came to the fore in the 1960s. Even over forty years later, there is much to praise in what we can now see was pioneering: the vision, the range of issues covered, the freshness and subtlety of much of the drafting, the clear focus on national action, and the first rush of goal-setting in that decade. There was also a more operational bent, the recognition of the role that the UN's expertise and its country representative, the world organization's agent in each country, should and could play. In 1966 the United Nations Development Programme began operations, and over time its resident representatives became the coordinators for the UN system in the field.

The UN had in fact already been providing support through the Expanded Program of Technical Assistance (EPTA), which was established in 1949. It had picked up on U.S. president Harry Truman's Point Four proposal in his 1949 inaugural address that expressed his belief that the United States should, by means of sharing its advanced scientific and technological "techniques," help less economically developed nations improve the living conditions of their people. The UN Special Fund was established ten years later to help fund UN development efforts. The fusion of these two institutions resulted in the UNDP.

During that time, the World Bank had doubled its capital and shifted its focus from post–World War II reconstruction of Europe to the development of newly emerging states. In 1960 it established the International Development Association, which provided low-interest loans on such soft terms as to amount to "grants" along the very same lines originally proposed years earlier for the United Nations. At the outset, the World Bank, in line with strong U.S. resistance, had opposed the creation of such a facility. But once it seemed that money would flow in its direction, the Bank shifted 180 degrees to support the proposal.[19] The World Bank's history noted that the IDA "carried the genes of its third world and United Nations parentage."[20] The Bank made its first IDA development credit to Honduras in 1961.[21]

The row over whether the UN or the World Bank would get the money figured in many recollections. Margaret Joan Anstee remembered the negotiations over a stillborn offspring, SUNFED: "That proposal stemmed from the need for developing countries, many of them recently independent, to have access to capital development finance at a cheaper rate than World Bank loans—especially the poorer countries. The 'S' [was] added when they discovered the acronym without it was 'UNFED!'" Like many of our interviewees, she recalled the rancor: "The argument went on for years until eventually a political compromise was reached. There wouldn't be SUNFED. Instead the UN Special Fund was set up to fund pre-investment studies, while the World Bank created a concessional arm to provide cheaper finance to poorer developing countries. . . . The idea behind the Special Fund pre-investment was an important one because it had been found that many countries could not obtain capital finance because insufficient preliminary studies had been done."

Max Finger looked back on Washington's distinctly negative stance toward SUNFED. It killed the idea because it "was described in Washington as a fund where the U.S. would put up practically all the money and everybody else would decide how to spend it. So naturally it was not popular with either the Treasury or Congress." Finger claimed that the origins of an alternative—that is, the creation of the UNDP to focus on technical assistance and pre-investment studies—were across First Avenue, at the U.S. Permanent Mission: "I came up with a notion which became the Special Fund and the

UN Development Programme. It was called 'pre-investment.' And here my Laos experience was very helpful. The idea behind it was that if we could help countries find their resources and then train people in how to use the resources, . . . capital would flow, either domestic or foreign, private or public."

He recalled the launching of the Special Fund: "Paul Hoffman was our delegate in the General Assembly in 1956. . . . Because of his reputation as head of the Marshall Plan, because of an article he had done for the *New York Times Magazine,* there was enthusiasm all over the place for Paul Hoffman. . . . We doubted that Paul would take it initially. And Lodge said, 'You know, Paul, it may have only about 15 million dollars.' Hoffman said 'I don't care if it is 15 cents, it is the principle.' . . . He had a lot of IOUs with the prime ministers of Germany and France as somebody who had headed the Marshall Plan. And the fund developed really quite rapidly and very well." Success, even relative success, has many parents!

The idea that investments in brick and mortar—everything from factories to roads and ports and communications—were necessary but insufficient led to an increasing emphasis on investing in people. The label technical "assistance"—which implied more of a one-way or top-down direction from the knowledgeable West to the rest of the world—gave way to the less paternalistic concept of technical "cooperation," which implied more equality. But the essential notion was a division of labor between the Washington-based international financial institutions and UN agencies. Hence, technical assistance began as a poor cousin's answer to the far more costly financial and structural investments that emanate from the World Bank and the IMF as well as from other bilateral donors and multilateral banks.

The evolution toward technical cooperation suggests that a certain leverage or multiplier effect for donor resources results from upgrading human resources. According to our voices, technical cooperation was more than just a rationalization for lacking the financial resources of the Bretton Woods institutions; it was a way to broaden the avenues toward development. Margaret Anstee, a prominent UN practitioner in Latin American and other field offices, looked back to the notion of technical assistance: "I think one of the things that went very wrong—and I used to have tremendous arguments with I. G. Patel about this when I came to work in UNDP headquarters for the first time in 1974—was the decision that UNDP fund national, rather than external, experts. That always seemed to me to be the beginning of the end. I. G. thought I was a dyed-in-the-wool imperialist. I said, 'It's not that. What added value are you giving when you fund national experts?' The World Bank gives capital assistance in the form of money. But what we are giving is know-how that doesn't exist in the country. In a poor country it can be very basic know-how. In more developed countries it can be something extremely sophisticated and done in different ways. But once you start funding national experts, what you are really doing is providing budget support, i.e., simply money. Therefore, the whole technical assistance raison d'être of the UNDP, which differentiates it from the Bank and other purely financial agencies, goes by the wayside."

Julia Henderson was one of the pioneers in getting the UN to do practical work and recalled the problems with a "soft" issue like community development, considered by many to be her singular contribution: "It rather changed our emphasis in our technical assistance work. We became more conscious of what could be done from the community level, not to have all of our concern about what the national governments were doing. And to encourage training people for that kind of work. The closer you were to the community, the better results that you could get. I know I was very enthusiastic about it at the time." She also acknowledged that economists at the UN often had no idea what she and her colleagues where doing.

Janez Stanovnik lamented missed opportunities in technical assistance: "I still maintain today that the reluctance of the West to turn towards the South was fatal. It is strange enough that only today, during the globalization, it is only private initiative and private capital which is going South, while public capital assistance is declining while according to economic reasoning it should have been the first to go South. But unfortunately it didn't. And I think the consequences are there. I think mainly that this project of sincerely helping the South on several scores—not only on the trade side but also on the financial side, and foremost on the advice of economic policies, technical assistance in administration, technical assistance in economic policies, et cetera—would have made the world entirely different from the one we are actually living in."

Many doubt the importance of analytical reports in the face of bureaucratic inertia, and the 1969 *Capacity Study* is often cited in this regard as both a negation and an affirmation of the proposition.[22] Few reports have been discussed with either such praise or such venom. Margaret Anstee, who drafted the report about the role of the UN system in development with Sir Robert Jackson, remembered: "The central thrust was the need for an integrated approach, the need for an end to fixed agency shares of the UN technical assistance pie in each country, the conviction that it shouldn't be the agencies or the headquarters who dictated the form of a program. We said, 'Development is homemade.' There should be a country program and that program should stem from the needs of the country as seen by that country and should be integrated into and synchronized with the national development plan, where one existed. The country program, as an integrated whole, was a central pillar of the *Capacity Study*'s thesis, around which everything else was developed. It was a big break with the past, when UNDP assistance consisted of separate, unrelated projects, often 'sold' by the specialized agency concerned and unrelated to the country's own priorities. . . . It should be one UN team with all its sectoral input as necessary, but geared to the country's needs. . . . The basic philosophy of the *Capacity Study* was maximum centralization horizontally, with the UNDP exerting 'the power of the purse' as the sole funder of technical assistance in the UN system and maximum decentralization vertically down to the field level."

Anstee, never bashful, had especially strong views about why the report's recommendations were never implemented: "A main reason why the *Capacity Study* did not achieve its aims was that the power of the purse fell down, and that, in the long run, was the downfall of UNDP. Many senior people in the UNDP opposed the study, among them Myer Cohen, in particular, and to some extent Paul-Marc Henry, because they also had their little fiefdoms. . . . They were aided and abetted, of course, by the agencies. . . . So those same centrifugal forces that the *Capacity Study* had sought to curb within the UN system as a whole came to prevail within UNDP itself."

Ignacy Sachs, for one, was unequivocal about the UN's failure to establish a powerful central development agency as Jackson had recommended: "It is perhaps the most important failure at the institutional level for the United Nations that on the pretext that everyone is concerned with development, the UN never even bothered to create a strong center capable of articulating and stimulating thinking about development. UNDP doesn't serve this function. Maybe today it tries to take on this role with its report on human development, but UNDP was conceived of as an executing agency, not as a think tank."

Paul Berthoud looked back at "the big bang of the Jackson report." He told us: "This is what we call the coming of age of the system—the recognition that the governments should be the masters of what they would receive from the international community and [that] there would be an integrated view of the way in which those contributions would enter the national development program of each recipient country. We moved to a program approach to technical cooperation, as opposed to a project approach, and one which at least theoretically—I insist on that—would be very much in the hands of the government. . . . Then we moved into programming exercises. We had programming cycles. We would, for periods of five years, decide how much money would be allocated to each country. Programming remained practically very often in the hands of the resident representative and his team, but it was theoretically the program of the governments and was certainly vetted by the government itself. In other words, we had definitely moved away from the sort of arbitrariness by which good brains in New York and in the agencies were deciding what we should do and what we should not do."

The strong personality of Sir Robert, known by friends and foes alike as "Jacko," was prevalent in many interviews. Berthoud recalled hearing Robert Jackson's exasperated voice saying: "It is generally said that people have the governments they deserve. It is also true that governments have the international organizations they deserve." Berthoud then commented: "He ruffled the feathers of many people by being critical—to my mind rightly so—of what had been a paternalistic approach to development assistance. It is obvious that up to that time, you had a brain trust in New York who basically were deciding what was good and what was bad. . . . Their diffidence was [attributable to] a genuine distrust of the possible effects of the system proposed by Jackson. But this was, of course, very much linked with a pique, with the fact they had been described as having been little lords running their own fiefs." Maurice Bertrand recalled the outrage of his friend, at the time the ILO's deputy director-general Francis Blanchard, who "was scandalized by Jackson's thinking."

Clearly he was not the only one. Sir Brian Urquhart remembered the almost uniformly negative reactions from senior UN officials to Jacko's recommendations that threatened agency turf: "He made a joke—well, he thought it was a joke—in the introduction of that report, saying, 'as far as I remember, . . . there were a number of dinosaurs and cavemen in the system.' And Paul Hoffmann, who was the head of the Development Programme, among others, took violent umbrage at this and rallied all of his fellow directors-general and others. It was ridiculous, because the *Capacity Study* was a perfectly sensible study, but, as so often happens, it was ruined by one sentence. One should have an anthology of such unfortunate remarks. Kofi saying that Saddam Hussein was somebody he could do business with is a sentence which will haunt him until the day he dies."

Whatever one's views about the style of the author, the key nonbureaucratic issue in the report was the focus on country specificity and country control. In looking back, Norway's Just Faaland argued that it is precisely the genuine application of this approach that is still missing: "I think a lesson from that, which the Bank at headquarters hasn't quite drawn—because it still happens everywhere—is that an effective support of an economy is very situation and country specific. Therefore, you can easily go very wrong when you have a general model of operation and even a general prescription for what needs to be done. . . . What you need to do and what it takes time to do is to make it country specific."

Influence of the Major Powers

The structure of the Security Council recognized the privileged role of major powers in the arena of international peace and security. The weighted voting procedures at the World Bank and the International Monetary Fund make a similar bow to Realpolitik. Money and military power talk. In the United Nations as well, Richard Gardner noted: "We have a UN of 191 countries, but there are ten or fifteen that really drive the organization." This is hardly a revelation. The influence of major powers is decisive in every decade.

However, the effective decolonization of most of what was soon labeled the Third World brought with it a different kind of competition between East and West, which itself resulted in the struggle for allies everywhere. In the effort to line up pro- or anticommunist allies, many aspects of UN life—New York debates, personnel matters, field assistance—provided convenient battle-fields. Equally serious, ideological lines were drawn within the organization, and even pragmatic attempts to analyze issues were often interpreted as pro- or anticapitalist or pro- or antisocialist.

Within the various economic and social arenas of the United Nations, there is a distinct effort to ensure that the voices of the "underdogs" are amplified, that the perspectives of the have-nots and haves are accorded equal time. "We cannot claim that there is perfect equality between member states, but the small and powerless do, on the whole, feel less *un*equal at the United Nations than in other international bodies," writes UN Secretary-General Kofi Annan. "Many of them believe, with Dag Hammarskjöld, that the UN's essential task is to protect the weak against the strong. In the long term, the vitality and viability of the world organization depend on its ability to perform that task."[23] Virtually all of those interviewed agree viscerally with the Secretary-General. There is a strong moral plea to emphasize the plight of the weaker states and an impatience with the strong-arm tactics of the major powers.

Sartaj Aziz weighed the importance of geopolitics: "The only place where the UN's contribution or overall performance may fall below par is in areas where the conflicts between member nations are very strong. So they are con-strained, whether it is the Cold War context or some other context where the big powers decide. So the UN has to withdraw because it can't push those things as much. The member governments are always restraining them, and they are always looking for space to do something here or there. . . . They are responding to what the members want them to do."

Needless to say, such problems certainly are not ancient history. In his inter-view, Rubens Ricupero stressed the plight of poorer countries in Africa today: "I recently went to a meeting in Addis Ababa, sponsored by our colleague from the Economic Commission for Africa, Mr. K. Y. Amoako. He calls it the 'Big Table.' It is an informal discussion of NEPAD [New Economic Partnership for African Development]. During this informal discussion, I was astonished to hear the representative of the IMF recognizing what we have been saying for years, that the Heavily Indebted Poor Countries [HIPC, the special category of countries whose foreign debt obligations have exceeded limits that the Bank judges reasonable] initiative had run into trouble because the IMF and the World Bank had been too optimistic in the projections they made of economic growth and export expansion. And he said—and this is what is great—'We were optimistic because we were under the pressure of some powerful countries to do so.'"

The United States, as the undisputed military and economic superpower—or *hyper-puissance,* according to former French foreign minister Hubert Védrine—was a favorite topic (or target) of our voices long before the harsh unilateralism of the George W. Bush administration came to the fore in the decision to go to war in Iraq in March 2003.[24] That the United States was in a similarly dominant position in 1945 and that the world organization's headquarters are located in New York mean that American predominance has always been a factor in UN affairs.[25] Our voices give some perspective to contemporary complaints about Washington's heavy-handedness. In some ways, however, not much has changed. Weaker countries, and sympathetic UN staff, have long complained about manipulation by the major powers.

James Jonah remembered that in 1965, the United States "lost" in the Article 19 dispute, the Charter article that penalizes countries that are more than two years behind in paying their bills. "People forget about what Goldberg, who was then the ambassador who had left the Supreme Court, said: 'If we cannot obtain a consensus on this issue of the obligation of member states to pay, whether they like it or not, it will come to haunt all of us. Because we, the USA, will decide what we can and cannot pay.' This was in 1965. I remember that speech; it struck me as a warning. So that is what the Americans did. They just said, 'We are not going to pay for this program or conference, which is the forum that would be used to denounce us.' And they didn't pay for it. . . . It was very painful for the Third World countries to accept, but they had no choice. In fact, the Americans . . . reneged on the payment of their debts. This has been the pattern. They always say, 'We will pay if you do this.'" Jonah moved from the 1960s to Washington's contemporary dominance: "What is happening now is that the Republicans, and the Bush-type Republicans, [feel] that the Democrats have not exploited 'the superpower role' of the United States. . . . They feel, 'We can do what we want. We cannot be challenged.'"

Richard Gardner noted the historical irony of not suspending voting rights for countries and the reasons why big powers get away with breaking the rules: "We were paying for the peacekeeping operations in the Congo and the Middle East. . . . The Russians weren't paying for either of these, and the French were withholding on the Congo. The Africans and Arabs weren't paying for anything. So we were actually paying seventy cents on every dollar, or some such number, and the Congress was absolutely furious about this. . . . Now, of course, it's rather amusing looking forty years later, when the shoe's on the other foot and the United States fails to pay its dues. But in those days, we were the great protagonists—the Kennedy administration—of collective financial responsibility."

Conor Cruise O'Brien, who left the organization after the UN Operation in the Congo (ONUC, after its French acronym), in which he had served, was unequivocal: "The United Nations is an institution which functions within well-defined parameters, and the parameters are not defined by any of the Third World countries at all. They are determined primarily to the extent of about 90 percent by the United States, working through its systems of alliances, including its relations with the other four permanent members. The whole thing, at the level of the Security Council or the Secretariat and to a great extent also of the General Assembly, is dominated by the U.S. . . . But there was once a time when the U.S. could automatically get a two-thirds majority in the General Assembly. That was at the time when Americans talked about the Security Council as paralyzed by the Russian veto and then defined the assembly—then run by the U.S.—as the moral conscience of mankind. It is very convenient to have a moral conscience of mankind which automatically approves of everything you do. But that ended with the Middle Eastern crisis of 1956, when the Arabs found that they could deny a two-thirds majority to a U.S. resolution. So from that day to this, the General Assembly ceased to be the moral conscience of mankind. The phrase was never uttered again."

When pressed about the UN's contemporary relevance in the post-9/11 world, O'Brien wryly commented: "Well, it's a very elastic institution. The people who bend it are mostly Americans, but on occasions it has been useful, in rather disreputable ways, at avoiding conflict."

When she was UNDP resident representative in Bolivia in the mid-1960s, Margaret Anstee discovered that the CIA was spying on her. At a party, the suspected CIA man of the embassy got drunk and said to her deputy, "Your boss has got to watch her step. We have got her telephone tapped. And we know who visits her." Anstee explained that "it was not hard to know who visited me because my house was on the only road that went down from the center of the capital, and anybody could see whose car or Jeep was outside."

Brian Urquhart recalled pressures from the United States on UN staff during the height of the Cold War when there were a "flurry of telephone calls from Dulles saying, 'You mean you are going to talk to the Chinese communists?' Hammarskjöld said, 'Yes, in human affairs it is very difficult to get anywhere if you don't talk to people. Of course, if you want to have a war with them, that's different.'" Urquhart added that "in the fifties and sixties, the United States believed that whenever they could delegate a serious international problem to the UN, they should do it. But ever since Kissinger, they believe, especially now, that if there is a serious international problem, they ought to get involved and solve it and get credit for it. So they only dump problems on the UN when they've made such a mess of it, like in former Yugoslavia, that they want to get rid of it."

What is the impact of such power on the flow of ideas in the world organization? Klaus Sahlgren provided an example when the UN Centre for Transnational Corporations, which he was directing, was asked by governments to set up a working party on the standardization of bookkeeping and reporting requirements of TNCs: "The U.S. government in particular felt rather strongly that it was not for the UN to set accounting and reporting standards for business." Hence the idea was killed, and Sahlgren wondered whether "perhaps today's Enron and similar scandals could have been avoided if we would have succeeded." A more direct impact is on U.S. decisions not to fund ideas such as population projects. Nafis Sadik, who headed the UNFPA in the 1980s, recalled: "Reagan had come into power, and they started asking for information, and we were providing it. They said we should not support abortion programs and we said we didn't. . . . And the U.S. always had a list of countries that it didn't want their money to go to. . . . We had to always show a segregated artificial account."

Robert Cox, whose scholarship focuses on so-called critical theory and the role of hegemonic interests and ideas, remembered the important influence that Washington exerted on UN secretariats, in his case on the ILO. He noted that its director-general was David Morse, a U.S. national who was at the helm of the ILO when it was awarded the Nobel Peace Prize in 1969. He resigned in a principled stand against U.S. pressure to reject the Soviet Union's application to appoint one of its nationals assistant director-general. The United States stopped paying its ILO bills in 1971 and withdrew from the organization in 1976, only to return in 1981. Cox remarked with irony: "The United States was more influential in the ILO after they had left than while they were there, because the ILO thenceforth was doing everything possible to bring them back and not doing anything that the United States might object to. I think that was at the point when the World Employment Programme became emasculated." He was referring to the WEP's efforts to formulate a new development strategy that diverged in key ways from the orthodox Western model. He concluded: "The UN can represent diversity, but when it comes to an important issue, the UN is sidelined. . . . As long as it is doing something that is not harmful to major national interests, that's fine. You can tolerate the expression of diversity."

Leticia Shahani recalled the behavior of the United States at the 1985 Nairobi conference on women: "Mr. [Alan] Keyes [the U.S. delegate] told us that if that word 'Zionism' ever appeared in the final document of the conference, their plane, waiting in the Nairobi airport, would leave any time should that word appear." She recalled a story from her boss, Under-Secretary-General Jean Ripert, who was told by the young African-American diplomat, now a conservative TV talk-show host in Washington: "You know, if this conference doesn't go the way that we have been saying it should go, you will lose your job; you can be fired because you are a member of the secretariat." Shahani went on to point out the obvious, that all states play the same game: "Oh, the Nairobi conference was very difficult. There were pressures from all sides— the Russians, the Kenyans, the Arabs, the Western Europeans and the USA. How it ended up by consensus is really a miracle."

At the same time, leadership by a major power can certainly make a positive difference, as we saw earlier for Washington's push on behalf of DD1. Richard Gardner remembered the ever-controversial topic of family planning and a Swedish initiative in 1962 to introduce a resolution in the General Assembly called "Population Growth and Economic Development." He continued: "Imagine that, it took sixteen years for the UN to even discuss population as an element of economic development! There was a silent conspiracy of the Vatican and a number of Catholic countries to keep this off the agenda." He also could have mentioned that another twelve years would pass before the first global conference was convened on the topic in Bucharest.

Gardner went on with his story: "There was a terrific fight in the UN committee that decides on the allocation of agenda items. The Argentines said, 'This item is out of order. We can't discuss this.' And Emma Lindstrom from Sweden, a formidable but rather tactless woman, started to lecture the Argentine representative, and the Argentine said in a loud stage whisper, 'Well, if all women in the world were like Emma Lindstrom, there would be no population problem.' That was the kind of male sexist joke that you could get away with in those days."

But the importance of leadership within a powerful country came to the fore, in Gardner's view: "Anyway, so here is the United States with a Catholic president, John F. Kennedy. The last president had said this is not a proper subject for government action. . . . The subject was so politically sensitive that Kennedy would have to approve it personally. . . . I went to New York and wrote the speech at the U.S. mission on Friday and Saturday, November 29 and 30, and then faxed it to the State Department. . . . Kennedy read the speech and said something like, 'Well, this is obvious, tell him to give the speech.' And apparently Ralph Dungan said, 'Mr. President, what will Cardinal Cushing say?' Kennedy replied, 'Ralph, let him give that speech. I'll take care of Cardinal Cushing.'"

Obviously, Washington did not have a monopoly on heavy-handedness. According to Mihaly Simai, there was "an understanding between the United States and the Soviet Union that the UN should not get greater authority to become much stronger. The Soviet Union was very keen to keep the UN alive and well up to the point which was in harmony with her interests. And the UN was an excellent forum for the Soviet Union for confrontation: a structured confrontation which . . . allowed several steps of escalation of confrontation. It also served as a forum for dialogue with those countries with which the Soviet Union did not have diplomatic relations. . . . This was not only the case of the Soviet Union. I remember in the case of Hungary, for example, there was a time when Hungary had no diplomatic relations with Israel. And the only important place to have direct negotiations with leading personalities of Israel was the United Nations."

Don Mills raised his eyebrows and repeated a question asked of him, "Are we subject to the British government in any way?" There was no need to answer that rhetorical question. However, he compared the role of the United States and Jamaica's former colonial metropole, the United Kingdom, in pressuring developing countries. He pointed to the existence of the Commonwealth, a free association of mainly former colonies and Britain, and said: "Not that they would not like us to support some things in which they are very interested, but they recognize that as a small country, a country like mine would, in a number of matters, be on the very opposite side, inevitably. Not in any hostile way. And that in some matters, like South African freedom, we would take a particularly strong position against them." Mills was dumbfounded by Washington's political bean-counting: "I think it was in the time of Mrs. Kirkpatrick as ambassador that the U.S. introduced this business about keeping score as to how each country votes in the UN and reporting to Congress—and votes not necessarily on resolutions which are put in by the U.S. but because the U.S. has an interest in the issue. The idea was to identify countries which voted 'against' the U.S.!"

Max Finger, ever the former U.S. diplomat, emphasized a minority view among our voices: "I can't think of any useful idea that was shot down by

Washington, except [the] Law of the Sea, which emerged anyway." Jan Pronk would certainly disagree and recalled his difficulties as a Dutch minister in the 1970s with U.S. ambassador Daniel Patrick Moynihan over the struggle for a New International Economic Order: "He had written brilliant books. In one of them, he was reflecting on the Seventh Special Session. In that book, he described me as 'dangerous,' because I believed in it. He was a very able negotiator, but he also understood that the U.S. should not isolate itself. And I did not want to get a resolution without the U.S., because without the U.S. cooperating, there would never be a new order."

At the same time, when Pronk was chair of the conference on climate change, he decided that it was better to get an agreement on global climate without the United States than no agreement whatsoever. And Sonny Rampahl agreed with that tactic: "I have always been predisposed to the principle of making progress where you can, with whomever will come with you. . . . It is not a wholly satisfying philosophy. And when the body that stands aside is the world's biggest culprit, and the world's biggest power, then it is easy to make what you are doing seem ineffectual. Yet I don't think that argument should carry the day. I am with Jan Pronk. And I am for shaming those who stay out."

Not all U.S. citizens working on UN issues, or the citizens of any country, for that matter, toe the party line from their capitals. Virginia Housholder, for example, had significant experience in Washington and in the administrative circles surrounding UN affairs in New York. She recalled: "Back in the olden days when I was there, an assessed contribution was a treaty obligation, and I don't think any time while I was with the State Department did we ever withhold any money from our assessed contribution. Well, then when I went to the Advisory Committee in 1977, I discovered that the U.S. was withholding odd little bits of money for things we disapproved of. And that's no way to run a railroad, because once you decide that your assessment is not a treaty obligation, then you can do anything with it that you want to." Echoing Householder's position, her compatriot Julia Henderson noted that even American international civil servants often tried to attenuate U.S. power: "I think I did my part [in] displacing the U.S. I made a point of not giving them any advantage because we were of a certain nationality."

James Jonah lamented Washington's weight in everyday operations: "The worst idea, to me, is the notion that the secretariat should realize that it has paymasters." He recalled one ugly moment when Madeleine Albright was the U.S. permanent representative prior to becoming secretary of state and she sought to banish the Japanese under-secretary-general: "Most people did not know that Akashi—when the Americans fought to get Akashi out— as a long-standing member of the Secretariat, stood to the principles of the international civil service and was run out of town. It was then that she said, 'Akashi does not know who pays his bill.' That, to me, is certainly wrong."

Gamani Corea put forward what to many might seem like hard-to-believe impressions of his relations with the Reagan administration while heading up what many in Washington viewed as an unabashedly pro–Third World lobby: "I must say that until the last period of the Reagan administration the Americans, including Moynihan, were broadly supportive and cooperative. They may not have agreed with what we were doing, but they did not sort of turn their guns on UNCTAD. . . . The Europeans were, in a way, allowing the U.S. to do the fighting for them, but without getting the visibility of standing in the way of things."

Corea went on to recount a story about U.S. secretary of state Henry Kissinger at the Nairobi conference in 1976. "We were sitting at lunch, he was next to me and talking, and then he made a remark which was rather complimentary to UNCTAD. I responded that I was very happy to hear him say that because most of the comments we heard on UNCTAD from the United States were rather distant or even hostile. Then he asked me, 'What makes you say that?' I said, 'I don't know. Maybe they think we are too partisan, that we are trying to mobilize forces to impose pressures on them beyond what they could do.' He said, 'No, no, no. You should not talk like that. That is your job. You do what you are doing because if you do not do it there will be no one to do it. Don't have this kind of inhibition. You go ahead.' I was very encouraged by that remark. It may have been tactful lunchtime diplomacy, but I think he meant what he said. I interpreted it to mean, don't worry about us, we can look after ourselves."

Samir Amin voiced his fear based upon his extrapolation from the current world situation and the historical parallel with the League of Nations: "The unilateral hegemony of the United States and its allies in the G-7 has replaced negotiations at the United Nations and its constituent bodies in a polycentric world, an unequal one certainly but still polycentric. . . . In my view, there exists a remarkable parallel between the collapse of the League of Nations that preceded the Second World War, beginning with the rise of the various forms of fascism, and the current collapse of the United Nations due to the hegemonism of the United States but with the complicity of the triad. Naturally, as with any historical comparison, there are many differences. But the essence is identical."

Still occupying the Presidential Palace in Brasilia during his interview, Fernando Henrique Cardoso echoed Samir Amin's thoughts on the implications of U.S. hegemony in world politics: "America is hegemonic in everything—in military terms, in technological terms, in cultural terms, in social terms, in economic terms. And America is now also affected by this sentiment of fear and a new kind of isolationism. It cannot be isolated from the world, but it now seems to fear the world and to believe that it is possible to control the world by unilateral actions. . . . In my opinion, only American public opinion can change this—no other force in the world, only American public opinion, and the world public opinion, maybe. But American public opinion must play a role because the Europeans have not, at least by now, enough leadership to provide a countervailing influence." This drumbeat will continue as background music in the remainder of the volume.

6

The 1970s: Creativity Confronts Geopolitics

- **The Environment and Sustainability**
- **Oil Shocks and the NIEO**
- **Transnational Corporations**
- **The Least Developed Countries**
- **Basic Needs and Redistribution**
- **Women and Gender**

The 1970s were a paradoxical decade: creative thinking and action on the one hand, mounting economic difficulties on the other. Creativity was evident in such fields as the environment, population policies, gender questions, employment creation, and development strategies—all themes of UN world conferences during those years.[1]

From the vantage point of the early twenty-first century, it might seem as if concerns about the environment, social development, the role of women, or the plight of poor countries have always been with us. In reality, the ways that we now talk and think about these issues would not be the same without the work of the United Nations during that decade. Moreover, perspectives about what now flows in the mainstream have moved substantially over time as a result of discussions in and around the UN beginning in the creative decade of the 1970s.

The decade also witnessed the two oil-price hikes, in 1973 and 1979. Initially, this stimulated hopes in developing countries for a New International Economic Order, and for a while, this led to lengthy negotiations on how it might be achieved, one of the first attempts to change what came to be called in a later decade "global governance." Transnational corporations were an important dimension of these negotiations. But the emergence of "stagflation," mounting debt and interest rates, and economic recession at the beginning of the 1980s killed the NIEO debate and reversed the alternative economic policies developed during the 1970s.

The Environment and Sustainability

The issues of global warming, the depletion of nonrenewable resources and the carrying capacity of the planet and concerns that consumption patterns of the wealthy are not sustainable are widespread in contemporary analyses by scholars, policy analysts, and the media. These issues emerged after a host of UN activities beginning in the 1970s and have assumed increasing importance in the period since that time.[2]

Although early General Assembly resolutions expressed concerns about the conservation of nature, the contemporary debate is usually dated to a Swedish initiative in 1969 to convene what later became known as the 1972 Stockholm Conference on the Human Environment. "Sometime during the late 1960s the term 'environment' began to take on its contemporary meaning," writes Maurice Strong, the secretary-general of that conference and champion of the cause at the UN since then, "complete with its undercurrent of urgent concern, and [it] emerged as a real issue in industrialized countries." Citing the publication of Rachel Carson's *Silent Spring* and the Club of Rome's *Limits to Growth*,[3] Strong points to the fundamental clash with developing countries because they believed that "pollution and environmental contamination were diseases of the rich."[4]

Richard Gardner recalled the language originally used to frame the issue and the importance of presidential leadership: "The word 'environment' was not one that was used in those early days. We talked about 'conservation.' I was very influenced by books like Rachel Carlson's *Silent Spring* and by other environmental pioneers. Indeed, I put into Kennedy's speech that he gave in the UN General Assembly in 1963 a reference to the conservation of wildlife in danger of extinction and to the protection of the forests, seas and atmosphere. It was just one paragraph. . . . It just said that these are issues that the UN should consider. . . . Sweden put the issue of the environment before the UN General Assembly—I believe it was 1968 or 1967. Sverker Astrom, who had been the Swedish permanent representative here and I think later had a major position in the Swedish foreign ministry, was the driving force in introducing the environment to the UN's agenda."

North-South divisions led to a new conceptualization. Developed countries were mainly preoccupied with the negative impacts of industrialization, while developing countries viewed the North's environmentalism as a blatant threat to their development objectives. Developing countries stressed that most environmental problems resulted from past industrialization of the North. They explicitly proclaimed the right to economic and social development and said that environmental concerns could not be used to limit this right. At her

opening speech to the Stockholm conference, Indian prime minister Indira
Gandhi captured the difference in a memorable sound bite: "Poverty is the
greatest polluter."[5]

Gamani Corea recalled that Maurice Strong was looking for support from
developing countries: "The developing countries at that time rather distanced
themselves, saying that environment is about pollution and pollution is a matter for the rich countries. Acid rain and things like that did not concern them.
Strong and his team were worried about this, and I recollect it was Prebisch
who told me in New York for the first time that Strong was asking about me and
that I should speak to him. Prebisch used the words, 'Next to the issues that
UNCTAD is pursuing, I think this is one of the most important.'"

In order to try to get the developing countries on board, Strong organized
a meeting in June 1971 of what he called his twenty-seven "gurus" at a motel
in Founex, Switzerland (just outside Geneva), to probe the interconnectedness of environment and development from a Third World perspective. This
meeting—which brought together Enrique Iglesias, Mahbub ul Haq, Gamani
Corea, and Ignacy Sachs along with a score of other experts—emphasized
that environmental issues should become an integral part of development
strategy.[6] These conclusions as well as the overall framing of the problem were
reiterated in Stockholm and in subsequent UN publications. One of the most
visible impacts of that conference was the creation of ministries of the environment embedded in governmental structures and the UN Environment
Programme to help ensure follow-up of its 106 recommendations.

Maurice Strong, recognized across the board as a genius in orchestrating
international negotiations, has written a memorable autobiography, *Where
on Earth Are We Going?* Many of our voices were eloquent about his gifts.
Mostafa Tolba—Strong's first deputy in UNEP, who was selected after his leadership in Stockholm as head of the Egyptian delegation—remarked: "One of
the things about Maurice Strong, he may not be the highest intellectual in the
world. But I have never seen anybody in my life who [better] chose or picked
people in the right place."

Paul Berthoud also worked for this "force de la nature." He described
Strong as "a very attractive personality. Bubbling with ideas. . . . Very dynamic. What struck me with Strong, because I had been all through my
career in public service . . . was the way in which he tried to project what he
was seeing as the merits of the private sector into the management of a
United Nations operation. . . . For instance, I heard Strong saying in a staff
meeting with all his senior staff, 'It is a very important matter. It is so important that we might even hire somebody from the outside to look at it.' . . . That
kind of openness and flexibility was a major strand of the way in which he

operated . . . a sharp contrast to the traditional bureaucratic approach. . . . He also would not mind in an administrative structure to leave some uncertainties, some vagueness about who should be doing what. You would go to him and say, 'But look, it is not very clear. You really want me to get in a fight with that guy? Why don't you tell him what he should do and me what I should do.' And Strong would say, 'A little fight from time to time is very good to know who is really the stronger.' It was another private business approach, which is so completely incongruous in the civil service that it was at times difficult to adjust to it. . . . He has been very successful financially in bubbling with his ideas, rather proud of the fact that he has had no formal education beyond the middle level, a self-made man." Richard Gardner echoed, "One thing that Maurice Strong did very well was to mobilize what we now call civil society and the intellectual community to help him."

Ignacy Sachs attended both the Founex and the Stockholm meetings and told us: "The Stockholm conference emphasized the idea that development and environment management are complementary. To those who claimed that to protect the environment it was necessary to stop growth, the conference replied that there was an alternative, namely to change the pattern of growth and the use of its benefits. The outcome of Stockholm was a comprehensive program integrating economic, social, and political dimensions." He also noted, somewhat more cynically, that "It's not with environmental ministers that you achieve sustainable development."

Gamani Corea, who chaired that crucial Founex session with Mahbub ul Haq as rapporteur, remembered: "One of the things we stressed in our report is that the environment issue is not only caused by the process of development, it is also brought up by the lack of development, particularly in a situation of population growth where people are cutting trees and getting into deforestation and overgrazing soils. Therefore developing countries need to focus on both the environmental aspects of the lack of development and the environmental aspects of getting onto the development path. . . . As a result of . . . the Founex report, the developing countries did come to Stockholm in all their numbers and did get intimately involved in it."

Michael Zammit Cutajar, who at the time was on the secretariat for the Preparatory Committee of the Stockholm conference ("PrepCom," in UN-speak), commented on the origins of the idea of integrating environmental concerns in development policy. "My recollection of the very specific driver for that conference . . . was the recognition of pollution." As pollution is a transboundary issue, its most typical manifestation of acid rain was an important rationale for the proposal to host the gathering. "Sweden was suffering from acid rain deposition in its lakes, acid rain coming from Britain, I guess, or from Poland, or wherever. So it was no accident that Sweden was the driving force and the host of the conference. It was not so much environment per se but the concept of its transboundary manifestation that got the conference going."

There was also a counterweight: "A second driving force," Zammit Cutajar said, "was, if you like, a counterforce, which was the developing countries led by Brazil, Amazonian superpower of the Third World, saying 'Hey, hey, hey, these are conditions on development, don't impose them on us. If you want to do things at home, that's fine. But we have to develop, for which we need to grow economically. So don't put any conditions on that.' And so that led to an attempt, starting with the Founex seminar, to link concerns about development with the drive for better environmental management."

Strong was instrumental in persuading French scientist René Dubos and British economist Barbara Ward, along with dozens of experts, to produce *Only One Earth*.[7] Strong recalled: "In doing so, I once again ran head on into the UN bureaucracy and rediscovered how it can sometimes act as a barrier to rather than a facilitator of initiatives." Strong put his business acumen and entrepreneurship to work and raised the money outside the UN, and the book promptly became a bestseller and made a profit in twelve languages. "*Only One Earth* was to become the theme and the rallying cry of Stockholm," he writes. He also remembered that because of the wide disparity in starting positions among countries, the first headline in the NGO newspaper published at Stockholm read "Only 113 Earths" (referring to the number of country delegations present).[8]

Fortunately, compromise was reached. The debates started with environmentalists arguing for a no-growth strategy, industrialized countries for business as usual, and the developing countries for expanded growth. At Stockholm, a consensus emerged that growth was necessary to alleviate poverty, while sovereign states acknowledged responsibility for domestic actions that affected the environments of other states and that a change in attitude, values, and behavior toward the ecosphere were clearly necessary. Moreover, a new institution was created, the UN Environment Programme.

Richard Gardner remembered the politics about locating the new agency: "The [G-]77 . . . took the position that UNEP had to be in Nairobi, which was a terrible mistake from which we are still suffering to this day. Their attitude was, 'Well, you have the headquarters of the UN in New York and in Geneva' (and by that time, they had put something in Vienna), 'now it's our turn.' I thought: 'That's your idea of economic development? To set up another UN organization in Africa to create jobs? You're not going to get the scientists down there.'"

John Ruggie agreed for the most part: "Maurice Strong clearly had in mind a model whereby UNEP would basically manage networks from some set of central nodes. Where those locations were didn't matter very much. But in order to do that, in order to have a system of cooperation based on interacting networks, you need to have very clear objectives. And the various actors need to share those objectives. You need to have a sufficient resource base to help build up the constituents of the network. None of those conditions ended up holding for UNEP, and it sort of sank into the morass of Nairobi, where it has been since. And as much as I appreciated the desirability of locating a UN agency in a developing country, I thought that UNEP was the one agency that should not have been [there]. If any agency should have been in a major UN center—Geneva or one of the European capitals—it should have been UNEP. You couldn't then, and cannot now, coordinate fast-moving networks from places that lack the communication and other infrastructure and that are so far removed from the thing they are supposed to be coordinating."

One of the key environmental issues was the status of the oceans, which cover 70 percent of the earth's surface. While UNEP encourages global and regional agreements to preserve the ocean environment, the UN itself has been involved in a long-term effort to codify what has become the Law of the Sea. Building on efforts in the 1930s, a 1958 UN Conference on the Law of the Sea (UNCLOS I) agreed to four multilateral treaties that essentially codified existing law but failed to agree on two of the most critical issues, the breadth of territorial sea and the extent of coastal state jurisdiction. In 1960 a second UN conference, UNCLOS II, failed to make any headway. UNCLOS III would eventually convene in 1973 and finish in 1982 with a treaty covering the remaining and disputed aspects with implications for the preservation of the marine environment. The initial impetus for this effort is usually traced to a remarkable speech before the General Assembly by Ambassador Arvid Pardo of Malta.[9] Malta's former president, Guido de Marco, pointed out that one powerful new idea arose during his country's first years of membership in the UN: "Arvid Pardo, our first permanent representative, started what everybody considers to be a seminal idea, the concept of the common heritage of mankind insofar as the riches of the sea and of the ocean floor and the seabed are concerned. I think that was a seminal idea which created a different approach also to what was previously the predatory concept into a common heritage of mankind."

In order to keep the issue of the environment alive, the United Nations set up the World Commission on Environment and Development in 1983. Norwegian prime minister Gro Harlem Brundtland—who subsequently was director-general of the World Health Organization from 1998 to 2003—headed this group, which in 1987 published *Our Common Future*.[10] This report, which was mentioned in a large number of our conversations, put environmental issues back at the top of the agenda and defined the notion of sustainable development—meeting the development needs of the present without destroying the environment and compromising the ability of future generations to meet their needs. It also stressed the essential needs of the world's poor and the limitations imposed by technology and social organization. It called for a world conference on environment and development.

Sonny Ramphal was one of the commissioners working under Mrs. Brundtland's aegis and explained why the idea itself was so consequential in squaring what seemingly had been a circle: "Sustainable development proved capable of carrying forward many of the ideas—ideas on climate change, ideas on the ozone layer . . . and of course the development dimension. It brought them all together. . . . That link between development and environment was really the essence of what sustainable development was about. Until then it had not existed."

Mostafa Tolba took over from Strong as the second UNEP executive director. He told us that the term "sustainable development" was not coined by the Brundtland Commission. "Sustainable development was actually coined by the governing council of UNEP in 1981. . . . We were not considering sustainable development in the context of what we are discussing now, that is social development, economic growth, and environmental protection. . . . We started back in 1973, one year after UNEP was established, with 'eco-development,' development that is ecologically sound. Then we came into the next year, 'development without destruction,' development without destroying the environment, the message I carried to the World Food Conference in my statement on behalf of UNEP. Then we came into 'environmentally sound development.' So all of it, in the context of environment. Then ultimately we thought that a sustained development would mean protection of the environment and its natural resources. So that is where we coined that."

The ideas of sustainability and the environment as well as the processes that led to them permeated many of our conversations. Victor Urquidi became a passionate supporter and analyst of sustainable development in the latter years of his academic research. He recalled the initial reactions to *Limits to Growth*, a report to the Club of Rome on the eve of the Stockholm gathering: "The critique of the study was tremendous. The economists in the U.S. just laughed at it, and in England, too." Shortly before his death in August 2004, the Mexico City newspaper *Reforma* recalled Urquidi's lifelong battle in favor of data and against ideology: "Urquidi did not publish rabid papers against capitalism, did not rant against the state. He was a rare bird, he moved against the tide. His papers carried hard facts, measurements, method, not just wishful thinking. The author was not up in arms against the world, he was not interested in siding with the 'politically correct' but in reasoning, proper reasoning, for the alleviation of poverty and inequality."[11]

What does the notion of sustainability mean in concrete terms? "We are being told that if all the countries of the world—if China, India—had today's per capita income of the United States based on present technologies and consumption patterns, the environment would collapse," replied Gamani Corea. "But what is the moral? Should the developing countries remain poor in order to save the environment or find some other pattern of development different to the North that does not put the same strains on the environment?" His solution is "to find a new pattern of economic and social change which puts less stress on the environment. The developed countries have to give the lead in this. I kept saying that what you want is not sustainable development, because one does not know whether development as we know it is sustainable; what we want is a kind of replicable development and a kind of sustainable lifestyle."

Twenty years after Stockholm, the Conference on the Environment and Development (UNCED), also known was the Earth Summit, was held in June 1992 in Rio de Janeiro. After several years of in-depth preparations, once again Maurice Strong headed the UN's team as secretary-general of the conference. The conference broke existing records in terms of both its size and the scope of its concerns. The participation of and contributions by NGOs were far more extensive than twenty years earlier in Stockholm, where their political participation in a parallel forum was a first in international conferencing techniques. As Just Faaland noted, "the environment is a field where civil society has, in a sense, led the politicians and gradually forced the politicians to take that at least a bit more seriously." The end of the Cold War facilitated the burgeoning of civil society throughout the Socialist bloc and many parts of the developing world. NGOs mobilized public opinion around the world and were able to shape to a large extent Agenda 21 (the final product of Rio). The Rio Declaration in many ways consummated the key ideas put on the table by the meeting of experts at Founex in 1971—namely, a global partnership between developing and more industrialized countries based on mutual needs and common interests in order to ensure a healthy future for the planet.

The range of environmental issues evolved in the twenty years following Stockholm. Now it is agreed that global problems include the ozone layer and global warming, the biosphere, and problems of permanent sovereignty of resources—all in the framework of sustainable development.

Sitting in the study of his townhouse in the historic center of Toronto, Robert Cox suggested that all issues of concern to the world eventually relate to the biosphere and the human environment. "One reason why I see it as a key central issue," he said, "is that I see all of the issues as being interrelated. If you want to take the ultimate holistic approach to the world, then the biosphere becomes your point of departure." The politics of seeing issues holistically is far from obvious. Nafis Sadik recalled the difficulties during the Rio preparations over whether population and demographic issues had a place in discussions of the environment and development: "A lot of work had to be done behind the scenes to get population issues into the environment. . . . There were several governments, including—I know Argentina was very much in the lead on this. Their view was that the world had been created by God for the use of humankind. . . . Therefore, to think about reducing numbers or having a balance just did not arise, because God had somehow created the earth. . . . They did not put it as a Catholic position. But, in fact, the Vatican and others also linked up with it. . . . The chapter on demographics didn't make recommendations because by this time the population conference had also been decided upon. So the way out was that these would be discussed and decided at the population conference . . . but no recommendations as such in Rio. . . . They gave in, in a way, to the conservative and the Catholic groups."

"The conferences of the Society for International Development, as well as one of its programs, the North-South Round Table, were very important spaces in which the development community met to bring together all the strands of development thinking and where I helped bring in the question of culture," Lourdes Arizpe told us. The reason she pursued this angle in her work was also fundamental: "I argued that there could be no sustainability—either environmental or economic—unless culture and social factors were taken into account in development. . . . In 1988, after a lot of working with governments and lobbying, the Group of 77 and other countries in the United Nations proposed a Decade on Culture and Development, 1988–1997."

Shifting from a macro to a microanalytical perspective, Arizpe drew on her research in Mexico to make the case for social sustainability: "You cannot save the trees in the Lacandon rainforest if you don't give farmers other options and if you don't promote convivial relations between local peoples. In Spanish, we have a much better word for it. . . . It's called *convivencia,* which means not only to live together but to experience things together, in a convivial way. So you need convivencia first so that farmers can act in a sustainable way towards the rainforest. . . . In the same way, at the world level, you need not only a concern for environmental sustainability, you have to transform all the political questions into a question of social sustainability. . . . Convivencia is the step previous to sustainability and it is highly dependent on culture. But at this moment, we still don't have the intellectual instruments to think about the need for a global social contract that encompasses environmental concerns and social sustainability."

Oil Shocks and the NIEO

Perhaps the most controversial in a series of efforts to develop new relationships between the North and the South emerged in the aftermath of the dramatic quadrupling of oil prices in 1973–1974. This led to a major shift in global income to the OPEC countries from both industrial and developing countries without oil—the latter are sometimes nicknamed the "NOPEC countries." The proposals to establish the NIEO were as much a shopping list as a single idea to level the economic playing field for the developing world. Yet the NIEO served to focus debate on a wide range of ideas put forward since the early 1960s by developing countries. Whatever their feasibility, they encapsulated the passionate call to change international economic relationships that privilege industrialized states, to enact some measures to level the international playing field.

However, "entrenched interest, national hubris, ideological divisions, and mindless militancy all played their part," Mahfuzur Rahman has written about the demise of the NIEO. "The idea of a new international economic order has long ceased to be a matter of serious discussion . . . [but] the story is worth recounting, if only to ponder the limits of international cooperation."[12]

As we saw earlier, stabilizing the prices of basic commodities had long been a fundamental piece of the platform of developing countries. But notions that strength would come in numbers were dismissed until OPEC managed to orchestrate a fourfold hike in the price of oil beginning in October 1973. The first efforts to regulate the price of oil began among Venezuela, Iran, Iraq, Kuwait, and Saudi Arabia in 1949. Following a reduction in prices in 1960 by international companies, oil-producing countries convened a conference in Baghdad to set up a permanent organization, which was formed a year later in Caracas. Other countries joined over time. OPEC demonstrated the power of solidarity when it imposed an embargo on the United States and the Netherlands, countries that had supported Israel in the Yom Kippur War. The successful resort to the "oil weapon" had direct repercussions on North-South affairs. Major development thinker Ignacy Sachs waxed nostalgic about the period: "I think that in retrospect the 1960s and 1970s were the productive ones in this fifty-year period. It was the time when the influence of the nations of the South was at its height. . . . It was a time when people were truly trying to think through the idea of development."

The bitter debates were mixed with the acute problems of countries that did not export oil. Jan Pronk, who was minister of development cooperation in the Netherlands in the 1970s, recalled: "I had sympathy for OPEC. . . . The G-77 needed an economic confrontation. Just to continue asking and talking would not have helped them at all. This confrontation could have helped if they would have been united, which means if the OPEC countries would have done more for the NOPEC developing countries, which they did not. In the end, they lacked a vision. Some did have—a country like Algeria, for instance, did have a vision. Most of them stayed apart. They had a chance at the World Food Conference, in 1974, in Rome. The outcome of that conference, a tripartite arrangement, was IFAD. It was a brilliant concept: oil for food. . . . It could have been a bridge. I cosponsored the resolution in Rome. . . . The result was that it was not an anti-Western resolution, because it was OPEC plus the Netherlands. Some Western countries followed by abstaining rather than voting against. However, IFAD never became the great 'oil for food fund.' Why not? OPEC remained hesitant and the West remained suspicious."

The so-called North-South dialogue was a central preoccupation of voices from North and South. Don Mills, the Jamaican ambassador who was chairman of the Group of 77 in New York in the 1970s, placed the origins of the NIEO within the context of broader trends in that decade. "The launching of the NIEO," he explains, "was closely associated with the Non-Aligned Movement and particularly with Algeria, seen at that time as a radical country, with President [Houari] Boumedienne and with Abdelaziz Bouteflika as the foreign minister, who became president of the UN General Assembly. Algeria had the chairmanship of the Non-Aligned Movement in that period and hosted the fourth conference of heads of state or government or the group in September 1973. Early in 1974 President Boumedienne, on behalf of the developing countries, called for the holding of a Special Session of the UN General Assembly . . . and the negotiations on that set of issues initiated. This was seen by some as a very radical set of proposals, introduced under the chairmanship of a country with a particular image, which added to the anxiety by many in industrialized countries."

Sartaj Aziz looked back at "one of the most interesting UN meetings I ever attended," the Sixth Special Session of the General Assembly in April 1974. He was referring to the dramatic moment when Algeria's President Boumedienne spelled out the NIEO in a memorable speech: "It was quite a remarkable concept of that time, developed by a group of bright Algerian officials. . . . He got a standing ovation of almost three or four minutes when he finished. I was a part of the audience and we all felt very good. So that evening, there was a dinner at the Pakistan minister's house. Ken Dadzie was there, and Donald Mills of Jamaica was there, and some other delegates. We were all talking about Boumedienne's speech and feeling very good about it. Somebody said, 'You know, Boumedienne is not alone. The Third World has come of age. Look at Nyerere of Tanzania, look at Michael Manley in Jamaica, look at Anwar Sadat in Egypt, look at King Faisal in Saudi Arabia, look at Bhutto in Pakistan, and Bandanaraike in Sri Lanka.' There were about eight or ten leaders who had become world-class statesmen in the Third World. . . . On the other side, in the developed world, there was a strange vacuum developing. Nixon had just been Watergated. Pompidou of France was dying. Wilson was not a very strong leader in Great Britain."

Aziz continued his recollection: "So we all felt very good and we agreed that the Third World had come of age again and the New International Economic Order could become a reality in a few years. . . . Five years later, in 1979, I was again in New York. I met Donald Mills at another dinner. He said, 'Sartaj, do you remember that meeting five years ago?' I said, 'Yes.' He said, 'Do you know that not one of those Third World leaders has survived?' King Faisal was assassinated by his own nephew. Bhuto had been hanged. Michael Manley was out. Sadat had been assassinated. Nyerere was tied in knots by the IMF. He said, 'Is it an accident that all those leaders have disappeared, or is there something more sinister?' I said, 'Who can tell?'"

The debate continued for awhile. For instance, the Charter of Economic Rights and Duties of States[13] was initiated in UNCTAD in 1972 and formalized at the 1974 regular session of the General Assembly. The Conference on International Economic Co-operation (CIEC) was begun by the French government in 1975 as a way to continue with fewer countries (twenty-five) than the entire UN membership. This continued under the appellation of North-South dialogue until 1981, and there were also the so-called global negotiations in a series of UN contexts (often called the *dialogue des sourds,* or dialogue of the deaf).

Ultimately, however, the South failed in its struggle to change the prevailing inequities in the global political economy through discussions. Our interlocutors were not of one voice in reflecting upon this failure, nor did they agree about the legacy of the NIEO. According to John Ruggie, "It represented the extension into the international realm of what a lot of these countries thought they were trying to do domestically, which is to pursue relatively statist policies. They were trying to construct a particular international political framework within which the global economy would be forced to operate. It was largely a nonstarter. And of course, it was abetted by a couple of factors.

One was the Soviets, who had a very strong interest—an ideological interest, if no other—in seeing this work, because it reflected their approach to things. . . . The other was the oil shocks, which gave the South a false belief that natural resource power could be manipulated to bring the negotiations around in their favor. The only problem with all of that was that it didn't reflect the laws of supply and demand and didn't make any economic sense. It ended suddenly."

Nonetheless, Ruggie thought that the legacy was not trivial: "There has to be a greater sense of social solidarity in the world; if we are going to live together on this planet, rich countries have to provide greater assistance to poor countries, particularly poor countries that are trying to help themselves. I think that lives on." Sadako Ogata added: "I think the big success of the United Nations was to present development, or the North-South issue, as a political issue."

Johan Kaufmann attributed the NIEO's demise to the radical "confrontational style" of the South and to semantics that were seen as "too aggressive and abrasive," which was a central theme in his *United Nations Decision Making*.[14] Don Mills's response to this proposition was that "it is really not surprising that the initial encounters on the NIEO would have had an element of hard talk and of deep concern on the part of those faced with a set of far-reaching proposals—the first international encounter on such a scale between one hundred or more countries, former colonies of a number of Western states. . . . In my situation, when two people come from very different points of view—if you would like to put it very roughly, advantaged and disadvantaged—anything you say could seem to be aggressive. . . . Refusal to budge by the other side in respect to any fundamental proposal in negotiation is also in its way confrontational and can be seen as 'aggressive' or 'abrasive.' . . . This does not justify excess, but it is not going to be a nice soft talk the whole way. So I found that whilst there were strong words, I thought that the term 'confrontation' was overdone. We talked quietly, for the most part. The situation was confrontational, if you were confronting an historical issue where you are asking for or demanding fundamental change. We put forward far-reaching proposals and there was deadlock. And a negative response is also, in a sense, confrontational."

A neighbor in the Caribbean, Alister McIntyre, disagreed wholeheartedly. He criticized the strategy of the South as "too maximalist." He added: "If you look at the Sixth Special Session, and even the Seventh—which was supposed to be consensus building—if you look at Paris, and CIEC, it was really, in a sense, asking for too much . . . [by] responding to perceived vulnerability in the North. It was saying, 'This is our chance to get what we have been waiting all these years and decades for.' . . . Not a great deal of attention was paid to building up support for Southern agendas among the peoples of the North in the way that NGOs are playing the game today. I think it was excessive confidence that they had the negotiating advantage, admittedly for a very short period of time."

Another son of the region, Sonny Ramphal, was more ambivalent: "I think we were unwise to over-radicalize NIEO. I don't think progress is going to be made by revolution in international issues. It is going to be made by conversion. I would hate to think that the Third World would see value in going back to a situation in which we were convincing ourselves that we could change the world because we were the majority or had a majority of votes. We won't. We can't. But we can help the world to change by demonstrating what the reality of the status quo is. I believe that this is how change will come. It will be very slow. It will be very painful. There will be greater suffering in the world because of it. But I don't think Don [Mills] is right in thinking that we will make progress if we go back to an ideological polarization of ideas." The political visibility was not matched, at least for Dharam Ghai, with a clear development focus: "I did not get too excited by NIEO because it was seldom linked to poverty eradication and social development."

Mihaly Simai explained three reasons why, in his view, the NIEO failed to achieve its objectives: "One reason was because the countries themselves which brought in the idea of NIEO were poor countries and they did not have any instrument beyond preaching. . . . The second thing was that it could not harmonize sufficiently with the interests of the developing countries themselves. The developing world was divided. . . . Then there was a third thing. With the end of the late 1970s, first Mrs. Thatcher entering to the British politics and her views on the market became dominant in Britain. It was basically an anti-trade union, anti-welfare state [view], but it influenced the global views. Then came the Reagan administration, which was equally anti-NIEO, anti-state, very much market-oriented. . . . [This] really washed away the ideology of the NIEO."

Other propositions were put forward to explain the failure of the South to establish a new global economic order. Max Finger offered a predictable dose of cold water, saying that any ideas considered "extreme" by the major powers would be doomed to fail: "The reality is that although the majority can pass resolutions, they cannot assure that the resolutions will be implemented, especially if it requires action by the industrialized countries. They can outvote us any time. But it becomes meaningless. . . . If you head down to the question about the New International Economic Order, as far as I was concerned this was not only a useless group of ideas but a damaging one. . . . The demands

were so extreme and their willingness to outvote the countries whose cooperation was necessary was so exaggerated that very little was done that was of
any help to the developing countries. . . . The essential lesson is that you can't
outvote people whose cooperation is essential and expect to achieve anything."

James Jonah remembered how those heady days of the 1970s and the NIEO
looked from inside the UN Secretariat: "It was never accepted by the Americans.
. . . It was again the Third World countries trying to find a niche for themselves. . . . And what were they saying? . . . 'You have things stacked against us.
All the economic decisions in the world are made at the IMF and the World
Bank. You have more voting there, and we have little say. We are helpless, and
we are going to stay where we are unless you create a new economic order.'"

Adebayo Adedeji, who in the midst of the brouhaha became the head of
the Economic Commission for Africa in 1975, recalled how these debates looked
in his region: "The founding of OPEC brought a paradigm shift into the oil
sector. Unfortunately, other primary commodities—agricultural and mineral—
have not been able to emulate the example of oil. . . . In 1977, I did say that we
needed a new national economic, social, and political order and a new regional order. And that from the NIEO, which was what the Third World was
asking for, Africa would achieve marginal benefit unless it first and foremost
put its house in order. I was regarded as being anti-NIEO. But within the
perspective of the African continent, I was clear in my mind that no matter
what new restructuring takes place in the world, Africa will be left out of it
unless Africa puts its house in order. That was as true then as it is today."

Javier Pérez de Cuéllar was very clear about the impracticality of the New
International Economic Order: "I think that if they had concentrated on trade,
for instance, and some aspects that were really important for developing countries, it would have been a success. But they wanted to make a revolution that
was tremendously dangerous for the developed countries. I was a member of
the Peruvian delegation and . . . was very much against the NIEO, but my
government instructed me to vote for it. But in the bottom of my heart, I
thought that it was absurd. The same thing happened in UNESCO. There
were all these ideas that are not realistic—the lack of realism within the developing countries is really sad. . . . It would be important to have an agenda in
which we start moving step by step. . . . A global approach is, in my opinion, at
the heart of many of the failures of the United Nations."

Don Mills, from his vantage point at the head of the G-77, explained that
developing countries had subsequently been unsuccessful at advancing their
cause: "I gradually developed a big question in my mind about the strategy.
When you ran into difficulties with the NIEO, and I realized the difficulties
we were going to have in making sort of significant headway, I said to myself,

'How in the name of heaven are we going to get any decisions worth anything at all [with a confrontational strategy] . . . when we achieved so little on the NIEO?'"

While Mills commented that "there are a lot of people who took the strategy very seriously and still do," he also recalled thinking to himself at a meeting in 1980 for the purpose of reviewing the NIEO, "Is this a tragic situation in terms of the use of time and energy and enthusiasm? . . . There are certainly elements which people regard as sacred. But really, how can you get agreement on a global strategy? . . . It is not possible."

Mills pointed to another shortcoming, the lack of constituency-building: "We did not create a sufficient constituency, either in our academic communities or even the NGO communities or the public. He contrasted this with another issue: "Decolonization was a street-corner issue in Jamaica and elsewhere. This was something that was taken up and people talked about it. People went to meetings and said, 'We want independence.' So it was a popular issue. The North-South matter was not a popular issue at all. . . . The NIEO—people know the name and have a very vague idea. But we have to learn that in any matter that is fundamental, you begin by getting your own people to understand it, to have some ideas, and have even some critical sort of consideration of it at home."

An even more criticized initiative—at the time especially by Western media and governments as well as by our voices—was the New International Information Order (NIIO), which sought to redress the imbalances and distortions in the flow of information resulting from the industrialized world's control of the media. Some circles worried that it was a means merely to legitimize even greater manipulation of the news media by repressive governments. Juan Somavía noted that there were two distinct explanations for efforts in UNESCO to develop this idea, "One of them was sort of the nonaligned [efforts, which were] heavily influenced by state domination of communication. . . . The other one was a demand for cultural pluralism, and for not having an ethnocentric view of the realities of the world." While he agreed that the former was an "easy enemy to attack" because it was so preposterous, he regretted that the second element had not been honestly debated. Somavía described advocates of this position as saying, "We want free flow of information. In fact, we want more free flow of information rather than less. And we want a freer flow for the perceptions and the ideas and the visions of society that are not out there today. Our criticism, from the point of view of liberty and freedom and democracy, is that this information system is simply limited to an ethnocentric perception guided by those who control the instruments of communications."

One of the key ideas UNCTAD pushed that was later enshrined in the NIEO was the creation of the Common Fund for Commodities. As many developing countries were dependent on raw materials for export earnings, the wild fluctuations in commodity prices were a perpetual concern. Alister McIntyre, who was UNCTAD's deputy secretary-general and had been the director of its Commodities Division, recalled a crucial missing element: "We had not consulted private financial institutions which were highly influential both with governments and the private sector. One of the things that we did was to have a group of quite senior executives from financial institutions come in to discuss the Common Fund with us—late in the day, I must confess. But they helped us out. They came out very strongly that the Fund had to have its own equity, because at one time the Group B countries [the West] were saying that no, it wasn't necessary for it to have its own equity; the Fund would pool the resources of the commodities agreements. The [senior executive] group came out and said, 'Yes, it should start with 500 million, but we expect it to grow.' . . . Once they had said that, it was clear that the United States government would not contest the view of the number two or the number three man at Chase Manhattan Bank, nor the British the man who had been head of the treasury and was in a very senior position with a private group, nor the Deutsche Bank, nor the Crédit Lyonnais, and so on. So once we had gotten that report out of the bankers, we were pretty much home and dry as far as the equity was concerned. Group B never again took up the position that the Fund did not need an equity. The question was how much. And around that the battle was centered. . . . We should have brought them in at a much earlier stage, at the stage of conception and design. But there was a prevailing mood against this kind of close interaction with the private sector."

For Gamani Corea, as for his predecessors and successors at the UNCTAD helm, the stabilization of commodity prices was an essential part of the work program. He used it to illustrate the trajectory of an idea: "Commodities were important to a large number of developing countries. . . . But in addition to that, the OPEC situation had emerged and was an example of producer countries pooling their strengths to get prices strengthened. . . . And I thought that the time was ripe to give a push to the commodity issue because of the history—my own personal history, the emphasis on commodities in the Havana Charter, and even the IMF, a short-term compensatory financing program. . . . I felt it had a certain theoretical support for all this based on economic analysis because in my Cambridge days we were taught that there was no mechanism in the market system to bring equilibrium to supply and demand in commodities. . . . So I thought that I had a sound analytical and theoretical basis for this—not just a demand that we want high prices."

Corea explained the final choice of a strategy that lay somewhere between two ideas—a plan that compensated for short-time declines in commodity prices or a commodity compensation scheme over the longer term: "The Common Fund itself, which was more controversial at the start, finally came to be accepted and it was ratified and has been set up in Amsterdam. But it is a bank without clients today because you do not have the commodity agreements to use it. . . . Third World countries did not really find it easy to coordinate their actions and take the drastic steps necessary. But still it is disappointing and rather inexplicable as to why this whole commodity initiative has more or less fizzled out for the time being."

Gerry Helleiner, perhaps Canada's foremost development economist, thought that "people caricatured the NIEO as a market-replacing, state-dominated plan for the functioning of the world economy. If it were all that, that was a bad idea. I don't think it was. I think that's unfair. Probably, in retrospect, it was a bad idea to try to organize the world's primary commodity markets in the way that the NIEO, the Common Fund, tried to. Probably the Common Fund was not a good idea, although I backed it at the time. It just wasn't likely to fly and would not have worked."

Some of our voices resembled Jan Pronk's, which still contains a residue of enthusiasm for the NIEO and what it tried to achieve: "I wrote about it. I defended it in Parliament. I spoke about it also in addresses to the United Nations. I still think that we need a change in the system." As Paul Berthoud noted: "We tried. We failed. But I don't think that we were wrong in trying. . . . I don't think there has been an intrinsic disavowal of the New International Economic Order—let's call that horrible cat by its name—through the demerits of its ability to achieve its goals. It has been discarded because it was displacing too many interests which nobody in place was prepared to sacrifice at the time."

Transnational Corporations

A key issue in the debate about addressing the needs of developing countries in the global political economy was the peculiar role of transnational corporations in the private sector. Surendra Patel's account of them and the code of conduct to regulate their behavior provides an interesting case study in the origins of an idea and what happened to it. UNCTAD began working on issues of private foreign investment and transnational corporations, largely as a counterpoint to the work of the World Intellectual Property Organization (WIPO), a UN specialized agency also based in Geneva but with a more pro-private sector orientation. The UNCTAD secretariat began to examine the effects of patents on developing countries at the third general conference in Santiago, Chile, in 1972. Patel told us: "[At the conference] I proposed three things, amongst which was the drafting of a Code of Conduct on Transfer of Technology. I was convinced that there should be a regulating code facilitating the transfer and access to technology for third world countries. . . . With Amartya Sen, Charles Cooper, Frances Stewart and K. K. Subrahmaniam, we were the first to analyze the way in which transfer of technology to developing countries was actually taking place. Of course we came across the predominant role played by multinational corporations. . . . We published a study entitled *Guidelines for the Study of the Transfer of Technology to Developing Countries.* Through that study we demonstrated that there was a need for the formulation of a reliable universal code facilitating the access to technology by developing countries. We were naturally re-questioning the entire licensing system. We put all the proposals saying . . . that there must be a way in which transfer of technology can be placed into some kind of a reliable system in which the developing countries could gain access to it rather than licensing."

Patel traced the call for a code of conduct to newly independent countries, which "were less developed and owned no patents. . . . Transnational corporations were concerned to establish worldwide recognition of developed country patents to protect their interests. James Enyart was director of international affairs of Monsanto Agricultural Company in the U.S. Monsanto built a coalition of key companies, including Pfizer, FMC, IBM, Dupont. This lobby aimed to create an enforceable minimum standard for protecting intellectual property. Lobbyists convinced their governments to develop the GATT Code on Intellectual Property. These laws were heavily slanted in favor of industrialized countries and have to this day continued to inhibit the industrial development of the South."

At the turn of the twenty-first century, considerable acrimony arose over the availability of AIDS drugs that were so expensive that people simply died because they could not afford access. But Patel noted that pharmaceuticals had always been part of the controversy over regulations and codes: "Several developing countries made lists of essential drugs in the mid-1970s and restricted imports to generic versions of these essential drugs. The first four were Sri Lanka, Bangladesh, Tanzania and Cuba. . . . The pharmaceutical companies and the developed countries reacted very strongly. In Sri Lanka, the companies interrupted the supply of vaccine during a cholera epidemic. In Bangladesh, three ambassadors, including from the USA and Switzerland, visited the president and threatened to withdraw development assistance if the essential-drugs policy was not reversed. . . . UNCTAD also supported local production of essential drugs. But drugs produced under license could only be used in national markets. The license contract did not allow them to be exported. And national markets were sometimes quite small. This was a way of maintaining high prices. . . . In Switzerland, for example, Bayer sells aspirin at ten times the price at which it sells in India. . . . Yet Indian enterprises cannot—are not allowed to—export to Switzerland or other countries where Swiss companies operate. . . . The discussions on which restrictions should be maintained and which should be dropped took place when we were negotiating the Code of Conduct on Transnational Corporations. . . . Unfortunately, this is one of the issues on which the negotiations on the code broke down. If we could have achieved this in the field of pharmaceuticals, it would have been a great precedent."

In 1971, ECOSOC asked the UN Secretary-General to appoint a group of eminent persons to study the impact of multinational corporations. The initiative was prescient because the topic would soon become hot following the involvement of International Telephone and Telegraph (ITT) in the overthrow in 1973 of the first elected socialist government in Chile of President Salvador Allende. Sotiris Mousouris worked on that effort and recalled: "The under-secretary-general of the Department of Economic and Social Affairs was then a brilliant Frenchman, Philippe de Seynes. . . . With enthusiasm and a lot of imagination, he responded to that mandate. He asked me to join his small team when I produced an outline of a study on multinationals, and I proposed a list of names to serve as eminent persons who were supposed to conduct hearings on the issue and submit proposals. Frankly, to produce the list, I consulted for a couple of hours a weekend in Boston with my professor, Raymond Vernon, who had published a year before *Sovereignty at Bay*."[15]

Mousouris stated the logic behind the UN's effort: "The multinationals had become new powerful actors in the world stage but they were not fully accountable to any state. They had their own logic and goals, and the impact of their operations on their home or their host countries was not understood. They were challenging the authority of elected governments and could influence international relations. And the big question, of course, was what effect they had on development, on developing countries."

Mousouris remembered a dinner with de Seynes in Geneva at the Hotel du Rhône: "He used the words 'demystification,' 'accountability,' and 'rules of the game.' We also talked about political intervention by giant corporations. The ITT case in Chile was very fresh in everybody's mind. They could overthrow regimes democratically elected. . . . That is the first thing that bothered him. The second is the effect they had on developing countries. He was uneasy that nobody knew exactly what was the result of their operations, the impact of their operations on the economies of these countries. We were worried that unless we clarified this impact, some developing countries would take extreme measures, like nationalization and appropriation . . . that would not have been beneficial to their economies. We wanted to identify the pros and the cons, what is good and what is bad, to maximize the positive and minimize the negative. And also to see what is the effect on labor, the effect on the environment, the effect on human rights, the effect on consumers. . . . We were pioneers. In fact, the issue of human rights was one of the provisions of the code of conduct that we started negotiations [about] soon after the commission and the center were established."

"I think, in retrospect, Philippe de Seynes saw a movement towards globalization and he thought that globalization needed some rules," Mousouris said. "The rules would be formulated, should be formulated, by the international community, taking into account the interest of all, both the host and home countries, and the interest of development, and the interest, of course, of private enterprises, because they create technology, they create jobs, they are engines of growth and so on and so forth. We wanted, let's say, an optimization of the functioning of transnationals in the world. . . . It was a pity. It was the first effort to introduce some rules of the game for what we call now 'globalization.' . . . Now, in retrospect, I think the developing countries made a big mistake in insisting on certain things, because we could have had a code of conduct by 1980, which would be extremely useful now."

Klaus Sahlgren, who served as the executive director of the UN Centre for Transnational Corporations from 1975 until the mid-1980s, praised the originality and quality of the intellectual work by the eminent persons: "A very original and welcome idea . . . a group of expert advisors coming partly from the academic world, partly from business, and partly from trade unions to assist the intergovernmental commission. This I found challenging and innovative. . . . As to the substance, there was among the eminent persons a kind of a feeling that we should start on a new foot. There was less talk about the New International Economic Order. It was a more businesslike approach, and I very much liked that."

Sahlgren recounted an anecdote from a different high-level gathering: "I can tell you a little story about the pope, who visited New York. Waldheim arranged a reception and everybody—all the ASGs [assistant secretaries-general] and USGs [under-secretaries-general]—could pay their respects to His Holiness. When my turn came, I said, 'I am Klaus Sahlgren, and I work on transnationals.' 'Oh, I heard about it,' said the pope. I said, 'Yes. Your Holiness is at the head of the biggest transnational of them all.' Then somebody from his staff interrupted me and said, 'Next one, please.'"

Sahlgren rued the decision in the 1990s to move what had been the independent unit of the Secretariat in New York to Geneva within the UNCTAD secretariat because it failed "to keep a neutral, impartial image in the eyes of its clients, which were both West and South, and also business. Now to put it in UNCTAD, which had and still has, I believe, a public image of being the part of the UN which mainly interests itself in the problems of the developing countries, was a tactical mistake."

The Least Developed Countries

By the late 1960s, the plight of the poorest and most disadvantaged countries became impossible to ignore in spite of the fear among developing countries that any weakening of Third World solidarity would open the way for the North to "divide and conquer" the South. In 1970 the UN's Committee for Development Planning established a working group to identify the hardcore poorest countries in order to make them eligible for special aid, trade, and investment measures. Statistics being statistics, country data was disputed. Equally controversial were the criteria used to identify the poorest countries. Finally, three dimensions were selected: low per capita income (less than $100 in 1968), low contribution of manufacturing to GDP (less than 10 percent), and low adult literacy (less than 20 percent). These led to the identification of twenty-four countries as "least developed" in 1971. Since that time, more accurate statistical measurements have become available. This, together with the economic setbacks and deteriorating conditions in many developing countries during the 1980s and 1990s, has more than doubled the number of least developed countries. Three ad hoc global conferences (in Paris in 1981 and in 1990 and in Brussels in 2001) have highlighted the problems of these countries and made agreements possible about a host of special measures on their behalf. What started as a controversial notion has become an accepted part of international policy.[16]

From the mid-1970s until 2001, the UN system's work on least developed countries was centered in UNCTAD, but after 2002 the special programmatic focus was transferred to the UN Secretariat in New York. Paul Berthoud recalled the origins of the idea: "Jack Stone is the father of the least developed countries concept. In terms of development of ideas, this is a fellow who has made a major contribution. That idea sticks. Much of UNCTAD's wash is gone, but the concept of the least developed countries is still there."

Jack Stone—who was director of the Research Division in UNCTAD when the category was launched and subsequently directed the Special Program for Least Developed Countries—recalled the struggle to get this idea accepted:

"There had apparently been resistance from the beginning to efforts to specifically identify these countries, which had been put forward in UNCTAD I in 1964 as a category requiring special measures. It was said that every agency in the UN system and every division in UNCTAD should emphasize work on the least developed countries [LDCs] . . . yet without specifically or officially labeling a group of countries as 'least developed.' Presumably, countries could put forward on their own their claims to have special measures apply to themselves. . . . Since such a system could only lead to merely paying lip service to the category without any meaningful action, the UN Secretariat tried a few initiatives to identify a list, but without immediate success. Any specific proposals put forward were at best taken note of and sent back for further study. In the early days, the opposition to formal identification was mainly from India and some of the large Latin American countries, who were afraid specific identification would leave them out and divide the Group of 77. . . . But eventually, later as the LDC group grew and got more political strength, the LDCs and the other 77 preached accommodations."

Surendra Patel recalled how the pragmatic emphasis on least developed countries emerged at UNCTAD III in Santiago: "It took a few more years to formulate trade policies and international aid programs for LDCs. It was from 1972 onwards that UNCTAD set up a unit devoted to assist LDCs in their negotiations. This provoked both good and bad results. One of the problems that emerged was that it divided the developing countries' stand. In my opinion it was nonetheless important to pay special attention to LDCs."

Dharam Ghai, who during much of this time was conducting research on basic human needs in East Africa and in Geneva, questioned the utility of such an idea: "Even if there were total trade liberalization, foreign capital inflows, good behavior by multinationals, and a transfer of technology, it would not make a hell of a lot of difference for the poorest countries. . . . I was not too popular, because they said, 'You are driving a wedge in the unity of the developing countries.' I always said, 'Unity has to be based on a diversified package which will cater to the needs of all.' And the least developed countries are the ones that need more help than anybody else. Not only from rich countries but also from developing countries as well."

Gamani Corea was a member of the CDP when it agreed on the criteria for what constituted a least developed country. He told us: "I myself had some misgivings about the political strategy of subdividing the Third World, of having a subgroup. Whether this was intended to create a special outlet for good treatment by the rich countries in order to show that they are meeting the most urgent cases, I don't know. . . . Well, one of the things I wanted to make sure of was that there would be no division within the developing country camp between the G-77 and the least developed countries. I suggested that all the proposals, resolutions and so on should be in the name of all the G-77, not just the least developed countries. . . . It is a tragedy that the number of least developed countries has increased. It is a very telling commentary on international cooperation for development."

Adebayo Adedeji was more cynical about the uses and misuses of this concept and asked rhetorically, "Poverty dehumanizes, doesn't it? What I have discovered to my horror was that many countries would very much like to be classified as LDC . . . so as to have access to soft loans and grants earmarked for this group of countries. And they are rather shameless about it." Perhaps, but acceptance of classification is also an indication of the power of an idea. Unlike Groucho Marx, who did not want to be a member of a club that would have him, being a member of the "least developed countries club" entailed benefits greater than the disadvantages of being stigmatized as such.

Basic Needs and Redistribution

Although "development" had already begun to be conceived more broadly than mere increases in GDP in the previous decade, nonetheless the 1970s marked a sea change in emphasis. The most fundamental needs of individuals on the bottom of the economic ladder became a central issue.[17] The ILO hammered out a basic needs-oriented development strategy, the World Bank adopted that approach and worked on redistribution with growth, and UNRISD did interesting work on a so-called unified approach. Social and cultural factors entered the game at par with economic considerations. The 1972 ILO employment report on Kenya[18] pioneered the notions of redistribution from growth and the informal sector, which inspired the work on redistribution with growth and basic needs.

The strategy that emerged amounted to an emphasis on meeting the needs of all of a country's citizens rather than being satisfied by an undifferentiated growth of GDP. Giving a priority to securing adequate food, elementary education, and primary health care was in many ways designed to compensate for earlier strategies that had merely emphasized growth without taking into account who benefited and how. In short, basic needs posited that it was important to consider whether aid and investment helped the proverbial man or woman on the street in urban and rural areas.

As a result of research and through a series of UN gatherings in the 1970s, basic needs were defined in terms of food, housing, clothing, education, and public transport. Employment was both a means and an end, and participation in decision making was included. The first task was to quantify basic needs for a target year, for instance twenty-five years in the future, which allowed the GDP to be quantified for that year.[19] This in turn made possible the calculation of the annual rate of economic growth required between the base and the target years as well as the necessary redistribution effort. This approach reversed conventional practice, which was to project a desirable annual rate of per capita economic growth into the future. The latter was a forward rolling approach while the basic needs approach was much more precise by setting specific production targets and deriving from those figures the desirable rate of growth and income distribution.[20]

Several of our voices were directly involved in analytical efforts to change the paradigm. In the mid-1970s, Amartya Sen went to work for the ILO and the World Employment Programme. Sen's research was part of the ILO's ongoing efforts to define what became known as "basic needs" and drew on his earlier experience with the Bengal famine. In his interview, Sen remarked: "First of all, let me say two positive things about basic needs. One is that it often makes excellent and immediate sense. Consider the idea that if you are dying of starvation, what you basically need is some food. This is surely an absolutely elementary point. So underlying the basic needs approach, there is a tremendous foundation of common sense. Not surprisingly, even though the term as such hadn't been used, the idea of minimum needs was very extensively written about by [Arthur] Pigou in his 1920s book *The Economics of Welfare*.[21]

"The second point to note is that the basic needs approach did a great deal in challenging both the focus of many theorists on something very abstract, like utility, and the focus of many worldly wise guys on something very concrete but very inadequate in coverage, namely just income and wealth. Of course, utility and income both can be very important in social analysis. But the basic needs approach told the world to focus on something more immediate, more elementary, and more directly relevant.

"All these approaches make good sense up to a point. Think of a famine. Obviously people suffer from starvation and may die, and a utility theorist may wish to see this all in terms of lack of utility. It is a possible view, but the basic needs approach asks us to be more specific. A famine is not only an epidemic of disutility, it is an epidemic of starvation. Similarly, income is central to famines. We know from the studies of famines that many of us have done that lack of income is often the basic reason underlying starvation. So the income approach does make sense too—indeed very good sense as well. And yet the basic needs approach is right to take us beyond the preeminence of income as a general-purpose means to more specific needs for food, clothing, shelter, medicine, and so on. While the income approach works well up to a point in famine theory (my own work on famines is very concerned with the generation of income, particularly through employment), we have to go beyond it in dealing with health care, medical arrangements, and ultimately ways and means of recreating a healthy economy with good educational and health services.

"The basic needs approach does, therefore, take us in the right direction. But we have to go beyond it as well, and in particular move away from its focus on commodities towards taking note of capabilities. Two persons may have exactly the same goods (same amounts of food, clothing, etc.), and yet one may have a physical disability or a proneness to illness, which can make him or her more deprived than the person who is not thus handicapped. The things we are able to do and be—our capabilities—depend both on the commodity basket that we can manage to get but also on our physical problems, our genetic differences, our environmental situations (related for example to local crimes and the presence or absence of epidemics in the region, in addition to physical climates), and so on. Also, the basic needs approach tends to see people as 'needy' beings—it is the view of human beings as 'patients' rather than as people whose 'freedoms' matter, the view of human beings as 'agents' who can do things. So we have to go beyond the commodity-centered basic needs approach without denying the important contribution it has made in advancing the public dialogues on social assessment and political priorities." Sen's intellectual journey in this area led to his prize-winning book *Poverty and Famines* (1981) and to *Commodities and Capabilities* (1985).[22]

Dharam Ghai also worked intensely on these issues. He underlined the 1972 report on Kenya because "it clarified the nature of the employment problem in developing countries—that we are not talking of people who are openly unemployed, as in industrial countries. We are talking about people who may be working, or apparently working, but with very low incomes and low-productivity jobs. There are also people who are grossly overworked, among them rural women, who obtain very low returns for their labor. . . . It argued that the major task of development policy is to ensure that everybody has a certain minimum standard of living. In fact, this was, if I may say so, my own idea. Subsequently, it developed into the basic needs approach."

Hans Singer's contribution to the Kenya employment report was critical, according to many of our voices. He was the first person to introduce the concept of "redistribution from growth." Singer recalled how he arrived at this: "Well, like any other economist I thought about the welfare effects of unequal income distribution and that, by redistribution of income, you could increase welfare. That was inherent in the Beveridge report. I'd been brought up to study Pigou and inequality quite carefully. I was very impressed by

Thorstein Veblen on conspicuous consumption, on the way in which inequality of incomes creates useless consumption. I was very impressed by Keynes' essays on the 'Economics of our Grandchildren'—where he also said that once you reach a certain income level, further increases in income become really useless. It's more useful to devote your mind to other things, to arts or leisure or philosophy.... The general idea (of redistribution from growth) was there, but with the hindsight of today, I would probably express it in a slightly different way—not redistribution *from* growth, not even redistribution *with* growth but . . . a certain *pattern* of growth. The pattern of growth matters. There are different kinds of growth; some of them reduce inequality and poverty and others don't. We want to create a certain pattern of growth which after all contains the essence of redistribution from growth."

Margaret Anstee claimed that the origin for the idea resulted not from work in Kenya in the 1970s but from Bolivia in the 1960s: "Yes, well the interesting thing about the National Economic & Social Development Plan (1962–71) was that it was—I know Louis [Emmerij] wouldn't mind my saying this—it was really about basic needs. That approach wasn't invented in the ILO conference or its employment conference some years later.... The whole matrix was built up on estimations of how many calories per day were needed, how many hospital beds, how many schools, how many yards of cloth, how many pairs of shoes." Anstee recalled the origins of early development plans as part of efforts to help identify priorities for basic needs: "The whole idea of the plan on which our UN team was working was to restart development, but development on a more equitable basis."

Whatever the origins, the basic needs development strategy was given a public policy boost when the ILO was in the midst of preparing for the World Employment Conference. Indeed, one could argue that the idea of "basic needs" can be dated back to the psychology literature of the 1940s. The best-known publication in this connection was the article by Abraham Maslow in the *American Psychological Review* of March 1942.[23] Later, in India during the 1950s, the concept of "minimum needs" was used within the Indian Planning Commission, with the creative contributions by Pitambar Pant. However, Paul Streeten stressed that "Pitambar Pant thought that the poorest ten or fifteen percent are the unemployables—the disabled, the lame ducks, chronically sick, the permanently ill, the mentally defective, the old. He thought that they had to be written off. He was not very interested in social services; he was interested in employment creation and growth. Therefore, he did not really consider how to meet the needs of those who cannot contribute to raising productivity; . . . he was very much a growth man. He thought that basic needs and employment can be achieved only through economic growth. He believed that income distribution was fixed." It is not surprising, therefore, that the idea of a basic needs–oriented development strategy did not become mainstream in those days.

In many ways the difficulty of giving credit to the birth of an idea to any one person or institution can be illustrated by the fact that the basic needs idea was elaborated in three different places almost simultaneously: in the Dag Hammarskjöld Foundation's 1975 publication *What Now?*;[24] in the 1976 Latin American Bariloche project;[25] and in the ILO's World Employment Programme in 1976.[26] Common to all three was an emphasis on the guts of the idea, namely that employment creation was not conceived as an end in itself but as a means to fulfill the basic needs of individuals—more or less equivalent to Maslow's first rung on his five-rung ladder, the last being the fulfillment of cultural needs. Many people were already on the second, third, fourth, and even fifth rungs, but others were not even in sight of the ladder. Designing a development strategy whose main objective was meeting basic needs, including those of the poorest 20 percent of the population, would eventually become a reality.

Not surprisingly, in most cases the required rate of economic growth to fully meet basic need targets was unrealistically high by historical standards— well over 8 percent per annum over twenty-five years. East Asia has subsequently achieved such rates, but in the mid-1970s the East Asian miracle lay ahead. And so the only alternative that could achieve the targets of basic needs was to work on the rate of economic growth *and* income distribution. Analysis at that time revealed that "redistribution from growth"—that is, marginal redistribution of future increases of income rather than redistribution of existing wealth—could satisfy basic needs targets with an annual rate of economic growth of 6 percent.

When this package was presented at the 1976 World Employment Conference, it was greeted with enthusiasm. The two exceptions were the U.S. delegation and some of the employer representatives from other industrialized countries, who were concerned that such an emphasis would slow overall growth and profits. By the end of the 1970s it looked as if a more appropriate development strategy had been designed that effectively combined economic growth, productive employment, and basic needs. At the core of the strategy was the shift to a pattern of economic growth that is both more employment-intensive, more equitable, and more effective in the battle against poverty. Several of our voices saw this as one of the most essential changes in thinking about development.

Francis Blanchard was the ILO's director-general at the time of its 1976 World Employment Conference that launched the basic needs development strategy. He looks back and ahead: "What's astonishing, without being encouraging, is to note that today, twenty-five years after the World Employment Conference, the World Bank and the IMF have taken on as part of their mandate the themes of poverty, that they have adopted the language the ILO used in 1976 to advocate voluntarist policies in the struggle against poverty and for satisfying the basic needs of the poorest. But today just as yesterday the political will is lacking, and there is no real coherence among the international agencies that make up what is referred to as the United Nations system."

Paul Berthoud grouped basic needs under what he called "collective economic security" and said: "This was an interesting idea. I think it was a sort of *feu de paille,* as we say in French, or a flare. But in any history of the ideas at the United Nations, I would hate to see it being omitted." Sartaj Aziz looked back at efforts to think about broadening the scope of basic needs at a 1965 conference of economists, where a key role was played by Lady Jackson (at the time Barbara Ward): "Surprisingly, it was Barbara Ward who brought out the neglect of the social dimension of development." He recalled her asking the group: "So you have achieved all this growth, but what has happened to income distribution?" Aziz recalled the group's response: "We said, 'We are looking at those things. We have a committee on this and a committee on that.' But it came out very clearly that income distribution had become worse and we had not devoted enough money to the social sectors. . . . The ideas that were scattered suddenly returned. All the economists, including many Western economists, conceded the same point, that development has to be meaningful in the larger interest of the people. There is a very beautiful quote in the Columbia [University] Declaration [of 1970] that says this in a very succinct way: 'Criteria are also needed which focus on the living standards of the bottom quarter of each country's population. We also suggested setting up of a special fund devoted specifically to the fulfillment of social objectives in the area[s] of education, health, family planning, rural and urban works, housing, and other related social programs.'[27] . . . So suddenly all the ideas, the conflicts, the contradictions that were floating around in our minds from 1965 onwards found a coherent framework."

Just Faaland devoted much of his career to economic analysis and noted that Norway's interest in development revolved "very much around [the] history of getting rid of poverty through development. And there is a built-in unhappiness in the realization that so many human beings live so miserably throughout the world, coupled with a realization that you can do something about it if we get ourselves organized. . . . Therefore, it was quite natural that a group working on development here at the [Christian Michelsen] Institute came to try to focus on what we later called 'basic needs.'"

Fernando Henrique Cardoso observed that "even without a revolution it was possible to make some progress. I was so sick of the discussion on dependency and development that I tried to create new labels to understand the realities in this part of the world." Why was basic needs so important a conceptual breakthrough? Because "during the 1970s, it was very difficult to have a nondeterministic approach."

There was a critical discussion about the basic needs strategy within the group of people who took responsibility for implementing it. According to Ignacy Sachs, "It is certainly legitimate to oppose the logic of needs to the logic of the market. And thus to argue in favor of real needs rather than of financial means, to argue in terms of the rights of one or another group and not whether they have the financial solvency that permits them to buy one product or another."

Dharam Ghai, considered at least a midwife of basic needs if not one of its originators, summarized the change in thinking over the course of the 1970s: "The notion of development has been expanded further to include emphasis on certain groups that are left out of the development process—women, children, ethnic minorities, racial groups, people in remote areas, indigenous people. All this has now become very much part of what we talk of as development. People never thought of those things. Environmental issues have also come in. You have to think of sustainability of natural resources. Human rights are becoming more and more central. . . . So in all these ways, the notion of development has been enriched. . . . Anyone who has worked in Africa knows that unless the political system is right, the government structures are right, that there is reasonable accommodation, that there is tolerance, that there is compromise and consensus among key groups—unless you are able to achieve this pluralistic system and a reasonable acceptance of the interests of different groups, you are in trouble. . . . So in other words, we now see development as a much more complex affair then it was thought of in the early postwar decades. Development has many dimensions. The very objectives of development are multifold. It is not GDP. It is not industrialization. It is a lot more complicated."

Women and Gender

Although they were scarcely visible on the UN's early agenda—except, of course, in the eyes of female staff members—women's and gender issues have become far more central to international relations, UN affairs, and development over the last three decades. The four world conferences on women convened by the UN changed the perspective of many people: in 1975 (in Mexico),

1980 (in Copenhagen), 1985 (in Nairobi), and 1995 (in Beijing). Each has marked a different stage of a process that has elevated gender equality to the center of the global agenda. These conferences on women have also highlighted the contribution of NGOs in advocating that a gender perspective and a feminist consciousness must be included in development policies and strategies. Devaki Jain, whose book in the UNIHP series is devoted to this topic,[28] summarized: "From women being a component, we are now of that view that women should lead development rather than women asking to be integrated into development."

Looking back at the century from his apartment in Paris, Celso Furtado told us: "If called upon to classify the most striking events of the century, the most profound, I would put in first place the evolution in the position of women." He added that in a globalizing world driven by the monotonous pursuit of commercial profits, "the emergence of women. . . . and more important still, of civil society as a whole" have been key elements.

Peg Snyder recalled the tenor of the times before the conferences: "About being a feminist, one must remember that we are speaking of the 1950s, a decade before the second wave of feminism rose in the U.S., which is usually identified as 1968. I think, therefore, that 'professional women' is a more appropriate identification—and that was revolutionary enough in the 1950s." However, she was quick to point out that her fieldwork in Africa in the early 1960s revealed that "there were roots of the global women's movement [there as well]. Each region—Asia, Africa, Latin America," she asserted, "had its own roots of what would become the global women's movement. Yet some people say that the global women's movement came from Western women. . . . [African] women were beginning to think of Africa as a whole, and they were beginning to think of women as working side by side with men in their independent countries and wanting to define what their roles would be."

Snyder noted that within the ECA's African Centre for Women, which she founded, "we were very, very careful in the vocabulary we used. We never used any of the women's lib vocabulary. We always spoke of women in agriculture or women in trade. We always used Africa's own kinds of vocabulary. And at that time, it was difficult because what was drifting back from the U.S. and in the Western press was all the extremist feminism. In Addis, we didn't talk about women *in* development, we talked about women *and* development, which is a distinction that keeps from using the acronym WID. I think the Americans claim the acronym, and well they might."

Elise Boulding chortled about another early change in language: "Margaret Mead and I used to, in those early years . . . make speeches about women as the housekeepers of the world. We wouldn't use that language now, but that was the right language at that time."

Leticia Shahani, a former UN assistant secretary-general who also served as secretary-general of the second global conference in 1985, noted with some irony the situation that had prevailed at the first UN World Conference on Women ten years earlier: "Mexico was the host government, and the bias of the Mexican government and the foreign ministry was obvious—they couldn't allow a woman to chair. Yes, Mexico was the host government of the first-ever World Conference on Women. But I guess that's how the world was then."

In the two decades between the first conference in Mexico City in 1975 and the last one in Beijing twenty years later,[29] the perception of the role of women in development changed substantially. With regional differences, the struggle for women's right to full and equal resources and opportunities met with some successes in the realm of public consciousness. A similar transformation was taking place in development thinking; the shift was from an earlier belief that development served to advance all people, including women, to a new consensus that development for all was not possible without conscious attention to gender (that is, socially defined roles for men and women that are only partially based on their sex) and equity—and that this would only be possible with the full participation of women. As the UNDP's *Human Development Report* argued in 1995, "unless development is engendered, it is endangered. . . . The new world order would thus put people—both women and men—clearly at the center of all development processes. Only then can human development become fully engendered."[30]

Despite the move toward this new consensus, the struggle to engender development was hardly monolithic. Noeleen Heyzer recalled the variety among her earliest female colleagues when she was a fellow at the Institute of Development Studies in 1979: "They inspired me with their courage to merge silent issues and women's analysis. They were also the people who first valued my work. But I also felt a kind of arrogance, which they had at that time, although it is so much better now. They felt that their interpretation of history and of their experience was universal. The whole struggle and dialogue on feminism at that time was the location of women's oppression. And the feminists' analysis in the West at that time was that it rested in the family. Yet in my experience, it was more complex than that. . . . There was a big discussion about women's biology, about motherhood, and children. I enjoyed motherhood and children when these were not fashionable in Western feminist circles. I eventually felt that I had to go back to Asia, because for me it was more than an intellectual discussion. I had to get out of 'are you right,' 'are you wrong,' and 'are we clashing because of ideology?' I was not interested in rigid ideological positions in feminism, in politics, nor in religion. I was more interested in bringing about better ways of living and interrelating in this world, working from grounded reality. I felt I needed to get back to the reality of women's lives, the stories, the textures, and the silences. Knowing the lives of both women and men, I did not want to ascribe power to men as an undifferentiated whole. Rather, I wanted to understand the dynamics of power, different kinds of power, as well as patriarchal power that devalued and commoditized women."

Making room for nuances in the women's movement reminded Heyzer of the continuum of religious institutions: "There is so much diversity, so many differences in practice, so that you can't talk about one Islam. It is the same with Christianity, with Hinduism, with Buddhism. That diversity has been extremely useful for women."

The voice of Leticia Shahani also did not minimize differing perspectives among women: "Western feminists," she recalls, "were saying [that] all you need are daycare centers, family planning, equal pay for equal work. But the Third World women were saying, 'Oh no, firewood is politics, water is politics, the North-South issues are politics, the conditionalities of the IMF are part of the lives of women and therefore women's issues.'"

Peg Snyder summed up the proliferation of approaches: "I think there are almost as many feminisms as there are people—not quite as many as that, but there are many feminisms." She also allowed that there were a variety of roles: "The more radical feminists—the bra-burning type of radical feminists—do a service: somebody has to be out there ahead and be shot at so that the others can move up."

Molly Bruce directed the staff and program of the Commission on the Status of Women from 1962 to 1977 and provided a different historical perspective. "Eleanor Roosevelt wasn't an ardent feminist," Bruce remembered. "Eleanor was one of those who thought that if you improved human rights, women's position would automatically be improved. . . . Eleanor's views changed somewhat, because [what] the women on the Status of Women Commission were saying was that the Human Rights Commission was so bogged down or had so big an agenda with the international bill of rights and the procedure they had set up for handling violations of human rights in the beginning that they wouldn't have time to deal with women's rights." Bruce also pointed out that the UN was not starting *de novo* because her staff "began from the point at which the League of Nations had left off and studied the legal status of women, particularly in family law. Very good work was done in setting standards at this time. Many recommendations were addressed to governments and three conventions were adopted on political rights of women, nationality of married women, and consent to marriage and minimum age of marriage, as well as both a declaration and convention on the elimination of discrimination against women."

At about the same time in Mexico, Lourdes Arizpe came to a realization that "grew out of the creeping perception we women had of being ignored and marginalized in leading and taking decisions, yet being equally tortured, imprisoned, and killed in 1968. . . . We were never listened to in the assemblies. Women were simply not given the floor, and we were not expected to have any ideas or to be able to express them. So feminism, sparked by the second wave in the U.S. and UK spread very quickly in Mexico among those of us who began to perceive the inequalities within the revolution. We began working in small *grupos de concientisación,* as they were called. We organized meetings; we started the first-ever Mexican feminist journal, *Fem,* which became the axis of the history of feminism in Mexico. . . . I had gotten very interested in women and development after I had found that the majority of rural migrants in Mexico were women. But when in Latin American meetings I insisted that tertiarization and informalization were a predominantly female phenomenon, I got benevolent smiles and unfunny jokes."

Although observers—especially those in the U.S. Congress and conservative think tanks in Washington—dismiss many international negotiations as the preoccupation of a developmental upper class, the four conferences on women have involved remarkable cross-cutting coalitions of socioeconomic groupings from North and South.[31] Undoubtedly, the effect on changing awareness and programs for women and men in many countries has been dramatic, although there is still more to do. Virendra Dayal admitted openly what clearly was the case for other voices: "I was pretty much an ignoramus on issues concerning women until one of these conferences did a bit of consciousness raising. . . . Whether it was the Bella Abzugs on the one hand or some nice genteel lady from India or from China, a kind of sisterhood came into existence—an awful lot of men began to understand what they were talking about."

Jan Pronk pointed both to the direct influence of these ideas on Dutch policy and the cumulative impact of conferences: "We had a strong feminist movement, here in the Netherlands, emanating from the 1960s. This resulted in much action around the UN women's conference in Mexico, 1975. I was asked to lead the Netherlands delegation, because the theme of the conference was women and development. We were able to focus on problems of women in the West as well as on often quite different problems of women in Africa, Asia, Latin America, and the Middle East. . . . On that basis, one of my successors as a minister for development cooperation, Eegje Schoo, made this a priority issue in development policy."

Similarly, Sartaj Aziz noted that the UN's conceptions about the role of women in development had a direct impact on the official policies at various governmental levels in Pakistan: "We have now a very strong women's move-ment fighting for their rights. There are women activists and NGO groups and also lawyers' groups which have been created primarily to protect women against violence and injustice. . . . We have implemented many of the conven-tions. For example, we now have women's police stations in all parts of the country. . . . We have the Women's Bank, which is the first bank that lends only to women. . . . The total number of female schools opened in this ten-year period is double the rate for males."

A number of the more outspoken voices on women and on gendering de-velopment, not surprisingly, are higher pitched. Elise Boulding spoke of ef-forts to link constituencies: "We met at Margaret Mead's office to talk about how to organize this women-to-women touring process so that women around the world would all get to learn about each others' lives, find out about each other's needs and how we could work together. . . . There was a continuing and growing volume of networking among women so that the ingredients for International Women's Year really came out of the International Year of Co-operation and the networking that happened then. . . . At the same time as the UN network was developing, there were national women's secretariats being set up in many member states of the UN. So for the first time you had women having something like a ministry of women's affairs in many countries. There was significant feedback between the processes of women being recognized by their own governments and UN recognition and the women's movement at the grassroots level. The timing was right and the levels were connected, so . . . the grassroots aspect counted."

"One of the things that happened as a result of International Cooperation Year—and that really prepared the way for International Women's Year—was the Women's Tribunal on Crimes Against Women," Boulding told us. "Women first began laying out for the world to see the practices of rape and violence against women, which was not a public issue before that time. UNESCO then held a conference on violence against women. . . . But that violence has been so much a part of the pattern of patriarchal society over the centuries that it is a very slow process to develop that kind of awareness. . . . The recent decision at the UN to declare rape a war crime is a great step ahead."

Lourdes Arizpe explained the discursive and conceptual shift from "women" to "gender": "The construction of gender in every society is a cultural con-vention. There are obviously—I would not deny it—biological, physiologi-cal, even psychological predispositions that are different between women and men. But the way in which these differences are constructed socially will de-pend on the culture of every society. In that sense, cultural analysis is a uni-versal instrument of understanding, because through culture you can see exactly how gender is constructed, how 'Indian-ness' is constructed, how race is constructed, how sexual preference discrimination is constructed."

Noeleen Heyzer agreed: "The word 'gender relations' grew out of the discussion by women who believed that you cannot just look at women's lives in isolation from the relationship between women and men. This relationship is culturally and socially constructed. Therefore, one needs to look at the social construction of this relationship. . . . This complex idea, in a sense, got incorporated into the work of development agencies, including the bilateral donors. They wanted a way of doing development work that would bring women in. They developed what was called 'gender analysis.'"

Heyzer also traced the debate about women and development: "The Mexico meeting looked at women and their roles. For the first time, Esther Boserup talked about women's role in the economy and women's participation. The debate focused initially on the lack of women's participation in the economic systems. Many people said, 'But women have always been participating.' The issue is not the integration of women into development or the economy. Women were already integrated, but they were undervalued. Their work was not recognized, they were not supported. . . . The issue became one of equal access: how do you make sure that women have equal access to the opportunities and the rewards of development? The focus then shifted to access over resources and benefits."

Some, however, like Heyzer herself, now question the move away from women to the idea of gender in development discourse: "Personally, I have a problem with the way that gender analysis has developed. I find it very static. Basically it is a quick fix. And this is a real problem. You generate an analysis and you train people in it—the tools of gender analysis. In every project you did your gender analysis. You mapped out access, the politics of access—who gets what, who did what, and so on. You keep in your head that there is a group 'men' and there is a group 'women.' And you are always looking at these two groups as though they were undifferentiated. You also set yourself up for dualistic confrontational categories—not all men oppress women and not all women are supportive of each other. The relationships between men and women are more complex. . . . Women themselves are differentiated, and so are men. Complexity and diversity are not captured. The dynamics of power is not really understood. I constantly try to go back and say, 'Let's try to capture the complexity, and the dynamics of different kinds of power.' . . . Also of human tendencies like jealousy and competition. In some cases gender analysis is useful, but in other cases you need to use other analysis to capture how patterns of social and gender subordination and emancipation are reproduced."

Devaki Jain also wondered whether the emphasis on gender had become counterproductive: "Many of us, including me, are thinking that the word 'gender' has been a problem. It has diverted attention from women's struggle for rights. It's an analytical tool, but it is now becoming a way of referring to women. So you do gender budgets—the question is have you gendered that, have you gendered this—which means that you are looking at the difference between men and women in data or in impact. But it has sort of become synonymous with women, which is a mistake because women is an identity based on gender, but it is not gender. So we are now hearing, here in New York as well as the South, that we should be careful because by not using the word 'women,' the unity building of the women's movement is getting distracted."

Indeed, the treatment of gender identity and expression and sexual orientation is an emerging battleground of ideas at the United Nations that is sustained by human rights NGOs, on one side, and opposed by coalitions of fundamentalist forces composed of governments and religious institutions, on the other. Although most international treaty-monitoring bodies have understood human rights conventions to prohibit discrimination on the basis of gender expression and sexual orientation and while several global conferences have debated whether these should be protected human rights, none of the major international human rights treaties specifically mentions sexual orientation. Most recently, in 2004, the battle moved to the UN Commission on Human Rights, where a Brazilian-sponsored resolution seeking to condemn discrimination on the basis of sexual orientation as a violation of human rights was deferred twice. Thus, questions of gender identity and expression as universal human rights have broadened the discussion of gender well beyond women's rights.

Some of our male voices reflected about when they first became aware of women's and, subsequently for some, gender issues. Many came to understand these issues within the larger context of human rights and social justice and pointed to personal encounters with women who helped raise their awareness. Bernard Chidzero—whose mother brewed and sold beer to help with his educational expenses—recalled that "from early childhood I would have been aware of the economic role of women in African society. They are the people who plowed the fields. They are the people who maintained the homes while men were hunting or discussing issues at the '*dare*,' which is the forum where the men meet and discuss family, tribal, as well as state matters. Women have always been a power, certainly in the Shona society. . . . When did it first become obvious to me that the role of women would need to be recognized centrally as part of the development perspective? I think partly at the university, because—not in Ottawa but in Montreal where I was doing postgraduate study—boys and girls were equals. . . . Perhaps I can go back earlier, to South Africa, when in the National Union of South African Students boys and girls mixed freely to speak. . . . But I think the turning point for me was when I was in UNCTAD. . . . It was then, when I participated in the Brundtland Commission . . . it was clear that women were as competent, if not more competent."

Gert Rosenthal, who grew up a continent away, recalled his experience with the role of women in his culture: "I have a deep conviction of—I don't know whether to call it equality or social justice, which probably is born from the highly unjust circumstances of Guatemala . . . [which], frankly, is a racist society, probably not that different from South Africa. So for me, the gender issue or the ethnic issue are really matters of social justice." Yet he noted, "I felt for many years that putting gender on the front burner in the UN context was trivializing the topic—the feminist movement, gay rights. There is an element of faddism involved in all this." Nonetheless, Rosenthal thought that "the UN has made an important contribution in Latin America in this area. So there has been both the frivolous aspect and there has been a real contribution, to the point that today it is politically incorrect for any government in Latin America not to have at least one or two women in the cabinet or in Congress."

Alister McIntyre's voice specifically credited his encounters with Caribbean women in politics and at the university for changing his thinking "pretty much before the Beijing conference . . . partly because a Jamaican woman was involved in it at the UN—Lucille Mair. So Lucille, of course, I had known on campus. . . . She had a habit of discussing all of these issues with me. But the whole issue of gender and development had, of course, surfaced because there were a number of activists in the Caribbean. Nita Barrow, who became her country's ambassador in the UN, was very well known internationally. So was Lucille. . . . A lot of them came through the church system. . . . So on issues of gender and development I first became aware that it was no longer a lobby. It was now an issue that had to be addressed in a very systematic way. And when I got to the University [of West Indies after leaving the UN], I was very pleased to discover that a lot of thinking was going on among the young people—meaning the women. Some of the men—thankfully a minority— still said that this was a way of downsizing them, and so on. Now, it has become an article of faith."

Stéphane Hessel recalled that his introduction to ideas of women and development was "when we set up under the auspices of my Department of Social Affairs a Commission on the Condition of Women. . . . That was in the early 1950s, or even late 1940s. . . . And there were some rather terrible women sitting on that commission and we were rather afraid of their enthusiasm and their emphasis. . . . I have never been a feminist in the way that I feel that one has absolutely to fight because women are so underprivileged. . . . I feel that women in positions of power are extremely capable and I feel, perhaps, they bring to their jobs a greater charisma than men, perhaps because they have to justify the fact that although they are women they are on top."

Yet Hessel also expressed some concerns about the evolution in the struggle: "The fight for gender seems to me a little bit of an alibi. I am not contesting that there are situations for women in many areas of the world, and perhaps even in our own countries, which are not what they should be. But it is more important to me to look at *all* vulnerable groups—children as well as women, the underprivileged, the disabled—and not only always gender, gender, gender. So you see, on that I am not as staunch a defender of gender as I should be." However, he acknowledged that disparities remain: "And for a country like France, where women only achieved the right to vote in 1945, very recently, women still have to fight for their status and it is a proper fight. It is good that this fight continues. If it is not too vocal and too offensive, I think it is proper."

At the University of Toronto, Gerry Helleiner recalls his awareness about women and development: "I think it probably did not get through to me and to this country . . . for another ten years or so beyond Nairobi. I cannot recall any projects or requirements in private analysis that gender be taken into account until the mid-1980s, about 1982. It is quite recent that this has been central. I guess in my graduate development class it never featured very prominently. . . . I had a section on it the first time about seven or eight years ago, in the 1990s. It wasn't all that popular. People didn't seem to be that interested. But it was late. For me it was late. As an international issue it was in the late 1990s before it was taken on board."

Adebayo Adedeji was unequivocal about his preference for a no-nonsense view toward this issue: "I have no sentiments about gender at all. I look at it purely from the economic perspective. Personally, in my family, I could not tell you whether the resources I needed for my education and living came from my mother or my father. But I knew that it was not one-sided. My father was not the only one looking after my education. Of course, that enhanced my respect for my mother. I had schoolmates whose mothers were passive in terms of their development. Even my grandmother, as old as she was, would pay for many things without asking my parents. So I grew up in that kind of environment. . . . But as I developed, I realized that if we really want sustainable human development, we cannot disenfranchise 50 to 51 per cent of our population. It is like riding a cycle on one wheel. You will never get there."

Adedeji, with some pride, noted for the record that "the ECA was the first in the entire UN system to establish a Centre for Women and Development.

That predated, by a few months, the 1975 Mexico conference on women in development. . . . In Africa today, most of the farmers are women. The men specialize in producing export commodities. The women specialize on producing food. But 80 to 90 percent of investments in agriculture, for half a century or more, have been concentrated on export production rather than on food production. We are paying dearly for that now. And it is because of the lack of empowerment for women that we are now dependent on food imports. Greater facilities are available readily and extensive services are available readily for farmers producing for export. Of course, we can argue that the colonial government did not really have gender discrimination in mind. But its effect is the same."

As mentioned earlier, Peg Snyder was on the ground at the creation of the ECA's African Centre for Women and went on to also be UNIFEM's founding director: "I think that the global women's movement would be lost or at least much weaker without the UN. . . . I have more and more respect for leadership in that sense, of what a few strategically placed people can do by cooperating. . . . I think women captured the UN and made it their own vehicle for their movement to make sure that their movement was going to go ahead. In many ways, the UN was far ahead, say, in its definitions of development as a concept and a movement whose long-range goal is the well-being of society, the community of men, women, and children. . . . Yes, the UN was very much ahead."

John Ruggie, perhaps reflecting his convictions as a scholar, told us: "I first began to take it seriously—and I suspect I wasn't the only one—when serious research became available that demonstrated the actual consequences of development policies that were aimed specifically at women: the consequences for the savings rate in the family, for nutritional standards for the children, for civic organization in villages. Norms don't really take a hold while they remain purely at the level of concept. I think there has to be an experiential basis for them before they take root. . . . My sense is that that was certainly in place by the mid-1980s, if I had to put a date on it. By then it was no longer simply, 'I would like this to be the case and therefore I believe it.' It was an acceptance that this was the case and we really ought to pay attention."

The actual measurement of women's contributions has become an essential research requirement, in which Devaki Jain played a pioneering role. She pointed to the importance of decisions about the parameters of such research: "You have to analyze poverty in a gendered way—the gendered analysis of poverty, that women are located in a different poverty than men. It is not just the feminization of poverty, which is an outcome, which is how there are many more women amongst the poor than men. . . . The poor woman's experience of poverty leads you to different types of public action and policy than the poor man's experience of poverty. Poor women's choices of development are different. You know that famous one of women wanting fuel and fodder trees and men wanting orchards?"

Jain continued her analysis by underlining that development and economics are "about politics. So in Beijing the biggest pledge was that women have to come into power because it is only through power that you renegotiate the discrimination which you face. . . . When you analyze it from a feminist point of view, you actually challenge the very facts and theoretical propositions of that particular theory—economic theory, statistical classificatory systems, measuring tools, measurement hierarchies. So you are opening up a new world of how to analyze. We also argue that this form of analysis is useful not only for women but for all forms of discriminated people. . . . It's a form of looking at a new picture of discrimination and how it is embedded."

Leticia Shahani noted that perhaps one of the most important contributions of the UN to development was the establishment of indices to measure women's work. "There was Esther Boserup—she's dead now—but she used to be Denmark's representative to the Commission on the Status of Women. She was the one I first heard articulating the need to quantify women's unpaid work." Nafis Sadik added, "I had always had this idea of linking women's rights with family planning. But [the idea] to broaden the whole subject from family planning to reproductive health and make it into a rights approach has evolved." Clearly research and measurement have political ramifications.

Noeleen Heyzer parsed the reasons for the value of such research and pointed specifically to the emphasis on "mainstreaming" that emerged from the Fourth World Conference on Women: "This reflected the failure of the women's machineries to achieve significant results or influence policies. . . . Mainstreaming signifies a push towards a more systematic way of incorporating gender perspectives at all stages of policymaking and development practice. It is not just getting women's participation; you wanted women's realities and perspectives to influence development. But there was concern that women's perspectives basically can flow—in the words of Bella Abzug—into the 'polluted stream.' What you want is not to mainstream into the pollution; you want a clean stream. . . . People started talking about transformation, about structures of transformation. How do you transform development to be more empowering of women? For example . . . the worker has always been the male head of a household with a wife who can take care of all the servicing. . . . Female-headed households were seldom part of the picture when one talked of families."

What, then, is the bottom line on this critical issue for all, not half, of the human species? Following the first UN Conference on Women held in Mexico in 1975, gender equity, according to Leticia Shahani, "went global," and agencies that once neglected gender issues took them seriously as governmental and not just NGO issues. Even though the idea entered the UN through NGO pressures, the world organization, Shahani noted, "has kept it alive as a global movement through the Commission on the Status of Women, the Commission on Human Rights, ECOSOC, and the GA [General Assembly]. Every time a foreign minister comes to the General Assembly, he hears something about gender. . . . It has reached the General Assembly as well as the highest levels of government." She concluded, "That's one of the wonderful things that the UN can do—to put pressure on national governments to think and act on global issues which also affect domestic policies."

7

The 1980s: Development Frustrated

- **The Death of the North-South "Dialogue"**
- **The Debt Crisis and Adjustment: A Lost Decade**
- **The Washington "Consensus"**
- **The End of the Cold War and the Socialist Model**

The confrontational strategy of the 1970s to level the global playing field successfully brought many ideas to the international agenda. However, the battle scars from various struggles to redress global trade, financial, and technological inequalities between the Northern and Southern Hemispheres were clearly evident in the 1980s. The simultaneous ascendance of conservative leaders in the United States and the UK brought to a halt any forward motion on the ideas of the NIEO—in discourse and in practice. Instead, a new hegemony of Western liberalism fatally cracked the South's solidarity of the previous decade. The North-South dialogue was effectively killed at the 1981 session of the Conference on International Economic Cooperation in Cancún—the last of its kind. As Robert Cox summarily concluded, "The NIEO was killed by neoliberalism."

The Death of the North-South "Dialogue"

"The tragedy of Cancún was that the West produced Reagan and Thatcher," remarked Sonny Ramphal. The temporary rhetorical advantage and muscle flexing by developing countries as a result of the enhanced power of oil producers soon clashed head on with the election of Prime Minister Margaret "Iron Lady" Thatcher in the UK and Ronald Reagan in the United States. Many observers argue that the handwriting had been on the wall for some time. But the final nail in the coffin of the so-called dialogue was hammered at Mexico's Caribbean resort. James Jonah quipped that Washington and London said, "You Third World countries go to the market economy."

In spite of the avalanche of ideas proposed in the 1970s, the reaction that congealed in the 1980s abandoned or simply ignored much of what had gone before. Development in the 1980s was built more on market ideology than on facts and figures or basic needs. Ignacy Sachs lamented: "The loss of momentum, or rather the disappearance of the Non-Aligned Movement, is one of the great tragedies of the end of the 20th century."

In retrospect, what can be dubbed the "neoliberal revolution" of the early 1980s grew from three factors in addition to the political triumph of Thatcher-Reaganism: the crisis of inflation and Keynesian policies in the North; the global recession, balance-of-payments problems, and the debt crisis that threw into disarray development strategies in the South; and the growing internal contradictions of the socialist economies of the Eastern bloc. The widespread acceptance of financial- and market-oriented orthodoxy in the 1980s was based not on clear evidence of its effectiveness—after all, many of its tenets simply reemphasized the core of earlier liberal doctrine. Rather, it came as a reaction against previous interventionist policies and their failures.[1] A cynical vision of the state as a mechanism for rent-seeking and self-interest replaced the more upbeat Keynesian and developmentalist visions in which the state was a legitimate and purposeful contributor to growth objectives.[2]

Gamani Corea remembered a light moment from his experience at Cancún; one day he suddenly saw Ronald Reagan walking toward him across the lawn: "I have always categorized VIPs into two types," said Corea, "those who remind me of waiters and those who are somewhat better. Those who remind me of waiters look straight ahead; they don't want to catch your eye in case you trouble them with something or another. Reagan was not like that. . . . I gave my name, and I said I am from Sri Lanka and that I am the secretary-general of UNCTAD. I had grave doubts about whether he was familiar with either Sri Lanka or UNCTAD. . . . I didn't want to exceed the limits of my position and talk politics with him. So I turned to make polite conversation and I asked him, 'Mr. President, have you had the opportunity of taking a morning's swim here in Cancún?' He said, 'Oh yes, I did it in the days before the conference started, but since that time I couldn't do it.'"

A visibly uncomfortable Corea had to figure out a way to make conversation, but fortunately he was saved by the personable U.S. president. "I have not been to your country, but you must know I come from California, and in California—let me tell you that we wear the same suits during the evening that you would wear in Paris or London. The evenings are cool and we often sleep under blankets. Nowadays, you would be surprised at the kind of blankets you have. You can get a blanket where you can set the temperature you want it to attain when you get under it. When it warms up and arrives at the temperature set, it holds it there."

A perplexed Corea was uncertain what to do next as the president of the most powerful country on earth moved from electric blankets to tourism and was upset that Corea was unable to visit Acapulco: "But this is your chance. You're here now. Why don't you arrange to go to Acapulco?" Corea's explanation that he was supposed to accompany the UN Secretary-General back to New York was seemingly not enough: "I imagined that if we had gone on much longer he would have put a plane at my disposal!" Corea recalled. "The upshot of it was that I ended up liking this gentleman very much. You could speak to him. He had no idea of imposing his authority. I felt he could go on chatting as long as I was available. He was very, very relaxed and taking a genuine interest in the person he was talking to. So I thought, whatever his politics, this is a very likable man."

At the meeting itself, Corea recalled Reagan's sense of humor. "Pierre Trudeau was in the chair and said, 'I want to make a proposal, and that is that in our interventions we dispense with two things: saying thank-you to the host because we should do that collectively rather than individually, and dispensing with applause after each speech.' Reagan put his hand up and said, 'Mr. President, I'm really disturbed by what you just said because I come from a profession where the absence of applause is the surest sign of failure.'"

In reflecting on the Cancún conference, Kurt Waldheim recalled: "The efforts on both sides to overcome the difficulties and to agree on the principles of that economic order did not work. There was a very sad atmosphere when the conference finished after two days of hectic debate and no agreement could be reached."

Clearly the climate within which, in an earlier season, more radical ideas had blossomed had changed. Our voices recounted that the euphoria about the possibilities for structural change had faded, if not evaporated. One of the few initiatives during the 1980s that was in line with the 1970s was the creation of the South Commission under the chairmanship of Julius Nyerere, which published its report, *The Challenge to the South*.[3] The central idea was that developing countries together should be more self-reliant and thereby gain bargaining power through mutual cooperation. An independent research secretariat for the South was a logical extension, and the South Centre was created and located in Geneva.

Sartaj Aziz sighed that the time for such romantic notions had passed, that in some ways these efforts were behind the curve: "The South Commission was stuck on the issues of the past and not so much the issues of the future. They were looking at trade preferences and they were looking at ODA and issues that had run their course and did not have support in the major donor countries. . . . First they had to present a more meaningful concept of development and put the responsibility for that concept of development—just like Arthur Lewis did in the Pearson report—squarely on the developing countries and not . . . make the developed countries feel that they are responsible for the development of the poor countries. . . . Secondly, they should have highlighted the discrimination implicit in the global system. . . . So to that extent, the conceptual and the innovative framework in which the commission should have operated was less than what was needed. But it did lead, positively speaking, to the G-15, which is a group of fifteen developing countries which is carrying out the South Commission's report. . . . They assess the situation as they face it today. They coordinate their position for various international meetings. And there is also a Group of D-8 now, of Islamic countries. They do the same thing. But the net impact is limited."

Adebayo Adedeji speculated: "The North-South negotiations would have had a different ending. . . . [But] Reagan and Mrs. Thatcher were there, and that was the end of it." One of the alternatives to the North-South axis was cooperation among developing countries, but Adedeji said: "South-South cooperation has really not progressed. Again, the inability to put one's money where one's mouth is very characteristic not only of Africa but of the South generally. The South Centre was established by Nyerere to set up a kind of South OECD. I think Nyerere died a frustrated man because he could not realize that goal. The South has the capacity of generating enough resources to do that. But it simply refused."

Reflecting on the meaning of African solidarity in this context, Adedeji recalled: "Julius Nyerere defined this to me very clearly once when African heads of state at an OAU summit failed to reach agreement on what actions should be taken domestically in their respective countries and I went to seek his assistance. He said to me, 'Bayo, the OAU summit is a trade union organization. All trade unions have solidarity against their employers, but between and amongst themselves they have various interest groups and consequently strong differences.' So solidarity is for facing the rest of the world, not necessarily solidarity within the continent. That is why dynamic economic cooperation has been unobtainable in Africa. That is why South-South economic and technical cooperation has made little progress."

The idea of a Third World secretariat was one that had been around for some time. Sonny Ramphal recalled: "We tried to turn UNCTAD into the secretariat, and of course the inevitable happened. The big countries who were paying for UNCTAD said, 'We're not going to allow you to do this.' So we don't have it in UNCTAD. Yes, UNCTAD makes brave attempts from time to time to help the South. But it can't function as a South secretariat ought to function." Paul Berthoud also lamented: "It never clicked. It never gelled, somehow, which is a big tragedy for the Group of 77, or for that matter for the Non-Aligned Movement, never having been able to develop their own intellectual capacity. . . . And unfortunately, the South Centre doesn't seem to be able to do it as much as we had hoped."

Devaki Jain has participated in various deliberations by the South Commission and the South Centre and expressed her dismay: "Nyerere provided space for that club in the same office of the South Commission which the Swiss had funded. . . . [But] Nyerere had many faults. . . . He never let the South Centre become the focal point for the energy that the South was generating. . . . I would be quite happy to let it die now."

What are the contemporary prospects for continuing the conversation? Not great, according to many of our voices. John Ruggie explained the politics of rhetoric: "Today, the North-South debate in the UN is largely a debate within the G-77. A group of fairly conservative G-77 members—Algeria, Cuba, Libya, Syria; they may consider themselves to be revolutionary countries, but I consider them to be quite conservative in the sense of being old-fashioned— frame the issue in this way. Other G-77 members will defer to them for the sake of the spirit of the group when their interests are not directly at stake. So you get replays of North-South debates. It involves a lot of deference for the sake of solidarity: 'We were all colonized at one point, and we were all victimized at one point. This doesn't cost us a whole lot, so why not?' When the issue at hand is important, you see less of it." Alister McIntyre noted that "one of the things that has happened is that the leadership of the Group of 77 has evaporated." Dharam Ghai added that "increasingly the notion of the Third World is becoming less and less meaningful in practical terms."

The Debt Crisis and Adjustment: A Lost Decade

The debt accumulated by non-oil-exporting developing countries was already a serious problem before what became known as the second oil-price hike in 1979. The burden of servicing this debt worsened substantially and some, like the World Bank's Robert MacNamara, warned that many countries were on a slippery slope. In spite of the initial euphoria about transferring wealth from North to South, the reality by the 1980s was that non-oil-exporting Latin America had transferred some $100 billion to Northern Hemisphere banks.[4] Some cynics called this a reverse Marshall Plan.

Increasingly, the economic conventional wisdom reflected concerns about price increases and gave priority to the fight against inflation. This led to a sharp increase in real interest rates, which, combined with the monetarist policy implemented by the U.S. Federal Reserve Bank, led to a considerable appreciation of the dollar. Concentration on budgetary and monetary discipline in the North and the accompanying recession led to a strong contraction of world demand and a further deterioration of the terms of trade for primary products in the South. Indebted developing countries faced what seemed to be an ever-deepening financial crisis, the combined result of the strong dollar, high rates of interest, and the drop in their export prices and incomes. This situation led to the beginning of the international debt crisis— Mexico declared its inability to service its debt in August 1982—and what became known as, after Enrique Iglesias coined the term, the "lost decade" for Latin America and Africa.

This crisis amounted to a major threat to international capital markets. With strong U.S. support, the IMF intervened massively to help reschedule Mexico's debt and that of other developing countries. But recourse to the funds of the lender of last resort came with severe conditions.[5] To gain access to IMF funds, borrowing countries were required to implement stabilization measures under structural adjustment programs, which became the major force for introducing economic liberalization to developing countries. Dharam Ghai observed the impact of the times on policy options: "If they did not have the debt crisis, I am not so sure these ideas would have spread so rapidly in developing countries. Because most of these countries, especially in Latin America, found themselves in a state of foreign exchange crisis and the debt crisis, they had no choice but to follow these policies dictated from outside." Samir Amin went even farther and redefined his thesis of "delinking": "The adjustment by the North to the development needs of the South rather than the adjustment of the South to the North's pursuit of its own development."

Although the debt crisis began in Latin America, its impact was perhaps most brutal in Africa, where most countries had little or no room to maneuver. Adebayo Adedeji discussed the battle of ideas between the Bretton Woods institutions and the UN: "The World Bank came out with the Berg report. I knew it was being prepared because Elliot Berg came to see me in Addis Ababa and I briefed him fully about the preparation of the Lagos Plan of Action. We urged the Bank through him to wait until at least the Lagos Plan of Action had been published and see the ways it can assist in its implementation. We felt that the Bank should put all its weight behind this very first serious effort being made by African governments to collectively come out with their own development paradigm and forge a future for the continent. Instead, Berg came out with a report which was the very antithesis of the Lagos Plan of Action and which was no more than a neocolonial development strategy. Hence the sharp reaction and the big row. The ECA conference of ministers rejected the report in its entirety because it was in fundamental contradiction with the economic, political, and social aspirations of Africa. . . . At the same time, the debt problem . . . got out of hand. The structural adjustment program was introduced, based on the Berg report, making it a condition for debt relief and debt forgiveness. So it became obligatory for the countries to opt for structural adjustment programs if they wanted anything to be done about their debt. This meant that African countries were forced under duress to pursue the World Bank's strategy and abandon their own paradigm."

Adebayo recalled the reaction by the U.S. assistant secretary of state for Africa: "Chester Crocker was no doubt more honest than most people when he . . . admitted that in the Western perspective, Africa is only one of a panoply of global concerns. . . . Crocker then concluded that the *Agenda for Action* reflects the Western perspective of Africa while the LPA reflects the African perspective." The Lagos Plan of Action, adopted by the OAU Summit in 1980, called for a self-reliant development strategy for Africa that included strong growth in both agriculture and industry and economic, social, and cultural integration for the continent.

The plight of Africa was obvious to many besides Africans. "I think it is really a kind of blindness not to take into account what is happening in Africa," commented Brazil's outspoken former president Fernando Henrique Cardoso. "It is tragic. It is possible to solve the problem, because it is not so much the amount of money that is necessary. The G-7 [Group of 7] took years and years just to cancel debts. We did it with Central America and Africa. If Brazil was able to write off debts, why not the Americans or the Europeans? And we did it because it is the only thing you can do, because they can never repay. But they suffer because they have to ask the International Monetary Fund for help, and the IMF then imposes rules on these poor people. This is ridiculous."

What was the standard prescription for reform by the Bretton Woods institutions? In order to qualify for financial help, a comprehensive program of structural adjustment was necessary. Belt-tightening required eliminating price subsidies, cutting public sector employment, and selling off state-controlled industries. It often led to major hardship and dissent in the streets. It also led our voices to reflect on this unsettling period.

Sartaj Aziz placed the ideas of that time in historical context and spoke of a "missed opportunity" of the previous decade: "We dethroned growth. But the alternatives were yet evolving. It took five, six, or maybe seven years. The 1974 World Food Conference provided one dimension for rural areas. ILO's World Employment Conference of 1976 provided another. UNESCO covered a third dimension. By 1980, we had a consensus but then came the Latin American crisis. The World Bank and IMF took over and the UN system took a back seat.... I initiated, in 1978, one year after IFAD was created, the idea of special programming missions in IFAD, which was to look at the target groups, analyze the causes of poverty, and then look at the overall policy framework in which they operate and live.... This approach was very similar to what is now being advocated for the poverty reduction strategies by the Bank/Fund.... So we did about twenty-two such programming missions. . . . They did bring out, in many cases, the conflict with the adjustment programs which were being launched at that time. I think if that kind of activity had continued in IFAD and IFAD had taken a leading role, probably the damage which the adjustment policies was doing on a one-size-fits-all kind of approach would have been minimized."[6]

Former ECA executive secretary Adebayo Adedeji pounded home the theme of Africa's own efforts in the face of debt-driven crises and recalled the publication of a seminal document entitled *Revised Framework of Principles for the Implementation of the New International Economic Order in Africa*: "We brought out four hypotheses—now very mundane but at that time [they] sounded revolutionary. . . . First, that aid could be anti-development. . . . Aid was anti-development because it distorts priorities and distorts the allocation of even domestic resources. . . . Second, that [in] Africa, going forward with the inherited colonial economic legacy would never achieve socioeconomic transformation. Third, that self-reliance and self-sustaining development was imperative. Fourth, that Africa must regain and reassert its self-confidence."

Adedeji once again commented on the power of ideas versus resources: "Meanwhile, in the face of the blatant failure of the structural adjustment program, the World Bank came out with its Long-Term Planning Strategy, which was closer to the Lagos Program of Action. But the World Bank is like an elephant. It takes it ages to turn around. Those who write its seminal documents are not those who operate the loans and disburse investments. Operationally therefore, the Bank continued with the structural adjustment program, even after the African governments and, I dare add, the General Assembly had endorsed the ECA's African Alternative [Framework] to Structural Adjustment Programmes." Indeed, it was a lost decade for development.

The Washington "Consensus"

The combined impact of a change in governments and philosophy in powerful countries of the West and the collapse of the Socialist bloc meant that economic liberalization and an accompanying political democratization were viewed as cookie cutters for the ills not just of the former socialist countries of Central and Eastern Europe and the Soviet Union but for the Third World as well. Beginning in the 1980s, the fulcrum of development debate and operations shifted away from the United Nations and toward the Bretton Woods institutions. Norway's doyen of development studies, Just Faaland, commented: "It wasn't because of some inherent weaknesses but more because of the international conjuncture that the NIEO fell down. Some people kept pushing it forward into the 1980s and so on, but it clearly was a dead horse. Therefore, the vacuum, if you like, was filled by the new orthodoxy. Could the UN proper have delayed or even avoided that setback? That's very speculative. I don't think the UN had the power to do it. . . . I doubt whether it had the intellectual and institutional capacity to do it."

Ignacy Sachs saw a historical continuity in the onslaught of neoliberal thinking: "After the invasion of Czechoslovakia [in 1968], the credibility of existing socialism became nonexistent, so that Western capitalism returned to its arrogance of the pre-1929 years and there was a surge of neoliberalism. The rise in inflation was cleverly exploited. They fought inflation while killing off at the same time the Keynesian inheritance. Paradoxically, the beginning of the 1970s was the time when the power, the political weight, of the Third World was at its most significant, but it was also the time when there occurred the switch to the phase in which we presently find ourselves."

The new orthodoxy was called by many the Washington consensus, which involved a somewhat limited view of the concept of consensus. A number of developing countries were, and consistently have been, actively opposed to the prescriptions emanating from the Washington-based international financial institutions that promulgated the so-called consensus. *Foreign Policy* asked its readers: "What better way to market your idea than to tag it a 'consensus,' suggesting that it's a grand unifying theory?"[7] One of our more radical voices, Samir Amin, lamented a missed opportunity to challenge this overall direction: "In this sad affair the European responsibility looms large since they agreed to align themselves with the strategies of American *hegemonism*. . . . In these circumstances, integrating European policies into American globalization—what I call the European rallying to neoliberal policies and acceptance of American hegemonism—brought about the disappearance of a distinct European vision so that one had what amounted to the European wing of the American strategy. . . . At the same time, there has always been in Europe a slightly nauseating discourse that says: 'We are the great power and will take the place of American hegemony.' In other words, the dream of one imperialism assuming the place of another."

John Williamson, a senior fellow at the Institute for International Economics and former World Bank staff member, described the shape of the cookie cut-ter.[8] "Consensus" actually reflected the prescriptions emanating from the Bretton Woods institutions. Williamson's original ten points fell into two major areas of policy.

The first was establishing a healthy base for growth through macroeconomic stabilization and austerity programs. This was seen as an important step on the road to the return of growth and prosperity. It included fiscal discipline to put an end to budget deficits, tight controls on public expenditure, and reliance on unified exchange rates in place of import controls or export subsidies.

The second was restructuring the economy toward export-oriented and market-oriented activities through liberalization, deregulation, and privatization. The objective was to strengthen the private sector as the main actor of growth and development through tax reform, liberalization of trade and finance, privatization, deregulation, and strengthening of property rights. Consensus thinking held that countries should also be opened to foreign direct investment.

Surendra Patel was clear about the geopolitical and geo-economic bases for the so-called Washington consensus: "The rise of the conservative governments of Reagan in the United States, Margaret Thatcher in the United Kingdom, Helmut Kohl in Germany and Nakasone in Japan had pushed the welfare state aside and adopted old neoclassic conservative financial policies. These policies were changing the profile of the world economy, and certainly not in line with our ideals. But, when you have four of the main powers combined, they are practically taking care of 75 to 80 percent of the world exports. They would naturally be a driving force."

IDB president Enrique Iglesias noted somberly: "We are now in a time of great confusion. While the Washingtonian paradigm was applied during a period of a spectacular worldwide expansion, the paradigm must now be corrected during the middle of a recession. Conditions are very difficult and painful."

Lourdes Arizpe emphasized the changing nature of what passed for conventional wisdom in Washington in the 1980s: "Latin American intellectuals played a very important role in bringing many of these ideas on culture into the United Nations, from Fernando Henrique Cardoso to Rodolfo Stavenhagen to Pablo González Casanova. The emphasis was on endogenous development, on collective movements, on center-periphery relationships, which worked out more in political and cultural terms. But it is not by coincidence that this thrust came from Third World politicians and thinkers, with strong support from the more enlightened European countries. So many of the mainstream development ideas now being taken up by the World Bank and other economic agencies originated in research and in schemes in developing countries. Just to mention a few: action research, poor people's loan schemes, the need to take into account social organization (now called 'social capital' or 'institutions'), the predominance of women in the pervasive influence of cultural norms and habits, the need for a responsive and accountable government (now called 'governance'). All these questions that were debated in developing countries in the 1960s and 1970s became mainstream in UN agencies in the 1980s. This is why it has been such a waste of time for the Washington consensus to have re-imposed narrow economistic policies in the 1990s, only to begin to re-introduce, once again, questions of governance, institutions and culture in the last few years."

Arizpe continued: "During the first half of the 1980s, most developing countries in sub-Saharan Africa and Latin America started to adopt policies based on universal IMF prescriptions; some would argue [and many of our voices agree] that they had no choice in the matter. Mainstream discourse swept all before it by emphasizing that the road to growth and development was open to any country ready to embrace structural adjustment and move toward an open economy and more rational market resource allocations."

The period following these policies was "different in one significant respect," wrote Moisés Naím, a former Venezuelan minister who edits *Foreign Policy*. "The world has been under the impression that there was a clear and robust consensus about what a poor country should do to become more prosperous."[9] Once again, growth received greater weight than income distribution and social objectives. The old hypothesis, now revived, was that policy reforms designed to achieve efficiency and growth would also promote better living standards, especially for the poorest.[10] The so-called trickle-down theory reigned supreme once again. The social costs of structural adjustment were inconvenient but temporary went the theme song. And in any case, they were inevitable in order to return to more rational and viable economic structures: TINA—There Is No Alternative!

However, the social cost was substantial. Cutting government expenditures often meant cutting back in such key areas as education and health. When in the early 1980s the IMF recommended policies that slashed public expenditures, both physical and human investment were also reduced. Economic growth often came to a grinding halt. For many countries in sub-Saharan Africa and Latin America, this was a period of stabilization and adjustment *without* growth. Worse still, the promise that growth would follow, perhaps after an interval, has frequently proved false. Recovery was often short lived, if it occurred at all.

The poorest of the poor often suffered the most, as they had less margin for maneuver. For the worst-off people in each country, the burden became intolerable. Per capita income in Africa fell to the level of the 1960s, while in

Latin America, on average, it regressed to levels that had prevailed at the beginning of the decade.

As the consequences became clearer, unease grew. The United Nations Children's Fund took the international lead, along with the Economic Commission for Africa. Few would have expected the counteroffensive to emanate from an organization charged with care for children and mothers. But children were among those hardest hit by the events and misguided policies of the 1980s. In its report *Adjustment with a Human Face*,[11] UNICEF argued that policies should safeguard the vital needs of a country's population. The basic rationale of economic policy was to put human concerns and people at the center of development.

The result was to move away from the brink, as ILO director-general Juan Somavía noted: "We still haven't been able to get to the point where the powers that be will actually acknowledge that a mere combination of privatization, deregulation, and the reduction of the role of the state is not going to produce the solutions. . . . Intellectually, today nobody would dare to say that those three elements don't contribute to a solution. But the intellectual arrogance you had in the 1980s in relation to those three elements as being the ultimate solution is no longer there. Yet the policies continue to be influenced by that thinking."

The pendulum had swung too far, according to many of our voices. There was a legitimate role for the state and governments in planning, setting rules, and ensuring a floor under the poorest. John Ruggie asserted: "The so-called Washington consensus really sold a bill of goods to the developing countries. The issue was not to do away with the state. The issue was to reform the state and to make it smarter, more agile, and more responsive to social needs. I am not sure the 'Washington consensus' exists anymore. But while it existed, it did a great disservice to developing countries who paid any attention to it, or were forced to."

Alister McIntyre summarized the ups and downs in the way that he and others had thought about the state's role in development over the course of his career: "We started with confidence that the problem of development can really be addressed by robust state action. This was the Rosenstein-Rodan 'big push' idea, and to a certain extent, Arthur Lewis was of that genre, although more pragmatic than others. Hirschman began to shift the emphasis, in a way, with ideas of unbalanced growth, which suggested more of a reliance on market mechanisms than the state. But basically, the Development Decades, the Hollis Chenery 'two gaps,' the big ideas of the 1960s on development all presumed a very vigorous role for the state. That persisted, of course, into the NIEO debate. . . . Where things began to go in a different direction was with the arrival of President Reagan in Washington. . . . There was almost exclusive reliance on the market. And of course, there was the disappointing performance of governments in practically all of the three regions of the Third World. Policy error was widespread and profound. So disenchantment with government action, together with new ideology, came to the fore—not so new, but the resurgence of an old ideology—changed the direction of development thinking towards less state action."

Gamani Corea cautioned that "the efforts to downplay the role of the state . . . have gone too far. I sometimes say, jokingly, that there is now a convergence of views between Wall Street and Karl Marx on the 'withering away of the state.' . . . The state needs to play a role, but it has to play not a confrontational role vis-à-vis the private sector but a cooperative role in which the state and the private sector reinforce each other. . . . This, I have suggested, calls for a different kind of planning. Not project-by-project planning, but the formulation of guidelines. A kind of roadmap which will tell the private sector where we can go five or ten years from now and then ask the private sector what contribution they can make to this, what their ideas are for investments in the periods ahead, what they can get from the state and so on. . . . I had the impression that this, in a way, was what was done by the success stories of Asia, starting with Japan and going to South Korea."

Dharam Ghai was equally skeptical of the salvation promised by the new orthodoxy: "I have never believed that this, in and of itself, will solve the problems of underdevelopment, of inequality, of poverty and of deprivation. I think we still need an active role of the state. I come back to planning. We ought to resuscitate the practice of planning so that a country can say, 'Over the next five or ten years, this is where we want to go. This is our mission. These are our goals. And these are the policy instruments we will use to get to that stage.' The pendulum has swung too far in the other direction. The state has been greatly weakened. Its capacity to deliver the things that it should be delivering—roads, utilities, power, transport, health, education, water supply— has been so debilitated that it cannot play that role. We have thrown overboard some very useful services that only the state can provide." Or, as Jan Pronk observed, "The relation between the state and the nation cannot only be judged with economic yardsticks, as seems to be the view based on the so-called Washington consensus."

Alister McIntyre pointed to the continual shifts in emphases culminating in the 1980s: "You have periods in the world of intellectual fertility, [when] ideas sprout. I think the 1960s was very much a decade of that sort of thing. The 1970s wasn't characterized so much by new ideas but simply by the propagation of old ideas with greater vigor. But the aridity came in the 1980s. . . .

The West virtually did a U-turn in shifting from development towards the immediate concerns of a rapidly crumbling Soviet empire. Maybe there were very good political reasons for this, but that's a fact. The 1980s were very difficult years in the UN. At one point, Pérez de Cuéllar called me to head a small group within the Secretariat on Secretariat reform. We did quite a bit of work on that. Out of that emerged a realization among most of the secretariats in the UN system . . . that political support for their work had dwindled, certainly in the West, and even in Southern countries that had begun to react to the changing political agenda. Development studies went into recession in most universities. So you had all of these forces, in a way, working against robust institutional support for intellectual innovation."

The 1980s marked the beginning of a new high watermark for a philosophical reliance on the virtues of the market. In the previous decade and in response to a growing uneasiness with the power of corporations and the realization of the importance of private investment, we saw that the UN created a special unit in 1974 to focus on transnational corporations. However, the Centre for Transnational Corporations was disbanded in 1993 and a few posts were moved to UNCTAD in Geneva. According to Sotiris Mousouris, this was probably inevitable and a reflection of the orthodoxy of the 1980s: "Well, a major part of the mission of the Centre was probably lost. The mission of the Centre was to analyze the effects of transnationals and try to introduce some rules of the game. We never called them 'dangerous beasts' or 'bad guys.' We just wanted to see how the animal works, what makes the animal click, and how to get the best out of it. There was of course a tacit attempt to regulate, to place limits. . . . Now the ideology, the objective, I believe, is how to attract foreign investment, how to persuade transnationals to invest in developing countries. This is the new philosophy."

Paul Berthoud recalled how the new orientation of the 1980s influenced UNCTAD: "I remember one day, at the height of the best days of UNCTAD, my making the nasty remark that while Karl Marx had said that religion was the opium of the people, we certainly had to be careful that UNCTAD did not become the opium of the ruling classes in developing countries. Not all my colleagues found it funny. But I had very strong feelings at times that we were so much nurturing our approach to the external dimension of development that it was becoming a sort of easy topic for the governments of the developing countries to concentrate on and in the process neglect their basic responsibility, which was to handle the problem of development at the national level. . . . I think that UNCTAD has really set a model of an alternative organization of the world economy, which has been a very important intellectual contribution.

Now the model has been shelved, basically, which is just a fact of life of the world in which we live."

More than resignation emanated from Berthoud's voice, however: "The model is one of reorganizing of the international economic relations on an acknowledgement that formal equality is not doing justice to the principle of equality among nations, that equality among unequals breeds injustice, and that you have to correct economic relations in order to instill equality at a real level of content and not in a purely formal way. It was built fundamentally on the old saying of Lacordaire in the nineteenth century that 'Between the rich and the poor, it is freedom that oppresses and justice that sets free.' . . . It is a fundamental element of the philosophy that you cannot handle relations among people who are placed in an unequal position in their relationship through principles of freedom of trade and activity in general. This entails legal adjustments. And, of course, interference in the freedom of trade. In other words, in a sense, it is a 'socialization' of the international economy. But one never used the word in UNCTAD because it was one of those red flags."

Gerry Helleiner concluded with a commentary about the relationship between the remedy and the original illness: "The legacy of the neoliberal thrust of the 1980s will be close to zero. They moved things back in the right direction but greatly overshot. It would have been wiser and less costly to move back in a gradual fashion rather than in the really roughhouse manner in which they did."

The End of the Cold War and the Socialist Model

Virtually side by side with the growing importance of liberalization as a panacea was the disappearance of the socialist model that had inspired many developing countries as they won independence from Western colonialism. Moscow itself has begun its own "revolution," and time will tell whether this upheaval will be as important on the world stage as the 1917 predecessor.

Arms reduction agreements between the United States and the Soviet Union and a gradual diminution in Soviet influence in Eastern Europe was given a boost by the ascension to power of Mikhail Gorbachev in 1985. Javier Pérez de Cuéllar attended the funeral of Soviet general secretary Konstantin Chernenko and recounted a personal realization that took place. He understood that radical change was on the horizon with the arrival of a different type of Soviet leader: "To my surprise, among the personalities Gorbachev wanted to see was the Secretary-General of the United Nations. I was surprised and flattered. I said 'It is wonderful.' Then he told me this in two words: 'I think the Soviet Union, from now on, will be very supportive of the United Nations, because we think that in the future all problems should be solved through your organization. You can rely on me. . . . We are going to pay all our arrears, which are very large.'"

Pérez de Cuéllar remembered a story that Gorbachev had called in the foreign minister and told him, "Listen, try to help the United Nations. Pay if possible our contributions." As the Soviet Union had dragged its feet on budgetary matters for years, the Secretary-General assumed, quite correctly it turned out, that massive change was under way: "My conclusion—perhaps I was wrong—was that he had, during his formation period, realized that they could not compete with the United States. They were no longer a superpower. They were, perhaps, not even a military superpower. But really, he realized that it was the end of the tremendous strength of the Soviet Union. And Gorbachev, I believe, thought that as they were permanent members of the Security Council, they could be part in the solution of all problems. At the United Nations, they have a voice as important as the United States."

Jan Pronk recalled his underestimation of the new Soviet leader: "In the beginning, for me, Gorbachev was just another Brezhnev, another Andropov. The language he used was different, but, I thought, not fundamentally, only a little bit adjusted to the circumstances of the 1980s. I remember how my son criticized me. He was a student at the international school in Geneva. They had had discussions at school, and he said, 'You are wrong. We believe in the man, he is different.' Clearly a person like Gorbachev did appeal to young people in the West, more than to a generation which had become cynical."

Virendra Dayal was serving as the fifth Secretary-General's chief of staff at the time and recalled a light moment on the 38th floor shortly after Gorbachev's arrival for the first time to UN headquarters: "Pérez de Cuéllar was a modest person who was always ready to praise others, and he said, 'Mr. General Secretary, it is all because of you and people like you that my hand has been strengthened. What is our achievement but that of member states? We would be nothing if it weren't for their cooperation.' . . . Gorbachev said, 'Well, let's just say that God is on the side of the United Nations.' I was sitting over there and I burst out laughing. I just burst out laughing. Gorbachev looked at me with a twinkle in his eye and he said, 'By which I mean the forces of history. The historical forces are on the side of the United Nations.'"

From his perspective in Budapest, the reasons behind the dissolution of the Socialist bloc were clear to Mihaly Simai long before Gorbachev: "The domestic problems of the Soviet Union reduced the capacity of the Soviet Union to help the solution of the economic problems of these countries [and] at the same time reduced the Soviet capacities to intervene militarily. . . . The Soviet intervention in Afghanistan was also a factor. None of these countries really was very happy with the Soviet involvement there, and the Soviet involvement in Afghanistan also weakened the military potential of the Soviet Union to intervene in Eastern Europe. So the disintegration, I would say, the 'cracks' . . . in the unity were growing; it was not yet disintegration but there were important cracks."

The collapse of the Berlin Wall in November 1989 is usually seen as the official termination of the Cold War. And certainly the implosion of the Soviet Union in 1991 marked the end of one historical period and the dawn of another. We are still searching for a label that explains its essence rather than its timing—"post–Cold War era" lacks clarity, especially after the terrorist attacks of September 11, 2001, added other dimensions.

The disappearance of the former superpower led to a predicament unimagined by the framers of the UN Charter, namely how to pass the mantle of a former permanent member of the Security Council. Viru Dayal recalled being in his office late on Christmas Eve in 1991, just before Pérez de Cuéllar's term came to an end at the end of December. Ill with the flu, the Secretary-General said to an insistent Ambassador Yuli Vorontsev of the Soviet Union: "Look, I would really like to see you, but I have got a fever and I cannot see you. My friend and *chef de cabinet*, Dayal, is there. Why don't you go and see him, give him the message and consider it given to the Secretary-General." Upon arriving in his office, Vorontsev presented Dayal with a note from Boris Yeltsin: "As of tomorrow, the Soviet Union ceases to exist, and the Russian Federation will be born. And the Russian Federation would like to assume the rights and responsibilities of the Soviet Union, including its place in the Security Council. And Vorontsev has been asked to present you with the flag of the new Russian republic. Could you kindly set the process in motion?" What would happen if someone questioned "who succeeds the Soviet Union when the Soviet Union itself was breaking into a multitude of states"?

Dayal read the draft of the short *note verbale* over the phone to the Secretary-General, which was then sent to all of the permanent missions on Christmas Eve: "Basically, it was working on the assumption that none of them would challenge the change. . . . I rang Ali Teymour, the chief of protocol, and said, 'Ali, we need a new flag to mount. The size we have got is wrong, but by Boxing Day just have these flags in shape to put all over the place.' . . . Yuli Vorontsev assumed his place the day after Christmas, sitting in the Security Council, as the ambassador of the Russian Federation. Nobody hounding him out of his chair. Actually, it was both the right thing and also we were lucky. All hell could have broken loose."

Vladimir Petrovsky became the highest-ranking Russian official in the UN Secretariat after trading his Soviet passport for a new Russian one. He brought his experience with him as Soviet foreign minister Eduard Shevaradnadze's deputy during the exciting first days of perestroika (economic restructuring) and glasnost (openness). Petrovsky was asked by Secretary-General Boutros Boutros-Ghali "to chair the task force to prepare *An Agenda for Peace.* . . . I was very proud. . . . We were able to put in *An Agenda for Peace* all of the ideas which were actually formulated at the end of the Cold War. One of my dearest ideas was preventive diplomacy, about which I started to speak very strongly already in 1986. It was not easy to advocate this approach for the Soviet Union in the Cold War. Preventive diplomacy looked very much suspicious because it meant to open up countries to early warning. But in the long run, in the process of change there was an understanding that it is very important."

Another thing became clear: The alternative of a centralized state, which owned certain means of production and which had provided a model distinct from capitalism for many developing countries, effectively evaporated. Our interlocutors, like virtually everyone, were surprised by the collapse of the Soviet bloc. It was hardly the "end of history,"[12] but the effective termination of East-West conflict certainly led to changes in thinking. The result of this dissolution, noted Celso Furtado, had one very clear effect: "The Cold War deformed the United Nations," he summarized. "The world was deformed by the imbalances of wealth on the one hand and of ideologies on the other. Today there is no longer a Cold War. This has caused an enormous concentration of power in the hands of the United States."

For the South, in addition to the disappearance of the Socialist bloc and the lost leverage in the competition for assistance from one side or the other during the Cold War, there was an accompanying shrinking in the ideas about available policy options. "The Cold War was fought in the name of democracy, and it was won in the name of the market," remarked Juan Somavía. "So having wagered on democracy, we should have reached conclusions on how to promote democracy in the world. Instead, we wound up seeing how to promote market principles around the world. . . . Markets have an incredible dynamism and can act as a stimulus. But as any good thing, if it is exaggerated, then you create problems. You cannot organize a society around market principles."

The disappearance of a development model that may or may not have had certain advantages, at least for some developing economies, was a real problem, according to Gamani Corea: "I always said that the emphasis on statism in Third World countries was not so much due to some kind of socialist ideological orientation but to the very practical fact that the state was the only strong actor in those countries. Many of them were too weak to rely on the private sector to do the things that developed countries encouraged them to do. I remember saying that when this talk of liberalization and deregulation came in, that it was not enough to clear the stage and remove the obstacles that were in the way and then expect that somewhere in the wings there was a wonderful '*corps de ballet*' waiting to give a great performance. I think you have to build up that team of performers. You had to encourage them, give them experience."

"After the collapse of the system, more or less people wrote off everything to do with the socialist kind of economies," noted Dharam Ghai. "I am not speaking just of state ownership of all means of production, and central planning, and doing away with markets, relying on direct allocation, but even in terms of [things such as] health and education that were relatively universal and egalitarian. There was a tendency to throw the baby out with the bath water. . . . The Reagan and Thatcherite revolution got massively reinforced as a result of the collapse of communism and the end of the Cold War. At a political level and in terms of bargaining power, it has been a loss for developing countries. I am not saying that communism was good for them. But in a sense, it gave them some leverage, some room for maneuver."

Former Maltese president Guido de Marco recalled the most dramatic early post–Cold War decision, the Chapter VII action in the Persian Gulf: "It was a United Nations in transition, trying to evaluate the effects of the Cold War, trying to think not within a Cold War corset, only to find Kuwait invaded in August 1990 by Saddam Hussein and a UN taking the necessary steps in a multilateral approach leading to the liberation of Kuwait. . . . The feeling in New York was that Saddam Hussein was simply a year too late. He did not notice that there was the Malta meeting of Bush and Gorbachev which ended the Cold War. He didn't notice that a new spirit had come over the United Nations and [that] this was best manifested eventually in the Security Council resolution which authorized the taking of such measures as were necessary for the liberation of Kuwait." At the same time, de Marco noted presciently the ominous residue of double standards: "We were living a contradiction. Kuwait, a state occupied, and by another Arab state. Palestine, occupied by Israel against resolutions of the United Nations calling on them to evacuate from the occupied territories. And in the case of Kuwait, the whole apparatus of the United Nations set in motion; in the case of the Palestinians, great abandonment."

Virtually all admitted to being totally surprised by the rapidity and the extent of collapse of the Soviet Union, and the memories were vivid about initial impressions and future repercussions.

James Jonah noted a link between postings of Soviet officials and their views about the nature of their system: "Petrovsky and I were very close friends, and he liked to get me to talk to his colleagues. So I got to know many of them there. And what happened, if you notice the people who brought about *perestroika* were either Soviet officials who had been in Washington, New York, or Ottawa. . . . I gathered from just talking to them, they said, 'Look, we are so advanced in science and technology. Why are we so backwards in other areas?' They were ashamed. . . . So they found somebody like Gorbachev. But the mistake that they made was that you cannot have openness and then maintain the Communist Party. It was a contradiction in terms. And if you read Karl Popper, you can see that. . . . There was just no way that you could have this kind of openness and free debates and everything. . . . And the war in Afghanistan was a big, terrible thing for them."

Premier Mikhail Gorbachev was slated to make a major speech at the General Assembly in 1987, but he ended up staying home because of a natural disaster. Reflecting on the contents that were eventually published in *Pravda,* Jonah remarked that it represented "fundamental changes in the Soviet attitude toward the UN and the role of the Secretary-General. So I said, 'This is a big change.' And Petrovsky was very much involved in drafting this. . . . This was the first time when, after so many years, the Soviet Union said, 'We accept the political role of the Secretary-General.' It was the first time. They never accepted that the Secretary-General had a political role. It was only an administrative role. . . . On peacekeeping they changed their position. These were fundamental changes." Clearly Pérez de Cuéllar's hunch at the Chernenko funeral had been correct.

The end of the Cold War led to disappointments as well. The one most often mentioned by our voices was the lack of incentive for aid and investments in many developing countries. "The biggest blow to the involvement of the West in the development of the South was that communism had ceased to be a threat," remarked Gamani Corea. "As long as communism was a threat, there was an attempt on both sides to see that the Third World countries did not get drawn into one camp or the other. Once that threat went away, there was no real motivation except the humanitarian, or charitable motivation, and that is never as strong as the geopolitical objectives."

At the same time, Gert Rosenthal suggested that the end of the Cold War "cleared the air" by leading to a greater sense of tolerance. In ECLAC, where he was executive secretary, it led to "a less ideologically conditioned view of both Cuba and the United States." The end of the Cold War also opened up the possibility for other initiatives within the UN system. Adebayo Adedeji remembered that "the collapse of the Soviet Union gave us the opportunity to drive home the point that you need a strong participatory political base for anything to become endurable and sustainable. And we took advantage of that. We organized the International Conference on Popular Participation in the Recovery and Development Process in Africa, which we could not have dared to organize a few years before. We couldn't call it democracy, because that would be confrontational. We called it 'popular participation for development.' . . . Without the collapse of the Soviet Union, we could not have done that. We were indeed far ahead of the curve."

John Ruggie felt that the impact of the end of the Cold War was immediate and stark, no less so for economic and social affairs than for peace and security: "At the level of the Secretariat, as long as the Soviet Union existed there was an enormous degree of self-censorship. There weren't a lot of people in the Secretariat who were utterly convinced by the NIEO negotiations, for example, but they felt obliged to go along with it, not only because the southern countries supported it but also because the Soviets supported it. Moreover, the whole development agenda was fundamentally warped by the existence of the Soviet Union because you couldn't talk about macro-fundamentals. The whole UN development effort was channeled into a project basis to avoid ideologically infused macro-debates. A project was a project; you drilled a well and water came out. It wasn't question of ideology. . . . But what you couldn't do was to frame those issues in the context of what the appropriate macro-conditions have to be to make all of it work. You couldn't talk about the constructive or productive role of the private sector without making an apology for state-owned enterprises and God knows for what else. So there was sort of Alice-in-Wonderland quality to economic discussions for much of the Cold War—not the very early days of the UN's history, but the further you got into the late 1950s and the 1960s. That nonsense obviously stopped with its demise."

A different kind of looking glass appeared. The range of ideas applied to transitions in the former socialist countries was extremely narrow. Indeed, one of the major intellectual debates that occurred was hidden from public view. What was variously called the "big bang," "one leap," or "shock therapy" model of rapid economic and social change was favored by the Bretton Woods institutions and promulgated by such economists as Jeffrey Sachs, Olivier Blanchard, and David Lipton and Central European politicians such as Leszek Balcerowicz and Vaclav Klaus. In contrast, the gradualist framework emphasized the necessity of carefully sequencing the reforms, societal consensus, and administrative capacity. This approach, which was advocated by the UN's Economic Commission for Europe, was largely ignored.[13] Putting forward a less orthodox and more human view went "against the stream of economic policy thinking in the leading market economies," Yves Berthelot and Paul Rayment write in the project's volume on that experience. "In 1989–1990, neoliberalism was triumphant and there was a widespread conviction that the policies of liberalization, deregulation, and privatization pursued in the 'Anglo-Saxon' countries provided an appropriate model for transition economies."[14]

Our voices reflected not so much on the painful transition process toward the market and pluralistic democracy but rather on the missed opportunity for a dramatic change in international relations. Unlike the ends of World Wars I and II that had led to the establishment of the League of Nations and the United Nations, there was no effort to launch a third-generation international organization. Hans Singer reported that the widespread hope for a new epoch of peaceful cooperation after the collapse of the Eastern bloc was quickly dashed by an "epidemic of hot war" and the decreased incentive for developed countries to provide aid to economically lesser-developed counterparts. "I was also bitterly disappointed," he recalls, "by developments in Russia. The hope was that Russia, with its tremendous resources, especially human resources, and knowledge of technologies, one of the leading countries in space technology and atomic technology, of course, the hope was that that country— also Eastern Europe and the Soviet bloc—would have great opportunities for development and in that way contribute and become a big aid donor. So developments within Russia, the rapid decline in output and the type of corruption and chaos that developed there was a terrible disappointment." Sadako Ogata was brief and noted with irony the "new world order," an expression coined by President George H. W. Bush in a euphoric moment after Russia's implosion and the unity of action in the Persian Gulf War. Ogata, who was responsible for ever-growing numbers of displaced people, said: "We looked and looked and there was no world order."

Margaret Anstee, who at the time was heading the UN's Office in Vienna, regretted that the West met the fall of the Soviet Union with inadequate responses: "I felt very strongly at that point that the complexities and the dangers—and I had seen them firsthand—of that situation were not fully understood in the West. It seemed to me that Western Europe, the United States, all the powerful countries, were treating the Soviet Union as I had always seen them treat developing countries, in the sense of saying, 'You show us first, and then we will see if we can help.' The problem was that when you are drowning, it is not helpful if someone on the shore says 'Show me you know how to do the breast stroke and then I'll come and save you.' You need them to throw you a lifeline so that you can at least support yourself for a bit."

Nobel laureate Lawrence Klein recalled his frustration: "I think that Russia got very shabby treatment after 1989, in terms of this way of looking at things. . . . We brought down Russia and then walked away from it. It could have been done so much better. All the calculations were wrongly based. The appropriate order of magnitude wasn't realized. . . . I went to a man who used to be the provost at the University of Pennsylvania, Vartan Gregorian [president of the Carnegie Corporation of New York], and I said, 'Would Carnegie consider putting up some money so we can do a study of how much Russia needs to get on their feet again?' He pushed it off to his underlings, who pushed it out of sight. They didn't even want to have a discussion."

8

The 1990s and the Dawn of the Twenty-First Century: Renaissance and Reform?

- **Globalization**
- **Human Development**
- **Human Security and the Responsibility to Protect**
- **Global Governance and the Millennium Development Goals**

The implosion of the Soviet Union at the outset of the 1990s confirmed the end of the Cold War and, as a consequence, the easing of East-West tensions within the United Nations system. In the area of international peace and security, the kinds of paralysis that had crippled the Security Council since shortly after the world organization's founding evaporated. At the same time, a host of UN peacekeeping operations began in areas of the world that had been off limits (Afghanistan, Iraq, Iran, Namibia, Angola, Central America). Almost simultaneously the Gulf War and overriding of Iraqi sovereignty in order to provide humanitarian access to the Kurds seemed to indicate a veritable "renaissance" in UN peace and security efforts. Although disillusionment set in (especially after 1994, following the Somali debacle and the failure of the UN to react in response to genocide in Rwanda), the profile of the Security Council remained highly visible over the 1990s. This continued with the handling of a number of issues—inspections and counterterrorism, for example—after September 11, 2001, despite Washington and London's decision to go to war in Iraq in March 2003 without the council's blessing.

Neither this book nor our project as a whole is about international peace and security, but the new atmosphere of guarded optimism also opened possibilities for the UN to play more active roles on the economic and social ideas front. The most visible multilateral gathering pushed the envelope with the lofty Millennium Development Goals (MDGs) agreed to by over 150 heads of state and government at the September 2000 Millennium General Assembly.[1] The eight goals covered a normative waterfront that placed poverty reduction

and people and the quality of their lives at the center of the global development agenda. They are not merely aspirations but also include concrete goals
that can be measured within a framework of accountability.[2]

The "mother of all summits" was an intellectual and logistical challenge to
the organization. John Ruggie recalled: "Frankly, most people, including member states, were horrified by what we proposed to do. The only thing we had
going for us was that everyone agreed that whatever we did, it shouldn't be
like the 50th anniversary, which everyone thought was an absolute flop that
accomplished nothing, wasted two years, cost a bunch of money, and in the
end produced a turd of a document which even the people who drafted it
couldn't remember."

Objectives are one thing, reality another at the opening of the twenty-first
century. Concrete failures of development have left the world with widening
extremes in wealth and income and with almost half the global population
surviving on incomes equivalent to less than $2 a day. The data speaks for
itself.[3] As a result of substantial progress in Asia (mainly in China and India),
the number of people living on $1 a day worldwide fell slightly from about 1.3
billion in 1990 to 1.2 billion in 2001, although in sub-Saharan Africa the figure
rose from about 230 to 315 million. While the global poverty rate fell, the absolute number of people living on less than $2 a day actually rose from 2.7 to
2.8 billion. The gaps between the richest and the poorest countries have wid-
ened over the past two centuries.[4] Malta's former president Guido de Marco
referred to "the poverty curtain, which can be a more difficult curtain to penetrate than the iron curtain itself."

Some six decades of UN development efforts have also led to genuine advances. Average life expectancy has increased to double the estimated level of
the late 1930s. Child mortality has been lowered by more than three-quarters.
Adult literacy has been raised to nearly three-quarters, with basic education
extended to over 85 percent of the world's children. Malnutrition has been
reduced in all regions of the world except Africa. Smallpox was eradicated by
1977, while the scourges of yaws, guinea worm, and polio have been virtually
eliminated. However, the poorest and least developed countries have gained
least, and in the last two decades a score or more have even slipped back from
levels achieved in the 1970s.

The aspirations expressed so vividly in UN circles from the earliest days
remain very much in the forefront of human endeavors in the contemporary
period as we struggle to fill the development glass a bit fuller, to reduce the
gap between human potential and actual performance. The voice of Rubens
Ricupero reminded us of the relevance of John Maynard Keynes's famous
quote about "scribblers." In updating it, Ricupero said: "My own impression

is that when people speak about the information revolution, or the information and communications revolution, they should not compare it to the Industrial Revolution, as it is often done. One should compare it instead to the first information revolution, the one by Gutenberg. This is not my own idea, but something I read first in a text of this famous thinker who lives in the U.S., of Austrian origin.... [Peter Drucker] said that the industrial revolution was mainly a new process of multiplying goods, like clothing, that already existed before. The information technology, as in the case of Gutenberg, was something deeper, because it created new possibilities that allowed the access of people to knowledge, to information, to communication, to newspapers. It had a tremendous impact on the mentality, on the way we would deal with ideas."

Ricupero provided a fitting conclusion: "We are again back to where we started—the power of ideas, the famous phrase by Lord Keynes. You remember when he said that even practical men that think they have no time to waste reading a book are often acting on the basis of theories of deceased economists. Ideas are always behind all these things. And the information technology makes the flow of ideas much easier."

Globalization

In the 1990s, "globalization" became a widespread moniker for what was happening in the world economy. Technological and communications advances gave a new twist to "interdependence," the term that had characterized earlier debates. The emerging dimensions of business, finance, trade, and information flows assumed planetary dimensions, which circumscribe how development is conceived and carried out.[5]

Globalization signaled new wealth and freedom for some, but to others the process seemed uninvited and cruel. While it may yield some benefits to certain groups, especially to those located in wealthier countries, its wake has brought inequality unprecedented in human history. Secretary-General Kofi Annan wrote about this paradox in his report to the summit: "The benefits of globalization are plain to see: faster economic growth, higher living standards, accelerated innovation and diffusion of technology and management skills, new economic opportunities for individuals and countries alike." In our conversation, Guido de Marco was more dramatic: "I think that the global economy is a *fait accompli*. . . . But what this global economy means [is] that certain countries may fall by the wayside. And when we say countries, we mean peoples, individuals, men, women, children." Samir Amin, one of our more critical voices, was more direct: "I am not against globalization. I am against neoliberal globalization."

Celso Furtado placed the dramatic "ideological turning point" in a slightly longer historical perspective: "We were leaving the Tinbergen era in which policy assumed primacy. It was becoming necessary to think of the world as being organized by human beings. So state responsibility took on enormous significance for developing countries. Now comes the primacy of the market, the monetary market that leads to globalization of the world economy, and Latin America finds itself condemned to go along with globalization too. With globalization, sovereignty becomes null and void."

But what exactly is globalization?[6] Supporters extol its virtues. Anti-globalizationists—especially social movement actors and transnational civil society organizations—traverse the globe in protest. On the one hand, globalization is viewed as a useful tool for understanding contemporary world affairs. On the other hand, the murkiness of the concept—there is no widely accepted definition—leads many scholars to argue that its utility is suspect. As UNCTAD's secretary-general at the end of the 1990s and beginning of the new millennium, Rubens Ricupero had an apt vantage point from which to view research about the phenomenon: "I believe that the main force behind globalization is a change in culture and in science—the changes that brought about the revolution in telecommunications and in information science. . . . Communication has always been . . . the way of spreading civilization through the inter-fertilization of cultures and civilizations. In this sense, globalization goes much beyond the unification of markets. . . . Many people take this dimension of the unification of markets, not only for trade but also for investment, or financial flows, as being the soul of globalization. I don't think this is true. The soul of globalization is communication."

In the popular imagination, globalization brings to mind certain images—such as worldwide dispersion and penetration, global change and transformation, and global geophysical and social processes that effect peoples' lives. Issues that once were meaningfully viewed as "domestic" now make sense only when conceived in worldwide terms. The global and the local, the international and the national blur.

The process of globalization is often assumed to be, as Emma Rothschild has written, "a phenomenon without a past."[7] Some have rightfully cautioned that such rapid increases in the frequency and density of international trade, for instance, are not new. Recent decades have, however, witnessed the significant acceleration and intensification of similar processes in earlier periods, reinforced especially by almost instantaneous communications.

The *United Nations Millennium Declaration*,[8] adopted at the close of the 2000 General Assembly Summit, identified challenges stemming from globalization as the key issue confronting the world organization's members: "We believe that the central challenge we face today is to ensure that globalization becomes a positive force for all the world's people. For while globalization offers great opportunities, at present its benefits are very unevenly shared, while its costs are unevenly distributed. We recognize that developing countries and countries with economies in transition face special difficulties in responding to this central challenge."

One of the central facets of discussions was the preponderant role of market forces. John Ruggie recalled the Secretary-General's efforts to reach out to the private sector and strengthen its link with the United Nations: "Toward the end of 1998, he was considering whether or not to accept an invitation to go to [the annual meeting of the World Economic Forum held in] Davos. We talked about it, and he said, 'I went last year. I don't have to go this year. But if you think we can put a major challenge to the business community, then I will consider it.' The Davos meeting was in January 1999. The first time the world heard about the Global Compact [the name given to the UN initiative to involve the private sector in its work on development] was in that Davos speech. It was essentially a critique of globalization as we knew it, arguing that among its major attributes today, globalization exhibits unacceptable patterns of inequality, both within and among countries. Secondly, there are fundamental asymmetries in global rulemaking that privilege intellectual property rights, for example, over fundamental human rights or environmental threats. That sort of rulemaking asymmetry is not sustainable, he warned. Thirdly, he sensed a growing fear among people of a loss of control, accountability and even identity."

Ruggie described the Global Compact as a direct response to globalization, which "is internally differentiated, in so many different ways, depending upon which company, which industry, which part of the world. In fact, I think companies are beginning to discover that while certain aspects of their operations can be global, there are others that can only be local, or national, or possibly regional, depending on circumstances. I read in the papers not long ago that Coke, which has a universally recognized brand, has recently decided that they have to back off on their global advertising campaigns because they just aren't working. So the most universally recognized of brands is going to be sold in highly differentiated ways in different markets, to be more responsive to the identities and preferences of different consumers. The slogan 'think global, act local' has been around for a while."

Noeleen Heyzer viewed globalization as one of three forces at work that we need to take into account if the UN is to respond adequately to the challenges of the twenty-first century: "There is no way of turning the clock back. But side by side with globalization is fragmentation in terms of the breakdowns of nation-states and wars at the community level. There were more break-downs in nation-states and communities after the Cold War as the crisis of leadership and legitimacy spread. But side by side with that has been the growth of 'problems without borders'—the fact that there are transnational criminalized networks which operate in drugs, in arms, in the trafficking of women and girls. . . . At the same time, other problems without borders have been transnational diseases and ecological crises. HIV/AIDS, as a problem without borders, must be addressed as part of international and national development. So if we are developing an agenda for development, we need to take all three sets of issues simultaneously. We need to take into account that as we are globalizing, we have transnational crimes and fragmentation. We have diseases. We have ecological crises that no nation and no community can handle on their own."

Enrique Iglesias also stressed realistic thinking: "In the globalized world in which we live it is very difficult to try to formulate a general model. I really believe in common sense, in pragmatism. We can't lose sight of the three great objectives, which are competitiveness, social justice and the internationalization of local economies."

Globalization processes are profoundly altering the nature of human social interactions. The nature, structure, geographical pattern, and magnitude of world trade and investment, for example, are in flux and have had an especially hard impact on poor people and poor countries. Many of our voices argued that within such societies the situation of marginalized populations has worsened. Sartaj Aziz was brief and to the point: "Globalization can work very well if the pie is expanding. When the pie starts shrinking, only those on top of the competitive ladder will benefit. But what about those on the lower end of the competitive ladder? They will be wiped out. And there is no protective safety net at the global level."

In the early 1990s, whether one liked globalization or not and whether one benefited from it or not, the world seemed to be becoming a smaller place. Or was it? The obvious movement toward greater integration was often in the headlines, but fundamentalist tendencies increased visibly in the 1990s. Weak state structures and crumbling national economies dominated international headlines and UN discussions, especially about Africa's future. Yet that continent's plight was by no means unique—for example, the implosion of the Soviet Union and the civil wars in the Balkans created similar dynamics. Fragmentation seemed at least as much in evidence as integration, a reality that James Rosenau dubbed "fragmegration."[9] Devaki Jain noted that "the world is much more fragmented. . . . Social groups are getting fragmented, feminist groups are fragmented. . . . I think it is destroying the capacity for unity and solidarity."

What else did our voices have to say about these seemingly conflicting trends? Rubens Ricupero was skeptical about benefits, based on the experience of Brazil: "I never swallowed this idea that integration into the world economy ... was per se a positive value, a positive goal. Unfortunately, most of the literature that we read makes this sort of simplistic mistake, to say that developing countries are not integrated in the world economy and the way for them to develop, to fulfill their potential, is to integrate fully into the world economy. ... My own country, Brazil, is perhaps the best example of how this theory is totally wrong. Brazil, from the beginning of its colonization in 1537, was totally integrated in the world trading system. ... You couldn't dream of a country more integrated in trade than one that practically exported 95 percent of its production. ... But the same process that integrated Brazil externally was the factor that disintegrated Brazil internally. ... What counts is not the quantity of integration, it's the quality of integration. Unfortunately, I think that many economists who are preaching the gospel of globalization forget this simple truth."

Drawing the lessons from his observations and interpretation of Brazilian history, Ricupero asserted: "Before the Mexican crisis, people had the illusion that financial liquidity was there to stay. After the Mexican crisis, we began to have crises more and more often and the intervals became shorter and shorter—in 1995, Mexico and Argentina; in 1997, Asia; in 1988, Russia and Brazil, one after the other. It is the impact of the financial crises that, in my opinion, has shown that globalization was in trouble—not that it would cease, would stop. I would like to go back to this image of Paul Valery, when he said about the first World War that 'we civilizations discovered that we are mortal.' It was in the Mexican crisis that globalization discovered it was mortal. ... I am persuaded that now, after September 11th ... all things that were considered as indispensable for globalization, like a free crossing of borders, not only for merchandise but also for persons, the fact that the nationality of a transnational company should not be a problem—all those things are now open to question. ... All things that were considered dogmas of globalization are now in jeopardy because of security considerations."

Fernando Henrique Cardoso, a distinguished scholar of development, added that "our understanding of globalization, as we used to say, was very poor. Even in our book,[10] [Faletto and I] spoke about the internationalization of the internal market. This was just a consequence of a different process of production, and then the internationalization of capital. So this was not perceived in the 1960s, you see. When some intellectuals discovered what we call today globalization, again it was a disaster because the idea was a new *deus ex machina*: 'Globalization will impose homogenous rules around the world, no alternatives. We are against globalization.' Some Americans and Canadians took the idea of center-periphery and generalized the idea and transformed the idea in a very poor way. Prebisch had never been an unsophisticated intellectual. He never proposed center-periphery ideas to stop analysis, but just as an instrument to understand reality. But they transformed it into something very rigid."

Brazil's former leader continued: "I don't believe the world could be managed just by international capital and NGOs. I think that the states will continue to play a role and that globalization is not necessarily opposed to national states or even to interconnections between national states. . . . So for us, globalization was not a disaster. But for several other countries, it was a disaster, because they are not yet engaged in the international market or in the new way of production. So they are in between. What I am saying is that it is possible to take advantage, but not for everyone. It depends on previous conditions. It depends on the capacity to stabilize the economy, to govern, and to exercise democracy."

What is the balance sheet? John Ruggie offered his thoughts: "There is a scale and an urgency now that is also a product of globalization, of an understanding that is very similar to the view the Secretary-General articulated in his Davos speech—that while we benefit from globalization, it is not sustainable in the way it is functioning. . . . I can see it on the part of their companies, as well. They got used long ago to being good corporate citizens inside their countries. It is increasingly becoming second nature for particularly Scandinavian-based companies and increasingly UK-based and other European companies also to understand the need to become good citizens globally. It is an enlightened self-interest. It is a definition of a self-interest that goes beyond the immediate self and stretches over a longer time horizon. The United States remains the exception, alas."

Adebayo Adedeji lamented the position of his continent: "When people talk of globalization and the future of the world, Africa is confined to the footnotes." Jan Pronk regretted the disappearance of the rights-based approach to development and social inclusion in Africa and other continents: "The forces of globalization had become so strong that this paradigm eroded. The idea of good governance came instead: good governance as defined by the West again on the basis of the Washington consensus, everywhere in the world the same, irrespective of the specific circumstances of the country concerned. Good governance also as a precondition for development and as a precondition for development assistance rather than as an objective and as a possible outcome of development policies assisted from outside."

Human Development

Starting in 1990, the UNDP began to publish the *Human Development Report,* which continues to put forth an annual view of development that places people at its center. "Human development" was defined as the process of strengthening human capabilities and broadening choices to enable people to live lives that they had reason to value. The model does not ignore the market, but it puts participation, empowerment, equity, and justice on an equal footing with growth. Kofi Annan went straight to the basics and the value of human development and why it provided the backbone for the MDGs: "The UN has provided intellectual leadership on the subject of economic development. I think there had been a tendency for everybody to focus on university education and on preparing intellectuals, forgetting that to get to the intellectual scene you need to have good primary schools. You need to put the kids through all the system. We tended to take for granted some of the essential services, like health, education, infrastructure, and others. But now, of course, everybody realizes that without good health, without basic education, and others, you are not going to move forward."

Mahbub ul Haq, the UN economist with the vision to create the *Human Development Reports,* died in 1998 before this project began. Many of our voices recalled the man and his thinking. Just Faaland was a member of what was then called the Harvard Advisory Group to the Pakistan Planning Commission when he encountered the young Mahbub in the mid-1950s: "I was well into my thirties and a father, and he was perhaps twenty-eight and a bachelor. I remember him, of course, as very bright. . . . He was, of course, technically well schooled. He was somewhat brash to begin with. . . . His relationship with the chief economist was difficult. . . . He obviously was a better economist. . . . It didn't take long before he realized that it was important to interact with and support other people. . . . Everyone knew that he was going to go far."

Sonny Ramphal recalled his late friend: "Mahbub was someone who advanced Third World causes in a very, very significant way. He did it without demagoguery, without descending into polemics. That of course was his strength with the industrial world. He commanded the respect of the industrial world. It led him into some difficulties with his own constituency, where they didn't feel that perhaps he was as radical as he ought to be. But of course, he was more radical than most of those who spouted radicalism."

Bernard Chidzero, in looking back at development over his forty years in the UN and the government of Zimbabwe, stated: "Thank God the UNDP and people like Mahbub ul Haq are promoting the whole concept of human development and sustainability of human development. Do we continue to define the development problem simply in materialistic terms? GDP, ten percent, fifty percent? Even if it means there is poverty and people die early? Or do we not find new measurements of development?"

In recalling the controversy surrounding the publication of the first report in 1990, Virendra Dayal articulated a lesson for future purveyors of ideas: "Wherever there has been a pathbreaking report of the UN, you can be sure there will be some people telling you how awful it is. It has been so every single time. When the capacity study was written by Jacko it happened. Take more recent examples—when *An Agenda for Peace* was written, people wrote . . . how bad it was. . . . I remember when Mahbub ul Haq wrote his first *Human Development Report*. It was trashed by everybody. But Mahbub ul Haq touched on an idea which nobody had ever thought of before and one which has absolutely transformed the way development is looked at now. . . . Many delegations, whether belonging to the so-called North or the so-called South, fell on his head as if he had committed a crime, saying, 'No, no, your indices are all wrong. You haven't taken this into account. You haven't taken that into account.' . . . It was a brutal affair. . . . But fortunately he had strong shoulders and could take that kind of rubbish. He persevered and the *Human Development Report* of the UNDP is, at least in my estimation, probably the most powerful bit of economic thinking that has come out of the UN system since it was created. But certainly if Mahbub had decided to fold his knees and pack his tent and go away after the first report, we wouldn't have had this."

A voice from Africa, Adebayo Adedeji, made a powerful point: "I regret to say that I am an economist, not a political scientist. But I have come to the conclusion that development is a subset of democracy and that an internalized and pervasive democratic culture is imperative. . . . Development calls for long-term perspectives. Development is not like instant coffee. You can only have long-term perspective if you are safe, if you know that your security is taken care of and that your human rights are inviolable and there is a judiciary that ensures the supremacy of the rule of law. Personal security, the security of the community, the security of the society and of property are *conditios sine qua non* for democracy and development. . . . We modern-day economists tend to forget that economics as a discipline used to be part of moral philosophy. The founders of economics—like Adam Smith and David Ricardo—put greater emphasis on the morality of development rather than on the quantities of development. Political environment was emphasized more in the early teachings on development."

A useful step toward more people-centered development was the creation of indicators that ranked countries in terms of their performance on the Human Development Index (HDI), a composite measure based on three indicators: longevity, as measured by life expectancy at birth; educational attainment, as measured by a combination of adult literacy and the combined gross primary, secondary, and tertiary enrollment ratio; and access to the resources needed for a decent standard of living, measured by real per capita income (in PPP$), with an adjustment factor. It ranks countries from 1 to 177. In 2004, Norway was number 1, the United States was in eighth place, and Sierra Leone came last.

As might be imagined, calling a spade a shovel in numerical terms did not make many friends among governments. In the *Human Development Report 1999*, Amartya Sen wrote about his initial skepticism about the merits of the HDI as an alternative indicator to mere growth. The intrinsic difficulty for Sen was the attempt "to catch in one simple number a complex reality about human development and deprivation."[11]

In our conversation with him, Sen spelled out in more detail what he meant: "The *Human Development Reports*, under Mahbub ul Haq's visionary leadership, consolidated the criticisms that had emerged in the literature on heavy reliance on the GNP and such commodity-based indicators, which was standard practice when Mahbub got going. I remember his first phone call to me on this in 1989. We had to focus instead, Mahbub argued, on the lives of human beings—their freedoms and well-being, their capabilities. I had starting work on capabilities from the late 1970s—my first formal statement on that was in my Tanner Lectures in Stanford in 1979, under the title 'Equality of What?' Mahbub was very kind to my book *Commodities and Capabilities*, published in 1985.[12] He wanted me to abandon pure theory and join him in making a perspective based on human lives rather than on commodities and incomes, the central approach to evaluating social progress and a powerful weapon for demanding more attention on people's deprivations and unfreedoms.

"I did work with Mahbub from the first *Human Development Report*—it came out in 1990. No one could tell the world, and had the ear of the world, with the kind of adeptness and success that Mahbub had. It certainly made those neglected issues very prominent. Mahbub was also a wonderful leader who always gave credit to others. He was a very generous man, and I was extremely privileged to have him as a lifelong friend. I remember his commitments and kindness from very early days, when we were undergraduates together in Cambridge. Aside from Mahbub's powerful intellect, his personality was exactly right for someone to serve as the leader of the team to which we were all (including Paul Streeten, Meghnad Desai, Keith Griffin, Gus Ranis, Frances Stewart, Sudhir Anand and many others) proud to belong.

"One slightly negative side of this approach, which relied heavily on public relations, was that in order to win the attention of the public, Mahbub had to simplify tremendously. He went on to do things which were exactly right for his purpose but also generated a good deal of problems for the intellectual respectability of the 'human development approach.' One of them was his insistence on having one very simple 'Human Development Index,' or the HDI.

"This is an index which has three complements, namely literacy and basic education, longevity, and a minimum level of income. These three were chosen out of many other concerns, and of these three, two—basic literacy and longevity—are more directly connected with capability than income is. But there are a lot of other capabilities that one can think of. So this selection involved considerable neglect as well. Secondly, these three were then merged into one index on the basis of weighting. And Mahbub was persuaded that the public would not be ready to accept any weight other than one, one, and one—all others would appear to them (Mahbub told me) as 'arbitrary.' But the equal weighting is itself basically arbitrary: its effects depend on the units in which each of the three variables is measured. Since I was given the charge of developing this compound index, I had to worry a great deal about all this.

"Anyway the HDI which we devised did become quite popular, despite its arbitrariness. Mahbub was immensely skilled in getting the attention of the world. He was out to 'get the GNP,' and he did. Even though I had been very opposed to having one simple Human Development Index, I ended up gladly helping him to develop it, since he persuaded me that there was no way of replacing the GNP unless we had another similarly simple index. But this index will be better in the sense that it will focus on human lives, and not just on commodities."

The HDI is now a widely quoted and influential indicator that provides a yardstick against which the impact of government policies and initiatives can be measured. One of our voices is a longtime contributor to these reports. Paul Streeten wrote that "there is considerable political appeal in a simple indicator that identifies important objectives and contrasts them with other indicators."[13]

"But so what?" a skeptic might ask. Lourdes Arizpe provided a response by making a passionate plea for widening the development agenda to include a host of such considerations, especially *culture,* which she defined as "the constant flow of meanings that people create, transmit, and transform, that allow them to build relationships with others, with family, with kin, with other citizens, which allows them to participate in economic activities, which allows them to create symbolic representations that, in turn, give them a feeling of security and certainty."

Given this perspective, she was pleased with the enhanced focus on people: "Development, since the 1950s, has been defined mainly by economists in terms of economics and development. And economics is the science of exchange, of the exchange of goods. I believe that human life is more than the exchange of goods and that in fact the meaning that this exchange has, is subject to the cultural conventions that give it form. . . . I began to realize this way back from my very first fieldwork in the sierra, because there I found a village where people were very poor in economic standards, where they lived mostly off their immediate environment but at the same time were extremely rich in their cultural, spiritual, ritual, and social life. That was when I began to realize that with these mainstream economic growth theories—in Mexico as well as in other countries—we were gaining something, but we were losing a lot more. I say this not to justify compensating poverty with cultural richness but rather to point out that economic wealth, as we are seeing more and more in the contemporary world, is now accompanied by social, cultural, and spiritual poverty."

"What I possibly regret the most is that the developing countries could not determine and pursue a systematic policy for their own development," Surendra Patel told us. "They were swept away by the powers of the developed world. They got divided and vulnerable. There was a time at the UN when the developing countries proposed a lot of conferences. Money was made available, a number of innovative and constructive proposals were put forward. But now most of these come either from the IMF or the World Bank, of which I am very critical, as you know. What also worries me is that the corporate sector has acquired enormous powers irrespective of the consequences, especially for the weaker groups in the societies. . . . And I may be wrong, but I have a fear that these economic forces will not contribute to improving the situation, especially for the common man. The economic distance between nations and within nations may not be bridged by the forces of market liberalization and globalization. . . . I fully agree with the concept of 'human centered development' that you put forward in the *Human Development Report*, but I sometimes wonder how far we are from the implementation of this noble concept."

In this regard, Viru Dayal contributed a more visceral reflection: "Two things have happened with the passage of time. One is a greater impatience. I don't have the time now for all kinds of refinements. I don't have time for trickledown effects and all that kind of stuff. . . . The other is . . . I have begun to view issues of economics as issues of rights. I have increasingly begun to think of these things as matters of rights—the right to education, the right to health, the right to food, the rights of the child, the rights of women. Here again, it is the UN that has given this concept."

"I keep saying that these social issues—women's rights, treatment of children, safety nets, better income distribution—should have top priority in the development agenda," Gamani Corea told us. "But you must remember also that these are not the issues that touch on the raw nerves of relations between states. In most cases, you can end up with a do-it-yourself kit for the developing countries: you look after everyone, you look after your children, your poor, distribute your incomes better. We will give you encouragement, we will give you technical assistance, we will give you a little money here and there. But it is not the same as the set of issues, like trade and aid flows, which affect the pockets and the economies of the developed countries. . . . So I have been saying to Third World countries, please be careful. By all means do these things because they are very valid. They are very important. You have to pursue them and to commit yourself to them. But don't make it an alternative to the more difficult hardcore issues of international economic relations—trade, aid, debt, tariffs."

For Adebayo Adedeji, taking human development seriously meant that "I had to unlearn a lot of what I was taught at Harvard, London, Leicester and Ibadan. I came to realize that development is more than mere economism, more than macroeconomic aggregates and indicators, that human beings are not mere economic beings. They are also political, social, and cultural beings as well, and these affect their behavioral patterns in the economic domain. Therefore, what is needed to launch the development process on a sustainable basis is a holistic human development paradigm, not a narrow economic growth strategy. While economic growth is no doubt important, it is insufficient to bring about a holistic sustainable human development."

While the human development approach has had an impact on thinking and some policy processes, not all of our voices were converts. Jacques Polak, a longtime research director at the IMF, bluntly stated: "The *Human Development Report* is not put on the agenda of the Executive Board [of the IMF]. I doubt many people in this building have even looked at it. I don't think it is generally distributed even."

Human Security and the Responsibility to Protect

Human security focuses on the security of individuals, in contrast with the national security of the borders of the countries in which such individuals live. Former Dutch minister of development Eveline Herfkens, currently a UNDP advisor on the MDGs, indicated why this concept makes a difference. She quoted Juan Somavía, who in 1999 questioned "why it seems to be more urgent for the United Nations to act when someone is killed by a bullet than when someone dies of malnutrition."[14]

As a Quaker and longtime peace activist, Elise Boulding noted: "I have always felt that peace was about human security. But using that language of human security is a relatively recent introduction. It is to remind us what security is about when we are talking about peace, because military security and very often politically defined security do not create the conditions for human security. . . . The old power paradigm simply doesn't cut it. . . . So it's been a very slow development from what pacifists meant by security, which has always been fairly inclusive."

Although the main purpose of the UN was to halt bullets and foster international peace and security, human security differs in two respects from what was foremost in the minds of the Charter's framers. First, it reorients discourse on security away from the state toward individual human beings and their communities. Second, it broadens the scope of analysis and policy beyond classical military concerns and engages a much broader range of issues (from the domestic and political through the environmental and economic to health).

Virendra Dayal offered his interpretation of the origins: "The genesis of these ideas has deep roots in the concepts of the Charter and of the Universal Declaration. The concept of human security is intrinsic to these great instruments . . . I think it came on the agenda because of the crassness of our performance and because of the vast numbers who were dropping dead in situations that were not acceptable anymore. Either it was brought on by political violence or violence stemming from language, race, religion, or the like or violence that came from natural calamity or from manmade disasters of one kind or another, of which we seem to have no limit. It's kind of a march of folly over decades in front of our eyes and a consciousness that doesn't permit us to accept that anymore."

Thus, a human security perspective has arguably been implicit since 1945 in much of the world organization's concerns. However, taking this view too literally would overlook what constitutes a substantial shift. The disappearance of the constraints of the Cold War and the growth in civil wars has increased the UN's attention to substate, group, and individual security concerns. The rise of gendered and human rights discourse has also contributed to the "humanization" of security, as has the evolution of the UNDP's discussion of development and security. Indeed, it is not surprising that two of our interviewees, Sadako Ogata and Amartya Sen, were co-chairs of the Commission on Human Security. Their 2003 report, *Human Security Now,*[15] tries to place these two notions—ensuring life as well as its minimal quality—side by side.

Amartya Sen articulated why, in spite of criticisms, he believes in the analytical utility of the concept: "There are perhaps three different reasons why the work on human security is so important today. One concerns economics. The world has been too captivated by the rhetoric of just economic growth or more broadly of economic growth and equity. Growth with equity is fine as far as it goes, but quite often we have to face the reality of an economic downfall. So in addition to growth with equity, we have to worry seriously about downturn with security, when a downturn cannot be avoided. The focus purely on growth with equity did not help the economies in East Asia and Southeast Asia when the economic crisis and slump came in 1998. The protective system was altogether lacking in these countries even though they have had such great economic success. Those who lost their jobs and were thrown to the wall hit the wall hard, with nothing to protect them from sudden penury.

"For example, South Korea was indeed very successful in economic growth, along with maintaining equity, but it had very little arrangement for social safety nets. That became a top priority only when Kim Dae-jung came to office as president during the economic crisis. Nor did the Republic of Korea have all the basic features of a functioning democracy. We do know that democracy is extremely important in order to be able to place the case of the underdogs in the active political picture and in order to make the government accountable. In fact, we do know that famines do not occur in functioning democracies, and something a little similar applies to the predicament of the less extreme but still very badly off victims of sudden downturn (like those in the Asian economic crisis). Not surprisingly, with the crisis, people who had not worried much about democracy in the past became very involved in promoting it in East and Southeast Asia. A veteran democratic campaigner like Kim Dae-jung suddenly had much more support; in fact, he won his election mainly on that ticket in South Korea. Democracy became a big issue in Indonesia, a bigger issue in Thailand and in many other countries. This was not unconnected with the recognition that democracy is not only important in itself, it has a functional role in giving voice to the victims of economic insecurity. This is, I believe, an important issue in the contemporary world. We have to worry about human security and not be too captured by the slogan of growth with equity.

"Secondly, in the world in which we live, with 9/11 and with many other atrocities committed across the world, it has become absolutely clear that people can suffer from insecurity even when in their normal day-to-day life they are quite well off. It is not the case that only the poor are insecure. The poor are, of course, quintessentially insecure (we must not lose sight of that basic fact), but insecurity can blast the lives of very rich people too. Some of the people who were killed in the financial offices in the Twin Towers were typically rich. Insecurity can invade the lives of even very well-placed people.

That's an important recognition. We have to recognize the fact that insecurity is not just concerned with poverty. The insecurity in the lives of human beings caused by violence and conflict deserves a fuller recognition, going beyond the concentration on just military security or defense expenditure. It is the insecurity of the people rather than the state on which we have to focus, in the approach that we have tried to follow.

"The third reason for the importance of the subject of human insecurity is the interconnection between different sources of insecurity. That war and terrorism can disrupt production systems, political arrangements, health services, schools and other educational institutions, and so on is obvious enough. But the causal connections go in the other way as well. Economic and social insecurity [do] have a role in generating violence. We should not think only in terms of simple slogans like 'Economic insecurity creates violence and war.' It is not an immediate or a mechanical relation like that. But it would be hard to deny that economic suffering and fear can actually cause violence in the long run. Just to give an example, the 1840s in Ireland, during the Irish famines, constituted one of the quietest periods in Irish history for a population not known to be particularly docile. But the famine-stricken Irish were indeed relatively docile through the famine period. Even when food was being shipped from starving Ireland to well-fed England, none of the boats laden with food sailing down the Shannon was subjected to attempted robbery or seizure. It was all very quiet in a famine-devastated and -debilitated country. But for a hundred years—indeed, much longer—after that, the famine dominated the thinking of the Irish, their understanding of neglect and callousness or worse, their grumble about English rule, their desire to be thoroughly independent. And the sense of grievance fed violence and terrorism, which has rocked Ireland and England over more than a century. Similarly, the economic and social insecurities in the contemporary world can have very far-reaching destabilizing consequences, in addition to being terrible in themselves.

"The subject of human security does need serious attention for all these reasons. Insecurity can take several different forms and they do interrelate. Along with Sadako Ogata, and also the other Commissioners, I strongly believe that this is a perspective that ought to receive much more attention. We have discussed some of the concrete steps that we should urgently take to try to reduce human insecurity in the world today. As always, I very much hope the UN system will be our big ally here."

The need to broaden definitions was given a boost when a U.S. foreign policy expert and former Pentagon analyst, Richard Ullman, pointed out in a 1983 issue of the journal *International Security* that traditional concepts were framed "in excessively narrow and excessively military terms."[16] Since that time, a human focus has entered the critical security studies literature and in the statements of liberal states and international organizations.

John Ruggie noted the extent to which human security is part and parcel of the UN's current approach: "The case we tried to make in the Millennium report was an outgrowth of the whole reform effort: you remember the SG's [Secretary-General's] statement there that we have to put people at the center of everything we do." At the same time, he remarked, "We have never applied the term 'human security' beyond the security realm." Ruggie explained his discomfort with the vagueness of the notion. "If it is pushed too far it becomes useless as a concept. . . . My worry about some of the more elastic definitions is that they don't mean anything. . . . I don't think there is a whole lot of sympathy up here for expanding the concept of human security to mean all the ways in which an individual can be adversely affected by anything."

In their forthcoming critical history of the idea, Neil MacFarlane and Yuen Foong Khong argue that the discourse on human security has two dimensions: questioning the traditional focus on the state in the security studies literature and focusing on the threats to individual human beings; and widening the discussion of threat beyond violence and toward economic, environmental, and other dangers: "The first has been useful in sensitizing the UN and member states to the protection needs of individuals and communities affected by conflict and in arguing that the sovereign rights of states depend in some sense on their capacity and willingness to ensure the physical security of their citizens. The latter seems less helpful. . . . But it is unclear what analytical traction is gained by subsuming these other issues under the rubric of security rather than addressing them in their own right."[17]

In a set of essays in 2004 on the topic in *Security Dialogue,* UNU vice-rector Ramesh Thakur praised the multidimensional quality of human security and recommended that "realists . . . get real." Don Hubert of Canada's department for foreign affairs, who worked with former foreign minister Lloyd Axworthy in making his government a champion of the concept, scratched his head and wondered about the value of analytical hairsplitting in light of the demonstrated policy relevance of human security for banning land mines and establishing the International Criminal Court: "One might have thought that it was only French philosophers who rejected concepts that 'worked in practice, but not in theory.'"[18]

The 1995 Copenhagen World Summit for Social Development focused on the *problématique* of human security. This meeting was a landmark in a shift by governments toward a people-centered rather than a state-centered framework for social development as well as for peace and security.[19] The summit's secretary-general was Juan Somavía. His voice resonated from his Geneva office as the current ILO director-general: "As far as my involvement is concerned, we started pursuing the issue in the middle of the 1980s with the South American Peace Commission. . . . I feel particularly proud. I think that this is one of my contributions. . . . We created the South American Peace Commission and began to have meetings around security questions. Some of my left-wing friends said, 'Juan, what are you doing? These are military questions. These are questions that have to do with the military.' I said, 'No, no, no. Security is too much of an important issue to be given up as a concept of the military.' . . . And I brought the human security perspective to the UN when I got there. . . . If we want stable and democratic societies, there is a whole linkage between work and family work and democracy work and social stability which we simply lost sight of; . . . there are linkages between all of these elements and the constitution of the ILO, which, already in 1919, says that peace is linked to social justice. . . . The Declaration of Philadelphia of 1944 makes statements that are common sense for us today, but it is one thing for common sense to be formulated and accepted, it is another matter for common sense to inspire policies. Already in 1944 it said that poverty anywhere is a threat to prosperity everywhere."

The award of the Nobel Peace Prize to the ILO in 1969 was a formidable recognition for that agency's efforts since 1919. Francis Blanchard remembered the links to what was then not yet called "human security" in a powerful presentation by Pope Paul VI at the annual conference in June of that memorable year when David Morse was at the ILO's helm: "It was in that speech that [the pope] proclaimed that 'Development is the new dimension of peace.'"

Margaret Anstee recounted Somavía's contributions to the idea: "With Juan Somavía, we worked out the whole thesis . . . supporting him on the Copenhagen summit and developing the idea that security is much more than a military or purely physical concept. Security embraces the whole question of the basic welfare of human beings. Nobody can be considered to have security if they don't have enough to eat or they don't have access to basic needs." Looking back on her experience on the front lines of wartorn Angola, she noted ruefully: "I didn't have time to make definitions. I was dealing with the problems of security all the time. Human security in Angola was at about the lowest ebb that you can possibly imagine by any possible definition. It still is. When people are under fire or not getting enough to eat or not having the real basics of life, you just don't define it. You deal with it. . . . It was easier for me to define human security when I was in Vienna than it was when I was in Angola."

One of the potentially overpowering contemporary threats to human security is not military; it is the AIDS pandemic. By January 2000, human security appeared as the new common ground when, with the United States in the chair, the Security Council declared that the disease was a threat to international peace and security in Africa. Kofi Annan explained how this happened: "We kept looking at the statistics, and we saw the havoc this epidemic is wreaking around the world. And I had a conversation with the council members just before they went to Africa. Holbrooke was going, and it was his first trip to Africa. He said, 'What should I do?' I said, 'Focus on AIDS. You will be surprised.' They came back, and he said, 'It's amazing what I saw. . . . I want to put this in the council.' I said, 'That would be great, but they may resist it.' The only way we could put it in the council was to say, 'It is a security issue, because it has security dimensions to it apart from the economic and health.' . . . The day AIDS was taken up in the Security Council, Al Gore was in the chair as president. Gore came to represent the U.S., and the room was packed and it really lifted the level. And we were also going to organize a high profile for the General Assembly's Special Session on AIDS. And our own public information and others really did a lot. And prior to that, there had been a meeting in Abuja, where lots of African leaders had participated. That was where I launched the Global Fund [to Fight AIDS, Tuberculosis and Malaria] and challenged all the leaders to speak out. Speak out, because when it comes to AIDS, silence is death. . . . I think sometimes it is one event that turns the tide—and I think that Security Council session and the General Assembly and the changing attitude of leaders really helped."

Michael Doyle observed Annan's efforts as an assistant secretary-general: "He was very successful in pushing forward HIV/AIDS. He was able to put that on the agenda in ways that had been difficult for others, to convene meetings of pharmaceutical companies, in effect, to embarrass them into better arrangements, to say that HIV/AIDS had to be a global issue for everyone, to bring home its importance and how deadly and debilitating it is."

Noeleen Heyzer added to the sense of urgency in confronting the menace head on: "I have said many times in my speeches that HIV/AIDS as a disease is a health crisis, but the epidemic is a gender issue. Unless we address the whole issue of women's status—the power of women to say 'no,' the reduction of sexual violence in women's lives, the unequal power relationships—unless all these are addressed, we are not going to stop the spread of HIV/AIDS. Younger and younger girls are getting infected by older men. The rate of infection among girls is five to six times higher than the rate of infection of boys in sub-Saharan Africa. Until you address the issue of gender, you are not going to stop the spread of this epidemic. Gender inequality in this particular case is not just a moral issue. It is fatal."

Elise Boulding went back in history to list the various movements that had contributed to human security: the women's movement; conflict and peace studies and its activist wing, the nonviolence movement; the human rights movement; the environmental movement; and economic justice movement. She recounted her direct encounters with that intellectual ferment: "There has been a gradual building up of understandings within and between initially separate movements. The peace research movement consisted of a very small group early on. Kenneth Boulding, for example, and Emile Benoit were really working on disarmament per se and the danger of threat systems. But that was it—just work on preventing arms races. But then people in the relatively early days of IPRA—they came from Scandinavia—said, 'Hey, there are economic issues involved.' Johan Galtung was the first to make the distinction between positive peace and negative peace. Negative peace was simply the absence of war. Positive peace involved social and economic conditions conducive to human welfare for all people and was a far more complex concept. And after Stockholm, positive peace came to include the environment too. . . . So each of these movements were developing separately, but some peace researchers were saying, 'Hey, these are all interconnected.' Ester Boserup, a Danish economist who was the first to report that women did all the farming in the Two-Thirds World, was an early discoverer of the interconnections. . . . Scandinavian peace researchers, in particular, were some of the first to call attention to that interconnectedness."

Devaki Jain reflected back on her interpretation of the origins of human security: "I find that women claim that it is they who gave this idea, because it's so crucial for women. If you take military security now it is very clear to everybody—but it has always been clear to the women's movement that the people who are affected most by war are women. The soldiers die, but the women are raped and [are] often homeless or abandoned, or going to prostitution. So now that the women have established that they are some of the prime actors in the war theater, human security—their own security, both in terms of war as well as poverty, hunger, deprivation, et cetera—is considered to be the central concern of women."

In May 1986, Vladimir Petrovsky was appointed deputy to the Soviet Union's new foreign minister, Eduard Shevardnadze, a ringside seat for the momentous changes under way in that country: "We introduced the new concept of comprehensive security. The reason for this was that we saw two major problems for the country. The country was too much militarized and the country was too much isolated from the world. The concept of a comprehensive security treated security not in the traditional way as only military but also as economic, environmental, humanitarian. . . . At the beginning there was a lot of suspicion. The first reaction of the U.S. and some Western countries was, 'It looks as if it is propaganda of the Soviet Union, a new propaganda.' For us, it was a really sincere attempt to start new approaches to international cooperation. . . . Talks were held on the high level between Gorbachev and Bush in 1988, and the assistant secretary of state, John Bolton, and myself. For the first time in its history, the United Nations made joint proposals on the new concept of security in all aspects."

Scholars often underestimate or ignore the impact of international organizations in translating intellectual developments into practice. The UN's role in operationalizing human security has been something of a mixed bag. Dharam Ghai voiced his skepticism, for instance, because the notion "is like motherhood. It is a good thing that nobody opposes. The question is how to go about it." Kofi Annan agreed for the most part: "One has to be able to define it more narrowly than is being done presently for it to be meaningful and helpful to policymakers. . . . On the other hand, it frightens governments. They think you want them to be responsible for somebody from cradle to the grave. And they keep saying, 'Where do we get the money for this?' So we have to find a way of defining it in a way that it will not frighten them, but they will come to see it as a useful tool and definition as to what they should aim for in terms of the welfare of the individual in their society. And I'm not sure we've done that yet."

A key moment in contemporary UN history was the first-ever Security Council Summit in January 1992, which led less than six months later to the publication of newly elected Secretary-General Boutros Boutros-Ghali's *An Agenda for Peace*. Peacekeeping and other conflict management tools were of course discussed, but perhaps equally interesting was an emphasis on the "non-military aspects" of international peace and security.[20] "If you read the report closely," Boutros-Ghali told us, "you'll note that I am discussing development as the best way to prevent war. My successor—and one of the great, sacred rules is never to speak of your predecessors or successors—held meetings of regional organizations, which I was recommending. They engaged in discussions. They held symposiums to talk about peace-building, about consolidating peace. The problem of preventing conflicts has been the subject of a hundred symposiums almost everywhere in the world. Subsequently, I wrote with Marrack Goulding the *Supplement to An Agenda for Peace* that is far superior."

"At the start of this new century, the protection of peoples is among the most important issues before us," summarized Lloyd Axworthy, who played a key role in the evolution of the concept. "Peace and security—national, regional, and international—are possible only if they are derived from peoples' security."[21]

What could be more crucial to human security than life itself? Axworthy wanted an answer to that question, especially in light of the furor that surrounded another key moment for ideas when Secretary-General Kofi Annan began speaking passionately about "the sovereignty of individuals." Within an organization composed of states that take their sovereignty seriously, a controversial set of speeches at the end of the 1990s about humanitarian intervention was definitely ahead of the curve.[22] The moral pleas from the future Nobel laureate that human rights transcended claims by states were put forward more delicately later at the Millennium Summit. The reaction was loud, bitter, and predictable, especially from China, Russia, and much of the Third World. "Intervention"—for whatever reasons, including humanitarian—remained taboo.[23]

Jan Pronk echoed words used by several Secretaries-General in his examination of state sovereignty and its relationship to human rights: "Sovereignty, as far as I am concerned, is not an absolute concept. Of course, you need it in international law. But you need it together with other concepts, which are human rights oriented. The sovereignty of a nation should serve the rights of its people. National sovereignty contributes to a nation's cohesion and stability. But it should do so in the interest of people and not disregarding them or subordinating human rights to the interests of the state. . . . Is humanitarian intervention justified? To answer that question with an absolute 'no,' under all circumstances would not only constitute neglect of human values but it would also be a kind of ostrich policy. . . . There is a mutual self-interest of all countries to both guarantee national sovereignty as well as to condition it."

Viru Dayal put it in more personal terms, speaking as an Indian and a human rights advocate: "I am not one to ride roughshod over sovereignty or the territorial integrity of states or anything like that. I am an Indian, my bones and my blood. And I know what it means to protect the borders of my country which have been regained after 250 years. So I am not going to be someone who says, 'Forget about sovereignty.' . . . When you take what have been described as the two great pillars of the UN—the pillar of sovereign equality of states and the sovereign equality of the individual and you rest this great edifice on those two pillars, you know the architecture that you want and that you need. That must be an architecture that accommodates a decent respect for the dignity and worth of the human person with a respect for the state."

No issue raises the temperature in UN conference rooms more than debates about sovereignty. John Ruggie helped us listen to in-house conversations: "That is an interesting story—the whole internal debate about humanitarian intervention and the Secretary-General's position. As you might imagine, there was a great deal of reluctance inside the house to go down that road. Most of the advice—not all—that he got from the traditional departments was to stay away from it. . . . We have tried to be very careful to pose it as a dilemma rather than as one principle clearly having driven out another. Essentially, most of the SG's pronouncements on this, including his speech of September 1999 and then again in the Millennium report, are posed very carefully as a dilemma. . . . We are an organization of sovereign states. The UN Charter speaks of noninterference in the essentially domestic affairs of member states. At the same time, humanitarian law and fundamental human rights have become more highly prized and robust. Yet we don't have good ways of reconciling those two sets of norms. The SG believes that we have reached the stage where it is no longer legitimate for sovereignty to be used as a shield behind which to butcher one's own people, but the organization hasn't resolved the dilemma."

Ruggie explained that many UN staff "came to work for the UN because they are pacifists. For them, any use of force, no matter what the purpose, is unacceptable; it is an admission of failure. And when the use of force is forced on them, as it were, they handle it badly, insisting that it be applied minimally. That position has gotten the UN into some deep, deep trouble in the past. . . . In the end, that debate was won by the, I wouldn't say 'pro use of force' position, but a more strategic, Charter-based view on the use of force."

Ruggie recounted his version of Raúl Prebisch's earlier reflection about the WHO's neutrality toward malaria or Dag Hammarskjöld's neutrality toward Charter values: "I remember on more than one occasion saying, 'A police officer isn't neutral with regard to a mugger and a muggee. But he or she is impartial.' That took a while to sink in. I think now we understand that impartiality means acting in a rule-based manner rather than being neutral. The humanitarian intervention issue is part and parcel of that same debate."

The use of military means for human protection purposes is an international policy option. A thoughtful way to respond to a contemporary Hamlet asking "To intervene or not to intervene?" came from the International Commission on Intervention and State Sovereignty (ICISS), an initiative of the Canadian government and Lloyd Axworthy. The commission's report, *The Responsibility to Protect,* was presented in mid-December 2001 to the Secretary-General.[24] As a result, the notion of "sovereignty as responsibility," framed earlier in the 1990s by the Secretary-General's Special Representative on Internally Displaced Peoples Francis M. Deng,[25] moved from legal journals into the policy mainstream. Secretary-General Kofi Annan mentioned how quickly the middle ground of public discourse had changed and referred to a closed retreat for the members of the Security Council that was held in May 2002 to examine the issues: "When I made the statement three years ago, if I had suggested 'let's go on a retreat and discuss this,' they would have all run away from me. But today, not only are they going to do it, they are bringing the authors of the report to participate."

Samir Amin judged these developments as unequivocally positive: "Today—and I consider this to be progress for humanity—the concept of absolute state sovereignty is no longer acceptable. Human beings—all human beings—feel involved in what is happening beyond their own borders; they have assumed the right to judge and even to intervene in favor of peoples other than their own. . . . In my opinion, this represents a step forward for universal conscience, not a step backward. It's an advance for universal culture."

Few ideas have moved so quickly from off stage to the limelight on the international policy agenda as "the responsibility to protect," the notion that military force can and should be used to protect human beings. Former *New York Times* columnist Anthony Lewis went so far as to describe it as "the international state of mind."[26] Jan Pronk noted that the idea "was brought to the UN from outside, by international lawyers and by Doctors Without Borders. . . . It may be possible to bridge two ideas which are supposed to be in juxtaposition—national sovereignty and individual rights—but which not necessarily are so." Cornelio Sommaruga, who was an ICISS commissioner, echoed these interpretations: "The sacrosanct sovereignty of states is no more what it was up to ten years ago. . . . What the international community has to do is to see that law and order are applied."

Sonny Ramphal was guardedly optimistic about human security and the growing acceptance of the need for multilateral cooperation in a post-9/11 world: "But what is happening now is awareness that we are all vulnerable. We are vulnerable to terrorism, but terrorism is itself compounded of all these elements—of hatred, of division, of exclusion, of lack of development, a sense of injustice. . . . And what we are coming to recognize through all of this is oneness. . . . So for my part, even within my lifetime, I believe I have seen the evolution of global opinion, world opinion, in this direction. Of course, it takes terrible events to catalyze these ideas, as it took a world war—World War II—to produce the UN Charter, to produce all the hopes and expectations. So September 11 is beginning to produce a renaissance of global thinking. We may suffer another setback, but it is an inexorable process."

Global Governance and the Millennium Development Goals

The principal objectives of the new world organization in 1945 was to prevent the reoccurrence of devastating world wars and then promote human rights and international economic and social cooperation.[27] The concept of world government was viewed by everyone, except for a few die-hard world federalists, as unattainable. Thus, Woodrow Wilson's vision of a system of collective security monitored by gradually growing intergovernmental organizations was presented as the more effective organizing principle.[28] Functionalists saw the creation of specialized agencies as a way to build "peace by pieces."[29] Having learned from the failure of the League of Nations, the UN was armed with the teeth of the Security Council's coercion power spelled out in Chapter VII of the UN Charter.[30]

When new issues such as the environment and population appeared on the global agenda, it was logical to think about expanding multilateral institutions to mitigate the adverse effects of interdependence. The UN system maintained a Keynesian flavor in that international regulation and more muscular intergovernmental organizations remained dominant in thinking.[31]

By the middle of the 1990s, however, discourse had switched to "global governance," and most would agree with two scholars that "since World War II, the United Nations has been the central piece of global governance."[32] This is a fuzzier but more accurate depiction of how greater order and justice, such as they are, could result from devising new ways to foster greater synergy among state and non-state actors engaged in solving global problems. The UN's traditional role—and a logical one for an institution whose members are states—of improving government policy and intergovernmental responses is giving way to broader emphases. In view of the increasingly transnational character of many problems and the importance of non-state actors, the concept of global governance encompasses both transnational market forces and civil society as regular UN bill of fare instead of an occasional snack.

John Ruggie recalled his boss's thinking in the lead-up to the Millennium Summit: "As far as the Secretary-General was concerned, he knew what we wanted to do as far back as early 1997. . . . We always knew that the summit was the second big step in the reform effort. The first focused on bureaucratic processes and creating an organization that was more flexible, responsive and better managed. But it didn't address the substantive priorities of the organization. That required mobilizing member states' political support. For us those two were always linked. And the Millennium Summit was always seen as the opportunity for the second."

What exactly is governance, and why do we need it? The concept of governance is centuries old and has been central in many theories that attempt to map the intersection of the political, economic, and social dimensions of public and private life. Traditionally, governance has been associated with governing, political authority and institutions, and political control.

In recent years, political scientists such as James Rosenau have used "governance" to denote the regulation of interdependent relationships in the absence of an overarching political authority, such as in the international system.[33] The most useful and widely cited definition comes from the Commission on Global Governance, which was co-chaired by one of our voices, Shridath Ramphal (with former Swedish prime minister Ingvar Carlsson): "Governance is the sum of the many ways individuals and institutions, public and private, manage their common affairs."[34] Sonny Ramphal spelled out why he felt the commission's work was crucial: "It brought together all the elements that were in need of being brought together globally. We were not, even in [the] Brandt [report], paying enough attention there, or in the Palme report on disarmament, or in the Brundtland report on the environment. We weren't paying enough attention there to changing the world . . . to international governance, to the evolution from the age of the nation-state." The commission's report appeared in 1995, the same year the journal *Global Governance* began publication.

The origins of global governance are the topic of another book in this series,[35] but many of our voices expressed their opinions about why the concept had emerged. First, there has been growing pressure and awareness of global, cross-border, and on-border problems, such as environmental pollution, transnational crime, terrorism, infectious diseases, and migration, which can only be resolved through international cooperation.[36] Second, aspects of globalization discussed at the outset of this chapter have created or exacerbated existing global problems while developing countries changed the UN's development agenda.[37] Third, not only did the number of states grow, so too did the number and importance of non-state actors; and at the same time, in some sectors confidence diminished in governments and the public sector. Fourth, states have ceded a measure of their sovereignty and authority to promote their economic interests.

For many of our interlocutors, the MDGs are a standard with which to measure global governance and whether or not we are moving toward the more equitable world that underpins the vision in the UN Charter. The lack of central authority in the UN system, at least for Nafis Sadik, works against coherently pursuing the MDGs: "Everything should be under one leadership. No one person can control everything, but there must be somewhere where overall policy is set. For example, if now the UN system has the Millennium Development Goals as its system goals, then it must be how the whole system is going to contribute to the goals. This should be reviewed and viewed together, not in the way it is done now—that this is the set of goals and each organization goes and does it in its own way and may be treading into each other's areas. And there is no clear-cut responsibility of what of each one will do and accountability for the results. All the normative agencies are running after project money, and the operational organizations are getting money for a lot of research and analysis and setting standards."

There was hardly an idea that was not on the agenda when the MDGs were agreed. John Ruggie explained the Secretary-General's orientation: "The report to the summit got our political masters mobilized behind a set of substantive priorities, things that we ought to be doing out there in the real world. And the Global Compact, and private-public partnerships in general, is his attempt to provide a platform for all the relevant social actors—not only governments, but civil society actors, the private sectors and others—to align themselves behind UN goals. 'All hands on deck,' as he likes to say."

Those on deck included NGOs and transnational corporations. When asked how it all began, Ruggie referred back once again to the January 1999 speech by Kofi Annan at Davos: "The reaction was so positive that we were compelled to make a program out of it. That's when we started to think seriously about which specific UN principles we would seek to promote: where they would come from, how they should be defined, how we would link it all together. Today we have a set of human rights principles, and Mary Robinson [high commissioner of human rights at the time] is on board. She has to carry the ball on human rights. . . . But in fact, Mary wasn't fully on board at the beginning. She was under enormous pressure from human rights NGOs to attack companies, not to work with them. The ILO was more or less on board although in the typical ILO tripartite fashion, which means you don't deal with business, you deal with business associations because that's what the ILO constitution says. UNEP was very excited because they had worked with companies in the energy and chemical industries in particular. They had the experience of the ozone protocol negotiations, and so forth. . . . So gradually we fleshed out a program, defined nine principles that we adapted from UN declarations that governments had adopted by consensus,[38] and allocated responsibility. We realized that what we were trying to do here, essentially, was to provide little pockets of voluntary global governance, if you will, in areas that were underdeveloped. The Secretary-General has considerable legitimacy, but he cannot claim to represent popular roots. So we brought in organized labor and NGOs. It became a partnership between the UN, the business community, the International Confederation of Free Trade Unions, and about a dozen or so NGOs in environment and human rights."

Michael Doyle recalled how the Secretary-General "was able to use his authority to convene the Bank, the IMF, and the OECD and stop the bureaucratic battle over what development means. The MDGs became a set of criteria for what development meant. The goals did not eliminate the bureaucratic conflicts, but [they] at least got development policy focused on a similar target. That was useful. Whether it should be GDP per capita or human rights or sustainability [was] a source of considerable tugging back and forth. He was able to bring them together on that. . . . His role was predominantly one of creating doctrine, identifying key issues, convening, and providing a stamp of legitimacy."

The need to create an economic security council was one of the ideas for UN reform in the early 1990s, but one that had little traction.[39] It was taken up by the Commission on Global Governance, and Sonny Ramphal recalled former IMF managing director Michel Camdessus telling the commissioners: "I sit in on the meetings of the G-7. I can tell you that the G-7—although it presents itself as a directorate of the world on economic issues—knows that it is powerless to implement its decisions. It recognizes the need for a different forum, a larger forum. But it is terrified of making the step without the assurance of how it will turn out. So you are right, the recommendation is on the right lines. Whether it is in the UN system or out of the UN system is in a sense a detail. The question is that the world badly needs management of the global economy if we are serious about the realities of globalization. And we haven't got it."

John Ruggie was one of the persons on the 38th floor responsible for pulling together the background documents for the summit. He described the effort to attract NGOs and the private sector into intergovernmental dialogue through the Global Compact as "the most complex political undertaking that I have ever been involved in." He continued: "The Global Compact is a partnership with the ILO, the High Commissioner for Human Rights, UNEP and UNDP, which leads the country-level efforts. . . . The human rights organizations still don't like the idea that Shell is a participant in the Global Compact, because of Nigeria. The environmental groups will say it doesn't make any sense to have a Global Compact that seeks to have business promote environmental issues that doesn't have Shell in it. . . . The model that we have selected is not a regulatory model; it is a learning model."

When asked to parse the difference from earlier efforts with the private sector, Ruggie added: "Through the power of transparency we hope that good practices over time will help drive out bad ones. . . . That learning forum already involves several business schools just to manage the cases. Somebody has got to put the cases together into comparable terms. There is so much activity going on as part of the Global Compact that it is almost mind-boggling to think that a small handful of people here, in the Secretary-General's office, are managing the process. . . . The thing to stress is that what we are doing is managing networks. . . . India was deeply suspicious of this effort at first. When we held our meeting in Bombay (Mumbai) last December [2000], twenty-two or twenty-four Indian CEOs showed up. They then told the Indian government what they were planning to do with this. When word got back to their UN mission, they became one of our staunchest supporters. So we are doing everything possible to promote activity in key developing countries. We even have a project starting up in China in the area of labor rights, believe it or not. That will blow you away, since there aren't a whole lot of labor rights in China. But we discovered one that they are willing to address—the problems faced by handicapped workers in the workplace, of whom there are 150 million in China. And our local champion is Deng Xiaoping's son, who, as you may recall, was thrown out of a window during the Cultural Revolution and is a paraplegic. He moves around in his wheelchair promoting the project."

"The Global Compact," Michael Doyle explained, "originated in the SG's understanding that there was an opportunity to add to the policy clout of the UN by mobilizing the private sector to promote UN goals. The key person who turned that idea into a reality was John Ruggie. The first purpose underlying the compact was mobilizing the private sector to make a difference on development, on human rights, on environmental protection, and [on] labor rights. The second purpose was that the very act of reaching out to the private sector would position the UN as an institution that was friendly to the more conservative powers—that is, the U.S., the Europeans, the Japanese—because it engaged with private enterprise. Previously, the UN had been regarded as an enemy of private enterprise. That made Washington more difficult and some of the other governments more difficult. From the political point of view and from the ethical point of view, this was a chance to find a new constituency."

Kofi Annan himself told us why the effort to push companies to be socially responsible and get them to apply universally accepted norms was an innovation that could work: "It is not a code of conduct which is enforceable. We don't have the means to enforce it. But what we have discovered is that transparency and dialogue can be powerful tools. . . . And let's not forget that when you talk of the Global Compact, the participants are the companies, and the companies include management and the trade unions and labor. And they are very much in the room with us, as well as the NGOs."

Opening the UN's embrace to include the private sector has encountered skepticism. On occasion, NGOs have called the entire effort "bluewash"—to indicate making the unacceptable acceptable by masking it with UN colors. In fact, a day prior to the Global Compact Leaders Summit in June 2004 at

UN headquarters, a group of NGOs gathered under the umbrella of the Alliance for a Corporate-Free UN. In our interview Adebayo Adedeji was passionate about his opposition: "I have still enough of that past in me to be rather guarded about the idea that one should open our gates to forces which are pursuing their own private interests in a way in which they might end up occupying too much space. I have the very strong conviction that in principle, as in a regulatory system of society, socialism is superior to liberalism. Let me put it squarely. I think that it is the function of government in society to ensure a decent place for everybody in that society. When you open too much the mechanism to forces which cater [to] private interests, you may frustrate that function. I have difficulty with the idea that the sum total of private economic rationality of all the powers will amount to a global rationality that will be conducive to the best organization of society. But this is all at a distance. I think there is *un temps pour tout* [a time for everything]—it is past for me to pass judgment on what is going on now. But if you ask me, I am sometimes concerned about the direction in which we are heading."

As Michael Doyle noted, the jury is still out on the impact of the Global Compact. "The compact still has not been able to demonstrate a strong impact on corporate good governance. We're still working on a 'leash' that they gave us. But there is still no better alternative. . . . The compact has gone out, to its credit, and commissioned studies—including one by Richard Locke and a few guys at Sloan who are doing a study to see whether the compact can make a difference. Frankly, I think the answer is going to be, 'Who knows?' But my view—what I say to the critics still when it comes up—is that I think we probably inspired some companies to do a little bit more. Second, we have provided a 'barefoot doctor' version of international corporate social responsibility for Third World companies who can now participate. There are all sorts of companies from Thailand, India, China, the Philippines, South Africa, Nigeria, and Egypt that have signed up. Third, if you have something better, put it on the table. This is the best we can do in today's world. That was the consistent defense that we of the Global Compact would give to the critics, and they never persuaded us that we were wrong. We always also said, 'Give us some time and we will prove that this makes a positive difference.' And frankly, we've never been able to prove that. Who knows what will happen next?"

Part Three.
The World Organization, Ideas, and Twenty-First-Century Challenges

The third and final part of this volume pushes us toward "future-oriented history." This seeming oxymoron to professional historians was part of our project's original justification and necessitates applying the relevant lessons from the past to contemporary problem solving.

This part begins with Chapter 9, "A Revolutionary Idea: The International Civil Service." It is supplemented by Chapter 10, "The Power of Ideas and People inside the UN," and Chapter 11, "Blending Outside Intellectual Energies." These three examine the role and contribution of actors and processes at the nexus of ideas, international public policy, and multilateral cooperation. Here we have pulled together commentaries about the nuts and bolts of international secretariats and discussions in a variety of international settings. Related comments on these topics have appeared throughout the book, but we wished to consolidate in one place a portrait of what often appears to outsiders, and actually to many insiders as well, like a Byzantine set of processes and a confusing array of players. At the same time, both UN insiders and outsiders are responsible for creating as well as transmitting or transforming (and sometimes distorting or suppressing) ideas, the heart of our intellectual history.

Senior UN staff may have risen through the ranks after having started at a very junior level (for example, Secretary-General Kofi Annan or Sir Brian Urquhart). Or they may be named to a junior- or senior-level international post from government (for example, Julia Henderson or Gamani Corea) or from an NGO or the private sector (for example, Noeleen Heyzer or Maurice Strong) or from the academic world (for example, Hans Singer or John Ruggie). Similarly, a member of the Secretariat may leave UN service and take up a position in government (for example, James Jonah or Bernard Chidzero) or an NGO (for example, Adebayo Adedeji or Sadako Ogata) or assume a university position (for example, Robert Cox or Alister McIntyre). Moreover, many so-called outsiders who have never been a UN official (for example, Gerry Helleiner or Sonny Ramphal) have been called upon as consultants or members of expert groups or commissions so many times that they are "inside-outsiders."

Chapter 12, "The Legacy and Future Intellectual Challenges," concludes this book. It attempts to shed light on the key assumption propelling this project—namely, that ideas matter. The voices help substantiate four propositions encountered by readers in the introduction. First, ideas can change the nature of international public policy discourse. Second, ideas can help states as well as individuals and non-state actors define and redefine their identities and interests, including providing a tactical guide to policy and action when norms conflict or when sequencing or priorities are disputed. Third, ideas can alter prospects for forming new political or institutional coalitions. Fourth, ideas become embedded in institutions and thereby can challenge not only the founding principles of those institutions but also help in setting future agendas.

In responding to our prodding to look toward the future, Secretary-General Kofi Annan joked: "I would not want to stay on for the next fifteen years. I may be a glutton for punishment, but not to that extent. In terms of ideas and where the organization should put the emphasis, quite frankly I would return back to the issue that you think we have tended to neglect. I would want to push for ideas in the economic and social area. How do we deal with the question of inequality within and between states? How do we bring in the marginalized and challenge economists and political scientists to try and come up with the idea and approaches that will free countries from poverty and the debt trap? . . . And finally, one area which I have pushed them to do something about, and I challenge every scientist I see, is to resolve the need for cheap and renewable sources of energy. And I am not talking about a renewable source of energy for the city dwellers like New York, but for the farmers and others who cut every tree in sight to heat water to cook—so that they will not have to do that. So it's energy, water, and sustainable economic development."

Although we continue to maintain that there is power in ideas and in the people who wield them, we do not ignore materialism. It would be foolhardy to overlook the importance of powerful states and organizations that flex their muscles and thereby circumscribe the potential of ideas to achieve significant change. At the same time, our voices put forward anecdotes and illustrations about the value of creative ideas and maneuvers, of imaginative and astute individuals in action in the international arena. People do matter.

9

A Revolutionary Idea:
The International Civil Service

- **Good Old Days?**
- **Cold War Diversions**
- **Geographical Representation**
- **Women at the UN**
- **Organizational Culture**
- **Reform Difficulties**

The possibility of constituting an independent group of internationally recruited people whose allegiance is to the welfare of the planet, not to their home countries,[1] is still much disputed. Many of our voices spent the bulk of their careers in international service—in many ways, it is what made them who they are professionally. For others, a stint within the world organization or working in close proximity to a UN institution was a significant professional experience.

During World War II, the Carnegie Endowment for International Peace sponsored a series of conferences to learn the lessons from what many believed was the "great experiment" of the League of Nations, namely creating a core of independent officials to attack international problems.[2] This legacy was carried over to the UN, and Charter Article 101.3 called for the "paramount consideration in the employment of staff" to be that of "securing the highest standards of efficiency, competence, and integrity" while paying regard "to the importance of recruiting the staff on as wide a geographical basis as possible." This chapter portrays the pluses and minuses of the heart and soul of the "second United Nations"—the staff—particularly the quality of the international civil service and its aptitude in the area of creative and productive thinking.

The foremost advocate for an international civil service was the second Secretary-General, Dag Hammarskjöld, whose speech at Oxford in the

Sheldonian Theatre on a muggy afternoon on May 30, 1961, spelled out the importance of an independent staff despite the fact that many thought this kind of "political celibacy" was "in international affairs a fiction." The most striking passage of his speech, which was crafted with the help of one of our voices (Oscar Schachter), asserted that any erosion or abandonment of "efforts in the direction of internationalism symbolized by the international civil service . . . might, if accepted by the Member nations, well prove to be the Munich of international cooperation."[3] The experiment is still under way and UN multilateralism is alive, if not always well, but Hammarskjöld's warning about the need to protect staff autonomy was prescient.

James Jonah, who headed the UN's personnel service from 1979–1982, has emphasized the critical importance of independence in his forthcoming memoir, *What Price Survival of the United Nations? Memoirs of a Veteran International Civil Servant.* In his interview, he recalled the "golden days" of the international civil service and its personification in the words of that Oxford address: "I still believe that the question which was posed by Hammarskjöld in his Oxford speech [the politicization of the international civil service] still stands. And I think people intuitively agree, but they feel it has gone so far that you can never change it. . . . But I am saying, 'Well, it may be practical politics, but the consequences down the road are very serious.' And I go back to what happened under the League system. I have looked at this book *The Enemy Within.*[4] . . . The book argued that the second secretary-general of the League killed the League from within. . . . Therefore, I still believe that if you kill this concept [of autonomy] . . . it will make the UN become what it was not supposed to be—an intergovernmental secretariat. . . . We are moving towards that, and I think it is not going to be very good for the credibility, as a corporate body of the UN. . . . I think it's deliberate. The Russians never bought the idea at all. At least they were clear about that. . . . The Americans, the British, they were sold on the idea. They really had complete faith in it, but they came to the position that the secretariat was detrimental to their interests."

Those employed by the UN system worldwide, both professional and support staff, today number approximately 50,000, which does not include temporary peacekeeping operations or the members of the IMF and the World Bank group because they are recruited and paid on different bases. This figure represents substantial growth from the handful, about 300, in the UN's first year at Lake Success. But "there is little realistic justification for describing this civil service as 'a vast, sprawling bureaucracy,'" wrote one of our interviewees in a widely quoted passage. Brian Urquhart, in collaboration with Erskine Childers (who died before we could interview him) noted that the organization that serves the globe's 6.5 billion people has a staff that was smaller than the civil service of the U.S. state of Wyoming (population 545,000), the employees of the Swedish city of Stockholm (population 672,000), the district health services of Britain's principality of Wales, and the combined civil services of Canada's province of Manitoba and its capital, Winnipeg.[5]

Numerous voices conveyed the importance of the "struggle" (not necessarily the "victory") for development and social justice that serves as a motivation to work as an international civil servant. Although disappointments go with the territory, and today a temporary shadow hangs over the Secretariat as a result of the oil-for-food inquiry being led by Paul Volcker, nonetheless a basic idealism and devotion was present in virtually all of our interviews. Juan Somavía spoke for many: "There is not a day in which you say, 'I am going to work throughout my life in order to make society better.' It doesn't happen that way. You get involved. You move forward." He saw that most of his colleagues had an approach to life but had made one crucial decision: "You took the decision to swim against the current. You took a decision to opt for very difficult things. . . . So the only thing you can't do is to complain that change is difficult. Of course it is difficult. Naturally it is complicated. The decks are stacked against making societies better and more just. But that's what it's about. . . . You help produce as much change as possible, and then others take over and continue the struggle. . . . Making societies more fair and more just is a damned difficult thing to do to. And we all just keep at it."

Good Old Days?

Many voices regretted what they saw as the deterioration in the standards of the international civil service and in staff morale and the fading of idealism over the last sixty years, largely due to systematic efforts to undermine the international civil service. The Cold War—and more particularly the blowback from McCarthyism that we heard about earlier—and growing pressures for great-power dominance in response to geographic representation from newly independent countries influenced all aspects of professional life at the UN. For instance, Janez Stanovnik told us: "I must tell you that the United Nations in my time, and before 1952 when I was in New York . . . was a true family of sincere believers, which it is not anymore." He did not conceal his admiration for the Secretariat during the first decade. Commenting that officials had "a brain and heart," he stated: "If I were to go on enumerating how many, practically I would say that there was no one single great name in economic writings in the period of 1945 to 1955 that was not in one way or the other associated with the United Nations. . . . All these illustrious, creative idea producers were in one way or another associated with the UN. In addition to this, none of them was ideologically infected by the great split in the world. But they were truly all mindful of catastrophe which we [had] been living through in the World War and were sincerely devoted to the ideas of the UN. I can, as an old man, just tell you what kind of emotional atmosphere it was working with the Secretariat."

Norway's Just Faaland went back even farther in reflecting on the nature of the UN's contemporary applied research: "I think it has decreased in quality and applicability. When you go back, as I think we did referring to the early 1950s, and even go back to the League of Nations, there were very important analyses of the world's future in the late 1930s. . . . It happened in a period when the world was getting organized in a new way, in all sorts of ways. I think there is a lot more such research going on now within and near to the UN, but it doesn't have the same impact and perhaps even vision that it had at the time—but maybe that's because of us, the people who are involved. Maybe it has to do with the general organization of world politics."

Robert Cox also remembered the optimism and energy that characterized his colleagues in the early years and praised the lack of technical specializations among that first group. "We were virtually all [what] you might call 'generalists' when we were recruited. We were recruited in order to become officials of an international institution and to work for the strengthening of the institution and the purposes of the institution. But subsequently it became much more a case of specializations and you wanted people who were technical specialists in this, that, and the other thing. And one could say that perhaps their commitments were towards their specialty rather than more towards the institution."

James Jonah waxed nostalgic about the start of his career in the 1960s: "When I joined the UN, I was exposed to people like William Jordan. Ralph Bunche used to speak to me at least once a week for at least an hour. Could you imagine? [I was] a P-2,[6] and all he wanted to do was to convey to me his experience. I was exposed to Brian Urquhart. So they were thinking ahead. These people were such well-established people, they were not afraid of a young P-2 coming and taking their jobs."

In reflecting on the difference between today's secretariats and those of yesteryear, Margaret Joan Anstee pointed to the inevitable problems of growth: "It has become very much bigger. I had grown up in UNDP where everybody knew everybody else. Senior people were more concerned about the staff. It is also the case that the organization has become demoralized by these constant attacks upon it. . . . People just don't seem to care so much about their staff. I do get depressed when I come back and see people in UN headquarters whom I know to be good people because they worked for me in the past—they all just want to get out. They say, 'The atmosphere has changed completely.'" Brian Urquhart agreed, "We lost our slim figure very quickly. And people and governments had their own hobbies that they were pursuing in the UN."

Stéphane Hessel, speaking about people of his generation who participated in the early years of the UN, allowed that "perhaps one tends to idealize in one's memory moments of that kind." Hessel recalled his bubbling enthusiasm at having unexpectedly landed a UN job: "I remember when I was sent to work on the WMO, the [World] Meteorological Organization, to bring it into existence. God knows that meteorology was not one of my favorite passions. But I felt that here again is something—the international is coming into being. We were, indeed, firm ideological internationalists. We were all secretariat, and we were terribly critical of governments. We were the ones who were supposed to see to it that the Charter was going to be put into effect and we knew that the governments were resistant. . . . The mood, the atmosphere in Lake Success, although the fact that we worked in this factory, that we were under the ground, it was really like a conspiracy. It was a plot to make the United Nations successful, and that is an atmosphere of great enthusiasm."

Enrique Iglesias looked back with nostalgia to a period when government interference did not undermine the staff: "The bureaucracy at ECLA in the fifties and sixties, for example, had a sense of mission. International bureaucracy had a soul; it lost its inspiration, turning its work into something more bureaucratic. The job gets done, some staff working harder than others. But the mystique that first inspired the United Nations has been lost."

As they compared the international civil service today with both national civil services and university faculties, two of our scholarly voices were measured. Robert Cox said: "I think it was a lot more diverse. . . . They are certainly up to the standards of the major national civil services. But there is a lot more variety and a lot more of what we used to call deadwood." Samir Amin commented about the nature of international administration: "I've met a good number of bureaucrats, both good and bad, of all kinds! . . . I don't share the impression—a notion commonly heard—that the United Nations is somehow more mediocre than other bureaucracies. Others are just as mediocre, if one is being harsh, or just as brilliant, if one wishes to be complimentary. It's an enormous machine in which there is a lot of waste in order to obtain modest results, but that's the price one pays in all bureaucracies."

Whereas most thought that the international civil service today is comparable in quality to the best-trained national civil servants, there was a range of opinion about comparisons between staff members of the UN system and those of the Bretton Woods institutions. The perception of the IMF's former director of research, Jacques Polak, was that the UN was less competitive in recruitment of staff, hampered largely by its lack of resources and its dependence on national governments: "The only place that economists were really appreciated was the Fund. The Bank had a very limited staff of economists and didn't quite know what to do with them. The UN was already a bureaucracy. . . . They hired a lot of good people, but in the end it did not amount to much."

In his view, the IMF secretariat has been an intellectual force: "The IMF started about ideas, and as circumstances in the world changed, new ideas were needed. It was really the duty of that organization to be alert to these issues. And because it had a good staff from the start, it was able to come up with new ideas and sell them to a certain extent to the membership. This is not obvious, I think, perhaps in other organizations. There, new ideas come from important member countries, who bring them in and then gather support from them and sell them. The interesting part in the Fund is that a lot of these ideas arose in the institution, or at least the staff of the institution was capable to pick them up from the air where they floated in a very general way and make a run with them."

This has been possible, Polak added, due to the quality of Fund's staff. "That goes back to the recruitment policy by Bernstein and other aspects of the Fund as a well-known place where interesting jobs could be had. One example of that was a young economist, who told me he had a chance of being considered for a job in the Fund or in the Bank, and he had decided on the Fund. And I said, 'Why?' And he said, 'Because the Fund publishes *Staff Papers*. That's why I joined the Fund's staff.' That was [Wim] Duisenberg. My recruiting of Bob Mundell fits in the same pattern. And Fleming for that matter. . . . We made major efforts to get the very best people. We had a good system of promotion, not based on nationality. And we allowed people to write. We had our own journal, in which they could publish if they wanted to, but also they could publish outside. And it took a staff large enough to produce ideas and to be able to sell those ideas to the Executive Board."

Margaret Anstee, when asked about Polak's view, responded: "He is certainly correct about being paid more and better conditions of service. That is not going to attract everybody. It doesn't necessarily attract the best people. I am not so sure about the quality of these two organizations now. They used to be, I think—well, they were insufferably arrogant sometimes, but they had really very, very good people. They drew away quite a lot of our own top people from UNDP, or from the UN. Quite a number of people went, although I do not necessarily think they went only for the higher salary."

In looking southward from New York toward Washington from his dining room on the 38th floor of UN headquarters, Secretary-General Kofi Annan was clear: "They are much better paid than we are. And because they are better paid, they perform better, because you are competing for talent internationally. And we should have the right incentives to be able to attract, recruit, and retain competent people over a long period. . . . We've lost quite a few people to the World Bank, but the reverse is not true. The traffic is one way. Their conditions are much better. I think the governments are reviewing it now. . . . I think it is also that once the conditions are improved, we ourselves should also aim higher and lift our standards of recruitment. We should also allow our staff to publish."

In responding to a question about why the Bretton Woods institutions have been more effective in recording their intellectual contributions, Gerry Helleiner's wry voice remarked: "I suppose, partly, it is the same reason the World Bank and the IMF have beautiful cafeterias. They have resources. They can have an in-house historian, an in-house archivist, and still eat well. Their ceilings aren't falling down. They are putting up new buildings. These are rich institutions. The UN literally has ceilings falling down. It is partly that, but it is also partly that the Bank and the Fund have had the luxury of fairly independent hiring practices and the quality of the people that they have is, on average, higher. There is less dead wood." Plans are finally under way and funding has finally been granted by the UN's member states to construct much-needed space for the UN in a new facility south of the present headquarters in New York. This will also provide a safer, cleaner work environment for UN staff there because it would permit the gutting and renovation of the original building, opened in 1951, which no longer meets any building codes and would be condemned were the UN subject to New York City standards.

As the head of the UN's internal watchdog, the Joint Inspection Unit, Maurice Bertrand was perhaps the most brutal critic of the international civil service, then and now: "My experience of the various secretariats that I visited gave me an impression of total anarchy in personnel management, of a generally low level of competence, and of a lack of rules."

Not all agreed. Lourdes Arizpe, based on her experience in Paris during the 1990s, was considerably more upbeat about contemporary intellectual productivity: "I was very impressed with many of the people of UNESCO because of their commitment, their conviction, and their sense of mission. Many of them I had met in the 1970s and 1980s, so there was this whole generation, including my generation of 1968, that, paraphrasing Virginia Woolf, I would say, 'We galloped through life behind ideals.' . . . Then there were other people who were well intentioned but perhaps did not have the training or the interest in developing projects more. And then there were those who where there because it was Paris. . . . I was especially struck at first because so many of the ambassadors told me, 'Oh, these bureaucrats in UNESCO are terrible. They don't work.' . . . Then I started knowing my colleagues more, and what I found is that some of them were terribly overworked, more like saints because they could accept conditions of work which would have driven anyone else out of their minds, and they were very capable of bringing out the work that could be accepted consensually by 186 member states! This is a huge feat."

After all is said and done, perhaps Sonny Ramphal's summary came closest to a middle ground and pointed the way toward a better future: "They need space in the UN. How do they find space in that system, in that highly structured, very institutionalized, almost rule-bound system? . . . In the early days, the UN system did gather some of the good minds. They had space there to work. Governments hadn't, as it were, taken over the system. Ambassadors hadn't trammeled the secretariat in the way that they were later to do."

Cold War Diversions

While some of the preceding judgments could perhaps be dismissed as typical reminiscences by old-timers, there can be little doubt that forces outside of the international civil service played an especially important role in diluting the original ideal. Janez Stanovnik, who carried a passport from Yugoslavia while a staff member, spoke about the overall impact: "So we have got, starting from about 1960, this disease of nepotism in the UN. I could cite examples which do not relate only to the Soviet Union—where of course the practices have been the worst—but also respected Western countries were often trying to get an influence on the secretariat of the UN by the way of 'political appointments.' The Charter's principle of 'just geographic representation' was greatly misinterpreted."

Another of the first UN staff members from the Eastern bloc was Hungary's Mihaly Simai, who remembered while some staff from the West were open to their colleagues from the East, others "considered us as a pain in the neck or a pain in the ass. . . . They said: 'What the hell are you doing here?' . . . But later on, even with these people, one could get along. I would say their views on Eastern Europeans had been basically shaped by Russians, and there were terrible Russians there. . . . Russians presented data on the Soviet Union in a way which was far from the realities and tried to block any effort to get out meaningful information."

Brian Urquhart, himself one of the great advocates of an independent civil service, pointed to the same issues: "To some extent, there is a gross lack of accountability for the secretariat, except in purely budgetary terms, and somebody has to correct that. We started off with an absolutely total belief in the rules of the Charter. We thought that we were there to serve the organization as a whole, that we did not take pressure or instructions from any government, and that any governments who tried to put pressure on us were to be rebuked. . . . Then the economic, social, and specialized agencies had all of these proliferating projects of one sort or another. The best-known one was UNESCO's project on sex at high altitudes, a project Julian Huxley introduced. So the secretariat—or some parts of it—became overstaffed and disreputable intellectually. . . . And we got a large collection of Soviet *apparatchiks*. The best of them were the KGB [Committee for State Security] people, who were at least reasonably intelligent. The remainder were the dregs of the foreign service and they were completely useless to any UN purposes. Right in the middle of the secretariat, there was this large inert mass of Soviet officials who nobody trusted."

Sir Brian at least found Moscow's attitude straightforward: "They said, we don't recognize the notion of an objective international service. As Khrushchev said to Hammarskjöld, 'We don't believe in angels. We don't believe there is such a thing as an objective international civil servant, particularly you.' Well, at least he was honest. Whereas the United States carried on about Article 100 and then really made it impossible."

The world's two most powerful countries were among the worst offenders during the Cold War in trying to undermine the integrity of the international civil service. Jack Stone recalled the problems of an American director who was trying to recruit the required staff member from the East: "In those days, recruitment from Soviet bloc countries was a Byzantine process negotiated through the personnel office and the East bloc." James Jonah pointed to the shoe being on the other foot with the painful imposition of an American staff member at the insistence of U.S. ambassador Jean Kirkpatrick: "Here was a woman who thought that she was an intellectual. . . . All she was there to do was to implement American interests. . . . So you can begin to see that once she's there, the staff are not going to be motivated to work. . . . This is going on around the secretariat now. It has gone too far."

Janez Stanovnik, whose exposure to Cold War pressures as executive secretary of the ECE was as acute as anyone's, looked back: "Member countries . . . [and] authorities within the UN secretariat . . . degraded the quality of the secretariat. All through my reign in ECE, if I may say so, I was time and again quoting Articles 100 and 101 to the ambassadors who were pressing on me for the appointments of their nationals. The article by Hammarskjöld in the *International Law Review* [his Oxford lecture] is a classic. You know that Hammarskjöld unfortunately yielded a little bit to McCarthy's pressure. In this article though, he formulates very, very clearly Drummond's—the first secretary of the League of Nations—principles on the recruitment of the international secretariat. . . . You see, in this first period it was mainly loyalty to the organization and the ideas of the organization and professional quality; [then] the so-called just geographical distribution. . . . became number one."

Geographical Representation

Javier Pérez de Cuéllar, who was the highest-ranking international civil servant during the period 1981–1991, argued that when he served the United Nations, "I put my nationality in the freezer. I felt that morally, ethically, I couldn't be an under-secretary-general of the United Nations and at the same time act as a Peruvian and try to be in touch with my ambassador. . . . I changed nationality in a way. In a sense, I was no longer Peruvian. I was international." The former Secretary-General described the ideal. The reality was often different.

Beginning in the 1950s and 1960s, new member states clamored for "their" quota of posts in international secretariats following the bad example set by major powers. The result was that competence was downplayed and the importance of national origins as the main criterion for recruitment and promotion was exaggerated.

Can anything be done? Kofi Annan maintained that it could. "You can have a geographic spread and still have very competent staff. . . . The difficulty is that we have tended, in the past, and even now, to rely on governments to give us names and good candidates for our positions. Sometimes they give you good candidates. Other times, they give you friends or people they cannot place in their own system." Annan concluded that honest searches and "just saying no" to governments could work wonders. Moreover, he argued: "We should try and get away from countries inheriting posts. There's a certain political reality, but I think as we move on into the future, when governments are cooperating a bit more, and the organization hopefully becomes stronger, we should be able to do more of that."

He then went on to illustrate how he implemented these ideas in concrete terms, using the example of what he did when it was time to replace Gus Speth as the UNDP's administrator in 2000: "I decided that the U.S. had held the UNDP job for too long. And at that time, they had UNDP, UNICEF, and World Food Programme [WFP], and I wanted UNDP to go to a European. So I asked the European Union [EU] to give me a list of candidates. They came with a list of one. So I called them, and I said, 'I asked for a list of candidates. You gave me one name. . . . Let me be clear. You may be embarrassed, because I will go outside your list of one. I will appoint a European, but it may not be yours. If you don't want to be embarrassed, give me a wider list.' They insisted on that person, and I did not appoint the person. I took someone who was from Europe—Mark Malloch Brown—but it wasn't the candidate the entire EU [had selected]. . . . And I think we should do more of that."

One of the ideas that Sir Robert Jackson proposed in his *Capacity Study* in 1969 was the establishment of a staff college to train personnel. The ILO's Training Centre in Turin, Italy, was transformed into the United Nations System Staff College in January 2002 in order to promote a common UN management culture. Jackson's original idea was to establish an essential career-development institution for those 50,000 people who serve worldwide. The Staff College is not that institution at present. Maurice Bertrand, who at the time headed the UN's JIU but had previously held senior positions in France's public administration, recalled an anecdote about the makeover. By chance he was sitting at dinner next to the wife of the French candidate whom he himself had proposed to head the agency, and she asked Bertrand, "But what happened with the Staff College? It seemed to me that this process was well under way, and then suddenly, everything stopped." Bertrand replied, "Madam, the Hundred Years War is still going on at the United Nations."

Ignacy Sachs went so far as to describe the principle of geographical representation as "a UN sickness" that had led him during a particular recruitment meeting to declare: "Since there is only one post and still so many groups to satisfy, we ought to find a woman who is secretary of a Latin American union of Catholic bishops!"

Brian Urquhart noted wryly: "On top of that, decolonization and the tripling of the membership posed a large geographical representation problem in the Third World. . . . So, if you were trying to fire a P-3, it became an international incident with the Non-Aligned Movement. It was ludicrous." Klaus Sahlgren agreed: "During my years in the UN, from the very beginning, the quota thinking became ever stronger. There were all kinds of quotas. I think that is poison. It destroys any organization if you have to take a person from that and that country because it is 'underrepresented.'"

Bernard Chidzero believed that political patronage contributed to the unnecessary fattening of the organization and to making it more complacent: "There are first-class brains in some of the organizations. People will go to them by conviction that things can be better, that things can be changed. . . . There are also people who have joined these organizations as providing comfortable jobs, good paying, no one breathing down your neck as you have more time and leeway than in private industry or in government. . . . Equitable distribution could lead to choosing the best people from a different country, but you could easily—and I think it is the latter—lead to countries chucking the people that they don't really need in their own countries. And this could lead, unless the contract is time specific, for those who are in service to stay put and be quite comfortable! Why make the United Nations secretariat thinner when the ax might fall on you?"

Some complained that promotions, especially to the most senior level, are often based more on political connections and government bean-counting than competence. Paul Berthoud recalled a conversation with Maurice Bourquin, a mentor who was a prominent Belgian international lawyer: "I went to him, and said, 'I would like to work for the United Nations.' He told me, "But Monsieur Berthoud, '*vous savez, les grandes carrières internationales sont des carrières nationales.*'" [You know, great international careers are national careers.] I have been quite aware of that through all my career. You can move up, doing a certain job, but the top jobs generally are being filled by people from the outside. . . . And it helped me a lot to be very happy with my career without having that striving to try and reach a political level."

The impact of excessive sensitivity to pressures from governments in recruitment and promotion clearly influenced the production and implementation of ideas. Janez Stanovnik illustrated how political patronage chips away at the professionalism of the international civil service and its credibility in the face of its critics: "A highly qualified expert in pharmaceutical sciences was the director of the Narcotics Division. He gets fired, and who gets the job? The daughter of the Secretary-General, who has absolutely not the slightest knowledge of the field but gets a D-2. . . . When scandals of this kind occur, this hurts not only internal morale, but how can I then stand eye to eye with an American senator who shoves these kinds of things into my face?"

For Sotiris Mousouris, as for many of our voices, successful recruiting is possible but depends on finding ways to bypass the normal administrative procedures: "The essential element of success was the quality of our work. The quality was high to some extent because we managed to get around the bureaucracy of the UN, especially for hiring people. The bureaucratic obstacles now at the UN are horrendous. . . . Because it was a new office, we had posts which could be filled also from outside the secretariat. We had some flexibility. That is very important for an office to function well."

Geographical background could help or, as in Klaus Sahlgren's case, hurt a career. "There were at that time actually five Finns in top-level positions at the UN Secretariat, clearly out of proportion. . . . The Secretary-General did not ask me whether I could be eased out. He contacted behind my back the Finnish government to find out whether it would object if my contract would not be prolonged. So I reacted by sending a polite but rather frosty cable to him, saying, 'I hear that you have been in touch with the Finnish government, and I hereby want to respectfully inform you that I am not available for any prolongation of my contract. I hope this will help you.' . . . Such is life at the UN."

In thinking back over his lengthy UN experience, Alister McIntyre emphasized the importance of quality rather than nationality if new thinking is the goal: "I'm afraid you can't forget the stars, because they are the people who, in the end, energize the whole organization with their ideas. So the question is, do you have good stars in the UN? I would say 'Yes,' but they are now less than they used to be. One should avoid generalizations, but I think the UN has been severely affected by this business of geography. As you know, a lot of attention was paid by the Ford Foundation report and other analyses of ways to install into the system, right from the bottom to the top, an ethic of competitiveness and of excellence. Secretaries-general and executive heads have tried. But they have been defeated by this passionate insistence by governments on geographic representation in secretariats. . . . I would say that because of the legacy of 'equitable' geographic representation, the UN is far less capable now of being an intellectual leader than it was before. That is not to say that good staff work is not going on. It is. But in terms of taking up an original idea and building it up and trying to influence governments and institutions to move with it, it is not sufficiently there anymore. We no longer live in the day of Prebisch, or even in the days of Jim Grant. . . . This is not a question of competence; it is rather to draw attention to the imperative of dynamic, intellectual leadership."

But it is not impossible to square this circle. Special recruitment efforts can be focused on underrepresented nationalities, including the use of quality-enhancing measures such as examinations for new entrants, without compromising the quality of the civil service. As with efforts to achieve better a gender balance, priority can be given to nationals of certain countries by casting the net widely enough to draw fully qualified candidates from those backgrounds. It is a fallacy that quality must suffer while moving toward a better balance in various types of representation. The real requirement is to limit pressures from outside influence and patronage—which come from donors and developed countries as well as from Third World countries. Klaus Sahlgren drew upon another source of inspiration that points the way toward a better policy for the future: "Mao Tse-tung used to say, 'It doesn't matter what color the cat has as long as it catches mice.' I can understand that the UN, in its own operations, will have to set an example to backward countries when it comes to gender or race discrimination. But that should not—and need not—happen at the expense of competence and efficiency."

Women at the UN

The Universal Declaration of Human Rights contained such language as "brotherhood" that would now be avoided as insensitive to the role of women.

But the meaning of the text is clear. Article 2 specified that "Everyone is entitled to the rights and freedoms set forth in this Declaration, without distinction of any kind, such as . . . sex." One might have expected the UN to be in the lead at integrating women into work compared with other institutions and to do so faster than many of its member states. This was not always the case.

James Jonah spent three decades as an international civil servant, and he remembered his efforts to alter the composition of the secretariat during his tenure as the UN's top official for human resources: "I raised the level of gender representation more than anybody else when I was head of personnel. And there was resistance. And I was very surprised, because some of my colleagues in the secretariat said they did not want women in their department. . . . They just couldn't accept it. But I think it can be overblown, too. Because I don't think, at least when I was in the UN, where you have two or three candidates and the woman is the best candidate, the woman is not taken. . . . At times it was more difficult. For example, we tried to include Russian women. You could not under the Soviet system. . . . Or any of the Eastern European countries. . . . It's different now."

Jonah also recalled the necessity of resorting to a tactic to which he was philosophically opposed: "We had the target of 25 percent. That's what I was concerned with. So I told the department, 'You have to make sure you have 25 percent. I don't care what your feeling is.' Then I began to do something which I didn't like to do. . . . I reserved 25 percent of the vacancies for women. There would be competition, but these posts would only be filled by women, my directive to every department."

Gamani Corea remembered a grilling from the floor by governmental representatives concerning the paucity of women on his staff during a session of the Trade and Development Board at the end of the 1970s: "I remember saying two things. First, I had no mental blocks whatsoever in getting more women into UNCTAD; those we have had have been doing well, and I'm sure there are others who can come and contribute. I said we would like to see more women. But I said there is one constraint, which I've faced, that has been put on us by you, the delegations. You have this system of overrepresented/underrepresented countries. Now you want to talk to me about an underrepresented sex. But what do I do when I get a claim for a job from an underrepresented sex from an overrepresented country? I tell you if countries cannot find the men to man the UN, those countries are not going to be the ones to provide women. So you have to give me some guidance. . . . The other thing I said was that I'd like to see more women amongst the delegations since almost all those people in the hall there that day were men!"

Kofi Annan pointed to gender as a key contemporary personnel issue with a longer history in the secretariat: "And gender came in, but it was rather timidly—there weren't enough women appointed in the professional category. How come they were mainly in the general service? . . . One of the Secretaries-General—but it was after 1976—said we would try and make a push to appoint more female staff. The women said, 'We want to make it fifty-fifty.' . . . In the meantime, the pressure became enormous after the Mexico conference and after constant pressure from the women's movement. And of course, if the UN is lecturing everybody, we had to lead ourselves. We can't go and tell people to have gender mainstreaming, to improve gender balance, when we don't have it in our organization. We are not at fifty-fifty yet, but at the professional level we are at about 42 percent. . . . And I have personally been determined to bring in as many senior women as possible. Apart from the contributions they make, they are good role models. It also really encourages others. And I must say they are very, very good. Talk to Gus Speth about it sometime. One day Gus came in and he said, 'Gosh, Kofi, I just came out of a meeting. . . . Tough women! There was blood all over the floor. I was lucky to get out.'"

Although many of our male voices commented on issues of gender and development, none discussed in any detail the constraints faced by female staff members in the organization. Not surprisingly, women were outspoken about longstanding shortcomings in the advancement of women within the organization. Hilkka Pietilä, the Finnish feminist development economist, wrote about her perception of change over time: "The United Nations has become a women-friendly global institution in spite of being a forum of governments."[7] However, the sense was that women's working conditions in the UN have improved since the early days of the organization, but mainly for those in high-level positions.

Readers may recall that Molly Bruce was in charge of the staff that ran the Commission on the Status of Women in Geneva. She was the deputy to Helvi Sipila, the first woman to be appointed with the rank of assistant secretary-general. Bruce remembered an occasion when members asked for statistics about the number and grades of women serving in the Secretariat. She chortled that "this was a very touchy issue" for her director and the UN Office of Personnel. She cabled immediately to New York "to tell him what was going on. Of course, he nearly had a fit because anything like that upset him. The personnel people sent instructions to me to reject the commission's request. . . . They didn't want to release any statistics to the Commission on the Status of Women or establish any targets for recruitment or promotion of women. These are readily accepted now."

Margaret Anstee, the first woman to be promoted to the level of UN under-secretary-general in 1987, had herself begun as a local hire in the Philippines in 1952. "It's a hell of a lot better, though problems do remain." She then offered some of her experiences with UN leadership in this area. Early in her UN career, Anstee was appointed as the first woman UNDP resident representative and was posted to Uruguay but was told that she could not get a promotion: "A telegram came from New York . . . saying, 'So sorry. We cannot promote you because the promotions board says that you are too young and don't have enough experience.' I sent back a cable saying, 'Okay. Then I am too young and too inexperienced to take over Montevideo.' After a long argument by cable I went—without promotion."

Mary Smieton, who was involved in personnel and recruitment in the early days of the UN, recalled that in the initial flurry of activity to launch the organization, she "was too busy" to ensure reasonable gender balance in the organization. She regretted the early absence of a common salary scale for men and women: "We were just unable, or at least I was unable, to attempt to really to bring the responsible people together to try and get a common set of procedures, and staff, and levels of salaries, and so on. I just couldn't do it. And it was a great pity, because then it painfully had to be readjusted in the years after."

Margaret Anstee recalled her unsuccessful bid to become UN high commissioner for refugees: "Pérez de Cuéllar decided to continue the incumbent for a short period. When that ended, the U.S. pushed Jean-Pierre Hocké but I was also a front-running candidate again. . . . Pérez de Cuéllar said to me, 'You know, you are my preferred candidate for this job.' I was always somebody's preferred candidate! He was a very cautious man, of course. He would never stand up over appointments. He went on, 'But I have been told that a woman could never be high commissioner for refugees.' I said, 'Why not?' He said, 'Because most of the refugees are in Muslim countries.' I nearly exploded. I said, 'Secretary-General, that is ridiculous. Has it occurred to you to put an equally ridiculous argument back? That is that no man could be high commissioner for refugees because most of the refugees are women and children and no man could deal with women and children?' He said that he had not thought of that."

She placed contemporary policy in a longer historical overview: "There were prejudices about all sorts of things. But now all these jobs (UNHCR, WFP, UNICEF, UNFPA) are being filled by women, as they should be. But that is at the top. I think there is a problem at the middle levels. I think it is difficult within the structure. In the case of very high-profile political appointments there is a feeling now that it has to be a woman here or there, and that is done. It is easier than it was, but it is still not easy for women to come up through the system."

The first woman actually to hold the job that Anstee had sought was Sadako Ogata, who served two five-year terms as high commissioner for refugees in the tumultuous 1990s. She looked back over the decades that preceded her appointment: "I never went to any of the women's conferences because there were plenty of women's groups who wanted to send delegates and so on. So that was fine. But during the 1975 conference in Mexico, I was here in New York as a delegate to the General Assembly. Whenever the United Nations comes up with an agenda, if you have powerful groups within the country to seize on the agenda and put it through, it works quite well. And the women's issue was very much an interplay between what the United Nations could do and what the domestic women groups could promote. In Japan, there was a ready response to that. I think it became a rallying point. They kept on saying that there were no women in the higher echelons of the foreign ministry. Suddenly I was appointed minister. It worked well with me because I could stay here with my family. So I became a minister in the Japanese permanent mission, and I stayed for almost four years."

When asked whether being a woman was an asset in the competition for the UNHCR's top job, she replied: "I think it didn't hinder. But in those days, there was hardly anybody. Nafis Sadik was head of UNFPA. . . . But I don't think Pérez de Cuéllar went around saying, 'I want a woman.' No, he was much more discreet in those days. . . . I don't know if I would have wanted to be a candidate on that basis." When asked when gender appeared on the UN's agenda, she answered: "Oh, I think Mexico had a lot to do with that. . . . Helvi Sipila, she was very good. She opened these gates. . . . There were many women who were very able, but somehow in the promotions they missed out. So I think I brought in the accelerated promotion of women and the way it's counted in the UNHCR. When I came, I think there was not a single D-2 woman in [the] UNHCR. There was one D-1 lady. I think there are a couple now, and they are all able people. No question."

Leticia Shahani blamed the culture at the UN for holding women back: "The bureaucratic lethargy of the UN is against accommodating these messy issues, like women and gender, because they do not fall within neat bureaucratic structures. . . . The women's issue has grown because of the UN and also despite the UN." Margaret Anstee raised another issue that made it difficult for her as a woman in the UN—her status as an unmarried person, which she believed had an impact on unmarried men as well: "I had always found that single people were treated with much less consideration than those who were married with children. It was assumed that you had no family responsibilities at all."

With regard to gender balance, "I would like to say that it is so thoroughly mainstreamed that it doesn't have to bubble up, but that wouldn't be entirely true," noted John Ruggie. "We have taken it very seriously in terms of senior appointments. That's where the SG has most direct authority. And he has been very serious in asking for women candidates, not only when we set up a deputy secretary-general's position, or in choosing a high commissioner for human rights, or supporting a candidate to head WHO, but also for panels and secretary-general's advisory groups. We don't always do a good job, but you would never send a list to this Secretary-General that didn't have an adequate representation of women on it. So that's the way in which it most directly manifests itself out here." Nafis Sadik echoed: "The Secretary-General, I think, is very conscious of gender issues. He makes it a point. One of his first statements was to try to get fifty percent of women in senior positions. He has tried to do that."

Of her experience as a pioneer in the world organization, first as chief of the Policy Division in the Bureau of Finance and later as director of the Bureau of Social Affairs, Julia Henderson recalled that "I wasn't conscious of being discriminated against. I really wasn't. Of course, if they give a woman a job as a senior administrator, they always do that and put her in charge of something social. . . . So that was a certain amount of discrimination. They think we're better suited for that."

Mary Smieton thought that establishing units within the organization to deal with issues of concern to women was not a solution. "I have always been against women's sections. It takes a feeling of responsibility from the departments that have to set overall policy. A women's section is a distraction, in my view. So I think whoever was in charge of the women's department was rather regarded as the 'statutory woman,' as we used to call it in this country." Sadako Ogata reinforced this view: "I don't know whether only women can deal with women's things. I don't think so."

Margaret Anstee shared a similar sentiment: "One of the things I did not like was that, initially, the UN thought it was adequately addressing the question of gender equality by appointing women to senior positions to cover women's issues. Necessary, okay, but not sufficient in itself." And it is because of that, she explained, that she decided to take on the job as special representative to Angola in 1992. She was "very conscious that it was the first time that a woman had been asked to lead a peacekeeping mission." Anstee recounts being told, again by Pérez de Cuéllar, that a woman could not deal with the military, a story with special irony because our interview with her occurred as she was about to travel to participate in a training program for the U.S. Southern Command. "It was the story of one's life all over again. Even the British ambassador, Tony Parsons, who was a dear friend, and I was rather furious with him but he sort of made amends later—said to my face, 'You cannot possibly have a woman in charge of the military.' And I said, 'What about Mrs. Thatcher?'"

At the same time, Anstee did not absolve women from the responsibility for their advancement, saying that "sometimes we women are our own worst enemies. Usually when challenges open up, a man, whether he thinks he is qualified or not, goes for it. A woman often worries whether she is adequately qualified even when objective observers think she is. The essence of my argument was that a lot of myths persisted about what women could not do, firstly because they had not been given the opportunity to prove otherwise, and, secondly, because . . . they had shrunk from accepting the challenge. I emphasized that women *must* accept challenges when offered."

Organizational Culture

The United Nations is a bureaucracy that is like and unlike others. Those who have worked in different types of administrations know that bureaucracies have similar characteristics, be they universities, national ministries, private enterprise, or international organizations. Organizational theorists document how organizations tend over time to develop cultures of their own. They adapt by adding new activities to their agendas, sometimes without examining why and sometimes as a result of questioning fundamental beliefs— "muddling through" or "learning," according to the late Ernst Haas, one of the most careful students of international organizations.[8]

The intensity of certain characteristics differs from one type of organization to another. Dharam Ghai noted that the "issue of diversity, tolerance, encouragement of dissent, and criticism are very important in any research organization. They are more difficult to realize in a UN organization." Despite this, Secretary-General Kofi Annan, was upbeat: "I must say that even though I have been a bureaucrat—I have been in bureaucracy all these years— I think I can honestly say that I've never seen myself as a bureaucrat. I've always challenged. I've always pushed the envelope. I've always sought to do things differently. . . . And that spirit has also helped me. I can try new things, I can reach out, I can challenge, I can test, and I can push the envelope, of course, without committing suicide."

His predecessor was less sanguine. Boutros Boutros-Ghali described his frustrations in rocking the UN boat: "So the difficulty lies in the fact that you have a bureaucracy that is very strong because it's been in place for decades and you are there for just five years. They know that you're going to leave. . . . These bureaucrats . . . are not really interested in the great problems of the planet or may not have access to experts who would enable them to take interest in these issues. So they fall back on personal contacts that allow them to act.... The heads of agencies often think of themselves as your equals. They come to see you and want to talk as equals.... It's the agreements among civil servants and national delegates that create logjams." Maurice Bertrand agreed wholeheartedly and pointed to the UN's structure "that makes it impossible or nearly so to take courageous positions. And besides, it's inherent in the very structure of all international organizations, not to mention the Bretton Woods institutions, where terror reigns because there is a doctrine from which one can not deviate."

Paul Berthoud reflected on the unavoidable and particular characteristics of the UN bureaucracy: "There is a coefficient of inefficiency which is built into multilateral operations. . . . the efficiency cost of being a multilateral setting [that] we have to be especially conscious of when we talk about UN reform." Berthoud warned "about too much of a 'Maurice Strong approach'— in other words, wanting to project indiscriminately a private-business concept of efficiency into the United Nations. Some concepts, like subcontracting, a sunset clause, or 'let those who can do it best do the job,' have in the UN very serious limitations due to the very texture and nature of multilateral intergovernmental cooperation. My cheap joke about that is that if we really wanted to use subcontracting in an efficient way, we would subcontract the Security Council to the American Arbitration Association. They would certainly do a much better job with fifteen of their lawyers than the council we have today with fifteen disparate ambassadors. . . . In other words, there are some intrinsic limitations which attach to multilateral cooperation."

In commenting on the quality of work in Addis, the cultures of the "two ECAs" figured prominently in remarks by Adebayo Adedeji: "We may have to distinguish between ECA as an intergovernmental body and the ECA secretariat. Because when both are . . . used interchangeably, confusion arises. The ECA that was antiapartheid and anticolonial was the intergovernmental council of ministers and their officials. They, not the executive secretariat, led the political debate; they took the political initiative. But in the field of development paradigm, analysis and strategy, member states looked up to the secretariat for leadership and for innovative ideas."

Every bureaucracy has internal procedures. Again, our voices contain much that would sound familiar to government administrators or academic deans. For instance, Margaret Anstee remarked that "grade inflation" in the evaluation and advancement of staff contributed to the tarnishing of the organization: "It is also, I suppose, for some people just a job like any other—though not for the people who go out on really tough missions. That is something that I was going to say 'divides the men from the boys,' but perhaps I should add 'the women from the girls.' In the traumatic experiences many of them go through, they show tremendous qualities. The problems are at the headquarters level and this terrible bureaucracy of personnel."

Klaus Sahlgren recalled "angering Waldheim once by sending him a memo pointing out this evaluation system of personnel is for the birds." His memo used strong language: "Ninety percent of the people are classified as 'outstanding.' . . . Ninety percent cannot be 'outstanding.' . . . This system undermines the UN from inside. You could not get rid of bad people." Sahlgren also had problems in public meetings where frankness was not the rule. As a colleague reminded him, "One must be polite even to idiots when they represent member governments."

Sadako Ogata lamented the impact of such a culture on management because "administrative issues and discipline issues are very complicated in the UN because there is a very heavy protection coverage of staff." The only way to overcome the deterioration is by leadership from the top.

Not long after John Ruggie arrived at the UN on leave from Columbia University, he found himself in an elevator with Secretary-General Kofi Annan: "'John, you seem to have adapted very quickly. I would have thought it would be harder for you." Ruggie replied, "You know, the UN is really very much like a university. Survival is all about ego management."

At the same time, Ruggie grew impatient with the obvious shortcomings in the system: "The problem with the UN is not a lack of good people, it is that the systems are still so screwed up. And the systems tend to be screwed up largely because of extensive micromanagement by government. I am talking about the personnel system, for example, or the reward system. . . . There are some really, really good people in the house. But they are good despite the systems, not because of them. We have no real incentive system. The UN is Lake Wobegone to the extreme. Everybody is above average. Everybody consistently exceeds expectations. That is what it says on everybody's personnel assessment form. So there are no incentives."[9]

Dharam Ghai was more upbeat in looking back over his research career in various parts of the world organization: "People find the UN environment not that open and receptive to new ideas. . . . But I was lucky. And I had a similar experience in UNRISD, when I became its director in 1987. I had the same freedom, the same possibilities—even greater because we were not intergovernmental. . . . It was much closer to university than even ILO, because ILO was still a tripartite organization. . . . UNRISD didn't have any of these things, so the degree of freedom was even greater. You set up global research networks. All that I was doing in ILO, I could do on an even bigger scale. In fact, we depended heavily on global research networks. At the ILO there were a lot of good people. We recruited a lot of very young bright people in the 1970s, many of whom are still there and occupy key positions in ILO today. . . . So I would say for me—but this is very personal—I found the environment in the ILO and the UNRISD very satisfactory and fulfilling. I had a lot of freedom. I could try out new approaches. I could take risks. I could innovate and so on. And my bosses were understanding. . . . But this is exceptional in my view. This is not a normal experience in working in UN agencies."

Among the factors that demoralized good staff, several of our interviewees spoke about self-censorship. A culture of vetting documents and publications and a lack of self-reflection can be major—although not necessarily fatal—obstacles for the organization's ability to challenge orthodoxies. Robert Cox recalled that in the 1970s: "The [World] Employment Programme was another thing that contrasted with the conventional ILO approach, and it was coming from within the ILO itself. So there were these tendencies that showed that there was some potential for a more critical approach to the rule of the ILO in those years."

Brian Urquhart, who brought to bear forty years of UN experience, remarked that "this discretion business is much overdone. In the early days of the UN, there was this idea that nobody could talk to the press and that we were some kind of Trappist order sitting there on the banks of the East River." He added that "the UN has a nucleus of wonderful people" who are "in the middle of a large mediocre group of coupon clippers." Like other voices, he believed such pressures reduce the chances for a vibrant professional staff that thinks in new ways.

Part of the culture is its relationship to those outside the "priesthood." Paul Berthoud emphasized the intellectual contributions that originated within the UN secretariat rather than outside: "One has to give a very important percentage of initiative credit to the secretariat. I don't know how many ideas really came from the other side of the dialogue. They were encouraged, but even when they came from a government it might often have been after a good chat which the delegate had with a member of the secretariat before the meeting started."

Emerging from many voices were the differences between the culture of staff members serving in the field and the culture at the main headquarters and that of the various UN specialized agencies. "You will find that in the field, the turf problems are much less than at headquarters," explained Juan Somavía, which is why most headquarters strongly advocate field experience for all staff. However, such guidelines are overlooked as often as they are enforced.

Brian Urquhart, for instance, urged that "staff members should expect to move into the field and to go to unpleasant places. They should gain experiences." Sadako Ogata, who headed an agency that spent a billion dollars a year on refugee assistance in the 1990s, noted: "There's a big gap between the UN and the field. And whenever I came to New York, I've said this many times to the senior management and the Secretary-General and the Security Council. The gap between the real world and the UN headquarters is very large."

Margaret Anstee elaborated such tensions: "There was a great divide between the field and the headquarters, and the field was much more inclined to work together as a team. . . . [But] nobody wanted to leave headquarters. Everybody wanted to stay in New York. . . . Headquarters is the center of power, and nobody wants to go outside. . . . There were so many people who never, ever wanted to go to the field. . . . It seemed to me that you had much more power at the field level."

There are too few incentives, as Dame Margaret explained: "People ought not to get a promotion unless they have worked in the field. There should be a rotation. I persuaded two administrators that that should be made a rule in the UNDP, and it was. And in each case they immediately breached it by giving people senior positions who had never been in the field. . . . The rule could so easily be enforced if willingness to go to the field was related to promotion prospects. Instead the reverse applies—UN headquarters staff who go to the field all too often actually lose their seniority for promotion instead of getting incentives and recognition for having done their duty, often at personal and family sacrifices, not to mention facing life-threatening situations."

As an outsider, Devaki Jain was less sympathetic to field staff. While admitting exceptions, she argued that overall UN field personnel were "poor . . . and bureaucratic." As an illustration, she told a story about South Africa's President Thabo Mbeki, which may have as much to say about differences between expatriate and local salaries as about the actual quality of field staff: "Apparently, he told this new UNDP administrator, Mark Malloch Brown, when he went to South Africa, 'Go away. You and your blue flags, and your people running around in huge Mercedes with blue flags, and your big houses, and ultimately we get one dollar for all that bombast. They want to be invited as ambassadors, they want pride of place in the functions. It's all very ceremonial, and the money is little. But they pay themselves very well, and they know how to handle that.' So this is a way of illustratively telling you that the secretariat has become a burden for the UN's vision."

The flavor of the world organization's culture does influence the quality of its intellectual output. A few days before leaving the 38th floor and returning to academia—this time to Harvard's Kennedy School of Government—John Ruggie thought about the reports during his four years as assistant secretary-general. He pointed to an improved in-house culture: "Well, this sounds like bragging, but most of the reports that have come out of the Secretary-General's office in the last four years are very different from reports in previous administrations. I think in Boutros Boutros-Ghali's time, *An Agenda for Peace* was very interesting. There were serious flaws in it, but it was provocative. But that was the exception rather than the rule. . . . In the last few years, whether it is the report on Africa, or the Millennium report, or Srebrenica, or Rwanda, these are very serious policy documents that are analytical at the same time as they are prescriptive. . . . And they have been honest—sometimes brutally. So I think the quality of the documents, most of them in any case, that have the Secretary-General's name on them, is considerably higher. At least that is what we hear from delegations, and it is my own impression. If the quality keeps up, I'm sure I'll keep reading them."

Reform Difficulties

There are legitimate and illegitimate calls to radically change international institutions, and our voices try to separate cheap shots at the UN from justifiable calls for reform. Some blamed ill-informed criticism for undermining the organization and its international civil service. This kind of pressure on the organization, Margaret Anstee suggested, is irresponsible and has a deadening effect on intellectual output: "One does sometimes get the impression in the reform process that there are governments that are constantly making the UN jump hurdles and then say, 'Okay, you jumped that hurdle nicely. Let's try a higher one. Now try that one.' . . . I don't see how the organization can continue never having even its basic approved budget fully funded and having a constant zero growth budget. It just is not feasible. . . . Anybody who is in a rather commanding position in the UN has to spend their whole time worrying about staffing and budgeting and how to meet the next day's payroll. So how can they be thinking great thoughts?"

Richard Gardner placed more responsibility directly on institutional inertia. As the rapporteur for the High-level Group on the Restructuring of the Economic and Social Machinery of the United Nations, he recalled: "So we put together a pretty good report, but Kurt Waldheim was utterly cynical. He got this report, and he had no interest in our recommendations because they all involved major changes in the status quo, and he didn't see how this would serve his purpose. And he had a couple of people on the 38th floor who didn't like our proposals because it would have shaken things up and maybe diminished their authority. So we worked our hearts out on this report and nothing happened—nothing."

Although Boutros Boutros-Ghali was subjected to what many thought was unseemly treatment by the Clinton administration that prevented him from serving a second term—which he detailed in his *Unvanquished: A U.S.-U.N. Saga*[10]—his voice expressed perhaps as much frustration with the difficulty, perhaps the impossibility, of making meaningful structural changes in the secretariat. He provided one ironic illustration: "The institute for the promotion of women that's located in Santo Domingo [International Research and Training Institute for the Advancement of Women (INSTRAW)]—I wanted to close it. I'd had occasion to visit it when I was minister of foreign affairs, and I knew for a fact that it wasn't working. . . . I failed and I had against me all the countries of the Third World—I, the champion of the Third World."

Robert Cox remarked on tensions within the staff during his twenty-five years of service, which ended in 1971: "In the International Labor Office, there was a kind of ideological struggle going on between what I call the traditionalists—the people who are concerned with the development of the conventions and recommendations and the whole sort of procedure for supervision of those—and the people who, growing perhaps out of technical assistance, were concerned with broader ideas of economic development and economic development as the basis for raising living standards."

Peg Snyder told a story that illustrates both why reform is difficult and that ideas and individuals can make a difference. She began with UNIFEM and how it had helped to transform UN development cooperation: "I came back to headquarters and said to the UNDP finance officers . . . 'We need to give these women a revolving credit fund.' The finance fellows said, 'Aha, you can't do that, madam. That's not possible. In the UN, we give experts, we give Land Rovers and you can write them all off the books at the end of the project. . . . We can't do that.' I said, 'We'll have to do that, because this is where women are and this is what they need. If we're going to talk about assisting the world's women, we must give them this credit fund.' We studied the rules and regulations and finally found a way to give it. I smiled not long ago when I saw something in one of the small newspapers that fly around the UN that UNDP had introduced revolving credit funds in 1979."

Given that even the friends of the world body have such strong views about the internal challenges facing the UN, it is not surprising that vocal external critics have called endlessly for budgetary and structural reform of the world organization. They have, to a large extent, achieved numerous changes, not always to the UN's benefit. Since 1945 there have been periodic calls for reform, but they became especially strident during the Reagan-Thatcher era and have continued virtually unabated since.

In the summer after taking office for his first term, Secretary-General Kofi Annan put forward a proposal with two tracks of reform.[11] Track one included those measures that are within the capacity of the Secretary-General himself to implement; these have been largely carried through, although even the Secretary-General's fans would probably not agree that they actually amount to what he called "the quiet revolution."[12] Track two included more striking reforms that depend on agreement and actions by member governments—and these have met with considerably less success; political agreement among 191 "bosses" rarely happens. Brian Urquhart commented on the politics of inertia: "Once you try to abolish parts of the UN, you run into all kinds of problems, because you have the government who has proposed it and the staff that is living on it. The concerned government is likely to go to its group, whether it is the nonaligned group or some regional group, and say, 'Look here, we can't have this, and mind you, the next time you have a project, I will certainly support it, provided.' . . . . This is one of the tendencies which [has] destroyed the credibility of a lot of the economic and social side of the UN."

The Secretary-General's call at the General Assembly in 2003 to set up a High-level Panel on Threats, Challenges and Change was intended to look toward the future and the adequacy of the UN as an institution. "The idea that the United Nations can stumble along in its atrophied condition has a powerful appeal in capitals around the world," writes Pulitzer Prize–winner Samantha Power. "But believing that the status quo will suffice is dangerous. . . . Dag Hammarskjöld, the United Nations' second Secretary-General, liked to say that the United Nations was not created to take humanity to heaven but to save it from hell. Even escaping hell requires an international organization that is up to the job."[13] The high-level panel's report was submitted for Kofi Annan's consideration in December 2004, and it promises to provide a major discussion item during what remains of his second term (2002–2006).[14]

One constraint circumscribing possible future efforts by the UN to counter threats, new and old, results from the horrific challenge to the UN's future work and personnel policy after the tragic bombing of UN headquarters in Baghdad on August 19, 2003. The death of twenty-two officials, including Special Representative of the Secretary-General Sergio Vieira de Mello, raised questions about the role of UN officials in complex crises. The second UN (the staff) confronts an extraordinarily difficult dilemma—to serve or not to serve—with implications that extend beyond Iraq. Gil Loescher, a university-based researcher who had long worked in and around the UNHCR, was waiting to interview Vieira de Mello on that day, and although he survived, he is today a double amputee. Loescher has written: "The attack on the UN in Baghdad brought a new and unprecedented degree of anti-UN hostility to the surface, probably changing forever the way the UN and others view the security context in which they have to conduct their operations."[15] A retreat behind fortified walls and a failure to confront the source of the threat is a de facto victory for terrorists, warlords, and insurgents. Plowing ahead without taking protective measures may result in more attacks on personnel. Either option contains the likelihood that the accessibility and efficacy of the world organization's field staff could be limited and even undermined. This has obvious implications for personnel policy, including the difficulty of attracting first-rate people as development workers increasingly find themselves in zones of conflict.

Nafis Sadik, who was a member of the high-level panel, reinforced the need for serious change by recalling her consternation when joining the Secretariat: "For me, when I first came to the UN, I was really at a loss. I knew a lot about those organizations that worked in Pakistan, but how the UN as a system works is not very clear. The whole division between the normative and the research and the standard setting and the operational is very unclear. Everyone seems to be doing everything." Jan Pronk added that: "It is high time to take UN reform seriously. Otherwise, the UN system would lose its relevance, become marginalized and replaced by new mechanisms set up by the big, rich, and powerful countries without a global constitution. That constitution—the UN Charter and its sequels—is a great achievement in world history. But we run the risk of losing that achievement if we do not reform the methods of global consultation and decision making."

Whatever the tasks to be undertaken, financing is necessary, and adequate resources are hardly ever guaranteed. "The UN really operates . . . with a good bit of efficiency," Virginia Housholder commented. "[But] the General Assembly will pass great big broad resolutions, then give them ten dollars and thirty-two cents to carry them out." In this regard, Guido de Marco recalled barking at a CNN reporter during the 1984 Ethiopian famine: "Do something to popularize and bring the problems of these refugees in[to] their peoples' homes through CNN. . . . The United Nations is as strong as the nations forming part of it want it to be. So don't lash out at the organization, lash out at the nations that don't want to give to the United Nations the capacity and the instruments to put these things into effect."

In this regard, Paulo Sergio Pinheiro, who has served as a UN human rights rapporteur in Myanmar and Burundi, felt compelled to comment on the conditions of UN staff working in Geneva: "The people who have worked with me, the members of the secretariat, are extraordinarily devoted and motivated people. But their situation is outrageous in terms of human rights. I think that 95 percent have temporary contracts. I can't image how you can intend to impose accountability for human rights if you are not able to succeed in promoting minimum ILO standards inside the OHCHR [Office of the High Commissioner for Human Rights]. . . . This is complete madness. If an American enterprise functioned like that, it would be outrageous. To the United Nations, I think that is scandalous."

The only genuine reform of the UN, Brian Urquhart said, was that undertaken by Dag Hammarskjöld: "He wrote integrity into the staff rules. On top
of that, he completely reorganized the secretariat. In those days he had time,
because he wasn't yet a famous international figure. He spent eighteen months
with people like Ralph Bunche looking at UN offices all over the world and
radically reorganizing the secretariat. He reduced the budget, he reduced the
staff, he got rid of a lot of people, and he pulled it all together. It was the only
reform of the UN which has ever been the remotest bit effective."

Noleen Heyzer agreed that "it was extremely difficult to break through"
on the reform front: "The top-quality staff are truly of the highest level. People
work long hours; they put in so much work that it is unbelievable. Their level
of commitment is extremely high. Then there are those that basically don't do
the work. Like every other organization, those who carry the burden carry
more than they should."

Perhaps we should go back to the basics, the independence of the international civil service institutionalized by the Noblemaire principles under the
League of Nations. "I think you need to build up a career service," said James
Jonah. "You really have to do that. Experience counts a lot." He indicated that
a lack of institutional memory was one unfortunate result and pointed to an
example, the explosion over the World Conference Against Racism in Durban
in September 2001. The lessons of an earlier conference on the same topic in
1982 had been ignored: "The people now . . . don't even have any clue of that
conference. But if you had a career service, that is what a career service does—
a body of knowledge, institutional memory. You are losing that now because
you are not strengthening the career service."

In spite of the litany of problems, many voices still would agree with the
bottom lines of Gert Rosenthal and Stéphane Hessel. "The intellectual history of the UN is basically a product of the UN secretariat," Rosenthal told
us. "I think that the intellectual heritage was formed from the people and
the teams that were at the disposal of the UN secretariat or its agencies or
programs. . . . They did make a difference." Hessel's voice echoed this sentiment: "Practically all new ideas about the working of the world economy or
the working of the world society have found a springboard within the United
Nations. . . . Some of these ideas had a short life and others a longer life. But,
that is really where they were put into words."

Here, whether they were optimistic or pessimistic, our voices spoke almost
in unison to say that however grim today's international order, the world would
have been far worse without the dedication and imagination of three generations of international civil servants. What does the future hold? Lourdes Arizpe
explained the challenge: "Someone once said that the United Nations is a dream

managed by bureaucrats. I would correct that by saying that it has become a bureaucracy managed by dreamers. Certainly you have to be a dreamer to work in the United Nations with conviction. It is only if you have this sense of mission that you can withstand the constant battering by governments who are afraid that the United Nations will become a world government. . . . So in the end, someone who works in the United Nations has to be a magician of ideas, because working for the United Nations is like working for a government in which all the political parties are in power at the same time. You have to be a magician of ideas in order to try and find that particular idea around which you can build the greatest consensus."

10

The Power of Ideas and People Inside the UN

- **Leadership**
- **The Secretaries-General**
- **Tensions in the System**
- **Country Groups and International Negotiations**

Reflecting on the role of the UN and ideas in an earlier conversation with the authors, Margaret Joan Anstee summarized six such roles with memorable alliteration. The UN can develop or promote ideas by serving as a *fount* (creating them), *font* (blessing or legitimizing them), *forum* (discussing them), *funnel* (channeling them into action), and *fanfare* (promoting them). Afterward, and with her usual sense of targeted irony, she added *funeral,* in recognition of the many ideas put quietly to rest after international debate. These various ways appear throughout the voices of people inside the United Nations.

Leadership

Leadership is critical to every human undertaking, and it is not surprising that it also feeds the creation, development, and adoption of economic and social ideas. Although bureaucracies are not known for risk-taking, many of our voices provided illustrations of leadership that supported new thinking within international secretariats.

"I hate to put so much emphasis on individuals," Gerry Helleiner told us. "It's a lousy theory of history." But in fact, individual human beings always play a variety of key roles in creating, legitimizing, discussing, channeling, promoting, and burying ideas. Helleiner continued: "I long to see somebody do a careful study, a sociology of knowledge person, who could try and track how ideas spread and in what circumstances. I haven't got a handle on it. . . . I don't like 'great men' theories of history, but I am increasingly driven to the thought that individuals are enormously influential. Politicians or people in key positions of authority, people like Elliot Berg, Anne Krueger, Joe Stiglitz, they do really matter. Their individual characteristics, their mindsets at particular times matter. Back in the 1940s, it was Paul Rosenstein-Rodan and Walt Rostow and Jan Tinbergen who had an impact. They influenced things. In the 1970s, Dudley Seers and the Sussex people and the ILO people—Louis Emmerij, Dharam Ghai, and a few others. In UNICEF, a little later, Jim Grant and Richard Jolly, whose sheer force of personality . . . did things. They marched upon the managing director of the IMF, told him that he was killing children, almost. They had an impact. And the fad, or whatever, began to move in a different direction."

A history of ideas must inevitably address those who shaped them, and our voices reflected on the management styles and intellectual contributions of some of those charged with leadership responsibilities at the UN. Robert Cox—a critical theorist of multilateralism—talked about it: "Leadership suggests sort of striding out in front and promoting things. I think it is less like that than trying to avoid conflict, trying to dress up the ideas for a new program in such a way as not to run into conflict with major interests in countries that can oppose them, or interest groups that have effect in opposing them. . . . It can have very little effect in changing the environment within which the organization works, but it can have some effect in having a sufficient understanding of the environment so as to avoid the institution getting into conflict that is going to be troublesome for it. And the best is being able to use that environment to sort of manipulate a situation so that you do advance your program of ideas a little bit."

Or to put it another way, Juan Somavía contrasted the approach of a researcher who says, "Look, let's go step by step" with that of a "political animal" who says: "Look, you are going to have a window of opportunity which will probably last for about six or eight months during which you need to respond to your feeling that people want change and that they are putting you there because they want the change. If you tell them that it will take three or four years to do some research to determine which way we have to go, we will not have change." But Malta's former president Guido de Marco warned about the limits of the political animal: "I always said that a politician who wants to be a prophet is a bad politician and a worse prophet."

Lourdes Arizpe thought that steering the way toward a consensus was the essence of international leadership: "That is the most important role of an international functionary—to help find strategies to dodge narrow political and personal interests and bullying tactics, to achieve the greatest good for the greatest number of people around the world."

But Margaret Anstee illustrated the need to have the right people in key positions by recounting the negative example of the creation and subsequent elimination of the post of UN director-general for development. "The people put into the job were not the most appropriate. We were thinking it should be somebody who was a Nobel Prize winner or that sort of thing—an Arthur Lewis. . . . Instead of this, there was Ken Dadzie and then Jean Ripert, both admirable and dedicated men but not exactly visionaries or strong leaders. Do you remember the joke, 'The UN system is beyond Ripert?'"

Ultimately though, as Gamani Corea noted, leaders cannot do it alone: "As the head of the institution you can play many roles—you can play an organizational role, you can give a kind of framework—but they have to pick this up and make things happen. . . . I think that the quality of the support staff in an institution is perhaps even more important than the quality of the head of the institution, because it is the support staff that provides the ideas, the thinking, the momentum, the contacts which make the institution relevant and come alive."

Drawing on his experience in the field and in headquarters, Virendra Dayal also emphasized those working collectively in the trenches: "I think that whenever the UN has done great things, it hasn't been just because of one person. It isn't the capacity of one or a few people to organize things properly, important as that is. I must confess that I have always been slightly skeptical of solo players, of prima donnas, because there are elements there sometimes of vanity and sometimes of an exaggerated expectation of reward, which warps their efforts. I have always felt that the strength of an organization must be in its capacity to play as a team."

In looking to the top tier, Samir Amin criticized every Secretary-General for not having used the position to push the envelope of acceptable ideas. At the same time, he noted political realities: "If the Europeans line up behind the United States and the Russians or Chinese, either out of fear or indifference, say nothing and Third World states stand silently by, clearly then the margin for maneuver is narrow. In those circumstances, what can a Secretary-General of the United Nations do?"

One of the themes across voices was how hard it was to make sure that economic and social priorities made their way to the top floor of UN headquarters. John Ruggie observed: "What you need is to have a Secretary-General who is interested, which this one is. And to have a critical mass of staff—it doesn't have to be large—that can formulate and polish his instincts, his intuitions and ideas and get him to sign off on proposals and go out and do something with them. . . . There are many reasons why it doesn't happen as often as it should. One is that Secretaries-General in the past have had little interest in economic issues. They haven't understood economic issues, and they haven't much cared about them, except politically or in a mushy moral way."

Kofi Annan was cognizant of the problem and instituted one solution in 1997, a second-in-command: "A lot of the crises we face in the political area have economic bases. . . . The way I have structured it, and to show you how the 38th floor has been actively involved—I have a division of labor with my deputy, who is down the hall from me. And Louise Fréchette [deputy secretary-general] is very actively involved in all these economic issues. . . . So in effect we have brought a certain equilibrium between the political and the economic and reduced the emphasis on the political. And besides, as an organization, about 80 percent of our budget is normally spent on economic and social issues. The political ones get the headlines. I cannot say that we are in a perfect equilibrium, but it is better and I am determined to push it further."

The Secretaries-General

The CEO of the world organization holds a particular place in folklore as well as in reality. And none more than Dag Hammarskjöld (1905–1961). A reader might be surprised that as head of the world organization (1953–1961) during the initial period of decolonization, the Swedish economist did not spend more of his time on economic and social development. Our voices made clear that these issues invariably took second place to political and security matters in the Secretary-General's office, regardless of the occupant. Brian Urquhart, who served under the first five, explained: "The 38th floor, under [Trygve] Lie and under everybody except Dag Hammarskjöld didn't really devote anything like enough attention to the economic and social side—partly because they weren't economists and didn't totally understand it and partly because there were so many political preoccupations. . . . It is very difficult, when you are Secretary-General, to focus on the economic and social side, because every day and every night something happens which preoccupies you on the political side." However, Hammarskjöld, according to Sir Brian, "believed that the UN was going to be the bridge over which the former colonial powers and the United States would be able, in a completely uncolonial way, to help in the development of the independent African countries."

Most of our interviewees echoed Urquhart's thoughts that Hammarskjöld, out of all of the Secretaries-General to date, had made the greatest intellectual impact on the organization—although comments on the current head were undoubtedly discrete out of respect for the incumbent and the critical juncture in the organization's history. According to Robert Cox, Hammarskjöld "was a key figure in that whole period and became kind of an icon because he did stand so much for the integrity of the international civil service and its role. Then he became the martyr, in a sense, the way he died over the Congo event."

Gert Rosenthal thought that the second Secretary-General was the only one who "broke the mold" of major-power control over the UN, although he did not know "how much he broke it." He added, however, that "there is also a legend about Hammarskjöld very much promulgated by Brian Urquhart. . . . It is the same thing as with Prebisch—this man who could do no wrong, and everything he did was perfect. Of course, he died in an airplane crash [in the Congo] so it is easier to martyrize him than Prebisch."

Brian Urquhart, whose biography[1] details those years, recalled that when Hammarskjöld first came to the UN, "he looked about fifteen years old. He was the youngest looking forty-five-year-old I have ever seen. He was extremely diffident and very shy and started off with all kinds of rather misguided gestures, like eating lunch in the cafeteria every day and turning down the Secretary-General's hospitality and living allowance." Urquhart added that he eventually became "a master with the press, and they liked him very much, because he talked very fluently and often said absolutely nothing, and it was sort of a game. But almost nobody understood what he had been trying to do. None of his officials ever talked to the press, and he was like a Delphic oracle—ask Hammarskjöld a question, you would get an answer which you could read under water, at 10,000 feet, backwards, forwards, and sideways. He was a brilliant intellectual, but he didn't really tell you what he was doing."

Oscar Schachter, who was in the UN's Legal Office under the first two Secretaries-General, compared them in terms of taking economic and social development seriously: "Certainly Trygve Lie did not. He was really out of it entirely. But Hammarskjöld came in with the idea that as an economist he wanted to meet the economists. He wanted to talk to Jack Mosak about the *World Economic Report*. He is the only Secretary-General who not only read but discussed the *World Economic Report*. He was critical of some IMF approaches. He had a kind of a stake in it, related to the fact that he wanted to be seen as an economist."

Schachter pointed to the political support that Hammarskjöld received from developing countries: "Psychologically, I think he identified himself with that movement. On the other hand, he . . . had very much an upper-class European view of people. While he certainly was respectful to individuals, he did not consider all cultures as equal. I saw him almost daily in the Congo situation, and he could be quite patronizing about Congolese figures and others from the Third World. . . . But he was also like that about many in the developed world. He referred to 'this young man' in the White House, Kennedy, whom I believe he should have gone to see about the Congo crisis. He relied too much politically on the support that he thought he was getting from the majority of members. And he really didn't take full account of the political importance of Khrushchev.

. . . But that's when it looked to many as though the new majority of Third World states were taking over. It looked, on the face of it, as if he would have a big majority in the General Assembly—as he did. But how much did that matter? This was, I think, Hammarskjöld's big miscalculation."

Conor Cruise O'Brien recounted why Hammarskjöld had selected him to work on the Congo: "He was much a 'horses for courses' person. He saw me as a horse who would be useful in certain circumstances, as being a westerner, but more well-disposed towards the emerging former colonial countries than most westerners were."

One of the results of the Secretary-General's leadership in the Congo, however, was Moscow's ire, which took the form of a proposal to replace the office of the Secretary-General with a *troika,* or a three-person square wheel to act as a check on the West. Vladimir Petrovsky recalled that the Kremlin thought that Hammarskjöld gave "the impression of a man with philosophical cast of mind who has his own vision of the world and of his role as the head of the international organization."

James Jonah had the following to say about the second Secretary-General: "I still believe that he is unsurpassed. I am convinced about that for three reasons. One, I think Hammarskjöld was a true intellectual of the highest and finest sorts. He was not a wishy-washy man. He had a good conceptual view of the UN. Secondly, he was a man of absolute integrity. . . . Thirdly, he had the quality of tremendous courage. The only person who really, to me, has come close to having this type of courage is Boutros-Ghali. Therefore, I believe, he remains, to me, exemplary as a Secretary-General. Of course, there has been so much revisionism. But again, I am convinced that we will never have another Secretary-General like Hammarskjöld. There is a determination among the veto powers that that will never happen."

Even though he was too young to have worked with him directly, nonetheless Hammarskjöld had an impact on Sonny Ramphal's internationalism: "He inspired me. He infused in me a bit of his vision . . . of 'one world to share.' And it is that kind of leadership that has to come from the Secretary-General to infuse successive generations of young people, particularly at a time when the UN is under siege and there are so many who would like to drag it down. I grew up with the basic conviction that the UN was the world's salvation. Not many people have that understanding today. . . . But it also has to come from the leading governments. And that, I am afraid, is the major disaster, the fact that the world's major power, the world's only superpower . . . sees the United Nations as there to be used for the advancement of its own national interests. That, of course, is the biggest threat that the United Nations faces, and the Secretary-General can't deal with that alone."

Our voices had considerably less to say in discussing the management styles or leadership of the first and third Secretaries-General, whose autobiographies and speeches are little known: Norway's Trygve Lie (1896–1968), who served from (1945 to 1953), and Burma's U Thant (1909–1974), who served from (1961 to 1971).[2] Brian Urquhart was not impressed by either: "Because of the Cold War, we got Trygve Lie, who was a mediocre and rather pathetic character, but he did his best. But Lie was somebody who had never been heard of, who had no moral authority, and who was intellectually totally inadequate for the job. That was the beginning of the end as far as the secretariat was concerned." He was equally unimpressed by U Thant, whom he described as "a good man but a terrible administrator."

From his office in Bergen at the Christian Michelsen Institute, Just Faaland had a different take on his compatriot: "We were, I suppose, proud. But you know Norway, when anybody makes it and comes a bit up compared to the rest of us, we all pull him down again. That is our tendency. . . . I have been in some meetings with him, after he was Secretary-General, when he came back and later became governor of a province here, in Oslo. He had come a long way, of course, from his own background. . . . I don't think he was ever someone I particularly wanted to emulate. . . . He grew up at Grorud . . . outside Oslo—as a trade unionist. And he got into party politics."

Indeed, few of our interviewees had worked with Lie, and very few commented about U Thant's legacy. James Jonah noted, however, that "one thing that U Thant did very well, he got out of the way. He allowed Bunche and others to run the show. That was very good, because you stretched the philosophy and temperament of others longer. So that was very good. He didn't manage to do anything, he just allowed the same intellectual things to continue." Among the major events that occurred under U Thant's watch, which perhaps explain his reticence, were the Cuban Missile Crisis and the Vietnam War.

Not surprisingly, our voices were outspoken on the fourth Secretary-General (1972–1981), who was subsequently elected in 1986 as Austria's president, Kurt Waldheim. They did not describe him as either effective or sympathetic. Most believed that the major powers must have known about his past—that he had concealed his allegiances to the Nazi Party and his involvement with war crimes while serving as a German officer in World War II. In spite of this hindsight, were it not for the relentless Chinese veto in December 1981, he would have had an unprecedented third term; he was supported by virtually all states. Among the most crucial events during his tenure were the Six-Day War and the accompanying oil-price hikes and the NIEO.

Margaret Anstee "felt that he had been wrongly treated, excessively punished. I never felt that he had been a war criminal—he had obviously lied, but

I felt that other people knew that he had lied long before it all came out. Major countries must have known [about that] when he was elected. And the extent of the reprisals that were taken against him seemed to me to be excessive. I did not think that the same thing would have happened had he been president of a larger country, such as Germany. His downfall was useful for some from a whole lot of points of view."

Max Finger, who worked at the U.S. mission at the UN in New York until a year before Waldheim's nomination, wrote a scathing book about him after retirement.[3] During his interview, Finger mused: "I think probably the CIA knew. Whether they told the State Department, I'm not sure. But it is interesting: Kurt Waldheim . . . was hired in the branch of the foreign ministry headed by Fritz Molden, who was the son-in-law of Allan Dulles. So I would not be surprised if Waldheim worked for the CIA and maybe also for the Russians. . . . It certainly gave the Soviets some leverage over him. . . . My own analysis of Waldheim is not that he was someone who hated Jews in his gut, that he was not a vicious anti-Semite. In fact, his family was part of the Catholic party of Austria that opposed the Anschluss. He was beaten up by some Nazi thugs when he was a teenager. But when he wanted to go to law school and you had to belong to Nazi youth organizations to do it, he joined Nazi youth organizations. That is why the title of my book was *Bending with the Winds*. He bent whichever way he had to to get where he wanted to go. That was the way he operated at the UN. . . . He would have been a good headwaiter in a fine restaurant."

Speaking directly about his experience with Waldheim, Klaus Sahlgren was equally straightforward: "He was clever, had a good political nose. But he was not a good administrator, and I think he was surrounded by sycophants who sort of hung to his lips and pretended to admire his every word, lacking the guts to criticize him." He also commented that cabinet meetings were a "waste of time" because the Secretary-General arrived invariably late and without an agenda: "It was according to Waldheim's whims. That illustrated two things—one, that Waldheim tried to keep control, sometimes without success. The other thing was that the UN was badly administrated. . . . I got more information from circulating unofficially in the corridors of the UN building than by attending these meetings."

Brian Urquhart was more generous: "To his credit, Waldheim did do a lot about the Jews in the Soviet Union. He got a number of agreements out of the Soviet government that probably wouldn't have been got by anybody else." Urquhart added, however, that "although he was the biggest bore on earth, if you pointed him in the right direction and gave him a push, he was usually prepared to do quite sensible things. He wasn't all bad. He didn't have any kind of originality, but he . . . wasn't a total disaster. As a personality, he was abysmal, but he was a very hardworking hack."

In thinking about Kurt Waldheim as a manager, Gamani Corea stated: "I found that from him I got no interference and maximum support. . . . He was very supportive of the G-77, independently of UNCTAD. I was appointed by him first in 1974 . . . [and] Waldheim began to pick up on issues that I had spotlighted in UNCTAD, particularly the Integrated Programme for Commodities, the Common Fund. He was Secretary-General at the time of the Sixth Special Session when the NIEO was proclaimed and so on. So he was there at a time when there was a certain Third World voice. . . . Those days we were a hive of activity. . . . Delegates used to come and complain to me that the tempo was too much. I used to tell them, 'You are living in a comfortable city, you are having good food, you are having good places to work, and you also want a good night's sleep?'"

Kurt Waldheim's defense of his past is in his autobiography.[4] In our conversation, he spoke about the operation of the world organization: "Governments sometimes try to send people who are not qualified, who have shortcomings, or who are just there in order to report back to their governments. . . . There were agents from the Soviet secret service. We knew it. But what could we do as long as we cannot prove that they have sent secret information from the UN secretariat to their governments?" As he sat in his office near the Ringstrasse in Vienna, where he retired after serving as Austria's president, he reflected on the UN: "It is not perfect, but it works. I also want to stress the fact that with a few exceptions, the international civil service is very dedicated, hard-working people. Unfortunately, they do not, in the execution of their task, always get the necessary support from member states, despite the fact that they have a clear mandate from the relevant organs of the United Nations."

The careful Peruvian diplomat Javier Pérez de Cuéllar was the fifth Secretary-General (1982–1991). He was at the helm for the move toward the right in the West and the reversal of the momentum toward dramatic change in international economic relations, as well as the thawing of the Cold War and the renaissance in UN peacekeeping. In his country's presidential elections in 1995, he was defeated by the incumbent, Alberto Fujimori. Our voices offered a variety of views about his record. James Jonah, for one, was unequivocal: "Pérez de Cuéllar, to me, was almost a disaster. It was not of his own making; he was a weak person. He is a man, I believe, who never wanted the job. I think he was a man who was pushed into a job by ambitious people. . . . He didn't want to get involved with dirty things. In fact, there was no leadership. . . . He was no fool, but he was not a very energetic person. He allowed a drift to take place."

Lawrence Klein, the 1980 Nobel laureate in economics, pointed to his direct experience with trying to get economic ideas discussed on the top floors at UN headquarters: "Pérez de Cuéllar had just been brought in. He assembled a group of people in New York and said, 'Let's just have a brainstorming session with no agenda.' We had about twelve people and the Secretary-General, and we had a conference room at the UN Plaza Hotel. Some of the people who were high in the hierarchy, under-secretaries-general, made foolish comments about the rich countries just rigging the exchange rates to rob the poor, et cetera. Amartya Sen was in that meeting, and I was in that meeting. We said, 'That's not how exchange rates are determined. That's not what the issues are. You can't just go out there and move them around and get the numbers that you want.' . . . It is very difficult to get sophisticated ideas through to some of the people who have power in the UN hierarchy. I think if there would be more of the thought sessions and if the Secretary-General would take them into account more effectively, they would do more good. The current situation is that the Secretary-General is so overburdened with the military action now going on in Afghanistan and the Middle East that there is very little opportunity to turn attention to anything."

After serving two terms as Secretary-General and as interim prime minister in Peru, Javier Pérez de Cuéllar finished his memoirs[5] and became Peru's ambassador to France, from which vantage point he looked back to his UN election in December 1981: "I used to say the United Nations Charter is my credo. . . . Still, I was wondering whether I was the best choice."

His modesty was complemented by second-guessing as to whether he should have exerted more leadership on development issues: "I wrote in my memoir that one of my frustrations, or my regrets, is that I didn't pay enough attention to the economic and social problems, despite my coming from a developing country which has social and economic problems. The question is that unfortunately my ten years—mainly the last five years as Secretary-General—were very tense. I had not much time to concentrate. In my time I had a number two who was a man from the First World. During my two mandates, I had two French, who dealt with these problems. Perhaps it would have been better to have a man from the Third World to sort out those problems, although both of them were excellent. . . . But one of the reasons is in fact that the social and economic problems were in the agenda of the other organizations. For the Secretary-General, what was needed was a kind of a political guidance from those organizations. . . . The Secretary-General used to make a statement on economic and social issues that was prepared in coordination with other officers of the United Nations. But actually, the secretary-general was not supposed to deal fully with those problems. But still . . . I should have made a strong effort in order to be involved in those economic and social problems."

In thinking about his role on the 38th floor (the top of the UN's "glass house" headquarters) as head of the so-called system, Pérez de Cuéllar recalled the expression *primus inter pares* (first among equals) and said: "If a Secretary-General wants to be a general, what prevails is *primus*. If he wants just to be passive, then he becomes one of the others ... [and] *pares* prevails." Indeed, Brian Urquhart sardonically commented that "the major powers can never decide whether they want a secretary or a general."

Boutros Boutros-Ghali, having been vetoed by the United States for a second term, became president of two Paris-based organizations, the International Organisation of the Francophonie and later the International Panel on Democracy and Development. From his Paris office in the 7ème *arrondissement,* he told us about arriving at the UN in January 1992: "I came with already well thought out ideas which were: in the first place, peace and the necessity of preventive diplomacy. To keep the peace, it's not enough simply to establish peace by preventing conflict; you have to promote peace before conflict arises—this is preventive diplomacy—during the conflict, and after the conflict—that's peace-building, the consolidation of peace. The second concept was that of development, for which I have always fought. Development does not mean economic development only, it has other dimensions, and it is the dominant problem of the twenty-first century: how to narrow the enormous gap between the rich and the poor. The third theme, which is ongoing, is reform of the United Nations. The fourth is democratization of international relations. You have to democratize globalization if you don't want globalization to pervert democracy. These themes, which I referred to in my inaugural address, I returned to during my term of office. They gave birth to my three plans for action, *An Agenda for Peace, An Agenda for Development,* [and] *An Agenda for Democratization,* which disappeared one week after I left the United Nations." Ever the ex-university professor, he recalled a story during a UNESCO commission meeting in which he was accused of being an "idealist." His retort: "Today's utopia is tomorrow's reality."

Boutros-Ghali's term was during the tumultuous first half of the 1990s when the organization was called upon to mount operations in an unprecedented number of civil wars at the same time that the UN system was collectively trying to revisit many economic and social issues through world conferences. He was characterized as a strong-willed, even arrogant intellectual who did not suffer fools gladly. Margaret Anstee pointed out one area in which, in her view, Boutros-Ghali did not demonstrate the necessary leadership. At the end of the Cold War, she tried to make the case to him that the

UN "should take a lead" in helping the former Soviet Union, adding that "they are rather like a developing country at this time." She recounted his reaction: "He did not think this was a good idea at all. And I was given a great talking to, that the priority was for developing countries. . . . I still believe that the West made many mistakes over the Soviet Union, and the UN did not take the lead that it should have done."

Among James Jonah's many assignments over his UN career was to head up a small think tank on the 38th floor, the Office of Research and Collection of Information (ORCI). It was established under the administration of Pérez de Cuéllar, but a weakened ORCI was then dismantled by Boutros-Ghali, who "was full of ideas. That's all he wanted from you. He judged a product on the ideas, and this was such an alien idea to some of these people. They didn't accept it. You could not go to Boutros-Ghali and say, 'We cannot do it because the African group is going to oppose.' He said, 'Don't tell me about the African group. Why are they against it? Do they have a rational reason? What matters to me is what they're saying, is it tenable in terms of the Charter and our mandate?' That's what Hammarskjöld used to ask. But these people [UN staff] don't ask, because it's too troublesome."

Jonah continued: "And I always said that you cannot understand Boutros-Ghali unless you know that there was a vacuum for ten years. Boutros-Ghali came in, saw this malaise, and wanted to shake things up. . . . He was not able to give leadership because he was baffled by the secretariat. He could not understand why people could be so incompetent. . . . It bothered him that there were people who could not write. But if you have gone for ten years where nobody questions you, this is true."

Many of our voices were not bashful about praising the seventh Secretary-General, the lifelong international civil servant from Ghana, Kofi Annan (1997–). Gert Rosenthal drew on his experience as a former senior UN colleague and as Guatemala's UN ambassador in New York: "He has a personality to go with his role of staying within the boundaries. The fact that he is African helps him, I think. He can get away with things that neither Boutros-Ghali nor Pérez de Cuéllar could have gotten away with because of the sensitivities of not being perceived as attacking a Secretary-General based on ethnicity. And the man knows the UN very well from the inside, which is his strong side. So he has done better than the other two, in my judgment. But he hasn't exercised the secretariat to its potential, basically because the powers that be wouldn't let him to begin with."

Viru Dayal, who spent the last decade of his UN career on the 38th floor but retired before Annan's arrival, speculated about an intriguing counterfactual regarding our concern with the creation and the translation into reality of alternative economic and social ideas: "Most of the Secretaries-General have come basically from the world of diplomacy. Therefore, they have been inherently stronger on diplomatic and political matters, on matters of war and peace, than on economic and social issues. For instance, had someone like Raúl Prebisch been the Secretary-General, I dare say his instincts would have helped him take the organization in different ways on economic and social issues, even if he was Secretary-General of the United Nations rather than of UNCTAD. . . . Let's just say there was a professional slant in this. But the reality is also that the exigent and the burning fires are not the kind of thing that can be ignored for five seconds. . . . Our present Secretary-General, Kofi Annan, has done what is the closest to putting together a cabinet way of thinking on these matters . . . a distinct improvement and advance on the way that preceded him. I am glad he has done this. Otherwise the 38th floor was deficient in its day-to-day leadership and understanding on economic and social issues."

John Ruggie gave a high grade to his former boss: "I should also attribute to [Annan] an understanding that the world needed to do much more to respond to certain social issues, including human rights and environmental concerns, but that pushing them onto the WTO agenda was highly dangerous."

Ruggie applied criteria that had been suggested by his former dissertation advisor, the late Ernst B. Haas at Berkeley, forty years earlier: "Haas had this set of concepts about what the possibilities are for decision-makers when faced with serious conflicts of interest. You can split the difference, you can settle on the lowest common denominator, or you can upgrade the common interest. And this guy—Kofi Annan—will invariably try for the latter. He will invariably pitch a principled answer rather than trying to compromise between conflicting interests. He will try for a principled answer that makes it damn hard for anybody to come out very strongly against him, because he isn't favoring one side over the other. He is promoting and favoring a principle for which the organization stands. . . . He wants to surround himself with good people. He is not threatened by anybody. He is so secure in himself that it is humanly impossible to threaten his ego. . . . There are leaders who rule by fear. There are others who rule by tit for tat. There are a variety of ways in which a leader leads. Kofi Annan rules by positive expectations, so everybody wants to do the right thing because you couldn't possibly want to disappoint him. You would be so heartbroken if you ever disappointed him."

Michael Doyle, Ruggie's successor as assistant secretary-general, added: "He is quintessentially a man of the Third World, a man of Africa, a West African, a Ghanaian. So these issues are not ones that he could ever, or would want to, escape from. So when we would have conversations like, 'What are your priorities?," he would always say, 'Addressing extreme poverty is priority number one.' Now, what he could do was a different story. The job of a Secretary-General is still overwhelmingly preventive diplomacy. That is three-quarters of his agenda and it's effectively the highest priority. Stopping wars—preventing and stopping them—are still ninety percent of his business. For the rest of the agenda, he knew that he could have a doctrinal effect and a facilitating effect. The money is in Washington. It's at the World Bank, it's at the IMF, it's with the separate countries of the OECD. All of the development work that takes place in the UN outside of the World Bank is a tenth of the World Bank's annual budget."

Sadako Ogata served as the UN high commissioner for refugees under two Secretaries-General: "I think the Secretary-General is trying to reach out in a very unique way. He alone is reaching out, instead of the Secretariat, to various areas, and I think he's rather good at it. . . . But he's not an intellectual like Boutros Boutros-Ghali was. . . . And I think he may come up with something that could be a breakthrough. He has really very strong instincts and courage."

Kofi Annan has often joked that the real meaning of "SG" is "scapegoat," but his as-yet-unwritten memoirs undoubtedly will emphasize how his voice speaks for others: "I sometimes say things in my speeches and statements, knowing that it will help those without voice. They can quote the Secretary-General, 'As the Secretary-General said'—and they will not go to jail. . . . I give them voice by putting my thoughts and ideas in a way that they can quote. . . . I think each of my predecessors operated at a different time, and they had to tackle the job in their own way. But I believe that anyone in this job has a unique opportunity and has a voice that should be used to assist those without voice and to lead in areas that are sometimes neglected. I have not hesitated to speak out. I know not everybody likes it, but it is something that has to be done. . . . You need to break that silence and wake people up and steer things in the right directions. I will continue to do that."

In recalling why he has cast the UN's participation net wider, he said: "I think one thing which has also helped is the fact that I came in determined to open the UN up and bring the UN closer to the people. And in the process, we are now dealing very effectively with NGOs, with the private sector, with universities, and foundations and realizing very early that the UN cannot achieve its objectives unless we reach out in partnership and work with others. I think there are times when—I won't say I have got into trouble, but there are times when some governments have not liked what I have said. But after a while, they get used to it or they come to accept it, although they may initially object to ideas I put forward."

The voices from and even near what can be the world's best bully pulpit have resonated over the years. People matter.

Tensions in the System

The usual nomenclature to describe the entire United Nations is the word "system." However, this term implies more coherence and cohesion than is present in the actual behavior of the world organization. Frequent use is also made of the UN "family," which at least has the advantage as a metaphor of leaving ambiguous the extent to which the United Nations is harmonious or dysfunctional, united or divided. Organizational relationships reflect over-lapping missions, the shared need for resources, and the desire to keep abreast of what is "popular" with donors. UN organizations are not unlike others in that they may innovate to exclude rivals or to cooperate with them, operating within a wider network of market forces.[6] The competition within and among secretariats is another factor—sometimes helpful, sometime hurtful—in the production and application of ideas.

In this regard, Cornelio Sommaruga recalled his consternation during debriefings by ICRC colleagues who had observed UN interagency meetings: "I saw my people coming back from these meetings in New York and in Geneva. *C'était une lutte de baronies* [It was a battle of feudal lordships]. . . . Everybody was fighting for his own mandates. And they were all part of the same fam-ily!" Francis Blanchard echoed the sentiment in describing the atmosphere in what was then the Administrative Committee on Coordination (ACC) and now is called the Chief Executive Board, which covers twenty-eight UN agen-cies and multilateral organizations: "It's also true that each one of them took care to defend the autonomy of the institution of which he was in charge. . . . Everyone speaks readily of the United Nations system or the United Nations family. I won't go so far as to repeat the phrase of Léon Blum: 'Family, I hate you.' The family can certainly be a center for interaction but also often for tensions. This is true as well for the United Nations system. This system is at the same time a non-system."

"I think it is vitally important that one achieves, say within the UN, a suf-ficient degree of intellectual coherence to encourage a free flow of ideas at the staff levels and above on development and coming to some kind of institu-tional strategy for the propagation of those ideas," said Alister McIntyre. He commented on interagency rivalries and their ultimate impact on this intel-lectual production: "I think that that situation hurt us in a number of ways. One, it prevented us from achieving critical mass. From the point of view of idea generation, one needs a certain critical mass of people working together, coming to the problem from a different regional or thematic perspective. So we lost that. Two, we lost the value of greater coherence in the propagation of the ideas themselves. All of the audiences for these reports were segmented, and we were not putting forward a consistent set of ideas, not in the sense of forcing uniformity but in the sense of bringing to bear on the ideas a diversity of experience."

Sartaj Aziz underlined a key issue that helps explain a UN weakness: "The General Assembly and ECOSOC were not decision-making bodies. They only provided a forum where delegates made speeches and expressed their points of view. The only decision-making body was the Security Council, which was confined to a very narrow agenda and was also subject to veto. . . . So in that way, the UN has retained global importance in the political and security fields. . . . There is nothing comparable in the economic and social field. The World Bank and the IMF annual meetings, by comparison, attract far greater attention at the world level than the UN meetings. It is partly because the UN system does not operate in a coherent, coordinated way. . . . The World Bank and IMF have become more important because the developed countries do not want the UN to take major decisions, because it is based on a one-country, one-vote system. They have themselves shifted the focus of economic decision making to more specialized forums where they can dominate, like the Group of 20."

In speaking about the relationship between New York headquarters and the specialized agencies, many academic observers echo the voices earlier in this chapter and point out the horizontal nature of authority in the UN system. "The orchestra pays minimum heed to its conductor,"[7] wrote Brian Urquhart and Erskine Childers. They pointed out the extent to which the UN is totally different from a government. The heads of agencies are appointed by different bodies with different priorities and budgets; they are located around the world and need not even attend "cabinet" meetings held a few times a year. This led Sir Robert Jackson, in his usual outspoken and picturesque fashion, to write at the outset of the *Capacity Study* in 1969: "Governments created this machine which is . . . unmanageable in the strictest use of the word; . . . like some prehistoric monster."[8] As noted earlier, this description made Jackson very few friends among the heads of UN agencies.

The World Bank and the IMF were originally envisaged to be part of the UN system, but this relationship soon became more de jure than de facto. The Bretton Woods institutions had more resources and clout. Although many of our voices resented their weighted voting—that is, major financial contributors have more to say—Janez Stanovnik suggested that it actually made the Bank and the Fund more effective institutions: "When it comes to the small nations, it is a great thing for the UN that you have in the UN this principle of one country, one vote. But . . . it is completely illogical that the operational decisions be carried out under the principle of one country, one vote, because this would then be against the basic democratic principle of one person, one vote. . . . You could have in the UN a very useful forum, but the moment when things have to be carried out, you must farm it to the bodies like the World Bank, the IMF, which have weighted vote systems and are there-fore more operational than the United Nations bodies."

Gamani Corea sustained this theme but with a twist for intellectual his-tory: "The developing countries can never look at the Bretton Woods institu-tions as ones in which they could exercise the kind of influence they have in the UN, where they have the strength of numbers. For that reason, any offset to the Bank and the Fund, which have the resources to offer in return for their policies, by the UN is good. . . . So this is all the more reason why the UN should emphasize the intellectual caliber and quality of its work."

James Jonah noted: "There was never much relationship, really, between the Bretton Woods institutions and the UN. . . . And if you remember, in the early years the Bretton Woods institutions would never get involved in politi-cal things. You just had to drag them to do that. They just kept saying, 'That is not part of our mandate.' . . . But the other areas where you have problems with the agencies is because it's a tough fight. And it's very strange that the Charter, on its surface, gives to the General Assembly a kind of a coordinating role; but because these agencies have their own independent budgetary sys-tems, they go their own way."

The relative power between New York and Washington was clear, at least to Boutros Boutros-Ghali: "Everyone turns to the Bank and to the Fund. First, the civil servants there are better paid—a very important point; then they have the financial wherewithal, whereas those in the United Nations system end up for all intents and purposes being marginalized." At the same time, the former Secretary-General saw the intimate link between peace and develop-ment, without which he would have proposed "abolishing the economic side of the UN and reinforcing the Bretton Woods institutions." He explained: "But since there's an interlinking, you can only really reestablish peace if you get the refugees back home, rebuild the infrastructure, reintegrate soldiers into society, find them a trade. It isn't Bretton Woods that's going to do that for you. . . . Bretton Woods has its own internal dynamic, its own concepts, its own norms that don't necessarily correspond to ours. To give an example: until recently, the institutions of Bretton Woods closed down as soon as a war broke out. They stopped working with the countries involved."

Boutros Boutros-Ghali talked about the budgetary problems of the UN system and pointed in the direction of UNESCO, "a laboratory for ideas" whose resources are totally inadequate: "When I asked what the budget was, they got angry. They said to me, 'Jesus Christ didn't need radio or public relations; neither did Mahomet.' I replied, 'Wait a minute! Jesus Christ walked the earth two thousand years ago.'"

But money is not everything. Looking back on his experience as deputy secretary-general of UNCTAD, Bernard Chidzero recounted how ideas can move from "poorer" UN bodies to the wealthier cousins in Washington. "We promoted very strong preferential treatment for the least developed countries. I think this aspect of development came only later into the Bank and the IMF." Chidzero provided another example of UN ideas being picked up by the Bank and the Fund: "I always argued with my colleagues there that we ought to pay more attention to social aspects of development. 'Yes,' they would say, 'but let's have the money first so we can tackle poverty realistically.' I see that they have changed somewhat, that instead of ESAF [Extended Structural Adjustment Facility] they now have . . . a Poverty Reduction and Growth Facility [PRGF]. In other words, the emphasis is now on poverty reduction." The discussions in UNCTAD while he was there were about the need for governments to determine their own development strategies. Chidzero noted that "it is interesting that the Bretton Woods institutions have not only embraced this but are championing the cause and even going beyond."

Although the resource disparities remained, there is consensus among our voices that under the current Secretary-General there has been movement to ensure closer collaboration between the UN system and the Bretton Woods institutions and the WTO. John Ruggie commented: "Well, if one is in the UNDP one looks over one's shoulder all the time at the World Bank, because the World Bank is the 800-pound gorilla while UNDP's resources keep shrinking. But having said that, the relationship between the UN and the World Bank is far better today than it was five years ago, and far closer. We do more things together. The IMF head now shows up at ACC meetings. The WTO head shows up. And, of course, the World Bank president does. That is unprecedented. It is again a reflection of the respect Kofi Annan enjoys and in part the recognition that the UN has legitimacy that can help those organizations. . . . We can certainly define initiatives and projects in such a way to get them very interested."

Nafis Sadik, who retired as the head of the UNFPA toward the end of Annan's first term, agreed that a procedural change had occurred but disputed its actual impact: "The Secretary-General has, in fact, cultivated the World Bank and IMF. . . . But I am not sure that the dialogue has yielded any steps of real collaboration. Take the example of the comprehensive development framework of the World Bank. Mr. Wolfensohn presented it to the ACC and then said that we were all invited to participate and [that] he wanted to have a good consultation. But in fact, what should be in that framework was already decided by the World Bank before they ever had any consultations with us."

While better links were generally viewed as a step in the right direction, Devaki Jain put forward a different dissent: "Kofi Annan has, in many ways, surrendered to the idea that the World Bank and the private sectors can be partners to the UN. By putting a partnership with an agency which is so different in its genesis, its funding, and its purpose, he is actually putting the UN into a mating which will hurt the UN's own values."

Few voices disputed the "dinosaur" images put forward by Urquhart, Childers, and Jackson to describe the system, with or without the Washington-based international financial institutions. Viru Dayal, for instance, lamented "the splintered character of the economic and social structures of the UN. There is far too much dispersal, too much interagency and interprogram competition. In this case, the aggregate was not greater, necessarily, than the sum of the parts. . . . There has to be a major concentration of focus and of energy. In Thomas Mann's book *The Holy Sinner,* there is this young hero who is extremely frail. . . . But somewhere along the line, he became a brilliant warrior. It wasn't his physical strength or prowess in arms. But he did have a tremendous capacity to focus his energies. It made all the difference. . . . Now the problem with, I think, a lot of the efforts of the so-called UN family is that we have an awful lot of ideas, one better than the other. But I sometimes wonder whether we haven't gotten so spread out that we might lose the big battle while winning small skirmishes."

While sitting down and discussing how to improve cooperation would seem an obvious solution, Margaret Anstee reminded us that "more crimes have been committed in the UN in the name of coordination than anything else, because all that happens is that you create more and more coordinating posts, until everybody is coordinating everybody else and no one is actually getting on with the job." Sadako Ogata noted the burden of coordination, or the price of keeping competition under control: "There are wasteful elements. Somehow in the 1990s, with the big humanitarian crises, humanitarian work became very popular. So the humanitarian space became very crowded. . . . You know, my predecessor, Mr. Stoltenberg, went to Jim Grant and wanted some assistance for refugee children. Jim said, 'Assistance by UNICEF stops at the entrance of refugee camps.' That's the way it was looked at. Now they're all over the place, everybody. . . . And then the machinery of coordination became very heavy all over the place."

Noeleen Heyzer agreed: "The turf fight in the UN is a very shortsighted one, because in an era of decreasing resources and decreasing levels of influence, people are fighting for whatever turf remains rather than trying to increase it. There is so much work to be done. Unfortunately, the concept of turf and the compartmentalization is very real in the UN. It has taken away an unnecessary amount of time, and there has been a terrible cost. This is something that needs to be addressed seriously because it is such a waste of productive time."

After all was said and done, James Jonah shrugged his shoulders and remarked that UN "un-coordination" resembled the governmental kind that he found when he took over the Ministry of Finance in Freetown: "Ministers do not coordinate. You have the secretary of agriculture going one way, the secretary of finance another. They don't even talk to each other. And the secretary of agriculture goes to FAO with a different policy." Leticia Shahani drew a metaphor from her work with women's issues and suggested that competition among agencies and between agencies and UN headquarters was partially a function of the organization's success: "It's like a mother which has given birth to many children. They don't go to the ancestral house anymore for family problems."

Above the din of complaints about the problems, two sets of views emerged about the roles of such bureaucratic conflicts for intellectual products—one view held that it was a plus, the other that it was a minus. Dharam Ghai put forward the advantages: "If we believe in competition in other spheres of life, we should believe in competition in the realm of ideas—even more, because nobody has answers to these complex questions." Oscar Schachter agreed: "I would say in general my prejudice is that competition is beneficial in these cases. And I don't see that competition in doing research—that is to say, two different offices, one in Washington and one here, tackling the same question could be harmful."

Likewise, Jan Pronk pointed out why duplication in the marketplace of ideas was not a problem when different approaches to solving a problem emerged from different institutions: "That is a continuous tension, not unhealthy, because it's a political debate. The issue of adjustment, which was dominant in the debate of the 1980s, needed such tension in order to challenge conventional wisdom as well as vested elite interests. UNCTAD helped, but so did ILO, UNICEF, and UNEP. . . . There were changes in both the World Bank and in IMF in the 1990s: the human face of adjustment, environmental impact of economic development, consequences for people of macro-programs, the willingness to accept safety nets. The second-generation adjustment programs are different from the first-generation programs. That is not only the result of thinking within Washington itself or of confrontation with governments but also of confrontation with bodies of intellectual thought in the UN family as a whole."

Based on his extensive experience in agricultural development in Pakistan and in the international arena, Sartaj Aziz provided a concrete example of the benefits of interagency competition, pointing out that it helped spawn a new policy favorable to the poor in the mid-1970s: "Considering the operational constraints that were inherent in its structure, IFAD did a remarkably good job in pursuing its mandate and in turning its focus on the poor, unlike many other UN agencies which treated governments as their clients.... So basically even the World Bank was persuaded to start looking seriously at the implementation problems of projects that deal with very poor people and to explore a more institutional approach to those problems."

At the same time, other voices pointed out that in their view the overall impact of institutional bickering on creative thinking within the UN system was negative. Lourdes Arizpe emphasized missed opportunities: "Instead of having a division of labor, you have a segmentation and a grabbing—what is the word in English for *arrancar* . . . a wrestling about certain turf areas, which does not help, which hinders the work of the agencies. But I also see something else, which is that in the 1950s, the work on economic development was first formulated at the United Nation headquarters so the debate on theories of development stayed in New York. What happened there, I think, is that the nineteenth-century disciplinary division between economics and the other social sciences—anthropology, sociology—became the blueprint for the division of labor between agencies. Economic development stayed in New York and more cultural, scientific, and educational aspects of development stayed in UNESCO, with very little communication between them. That was unfortunate, because there should have been much more multidisciplinary work between these different social sciences." Margaret Anstee noted an obvious problem for seasoned observers: "You have the paradox of a UN system originally conceived on sectoral or thematic lines having to struggle with issues that require a broader comprehensive response."

The nature of rivalry in the trade sector can be gleaned from numerous voices. Klaus Sahlgren commented sardonically that "UNCTAD was considered sort of second rate in the GATT, a nuisance, actually." Rubens Ricupero spoke about the creation of the WTO while the trade-oriented organization that he headed, UNCTAD, continued to function and by definition continued the interinstitutional tensions that had existed earlier with GATT: "The fact that for the first time in history we would have an international organization dealing with trade was new. Of course the GATT, to some extent, was already playing that role. But the GATT was a fiction, a fiction in the sense that people said that it was more a contract than an organization. The members were called Contracting Parties. It was not a fully realized international organization. When finally it came into being, of course people began to ask, 'Why should UNCTAD continue to exist if you have a trade organization that should represent all countries in the world?' . . . There was serious consideration for the abolition of UNCTAD."

He recalled that the tenth UNCTAD conference took place in Bangkok only a few weeks after the eruption by anti-globalization and anti-WTO critics in Seattle in late 1999. "There is no denying, everybody recognized that it was a contribution to the healing process, because it was organized with the idea of bringing everybody together. Michel Camdessus was there, alongside Mike Moore, Jim Wolfensohn. Everybody discussed what had taken place in Seattle. And although it didn't deal directly with that, I think it helped pave the way for a recovery, because it was not done in a spirit of confrontation. We were not going to launch any process of negotiation, so people could come and discuss in a relaxed way. So I don't think it is bad to have a place where you can test ideas, where you can discuss them."

"I am under the impression the whole international system has weakened," mused another old UNCTAD hand, Surendra Patel. "Things are now discussed at WTO and other forums where it is obvious that the interests of the developing countries are not safeguarded. When you leave the issues with the World Bank, the IMF and WTO, the other agencies' role becomes almost irrelevant. At the annual conferences there is a dramatic speech by the president of the World Bank and by the managing director of IMF and the show is over. Real issues are not discussed even at the development and interim committees, where it is business as usual."

Indeed, the intellectual tensions between the international financial institutions and the UN system was a theme to which our voices returned. Victor Urquidi, who attended the Bretton Woods conference in 1944 as a member of the Mexican delegation and then was a World Bank staff member for two years in the late 1940s, was adamant. "I think the tensions were very deep," he said. The World Bank "did not want to join any opinion that was near what the less developed countries were saying at the United Nations." In its early years the Bank "did not consider development as development. They considered it as projects. Bankable projects—that's what they called it: money for electric power development, money for railroads, money for irrigation districts. But no overall concept of what they were doing in a country in which they were lending money for development as they defined it, which was just projects."

Richard Gardner recounted an anecdote that suggested the distance between the UN in New York and the World Bank in Washington: "I remember there was a proposal to have a UN postage stamp. They wanted to put in the postage stamp the alphabet soup of the different specialized agencies, and the World Bank did not want 'IBRD' on that postage stamp." Gardner's story illustrates the difference between de facto unity and the de jure unity implied by a nicely constructed organigram at the end of a textbook.

Adebayo Adedeji bristled about the so-called expertise of the Bretton Woods institutions and remembered a visit by Jean Ripert, who was the director-general and who accompanied the Secretary-General on his 1984 visit to drought-stricken Ethiopia: "After see[ing] children, men, and women dying every minute before believing the severity of the crisis, . . . said he at the sight of the drought-affected displaced persons, 'Adebayo, I am sorry. I wish I had believed what you said.' I was so angry with him, I couldn't say anything. I simply walked away. But here was the director-general for economic and social affairs in the UN. Even the biblical doubting Thomas was not that vicious or churlish. It seemed there was a tacit understanding that the UN headquarters should not question the programs of the World Bank which result in so much tragedy in Africa, even when claims of success are being made in the face of large-scale tragedy. . . . We didn't think of ourselves as a rival to the World Bank. It is like an ant pretending to rival an elephant. It was not rivalry. We just felt that they had got it wrong in terms of Africa because they simply do not know Africa well. They look at the continent with the lenses of North America and Western Europe."

Clearly there was an enormous gulf between the view of the Bank and the Fund and the UN's mainstream thinking, as Gerry Helleiner noted: "If you regard the Fund and the Bank as integral parts of the UN, I think there are a lot of bad ideas coming out of both. The Bank, in its neoliberal excitement in the 1980s, was mistakenly pushing universal prescriptions for all and liberalizing everything and privatizing everything and reducing the role of the state in all circumstances and charging user fees to everyone on everything. I think those were bad ideas. They were not much shared by others in the UN system, so UNICEF and UNDP and ILO were not in on that set of ideas. The IMF's insensitivity to distributional and poverty issues and its overarching anxiety to stabilize economies also, I think, was fomenting bad ideas and bad practices. But again, it was the UN agencies that led the attack—UNICEF above all—on those bad ideas."

What is the bottom line as we move farther into the new millennium? Perhaps the UN family is not worse than most families or administrations, but should it not be a better incubator for ideas? In looking toward future problem-solving, Juan Somavía commented about the downside of tensions in the system by speaking as the head of the ILO: "No significant issue for our societies today can have a single institutional basis. . . . So the problem is that an animal that is becoming increasingly integrated, the global economy, is affecting the whole of the United Nations system in different ways. But each one of the UN organizations—I include the Bretton Woods institutions—[is] looking at this global animal from its own perspective and trying to suggest solutions in its own specific area. This sectoral approach to an integrated phenomenon has reached its limits. . . . I think that the UN is clearly underperforming today in terms of its capacity to contribute to solving many of the problems that this model of globalization poses, because there is no system. There is no capacity to make the system work together, and that is a reality."

Country Groups and International Negotiations

The framing of ideas within UN debates reflected the emergence of the Third World as a consolidated force for advocacy and change in international public policy. The creation and growth of the Non-Aligned Movement and the Group of 77 were prominent in earlier voices. This Third World of about 130 developing countries created a formidable forum for promoting and debating ideas, especially during the Cold War. The others on the stage were the so-called First and Second Worlds—the members of the Organisation for Economic Co-operation and Development and of the Soviet bloc, respectively.

Geographically challenged readers may get lost trying to follow the curious Cold War compass. Although the main political conflicts of the day were characterized across the East-West ideological divide (communism versus capitalism), the main economic issues within the UN were framed across the North-South divide. When the debates began in the 1950s and 1960s, wealthy countries were mostly located in the Northern Hemisphere and the poorer countries in the Southern Hemisphere. The "North" thus included the developed-market countries from the industrialized "West" as well as the socialist countries from the "East." In reality, the East almost always sided with the South during international economic and social negotiations during the Cold War, but then these countries clamored to be part of the West beginning in the late 1980s—and many joined the European Union in 2004.

The presence of subgroups within a larger group invariably means that complex ideas get simplified in order to be acceptable to all parts of the larger group.[9] The dynamics of negotiations can lead to compromised ideas and positions that occupy the middle ground or extreme positions in order to satisfy lowest and highest common denominators. However, two scholars examined the results of ideas in the 1960s and 1970s and argued that solidarity among developing countries "could, and did, steer the United Nations in directions that it wanted to move, it could, and did commit the United Nations to principles that it wanted to legitimize, and it could, and did, demand global actions conducive to its interests. The Group of 77 ultimately could not enforce compliance with its demands, but it could bring attention to them and impressively argue for their rectitude."[10]

"The spread of the group system in the UN has some similarity to the invention of political parties in early U.S. history," Jack Stone noted. "Neither was contemplated in their founding charters, but both flourish." One of the more intriguing units was also not expected, the "like-minded group" of Western countries that were sympathetic to Third World views. From his vantage point in Bergen, Just Faaland explained: "Norway very soon, I think already in the early 1950s, found its place in the debate more on the side of the developing countries than on the side of the rich countries, always trying to strengthen, intellectually and by vote, the developing country position, and trying to explain, mediate, with the other groups."

Johan Kaufmann, whose career in the Dutch foreign service was complemented by his interest in writing about the procedures for multilateral deliberations,[11] pointed out that this so-called like-minded group of Nordic countries pursued an approach that was not a stretch for the Netherlands: "Dutch domestic politics also has a tendency to find common solutions rather than confrontation. . . . The like-minded countries idea goes naturally with a great many people at the same time as being one way out to avoid confrontation. And I don't think it can be said it originated at one particular point. It was a natural idea to come up." His obituary in December 1999 captured the charm of this diplomat-analyst: "Kaufmann was an active participant in—as well as a fascinated observer of—international negotiations. His often somewhat absentminded appearance, his vast knowledge of the matters at hand and his modesty, appealed to many from the East, the West and the South. He was in total control of the diplomatic box of tricks, starting with asking too much and offering too little and then, with great elegance, making concessions, giving opponents space, letting the debate follow its own rhythm and emotions, listening carefully as chairman and, if needed, seeming to doze off but being able, at the right moment, to pull a proposition out of his sleeve. He described these tactics, as if in a recipe book, in *Conference Diplomacy*, which was twice reprinted."[12]

Smaller countries and middle powers can benefit from group negotiations, as Guido de Marco reminded us: "It does happen that a country can punch beyond its size. So when you come to ideas and ideals, it is not true that a small country necessarily finds itself at a loss. A small country agitates itself with more difficulty. A small country may not have the right kind of backup.

But if it has an idea and [if] it has a sense of direction with that idea, I think, within the United Nations it can work a great deal."

Janez Stanovnik cited the ironic but accurate Orwellian view that "we are all equal, but some are more equal than others. And it has to be accepted that unless there will be an understanding among the smaller countries for the greater responsibility which is carried out by the larger countries, I am afraid to say I don't see a smooth and happy world order. There must also be an understanding on the other side of course."

Samir Amin pointed to the ultimate "group," the seven richest countries of the G-7 (Canada, France, Germany, Italy, Japan, the UK, and the United States), which has subsequently become the G-8 with the addition of Russia: "[Valéry] Giscard d'Estaing played a very important role at that time, a negative one, when he came up with the G-7. His proposal would never have been accepted had the Americans not been in agreement, but they were. In effect, this proved a way of replacing the influence of UN member states, the Security Council, the General Assembly—despite all their weaknesses—with another level of international decision-making by giving a monopoly to the wealthiest nations."

One of the more colorful stories about finessing group procedures came from Klaus Sahlgren, who was elected to chair the GATT working party on a particularly difficult proposal from Washington. Toward the end of one set of all-night negotiations "we had bottles of whisky on our desks and sandwiches," he remembered. After everything was finally hammered out, there was one dissenting view, from Greece's ambassador, "who, at three o'clock in the morning announced that he cannot accept the result. As you know, in GATT you work by consensus." Washington's delegate "said loud and clear, 'That fucking Greek.' I came up with a slightly more elegant suggestion: could the distinguished ambassador of Greece perhaps go out and wash his hands while we take this decision? And, taken by surprise, he did." Thus, consensus could be reached and Greece could be spared a struggle.

Alister McIntyre noted that groups had a perverse and unwanted influence on UN staff who were supposed to be doing research: "I hated this political division of the staff into who's in the B Group and who's not. I never paid the slightest attention to it. It got me into a fair amount of trouble with the [G-]77, but I managed to survive that."

Hans Singer recalled that UNCTAD, where developing countries launched so many ideas, did not succeed in serving as a consistent research organ for the G-77, at least in part due to the very "size and diversity of the G-77." Agreement among developing countries was rarely possible. Gert Rosenthal concurred that such heterogeneity among the G-77 makes decision making difficult and even calls its credibility into question. What often happens, he notes, is that the group of developing countries tends to express the views of more radical members in part because the other members do not wish to alienate the leadership. "But this degrades the G-77," Rosenthal stated, "because it goes around making statements which are not taken too seriously. In other words, non-G-77 countries tend to view those positions as posturing." Rosenthal noted that, perhaps of even greater significance, such "posturing" ultimately weakens the UN vis-à-vis the Bretton Woods institutions because it makes the UN appear as if it is a platform for denunciation while the IMF and the World Bank are places to conduct real business. Ministers of finance approached the Bretton Woods institutions "in a very business-like manner, while their foreign ministers went to the UN and ranted and raged." He observed that the North-South cleavage has ebbed and flowed—the more cooperative atmosphere in the 1980s followed the confrontational 1970s—and speculated that the level of tension may be once again on the rise.

In this regard, Michael Zammit Cutajar insisted on using "Southern solidarity" in spite of obvious divisions and vast differences in wealth among so many countries. This reality may be hard for many Westerners to fathom, especially when several Third World countries have per capita incomes that surpass those in some First World countries: "People will decry the lack of logic, of economic logic, in the Group of 77, or the concept of 'North-South' or of 'developing countries.' But it is not a question of logic. There is a sense of not being in the club. Saudi Arabia may be rich, but it certainly is not accepted as a member of the inner circle. It's foreign, it's not Christian, it's not 'white,' it's not Western, it's 'the other.' It's a most fundamental feeling, I'm speaking with some emotion now, because . . . I'm Maltese . . . you could say almost European. Most of my countrymen would burn me, they would say of course we're European! But this feeling of not belonging or of being excluded still comes through if you're in a country like England where there are definite barriers as to who is in and who is not. That's a rather peculiar case, but the feeling of exclusion is a very strong phenomenon in the world and anyone who can share that feeling with somebody else has an immediate solidarity."

Devaki Jain, one of the founding members of DAWN, recalled a similar logic behind a controversial decision, or "a troubling thorn," which "was to limit our membership or informal belonging to women actually living in the South. . . . We felt that location was as important an experience as learning from the field and academy for that particular political veneer which comes out of participation in citizenship under a given constitution. When you are struggling, politically located in your own political fabric, the incentives, the vibes, your priorities, your capacity to do is very different than when you are living in a country with a social security base; where your gas and water supply works and every morning you read the *Times* of London."

11

Blending Outside Intellectual Energies

- **Outside Academics and Consultants**
- **Independent Commissions of Eminent Persons**
- **Nongovernmental Organizations and the Private Sector**
- **Global Conferences**

Many people who have been affiliated with the United Nations and have played an essential role in the organization's intellectual activities have not been international civil servants. Many of our voices had significant associations with a university or independent think tanks before or after their UN service. Many have served as members or chairs of high-level and independent panels and commissions that have studied a new or emerging problem that was not yet on the international radar screen. Many have also served as a staff or board member of a nongovernmental organization, and most have attended global ad hoc conferences that pull together a range of actors on the international stage.

This chapter is about "outsiders" and begins with academics and consultants who complement the UN "insiders" of the previous two chapters in collective efforts to generate, implement, and disseminate ideas. Other sections of this chapter concern independent commissions and non-state actors (NGOs and the private sector) before concluding with UN global conferences, at which UN staffers who organized them are joined by governments and increasingly by an "army" of NGOs, think tanks, and academics—for example, over 10,000 in Beijing in 1995. Outside and inside intellectual energies often come together, or "blend," at the United Nations; indeed, there often is synergy between them.

Outside Academics and Consultants

"Knowing that I've been in the house for a while, I've always reached out to talk to others," Kofi Annan told us. "There is a tendency for people in this house to say, 'We are special. We are different. The rest of the world does not understand us.' And you can really get into a cocoon." His openness to outside expertise is refreshing: "There are times when I bring in groups to advise me on issues—use experienced leaders to give me advice. . . . So it's an extensive network, and it depends on the issue. For example, when I'm dealing with AIDS, I reach out to experts in that field. And you go to a different group depending on the emphasis. I'm also happy, too, that lots of institutions and excellent intellectuals are very happy to work with us. It's quite remarkable how they are always ready to help."

In a rare moment of self-criticism, Annan's predecessor, Boutros Boutros-Ghali, told us: "One of the flaws of an academic who becomes a politician is that he no longer has the time to renew and enrich his intellectual capital. You live on your past. Physically, you don't have time. To be a good academic you need to do four or five hours of reading every day, keep up with the latest theories, meet with colleagues, have time to discuss with them." When asked about the UN University in Tokyo, Ignacy Sachs pointed to the disconnect between the label and the actual capacity of that institution: "It's an institution that does not have the size it was supposed to have, and it's little ridiculous to refer to the United Nations University when in reality it's merely a little research foundation."

Experts may influence a broad spectrum of international politics through their ability to interact with policymakers irrespective of location and national boundaries. They can frame the debate on a particular issue. They can provide justifications for alternatives. And often they can catalyze national or international coalitions to support chosen policies and advocate change. By diffusing ideas from beyond as well as within UN decision-making structures, "epistemic communities," as Peter Haas calls them, influence policy most during times of uncertainty and change when the demand for expertise increases, which empowers knowledgeable specialists.[1] Much literature relates to scientific elites with particular expertise in areas such as the AIDS pandemic[2] and the environment.[3] A related approach is Peter Hall's study of the cross-national spread of ideas among experts in the postwar period, when Keynesianism spread largely because it "acquired influence over the economic policies of a major power and was exported as that nation acquired increasing hegemony around the world."[4]

Ahead of the Curve? UN Ideas and Global Challenges examined the early resort to outside expertise in helping to define the future international development agenda.[5] Early reports contributed prescient thinking by such people as Gunnar Myrdal, the Nobel laureate who was the first head of the ECE, and Arthur Lewis and Theodore W. Schultz, both of whom would later also receive Nobel prizes. They also pioneered a pattern for blending outside expertise into the work of the world organization. Each development report was prepared by a team of prominent outside economists from different parts of the world with support from the UN Secretariat. There also was a strong ethical dimension to them, as these economists accepted that their purpose was to contribute to a world of greater economic and social justice with less poverty and that work for the United Nations was a service to the larger community of states and peoples in addition to being an honorable part of a professional career.

With her usual irony, Margaret Anstee remembered discussions about what to call outsiders with knowledge: "Experts were at first called specialists. But there was an American book called *The Specialist*[6] by a chap who was a specialist in country privies [toilets]! So it was decided that *specialist* was not a very happy name to give to people, and they were called experts. Somebody then pointed out that an expert is somebody who is a long way from home!" Whatever they are called, our voices contained a range of views about the impact of using expertise from outside secretariats.

The value and shortcomings of scholars for the UN's work were present in many voices. What Nobel economics laureate Lawrence Klein told us probably matches what most scholars would say: "I believe that it would be quite valuable if the UN had a better academic world contact. The IMF, the World Bank, and the OECD have very good rapport. It is partly because they are much better financed." Cornelio Sommaruga was more impatient with scholars: "Academics have also to understand that *l'art pour l'art* [art for art's sake] may be of interest for them but not necessarily for governments and for organizations. . . . We need texts with sex appeal."

While the approaches of scholars and policy people in the UN are distinct, there was agreement with Sommaruga's caricature from an unexpected source. "In retrospect, I am embarrassed by some of the things that I used to do, like sending somebody who is in public office a book, as if that person ever had time to read a book," chuckled John Ruggie as he was about to leave the 38th floor and return to a new ivory tower. "Or sending papers off to them and suggesting that answers they were seeking to their problems could be found in these thirty-four pages if they only worked at it hard enough. The influence of outside thinking on policy is far more problematic. . . . The most direct carrier, obviously, is people. There is no substitute for doing what I am doing here at the UN: simply leaving the one world and entering the other world. You bring with you ideas, and there is a contagion effect among the people you're working with. For example, I can trace back some of our early ideas here in the Secretary-General's office that led to the Global Compact. I can trace that back to my 'embedded liberalism' article in 1982.[7] The first time

I gave that article to some of my colleagues, they had absolutely no idea what I was talking about. But after a while, going back and forth in a dynamic way, there was that contagion effect. And, of course, I learned enormously from them in the process, because they saw the institution and the system from a gears and wheels point of view, from the inside."

Ruggie mentioned timing as another variable. "Seminars and conferences that policymakers attend can also be important carriers, particularly if they happen to be struggling with a problem at the time and luck has it that you're addressing that problem. The critical issue there is an issue of framing, however. . . . But if you are lucky enough, and you frame the issue in a way that is meaningful and useful to the policymaker, then direct interaction in seminar settings also can be extremely helpful. . . . What I mean by framing is that you can lock up Kofi Annan with Kenneth Waltz's *Theory of International Politics*[8] forever and there won't be much cross-fertilization, because the way Waltz frames international politics is not very useful to a Secretary-General of the United Nations. . . . Understanding balance-of-power politics in a sophisticated way . . . doesn't help you make specific choices or pursue specific courses of action if you are sitting in that office."

Michael Doyle agreed: A hard-nosed realist . . . wouldn't flourish in the UN environment. John Mearsheimer,[9] whom I admire greatly, would be a disaster in that environment. The cultural disconnect would be so enormous. At that same time, my friends who are strong postmodernists, for whom there is no text that doesn't need to be subverted and no term that doesn't have to be parsed in twelve incompatible directions, [also] would not flourish in the UN public policy environment. You need a political scientist who [has] ordinary language, attitudes, and some experience with policy—and a practical orientation—the kind of a person, the kind of work that you do, I do, John Ruggie, Andy Mack. You could go down the list. That was the kind of person who could operate in the environment I entered. It wasn't a place for highfalutin political science of any form. It just wasn't compatible with it."

Now a retired and still-prominent professor of development economics at the University of Toronto, Gerry Helleiner has frequently been consulted by the UN and other international institutions. He remarked that "these expert groups are devices for demonstrating that ideas can be shared among people of quite different interests and origin when they gather as independent people, not representing their constituencies. . . . I prefer expert groups to jamborees. If I had my druthers, I think that is a much better use of money. Now I show utterly my biases. I show support for research. I guess that goes without saying or I wouldn't be in academia."

He assessed the impact of academics on UN staff: "When you do go and testify, invariably no one has ever heard of you or knows anything about anything you have ever done in the past. You can assume nothing. And it's good for you to realize that nobody knows anything or gives a damn about the things you have been sweating your guts over for the past fifteen or twenty years. . . . And these are the people that are supposed to be making decisions in the area you think you have been making contributions in." He continued: "There is nothing worse than people who are very bright and analytically capable but who are talking at much too general a level and who spin general approaches to things and are unable to be specific about anything. If you really have a practical idea as to what needs to be done in a particular commodity sector or with a particular intellectual property provision and you can articulate it in a way that is intelligible to a person whose field this is not, if you can translate the theory and the arcane details into a language that is intelligible to the intelligent layman—and a lot of people don't have that— then an academic can be very useful."

Gamani Corea specifically mentioned the influence of academics from both the South and the North: "There was a certain tradition coming from socialist thinking about the role of the state, the role of social justice, and so on, which was reflected in the thinking of intellectuals in developing countries who came from universities abroad . . . big names associated (I'm going back to my young days) people like Harold Laski and intellectuals on the British left. Those names were quite well known and their ideas were very influential. Most of the people were associated with the Left Book Club, even people like Beveridge, John Strachey and the Webbs. That whole generation of thinkers, at that time, were not formulating policies as such for developing countries. They were pointing to shortcomings and gaps."

Wishing to balance some of his earlier comments about the UN's intellectual shortcomings, Alister McIntyre said: "I am not entirely pessimistic about what the UN can do in generating new ideas. Today, it can draw ideas from outside. For example, the UNDP with Mahbub ul Haq and the *Human Development Report,* which was a very good use of outside expertise. I used to try my best to encourage that in UNCTAD and again when I was in the Office of Director-General, to bring in people to help us think through problems."

Nafis Sadik, executive director of the UN Population Fund in 1987–2000, pushed this argument further: "I think population work has always come from outside of the UN. . . . Outside organizations put a lot more pressure on the UN, but also on governments. I think the work of the Pop[ulation] Council, the work of many of the scholars at Princeton University, at Stanford University influenced very much the eventual outcome of setting up a UNFPA and having a population program. Those influences came from outside, because in fact many members of the UN itself in fact resisted it." Michael Doyle, who was a professor at Princeton and Columbia Universities before joining the

Secretariat and after leaving, agreed: "If you want genuinely fresh ideas, you've got to go outside the system altogether. You have to go to commissions, panels, academics, and NGOs and a few governments—mostly academics and NGOs."

"The incentive for a serious intellectual to leave a university or government service [for] the UN is very limited," said Brian Urquhart. "Greatly to Boutros-Ghali's and Kofi Annan's credit, they have managed to get serious people into their immediate office." But Leticia Shahani cautioned that "academics have their own way of looking at the future, but they are not in the electric chair of policymaking and budget allocation, which are political responsibilities."

Robert Cox pointed to the discomfort between academics and specialists within the international civil service: "I could begin to think of myself as something more like an anthropologist. That is, you live with the tribe and you understand the tribe, but you are not really of the tribe. And that is okay as long as you keep that pretty much to yourself. But as people begin to see that you are not really one of them, one hundred percent, then there is a sort of resentment that can grow up about it as well."

In 1971, he chose to retire from the ILO and pursue an academic career. He explained: "I don't regret it, and I think in effect that I probably have had more influence through my students than I have had with anybody in the ILO or with any government representatives in the ILO." In his view, experts often are brought in not for new ideas but to legitimize a desired program or approach: "I learned that you don't invite a consultant in when you want good advice about management. You invite them in when you want to do something and they're going to help you to make the recommendations that will result in a structure coming out which is the one you wanted to begin with." While on occasion he sees a role for independent analysis, Mihaly Simai agreed that "academics are used for window-dressing by the secretariat, where the secretariat is already familiar with the outcome of the given work done by an academic and they want the consent or they want to strengthen their views by external academic expertise."

Others were less cynical about the UN's use of experts. For example, Just Faaland, who spent most of his career at a Norwegian development institute in Bergen, emphasized the critical importance of injecting outside intellectual grist into the mill: "The UN would be a much poorer organization if it hadn't been for . . . consultancies and other ways of mobilizing the outside world. . . . Some of the academics who are in this, they are in this for a quickie. Then they move back to their research and back to other interests. The constant pressure is not really there. But that, in a way, is a function that UNRISD,

WIDER, the OECD Development Center, and such institutions can perform. They can, in a sense, be a channel for such inputs and see to the continuation of pressure to change."

Lourdes Arizpe articulated a theme that others touched upon, namely the need for a division of labor between academics and practitioners: "You do need pure intellectual research. Think of the way in which Claude Levi-Strauss, who did not do very much fieldwork nor was engaged in social action, changed our perception of societies. For this reason, universities such as the National University of Mexico is essential in terms of an institution that looks at the long term in developing very precise instruments of understanding. But then you need an institution like the Institute of Development Studies in Sussex, where the theoretical conclusions can be translated into elements to guide policy. . . . And finally, there must be the institutions such as UNESCO, where such ideas that guide policy are negotiated among many governments and civil society groups so that the end result is a consensual outlook on actions. . . . The problem that I see is that there has been a denial of the need for theoretical thinking in the last two decades and an insistence that we should only respond to demand, to what people want or to what people say they want."

Precisely this kind of merging of practitioner and scholarly approaches at the IDS and other development institutes was what made the work on basic needs in the 1970s at the ILO so creative, according to Dharam Ghai: "One of the reasons why the World Employment Programme became so successful was that it linked, in a very integrated way, technical cooperation with research. In fact, the boundary between the two disappeared. There was a lot of research going on in the World Employment Programme of all kinds. But these missions were, if you like, an integration of research and policymaking. Participants included some of the leading academics and development specialists. And they applied their accumulated knowledge and research to a very concrete issue—how to generate productive employment for everybody and for everybody to have minimum living standards."

An example of Ghai's model researcher is certainly Samir Amin, who described the three mutually reinforcing and inseparable activities in his own career: teaching, work in economic management, and politics. They are why, he told us, he "knew the United Nations well." He described his own well-known radical criticism of the global economy, which he believed resulted from mixing theoretical reflections and practical exposure, in the following way: "I set myself the task of looking at capitalism not as an abstract means of production, which characterized Marxism's historical drift off course, but rather as a world system that produced, among other things, what we have come to call 'underdevelopment'; that is, polarization on a world scale." He defended his doctoral thesis in 1957, and Walt Rostow's famous book *The Stages of Economic Growth* was published in 1960.[10] Amin asserted: "I wrote an anti-Rostow before Rostow."

While agreeing that outside scholars add value, James Jonah nonetheless lamented the seeming necessity to go outside because of the incapacity within the secretariat to produce high-quality research: "Most of the reports of the Secretary-General are produced outside, in academic institutions. . . . Many of the donors have accepted, reluctantly, that the UN cannot do it. . . . It shows you that the secretariat is not there, whereas if you look at the World Bank, they have people in there who are very, very good." In Jonah's view, the ability of the secretariat to push the envelope depended on one condition: "The Secretary-General must want it. If you know he wants it, it will be delivered. If he makes it a requirement, it will be delivered." While noting openness at present, he also regretted that research was "biased, because it is mostly Western institutions, which is why most of the things the Secretary-General does are not embraced by the Third World countries."

Secretary-General Kofi Annan articulated why going outside, even if inside expertise is available, may be preferable: "There are certain issues that are better done outside and there are certain issues that can only be done inside. . . . But take a look at the intervention issue. I couldn't have done it inside. It would have been very divisive. And the member states were very uncomfortable because, as an organization, sovereignty is our bedrock and bible—here is someone coming with ideas which are almost challenging it. So I had to sow the seed and let them digest it but take the study outside and then bring in the results for them to look at it. I find that when you are dealing with issues where the member states are divided and have very strong views, and very strong regional reviews, if you do the work inside the discussions become so acrimonious that however good a document is, sometimes you have problems. . . . But if you bring it from outside . . . they accept it."

In evaluating the UN's internal research capacity, the critical voice of Devaki Jain indicated the impressions about one unit, the International Research and Training Institute for the Advancement of Women: "INSTRAW is dying, as you know, and should be allowed to die, because INSTRAW was supposed to be an intellectual powerhouse for the UN, but apart from the fact that no intellectual was placed there to lead, bureaucracies cannot be the source of intellection."

One of the first such bodies was the UN Institute for Training and Research, established in 1963. In the halls of its offices across from UN headquarters in New York, an oft-heard alternative for its UNITAR acronym is the "UN Institute for the Tired and Retired." But informed by his experience as the director of research in the late 1960s, Oscar Schachter recalled this institute's lofty origins: "UNITAR started, in a way, from Hammarskjöld, with a statement that the Secretariat was not a proper research body, that they were being asked to do research which they were not competent to do or were not supposed to do. He had the idea that research people were, so to speak, scientists. They worked as scientists. They had their own canons to follow."

Max Finger argued that it was difficult to ensure independent research within the organization, offering UNITAR a case in point: "We had originally envisaged it to be a kind of Rand Corporation for the Secretary-General. But at any rate, we wanted UNITAR to be a group of experts who could advise the Secretary-General on policy and report directly to him. . . . Unfortunately, that part of it never developed. In part, I think [Under-Secretary-General] C. V. Narasimhan buried it. Dick Gardner and I went to see Narasimhan to propose that John Holmes or Kenneth Bailey . . . be the head of UNITAR because of their academic background and credentials. . . . We wanted somebody of that stature. Instead the Secretary-General apparently decided that he needed somebody with under-secretary-general rank from black Africa. And he appointed a guy named Darbusier, who is really a dark-skinned Frenchman—a very nice guy, but he didn't have the standing with foundations. . . . Narasimhan said to us straight out, no he can't be from any NATO country when we mentioned John Holmes. . . . The result is that Joe Slater at Ford, who had originally talked about $2 million as a nest egg, withdrew the offer and they put the money from the Ford Foundation into the Hammarskjöld Library. . . . UNITAR has not been a favorite of Washington since then."

The heightened visibility of the controversial issue of transnational corporations in the 1970s was an illustration of why outsiders were essential intellectual resources, according to Sotiris Mousouris: "We had a close cooperation with the academic world. As you know, Raymond Vernon from Harvard helped us on several occasions, often as informal consultant. Others came to work at the Centre [on Transnational Corporations]. For instance, professors John Dunning, Charles-Albert Michalet, John Stopford, Norman Girvan, and others worked for some time at the centre and helped with the research. Those who were doing research on transnationals were often seeking to work with us. We had a good reputation. And of course we had collected enormous data. They felt the centre was dynamic and was doing something important." Unlike other voices, Mousouris judged that there was more synergy than competition: "So it is difficult to tell you how much came from the secretariat, how much came from the academic world. I cannot even remember how many ideas were mine. I remember writing on yellow pads outlines of research topics and giving them to consultants and to staff."

The former head of the CTC, Klaus Sahlgren, recalled his decision "to put most of our money into high-level consultants. So we had a big budget for hiring consultants. I figured that if we invested our resources into recruiting ordinary international civil servants, we would not get the best results. What we wanted was expertise. One important consideration was that in hiring consultants, the unfortunate national quota system would not apply."

In terms of inputs from academics and consultants, some of our voices argued for a mutually reinforcing process. Sartaj Aziz, for instance, saw the importance of injecting external ideas but also of inside massaging: "Obviously there is a lot of cross-fertilization of ideas. All the UN agencies which have people who are either from an academic background or interact with the academic community do manage to pick up a number of ideas. And the academics, if they come up with major breakthroughs in ideas, like Arthur Lewis's book *The Theory of Economic Growth,* or Schumpeter's *Strategy,* or Gunnar Myrdal's *Asian Drama,* all had a major impact on development thinking. . . . But below that, even less important ideas in institutions which have close interaction with the academic community can become significant. More agencies invite members of the academic community to lead missions, for example, to different countries."

According to Aziz, "The 1960s and 1970s were, from that point of view, a very productive period, a creative period for both the UN and the academic community. Then suddenly in the 1980s, interest in development as a subject started declining. On the one hand, for example, in Boston and Harvard, the number of people taking up development courses declined because aid was declining and the need for advisors was diminishing. . . . But what is more, at that time the whole emphasis shifted to the free market system and the 'structural adjustment' process. Now you require a different kind of advisor—monetary specialists, investment specialists, rather than social scientists. But there were a lot of related subjects which started getting attention—women's issues, the environment, disarmament, nuclear issues. The debate therefore moved away from development, poverty, employment, basic needs to more macroeconomic adjustment. . . . The official UN system and the academic community's role were diminishing."

Sadako Ogata was a university administrator and instructor when she arrived in Geneva to assume the UNHCR's helm. She recalled her own efforts to set up the Center for Documentation and Research (CDR) to put archives in order and build up a better database inside and outside of her headquarters: "Then I thought maybe we should have some visiting scholars. . . . I also thought about taking in people who had field experience to spend some time reflecting and analyzing. Several people had that opportunity, and some produced good monographs. But you see, UNHCR is a very busy office, and having the time to think and write is regarded as a luxury. . . . The CDR did manage to establish contacts with think tanks and academics. And in that sense, it was rather useful. . . . At the same time, the utility was never really proven to the organization widely enough. It was disbanded after I left. I rather thought it might happen that way."

She reflected on the contrasts between the two worlds: "I still associate myself with the academic community and feel a part of it, but you cannot really live in the ivory tower. If you really want to solve the world's problems you have to reach out much, much more."

Independent Commissions of Eminent Persons

A particular type of expertise—which combines knowledge and political visibility—has been influential in nourishing economic and social ideas. It emanates from reports of independent commissions composed of eminent persons, usually with a high dose of former politicians. These efforts are intended to help raise the visibility of a particular global challenge by putting forward a consensus view from prominent individuals who represent a spectrum of opinion and nationalities. But unlike official or semi-official UN reports, the commissioners speak in their individual capacities and may be able to move beyond what passes for politically correct conventional wisdom in UN circles—although some have also argued that UN-backed panels, when properly composed and staffed, can also push the envelope of ideas.[11] Although the reports are normally presented to the Secretary-General, who decides whether or not they will be followed up, the production of a cornucopia of ideas outside the confines of the UN Secretariat provides more room for imagination.

Normally such commissions' reports are named after their chairs. This technique was launched with *Partners in Development,* headed by former Canadian prime minister Lester B. Pearson.[12] The so-called Pearson Commission was followed by a host of others, including the two commissions on development issues chaired by former German chancellor Willy Brandt,[13] the commission on common security chaired by former Swedish prime minister Olaf Palme,[14] the commission on environment and development chaired by serving Norwegian prime minister Gro Harlem Brundtland,[15] the commission on humanitarian problems chaired by Iranian and Jordanian princes Sadruddin Aga Khan and Hassan Bin Talal,[16] the commission on South-South cooperation chaired by serving Tanzanian president Julius Nyerere,[17] the commission on global governance chaired by former Swedish prime minister Ingvar

Carlsson and Guyana's Shridath Ramphal,[18] the commission on humanitarian intervention and state sovereignty chaired by former Australian foreign minister Gareth Evans and former Algerian ambassador Mohamed Sahnoun,[19] and the commission on human security chaired by Sadako Ogata and Amartya Sen.[20] Some commissions are recalled more by the names of their sponsors rather than of the chairs—for example, the first report to the Club of Rome[21] and the report of the Carnegie Commission on preventing deadly conflict.[22]

"I think you need a team," said Michael Doyle in explaining what constitutes a successful commission. "There are very few people—none that I can think of—who have all the talents, but a team can make a difference. I think it is useful to have two sorts of people, especially. One is an academic who can of think the big thoughts and has credibility doing so. . . . The other type of team member you need is somebody who has slogged away in the trenches for enough years that he or she knows where all of the bodies are buried bureaucratically. They know about all the failures that have taken place, of previous people trying to reform the system. A good commission brings both kinds in."

Judgments about the quality of the analyses as well as the ultimate political impact of such commissions vary substantially across our voices. At one end of the spectrum, a glum Sonny Ramphal quipped: "The Brandt Commission produced Cancún, and the Brundtland Commission produced Rio. What did Rio produce? Rio produced the UN's sustainable development commission. What has that commission produced? Disappointment." Notwithstanding his harsh judgment based on experience, Ramphal subsequently agreed to serve as co-chair of another commission.

What is a fair way to evaluate the thinking and impact of these commissions? Most interviewees viewed their reports as elements of a multifaceted effort that results in alterations in worldviews and values, in new policies and concrete actions—in short, as other pieces in the mosaic of global governance. The way reports from high-level commissions are received and used usually depends on factors that are impossible to control, including changes in the world economy, domestic politics, and elections in major powers. The three functions of such commissions that emerged from the interviews are increasing awareness and raising consciousness, advocating for particular ideas, and lending legitimacy to programs and ideas. Some interviewees qualified their judgments by arguing that they could be successful if initiatives were backed by major powers and if the subject matter was narrowly focused.

Two of our interlocutors—Sartaj Aziz and Dharam Ghai—served on the staff of the commission that began it all. Aziz looked back: "The Pearson Commission was actually conceived by Robert McNamara to gain more support for aid—aid generally, but better funding for the World Bank. So he thought that if a group of people were to evaluate twenty years of development experience it would provide further rationalization. In the Pearson report, we introduced the concept of self-sustaining growth . . . [which] means a process that can be sustained, even if aid goes away, and that is not possible without human development. . . . That was, at that time, I think, quite innovative."

Partners in Development "made a contribution by a systematic review of the history of development cooperation, what it had achieved, its limitations, what its rationale was, and how to put forward the case for renewed interest in assistance," Ghai told us. "There is one idea put forward in the report—it was Arthur Lewis's idea that I find still very relevant. The argument was that development cooperation is a joint enterprise. . . . Developing countries have to perform. The aid must be used effectively. The developing countries must be held accountable. But the donor countries also have responsibility and must also be held accountable. . . . The commissioners were eminent and responsible people. They were not the kind of people who would scare anybody. They were members of the establishment."

James Jonah emphasized the political climate rather than the quality of ideas. He pointed out that "big studies like the Brundtland report—she was prime minister of Norway with a high political profile, therefore the media seizes it, and it gets in. But in the long run, it is the member states who have to decide whether they are going to implement it or not. . . . All the ideas are there, but they don't get through. . . . I don't think it is intellectual quality. I don't think governments go that way. . . . When the appropriate ripeness is there, then they will approve it. It is good, in a sense, because if you get the media to accept it, then the local population can put pressure on their governments one way or the other to go along with it." Adebayo Adedeji agreed: "I don't think most people have ever read cover to cover *Partners in Development.* Nor did they read Brandt's *Common Crisis: North-South Cooperation for World Recovery.* But the ideas put there—particularly as publicized by the media—stuck in the minds of people."

"We have run into an era of fatigue with grand commissions, especially commissions that keep saying the same things," said Alister McIntyre. "They are not news from the point of view of the media. The Brundtland Commission had an impact. It was saying something different. Brandt, although it was separated by some years from the Pearson Commission, was more or less covering the same area. The Commission on Global Governance again was— I regret to say that some of my friends were on it—repeating ideas that had surfaced before in less grand style."

"Such reports were certainly helpful," argued Kurt Waldheim. "Prestigious people drafted them and underlined the importance and urgency of solving burning issues. Governments had to think about those problems. They gave also the possibility to developing countries to draw the attention of the international community to these issues. This is one side of the coin. The other side is that governments usually are not ready to act on matters which are not ripe for decisions. . . . And here I come to a very delicate subject—that is, power politics. Having gone through this experience for ten years, I have to say that power politics of the nineteenth or twentieth century hasn't really stopped. The belief that problems can be resolved through important intellectual reports with good ideas is wrong. . . . I learned it the hard way because I was an idealist."

Brian Urquhart, who served on numerous commissions, cautioned that "the big commissions always claim a great deal of credit." Rolling his eyes, he said: "I just got a five-page letter from David Hamburg [then president of the Carnegie Corporation of New York, which had funded the commission] saying how absolutely stellar the repercussions of the Commission on the Prevention of Deadly Conflict have been. I am glad he thinks so, and I hope it's true. But a high-level commission is a huge, heavy piece of machinery. It is enormously expensive. It takes a hell of a lot of time, and I wonder really how much effect it has. . . . I don't really believe that these problems (globalization, poverty, etc.) are susceptible to thirty distinguished old fellows deliberating on them and producing a report."

From his point of view as a government consumer of such reports and a participant in commissions, Stéphane Hessel agreed. "Whenever I work on such groups, I have the feeling that what we say is listened to by a limited number of people and that it is then set aside by those who represent the important governments. I have never heard an ambassador of an important country . . . really quote one of those reports."

As someone who not only participated in several commissions but also invested in them while minister of development cooperation in the Netherlands, Jan Pronk clearly thought that they were cost-effective ways to improve the intellectual basis for global problem-solving: "Timing is very important, and the choice of a political concept which all of a sudden is being seen as eye-opening. Such an example is the Brundtland report, *Our Common Future*. It came at an appropriate moment, when the world was recuperating from the economic crisis and people were searching for a new perspective. The definition of sustainability: 'No future generation should have less choice options than any present generation, due to choices made by the present generation.' That is a value applicable to each and every individual and nation. And it is the responsibility of any present generation. A great concept and good timing . . . made a difference. . . . The Brandt Commission report had experienced bad timing, because we published our report in the midst of an international economic low. The concept of interdependence and mutual interests was good, but the times were not conducive for a new approach."

Most agreed that these commissions and their "blockbuster" reports were of some significance regardless from whose "club" the commissioners came. Bernard Chidzero said: "I think these commissions were not just academic exercises. They were intended to produce results which would be applicable to real situations and which would necessitate governments' policies and institutional arrangements. . . . [They] have generated an awareness of the real problems which we face, not just of academic ideas. They have underpinned the necessity for governments to take action." For example, "the world has become one," he said, "in the sense of global governance and the many issues of effective neighborhood as raised by the Commission on Global Governance. It is no longer just a theoretical, nice, moral issue about neighborhoods; it is a question of survival for countries to work together."

In thinking about specific examples from eminent commissions, John Ruggie commented on their pluses and minuses by using the Club of Rome report as an example: "It was a mixed blessing, as are many reports like that. On the one hand, they often encapsulate a particular set of problems in a way that is very useful for social mobilization and activist purposes. They have a relatively simple approach that allows you to grasp a complex reality that you, as a citizen, only vaguely understood before. Now, all of a sudden, it is put together in a nice coherent package. That is essential for mobilization purposes, which has spillover effects on the policymaking process. . . . The downside of that particular report, and some others like it, is that they have been wrong—badly so in the Club of Rome case. So they also trigger a backlash. The Club of Rome report was patently wrong and triggered a generation of resistance to environmental doom-and-gloom theories, some of which were right!"

"I happen to think that [they are] one of the things the UN does best," stated Gert Rosenthal, who pointed to the need for the repetition of certain topics. "Sooner or later, people start repeating certain basic propositions. Usually they are born in the UN Secretariat, or the UN Secretariat buys in when they are developed somewhere else and popularizes them. The UN does that very well. It takes time. No single document, no single conference is a watershed event. Oftentimes a report's ideas find sudden wide repetition in public circles up to five years after a report's release." Gerry Helleiner agreed: "If you put the right kind of group together, a mixed kind of group, it does have an impact on people. It is like social scientific research. The impact may not occur for twenty-five years and you don't really know whether any or all of this research has an impact."

Janez Stanovnik noted that "these reports had tremendous impact, not only on the General Assembly but also on thinking outside. . . . I was called to the cabinet meeting of the Yugoslav government to give them a brief report. I was given only five or ten minutes, but the question which the president of the government would put to me [was] 'You just tell us now in just five minutes, what are your impressions? Where is the world going? What is happening in the world which we must be aware of?'" Stanovnik was able to refer to a UN report for his answers, as "there was a connection between what was going on in the General Assembly and what was going on in national governments."

Former Secretary-General Javier Pérez de Cuéllar commented: "Do you remember one expression that was very naughty, from a famous French politician, [Georges] Clémenceau: 'If you want to solve a problem, just create a commission.' . . . It is very witty to say such a thing, but it is not true. But I think those commissions were very important, because actually they attract the attention of the international community to some very important problems—human development, for instance. And in the case of my commission, this Commission on Culture and Development[23] was very important because it was one dimension of the problem of development that has been disregarded—I wouldn't say forgotten, but in a way considered as a kind of a second- or third-degree problem. And it was very important that we provided lots of ideas. Some of them were, perhaps, too bold. But it is much better to be too bold in those cases than to be shy. . . . The problem is the follow-up."

Lourdes Arizpe was a member of that UNESCO commission and judged that it had "made an extraordinary achievement, which was to organize the international debate on culture." She noted with satisfaction that "the anthropological viewpoint had strongly influenced the commission's report, because we were able to give a broader definition of culture than had hitherto been used in defining cultural programs in the United Nations. . . . Even though, in terms of projects, UNESCO in the 1970s and 1980s did bring in a much broader range of topics on culture, such as cultural policies and indigenous cultures, there had never been a formulation which linked culture to sustainability, democracy, human rights and gender equity, encompassing many more social and political aspects than had been included up to then in cultural programs."

So are these commissions worthwhile? The composite ambivalence from our voices probably means, as for many questions, that the answer is, "It depends." Sadako Ogata recalled her own extensive involvement in both the Commission on Humanitarian Issues and the Global Governance Commission: "The utility of the big commissions has receded in the 1990s. That's my impression. So in terms of agenda setting, I don't know how far commissions can provide impetus. Is it because the world is saturated with too much information? Globalization? Maybe, but I think it is difficult to see who is really setting the agenda now." Mrs. Ogata (as she prefers to be called) agreed to co-chair the Commission on Human Security. Perhaps, in retrospect and echoing Sonny Ramphal's own decision to overlook his ambivalence and chair such a group that we cited at the outset of this section, she too thought that they could make a difference.

Nongovernmental Organizations and the Private Sector

The UN Charter begins with the words, "We the peoples," when one might have expected an initial and resounding emphasis on "We the [Sovereign] Member States." Charter Article 71 specifically makes provision for the inclusion of perspectives from non-states in the form of "suitable arrangement for consultation with nongovernmental organizations which are concerned with matters within its competence." There has been a slow and dramatic growth in the role and influence by NGOs in UN corridors and elsewhere. The private sector's role has always been huge in the world economy, and it is increasingly part of the UN's agenda as well. "I think life would be duller without the NGOs, and there would probably be much less point to it also," said Viru Dayal. "I think that the work of the world—if that doesn't sound too pompous—can only benefit from the involvement of civil society. It is increasingly getting better and better informed itself. There is so much talent that the governments must draw on. Besides, civil society knows where the shoe pinches. They know when to laugh and they know when to cry."

Henrique Fernando Cardoso chaired the Panel of Eminent Persons on United Nations–Civil Society Relationships, whose 2004 report addresses directly the multiconstituency process that is increasingly central to deliberations: "The most important contribution of the United Nations has always been its convening power, bringing together Governments. . . . The same applies today, except that some of the world's major players are not governmental. Few of the most pressing battles today—whether they involve hunger, poverty, illiteracy, global pandemics, terrorism, narcotics, climate change, natural disasters, environmental threats, abuse of women and children, sectarian and ethnic divides, unemployment, economic crises or inequity of wealth, power and information—can be resolved by central Governments alone. Others are needed in these battles—from civil society, the private sector, local authorities and elsewhere. Why? Because they have essential knowledge, abilities, experience and links to key constituencies."[24]

After leaving New York, Boutros Boutros-Ghali headed the International Organisation of the Francophonie (an NGO that groups French-speaking countries) in Paris. In examining the role of such institutions in international discussions, he pointed to the pluses and the minuses: "All these non-state actors are much more developed in the North than in the South. When you get them involved, you increase the influence of the North over the South. But I'd say that it still has a democratizing effect: instead of the North's being represented by a superpower—that is, Washington—the North is represented by five or six different players: you have Washington, you have the nongovernmental organizations, you have big business, you have parliamentarians, you have the mayors of certain cities. You have, so to speak, broken the monopoly of the sovereign state, and this in itself is a step toward democratization."

The sixth Secretary-General also was not bashful about calling into question the ability of certain NGOs to really understand the societies in which they were working: "For instance, when they say that one must forbid child labor. That's a mistake of the Western idealist who understands nothing about reality in the Third World: they'll be ten times poorer without work. On this issue alone I could tell tales until tomorrow. When I was minister of foreign affairs, I saw these representatives of Amnesty International or the blue-eyed gentlemen from Scandinavia who came from another world and did not know anything about life in this part of the globe. To be completely honest and objective, I'll tell you something else, and that is, if I spend six months in the rich world, I marginalize the problems of the poor world. Six months are enough for me to forget them, for me who have lived in the poor world and have spent my life on its problems. But believe me, when you live in poor countries, you develop a certain sensitivity. I think it is easier to live as a poor person among the wealthy than to live as a rich individual among the poor."

Virendra Dayal diluted his earlier enthusiasm a bit: "NGOs have got to watch their step a little bit; . . . they must have a way of filtering out, as it were, the entrepreneurs of hate from their own councils and from their own drafting processes. There must be some decency to it. In other words, the NGOs that come must also be guided by the same Charter that is meant to be guiding everybody else there. . . . They shouldn't be wrecking the temple because of their private hatreds or grievances."

But Jan Pronk observed the importance of such clashes: "It was important to strengthen nongovernmental organizations as part of the civil society. In international conferences, you need the participation and contribution of civil society—all major groups. In the end, governments will have to take decisions. In democratic countries, they are fully representative and accountable. But governments would be wise [to involve] civil society fully in the definition of issues, in the development of options for solutions, in a discussion of the pros and cons, in the process of implementation and in reviews thereafter. If not, decisions by governments will not reflect people's opinions, because governments have a tendency to bureaucratize and to alienate themselves from citizens."

One image that immediately comes to mind is tens of thousands of people filling the streets of Seattle in December 1999 in one of the more violent manifestations of civil society in recent memory. This example helped set the stage for a less raucous but dramatic and significant walkout by many countries from the 2003 WTO Summit in Cancún. NGOs used Seattle to oppose the broad forces of globalization and specifically to protest the World Trade Organization, which was meeting to set a new agenda for a proposed new round of global trade negotiations. For days the media displayed images of protesters engaging in violence and vandalism and of public authorities gassing and arresting them.

"I am aware that after what happened in Seattle, governments are hesitating to involve NGOs," Pronk said. "But excluding them would not be a sensible reaction. Seattle was not new. Similar violent protests took place in Copenhagen in 1970 and in 1982 in Berlin at the annual meeting of the Bank and the Fund. The violence in the streets has to be addressed, but the protests should be taken seriously. International organizations, including the UN, are no islands far away from world city life. They are part of the political reality and should not be afraid to be confronted and not afraid to answer. Confrontation can lead to a breakthrough thereafter."

This is not the first time such groups have inserted themselves into state deliberations and decision making. Although commentators tend to emphasize the last few decades, the NGO phenomenon has been gaining momentum for two centuries.[25] Although Charter Article 71 carved out space for NGOs as observers of UN deliberations, during the Cold War the Socialist bloc and many developing countries with totalitarian regimes resisted the intrusion of independent and dissident voices. Since the thawing in East-West relations began in the mid-1980s, however, human rights advocates, gender rights activists, developmentalists, and groups of indigenous peoples have become more vocal, operational, and important in contexts that were once thought to be the exclusive prerogatives of states.

The sheer growth in NGO numbers has been nothing short of remarkable. The Union of International Associations estimates the number of international NGOs (those that operate in more than two countries) at about 25,000.[26] A more cautious estimate is some 13,000, all but one-quarter of which have been created since 1990.[27] National NGOs have grown faster still in both the South and the North.[28] Throughout the Third World, grassroots organizations are said to number in the millions.[29] For example, in France there was a fivefold increase in less than thirty years after 1960 (to 54,000), and across the

English Channel, some 4,000 new charities were established yearly in the UK during the 1980s and 1990s.[30] By one estimate there may be some 2 million in the United States alone; and in Russia, where there were virtually none a generation ago, there were some 65,000 as the millennium dawned.[31]

NGOs and other looser associations of what increasingly is called "global civil society"—defined as "the sphere of ideas, values, institutions, organisations, networks and individuals located between the family, the state, and the market and operating beyond the confines of national societies, polities, and economies"[32]—are thus inserting themselves into a wide range of intergovernmental deliberations. But how significant is this flurry of activity in terms of generating new ideas, norms, and principles? According to one observer, "NGOs are an increasingly important piece of the larger problem of global governance. Although the state system that has governed the world for centuries is neither divinely ordained nor easily swept away, in many ways that system is not well suited to addressing the world's growing agenda of border-crossing problems."[33] The presence of alternative voices has become an integral part of the UN system's processes of deliberations and of world politics more generally, what some would call the third UN. Virtually all of our voices commented about the importance of non-state actors for the UN's intellectual output.

When Maurice Strong was secretary-general of the 1972 Stockholm conference on the Human Environment, he insisted on the presence of NGOs. Thereafter, NGO parallel meetings, usually called forums, have become a prominent part of conference deliberations and have been an important force in pressing for more-forward-looking approaches. In the 1990s, for instance, thousands of NGOs attended the Rio and Beijing conferences. Moreover, NGOs had become primary executors of UN-funded projects, in both the humanitarian and development fields, by the time ECOSOC agreed to more flexible accreditation standards in 1996 that opened the way for easier NGO access.

Kofi Annan was impressed by the growing range and influence of NGOs in the information age: "What is important is that through information technology and the ... IT revolution, they are coordinated and linked up in a way that we couldn't have imagined a few years ago. So you have a global civil society that is connected by the web and can really move issues. We saw their strength in the campaign for the ban of landmines. We saw the contribution they made for the ICC [International Criminal Court]. . . . Quite frankly, on some of the issues they are ahead of the curve. They can say and do things that we cannot say or do. And eventually we will catch up with them."

Oscar Schachter used an historical perspective to evaluate the appearance of ideas from the UN's founding: "On issues like women's rights, and to some degree human rights and disarmament, NGOs certainly do exercise continuing pressures. I think women's rights have been their most successful effort. And then with the change in the world which everybody notices—the communication change, the ability to mobilize action quickly—NGOs have greater sophistication. . . . The interesting thing for me, looking back from the point of view of someone who was there fifty years ago, the big point is how the NGOs have become professionalized. They have large numbers of people and they developed international linkages."

Many of our voices recalled their own roles in NGOs. In recalling her involvement in NGOs prior to assuming the helm at UNIFEM, Noeleen Heyzer looked back at some of the challenges and rewards of pushing the envelope on women's issues: "I wanted to bring academic rigor to the activism that was developing from the ground. At one stage, there was a big divide between research and activism, and I wanted to bridge that gap. I felt that it was important to have very solid analysis to influence activism. Activism without knowledge and without analysis can go astray. But at the same time, research without the kind of activism and commitment that I saw on the ground could not bring about the transformation needed to improve the lives of people marginalized by development." She illustrated her point with her experience in DAWN: "To understand what was happening to development in the 1980s and early 1990s and to develop a new framework of thinking and articulation . . . DAWN did manage to develop a new kind of thinking and analysis that pulled in the experience of women and of activism, and then converted that into policy changes. DAWN played a big role in the Third World Conference on Women. . . . We managed to change paradigms of thinking."

Devaki Jain asserted that such networks "have played a very important role in the process of linking women to the UN, generating ideas, and enabling their entry into the UN. Even today, they are the most lively in organizing around a conference—more than individuals. . . . DAWN was the first interregional network of the South. It networked the regional networks. Therefore, when we were asked why we were there, [we said that] we were the umbrella for all the networks."

Paulo Sergio Pinheiro, who founded his own human rights NGO and worked as a special rapporteur for the UN Commission on Human Rights, observed: "How do you call in English the actors that are not the main actors? Supporting actors—in Portuguese, it is *figurantes*—the people that go to be at the scene of a ball but they are not the main actors. . . . Civil society cannot continue having this bit part. You have to integrate. . . . At least in the human rights structure, I think that the United Nations could do some progressive reforms. The present arrangement is not convenient—that you have a General Assembly, but you don't have a General Assembly of the peoples."

Enrique Iglesias was more cautious: "NGOs believe that governments have no respect for them, don't listen to them. . . . Governments believe, also legitimately, that NGOs are political intruders, trying to set forth hidden agendas in battles they can't win in either the political arena or in elections." James Jonah pointed to the "two United Nations," member states and the secretariat, which are both "very ambivalent" about the role of NGOs: "In the early years, up to the mid-1980s, or when Boutros-Ghali got in, the Secretariat viewed NGOs as useful instruments in the area of disarmament, apartheid, and Palestinian issues. . . . [But now] governments are beginning to raise questions: 'Who are these unelected people? Why should you give them a voice in the General Assembly? Who elected them?'"

Robert Cox also raised the issue of NGO claims of representation: "I am not convinced of the idea of a kind of representative body of NGOs, because I think NGOs are very skewed in terms of their actual representation of, let's say, the grassroots. Some are more effectively representative than others, perhaps, but you cannot just assume that because they are NGOs they represent humanity at large." He further explained: "Some of these movements are movements of generosity, in the sense of aspiring to social equity and compatibility and peaceful relationships. And some of them are xenophobic and racist and just antagonistic towards other social groups. So civil society covers all of these things, and, as I would prefer to say, it's a terrain of conflict rather than something that one ought to think of as a good thing in itself. . . . So you have to look critically at the nature of these organizations that proclaim themselves as representative of civil societies."

Others, especially our Third World voices, expressed additional qualms. Bernard Chidzero's interview took place in Harare during a tense moment when the government of Zimbabwe, for which he still was a consultant, was under siege from a veritable army of both local and international NGOs. He expressed his preoccupation: "We have certain peculiar developments, such as the urge on the part of some civic groups to change government for the sake of change. That role is not the main permanent role of NGOs. They have a development role to play. There may be a tendency for nongovernment organizations to become instruments of their countries, to promote the interests of their home countries, or to become agents of political parties. There may be a tendency on the part of some NGOs to operate as agents of multinationals. . . . If they can remain in the areas of serving mankind without taking sides with political groups, they will serve a very useful purpose. But if they become associated with eroding or opposing parties, they become part of a political system. They become political agents. And, I think, this would destroy or minimize their roles . . . [and] bypass certain market forces and civil government bureaucracy. That is a virtue but it is also a danger, because the NGOs . . . may be promoting projects which are not those of government, or which are even antigovernment."

James Jonah noted that uniform categories of "saints" or "sinners" are hardly sensible—at least for someone who attempted to coordinate NGOs in Somalia as a UN official and in Sierra Leone as a governmental one: "Not all of them are solid. Some of them are outright crooks, sorry to say, engaged in smuggling commodities and diamonds. In Africa in particular, some of these NGOs have links with rebel movements. I think that raises questions. Thirdly, governments are raising questions—and I know we did in Sierra Leone— about the accountability of NGOs in terms of how they run their show. Because they are politically powerful in many countries like the United States, and in Europe, these governments channel their assistance through NGOs. But who measures how the NGOs dispense these funds? You hear from the Americans that they have given to Sierra Leone $15 million. But it is given to NGOs. We don't know what amount they spent in our country and how much is overhead. There has to be proper monitoring."

Ponna Wignaraja echoed the concerns about NGO incoherence: "Each one is saying and doing their own thing and is a babble of voices. They don't have a single set of coherent messages to give a government or donor as far as it matters to the poor. And some of them are very money-grabbing also." Michael Doyle pointed to a picturesque image borrowed from his colleague, Under-Secretary-General Nitin Desai: "He said that right now NGOs are organized— or disorganized—like a medieval fair. There are all sorts of activities going on. It's very entertaining and quite confusing. How do you move from that medieval fair to a supermarket where you have aisles and shelves and reliable goods and you know where to find them and you restock it when it runs out?"

Sadako Ogata commented on the difficulties of working with so many moving parts in field assignments. She said that UN organizations that subcontract to private groups "cannot work with NGOs all over the place, trying to influence everybody. It's just too much." Drawing on her experience in Geneva, she continued: "We need them. But you see, the UNHCR has more than 400 contracts with more than 200 NGOs; they are there to help and to do things. They are not there to politicize, although some of them politicize."

"NGOs have become increasingly prominent in the North, and they are beginning to emerge in the South, too, and link up with like-minded NGO groups in the North," remarked Gamani Corea. "There is still a feeling that the priorities that determine the establishment of NGOs are still a bit too heavily influenced by the North." Corea went on to ponder: "I was puzzled; what is the composition and role of this international civil society? . . . It included media, academics, transnational corporations and NGOs. I said, 'This is fine, but don't you see you are leaving out the authentic civil society of Third World countries? The mullahs, the swamis, the Buddhist clergy and the like. Why are they left out? They are still part of the cultures of those countries.' You get the feeling that 'international civil society' has become a kind of adjunct to be manipulated in support of whatever thrusts are being made by governments and international organizations and [that] they have not yet acquired any independence of their own."

Elise Boulding was quite aware of the criticism of dominance from NGOs in industrialized countries over their counterparts in the South: "It has been too often a one-way traffic of ideas from the West to those 'backward' countries of the South, rather than a dialogue with a mutual listening and learning as a result." And in addition, she pointed to the obvious fact that the UN hardly has a monopoly on interagency rivalry: "There's not enough cooperation among NGOs. They are too competitive, too turf conscious. They have got to learn to cooperate."

What then are the appropriate roles for them in relationship to the UN system? John Ruggie offered his assessment of their operational and advocacy roles: "NGOs and the UN interact most effectively . . . in the humanitarian areas, in human rights, in peacekeeping, in the World Food Programme, in natural disaster responses. . . . The UN would have to shut down some of its activities if it weren't in partnership with NGOs in many of these areas. . . . Here at headquarters, it's a little bit different because the NGOs that gather here tend not to be field oriented. What they really want here is to have access to the policymaking process of the organization as a whole, specifically the General Assembly. Whereas the Secretary-General has been, as you know, very supportive of closer relationship between the UN and civil society organizations, most member states, most of the time, have been deeply resistant to getting them involved in the policy process. Yes, we will have hearings and they can express their views, briefly and late in the evening. . . . So the big issue here, at headquarters, is how to square the circle of wanting to be more open to NGOs but maintaining the boundaries of intergovernmental governance. It varies by issue area too. The U.S. will say, 'Oh yes, civil society actors are wonderful,' until you begin to discuss issues related to disarmament or arms control. Then they want them to go away."

Lourdes Arizpe looked over the horizon: "If you see that in the last thirty years the ratio of wealth of the twenty percent richest people to the poorest twenty percent has doubled, you really wonder what all of these development institutions have done. So major changes have to be carried out. And the hope—I believe it is only a hope—is that by bringing in civil society, there will be more accountability of governments in terms of their actions. . . . There has to be more accountability of the powerful in bringing about more and more blatant structures of inequality."

The role of the private sector, as we said earlier, remains controversial. But certainly if the UN is to begin to reflect the complexity of actors necessary to address global problems, the for-profit sector is as important as not-for-profit NGOs. The Global Compact, an idea that emerged from the Millennium Summit, placed transnational corporations at the center instead of the periphery of UN discussions and brought NGOs into the picture to measure best practices. Some argue that the closer association with the market represents a maturing of the United Nations, while others assert that it amounts to selling out or "blue-washing for capitalism."

John Ruggie was one of the sources behind the idea of the Global Compact while in the Secretariat,[34] and he continues to work as an advisor on it from his Harvard University base. He mentioned the anticorporate views about the initiative: "Essentially, their slogan is that they want to save the UN from corporate takeover. What's interesting is that this is really just the tip of the iceberg of a very, very important development in civil society. A major cleavage is emerging between NGOs that have actual responsibilities on the ground—whether it is Amnesty in human rights, or Greenpeace in the environment, or Save the Children, or what have you—and pure activist groups. The NGOs that have actual responsibility on the ground almost invariably have decided that they cannot do what they need to do if they haven't worked out some sort of relationship with the private sector. There are just too many resources there and too much capacity to ignore. . . . The anti-globalization activist groups, of course, aren't doing that, because their whole rationale is to oppose what they call 'corporate globalization.' So some of the NGOs that are in the Global Compact feel a little heat from their brethren."

A number of conversations pointed to the possible role of an often-overlooked private actor, the media. Amartya Sen drew upon memories of the Bengal famine that informed his *Poverty and Famines:*[35] "I think I was nine in the spring of 1943, when the famine began. It finished by the time I was just turning ten, in November. Yes, there were a number of striking aspects of that. One was, of course, I had never seen people dying in such numbers. I had not, in fact, even seen people dying anyway. But then in 1943, I suddenly saw hundreds of thousands of people starving and dying. It was naturally a remarkable and a harrowing experience. It seemed incredible that there could be no way of saving them.

"Second, as you say, I was struck by the fact that while so many people—what seemed like millions of people—were roaming the streets and falling and perishing, I did not know anyone whatsoever among my circle of friends or in the school or anyone connected with the family in any way who had the slightest difficulty living on. So I was struck by the divisiveness of society—its class character—and the extreme contrast between some people not being able to afford food at all to survive while others were not having any difficulty at all. I was beginning to understand a little about class divisions. And it wasn't class only, in the very broad sense. The divisions were much more detailed and more fine, linked to occupation groups and locations and so on. So later, many years later when I would study famines, that elementary understanding played a big part: that class and occupation groups had to be linked firmly to what one is trying to explain.

"Also, there was the oddity of the extreme suddenness of the famine. That was a big surprise. Nothing was being reported, and there was very little discussion of any kind of storm that was coming. Because of censorship that the Raj had imposed over those years, connected mainly with the war, the Indian newspapers were not allowed to print anything disparaging about the Raj which could inflame criticism. But the main English paper in Calcutta, *The Statesman,* a distinguished daily then, was left uncensored. It was a British-owned paper, edited by an Englishman called Ian Stephens who later was a Fellow at Kings whom I came to know—much later—quite well. But at that time, I didn't even know who the editor of that newspaper was. Ian Stephens initially toed the line in not reporting anything much on the famine. The justification was that the Japanese were in Burma and the war was going on and they did not want to do anything which would undermine the war effort. But it also meant, of course, little notice was taken of—and nothing much was done to save—the millions who perished.

"But eventually, Ian Stephens could not keep himself silent any longer. This was in October, by which time the famine had gone on for many months. On October 14 and 16 of 1943, *The Statesman* published agonizing reports and stinging editorials on governmental policy. This, of course, immediately got the attention of Parliament, in Britain, in London. Within a few weeks, relief began. And within a month the famine was over. The experience brought out clearly the power of the press and why public discussion is an enormously important way of promoting justice in the world. The idea is not, of course, unrelated to what the UN stands for.

"That is, if the newspapers in the developed countries took greater interest in what is going on in the developing countries, there might be more involvement. And we know that attempts to get the public informed and aroused can produce big reactions, big positive reactions, whether you take things like Live Aid and responses connected with that or you look at more literary involvement with disasters elsewhere. For example, the Ethiopian famine was completely neglected, then suddenly there is a good report by the BBC, followed by strong accounts in the newspapers. It aroused immediate interest and concern, because human beings have sympathy for each other."

Sen built on that illustration as he discussed ways to think about levers for change even in the United States: "The issue of public discussion is important also for deprivations in the richer countries themselves. It is not just a question of whether these journalists or broadcasters take an interest in things abroad but also whether they take an interest in social affairs even at home. I have sometimes tried—as have many other people—to draw public discussion into domestic ills in, say, America or Britain, with little success. Some year ago, I think it was in 1993 (ten years ago, really), I wrote an article in the *Scientific American* called 'The Economics of Life and Death' showing that even in rich countries like the United States, because of various social and economic deprivations (including social inequalities, lack of medical insurance, bad schooling, etc.), life expectancy at birth of large societal groups (such as African Americans living in big U.S. cities) can be lower than that in very poor countries, like China, India, Sri Lanka, not to mention Costa Rica and Jamaica. Others have written on these issues also. But while they generate interest among academics and such, they are hardly ever taken up in more general public discussion in a way that could make a difference to policy.

"It is very difficult to get newspapers interested in all this, except to note the point in a low-key item. You would occasionally get one of the higher-brow papers, like *The New York Times* or the *Los Angeles Times* or the *Washington Post* or the *Chicago Tribune,* writing an article on such a problem. But there is no sustained onslaught on what are gigantic deprivations. Even if charity begins at home, it could begin more firmly than it tends to do. So I think yes, there is a big problem here. It is not just a failure that applies across the borders, dealing with the poorer countries, but even within the borders of a rich country."

In trying to assign responsibility for ideas, Juan Somavía noted: "You always have this combination of issues and people who are the bearers of the torch and who dare to go forward and go beyond the accepted." He pointed to the same explanation for human rights and gender: "If it had been left to the UN system alone, it would have been a complicated thing to move forward. . . . The instrument was generated by the UN, but the actual capacity to promote it and develop it had to come from civil society."

So both members of the private sector and NGOs have assumed a growing importance in world affairs and as lobbyists at the UN. For example, most interviewees attributed the recognition of gender and human rights concerns to NGO advocacy work. Leticia Shahani noted that the UN's influence "moves like an iceberg. But eventually, again because of the pressure of people and NGOs, the women's issue emerged."

"The NGOs, god bless them, have made life unsafe for established international bureaucracies," said Brian Urquhart.

Global Conferences

Viewed from the vantage point of the twenty-first century, it may be difficult to believe that in the 1960s environmental degradation, population growth, urbanization, and women's rights were largely invisible on the international radar screen. This changed during the 1970s, and one reason was that the United Nations system launched a series of global conferences on emerging global challenges. They publicized new issues and mobilized governmental and nongovernmental support for new policies and actions. Many of these themes were revisited in the 1990s on the assumption that ideas needed to be updated and revitalized.[36]

International conferences are, of course, nothing new. Since the Congress of Vienna before and after Napoleon's defeat at Waterloo, conference diplomacy has been a common device states have used to address new challenges. The League of Nations convened them during the interwar period to address economic as well as political crises. And of course, the UN has the General Assembly. So what is the purpose of special meetings? Viru Dayal: "I think that the global conferences have been very good in stimulating ideas. Even more important, they stimulate civil society. That is why if you were to ask me whether five General Assemblies are worthwhile or one global conference, I am almost inclined to say one global conference. . . . They create an enormous rumpus. . . . The racket is important for the spread of ideas."

When asked to be more specific about the General Assembly, he pointed to "the sheer tedium of these speeches, you know—it's just hellish. And you can see and hear, from year to year, the speech that has been written before. You can hear the wretched thing before it's been pronounced. . . . So I think, actually, if you were to ask me whether global conferences are a good idea, I think they can be a wonderful idea for consciousness-raising. . . . That whole racket, that disorderly mess is really what energizes the mobs! That is what democracy requires."

The UN has institutionalized the conference system as a transmission device for ideas about common, global concerns. It is the most central location to observe the blending of "outside" and "inside" intellectual energies. The UN pioneered what became a template: establishment of a temporary secretariat headed by a secretary-general, often from outside the UN system; a series of preparatory committees; participation of NGOs; and standard outcomes (final declarations and programs of action). And, increasingly in the 1990s, follow-up and monitoring meetings and institutions became part of the recipe. These conferences are ad hoc; they are not regular events but are especially authorized to draw attention to an emerging issue or an older one that has moved to the back burner. A number of them have scheduled a review after a fixed term, a tactic that, as we will see, is questioned by some of our voices.

Most of the specific gatherings mentioned here figured individually in many earlier voices. Dharam Ghai gave us his bottom line on their composite value: "Global conferences have done a hell of a lot in increasing awareness and sensitivity to gender, the environment, and population issues—promoting national and international action." Nafis Sadik pointed to the same issues, as well as human rights, and argued that global conferences were not "talk shows" but rather were essential: "UN conferences have been absolutely dramatic in the way they have changed thinking around the world. It might be a slow process. It is a cumbersome process. After all, there are so many governments. And it looks like it doesn't get anywhere. But in fact, the slow process of arguing and dialoguing and giving in, et cetera, leads to a consensus and moves the issues along. . . . Many difficult issues that we never talked about are now being talked about by the same governments who would never even utter some of the words."

After a hiatus, the UN system in the 1990s resumed an intense round of conferences that built upon those of the 1970s, but this time as summits and media events for heads of state and government rather than for "mere" government ministers. With a larger dollop of international civil society, they sought consensus around alternative approaches to development and centered on human beings and the protection of the environment. Toward the end of his term, which also coincided with a fatigue for such gatherings, Secretary-General Boutros Boutros-Ghali triumphantly proclaimed: "Through these conferences, development cooperation will be revitalized and reinvented. The United Nations, its Member States, and you, the delegates at the conferences, are deciding development patterns for future generations. You are deciding the form of development cooperation to be adopted by the United Nations; you are setting the standards by which the actions of States, Organizations and individuals will be judged."[37]

Michael Doyle pointed out their utility in the 1990s: "Forty-five, fifty years after the founding of the UN, we needed a new burst of goals. At the end of the Cold War, there was an opening to redefine what the international order was going to be about. We had to have broad participation. . . . I think the problem started coming when you got to Durban [site of the World Conference Against Racism in 2001], where, in my view, the conference did as much harm as good. It provided a platform for nasty anti-Semitism and very bad Third World rhetoric. It generated contempt in the North. The fact that there was a bit of progress on caste issues and a couple of other things was not worth it, to my mind." He added that in the future, "we have to make sure that something constructive can be done, not just have a conference in the *hope* that something constructive can be done. We need to say that only if this PrepCom is very good will we go ahead, otherwise not."

Our interviewees thus were hardly of one voice; many were supportive but usually less enthusiastic than Boutros-Ghali. They agreed that public opinion was mobilized and long-run dynamics altered, but some were dubious about the precise impact and cost-effectiveness of such gatherings. Most especially, most saw follow-up action as inadequate to address the dimensions of the challenges.

While pointing to the fact that "the conferences of the 1990s did a great job," Noeleen Heyzer was one of several voices who belonged "to the school that the 'plus fives' [periodic reviews of conference commitments at five-year intervals] have been a disaster, because after working so hard to have strong agendas the concentration should be on implementation. The time should be used to share good practices that emerge, rather than negotiating documents. It has become a ritual whereby a lot of energy is focused on the negotiation of words. I don't find that exciting at all. So much energy is used to just maintain the gains that people have made. New players have come in and now the whole agenda is being reopened again and again. It has become a fight over words and a waste of so much energy."

Jan Pronk agreed: "To start all over again, already five or ten years later, is risky, because those who feel that the summit outcome did not fully reflect their views will see the review conference as a second chance. . . . Rather than focusing on future implementation, these meetings tend to concentrate on renegotiating the past."

Kofi Annan expressed a nuanced opinion: "I think the conferences that put new ideas on the table and provide intellectual leadership and sensitize the public to issues that they are not aware of are very, very good. Where we have a problem is going back. It's like moviemakers. They repeat it. They have a good movie and then they have to have movie number two. And we are going through the plus fives and the plus tens. . . . We ought to be able to review progress without having to hold these massive conferences. And sometimes they come to these conferences and try to dilute positions they agreed to five years ago or ten years ago."

Thinking specifically about human rights, Paulo Sergio Pinheiro said: "On the conferences, I am completely with the group of people who think they are tremendously useful. Of course, perhaps Vienna was not the best place to organize the human rights conference. . . . But in any case, I think it is great to have the human rights conference in Beijing, in Durban. . . . The impact is enormous, because when you organize this in Asia or when you organize this in Africa, it is extraordinary the effect of mobilization. . . . You have states more compelled to bear or to tolerate the presence of NGOs."

But what actually makes them work? Sartaj Aziz was deputy secretary-general of one of the first such conferences, the 1974 World Food Conference. "Let me start off by summarizing five elements that I think constitute the prerequisite for the success of any international conference. First, to present the issue in a manner that creates global awareness and a different way of looking at the issues. The food conference did so very successfully. Second, to propose an action strategy which is acceptable to both sides and broadly covers the range of views that surround an issue. Third, to evolve within an overall conceptual framework or strategy an action plan which is negotiable and yet meaningful. Fourth, a clear articulation of financial resources required for implementing the action plan. Fifth, a follow-up mechanism which can monitor the progress at the policy funding level, and implementation levels. The WFC was successful on the basis of all these five criteria. . . . In the case of the World Food Conference, the ground situation also assisted the first objective because there was a crisis. People were dying. And there was a tremendous interest in the subject, particularly by NGOs and various church organizations."

Richard Gardner stressed the importance of timing and leadership: "I think the Stockholm conference came at the right time. I think probably the Beijing women's conference came at the right time. I think the Cairo population conference in 1994 came at the right time. Of course, a lot depends on the leadership, who is the secretary-general, what kind of team he assembles, whether he is as effective as Maurice Strong in reaching out to the scientific and scholarly communities as well as to business leaders and NGOs. The commitment of key governments is critical."

Mostafa Tolba also was supportive of convening global gatherings: "I have no doubt that international conferences are necessary if we really want to solve any global problem, whatever it is—population, social justice, environment, women, whatever. How to ensure that they are successful or useful is a million-dollar question which I have been pushing over the last thirty years. That is, to set specific goals and targets. . . . And what are the yardsticks by which we can measure every two or three years whether we are moving in the right direction or not and then adjust accordingly? . . . But nobody wants to have targets, nobody in the governments wants to commit themselves to anything that is called a target. I tried it for twenty years in UNEP, and the governments are just allergic to having targets."

Kofi Annan reflected back on the 2000 Millennium Summit, what many described as the "mother of all conferences": "Quite frankly, quite a lot of the ambassadors and the people in the house didn't believe it was possible when it was mentioned in 1997. As we got closer to it and more and more of their leaders decided to come—because we were writing to them, phoning them—they all got quite excited about it. And we also did the report in such a way that the last few pages could form the basis of the declaration. So we had a situation where the process was quite well managed and focused and not diluted, as sometimes happens with these conferences. In fact, that leads me to wonder if we shouldn't find a way of planning future conferences leaving the document to one organization, one individual, rather than getting the member states together to write the document and agree on the document. Really, it wastes lots and lots of time and energy."

In speaking about the reactions of the heads of delegation, the Secretary-General recalled: "To have 150 heads of state and governments and kings here, under one roof, was quite an achievement. Then they participated, for the first time, in roundtables where the heads of state talked amongst themselves, without aides, without assistants. One of them chaired and then reported the findings to the plenary. What struck me was how much these people miss by not interacting with each other, talking to each other without aides and advisors. They loved it, and said, 'Can we have more of this?' . . . And some of the things that came up were incredible. I recall we were discussing the debt issue. . . . As we were discussing this, the DRC [Democratic Republic of Congo] foreign minister—his president wasn't there—took the floor, and said, 'I agree with you, Mr. Secretary-General, and all those who have spoken. I think that debt is the real problem, and I believe the real solution is to get rid of all the creditors.' There was silence in the room, and then he added, 'I don't mean kill them all.' It was incredible."

Even if they "work," what makes them worthwhile? Devaki Jain made the point that networking was an essential impact of the series of global women's gatherings that began in Mexico City in 1975 and "was a turning point in the lives of many of us. . . . It gave us a huge understanding that there was a world of women with whom you could identify yourself. . . . The UN provided us with the international platform to universalize issues which we earlier thought were only country specific."

Taking the perspective of the prominent public international lawyer that he was, the UN's former legal counsel and Columbia University professor of law Oscar Schachter looked upon the products of such conferences as constituting elements of global governance: "While they wouldn't be considered hard law, they are a source that advocates often refer to as though they were law or as though they were accepted policy. So that repetition may be a significant factor, subject of course to an assessment about whether the repetition of generalities makes a difference in concrete practice." He cited the Fourth World Conference on Women in Beijing, the final resolution of which is taken more seriously "because there are the organized women's bodies in a lot of countries of the world that give the conference resolution a very high priority. They make their positions felt in local politics."

After earlier recounting how Mexico, as host country, was not yet ready to have a woman head the conference for women, Leticia Shahani nonetheless pointed out some of its accomplishments: "I think the main accomplishment of the first United Nations World Conference on Women was that for the first time, governments accepted the issue of women, the status of women, as a governmental concern. It wasn't just a social welfare handled only by NGOs. Now governments took a serious look at how half of the population in their societies live." Ten years later, Nairobi was "a major breakthrough in what we can call the integration of women in development and [in] making the women's issue now a part of the entire development and peace process. And, of course, human rights . . . Nairobi was the first successful attempt in a UN global conference to put women's issues within the major concerns of the UN, as part of the economic and political picture. Women's issues became part of the major development issues like population. They became part of the North-South dialogue. They became part of the peace process."

Sadako Ogata viewed conferences merely as a first step in the arduous process of social change: "I think in the 1970s the UN was on the vanguard of new ideas—world conferences on the environment, population, women, food. I think the UN was able to get hold—when you say 'UN,' it really means some of the member states—and it took the issues and presented them as a global agenda. So I think it played a more constructive role in the 1970s as an agenda-setting forum. The secretariat is usually cautious. . . . I think a lot of agenda setting was fine, but actually, I think follow-up was much more formalistic."

Just Faaland agreed: "I think the issues they take up do get higher priority for while. But in every one of them, and also for the UN system itself, I feel that follow-up is miserable. What is the point of having all these policies agreed if you don't follow up how far you have been able to do it, and perhaps more importantly, what are the particular reasons and circumstances you have that don't allow you to meet these ideals? . . . I am not saying necessarily that we should have done less on these things, these events. But we should have done more in between."

Adebayo Adedeji agreed that conferences provided the basis for action but not the resources to do so. At the same time, there are other ways to measure success: "These conferences have their own uses. You can argue at home, on your own, about the need to take certain actions but if you have a global conference resolution to back you up, that strengthens your hand and your claim for resources. . . . Global conferences are also vital for developing global ethics, values, and consensus."

Rubens Ricupero distinguished the 1990s from the 1970s: "I found that they have been very useful, particularly in some areas, like the environment and human rights, where you needed a sort of codification. After a period of enormous creation, you needed to organize a little bit what was the consensus on those matters. But I must say that although they have been very useful on subjects of this kind, such as women, as well as population, the social summit—all those conferences were landmarks—they are now suffering from a different danger. The world has entered into a period where, I am afraid, the atmosphere is no longer propitious for those large conferences. Why is that? Because the conferences were, by and large, the product of a period where some ideas were maturing and were reaching, not total universal consensus, but a very widespread consensus on the need for multilateral approaches. And unfortunately, in the last few years—mainly in the U.S., but the U.S. is absolutely vital in this matter—we saw a contrary trend away from this recognition of the usefulness of a multilateral approach."

John Ruggie also distinguished between conferences then and now: "I think many of the conferences, going back to 1972, were very useful as agenda-setting devices. . . . Even if the action plans never fully materialized, issues became better defined. Secondly, they provided a venue around which social groups who cared about the issues could coalesce. They helped generate transnational networks of social groups in the different issue areas, whether it was environment or women or human rights. . . . Thirdly, they affected at least the structure of the domestic policymaking process, if not always the content. Before Stockholm, there were relatively few environment ministries in the world. As a result of having to prepare for Stockholm and then having to follow up on it, governments created environment ministries. . . . So from a process point of view and from an agenda-setting point of view, the conferences were extremely useful. But I think we have overdone it now. The plus-five phenomenon is out of hand. It is even getting dangerous because in several recent instances attempts were made to roll back the things that were actually agreed to at earlier conferences rather than to build on them. The whole thing by now has become quite formulaic, having lost its creative impulse. . . . The routinized plus-five phenomenon should be abolished, and the sooner the better."

Lourdes Arizpe spoke persuasively about the importance of conferences in a globalizing world: "I believe that the United Nations is driven by the art of the possible, just as politics is defined as the art of the possible. But what these global conferences have done is push forward, as far as possible. And in many ways, they push forward in a way that leads the world in a given direction. If this had not been done, I do believe that economic globalization would not have been possible, because you need some sort of larger, overarching view of the connections between nations, between peoples, in order to set up trade systems, or telecommunications systems, or whatever. If you do not have that, if everything becomes regionalized and localized to the extent that it fragments, you cannot have globalization. And you cannot have economic globalization if you do not have some sort of globalization of the minds. And that you can only do through culture. World conferences create a culture of seeking world consensus."

Paul Berthoud noted a fundamental bottom line for world conferences, one that would have received an affirmative nod from most of our voices: "They are eminently useful in putting ideas on the map and sometimes institutions on the map to cater [to] those ideas. . . . So I would say that those events—they are big bangs, in a sense. . . . The normal process of deliberations, regular meetings of permanent bodies, would not be nearly as equipped to bring matters to the fore as those conferences are. I see them as important points of anchorage in the evolution of ideas."

In examining the evolution in international conversations, Brian Urquhart (who probably has participated in more international gatherings of all sorts than any of our other voices) reminded us: "In 1945 there was no such thing as global problems. There were political problems, and political problems were the dirty stuff which the UN did, and then these sea-green incorruptible special problems like labor or food and agriculture were nonpolitical and were dealt with by specialized agencies. Nobody thought of global problems which affected everybody. . . . So it is a great achievement to have gotten those global conferences going. Of course they're talking shops. . . . Human enterprises, unless they're war, start by discussion and usually end by discussion."

12

The Legacy and Future Intellectual Challenges

- **Ideas Change International Discourse**
- **Ideas Redefine State and Non-state Interests and Goals**
- **Ideas Facilitate New Coalitions**
- **Ideas Become Embedded in Institutions**
- **The UN's Future Intellectual Challenges**

This final chapter sheds light on the importance of ideas in international public policy. It does not definitively portray the exact nature of the interplay between politics, power, institutions, and ideas. The voices in these pages do begin, however, to suggest that the United Nations has provided an essential space in which powerful normative and policy agendas have been articulated. In the first four sections of this chapter, the voices help substantiate the four key propositions about the power of ideas adapted from what is, somewhat awkwardly, called the "ideational" literature that we summarized in the introduction.[1]

The final section looks to the future. We permit our own voices to intrude here more than elsewhere in the volume. What are the most pressing intellectual challenges for the United Nations? What is the UN's comparative advantage in the marketplace of ideas? Indeed, will there be a United Nations, or is multilateralism a quaint notion left over from the pre–9/11 world? In short, where are we headed and what can be done intellectually to succeed in the struggle for development and social justice?

"In some sense, ideas are the currency," Michael Doyle explained. "The UN has no power. It has good ideas. It convenes, it mobilizes, it inspires, it provides legitimacy. It is an idea shop. So at that level, ideas are very important. But at a different level, no one should think that you apply political science in public policy. It's just not what happens. We're responding, on the Secretary-General's staff, to what is happening out there in the world—to 9/11, Afghanistan, Iraq, to global poverty, the HIV/AIDS epidemic, to the need to protect children, the human rights agenda. It's a responsive institution. There is only so much ability to lead out of the blue. What the Secretary-General and the best members of his staff are good at is seeing where these waves are coming from and identifying the ones to which the UN would add value, where the leadership of the Secretary-General could make a difference, as it did on HIV/AIDS; on development issues, at least intellectually; on preventive diplomacy—trying to bring things together. . . . For that, ideas were useful."

"The UN is, of course, a practical body, and it is right that it would be mainly concerned with the urgent and the immediate," added Amartya Sen. "Yet it is also necessary not to be boorish in ignoring the ancestry of many of the ideas that the UN stands for and tries to promote. I think the UN has, taking the rough with the smooth, made good use of ideas, generally. But it varies a little between different parts of the UN system. As I have worked over the decades with different parts of the UN system, I have been impressed how some of them have been more explicit and more keenly aware of the sophisticated ideas that lie behind the day-to-day work and commitments of the UN. This can make a difference in giving intellectual depth to practical strategies."

Ideas Change International Discourse

Ideas substantially influence international public policy by transforming the acceptable middle ground for intellectual engagement. Stated in another way, they can change the nature of international discourse—a necessary, albeit insufficient, step in a path leading to new policies and eventually to altered behavior. As earlier chapters have illustrated, the intellectual agenda, the public policy lexicon, and the language of diplomacy look very different over time as a result of ideas promoted and implemented by the UN. What earlier was unthinkable may have become mainstream, and what earlier was conventional wisdom may have become obsolete. Dharam Ghai told us when ideas fly: "The idea has to have some power. It must be relevant. And it should fit the time. These days, things go very fast. The international development community is well connected. So when some good ideas come, either from within or from outside, and they are relevant and they make sense, people try to join the bandwagon. . . . A lot of the time these things are in the air. . . . A concept emerges which captures this. . . . Then it spreads very rapidly."

Ideas—even when misunderstood, distorted or misused—can be important, which is why we have tried to get a better handle on the UN's impact on the international marketplace of ideas. Samir Amin pointed to what had happened to his notion of "de-linking" and its subsequent influence on scholarly debate: "I am among those who are responsible for this expression. . . . It strikes me as controversial and a poor choice. I mean the choice of the word, because in the social sciences, one inevitably uses the terms used in daily discourse which have a generally accepted meaning but may not have the same significance in the analysis that one is undertaking. . . . I'm pressing my point of view because I have always, at least early on, defined what I meant by 'delinking' by making clear that it is not autarchy. It doesn't mean 'good-bye, we're emigrating to another planet, we're breaking off all relations.' . . . It's not that at all. It's a strategic choice that involves subordinating foreign relations to the imperatives of progressive domestic change. . . . I've had the experience of discussing this with [former Tanzanian president Julius] Nyerere, who really appreciated the term . . . and I was quickly persuaded that he really did not understand it. . . . The term 'de-linking' has thus been totally integrated into the national-populist discourse . . . but in the process completely lost its rigor."

At a minimum then, vocabulary changes the way we talk about things, as Jack Stone noted: "You have to adjust your vocabulary every decade to the new buzzwords." Noeleen Heyzer illustrated this reality with an example: "The environment conference managed to get people from the grassroots to talk about the way the environmental erosion and the ecological crisis affected them. And it definitely changed the whole dialogue."

Stéphane Hessel argued that changes in language are important even if they do not get translated immediately into action: "It is useful to have words, even if they are not followed by deeds. . . . There is a tendency . . . to say that it is better not to have words if you don't have deeds. . . . People who are not capable of having their words followed by deeds, should they therefore shut up? I would say the opposite. I would say that words carrying ideas have a long-lasting effect. If it had not been for people like Socrates or Hegel, we would not have the kind of view of the possible future of humanity that we do have. Therefore, it is good to have the Universal Declaration. It is good to have even a strategy for the Third Development Decade. They carry something which is wishful—wishful thinking. And one should, perhaps, not underestimate the fact that they do carry forward hopes and potential." Adebayo Adedeji underlined the need for a long-term perspective: "Good ideas never get forgotten. It may take a long time for them to impact on policy, but as long as they are sound they keep bouncing back until something is done."

Leticia Shahani also spoke about the great need for the UN to remain relevant intellectually: "I think this is a challenge before the leadership of the UN, to really seize those opportunities where its programs have international relevance. Some issues are flavors of the year or of the decade, and then other concerns replace them."

Virendra Dayal pointed to the evolution of human rights discourse as having implications for future ideamongers: "If you take, for instance, the ideas on human rights, there you can hardly say that the timing was perfect, and nor could you say that there was a great deal of packaging that was done. In fact, the ideas managed to survive in spite of the bad timing, and in spite of the third-rate packaging. They survived in spite of the Cold War and the apprehensions they caused among despotic regimes the world over. And the circumstances, in a sense, could not have been worse. . . . Yet because the ideas themselves were so remarkable, we have a body of normative law the likes of which the world has never seen before in respect of how human beings should be treated."

The balance between the practical and the ideal in the battle of ideas was "not a false dichotomy" but a preoccupation for Jan Pronk: "I have seen so many proposals, publications, ideas based only on what ought to be the case, in the view of the author. Most of them are non-starters from the very beginning, not taking into account power realities nor the economic reality of the day. So you have to make a combination between what you think is feasible and what you want to be done." Pronk recalled the advice of his mentor, Nobel laureate Jan Tinbergen, who always said to his collaborators: "I want to change reality, but my time horizon is the next five years. I won't set targets for twenty years from now. They would be just theoretical aims, and I wouldn't know how to accomplish them because the instruments are not yet available. Then I'll refrain from it, let others do it."

Janez Stanovnik provided us with his interpretation of how the discourse about development within the UN had evolved. "The route in between the idea to the action," he said, "is not very straight. You may have, among academics, a certain line of thinking. Let me say Keynes's doctrine is suddenly affecting the entire academic world. Everybody was Keynesian in the 1950s and the 1960s. This then got translated into development policies . . . [by] Robert Solow or Hans Singer or Raúl Prebisch or Sumitro [Djojohadikusumo] in Indonesia or Evsey Domar. . . . This then influences also the delegates who are all educated in universities or by their own life experience. They are part of this intellectual atmosphere which is being created. Then, of course, this is reflected in UN discussions. The dialogue among the delegates in the UN leads to intellectual compromises."

Gert Rosenthal earlier described how the UN and its ideas helped influence popular language by repeating basic propositions. He continued: "It is usually a cumulative process, where some seminal ideas which tend to be discussed among a very limited group of people sort of bursts into the public consciousness through media, through word of mouth, through documents. And all of a sudden, maybe two, three, five years after the document came out, everyone is repeating some of its main points as if they were gospel. . . . For example, in all capital cities of the world today, you will see special arrangements for handicapped people on curbsides, access to buses, and preferential parking. And those are ideas and commitments that were born in the UN."

Juan Somavía emphasized that for most issues civil society had led but that the UN had played "a very fundamental role as a legitimizer of ideas that are nascent, of things that are out there. . . . The moment the UN begins discussing an issue and it becomes part of programs and institutional debate, et cetera, then it legitimizes something that otherwise could be perceived of as marginal in society."

Kofi Annan listed a number of areas in which the UN shaped discourse—the environment, development assistance, governance—but pointed to one in particular: "We have defined what development means, what development should mean for the individual through our *Human Development Reports*. It is not a question of statistics. You are dealing with health, you are dealing with clean water, you are dealing with education, and all that. So we have given a functional and meaningful definition to poverty and development which wasn't there before. And I think this is very important for policymakers and for people who want to measure progress."

John Ruggie mused about the difference between using ideas in a classroom at Columbia University on New York's Upper West Side and using them in a conference room at the UN on the East Side: "That's what you do with ideas, you try to persuade. But in the first instance, as an academic, you can live with just persuading yourself. You can convince yourself that sooner or later others will catch on to how smart this really is. But you can't do that here. If you don't persuade others right away there isn't any tomorrow."

Fernando Henrique Cardoso stated that the broadening of the concept of development to include social aspects was "a consequence of United Nations presence across the world in order to enlarge views on what the government role is and also the concept of equitable development and the Stockholm conference, the Rio conference, and now the Johannesburg conference, plus the women's conference in China. . . . All this, I think, has a direct effect on social science in general, even when the persons are not aware of the fact. But the renewal of the issues and themes was very important, a subject matter to be taken up by universities and by political parties. I think this was a very important role played by the United Nations."

Whether our voices thought that UNCTAD was a target for praise or scorn, it clearly was in the eye of many intellectual storms. At the end of the day, its main contribution undoubtedly was as an incubator for many dramatic changes over forty years in the way that we talk about trade, finance, and development. Rubens Ricupero, its secretary-general when we interviewed him, who spearheaded the recent published history of the agency,[2] placed his description in an historical context: "Fifteen years ago, when I was working in the Uruguay Round, very few people in the industrial countries would admit in public that the world trading system was full of imbalances that worked against the poor. Even today, the Americans don't recognize it officially. Despite this, nowadays, it has become so widely accepted that it is practically what Antonio Gramsci would describe as a philosophy that became commonplace. . . . Nowadays, not only all the NGOs are saying that but the World Bank, the IMF, Clare Short [then UK international development secretary], all the ministers of development cooperation are saying that. I hope that UNCTAD was in part responsible for the change." With an element of satisfaction, he concluded: "Much of what the World Bank is doing now on trade is very close to what we have been saying."

Ideas Redefine State and Non-state Interests and Goals

As a former head of state, Guido de Marco had an excellent vantage point from which to observe the impact of human rights ideas, both universal and European, on Malta: "I think I was strongly influenced by the Universal Declaration of Human Rights. I was even more influenced by the Charter of Human Rights of Strasbourg. Here we have a court for human rights whereby human rights are not only something for domestic application, but nations agree to subject themselves to a court of human rights, which has its seat in Strasbourg. Indeed, the very first act which Parliament approved, when I became minister for justice and the interior, was that the Charter of Human Rights, the Charter of Strasbourg, the European Declaration of Human Rights, became part of domestic law in Malta. I wanted to ensure not only that Malta is bound internationally through the Charter of Human Rights but that Malta is also bound domestically by the Charter of Human Rights."

The United Nations has pushed ideas about more inclusive, or less particularistic, values to advance the struggle for development and social justice. Are there ideas that provide a tactical guide to policy and action when norms clash or when sequencing or priorities are disputed and the common good inevitably takes a back seat?

An interesting example is the notion that democratic states have a long-term national interest as well as moral responsibility to promote human rights. This was christened "good international citizenship" by Gareth Evans, Australia's foreign minister in the late 1980s.[3] It is this vision that underpins

Canada's human security agenda with its conviction that there is a relationship between the provision of basic rights and wider international security.[4] The challenge facing enlightened state leaders is to build an international consensus behind policies that address the underlying cause of human rights deprivations and defend basic rights whenever they are threatened. For advocates of good international citizenship, the promotion of justice is the key to lasting order even if they also "must convince others of their case, their competence, and their motives."[5] The UN Charter, of course, was a clear statement of the need for calculations of common interests rather than narrower mathematics that stopped at national borders.

Ideas are slender arrows in the quiver of those seeking to take aim and ultimately reach an important enough issue to engage state interests. Nonetheless, a number of UN arrows have struck home. Nafis Sadik pointed to a prime example: "We say that population and family planning is a huge success story for the UN. To get government to change policy is very difficult, and in a sensitive area where there were so many hangups, so many different points of view, so many sensitivities. There were religious sensitivities, social-culture, there was also this North-South suspicion. There were customs and norms. To have made the change in getting all countries to have a family planning program without imposing anything on them, just by advocacy and demonstrating to them the need—that was quite a big achievement."

Speaking about his experience with the National Human Rights Commission of India, Viru Dayal spelled out the concrete link between ideas bandied about internationally and their local impact in South Asia: "These are ideas which, I think, have grown in our souls because of our work in the UN. But the interesting thing is this; they are not ideas which have grown only in the soul of UN people. They have radiated from the UN. My colleagues in the commission are, after all, justices of the Supreme Court of India. The chairman of my commission wrote a judgment when he was still Supreme Court chief justice, saying that even if India is not a state party to X or Y international instrument, if there is nothing to the contrary in domestic law, India must consider itself bound in its conduct by those international laws and treaties. . . . We were not a signatory at that time to the relevant convention having to do with the rights of women. . . . He said, 'If there is nothing to the contrary in domestic law, then we must consider ourselves bound by international treaties on these matters.' So the UN's centrality as a kind of a center of the planetary system from which radiate great ideas must never be underestimated."

Lourdes Arizpe built on this comment and pointed to the political relevance of such norm-building efforts in Mexico: "Even though it brings out resolution after resolution, so that you can paper the whole building with them, as I've heard it said, these resolutions place a mirror in front of governments and people. . . . I've seen it in many meetings, where the powerless Indian groups or women's groups have actually taken documents from . . . the United Nations and presented these to the officials from their governments and have forced their governments to be more accountable because there exists this document which has been signed and ratified by a majority of countries in the world, showing that this is the way that governments should behave or corporations should behave or men should behave."

Leticia Shahani reported how many UN ideas had been instrumental for her country: "The North-South dialogue had helped the Philippines, a state that has been tied closely to the United States, sharpen our identity with the developing world." Dharam Ghai referred to his experience in Vietnam as part of a team assessing the UN contribution to capacity-building for poverty reduction from 1985 to 1997. The impact of ideas jumped out: "One of the things that came out was how seriously the Vietnamese took the world conferences. . . . First of all, advocacy was very important, on environment, gender, participation, poverty, and governance. As recently as the late 1980s, in Vietnam, poverty reduction was regarded as a diversion from economic development. They used to say, 'This poverty thing is the product of global imperialism. The moment imperialism is brought to an end, poverty will disappear.' Subsequently, they became converts to poverty reduction, and they have done an excellent job. I think the UN conferences and advocacy played an important role in their conversion."

Another specific illustration of the impact of ideas came from Janez Stanovnik: "The Brundtland Commission has had tremendous impact on governmental policy thinking. Documents of my little country's government now always speak of 'sustainable development.' . . . These I wanted to give as examples where ideas which are being germinated within the secretariat or with the secretariat's wisdom by appointing the right persons from outside the world to write the right kind of reports, which then come on the governments' table."

As many of our voices found themselves in national administrations at some point in their careers, other personal experiences illustrate this kind of impact. One of the more disputed notions over the years has been setting targets. This quintessentially operational idea, which some dismiss cavalierly as useless, actually has influenced the way that governments do business.[6] For example, Jan Pronk indicated how they mattered while he was minister: "Targets help, if they are the results of a political process involving not only bureaucrats but also civil society. In countries where that has been the case, the

0.7 percent target for ODA has been reached and maintained. That is how we did it in the Netherlands. . . . Quantitative targets also help countries to scrutinize each other. That is true, for instance, for trade liberalization targets, but also for climate change targets. . . . Finally, targets should not be input oriented, but result oriented. The ODA target is not ideal because it refers to an input—aid. Citizens will be much more convinced about the need of setting output targets, to halve poverty, to eradicate disease, to decrease child mortality, and so on."

Bernard Chidzero referred to the utility of UN target-setting as causal ideas to guide policy: "I think it is a useful exercise. It draws attention to the objective in measurable terms—time and quantity, the speed at which we must move." In commenting on the impact of UN reports on his country, Chidzero recalled: "The study or review that we called *Zimbabwe: Towards a New Order, an Economic and Social Survey*[7] . . . was in response to a request by the co-leaders of the Patriotic Front . . . that would assist the nationalists to take over the country and run the economy. The task was handed over to UNCTAD to conduct this study with financing from UNDP. . . . It's a very important study which influenced the thinking in this country decisively. . . . It was on the basis of that study that the first development conference in Zimbabwe, which we called ZIMCORD [Zimbabwe Conference on Reconstruction and Development], was prepared in order to rally resources from the international community, to promote development in Zimbabwe. . . . When people say the Marxists succeeded the Ian Smith government, they don't understand what they are talking about." When he died in August 2002, opponents on both sides of the political spectrum in Zimbabwe were effusive about Chidzero's contributions. Chidzero was the first person President Robert Mugabe called in 1980, when Zimbabwe achieved independence, to come home and serve his country. Mugabe recalled that "even after he retired as a Cabinet Minister, I retained him as my economic advisor because of his unparalleled brilliance."[8] Mugabe's bitter rival, Morgan Tsvangirai, also was full of praise: "He was never a *pasi nanhingi* (down with) politician. Chidzero was a truly selfless son of this nation who played a big part in our independence. He never in his illustrious career ever uttered a single word that sought to alienate any section of Zimbabwe's population in a bid to gain political advantage."[9]

The voice of Lourdes Arizpe was careful to make clear that while UN organizations contribute to shaping national policies, governments are mainly to blame for the world organization's shortcomings: "I find it terribly unjust to blame the institution when many of the faults that are criticized do not come from the institution but from the governments because they have certain interests and therefore pressure the institutions to behave in a certain way. . . . It happens where governments put their national interests above the interests of having an institution that can manage spaces of negotiation in a global environmental. But I think it is this myopia—shortsightedness of some countries that think it is in their interest to weaken the United Nations, because it gives them a greater power of acting without being accountable. . . . In the long term, it's going to be detrimental to that power because there is going to be no way of rationally solving all the conflicts that they are giving rise to in an interdependent world precisely by ignoring the human rights and the democratic principles that they supposedly espouse."

As ideas move from the international to the national level, the path they take and the speed with which they are transmitted varies depending on the issue. Noeleen Heyzer commented, for instance, that "the UN became the place where women could bring issues ignored at the national level into the international spotlight to be addressed by national governments." And she pointed out why that mattered: "When the ideas took a powerful form, they got recognized and accepted, because it spoke about women's lives. . . . With these international norms, women pressured for the revisions of national norms and policies based on international standards. We worked so hard to ensure that decision making in the courts and in the criminal justice system also changed because of new legal standards and norms. So ideas became action which changed people's lives."

Rubens Ricupero noted how the contents of discussions in Rio de Janeiro—no longer the capital but still the heart of his home country—had had an impact on national policy: "The United Nations Conference on the Environment and Development, the Rio summit, in 1992, was a very important event in Brazil, because it was the first time Brazil abandoned a defensive attitude on the environment. Brazil has many problems on the environment, both in the Amazon and in the big industrial cities. There had been a tradition of defensiveness. This time, Brazil decided to host the conference as a way of raising public awareness for the issue. It had a tremendous impact. It helped give a boost to this environmental movement in Brazil."

Gert Rosenthal noted that during the "fever of the Chicago School's ascent, one of the things that was being said about ECLAC was the enormous damage that the commission caused in Latin America by pointing governments in the wrong direction. Mario Vargas-Llosa used that accusation a lot when he was running for president of Peru—a little like satanizing ECLAC for having condemned Latin America to poverty. And that is a little unfair, because what ECLAC did was interpret what was happening and wrapped it up in a conceptually coherent proposal. And to think that they were that influential that they could push all the governments off in the wrong direction is crazy." In Rosenthal's judgment, Latin America's powerful industrial entrepreneurs, along with a small but highly paid segment of the blue-collar working class, pressed for and received protective measures for a longer period than was economically healthy. Thus, Rosenthal concluded, "there is a lot of misconception also as to what the UN did and didn't do. And there are also misconceptions on what the original ideas of the UN were and what sort of adaptations of those ideas were that somebody borrowed heavily from outside but put them in a nicer wrapping."

Max Finger remarked that ideas mattered even in the capital of the remaining superpower: "That is where I think the main role of the UN should be. Not in overriding Washington, which is the spirit of NIEO, but in feeding ideas that Washington can think about and come up with a response. . . . IDA happened. Trade preferences happened. The World Food Programme happened. And these were all ideas that came from the UN environment and penetrated Washington."

Noeleen Heyzer provided another illustration about the impact of ideas on government policy. She pointed to women and the mechanisms that enabled NGOs to help brief the Security Council: "We worked extremely hard to put the whole issue of women, peace, and security onto the Security Council agenda. The Security Council is an extreme case of a highly controlled arena and it is very difficult to put various issues on their agenda. To change the dialogue and to put in new issues that changes people's thinking is not easy. . . . We used what is called the Arria Formula . . . to allow real consultation. . . . We brought women—the nongovernmental groups and women themselves who were affected by conflict—to talk to the members of the Security Council to prepare for the Security Council resolution 1325 on women, peace, and security.[10] UNIFEM's role was to get the space and to help women clarify their messages. We became the mediator of different worlds. It is not easy for different worlds to understand one another, I've learned. Therefore, we try to prepare the ground, help the women to crystallize their voice, make sure that their message is heard by members of the Security Council, and determine what the Security Council needs to hear before they can make certain kinds of decisions. . . . When that happened, a synergy took place. . . . Members of the Security Council after that said, 'We will change our statement.' Up to that time, they were not even willing to come up with a short resolution."

"In a funny way that isn't always clear and certainly does not have a uniform pattern, the ideas percolate through and eventually influence outcomes. That is a very Keynesian view," Gerry Helleiner noted. "The power of ideas is greater than the power of vested interests." He then quoted Lord Keynes's statement that "in the long run we are all dead" as a prelude to his bottom line: "But that doesn't alter the fact that ideas do move things as well as interests."

Ideas Facilitate New Coalitions

Ideas can catalyze political and institutional forces. Once this occurs, the prospects are altered for forming new coalitions that tip the balance in favor of modest, and sometimes more dramatic, changes in policy to address global problems. In thinking about sustainability, for example, Jan Pronk told us: "A new coalition [emerges], with the help of different groups which in the past were antagonizing each other."

Noeleen Heyzer noted the importance of new partners coming together around an idea as part of the process of crystallization: "How do you create solidarity for the idea? How does it emerge? If I use the experience of the women's conferences, it was trying to birth an idea out of collective discussion so that it is alive and when it finally emerges everybody recognizes it as their own. It is creating a space, it is valuing different perspectives and creative discussion for the emergence of that idea. . . . And then it is also the timing. . . . But it is more a site, a space issue, and also a legitimacy issue. The UN system provides legitimacy for marginalized groups to have a powerful space for the articulation of their ideas."

Alister McIntyre pointed out that putting together coalitions is unpredictable: "So the whole business of orchestrating a conference, and bringing an issue to international attention, requires much more attention to the marketing side than international institutions are typically capable of doing. And they don't build coalitions that can do it for them. . . . NGOs can help; but you can't rely on NGOs alone. . . . You have to try to find other constituencies—the private sector, the labor movement, farming communities, farming organizations. You have to disentangle the whole web of organizations in a country and see what is the best combination of forces you can mobilize for your particular aim. But we don't have that kind of capacity in the UN at all."

Bernard Chidzero provided the example of how the Integrated Program for Commodities and the Common Fund helped foster South-South cooperation and thus helped to solidify an emerging coalition—in spite of the fact that the Integrated Program for Commodities itself was never adopted: "In failure we succeed, because it lets us know our weaknesses and therefore how to overcome those weaknesses by taking necessary remedial measures. I do not think that this thrust of effort on commodities or generalized preferences, for instance, to allow products of developing countries, particularly processed products, into markets of industrialized countries . . . was to no purpose or achieved no results. No, on the contrary, it coordinated the different positions of developing countries so that when they went to negotiate, either bilaterally or within the multilateral institutions, such as the GATT, they would be singing the same tune, if you want—or making sure that the consensus was not eroded by individual interests creeping in."

Michael Doyle offered the Millennium Development Goals as an illustration of an idea that brought together disparate elements around a same set of goals for development: "The MDGs are the platform under which the UN Development Group [UNDG] convenes. This is UNDG's work. UNDG is the place where the World Bank, the IMF, UNDP get together for their policy meetings. The MDGs provide a 'constitution,' if you will, for the UNDG. That was one part. The MDGs also provide the agreed-upon country framework for development planning. This is the template through which the World Bank, the IMF, the regional banks, the bilaterals, and UNDP talk to a member country about its development strategy. This is the template by which a country's development is measured. . . . And there were compromises. The most notorious one was that we had to leave out reproductive rights. I've had dozens of women's organizations write me letters, cc'd to the Secretary-General, explaining why this was a retrogressive step: How could you possibly justify leaving out reproductive rights? And that was a very hard one. The reason was, reproductive rights were not in the Millennium Declaration, Catholic countries and the Islamic countries said, "No," and the United States wasn't very much in favor either."

The coagulation of new coalitions and partners around various environmental issues has been continual since the Stockholm conference. Paul Berthoud, who was part of the initial team in Nairobi assembled by Maurice Strong, looked back: "One of the things which fascinated me in UNEP—and it is very much relevant to the evolution of ideas—was the way in which . . . developing countries were brought into this venture of the environment. It is quite on the record that developing countries had been very skeptical about the whole idea. . . . 'Why don't you do that in OECD? That's your problem, not ours.' Now the genius of Maurice Strong was to go to them and tell them, 'Look, poverty is your worst pollution, so why don't you come and join. We are talking about the same thing.' And it worked."

Perhaps the best indication that ideas are important is when they are seen to endanger fixed positions that mobilize groups for and against them. Nafis Sadik told us a story about traveling to Rome to see the pope on the eve of the Cairo conference. In spite of the Vatican's well-known hostility to most population-control measures, she was not really apprehensive because the Holy See had participated in all of the preparations: "So I went in, and the pope was really not—you could see that he was not very happy. He started by asking me did I know that this was the year of the family. To him it seemed like this was the year of the disintegration of the family. . . . 'Why have you taken this different approach to your predecessors?' [he asked] . . . I said, 'No, not really, except that I have moved from a top-down demographic approach—and this has evolved in the two years of the preparatory process, with NGOs and expert-group meetings—to an individual needs approach.' He said, 'That is what I mean. There is no such thing as individual needs and rights in this. It is couples' needs.'"

Sadik continued her observations about strange bedfellows: "The Vatican then organized meetings with Muslim groups in Rome—several of them. They called all these very conservative religious leaders. They sent out delegations to all the Muslim countries. I mean, they carried out a huge demarche around the world against the conference. . . . And there were some threats that the UN received against me. I had strict security. They had a guard assigned to me around the clock. These guards checked the bathrooms before I could use them."

A reflection from Jan Pronk about coalitions is intriguing for those who think about change from the top down: "No idea is sustainable in itself if it does not have an appealing value to people who are not in the system. Anti-apartheid and nondiscrimination are examples of issues raised from below, not by the elite, not by intellectuals, but by people and victims themselves."

Lourdes Arizpe embroidered this theme by arguing that it was essential to create space for groups, at both the elite and grassroots levels, to come together in new ways around issues: "I would strongly argue that respect for other cultures does not imply discarding a global vision," she said. "We need both. . . . It is a question of negotiating how the two come together. And there are all the mediating levels of the nation-state, of the regional unions or trade agreements, and of international institutions. This is why I think it's so risky that the United Nations has been left aside on so many questions in the last few years, because the United Nations is there to create the spaces so that the different powers can negotiate. If this space is forced to become subordinate to other powers, then there is no longer any space for negotiations to take place. The greatest risk for the world today is that negotiation becomes impossible."

Ideas Become Embedded in Institutions

Ideas matter, especially once they take concrete form. In the jargon of social scientists, ideas can become "embedded" in an institution and influence its agenda. Thus, they can challenge not only the founding principles of institutions but also set future agendas. In fact, ideas embedded in an organization often can take on a life of their own and then foster or impede further changes. Enrique Iglesias, for instance, mentioned that some of the earliest ideas in his regional commission inhibited creativity by becoming "ECLA's Talmud." He went on to say that "social ideas deal with real-life problems that are very different from the ones envisioned in laboratories." He referred specifically to the experience of his friend Fernando Henrique Cardoso, whose ideas on dependent development ran into "limits of power and the difficult circumstances of the national and international reality."

An institution thus is a visible manifestation that an idea has arrived. As earlier voices underlined, institutional building (or "aggrandizement," according to critics) is the stuff of bureaucratic battles. Ideas can be used to build empires, however small or large.

Robert Cox suggested that on occasion the very existence of new institutions could challenge the rigidity of existing norms. He also noted that pursuing such a strategy inevitably entailed risks. "I guess the reason why new institutions are created," he states, "is that those people who feel that the new idea is important are doubtful that they are going to be able to put it into action through the existing institutions. It is the rigidity of existing institutions that leads to the idea that if you want to start something new, you have to create another institution. Then the hope of some people would be that by creating another institution, you can inject some part of that idea into the existing institutions—that they should play along with it. And they should be influenced by its existence and take account of it in their programs and work out collaborate relationships and so forth, which is sort of an ideal formula."

Leticia Shahani noted two crucial examples of the institutionalization of ideas that resulted from the First UN World Conference on Women in 1975. UNIFEM and INSTRAW "were children of the Mexico conference," she said. Jan Pronk, who served as a Dutch minister of development cooperation on several occasions, told us why the ideas from new institutions and various women's gatherings made a difference to him and his government: "Gender became an essential aspect of the criteria for the allocation of aid, because it was generally understood that poverty had become feminized—with consequences for children—and also that women are the one and only driving force in a people-centered, bottom-up development process."

The "C" in UNCTAD refers to what amounts to a perpetual conference. On the face of it, an observer might very well ask, "What is a better proof of waste?" But Rubens Ricupero saw the creation in 1964 of a "counter-GATT" as an essential institutional development in world politics: "UNCTAD had to be motivated by an ethical imperative—that is, to try to always look at things from the development perspective and giving more attention to the weak and vulnerable. . . . This idea, this ethical imperative, this search for more justice in trade relations, had been at the origin of UNCTAD and would have to be there always."

Gamani Corea, who preceded Ricupero as head of UNCTAD, built on those thoughts. Corea recalled his first conference at the helm, UNCTAD IV in 1976 in Nairobi: "There were ideas which were not on the negotiating table; they were not winners, as you said, but were kept alive in one form or another and kept popping up from time to time." Corea also recalled the importance of keeping his institution's ideas away from financial decisions: "The idea of converting UNCTAD into a specialized agency, to the best of my knowledge, arose after the UNIDO [United Nations Industrial Development Organization] example in the later 1970s. Some of the leaders of the G-77, the stalwarts, thought that UNCTAD too should follow suit and become a specialized agency. I remember resisting. . . . UNCTAD got its strength from its link with the General Assembly and the UN. Our influence and our ability to be effective would be greater if that link was kept. If it became a specialized agency with its own budget there was the prospect of people being able to withdraw from the membership and to cut the budget."

Johan Kaufmann, speaking from the Dutch Foreign Ministry's perspective, took exception to the crack that UNCTAD really stood for "Under No Circumstances Take Any Decisions." He valued the ideas advocated by the first conference, pointing out that they continued to be discussed precisely because a permanent secretariat was established in 1964.

Robert Cox recounted how a useful idea, once institutionalized, can become trapped and perhaps ultimately be killed, depending on the organizational culture. He pointed to an antidote, the proposal to launch an Institute for Labor Studies, an idea supported by David Morse, the long-serving ILO director-general (1948–1969), to push the ILO to be more self-reflective. "The idea there, in my mind, was that an institution that has become successful in its routine becomes, in some ways, a prisoner of its success and goes on doing the same thing in the same way because it has worked. But if it no longer is really dealing effectively with the issues that you can now perceive, then maybe it needs to be changed. And the idea was that you set up an institute which is geared to research primarily but also to a kind of—training is not really the right word—educational effort among people who might be in key positions in the social policy field. Then you could develop a kind of critical mechanism to which the ILO, in its routines, might react in some way and be a means of introducing change."

In looking back over the UN's experience with ideas taking institutional forms, Sartaj Aziz drew on his experience as an international and national civil servant: "Obviously all of the things that have happened—positive things that have happened—have their base in some bright, brilliant ideas, like the basic needs approach, for example, or World Employment Programme, or the link between poverty and hunger, or a new initiative to bring OPEC into the mainstream of funding for IFAD. . . . But the task of converting ideas into an operationally meaningful framework requires an opportunity to develop the idea. . . . In the case of the World Food Conference, for example, although the conference accepted the link between poverty and food, if IFAD had not been created how would you operationalize that idea?"

In retrospect, Peg Snyder noted that her instincts had been correct in getting an institutional base for women's research: "Aida [Gindy], Molly Bruce, and others planned—I believe it was 1972—the very first headquarters expert group meeting anywhere on Women and Economic Development. It was chaired by noted economist and Nobel laureate Sir Arthur Lewis, and the expert was Ester Boserup. . . . We were beginning to help put women on the world's agenda and certainly to make order out of all that was done in ECA." In reflecting back on the work of what would, in 1975, become the African Training and Research Centre for Women, she recognized that measuring women's unpaid work contributions was important but that the organizational platform was even more crucial: "We had data in all those areas; it was at the time the only work being done on a regional basis. It just wasn't done. . . . I guess I had the instinct not only for economic and social justice but also for institutionalizing so that there would be a long life for whatever was being done."

Ideas once embedded within an institution can sometimes burst forth in unanticipated ways. Paul Berthoud earlier argued that the expansion of the environmental agenda to include poverty was crucial at Stockholm: "But the consequence of that was, of course, that UNEP started with a very broad agenda. . . . We inherited a broad sector of activity under the heading of 'human settlements,' which was really what developing countries largely considered as their share in what UNEP was to be doing in the field of environment. . . . In 1977 already, the Vancouver conference disassociated human settlements from the environment and created for that field a separate unit, [which] was a surprising move, and I have always been fascinated about the forces which were at play in that game. First of all, there was a very clear broadening of the concept of environment by bringing human settlements within the realm of UNEP as an important element of an environmental program, and then, five years later already, one saw that this was really not congruent and human settlements had to be detached, separated. . . . It is a fascinating tale about the clipping of wings of ideas within the UN system."

Sotiris Mousouris recounted how the Centre on Transnational Corporations and its intellectual products took shape: "Again, the idea of researching and eventually regulating them had been in the air for some time. The first step was convening the Group of Eminent Persons. Among the fifty or so witnesses was Gianni Agnelli of Fiat, who arrived at the Palais de Nations in Geneva by helicopter, and a host of others, including the president of IBM; the chairmen of Pfizer, Du Pont, Unilever, Pechiney, and Nestle; the vice-chairmen of General Motors, Siemens, Exxon, and Shell; labor leaders from the WFTU [World Federation of Trade Unions] and AFL-CIO; ministers; and last but not least professors. . . . When we started drafting the report of the group, we also went for a couple of weeks to New Delhi. The chairman of the Group of Eminent Persons was a very wise Indian, L. K. Jha, who was governor of Kashmir. We worked with him, along with Somavía and the British professor John Dunning. . . . The first disagreements and conflicts appeared then. . . . The report of the group recommended the establishment of a commission on multinational corporations and a center in the secretariat to be the focal point in the UN on the subject, to collect information, make studies, and prepare a code of conduct and other international agreements. The center was to be independent, autonomous."

While agreeing that institutions were key manifestations of the importance of ideas, Adebayo Adedeji also put forward a note of caution: "If all ideas were institutionalized, you would have too many institutions around. There is no doubt that once you establish an institution, in this society of ours in the world in which we live today, they are like cemeteries. You can't remove the graves. They become permanent. But that, in itself, may mean that even when experience has proven that the particular idea needs to be drastically reformulated, if not forgotten, the institution remains. . . . So one must be very careful and not rush to establish institutions."

The UN's Future Intellectual Challenges

An essential challenge for the United Nations, as we have argued elsewhere,[11] is to establish and maintain an environment in which creative thinking and policy analysis can flourish. As such, the world organization should employ professionals of outstanding quality and give them the space to think and write independently, support research adequately, reward originality as opposed to routine report-writing, strengthen multidisciplinary and multiagency dialogue, enrich analysis with field experiences, and avoid political correctness and orthodoxy of all stripes.

Why do these recommendations make sense? Because people evolve and ideas evolve. Many of our voices spoke about how their ideas had changed over the course of their careers—reflecting new information, new insights, world crises, and learning. This brings to mind a comment reportedly made by John Maynard Keynes when asked about inconsistencies in his ideas. He replied, "When I get new information, I change my views. What do you do, Sir?" Foolish consistency in the face of new problems or new data is, indeed, the hobgoblin of little minds or of ideologues, as the case may be.

Many of our voices looked over the horizon and spelled out the most pressing intellectual challenges in the first decades of the new millennium. They were not reticent about the crisis in multilateralism itself. We listen to them and point to lessons learned and future challenges. Most of the interviews were completed before the tragic events of September 11, 2001. The nature of international security threats, the role of the UN in this new climate, and the preponderance of U.S. power are topics for other books.[12] These issues undoubtedly would have figured more prominently in our interviews had our timetable been different. Nonetheless, our own conclusions necessarily take into account the politics of 2004.

"I think the crying need is to have a pattern of development in the rich countries which stops the progressive erosion of the global ecological system," Gamani Corea replied when asked about future research challenges. "I also think that within countries there is still a challenge to which no intellectual answer has yet been formulated. That is how to design a mutually reinforcing process, a positive relationship, between social progress and economic progress. Because often each has its own champions, and they become antithetical. There can be a dichotomy between social progress and economic progress. I mentioned yesterday that we were told that in looking after the social sector we were taking resources away in Sri Lanka from development and hence being premature. We were trying to eat the fruit before we planted the tree. So today there is a big demand for social safety nets: for the spread of education, the spread of improvement in health services, access to transport, participation of women. And I think there is big need to see how this can also support and help economic development and growth."

Robert Cox elaborated on a similar theme in thinking about the biggest intellectual challenge to the UN system, neoliberal orthodoxy: "I would put my bets on what you could call 'deep ecology': the sense of the interdependence of humanity with nature and the constraints on the survival within nature. I think that out of that could come the kind of alternative thinking that would affect the way we organize society, the economy, and even politics. But that's a long road and, as I say, I'm inclined to be more of a pessimist than perhaps I was in 1948, so I wouldn't make any predictions. But if you asked me where is the intellectual crux of a change of thinking, then I think that's maybe where it could come from."

"It is consumption more than anything else that is going to lead us to disasters, because we are not showing a capacity in the world to come to grips with consumption," said Sonny Ramphal. In criticizing industrialized countries and the United States in particular, he said: "Their knee-jerk reaction to the consumption issue is: 'Well, we've got to find other ways in which we can sustain consumption or make consumption at this level sustainable.' . . . An absolutely essential attitudinal change must be to reduce consumption in absolute terms. . . . The consumption issue is inseparable from development, because it is impossible to conceive of development, certainly on the basis of the best science that we have at our disposal, to conceive of development across the board at present levels of consumption in the West. If the rich countries continue to consume at their present rate, then it is not going to be possible for the poor countries to develop to a tolerable level of consumption. That, I think, is the great threat, the great challenge, and I do not believe that we are dealing with it adequately." Dharam Ghai was more succinct: "I think the big challenge at a global level, and therefore for the UN, is to ensure that there is equitable distribution of benefits brought about by globalization."

Alister McIntyre emphasized a different challenge, one that was echoed by several other voices: "I would think that the most fundamental problem facing the UN, and the international community, is [how] to deal effectively with the issue of . . . the 'knowledge divide' . . . now coming to occupy a central place in the discussion of international development and the whole business of closing the gaps between North and South. It is not something that the UN is particularly well equipped to deal with, for the simple reason that there is no single agency that would have a sufficiently strong jurisdiction to exercise leadership on that issue, and with that would come concomitant expertise. And then it requires a fairly close relationship with those parts of the private sector that are involved in knowledge development. How to bring the two together and get a good interface is going to be an exceptional challenge."

Although McIntyre was careful to specify that although he was speaking about more than the "digital divide," that issue was certainly central. Boutros Boutros-Ghali characterized the vast differences between the North and the South as a "new Berlin Wall," and he asked rhetorically how it was going to be possible to reduce the digital divide "if in 50% of the villages there is no electricity, if 50% of the population is illiterate?"

Sartaj Aziz also looked to knowledge creation as the essence of the UN's future intellectual agenda in a troubled and fast-changing world: "The twenty-first century is not going to be a century of capital, but the century of knowledge. In other words, progress, and who makes it and who doesn't, will depend on knowledge and communications. . . . I feel that it will be quicker and easier to close the knowledge gap than it was to close the capital gap. India has caught up with the rest of the world in information technology, for example. Pakistan is also catching up. China is also doing the same. The process can be telescoped. You don't have to start with technology at the lower end and then go forward, as generally happens with industrial technologies. Late students can start at the latest rung on the technological ladder.... If this digital divide can be bridged quickly and there is a concerted effort on the part of all the stakeholders, governments, NGOs, the academic community to do so, we can start closing the income gap. We will not totally close the gap, but [we will] reduce it. Partly the gap will be closed at the other end because the present consumption patterns cannot go on the way they have been. So the upper limit will keep coming down in real terms, although in monetary terms or in dollars the gap will appear larger. But in terms of purchasing power parity, it will be much lower."

Lourdes Arizpe reminds us about another dimension of two pressing intellectual challenges: "The first is the worrying loss of the diversity of knowledge that humanity has taken millennia to accumulate, a fraction of which is being conserved only for instrumental purposes, [by] exploitation through patents. The second is that market-driven societies tend to be culturally and spiritually barren. The consequences of this in terms of loss of sociability and cultural meanings can be seen in developed countries coupled with the trivializing effects of the media. And this is beginning to happen in the middle-income developing countries. Thus, the social and cultural dimensions of sustainable development must be an intrinsic part of any model of development."

"I think the women's revolution has made women a force, has made development a women's issue, and made the UN the guardian and advocate of their global movement," Peg Snyder told us. "But I would like to see the United Nations itself have a new kind of strength in the face of globalization and not just have to do peacekeeping and cleaning up the mess that bombing makes for societies.... I'd like to see the UN get a better grasp on the underlying issues of globalization.... I don't think the UN has spoken out particularly well."

In thinking about future research challenges, Lawrence Klein said matter-of-factly: "Well one that I clearly wanted to see get off the ground is to look at AIDS because the economic feedback from AIDS in countries that need people in good health, who are sturdy and between the ages of twenty and fifty, who are being hit hard by AIDS, is having a very perverse productivity effect. The payoff on an AIDS analysis could be enormous if that were studied carefully. The *New York Times* had a very interesting editorial a few months ago saying that the pharmaceutical companies are much more interested in treatment medicine than vaccination and preventive medicine because it is more profitable. Things like that could be investigated in terms of what would be saved if you did it one way or put resources in another direction."

In the post–Cold War era there has been much discussion about the erosion of the state and state sovereignty. Bernard Chidzero told us that "the concept of national sovereignty remains very real. And this, in my view, further emphasizes the need to strengthen the UN as a point of reference where we can all meet to exchange views and see whether we can moderate the negative forces or effects of such phenomena as globalization." He continued: "Sovereignty we cannot do away with. . . . We have not reached the stage of free movement of people without regulations, for reasons which may not do with security of protection of jobs. There are other challenges—disease control, for instance. . . . But I think that the concept of sovereignty of a state as an autonomous unit, self-sufficient, interacting with other autonomous, self-sufficient units, is becoming an obstacle. We have got to find some other ways of doing things. Already we are making attempts at greater regional cooperation, in which we surrender certain aspects of sovereignty and retain others and evolve a new regional sovereignty, so to speak, in a dynamic process. I do not imagine God was sitting on high, saying, 'You are sovereign. You have inherited that territory; I have determined that you shall stay there.'"

Chidzero concluded, "I think that some of the intellectual challenges would be to evolve a UN system in which voting as voting would be unnecessary except on matters of life and death, so to speak. We must attempt to reach decisions by consensus. This does mean reforming, in a sense, the Security Council, where power is in the hands of the few who make decisions. If we maintain the Security Council, can we democratize it? If we do, will it operate? . . . More civic participation in the UN itself and the specialized agencies is what I am trying to underline."

"I think that the biggest challenge is to change the status of social and economic rights for progressive rights that can be accountable," argued Paulo Sergio Pinheiro. "Of course another area is democracy—not only rule of law, but how to make democracy something more alive, more real for the peoples of Eastern Europe, of Africa, and Asia. . . . I think that the challenge of this century is how to make more operative social and economic human rights standards."

Ever the practical politician, Jan Pronk suggested that creating appropriate mechanisms should be the top priority: "We need what I call an Economic Security Council or a second chamber of the Security Council dealing with problems related to economic, social, and environmental security. . . . Next, a civil society chamber within the UN, in order to connect world civil society directly with the UN, not only through their respective governments. And thirdly, establish a right for minority groups to appeal directly to the UN, not through the government concerned. . . . Such reforms could strengthen international democracy."

Shortly before he died in 2003, Oscar Schachter listed three intellectual challenges: "First would be the use of force, roughly the legitimizing acts of force in the humanitarian interests or in common interests. . . . The future, I think, will involve the pressures to use armed force in cases where the Security Council does not authorize it. That, I think, calls for a development of both normative notions and procedural actions to go along with that. . . . Secondly, I would select the problem of resources. I mean in the broad sense of the economic resources, especially for the poor countries. I would think that there too we should have an important international institutional role. I can't formulate it as I would a more legal or institutional problem. But I think that I would put that close to the top, the premise that the present economic order does not satisfy the needs of the poor people and the basic value of equality. . . . And a third thing, out of the top of my head, would be a difficult objective, namely meeting the so-called democratic deficit in international matters. This brings up the importance of power in the development of international law. Most international lawyers regard power as an intrusion, if not an 'enemy' of law, but I regard it as critical to building international order."

Janez Stanovnik highlighted how important it is for the UN to continue to create new ideas as an antidote to the dominant mood of pessimism about its relevance in world politics: "The United Nations in my view is primarily a world forum. This is where different ideas, policies and interests meet. The principal purpose is not passing the resolutions with a majority vote. [The] principle purpose is reaching the compromises by confronting the arguments. . . . The power of the UN is not in majority of votes, nor in coordinated economic power, and even less [in] military power. Its authority is in moral power, in the fact that the people of the world believe that this is an organization which stands for peace, justice, for equality, for development, for human rights—for survival of humanity."

Fernando Henrique Cardoso thought about the relationship between ideas and accomplishments: "You have to try to move ahead, to create the conditions for what at the beginning appears as impossible. . . . This is the main challenge for me in political life. If I believed in remaining limited to the possible, I would never have started up a stabilization program in Brazil, because in political terms it was impossible. In economic terms it was impossible. The economists surrounding me were insisting all the time that it would be impossible, because the president at the time was a weak president, because the Congress was in a situation of disarray, because everyone was to some extent motivated by the inflationary culture. My opinion was the contrary—let's try to do it. . . . So I think that we should not always assume that what is a limit will remain a limit."

Mostafa Tolba looked from his balcony overlooking the Nile and across a sprawling Cairo brimming with unemployed youth and said: "The one thing that I sincerely hope that the UN will turn its eyes to is the youth, the people of tomorrow, the leaders of tomorrow. Who is going to really help these people and adapt their views at the national, regional or global level? . . . [There is a] tremendous political vacuum in most of the developing countries. . . . They are barred from getting into parties, into the political system. Where do they learn their political agenda? Where do they learn how to lead, I do not know. . . . We are sitting over there, blocking their ways, keeping them from saying what they want, running the show the way we want. We can have a United Nations conference *of* youth, not *on* youth. Let them talk and come with their own aspirations. How do they want to see the world? We will probably have some reasonable, some meaningful recommendations and ideas rather than the things that are becoming stale, that are becoming clichés of the old generation."

In looking toward the next generation, Juan Somavía challenged us to emphasize "integrated thinking," comprehensive and transdisciplinary approaches: "It begins with our educational system. . . . You are taught as a lawyer. You are taught as an economist. You are taught as a sociologist. And you have been requested for the last twenty years to become more and more specialized. . . . The whole system has pushed, pushed, pushed, in educational terms, towards specialization, when the reality of the world has been pushing more and more towards integration. So to begin with, the educational system is totally dysfunctional in this capacity for integrated thinking. . . . We don't teach holistic approaches. We don't teach how it is that one thing depends on another if you want to have a balanced society."

Ever the teacher, Elise Boulding extended Somavía's comments and put forward her vision: "We just have to develop ways of teaching about these issues of the world in such a way that more people will be literate about the state of the planet. I would start with the elementary schools, right from kindergarten through the Ph.D. . . . We have to find ways to prepare the public who only watch TV and play on e-mail and don't have any first-hand exposure to actual policymaking processes. You have the small group of activists and you have an inert audience. . . . So I think the entire educational community has to go on the alert."

Michael Zammit Cutajar stressed a different challenge for the UN in the next decade—"to stay alive." This had resonance with other voices, who also thought that the survival of multilateralism is anything except a foregone conclusion in either operational or intellectual terms. "To find ways of remaining relevant and to avoid being gobbled up by a combination of the U.S. and the private sector. The push towards involvement of the private sector and the need to keep the U.S. on board are so strong, they boil down to one thing. The UN based in the U.S. has this need to keep the U.S. on board, to look good in the *New York Times,* so to say, and that can, if not balanced, lead to the organization becoming quite skewed."

Indeed, remaining steadfast in the pursuit of unpopular ideas—for instance, of multilateralism in the face of the rampant unilateral tendencies unleashed in Washington by the war in Iraq or in the U.S. decision to opt out of the Kyoto Protocol to the United Nations Framework Convention on Climate Change—was clearly a preoccupation for many of our voices, and for us. Rubens Ricupero provided an important set of reflections about the near future: "The problem is the future of multilateralism—even of the United Nations. . . . The UN is but a stage in a long process of evolution in human history—the search for an international organization of states. The UN only became feasible because it had behind it the power of the United States. . . . The two occasions when the world tried to organize an international institution of states—in Paris after the First World War and in San Francisco after the Second World War—the idea came from the United States. The difference was that in the first case, the U.S. was not entirely persuaded. It was mainly a personal idea of President Wilson. The U.S. finally did not join, and this was one of the major reasons why the League of Nations became a sort of European organization and finally died away. The UN had a better destiny because it was not just an idea of Franklin Roosevelt, but it was also the expression of the thought of an outstanding generation of U.S. diplomats, politicians, and statesmen. It was an entire generation from the East Coast establishment, internationalist in outlook—that generation . . . [that] had lived through the Great Depression, that had created the New Deal, that had fought the Second World War and was about to create the Marshall Plan. That generation was able to generate a bipartisan support for its ideals and goals."

"This bipartisan support for a multilateralist diplomacy no longer exists," Ricupero continued. "I don't think Iraq will be for the UN what Abyssinia was for the League of Nations, because I believe that the UN will be able to survive. . . . I believe that we are living in a very somber moment, and by no means am I trying to put a brave face on it. But it is important to make sure that, though fragile, the UN survives. It is important to keep it alive and hope that this trend in the U.S. will pass, because if it doesn't pass we will be in trouble. . . . If the major power in the world loses its interest in the multilateral approach, then there is no future for multilateralism."

In late 2003, when he established the High-level Panel on Threats, Challenges, and Change, Secretary-General Kofi Annan's none-too-hidden agenda was how to engage the United States. Washington's hubris about the value of going it alone seems to have faded somewhat over time with its appeal to the Security Council in October 2003 in pursuit of a blue-tinged resolution 1511 on Iraq, Lakhdar Brahimi's efforts on the ground, and the passing of sovereignty to Iraqi authorities at the end of June 2004. The Bush administration's "strategy is one of partnerships that strongly affirms the vital role of NATO and other U.S. alliances—including the UN," according to Secretary of State Colin Powell. Although it is hard to take this assertion at face value, nonetheless the occupation of Iraq seems to have had a sobering impact on many inside the Washington Beltway, even on some neoconservatives.

Theodore Sorensen, a former speechwriter for John F. Kennedy, posed a rhetorical question in mid-2003 (the answer to which had become more obvious in 2004) that seemingly was behind Security Council resolution 1546: "What is more unrealistic than to believe that this country can unilaterally decide the fate of others, without a decent respect for the opinions of mankind, or for the judgment of world institutions and our traditional allies?"[13] The existence and viability of Iraq's interim and then transitional (after January 2005) government will depend largely on the United Nations.[14]

No U.S. administration will permit the Security Council or any other part of the UN system to stand in the way of pursuing its perceived vital interests. At the same time, the council and the UN system often serve American national interests and give the United States cause to proceed cautiously and with international acquiescence, if not jubilant support. Depending on the issue, the stakes at hand, the positions of other potential allies, and the plausibility of collective action, Washington has the power to act either unilaterally or multilaterally.[15] As the George W. Bush administration discovered, however, "even imperfectly legitimated power is likely to be much more effective than crude coercion."[16]

In light of the sobering experience in occupied Iraq, perhaps the United Nations will become more appealing to Washington.[17] There are numerous other examples of shared interests, which include fighting terrorism (sharing intelligence and working together on anti-money laundering efforts), confronting the global specter of infectious diseases (HIV/AIDS, Ebola, and SARS), pursuing environmental sustainability, monitoring human rights and criminal tribunals, providing humanitarian aid, as well as pursuing weapons inspections and a host of other tasks in post-conflict reconstruction in Iraq.

Princeton University's John Ikenberry pointed out an irony in the widespread negative reactions against Washington's actions: "The worst unilateral impulses coming out of the Bush administration are so harshly criticized around the world because so many countries have accepted the multilateral vision of international order that the United States has articulated over most of the twentieth century."[18]

The unfortunate reality of power means that if the United Nations and multilateral cooperation for development or any other purpose are to flourish, the United States as the globe's remaining superpower must be on board, which is why elsewhere one of us argued for ways to stimulate "tactical multilateralism."[19] The record of the first Bush administration gives pause even to inveterate optimists, however, amounting to what K. J. Holsti summarized as "major assaults on [international] community projects."[20] The list is long, which in addition to the war in Iraq includes: abrogating the ABM Treaty, withdrawing from the draft protocol for verification of the Biological Weapons Convention and from the Kyoto accords on global warming, subverting the International Criminal Court, rejecting the Comprehensive Test Ban Treaty, failing to sign the Convention on the Rights of the Child (one of only two countries not to do so), and resorting to predatory trade practices.

Nonetheless, we hasten to recall an often forgotten fact—namely that the United States raced to be the first country to ratify the UN Charter, with the Senate's approval coming on July 28, 1945, scarcely a month after the end of the San Francisco conference. But the sun of such earlier enlightened American leadership of the world organization set during the first administration of George W. Bush. An emboldened Bush White House, after the results of the November 2004 election, does not augur well for much multilateral sunshine in the near term. Indeed, while the second Bush administration, for its own tactical purposes, may well engage in some multilateral efforts, it is likely to do so either by attempting to pressure the UN into rubber-stamping a U.S. security and "values" agenda or by sidelining the organization altogether if such acquiescence is not forthcoming.

Either way, one of the legacies of the Bush administration may be, in the short term, undermining the world organization's ability to generate and implement progressive development ideas. At the same time that the current moment and our own mood are dark, the kind of political commitment and internationalist orientation that existed the last time that the United States was as dominant on the world stage, right after World War II, could dawn again with appropriate vision and leadership.

We close this volume with several voices that reflect on the precarious present. Speaking from South Asia, no stranger to violent strife, Viru Dayal cautions: "While we have fought all through human history in the name of religion, I think people have suddenly gotten wind of the fact that we can finish ourselves off now if we carry on in our manic-depressive way on this subject any longer. . . . I don't speak in terms of Islam and the so-called conflict of civilizations. But I think that what we have is a very serious truth that has come up to confront all of us—that we can do great harm in the name of faith. And we better all shape up in our respective societies, whether India, America, Pakistan, Israel, or Egypt. We better have the voice of reason triumphing over lunacy. . . . [September 11] was a moment of pivotal importance, both in respect of the issue of religion gone amuck and in respect of the need to defend rights more critically, and with greater determination, both because of the possible onslaught on rights by the state acting in the name of security and by those professing to act in the name of religion."

As a Mexican citizen, Lourdes Arizpe spoke of the momentous challenges in the cultural relationships between the West and the rest: "It is the greatest challenge after the advent of industrial capitalism, because it is first of all capitalism transformed into a world system, which means that everything that was guaranteed in industrial capitalism in the West must now be guaranteed for the rest of the world. And this is very problematic. . . . The first challenge of the United Nations is to create a new scheme for the coexistence of different cultures that are no longer juxtaposed as a mosaic of cultures but as currents in a single river . . . to create the spaces, identify the people who would be able to develop these concepts and perspectives, and put them in positions where they can lead this world debate on how different cultures and religions can coexist."

The former president of Malta, Guido de Marco, spoke for all of us in thinking about the future of the world organization: "If the nations forming part of the UN want to give relevance to the UN, the UN is a very relevant body. If the nations forming part of the UN do not want to give it relevance, then the UN slowly moves into irrelevance. . . . I'm afraid that the present one is not a United Nations for all seasons. It's a United Nations which [is able to act] on some issues but . . . is bypassed on other issues. . . . How are we going to view the future? Do we have the courage to change or not? Do we want the United Nations to meet the challenges of this century or do we want the United Nations to be there as something that can be useful, an umbrella which we can hold in our hands but which doesn't open if it starts raining?"

Finally, UNIFEM's executive director Noeleen Heyzer gazed up a steep incline as we climb toward the future: "Most of the real talk happens along the corridors. In the formal context, people prepare country statements and then deliver these five-minute statements to half-empty rooms. And you bring in heads of state to do that. . . . If the UN is to play the role that it has been set up to do, then we have to find other ways of doing work. How do you generate real conversations and real dialogue? If we don't do that, then other people will take that space because real dialogue is needed, especially today. . . . Because the UN is such a compartmentalized structure, there is still a divide between the normative side of the house and the operational side. . . . It is extremely important that what happens on the ground—which is some of the best work of the UN system—gets reflected in the debates at the intergovernmental level and that the recommendations and the norms that are created there get brought back to the local level. This kind of feedback process and linkages are still not strong enough."

Future intellectual challenges reinforce the point that we are all probing for answers and help anywhere we can find them in the current chaotic atmosphere. Moreover, it is in this context that the personal backgrounds explored in the first three chapters of this book remain pertinent for our voices themselves and for the future. Heyzer paused for several moments and drew upon her past in multicultural Singapore to continue to look forward: "The battlefield is actually the human soul, and this is now the fight—this whole area of religion and spirituality. I think there needs to be a deeper understanding that as we are globalizing, as we are generating wealth, as we are developing all these development alternatives, there is an area that we still do not understand. And this is the very deep spiritual nature of the human experience as well. . . . How do you touch a human being in such a deep way that dying becomes a sign of pride? To go beyond even the human instinct for survival for a cause that they feel gives them dignity? How do you provide human dignity and human respect at a time when there are all these devaluations that are taking place? Current legitimacy has been broken and people are going back to their 'roots,' to their 'gods,' to create more secure futures, even their past. People are questioning the whole framework of meaning and human existence. This is going to be a huge challenge intellectually."

When it awarded the 2001 Nobel Peace Prize to the United Nations and its Secretary-General, the Norwegian Nobel Committee stated why ideas and people, and the UN as an institution with both, matter: "Today the Organization is at the forefront of efforts to achieve peace and security in the world, and of the international mobilization aimed at meeting the world's economic, social and environmental challenges . . . The only negotiable route to global peace and cooperation goes by way of the United Nations."[21]

The collective experiences and testimonies of our voices provide ample evidence of this reality.

Appendix 1

Biographical Notes of Persons Interviewed

Adebayo Adedeji (1930–) was executive secretary of the UN Economic Commission for Africa from 1975 to 1991. Before that, he was a member of the Nigerian civil service, professor of administration in the University of Ife, and minister for economic development and reconstruction of post–civil war Nigeria (1971–1975). He was born in Nigeria and educated at University College in Ibádan, Nigeria, and at London and Harvard Universities. He is currently founder and executive director of the African Centre for Development and Strategic Studies and member of the Advisory Board of the UN African Futures Project.

Samir Amin (1931–) was director of IDEP for ten years, executive director of CODESRIA in Dakar (1973–1980), and since then has been director of the Forum du Tiers Monde (1980–). He was born in Egypt and educated at the Institute of Political Science and the National Institute for Statistics and Economic Studies in Paris. His most recent publications include *Spectres of Capitalism: A Critique of Current Intellectual Fashions*; *Capitalism in the Age of Globalization: The Management of Contemporary Society*; *Obsolescent Capitalism*; and *The Liberal Virus*. Oral history conducted in French.

Kofi Annan (1938–) is the seventh Secretary-General of the United Nations and winner of the Nobel Peace Prize in 2001. He was elected Secretary-General in 1996 and reelected in 2001. A career international civil servant, he joined the world organization in 1962 and has worked in various capacities, including as assistant secretary-general for human resources management, programme planning, and budget and finance and as under-secretary-general for peacekeeping operations. He was born in Ghana and educated at the University of Science and Technology in Kumasi, Ghana, Macalester College and Massachusetts Institute of Technology in the United States, and at the Graduate Institute of International Studies in Geneva.

Margaret Joan Anstee (1926–) served the UN for over four decades, rising to the rank of under-secretary-general in 1987, the first woman to hold a position at this level. She has worked on operational development programs in all regions of the world, mostly with the UNDP. She was director-general of the UN Office in Vienna (1987–1992), head of the Centre for Social Development and Humanitarian Affairs, and coordinator of UN narcotic drug control. In 1992–1993, she was the Secretary-General's special representative to Angola, the first woman to head a UN peacekeeping mission. She was born in the UK and educated at Cambridge and London Universities. Her extensive writings on UN peace operations, reform, and economic and social development include *Orphan of the Cold War* and her autobiography *Never Learn to Type: A Woman at the United Nations*.

Lourdes Arizpe (1945–) was assistant director-general for culture at UNESCO (1994–1998), a member of the World Commission on Culture and Development, and director of the *UNESCO World Culture Report* (1998 and 2001). Since the 1970s she has worked as a consultant for the ILO and the UNDP and was a member of the Advisory Group for Social Affairs for Latin America and the Caribbean Regions for the World Bank. A Mexican national, she was educated at the London School of Economics and the National School of Anthropology of Mexico, and she received Fulbright-Hays and Guggenheim grants. She is president of the International Social Science Council and the former vice-president of the International Society for Development. Her most recent publication is *Culture and Global Change*.

Sartaj Aziz (1929–) was a civil servant in Pakistan, mostly in the Planning Commission, where he was joint secretary (1967–1971), before starting his UN career in 1971 as the FAO's director of commodities and trade. In 1977 he became assistant president of IFAD, the agency he helped create as deputy secretary-general of the 1974 World Food Conference. In 1984 he began a political career that included minister of state for food and agriculture (1984–1988), finance (1990–1993 and 1997–1998), and foreign affairs (1998–1999). He was also secretary-general of the Pakistan Muslim League (1993–1999). A native of Pakistan, he was educated in Hailey College of Commerce, Lahore, and Harvard University. He is vice-chancellor of Beaconhouse University in Lahore, and his publications include *Rural Development: Learning from China*; *Hunger, Politics and Markets*; and *Agricultural Policies for the 1990s*.

Paul Berthoud (1922–) joined the UN in 1951 and held positions in New York, the Middle East, Latin America, Africa, and Geneva before finishing his career as UNDP resident representative in Venezuela (1981–1983). He was legal adviser to UNTSO and ONUC, chief of the Social Affairs Division in ECLA, director of UN Economic and Social Office in Beirut, secretary of the board and the conference and director of Programme Support Services at UNCTAD, and director of the Fund of UNEP. After retirement he has served as a consultant to several UN agencies and as a UNITAR senior special fellow. He headed the team that assessed the feasibility of establishing a UN Staff College. He was born in Switzerland and educated at the University of Geneva.

Maurice Bertrand (1922–) was a member of the UN's Joint Inspection Unit (1968–1985) and a member of the high-level expert group on the restructuring of the UN in 1986. Before joining the UN he was professor at the Ecole Nationale d'Administration and conseiller at the Cour des Comptes in France. He was born in France and educated in law and politics at the Universities of Lyon and Montpellier. After leaving the UN he became a guest professor at the Graduate Institute of International Studies in Geneva. He has written many publications about reform of the UN system, including *The UN as an Organization: A Critique of Its Functioning.* Oral history conducted in French.

Francis Blanchard (1916–) joined the ILO in 1951, becoming assistant director general in 1956, deputy director general in 1968, and director-general for three terms (1974–1989). After leaving the ILO, he prepared a number of reports on coordination within the UN. Before he joined the ILO, he worked for the International Refugee Organization, the predecessor of the UNHCR. He was born in France and educated in law and politics at the University of Paris. His memoirs is entitled *L'Organisation International du Travail: De la Guerre Froide à un Nouvel Ordre Mondial.* Oral history conducted in French.

Elise Boulding (1920–) has worked as an advisor, consultant, and council member for UNESCO and the UN University on peace education, women, and human development. She also served on the Committee for the Quaker United Nations Office. She was an advisor to the Human and Social Development Program and consultant to the Household Gender and Age Project at the United Nations University. She is currently professor emerita at Dartmouth College. She was born in Norway and is a naturalized U.S. citizen and was educated at Douglass College, Iowa State College, and the University of Michigan. Her most recent publication is *Cultures of Peace: The Hidden Side of History.*

Boutros Boutros-Ghali (1922–) was the sixth UN Secretary-General (1992–1996). He was professor of international law and international relations at

Cairo University (1949–1977), and he was a member of Parliament and minister of state for foreign affairs and deputy prime minister for foreign affairs (1977–1991). After his term as Secretary-General at the UN, he became secretary-general of the International Organisation of the Francophonie (1997–2002). He is currently president of the International Panel on Democracy and Development at UNESCO and president of the Egyptian National Commission for Human Rights. He was born in Egypt and educated at Cairo University and the Sorbonne, Paris. His many publications include *The Papers of United Nations Secretary-General, Boutros Boutros-Ghali* and *Unvanquished: A U.S.-U.N. Saga.* Oral history conducted in French.

Margaret Bruce (1918–) entered UN service in November 1945 in London and continued when the Secretariat first moved to Hunter College in the Bronx. She worked on human rights and women's issues (including the Universal Declaration on Human Rights with Eleanor Roosevelt). She rose from junior human rights officer to assistant director of the Human Rights Division, later becoming deputy director of the Centre for Social Development and Humanitarian Affairs. She retired in 1977. She was awarded the Order of the British Empire in 1979. She was born in England and educated at Cambridge University and currently holds joint U.S.-UK citizenship.

Fernando Henrique Cardoso (1931–) was president of Brazil from 1996 to 2003 and earlier minister of finance and economy and minister of foreign affairs. He was a professor in ECLA (1964–1967). Before starting on his political career as a federal senator in 1983, he had been a professor of sociology and political science at several universities, including in São Paulo, Paris, Cambridge, and Stanford. He was born in Brazil and educated at the University of Paris and the University of São Paulo. He chaired the Panel of Eminent Persons on United Nations–Civil Society Relations (2003–2004).

Bernard T. G. Chidzero (1927–2002) worked for UNCTAD from 1968 to 1980, for the last three years as deputy secretary-general. His UN career began in 1960 as an economic affairs officer in ECA; later he was the first black African to be named UNDP resident representative (in Kenya, 1963–1968). He returned to Zimbabwe on independence in 1980, becoming successively a member of Parliament and minister of economic planning and development and later senior minister of finance; he was still working as an advisor to the government when he died. He presided over the seventh session of UNCTAD and chaired the Joint Ministerial Committee of the World Bank and the IMF (1986–1999). He was born in Zimbabwe and worked in the tobacco fields and as a tailor's assistant until age thirteen, when he learned to read and write. He was educated at the University of South Africa, the University of Ottawa, McGill University, and Oxford University.

Gamani Corea (1925–) served as UNCTAD's third secretary-general (1974–1984). Earlier he served as ambassador of Sri Lanka, deputy governor of the Central Bank, and permanent secretary of the Ministry of Planning and Economic Affairs and held various positions in the Bank of Ceylon. His other UN affiliations have included being secretary-general of several UN conferences and member or chairman of several UN panels of eminent persons, including the UN Committee on Development Planning, the UN Cocoa Conference, the Expert Group on Development and Environment, and the ECAFE Expert Group on Regional Performance Evaluation. He was born in Sri Lanka and was educated there at the Royal College and the University of Ceylon and at Cambridge and Oxford Universities. He is chancellor of the Open University of Sri Lanka, senior advisor to the Sri Lanka Ministry of Foreign Affairs, and president of the Association of Former International Civil Servants in Sri Lanka.

Robert Cox (1926–) started work in the ILO in 1947 and retired in 1971 after serving as director of the International Institute for Labour Studies (1965–1971). After leaving the UN he held various professorships including at Columbia University, University of Toronto, Yale University, and the Australian National University, and he is currently professor emeritus of political science and social and political thought at York University. He was born in Canada and was educated at McGill University. His most recent book is *The Political Economy of a Plural World: Critical Reflections on Power, Morals and Civilization.*

Virendra Dayal (1935–) worked at the UN from 1965 to 1993, retiring after serving as *chef de cabinet* for Secretaries-General Pérez de Cuéllar and Boutros-Ghali. Other UN positions included UNHCR's relief operation in Bangladesh and elsewhere and director of the UN's Office of Special Political Affairs. He served on the Indian delegation to the World Conference on Human Rights and was a member of the Carnegie Commission on Preventing Deadly Conflicts. He is currently the executive director of India's National Human Rights Commission. Before joining the UN, he was a civil servant of the government of India. He was born in India and educated at St. Stephen's College in Delhi and at Oxford University, where he was a Rhodes Scholar.

Leila Doss (1921–) joined the Radio Division of the UN in 1947 and worked in various information centers until she was appointed assistant secretary-general for personnel services. She retired in 1982. During her UN career, she was director of the UN Division of Economic and Social Information and head of the information campaign for the International Year of the Child. Before joining the UN, she worked in Egyptian State Broadcasting and as professor of English literature and creative writing at the University of Cairo. She was born in Egypt and educated at the American University in Cairo. After leaving the UN she remained active as a lecturer in international affairs and headed "The World at the UN," a field study program at Fordham University.*

Michael W. Doyle (1948–) served as assistant secretary-general and special advisor to UN Secretary-General Kofi Annan (2001–2003) and continues as an advisor. He is the Harold Brown Professor at Columbia University with joint appointments in the School of International and Public Affairs and the Law School. He was born in the United States and educated at the U.S. Air Force Academy and Harvard University. From 1977 to 2001, he was a professor of politics and international relations at Johns Hopkins and Princeton Universities and was director of Princeton's Center of International Studies (1997–2001). He has served as a member of the External Research Advisory Committee of the UNHCR and the Advisory Committee of the Lessons-Learned Unit of the Department of Peacekeeping Operations. His recent books include *New Thinking in International Relations Theory* and *The Globalization of Human Rights.*

Just Faaland (1922–) created the development wing of the Christian Michelsen Institute in Bergen, Norway, and has worked as an economic consultant for many parts of the UN and other international organizations and in many countries since 1949, when he started as an economist with OEEC. Subsequently he worked for the World Bank, the ILO, IFAD, the FAO, the WFP, the UNDP, and the Asian Development Bank. He has been resident advisor to the governments of Pakistan (1957–1960) and Malaysia (1968–1970) and was World Bank resident representative in Bangladesh (1972–1974). He served as president of the OECD Development Centre (1983–1985) and chairman of the UN Committee for Development Planning (1999–2000). He was born in Norway and educated at the Universities of Oslo and Oxford. His numerous publications include *Growth and Ethnic Inequality: Malaysia's New Economic Policy* and *The Political Economy of Development.*

Seymour Maxwell Finger (1915–) was a career U.S. diplomat, serving from 1956 to 1971 at the U.S. Mission to the UN as economic advisor, minister-

---

*Transcript not finalized in time to be included in this volume.

counselor, and ambassador. He served in the European theater in the U.S. Army (1943–1945) and in the foreign service in various countries (1946–1956). He was born in the United States and educated at Miami University of Ohio. Currently he is a senior fellow at the Ralph Bunche Institute, adjunct professor of political science at The CUNY Graduate Center and at New York University, and president of the Institute for Mediterranean Affairs. He is author of *Your Man at the UN: People, Politics, and Bureaucracy in the Making of American Foreign Policy; American Ambassadors at the UN;* and *Bending with the Winds: Kurt Waldheim and the United Nations.*

Celso Furtado (1920–2004) was director of ECLA's Economic Development Section (1949–1957) and subsequently a member of many UN committees and commissions, including the Academic Council of the UN University, the UN Committee on Development Planning, and the World Commission for Culture and Development. Outside the UN, he was director of the Brazilian National Economic Development Bank, director-general for the development of the Brazilian North East, minister of planning; minister of culture, and Brazilian ambassador to the EEC. He was a visiting professor of economic development at many universities and was a member of the South Commission. He was born in Brazil and educated at Brazil University (Rio de Janeiro), Paris University, and Cambridge University. *Development and Underdevelopment* was one of his most influential publications among the thirty books he has written on the economic history of Brazil and the Americas; his autobiography is *La fantaisie organisée.* Oral history conducted in French.

Richard N. Gardner (1927–) has been closely involved with international affairs and the UN as a U.S. official, a university professor, a lawyer, and a consultant. From 1961 to 1965, he was deputy assistant secretary of state for international organization affairs and was twice ambassador (to Italy, 1977–1981, and to Spain, 1993–1997). He was a public delegate to the Millennium General Assembly in 2000 and special advisor to the UN at the 1992 Earth Summit in Rio. He was born in the United States and was educated at Harvard College, Yale Law School, and Oxford University, where he was a Rhodes Scholar. He is currently professor of law and international organization at Columbia Law School and counsel to the law firm Morgan Lewis. He is the author of several books on international affairs, including *In Pursuit of World Order: US Foreign Policy and International Organizations* and *Sterling-Dollar Diplomacy in Current Perspective: The Origins and the Prospects of Our International Economic Order.*

Dharam Ghai (1936–) joined the ILO World Employment Programme in 1973 and retired as director of UNRISD (1987–1997) and later returned as an adviser to ILO and to the International Institute of Labour Studies. He was a senior economist on the staff of the Pearson Commission, prior to which he had been a lecturer in economics at Makerere University in Uganda (1961–1965) and Visiting Research Fellow at Yale University (1965–1966) and research professor and then director of Nairobi's Institute for Development Studies (1967–1974). He has served as consultant to UNCTAD, UNIDO, IFAD, the UNDP, UNICEF, the WHO, and the FAO and to various governments. He was born in Kenya and educated at Oxford and Yale Universities. His latest publications include *Building Knowledge Organisations: Achieving Excellence*; *Social Development and Public Policies*; *Economic and Social Progress in Africa*; and *UN Contributions to Development Thinking and Practice.*

Sven Hamrell (1928–) was founder and executive director of the Dag Hammarskjöld Foundation (1967–1995), at which he remains a senior advisor. He was chair of the Rural Advancement Foundation International and member of the Swedish Government Commission on Humanitarian Aid and the Commission on Aid to African Refugees. He was born in Sweden and educated at Bowdoin College and the New School for Social Research in the United States and at Uppsala University in Sweden.*

Gerald Karl Helleiner (1936–) is a distinguished economist whose career has been devoted to research, teaching, and advisory work about development, especially in Africa. He has been chairman of the North-South Institute, leader of the International Development Research Centre Mission on Economic Policy in a Post-Apartheid South Africa, and a member of the UN Committee for Development Planning, the Secretary-General's Advisory Group on Financial Flows for Africa, and UNCTAD's Expert Group on Economic Group on Economic Cooperation among Developing Countries. He was born in Austria and is a naturalized Canadian citizen. He was educated at the University of Toronto and Yale University. He is currently professor emeritus at the University of Toronto. He is a member of the Executive Board of the African Capacity-Building Foundation in Zimbabwe and the Board of Trustees for the Economic and Social Research Foundation of Tanzania. His many books include *Poverty, Prosperity, and the World Economy: Essays in Memory of Sidney Dell*; *The New Global Economy and the Developing Countries: Essays in International Economics and Development*; and *The IMF and Africa.*

*Transcript not finalized in time to be included in this volume.

Julia Henderson (1915–) served with the United Nations from 1945 to 1970, including as director of the UN Division of Social Welfare (1950–1954), the Bureau of Social Affairs (1955–1967), and Bureau of Technical Operations (1967–1970). For much of this time, she was the most senior woman staff member. She started her career in late 1945 as a member of the UN Preparatory Commission staff, working in London prior to the first session of the General Assembly in January 1946. After retiring from the UN, she became secretary general of the International Planned Parenthood Federation (1971–1978). She was born in the United States and was educated at the University of Illinois, the University of Minnesota, and Harvard University. Her memoirs are titled *Around the World in Eighty Years.*

Stéphane Hessel (1917–) started his UN career as a colleague of his compatriot Henri Laugier and as the first assistant secretary-general for social affairs (1946–1950). Later he was the UNDP's deputy administrator for policy and evaluation (1970–1972). Between these assignments, he worked for the French Ministry of Foreign Affairs and was in charge of human rights and social affairs. From 1976 to 1981 he was French permanent representative in Geneva, the UN's economic and social capital. He was a member of the Independent Working Group on the Future of the UN (1994–1995) and was the French representative to the 1993 World Conference on Human Rights in Vienna. He presided over the French delegation to the Human Rights Commission on other occasions. He was born in Germany and became a French citizen; he was educated at the Ecole Normale Superieure in Paris.

Noeleen Heyzer (1948–) has directed UNIFEM since 1994, the first director from a developing country. Before this, she worked for the ILO and ESCAP and was director of the Gender Programs of the Asia and Pacific Development Centre (1984–1994). She has chaired a number of UN task forces and committees, including on women's empowerment for the UNFPA, on implementation of the Platform for Action of the Fourth World Conference on Women, and on others on microcredit and gender equality. She has headed the international delegation to engender the peace process in the Middle East and was co-convenor of the Round Table on Human Rights and HIV. She was born in Singapore and educated at the Universities of Singapore and Cambridge.

Virginia Housholder (1918–) worked for the UN Relief and Rehabilitation Administration (1945–1947) and UNESCO (1947–1949), after which she was with the Bureau of International Organization Affairs of the U.S. State Department from 1950 until her retirement in 1968. In 1977 she was recalled from retirement to serve as U.S. member of the UN's budgetary watchdog, the Advisory Committee on Administrative and Budgetary Questions, where she served from 1977–1978 and 1981–1985, the first woman so elected. She was born in the United States and educated at MacMurray College for Women, the Bradley Polytechnic Institute, and the University of Wyoming.

Enrique Iglesias (1931–) is president of the Inter-American Development Bank, a position he has held since 1988. From 1972 to 1985, he was executive secretary of ECLAC. Between these assignments, he was Uruguay's minister of external relations, representative to ECLAC, and president of the Central Bank. In 1981, he served as secretary-general of the UN Conference on New and Renewable Sources of Energy, and in 1986 he was chairman of the conference that launched the Uruguay Round of Trade Negotiations. He was born in Spain and is a naturalized Uruguayan citizen. He was educated at the University of the Republic of Uruguay. He is also currently the president the Society for International Development. Oral history conducted in Spanish.

Devaki Jain (1933–) moved from being a lecturer in economics at Delhi University to found The Institute of Social Studies Trust, which pioneered analysis of gender in poverty. In 1984 she convened the first meeting of Third World women social scientists and activists in Bangalore, which led to the founding of Development Alternatives with Women for a New Era. She has been a member of advisory committees and expert and eminent persons groups for such UN organizations as UNIFEM, the WHO, the FAO, ILO, UNESCO, UNICEF, the UNDP, and the UNFPA as well as for national committees in preparation for the UN world conferences on women. She was born in India and educated there at Mysore University and in the UK at Oxford University. Her many publications include *Women Enrich the UN and Development,* a book in the UNIHP series.

James O. C. Jonah (1934–) retired as under-secretary-general for political affairs (1992–1994) after more than three decades in the UN Secretariat, including as political advisor in the Office of the Secretary-General (1970–1979) and as assistant secretary-general for personnel services (1979–1982), of the Office for Field Operations and External Activities (1982–1987), and for special political questions (1991–1992). After leaving the UN, he became Sierra Leone's permanent representative to the UN (1996–1998) and minister of finance, development ,and economic planning in Freetown (1998–2001). He was born in Sierra Leone and educated at Lincoln University, Boston University, Harvard Law School, and MIT. He is currently a Senior Fellow at the Ralph Bunche

Institute for International Studies of The CUNY Graduate Center. His publications include his forthcoming memoir, *What Price Survival of the United Nations? Memoirs of a Veteran International Civil Servant.*

Johan Kaufmann (1918–1999) was economic counselor (1956–1961) and then permanent representative of the Netherlands to the United Nations in both New York and Geneva (1961–1969 and 1974–1978). He was also permanent representative to the OECD (1969–1974) and ambassador to Japan (1978–1983). He was born in the Netherlands and educated in Amsterdam and at the University of Geneva. He wrote prolifically about multilateral diplomacy at the UN, including *The Diplomacy of International Relations: Selected Writings*; *Conference Diplomacy: An Introductory Analysis*; and *The Evolving United Nations: Principles and Realities.*

Lawrence R. Klein (1920–) won the Nobel Prize in Economic Sciences in 1980 for creating econometric models and applying them to the analysis of economic fluctuations and economic policies. He played a major role in establishing the LINK econometric model, which is used by the UN for global forecasting. He has also been a consultant to UN agencies, including UNCTAD and UNIDO, and to the UN on the economics of disarmament and development. Currently he is Benjamin Franklin Professor of Economics (emeritus) at the University of Pennsylvania, and for the last twenty years has been a director of W. P. Carey & Co. He was born in the United States and educated at the University of California, Berkeley, and MIT. His many publications include *Econometric Modeling of China*; *Principles of Macroeconometric Modeling*; and *Arms Reduction: Economic Implications in the Post–Cold War Era.*

Stephen Lewis (1937–) started his career as an elected politician and broadcaster. He was Canada's permanent representative to the UN (1984–1988) and was UNICEF's deputy executive director (1995–1999). He has served as chair of the UN committee which drafted United Nations Programme of Action for Africa Economic Recovery and Development, as the Secretary-General's special advisor on Africa, as chair of the first International Conference on Climate Change, as UNICEF's special representative, and as UNICEF's coordinator of the Graça Machel study on the Impact of Armed Conflict on Children. He has been a consultant to USAIDS, UNIFEM, and the ECA. In 2001, he was appointed the Secretary-General's special envoy for HIV/AIDS in Africa. He was born in Canada and educated at the Universities of Toronto and British Columbia.*

*Transcript not finalized in time to be included in this volume.

Guido de Marco (1931–) was president of Malta from 1999 to 2004, during which period he served as vice president of the Independent World Commission on Oceans. Earlier he had been minister of foreign affairs, deputy prime minister, and minister of the interior and justice for Malta. From 1967 to 1987, he was Malta's representative in the Parliamentary Assembly, Council of Europe. He was born in Malta and was educated at the Royal University of Malta. His publications include *A Second Generation UN: For Peace in Freedom in the 21st Century* and *Malta's Foreign Policy in the 90s: Its Evolution and Progression.*

Alister McIntyre (1930–) worked in UNCTAD from 1977 to 1987, first as director of the Commodities Division and then as deputy secretary-general and officer-in-charge. After this he joined the secretariat of the Caribbean Community, was assistant secretary-general in the UN's Office of the Director General for Development and Economic Co-operation, and was secretary-general of the Caribbean Community. Currently he is the chief technical advisor for the Caribbean Regional Negotiating Machinery in Jamaica and personal representative of the UN Secretary-General on the Guyana/Venezuela border controversy. He has been chairman of the Commonwealth Group of Experts on the New International Economic Order, the International Forum on Debt and Development, and the IDB/OAS Independent Group of Experts on Smaller Economies and Western Hemispheric Integration. He was born in Grenada and was educated at the London School of Economics and Oxford University.

Donald Owen Mills (1921–) was the Jamaica's permanent representative to the UN (1973–1981), during which time he was its representative on the Security Council (1979–1980), vice chairman of the Group of Experts on Restructuring of Economic and Social Sectors of the UN, president of ECOSOC, and chairman and chief negotiator for the Group of 77. Before this he worked in Jamaica's civil service, including as head of the Central Planning Agency. He is presently chairman of the Commonwealth Foundation and a member of the Judicial Service Commission, the Privy Council, and the Jamaica Council on Ocean and Coastal Zone Management. He was born in Jamaica and educated at Jamaica College and the London School of Economics.

Sotiris Mousouris (1936–) served as assistant secretary-general heading such UN departments as the Centre Against Apartheid, Political Affairs, Secretariat Services for Economic and Social Matters, and the Office of the Personal Representative of the Secretary-General for Afghanistan and Pakistan (1982–1995).

He joined the UN in 1966 as economist in the Department of Economic and Social Affairs and as assistant director at the Centre for Transnational Corporations, which he helped establish. Born in Greece, he studied at the University of Athens and at Harvard Business School. Since retirement from the UN, he has been appointed president of the Organization for the Construction of the New Museum of Acropolis and as special envoy of the Greek foreign minister. He currently is president of the Greek-African Chamber of Commerce and Development.

Conor Cruise O'Brien (1917–) was Ireland's permanent representative to the UN and head of the International Organizations Section of the Irish government (1956–1960). In 1961–1962, he served as the Secretary-General's representative to Katanga. He was born in Ireland and educated at Trinity College. He continues to write as a columnist for Irish and British newspapers and was editor-in-chief of the London *Observer*. He was a university president and has been a visiting professor at universities around the world. He has at one time or another also been a diplomat, politician, government minister and member of Parliament, historian, biographer, antiwar activist, intellectual, playwright, and prose stylist. His numerous works of analysis and fiction include *The United Nations: Sacred Drama*.

Sadako Ogata (1927–) was UN High Commissioner for Refugees (1991–2000) and has over three decades of involvement with the UN. She was six times delegate of Japan to the General Assembly (1968, 1970, and 1975–1978), chairman of the Executive Board of UNICEF, and minister plenipotentiary at the Japanese permanent mission. From 1982 to 1985 she represented Japan on the UN Commission on Human Rights. The rest of her career has mostly been spent in teaching and administering international relations at the International Christian University and Sophia University, both in Tokyo. She was co-chair of the Commission on Human Security (2002–2003). She was born in Japan and educated there at the University of the Sacred Heart and in the United States at Georgetown University and the University of California, Berkeley.

I. G. Patel (1924–) was the UNDP's deputy administrator (1972–1977). From 1958 to 1961, he was executive director for India at the IMF. Before that, he worked as an economist at the IMF (1950–1954) and in the Indian Ministry of Finance (1954–1958, 1961–1967), after which he became secretary for economic affairs for the Indian government (1968–1972). After leaving the UNDP, he was governor of the Reserve Bank of India, director of the Indian Institute of

Management, and director of the London School of Economics. In 1995 he was a member of the Commission on Global Governance. He was born in India and educated there at Baroda College and Bombay University, as well as at the University of Cambridge and Harvard University. His recent publications include *Economic Reform and Global Change.*

Surendra J. Patel (1923–) is one of India's most distinguished economists. In his rich and varied career, he was senior advisor at the World Institute of Development Economics Research (WIDER) and visiting professor at the Institute of Development Studies. He joined the United Nations in 1950 and retired in 1984 as the director of UNCTAD's Technology Division. He was born and educated in India and is the author of several books and scholarly articles focusing on development issues.

Javier Pérez de Cuéllar (1920–)was the fifth UN Secretary-General (1981–1991). His involvements with the UN began in 1971 as Peru's permanent representative to the UN; during his tenure he was also vice-president of the General Assembly, chairman of the Group of 77 and president of the Security Council. In 1975 he became under-secretary-general for special political affairs and at times served as the special representative of the Secretary-General in Cyprus and Afghanistan. After leaving the post of Secretary-General, he became chairman of the UNESCO/World Commission on Culture and Development. During an electoral transition, he acted as prime minister of Peru (2000–2001) and is currently Peru's ambassador to France. He was born in Peru and educated at the Catholic University in Lima. His UN memoirs are titled *Pilgrimage for Peace: A Secretary-General's Memoir.*

Vladimir Petrovsky (1933–) became under-secretary-general for political affairs in 1992 and director-general of the UN Office in Geneva (1993–2002). He had earlier worked in the UN Secretariat (1964–1971) on leave from the Soviet Foreign Ministry, after which he worked in Moscow on Soviet/U.S. relations in the Foreign Policy Planning Department, headed the Department of International Organizations (1979–1986), and was Russia's first deputy foreign minister (1986–1991). His other UN affiliations include secretary-general of the Conference on Disarmament, chair of the task force that drafted *An Agenda for Peace,* and the Secretary-General's special envoy to Libya (1992–1993) and Albania (1998). He was born in Russia and educated at the Moscow State Institute of International Relations, and he is a member of a number of academies and the author of seven books in Russian.

Paulo Sergio Pinheiro (1944–) is an independent expert for the UN Secretary-General's study on violence against children and special rapporteur on the situation of human rights in Myanmar and previously in Burundi. He is a member of the UN Sub-Commission for the Promotion and Protection of Human Rights and the Interamerican Commission on Human Rights. He was secretary of state for human rights in Brazil (2001–2002), where he had taught and conducted research at the University of São Paulo; he also has taught at the Ecole des Hautes Etudes en Sciences Sociales, Paris, and at the University of Notre Dame and Oxford and Brown Universities. He was born in Brazil and educated at the Catholic University, Rio de Janeiro, and at the University of Paris. His publications include *Brasil: Um Século de Transformações*; *Brazil and the International Human Rights System*; and *The (Un)Rule of Law and the Underprivileged in Latin America*.

Jacques J. Polak (1914–) worked as an economist in the League of Nations secretariat (1937–1943) and in the Netherlands Embassy in Washington (1943–1944), in which capacity he attended the Bretton Woods Conference. He joined the IMF in 1947 and served as director of the Research Department (1958–1980), as economic councillor (1966–1980), and as an executive director (1981–1986). From 1987 to 1989 he was senior advisor to the Development Centre and World Bank consultant. He was born in the Netherlands and educated at the University of Amsterdam. His many publications include *The World Bank and the IMF: A Changing Relationship*.

Jan Pronk (1940–) served three times as minister for development cooperation for the Netherlands (1973–1977, 1989–1994, and 1994–1998) and as minister of housing and the environment (1998–2002). He first became member of Parliament in 1971. In 1980–1986 he was UNCTAD's deputy secretary-general. He was born in the Netherlands and educated at the Netherlands School of Economics (now part of the Erasmus University at Rotterdam). From 1965 to 1971, he was research assistant to Jan Tinbergen at the Netherlands Economic Institute, and in 2003 he assumed a research professorship at the Institute for Social Studies in The Hague. In 2004 he was appointed the Secretary-General's special representative for Nafur.

Shridath Surendranath Ramphal (1928–) was secretary-general of the Commonwealth from 1975 to 1990. During this period he served on five independent international commissions on global issues: the Brandt Commission on International Development Issues, the Palme Commission on Disarmament and Security Issues, the Brundtland Commission on Environment and

Development, the Independent Commission on Humanitarian Issues, and the South Commission. He was also co-chair of the Commission on Global Governance. He also served as special advisor to the Secretary-General for the UN Conference on Environment and Development, president of the World Conservation Union, and chairman of the UN Committee on Development Planning. He was born in Guyana and educated there at Queens College and at Kings College, London, and Harvard University. His publications include *Our Country the Planet: Forging a Partnership for Survival.*

Rubens Ricupero (1937–) was UNCTAD secretary-general (1995–2004). Earlier he was Brazil's minister of finance, minister for the environment and Amazonian affairs, and ambassador to Italy, the United States, and the United Nations in Geneva. He was chairman of the Finance Committee at the UN Conference on the Environment and Development as well as governor for Brazil at the World Bank, the IMF, and the African Development Bank. He also has headed Brazilian delegations to the Conference on Disarmament and at the UN Human Rights Commission. Between 1966 and 1985 he was a diplomat at the Ministry of External Relations and was professor of international relations at the University of Brasilia. He was born in Brazil and educated at the University of São Paulo.

Gert Rosenthal (1935–) was executive secretary of the Economic Commission for Latin America and the Caribbean (1988–1997). He was Guatemala's permanent representative to the UN (1999–2004) and previously was a member of the Follow-up Commission of the Guatemalan Peace Accords. He joined ECLAC in 1974 as director of its Mexico office and in 1987 was appointed its deputy executive secretary. He was born in Guatemala and educated at the University of California, Berkeley. He has written extensively on development issues, including the history of ECLAC for the UN Intellectual History Project's volume edited by Yves Berthelot, *Unity and Diversity in Development Ideas: Perspectives from the UN Regional Commissions.*

John Gerard Ruggie (1944–) was assistant secretary-general and senior advisor for strategic planning to Secretary-General Kofi Annan (1997–2001). Before this he had been a consultant to the UN on peacekeeping operations, international development, science and technology, and the environment. From 1973 until he joined the UN, he was professor of political science at the University of California, Berkeley, Colombia University, and the University of California, San Diego; from 1991 to 1996 was dean of the School of International and Public Affairs at Colombia. After leaving the UN he became

Kirkpatrick Professor of International Affairs at the Kennedy School of Government at Harvard University. He was born in Austria and is a naturalized U.S. citizen; he was educated at McMaster University, Canada, and the University of California, Berkeley. His numerous publications include *Multilateralism Matters*; *Constructing the World Polity*; and *Winning the Peace.*

Ignacy Sachs (1927–) acted as a special advisor to the Secretary-General for the UN Conference on Human Environment in Stockholm in 1972 and for the UN Conference on Environment and Development in Rio in 1992. He was director of studies and professor at the Ecole des Hautes Etudes en Sciences Sociales in Paris, where he founded the International Research Centre on Environment and Development in 1973. He directed that centre until 1985, since which time he has been director of the Research Centre on Contemporary Brazil. He is a founding member of the International Foundation for Development Alternatives. He was born in Poland and educated at the Universities of Rio de Janeiro and Delhi and the Central School of Planning and Statistics in Warsaw. Oral history conducted in French.

Nafis Sadik (1929–) began working with the UN Population Fund in 1971 and served as its executive director from 1987 to 2000. She served in 1994 as secretary-general of the International Conference on Population and Development. She is a member of the Board of Governors of the Foundation for Human Development and a member of the South Asian Commission on the Asian Challenge. She was the president of the Society for International Development (1994–1997). She was a member of the Secretary-General's High-level Panel on Threats, Challenges, and Change. She was born in India and educated at Loreto House in Calcutta, Dow Medical College in Karachi, and the Johns Hopkins University. Among her publications are *Making a Difference: Twenty-five Years of UNFPA Experience.*

Klaus S. Sahlgren (1928–) was executive secretary of the UN Centre for Transnational Corporations (1975–1983) and executive secretary of the Economic Commission for Europe (1983–1986). Before this he was the permanent representative of Finland to the UN and other international organizations and chair of the GATT and EFTA councils. He was born in Finland and educated at Åbo Akademi and the Officers' College of Marine Warfare.

Oscar Schachter (1915–2003) was UN legal advisor from 1946 to 1953, worked at the United Nations Relief and Rehabilitation Administration from 1946 to 1966), and was director of the General Legal Division (1953–1966). From 1966 to 1975 he was director of research at UNITAR. During much of this period, he held appointments at Yale Law School and Colombia Law School and in 1966 joined the Columbia faculty, where he taught until shortly before he died. He served as the president of the American Society of International Law (1968–1970) and in numerous consultant capacities: to the UN Commission on Transnational Corporations, to the panel of arbitrators of the International Center for the Settlement of Investment Disputes at the College de France (a presidential appointment), at the U.S. State Department, and as attorney for several U.S. government agencies. He was born in the United States and was educated at City College and Columbia University Law School. His publications include *Who Owns the Universe?* and *UN Legal Order.*

Amartya Sen (1933–) won the Nobel Prize in Economic Sciences in 1998. He has served as an advisor and consultant to the Secretary-General and many parts of the UN system, including the ILO, UNIDO, UNICEF, UNCTAD, the WFP, UNIFEM, WIDER, and (extensively for) the UNDP, beginning with the first *Human Development Report.* He was co-chair of the International Commission on Human Security (2002–2003). He has served as president of the Econometric Society, the American Economic Association, the Indian Economic Association, the International Economic Association, and Oxfam. He is Lamont University Professor and professor of economics and philosophy at Harvard University after having been master of Trinity College, Cambridge University (1998–2004). He was born in India and educated at Presidency College in Calcutta and Trinity College, Cambridge. His many publications include *Collective Choice and Social Welfare; On Economic Inequality; Poverty and Famines; On Ethics and Economics; Development as Freedom* and *Rationality and Freedom.*

Leticia R. Shahani (1929–) was assistant secretary-general for social development and humanitarian affairs (1981–1986), during which time she served as secretary-general of the Third World Conference on Women in Nairobi in 1985. Prior to that she had worked in the UN's Division of Human Rights (1964–1968) and in 1974 chaired the Commission on the Status of Women. She also served as secretary-general of the UN Congress on Crime Prevention and the Treatment of Offenders. She has held positions in the Philippine Senate for over ten years and has been undersecretary of foreign affairs, chair and commissioner of the National Commission on the Role of Filipino Women, and ambassador to Australia and Romania. She was born in the Philippines and educated at Wellesley College, Columbia University, and the University of Paris.

Mihaly Simai (1930–) served in various UN capacities for over three decades. In 1959–1960 he was with the ECE and in 1964–1968 with the Centre for Development Planning, Projection, and Policies. In 1993–1995 he was director of the UNU's World Institute for Development Economics Research. He has also served as a member and officer of various UN groups and bodies, including the UN Committee on Public Administration, the UNICEF Executive Board, the Committee on Development Planning, and as a member of the Advisory Board of the UN Staff College. He has been a consultant for the UNCTC, UNIDO, UNCTAD, the UNDP, and UNITAR. He is currently professor at the Institute for World Economics of the Hungarian Academy of Sciences and the Budapest University of Economics. He is also president of the Hungarian UN Association and the Hungarian National Committee of UNICEF and honorary president of the World Federation of UN Associations. He was born in Hungary and educated at the Budapest University of Economics (formerly Karl Marx University).

Hans Singer (1910–) joined the UN as an economist in 1947 and for twenty-two years played a pioneering role in the economic work of many parts and agencies of the UN, including UNICEF, the Department of Economic Affairs, the WFP, UNRISD, the ECA, and the African Development Bank. He was director of the Economic Division of the UN Centre of Industrial Development (1967–1969), after which he left the UN and joined the Institute of Development Studies at the University of Sussex, where he remains an Honorary Fellow. His prolific output of publications covers almost all aspects of the UN, the international system, and development, but he is best known for his pioneering work on the Prebisch-Singer thesis. He was born in Germany and educated at the University of Bonn and Cambridge University. His biography is *Sir Hans Singer, the Life and Work of a Development Economist,* by John Shaw.

Mary Smieton (1902–2005) was the first director of personnel in the United Nations (1946–1948). She held this position on secondment from the Ministry of Labour in the United Kingdom, returning to the ministry as permanent secretary. She was made a Dame for her contribution in 1949 and retired from government service in 1963. During the 1960s she served as the UK representative on the board of UNESCO. She was born in the UK and was educated at Cambridge University.

Margaret C. Snyder (1929–) was founding director of UNIFEM (1978–1989) after serving as regional advisor for the Economic Commission for Africa, co-founder of its African Centre for Women, and head of its Voluntary Agencies

Bureau (1971–1978). She was an international election observer in Ethiopia, Uganda, and Tanzania and continues as senior advisor to the UN and the UNDP and on UNIFEM's Assessment Advisory Committee. She sits on several university and NGO boards. Born in the United States, she was educated at the College of New Rochelle, Catholic University of America, and University of Dar es Salaam, Tanzania. Her most recent books include *Transforming Development: Women, Poverty, and Politics* and *Women in African Economies: From Burning Sun to Boardroom.*

Juan Somavía (1941–), director-general of the ILO since 1999, launched the concept of decent work in a fair globalization. He has been a lecturer on trade policy and was involved in the GATT Kennedy Round in 1966. He was ambassador and advisor to the Chilean foreign minister on regional and multilateral issues (1968–1973) and permanent representative to the UN (1990–1999), during which time he proposed the 1995 World Summit for Social Development and chaired its preparatory committee and was twice president of ECOSOC (1993–1994, 1998–1999) and the Security Council (1996 and 1997). He chaired the board of UNRISD (1996–1999) and was founder, executive director, and president of the Latin American Institute for Transnational Studies (1976–1990) and secretary-general of the South American Peace Commission (1986–1990). A staunch opponent of the Pinochet dictatorship, he was actively involved in the restoration of democracy. He was born in Chile and educated at the Catholic University of Chile and the University of Paris.

Cornelio Sommaruga (1932–) was a diplomat of the Swiss Department of Foreign Affairs (1960–1986), reaching the position of state secretary for external economic affairs, after which he was elected as the president of the International Committee of the Red Cross (1987–1999). In 2000, he became president of the Geneva International Centre for Humanitarian Demining and of International Association of Initiatives of Change. He was a member of the High-level Panel on United Nations Peacekeeping Operations and the International Commission on Intervention and State Sovereignty. He was born in Rome as a Swiss citizen and was educated at universities in Zurich, Paris, and Rome. He has written extensively on human security and humanitarian action.

Janez Stanovnik (1922–) was executive secretary of the Economic Commission for Europe (1967–1983). Prior to that, he was a member of Parliament, chief of staff for the first vice president of Yugoslavia, and director of the Institute for International Economics and Politics in Belgrade. In 1964, he was chairman of the Economic and Financial Committee at the First UNCTAD

Conference and in 1965 was special advisor at UNCTAD. After leaving the UN, he was elected president of the Republic of Slovenia and retired when Slovenia became independent from the former Yugoslavia in 1990. He was born in Slovenia and educated at the University of Ljubljana and the Institute for Social Sciences in Belgrade.

Jack I. Stone (1920–) was UNCTAD's director of research (1970–1977) and of its Special Program on Least Developed, Land-Locked and Island Developing Countries (1977–1981). Since 1981, his consultancies have included economic research for the UNDP, the Eastern Caribbean, the UN, UNCTAD, and the World Bank. He was head of financial policies in the OECD's Development Assistance Committee (1967–1970) and a senior economist for USAID (1963–1966). Earlier, he was an analyst with the postwar military government in Germany, the Marshall Plan, and Fomento Economico in Puerto Rico and deputy director for the Upper Midwest Economic Study at the University of Minnesota. He was born in the United States and was educated at the University of Chicago and Harvard University.

Paul Streeten (1917–) is professor emeritus at Boston University and has been a distinguished teacher and writer on development for over five decades. He has served as the editor of *World Development* since its founding in 1972. In the 1960s he was deputy director general of the Economic Planning Staff of the UK's new Ministry of Overseas Development. In 1976–1980 and 1984–1985, he was a senior advisor with the World Bank, where he helped formulate policies on basic needs. Since 1990, he has provided intellectual inputs into the UNDP's *Human Development Report* and UNESCO's *World Culture Reports*. Born in Austria and a naturalized UK citizen, he was educated at the University of Aberdeen and Oxford University. His recent publications include *Thinking about Development* and *Globalisation: Threat or Opportunity?*

Mostafa Kamal Tolba (1922–) joined UNEP as deputy executive director in 1973 and served as its executive director from 1976 to 1992. He is professor emeritus of the Faculty of Science at Cairo University, president of the International Center for Environment and Development and Environment and our Common Past, chairman of the Egyptian Consultants for Environment and Development, and an alternate member of the executive board of UNESCO. He was born in Egypt and educated at London's Imperial College and Cairo University. He has written extensively on the environment; his most recent book is *Global Environmental Diplomacy: Negotiating Environmental Agreements for the World, 1972–1992*.

Brian Urquhart (1919–) joined the UN in 1945, serving as personal assistant to Gladwyn Jebb and then the first Secretary-General, Trygve Lie, and subsequently in various capacities related to international peace and security under Ralph Bunche between 1954 and 1971. He was involved in conferences on peaceful uses of atomic energy and in all of the major crises ranging from the Congo to Cyprus, from Kashmir to various hot spots in the Middle East. He took over after Bunche's death in 1971 as under-secretary-general for special political affairs and remained in this position until his retirement in 1986. He was born in England, educated at Oxford University, and served in the British Army from 1939–1945. He has written several books, including biographies of Dag Hammarskjöld and Ralph Bunche and volumes on decolonization and on reforming the UN system. His autobiography is titled *A Life in Peace and War.*

Victor L. Urquidi (1919–2004) attended the 1944 Bretton Woods Conference and from 1947 to 1949 worked in the World Bank. He joined the Mexican Regional Office of ECLA in 1951 and become its director (1952–1958). From 1964 to his death he worked at El Colegio de México, as its president from 1966 to 1985 and subsequently as research professor. He wrote extensively about Latin American development, trade, education, science and technology, and, more recently, economic aspects of the environment and sustainable development. He was born in France in 1919 as a Mexican citizen and educated at the London School of Economics.

Kurt Waldheim (1918–) was the fourth UN Secretary-General (1971–1981). Previously, he was Austria's permanent representative to the UN (1964–1968) and its foreign minister (1968–1971). He had earlier served as chairman of the Safeguards Committee on the International Atomic Energy Agency and on the UN Committee on Peaceful Uses of Outer Space. He was elected president of Austria in 1986. He was born in Austria and educated at the Vienna Consular Academy and the University of Vienna. He is the author of *The Austrian Example* and *Kurt Waldheim: In the Eye of the Storm.*

Ponna Wignaraja (1926–) was a development advisor in the UN system for some thirty years, beginning with the IMF (1951–1953) and the World Bank (1962–1967) and later with the UN itself. He was secretary-general of the Society for International Development (1981–1986). In 1991 he was appointed vice chairman of the Independent South Asian Commission on Poverty Alleviation, and he currently is chairman of the South Asian Perspectives Network Association. He was born in Sri Lanka and educated at the University of Ceylon and at Yale University. His publications include *Towards a Theory of Rural Development*; *New Social Movements in the South*; and *Pro-Poor Growth and Governance in South Asia*.

Michael Zammit Cutajar (1940–) was executive secretary of the UN Framework Convention on Climate Change (1996–2002), after having set up and directed the secretariat supporting the UN's climate change negotiations. He began his UN career in UNCTAD and returned in several senior capacities (1967–1971, 1974–1978, and 1986–1991). He also worked for the UN Conference on the Human Environment and UNEP (1971–1974). In the 1980s, he joined the International Foundation for Development Alternatives and was a consultant to the UN Office for Emergency Operations in Africa and the Office for Special Political Affairs. He was born in Malta and educated there at St. Edward's College and at the University of London.

Appendix 2

A Methodological Note: Making This Oral History

For those who are interested in the way that we conducted the oral history component of the United Nations Intellectual History Project, we spell out here relevant details. We touch upon the selection of the persons interviewed, the formulation of our questions, the conduct of the interviews themselves, and the finalization of the texts that appear in the preceding pages.

We began by examining, literally and figuratively, the persons whom we have encountered in what amounts collectively to a century of exposure to development debates in and around the United Nations. This list of potential contacts was constantly refined to fill gaps and reflect oversights or suggestions, particularly those emanating from our International Advisory Council and group of authors. We sought balance and diversity—countries of origin, backgrounds, gender, and viewpoints.

In the end, our budget and a publishing deadline limited the interview pool to seventy-three individuals. We ourselves accept responsibility for the final composition of the list. Our goal was not to create a sample that was, in a conventional sense, scientifically representative. We are not even sure what that would mean, given the many individuals who have participated in UN development work. Rather, we sought to find individuals with an openness of mind and a broad enough exposure to intellectual currents and UN debates who would reflect candidly on what was an utterly unusual and intense period of experimentation with multilateral cooperation—the last sixty years. We believe that we have succeeded.

We also made another fundamental decision at the outset, and one that distinguishes this oral history from many others. We not only rejected the anthropological and sociological convention of anonymity for interviewees; we also insisted that everything in the approved transcripts could be used *immediately* by us and other researchers. We believed that much would have been lost in hiding identities or in closing what was available until after the deaths of those interviewed.

No decision comes without a price. Without the shield of anonymity or the promise of confidentiality until some distant date, it is certainly likely that some elements of frankness were sacrificed in the voices that appear here. Readers should also be aware that, paradoxically, the definitive "oral" history is what appears in the approved and revised written transcripts rather than what originally was recorded during interviews. Because we insisted that no material would be sequestered even temporarily from public scrutiny, there is occasionally, although not all that frequently, a substantial discrepancy between what was recorded and what is found in the approved transcription.

Following the procedures suggested by Columbia University's Oral History Research Office, we offered all the persons with whom we spoke the opportunity to review and correct the interview transcripts. We thus gave everyone the option of amending or adding material. In the vast majority of cases, modifications actually heightened the historical accuracy and added clarification to the oral interview. In only a few cases was lively and highly critical material lost.

Our first interviews took place at the end of 1999, and by the end of 2003 virtually all were completed. On average, our interviews were four hours long. The briefest lasted an hour; some were as long as twelve hours, taking place over several sessions. In all, we spent some 325 hours with those whom we interviewed.

Interviewing was not new to us. All four of us over the course of our careers have continually relied on colleagues, friends, and informants for supplemental data and insights about contemporary events. Our analyses, either as scholars or members of international secretariats, have relied most heavily on conventional documentary material and statistics. Oral history, and this project in particular, was different in many respects. These interviews were longer and more intense than anything that we had ever done. And the resulting interviews provide the core material for this book rather than supplement other sources.

These interviews were also far more intimate and less focused than our previous interviews had been, in order to permit the interviewee's voice to permeate and that of the interviewer to recede. The burden of appropriately conducting such conversations was enormous—especially because we invaded the personal space of interviewees in a most exhausting fashion.

Our colleagues at Columbia University's Oral History Office had advised that for the "conversational narrative" to emerge, it is critical for the interviewer to be well prepared.[1] For almost every interview, a project researcher helped scour archives, personal papers, and secondary material to ready us to make the best use of limited time with an interviewee. Only by reading what had been written either by interviewees or about them and their contributions were we able to construct questions that guided the conversations. Our conversations were informed by our own understanding of, as analysts of and participants in, the history of UN ideas. Our own sense of what was of particular salience for the story and the period that we were investigating is present in the dialogue as well.

As is supposed to be the case, our lengthy sets of prepared questions often gave way to the flow of a conversation, which gathered a momentum of its own. Interlocutors often responded with unanticipated but rich information that sparked a different line of questioning than we had anticipated. Additional facts may have been lost in this process, but they were offset by increased intensity and emotion. Above all, an oral historian learns to listen. We always wanted more, and we wanted to push deeper. A sense of intimacy made certain questions easier to ask, others harder. At the end of the day, however, the controls were in the hands of the interviewees. We have the impression that significant numbers of our participants spoke with a refreshing candor about their experiences, their colleagues, and themselves. A sense of self-criticism was evident much of the time, and we also felt the presence of emotions and thoughts that had rarely been shared with others or certainly not in public.

All except seven of the interviews took place in English. This was not "linguistic imperialism" on our part but a pragmatic decision to use a commonly used research language. The passages used here of interviews conducted in French or Spanish were translated into English, but the complete transcripts are available in the language in which the interview was conducted.

Finally, and as we noted in the introduction, this is not a hagiography. Our colleagues appear in these pages, warts and all. Every story is different; each voice is unique. The complete transcripts are separate documents to be remembered as such. The recorded conversations and corrected transcripts encapsulate a story within our story. The structure and subtlety of language in each interview, including each interviewee's sense of irony and of imagery, provide a firsthand account of a personal and professional voyage through the intellectual history of the United Nations.

Notes

Introduction

1. For a discussion, see Morten Bøås and Desmond McNeill, *Global Institutions and Development: Framing the World?* (London: Routledge, 2004).

2. Judith Goldstein and Robert O. Keohane, eds., *Ideas and Foreign Policy* (Ithaca: Cornell University Press, 1993).

3. Kathryn Sikkink, *Ideas and Institutions: Developmentalism in Argentina and Brazil* (Ithaca: Cornell University Press, 1991).

4. Peter M. Haas, "Introduction: Epistemic Communities and International Policy Coordination," *International Organization* 46, no. 1 (Winter 1992): 1–36; and Peter M. Haas, Robert O. Keohane, and Marc A. Levy, eds., *Institutions for the Earth: Sources of Effective International Environmental Protection* (Cambridge, Mass.: MIT Press, 1992).

5. Peter A. Hall, ed., *The Political Power of Economic Ideas: Keynesianism across Nations* (Princeton: Princeton University Press, 1989).

6. Ernst B. Haas, *When Knowledge Is Power: Three Models of Change in International Organizations* (Los Angeles: University of California Press, 1994); and see Peter M. Haas and Ernst B. Haas, "Learning to Learn: Improving International Governance," *Global Governance* 1, no. 3 (September–December 1995): 255–284.

7. Kathryn Sikkink, *Activists beyond Borders: Advocacy Networks in International Politics* (Ithaca: Cornell University Press, 1998).

8. Thomas S. Kuhn, *The Structure of Scientific Revolutions,* 2nd ed. (Chicago: University of Chicago Press, 1970).

9. Alexander Wendt, *Social Theory of International Politics* (Cambridge: Cambridge University Press, 1999).

10. John G. Ruggie, *Constructing the World Polity* (New York: Routledge, 1998).

11. See, for example, Robert W. Cox, ed., *The New Realism: Perspectives on Multilateralism and World Order* (New York: St. Martin's, 1997); Robert W. Cox with Timothy J. Sinclair, *Approaches to World Order* (Cambridge: Cambridge University Press, 1996); Quintin Hoare and Geoffrey N. Smith, eds. and trans., *Selections from the Prison Notebooks of Antonio Gramsci* (London: Lawrence and Wishart, 1971).

12. See, for example, Studs Terkel, *The Good War: An Oral History of World War II* (New York: W. W. Norton and Co., 1984); *American Dreams, Lost and Found* (New York: Pantheon, 1980); and *Hard Times: An Oral History of the Great Depression* (New York:

Pantheon, 1970). For an overview of methods, see Ronald J. Grele, *Envelopes of Sound: The Art of Oral History,* 2nd ed. (New York: Praeger, 1991).

13. Ronald Bayer and Gerald M. Oppenheimer, eds., *AIDS Doctors: Voices from the Epidemic* (Oxford: Oxford University Press, 2000).

14. Louis Emmerij, Richard Jolly, and Thomas G. Weiss, *Ahead of the Curve? UN Ideas and Global Challenges* (Bloomington: Indiana University Press, 2001), 214. This is a volume in the United Nations Intellectual History Project series.

15. "Ideas to Live (and Die) for," *The Economist,* January 17, 2004, 72.

16. Quoted by Mary Marshall Clark, "The September 11, 2001 Oral History Narrative and Memory Project: A First Report," *The Journal of American History* 89, no. 2 (September 2002): 575.

1. Growing Up

1. The term "third culture children," "third culture kids," or simply "TCKs" was coined in the 1960s by Ruth Hill Useem, an American sociologist who sparked an entire field of study about children of one culture who grow up in a different one either because of their parents' career choices or because they were refugees and who subsequently develop a "third," and often global, cultural identity. See David C. Pollock and Ruth E. Van Reken, *Third Culture Kids: The Experience of Growing Up among Worlds* (Yarmouth, Maine: Intercultural Press, Inc., 1999).

2. Johan Kaufmann, *United Nations Decision Making* (Netherlands: Alphen aan den Rijn, 1980).

3. The bohemian lives of his parents figure prominently in his own autobiography; Stéphane Hessel, *Danse avec le siècle* (Paris: Seuil, 1997).

4. In addition to his reports for the JIU, see, for example, Maurice Bertrand, *Refaire l'ONU! Un programme pour la paix* (Paris: Editions Zoé, 1986); and *The Third Generation World Organization* (Dordrecht: Nijhoff, 1989).

5. Celso Furtado, *La fantaisie organisée* (Paris: Publisud, 1987).

6. The Maginot Line was a line of concrete fortification, machine-gun posts, and other defenses erected by France along its borders with Germany and Italy in the wake of World War I. It failed to stop the German invasion of France in 1940. It was not so much "pierced" as circumnavigated by the German offensive through Ardennes.

7. These reports were published twice before being discontinued as an independent publication. See UNESCO, *World Culture Report 1998: Culture, Creativity and Markets* (Paris: UNESCO World Reports Series, 1998); and *World Culture Report 2000: Cultural Diversity, Conflict and Pluralism* (Paris: UNESCO World Reports Series, 2000).

8. At the time, about $40 a year.

9. Actually published as Margaret Joan Anstee, *Never Learn to Type* (London: John Wiley, 2003).

10. "Joint Resolution of Appreciation to Dr. Gamani Corea, Adopted on 16 May 2003 by the Board and the Council of Representatives of the South Centre," reproduced in *South Letter* 39 (2003): 92.

11. Amartya Sen, *Development as Freedom* (New York: Knopf, 1999).

12. On May 15, 1932, the prime minister of Japan, Inukai Tsuyoshi, was assassinated in an attempted coup d'état by eleven young naval officers. This incident is considered one of the main reasons that the military assumed a prominent role in ruling the country until World War II.

13. A Dutch burgher is a person who left Holland and went to Ceylon many generations ago.

2. Formal Education

1. After the 1938 Anschluss by the Nazis, Austria became part of the Third Reich and its citizens who had escaped to the United Kingdom were considered "enemy aliens."

2. George Weidenfeld, *Remembering My Good Friends: An Autobiography* (New York: Harper Collins, 1995), 62–64.

3. This right-wing demonstration, which marked a generation, turned violent.

4. The Bandung conference, formally titled the Asian-African Conference, was held in Bandung, Indonesia, in 1955. Convened in a period of decolonization, the conference explored common problems within these regions and strategies to foster economic and political cooperation among Third World states. The Non-Aligned Movement emerged out of the Bandung conference and held its first summit in Belgrade in 1961.

5. This was an anti-fascist group in the UK that aimed to widely disseminate left-wing literature during the interwar period. For more information see http://books.guardian.co.uk/departments/politicsphilosophyandsociety/story/0,6000,517876,00.html

3. Serendipity and International Careers

1. Brian Urquhart, *A Life in Peace and War* (New York: Harper & Row, 1987), 55.

2. This was the highest-ranking title, next to that of Secretary-General, at the time.

3. The Organisation for European Economic Co-operation became the Organisation for Economic Co-operation and Development (OECD) in 1961.

4. Readers may have noted that even English-speaking voices often use the Spanish acronym for ECLA.

5. For details, see John Toye and Richard Toye, *The UN and Global Political Economy* (Bloomington: Indiana University Press, 2004), 110–137. This is a volume in the United Nations Intellectual History Project series.

6. Richard N. Gardner, *Sterling-Dollar Diplomacy* (Oxford: Oxford University Press, 1956).

7. Fernando Henrique Cardoso, *Empresário industrial e desenvolvimento econômico no Brasil* [*Brazilian Industrial Entrepreneurs and Economic Development*] (São Paulo: Difusão Européia do Livro, 1964).

8. Fernando Henrique Cardoso and Enzo Faletto, *Dependency and Development in Latin America* (Berkeley: University of California, 1979).

9. Gunnar Myrdal, *The Political Element in the Development of Economic Theory* (New Brunswick: Transaction Publishers, 1990), with a new introduction by Paul Streeten.

10. Richard English and Joseph Morrison Skelley, eds., *Ideas Matter: Essays in Honour of Conor Cruise O'Brien* (Lanham, Md.: University Press of America, 2000).

11. Conor Cruise O'Brien, *The United Nations: Sacred Drama* (London: Hutchinson, 1968).

Introduction to Part Two

1. Ngaire Woods, "Economic Ideas and International Relations: Beyond Rational Neglect," *International Studies Quarterly* 39 (1995): 164.

4. From 1945 through the 1950s

1. In 1945 there were sixty-three states in the world. Fifty met in San Francisco from April to June 1945, signing the founding documents on June 26th. Poland signed soon afterward, thus becoming a founding member. At the end of the nineteenth century, there were some fifty states in the world, but only twenty-six participated in the 1899 Hague Peace Conference. At the Second Hague Peace Conference in 1907, forty-four participated. Following World War I, some ten to twelve new states were created or old ones had their borders redefined. As the millennium dawned, 191 states were members of the United Nations, and the number is likely to grow.

2. John Maynard Keynes. This sentiment is echoed his own book, *The Economic Consequences of the Peace* (London: Macmillan, 1919), which was very unpopular with the establishment when it was first published.

3. See Craig Murphy, *International Organization and Industrial Change: Global Governance Since 1850* (Cambridge: Polity Press, 1994).

4. John Maynard Keynes had proposed a three-legged stool for postwar economic management. While two of them, the World Bank and the IMF, were agreed at Bretton Woods during the war, the International Trade Organization was not negotiated until 1948 in Havana at the UN Conference on Trade and Employment. Although sponsored by the United States, the Havana Charter was not ratified by the U.S. Senate, where protectionists dominated. While negotiations were under way for the ITO, however, twenty-three countries met in Geneva in 1947 and agreed to the General Agreement on Tariffs and Trade (GATT), which remained in force until 1995, when the World Trade Organization (WTO) was established.

5. Quoted in William Korey, *NGOs and the Universal Declaration of Human Rights: "A Curious Grapevine"* (New York: St. Martin's Press, 1998), 9.

6. See Roger Normand and Sarah Zaidi, *A Critical History of Human Rights at the United Nations* (Bloomington: Indiana University Press, forthcoming). This is a volume in the United Nations Intellectual History Project series.

7. E. M. Miller [Oscar Schachter], "Legal Aspects of the United Nations Action in the Congo," *American Journal of International Law* 55, no. 1 (1961).

8. Thomas Risse and Stephen C. Ropp, "International Human Rights Norms and Domestic Change: Conclusions," in *The Power of Human Rights: International Norms and Domestic Change,* edited by Thomas Risse, Stephen C. Ropp, and Kathryn Sikkink (Cambridge: Cambridge University Press, 1999), 273.

9. See, for example, Danish Institute of International Affairs, *Humanitarian Intervention: Legal and Political Aspects* (Copenhagen: Danish Institute of International Affairs, 1999); Jonathan Moore, ed., *Hard Choices: Moral Dilemmas in Humanitarian Intervention* (Lanham, Md.: Rowman & Littlefield, 1998); James Mayall, ed., *The New Interventionism* (Cambridge: Cambridge University Press, 1996); Oliver Ramsbotham and Tom Woodhouse, *Humanitarian Intervention in Contemporary Conflict* (Cambridge: Polity Press, 1996); John Harriss, ed., *The Politics of Humanitarian Intervention* (London: Pinter, 1995); Stanley Hoffmann, *The Ethics and Politics of Humanitarian Intervention* (South Bend, Ind.: University of Notre Dame Press, 1996); and Thomas G. Weiss, *Military-Civilian Interactions: Humanitarian Crises and the Responsibility to Protect,* 2nd ed. (Lanham, Md.: Rowman & Littlefield, 2004).

10. For a snapshot of the changes, see UNDP, *Human Development Report 2000* (New York: Oxford University Press, 2000). For examinations of the historical developments, see: Jack Donnelly, *International Human Rights* (Boulder: Westview, 1993); Tim Dunne and Nicholas J. Wheeler, eds., *Human Rights in Global Politics* (Cambridge: Cambridge University Press, 1999); and David P. Forsythe, *The Internationalization of Human Rights* (Lexington, Mass.: D. C. Heath, 1991).

11. For an overview of these developments, see Thomas G. Weiss, David P. Forsythe, and Roger A. Coate, *The United Nations and Changing World Politics,* 2nd ed. (Boulder: Westview, 2004), Chapters 5–7.

12. *World Conference on Human Rights: The Vienna Declaration and Programme of Action* (New York: UN, 1993).

13. The UN was snubbed at this occasion. The UN Economic Commission for Europe was of course perfectly qualified to undertake the coordination of the Marshall Plan, and this was in fact proposed by Walt Rostow, a prominent American economist. But the United States rejected this proposal. See Yves Berthelot and Paul Reyment, "The ECE: A Bridge between East and West," in *Unity and Diversity in Development Ideas: Perspectives from the UN Regional Commissions,* edited by Yves Berthelot (Bloomington: Indiana University Press, 2004), 59–62. This is a volume in the United Nations Intellectual History Project series.

14. Dean Acheson, *Present at the Creation: My Years in the State Department* (New York: Norton, 1969), 698.

15. See David A. Kay, *The New Nations in the United Nations 1960–1967* (New York: Columbia University Press, 1970).

16. "A Conversation with Oscar Schachter," *American Society of International Law Proceedings* 91 (1997): 344. For a substantive and personal obituary, see Lori Fisler Damrosch, "Oscar Schachter (1915–2003)," *American Journal of International Law* 98 (2004): 35–41.

17. See Robert Aldrich and John Connell, *The Last Colonies* (Cambridge: Cambridge University Press, 1998).

18. Julius Nyerere, "Foreword," in Chakravarti Raghavan, *Recolonization: GATT, the Uruguay Round & the Third World* (London: Zed Books, 1990), 19.

19. Richard Wright, *The Color Curtain* (Jackson, Miss.: Banner Books, 1956), 13–14.

20. Mark T. Berger, "After the Third World? History, Destiny and the Fate of Third Worldism," *Third World Quarterly* 25, no. 1 (2004), 13. Berger was the guest editor of this special issue, which reviewed the problems and prospects of the so-called Third World. Interested readers may also wish to consult other recent works: R. Malley, *The Call from Algeria: Third Worldism, Revolution and the Turn to Islam* (Berkeley: University of California Press, 1996); and G. Lundeestad, *East, West, North, South: Major Developments in International Politics Since 1945* (New York: Oxford University Press, 1999). Older references include R. Abdulgani, *Bandung Spirit: Moving on the Tide of History* (Djakarta: Prapantja, 1964); C. P. Romulo, *The Meaning of Bandung* (Chapel Hill: University of North Carolina Press, 1956); and P. Worsley, *The Third World* (London: Weidenfeld and Nicolson, 1964).

21. Literally, the term means five principles of foreign policy (mutual respect for territorial integrity and sovereignty, mutual nonaggression, mutual noninterference in internal affairs, equality and mutual benefit, and peaceful coexistence). They were enunciated by Jawaharlal Nehru in April 1954 in a trade agreement with China and adopted as a keystone of relations among nations at the Asian-African Conference (the Bandung conference).

22. This is made clear in Berthelot, ed., *Unity and Diversity in Development*.

5. The 1960s

1. Adam Smith, *An Inquiry into the Nature and Causes of the Wealth of Nations* (Oxford: Clarendon Press, 1969). The original was published in 1776.

2. These topics have provided a springboard for analysis in another book from the United Nations Intellectual History Project series: Richard Jolly, Louis Emmerij, Dharam Ghai, and Frédéric Lapeyre, *UN Contributions to Development Theory and Practice* (Bloomington: Indiana University Press, 2004).

3. For a discussion, see Hall, ed., *The Political Power of Economic Ideas*.

4. Paul Samuelson, *Economics* (New York: McGraw-Hill, 1948). This point was made by Devesh Kapur, John P. Lewis, and Richard Webb, *The World Bank: Its First Half Century*, vol. 1, *History* (Washington, D.C.: Brookings Institution, 1997), 67.

5. United Nations, *Measures for Full Employment* (New York: UN, 1949); *Measures for the Economic Development of Under-Developed Countries* (New York: UN, 1951); and *Measures for International Economic Stability* (New York: UN, 1951). See Emmerij, Jolly, and *Ahead of the Curve?* 26–42.

6. For a discussion, see Peter Willets, *The Non-Aligned Movement: The Origins of the Third World Alliance* (London: Pinter, 1978); J. W. Burton, *Non-Alignment* (London: Deutsch, 1966); C. V. D. Crabb, *The Elephants & the Grass: A Study of Non-Alignment*

(New York: Praeger, 1965); L. W. Martin, ed., *Neutralism & Nonalignment: The New States in World Affairs* (New York: Praeger, 1962).

7. Robert W. Cox and Harold K. Jacobson, *The Anatomy of Influence: Decision Making in International Organization* (New Haven: Yale University Press, 1973), 425.

8. United Nations, *The United Nations Development Decade* (New York, UN, 1962), vi.

9. Ibid., 6.

10. Ibid., 7. In fact, by 1965, it seemed that growth in the developing countries had been more like 4.5 percent per annum from 1955 to 1960 but had slowed to 4 percent from 1960 to 1963. See United Nations, *The United Nations Development Decade at Mid-Point* (New York: UN, 1965), 6. For a discussion of the entire period, see Colin Legum, ed., *The First U.N. Development Decade and Its Lessons for the 1970's* (New York: Praeger, 1970).

11. UN, *The United Nations Development Decade* (New York: United Nations, 1962), 11.

12. Wolfgang F. Stolper, *Planning without Facts* (Cambridge: Harvard University Press, 1966).

13. For a recent official history of the institution's contributions to UN development ideas, see Shigehisa Kasahara and Charles Gore, eds., *Beyond Conventional Wisdom in Development Policy: An Intellectual History of UNCTAD 1964–2004* (Geneva: United Nations, 2004).

14. Georges Balandier and Alfred Sauvy, *Le "Tiers-Monde," Sous Développement et Développement* (Paris: Presse Universitaire de France, 1961).

15. For details, see http://www.g77.org/

16. See Joseph S. Nye, "UNCTAD: Poor Nations' Pressure Group," in *The Anatomy of Influence—Decision Making in International Organization*, edited by Robert W. Cox and Harold K. Jacobson (New Haven: Yale University Press, 1973), 334–370.

17. For details, see especially Toye and Toye, *The UN and Global Political Economy*. See also Michael Zammit Cutajar, ed., *UNCTAD and the South-North Dialogue: The First Twenty Years* (London: Pergamon, 1985); Robert L. Rothstein, *Global Bargaining: UNCTAD and the Quest for a New International Economic Order* (Princeton: Princeton University Press, 1979); Branislov Gosovic, *UNCTAD: Compromise and Conflict* (Leiden: Sijthoff, 1972); Diego Cordovez, *UNCTAD and Development Diplomacy: From Conference to Strategy* (London: Journal of World Trade Law, 1970); Kamal Hagras, *United Nations Conference on Trade and Development: A Case Study in UN Diplomacy* (New York: Praeger, 1965); and Thomas G. Weiss, *Multilateral Development Diplomacy in UNCTAD: The Lessons of Group Negotiations, 1964–84* (London: Macmillan, 1986).

18. Dag Hammarskjöld, "The International Civil Servant in Law and in Fact," lecture delivered to congregation at Oxford University, May 30, 1961, reprinted by permission of Clarendon Press, Oxford, 351. Available at http://www.un.org/depts/dhl/dag/docs/internationalcivilservant.pdf.

19. See Sidney Dell, "Economics in the United Nations," in *Economists in International Agencies,* edited by A. W. Coats (New York: Praeger, 1986), 44–45.

20. Kapur, Lewis, and Webb, *The World Bank: Its First Half Century,* 1: 154.

21. See Jolly, Emmerij, Ghai, and Lapeyre, *UN Contributions to Development Theory and Practice,* chapter 3; and Olav Stokke, *International Development Assistance*

(Bloomington: Indiana University Press, forthcoming). Stokke's volume is part of the United Nations Intellectual History Project series.

22. *A Capacity Study of the United Nations Development System* (Geneva: United Nations, 1969) volume I, document DP/5.

23. Kofi A. Annan, "Democracy as an International Issue," *Global Governance* 8, no. 2 (April–June 2002): 135–142.

24. Interested readers might consult Rosemary Foot, S. Neil MacFarlane, and Michael Mastanduno, eds., *US Hegemony and International Organizations* (Oxford: Oxford University Press, 2003); Michael Byers and Georg Nolte, eds., *United States Hegemony and the Foundations of International Law* (Cambridge: Cambridge University Press, 2003); and David M. Malone and Yuen Foong Khong, eds., *Multilateralism & U.S. Foreign Policy: International Perspectives* (Boulder: Lynne Rienner, 2003).

25. See Stephen C. Schlesinger, *Act of Creation: The Founding of the United Nations* (Boulder: Westview, 2003).

6. The 1970s

1. See United Nations, *The World Conferences: Developing Priorities for the 21st Century* (New York: United Nations, 1997), 35–36; Michael Schechter, ed., *United Nations-Sponsored World Conferences: Focus on Impact and Follow-Up* (Tokyo: UN University Press, 2001); and Jacques Fomerand, "UN Conferences: Media Events or Genuine Diplomacy?" *Global Governance* 2, no. 3 (September–December 1996): 361–375.

2. See Nico Schrijver, *The United Nations and Global Resource Management* (Bloomington: Indiana University Press, forthcoming). This book is part of the United Nations Intellectual History Project series.

3. Rachel Carson, *Silent Spring* (Boston: Houghton Mifflin, 1962); and Donella H. Meadows, Dennis L. Meadows, Jorgen Randers, and William W. Behrens III, *The Limits to Growth: A Global Collapse or a Sustainable Future?* (London: Earthscan, 1972).

4. Maurice Strong, *Where on Earth Are We Going?* (Toronto: Knopf, 2000), 115 and 121.

5. Quoted by Maurice Strong, "Policy Lessons Learned in a Thirty Years' Perspective," in Ministry of the Environment, *Stockholm Thirty Years On* (Stockholm: Ministry of the Environment, 2003), 16.

6. See *Development and Environment: Report and Working Papers of a Panel of Experts Convened by the Secretary-General of the UN Conference on Human Environment* (New York: United Nations, 1972).

7. René Dubos and Barbara Ward, *Only One Earth: The Care and Maintenance of a Small Planet* (New York: W.W. Norton & Company, 1972).

8. Strong, *Where on Earth Are We Going?* 126 and 129.

9. See Robert E. Riggs and Jack C. Plano, *The United Nations: International Organization and World Politics* (Belmont, Calif.: Wadsworth, 1994), 219–222.

10. World Commission on Environment and Development, *Our Common Future* (Oxford: Oxford University Press, 1987).

11. Federico Reyes Heroles, "Victor Urquidi: No Concessions," *Reforma*, August 10, 2004.

12. Mahfuzur Rahman, *World Economic Issues at the United Nations: Half a Century of Debate* (Dordrecht: Kluwer, 2002), 145.

13. See General Assembly Resolution 3281 (XXIX).

14. Johan Kaufmann, *United Nations Decision Making* (Alphen aan den Rijn: Sijthoff and Noordhoff, 1980).

15. Raymond Vernon, *Sovereignty at Bay* (Cambridge: Harvard University Press, 1977).

16. For a discussion of the early developments, see Thomas G. Weiss and Anthony Jennings, *More for the Least? Prospects for Poorest Countries in the Eighties* (Lexington, Massachusetts: D. C. Heath, 1983). The United Nations has brought out periodic reports on the situations of these countries. For the latest example, see UNCTAD, *The Least Developed Countries Report 2002* (New York and Geneva: UNCTAD, June 2002).

17. See Emmerij, Jolly, and Weiss, *Ahead of the Curve?* Chapter 3.

18. ILO, *Employment, Incomes, and Equity: A Strategy for Increasing Productive Employment in Kenya* (Geneva: ILO, 1972).

19. Glen Sheehan and Mike Hopkins, *Basic Needs Performance: An Analysis of Some International Data* (Geneva: ILO, 1979).

20. ILO, *Employment, Growth and Basic Needs: A One World Problem* (Geneva: ILO, 1976), also published commercially as *Employment, Growth and Basic Needs: A One World Problem—the International "Basic Needs Strategy" against Chronic Poverty* (New York: Praeger Publishers, 1977).

21. Arthur C. Pigou, *The Economics of Welfare* (London: Macmillan, 1920).

22. Amartya Sen, *Poverty and Famines: An Essay on Entitlement and Deprivation* (Oxford: Clarendon Press, 1981); and Amartya Sen, *Commodities and Capabilities: Lectures in Economic Theory Policy,* vol. 7 (New York and Amsterdam: Elsevier Science and Technology Publishers, 1985).

23. Abraham H. Maslow, "A Theory of Human Motivation," *Psychological Review* 50, no. 3 (March 1942): 370–396.

24. Dag Hammarskjöld Foundation, *What Now? Another Development* (Uppsala: Dag Hammarskjöld Foundation, 1975).

25. Amilcar O. Herrera, *Catastrophe o Nueva Sociedad: Modelo Mundial Latino-americano* (Buenos Aires, 1976).

26. ILO, *Employment, Growth and Basic Needs.* See also Dharam Ghai, *The Basic-Needs Approach to Development: Some Issues Regarding Concepts and Methodology* (Geneva: ILO, 1977).

27. Barbara Ward, *The Widening Gap* (Columbia University Press, 1971), 12.

28. Devaki Jain, *Women Enrich the United Nations and Development* (Bloomington: Indiana University Press, forthcoming). This book is part of the United Nations Intellectual History Project series.

29. *Platform for Action and the Beijing Declaration: Fourth World Conference on Women* (New York: UN, 1995).

30. UN Development Programme, *Human Development Report 1995* (New York: Oxford University Press, 1995), 1–10.

31. See Martha Alter Chen, "Gendering World Conferences: The International Women's Movement and the UN," *Third World Quarterly* 16, no. 3 (1995): 477–494; and Jane Connors, "NGOs and the Human Rights of Women at the UN," in *"The Conscience of the World": The Influence of Non-Governmental Organizations in the UN System,* edited by Peter Willetts (Washington, D.C.: Brookings Institution Press, 1996), 147–180.

7. The 1980s

1. Albert Hirschman, "The Rise and Decline of Development Economics," in Hirschman, *Essays in Trespassing: Economics to Politics and Beyond* (New York: Cambridge University Press, 1981), 384.

2. David C. Colander, ed., *Neoclassical Political Economy: The Analysis of Rent-Seeking and DUP Activities* (Cambridge: Ballinger, 1984); T. N. Srinivasan, "Neoclassical Political Economy, the State, and Economic Development," *Asian Development Review* 3, no. 2 (1985): 40–45; James M. Buchanan, *Liberty, Market, and State: Political Economy in the 1980s* (New York: New York University Press, 1985); Charles K. Rowley, Robert D. Tollison, and Gordon Tullock, eds., *The Political Economy of Rent-Seeking* (Boston: Kluwer Academic Publishers, 1988); James Buchanan, Robert Tollison, and Gordon Tullock, eds., *Toward a Theory of Rent-Seeking Society* (College Station: Texas A&M University Press, 1980); Deepak Lal, "The Political Economy of Economic Liberalization," *World Bank Economic Review* 1, no.1 (1987): 273–285; Anne Krueger, "Government Failures in Development," *Journal of Economic Perspectives* 4, no. 3 (1990): 9–24.

3. South Commission, *The Challenge to the South* (Oxford: Oxford University Press, 1990).

4. ONU/DASEI, database, 1986.

5. See, for example, John Williamson, ed., *IMF Conditionality* (Cambridge: MIT Press, 1983).

6. These missions stopped in 1986, after Idris Jazairy came aboard as the new president of IFAD.

7. "Too Much Consensus," *Foreign Policy* 144 (September/October 2004): 16.

8. See John Williamson, ed., *Latin America Adjustment: How Much Has Happened?* (Washington, D.C.: Institute for International Economics, 1990); and John Williamson, "The Washington Consensus Revisited," in *Economic and Social Development into the XXI Century,* edited by Louis Emmerij (Baltimore: Johns Hopkins University Press, 1997), 48–61.

9. Moises Naim, "Fads and Fashion in Economic Reforms: Washington Consensus or Washington Confusion?" *Third World Quarterly,* 21, no. 3 (June 2000): 505.

10. For a presentation of SAPs see, for example, Vittorio Corbo and Stanley Fischer, "Structural Adjustment, Stabilization and Policy Reform: Domestic and International Finance," in *Handbook of Development Economics,* vol. 3, edited by Jere Behrman and T. N. Srinivasan (Amsterdam: North Holland, 1995), 2845–2923; Paul Streeten, "Structural

Adjustment: A Survey of the Issues and Options," *World Development* 15, no. 2 (1987): 1469–1482.

11. Giovanni A. Cornia, Richard Jolly, and Frances Stewart, eds., *Adjustment with a Human Face* (Oxford: Clarendon Press, 1987).

12. Francis Fukuyama, *The End of History and the Last Man* (New York: The Free Press, 1992).

13. 'See Emmerij, Jolly, and Weiss, *Ahead of the Curve?* Chapter 6.

14. Yves Berthelot and Paul Rayment, "The ECE: A Bridge between East and West," in Berthelot, ed., *Unity and Diversity in Development Ideas,* 118.

8. The 1990s and the Dawn of the Twenty-First Century

1. For an overview, see UNDP, *Human Development Report 2003* (New York: Oxford University Press, 2003).

2. See Sakiko Fukuda-Parr, "Millennium Development Goals: Why They Matter," *Global Governance* 11, no. 4 (October–December 2004), forthcoming.

3. Figures here are based on World Bank, *Global Poverty Monitoring,* available at www.worldbank.org/research/povmonitor/index.htm (accessed July 2004).

4. UNDP, *Human Development Report 1999* (New York: Oxford University Press, 1999), 3.

5. See, Anthony Giddens, *Runaway World: How Globalization Is Reshaping Our Lives* (New York: Routledge, 2000); and David Held, Anthony McGrew, David Goldblatt, and Jonathan Perraton, *Global Transformations: Politics, Economics, and Culture* (Stanford: Stanford University Press, 1999).

6. For a discussion, see Thomas G. Weiss, David P. Forsythe, and Roger A. Coate, *The United Nations and Changing World Politics,* 4th ed. (Boulder: Westview, 2004), Chapter 10.

7. Emma Rothschild, "Globalization and the Return of History," *Foreign Policy* 115 (Summer 1999): 107.

8. UN document A/RES/55/2, September 18, 2000. For a discussion of these issues, see Roger A. Coate and Gail Karlsson, "Mobilizing Support for the Millennium Development Goals," in United Nations Association of the United States of America, *A Global Agenda: Issues before the 58th General Assembly* (New York: Rowman & Littlefield, 2003), Chapter 5.

9. See James Rosenau, *Turbulence in World Politics* (Princeton: Princeton University Press, 1990).

10. Fernando Enrique Cardoso and Enzo Faletto, *Dependency and Development in Latin America* (Berkeley: University of California Press, 1979).

11. Amartya Sen, "Assessing Human Development," in UNDP, *Human Development Report 1999* (New York: Oxford University Press, 1999), 23.

12. Amartya Sen, *Commodities and Capabilities* (Amsterdam: North-Holland, 1985).

13. Paul Streeten, "Human Development: Means and Ends," *American Economic Review* 84, no.2 (1994): 236.

14. Eveline Herfkens, "Foreword," in Juan Somavía, *People's Security: Globalizing Social Progress* (Geneva: ILO, 1999), viii.

15. Commission on Human Security, *Human Security Now* (New York: Commission on Human Security, 2003).

16. Richard H. Ullman, "Redefining Security," reprinted in *Global Dangers: Changing Dimension of International Security,* edited by Sean M. Lynn-Jones and Steven E. Miller (Cambridge: MIT Press, 1995), 15–39, quote on p. 39.

17. S. Neil MacFarlane and Yuen Foong Khong, *Human Security and the UN: A Critical History* (Bloomington: Indiana University Press, forthcoming 2005), Chapter 8, "Conclusions." This is a book in the United Nations Intellectual History Project series.

18. "What Is 'Human Security'?" special section of *Security Dialogue* 35, no. 3 (September 2004): 347–371, quotes on pp. 347 and 351.

19. *Copenhagen Declaration and Programme of Action* (New York: UN, 1995).

20. Boutros Boutros-Ghali, *An Agenda for Peace* (New York: UN, 1992).

21. Lloyd Axworthy, "Human Security and Global Governance," *Global Governance* 7, no. 1 (January–March 2001): 23.

22. Kofi A. Annan, *The Question of Intervention—Statements by the Secretary-General* (New York: UN, 1999); and *"We the Peoples": The United Nations in the 21st Century* (New York: UN, 2000). For a discussion of the controversy surrounding the speech in September 1999, see Thomas G. Weiss, "The Politics of Humanitarian Ideas," *Security Dialogue* 31, no. 1 (March 2000): 11–23.

23. For an overview, see Mohammed Ayoob, "Humanitarian Intervention and International Society," *Global Governance* 7, no. 3 (July–September 2001): 225–230; and Robert Jackson, *The Global Covenant: Human Conduct in a World of States* (Oxford: Oxford University Press, 2000).

24. International Commission on Intervention and State Sovereignty, *The Responsibility to Protect: Report* (Ottawa: ICISS, 2001). See also *The Responsibility To Protect: Research, Bibliography, and Background* (Ottawa: ICISS, 2001), primary authors Thomas G. Weiss and Don Hubert.

25. Francis M. Deng, *Protecting the Dispossessed: A Challenge for the International Community* (Washington, D.C.: Brookings, 1993); Francis M. Deng, Sadikiel Kimaro, Terrence Lyons, Donald Rothchild, and I. William Zartman, *Sovereignty as Responsibility* (Washington, D.C.: Brookings Institution Press, 1995); and Francis M. Deng, "Frontiers of Sovereignty," *Leiden Journal of International Law* 8, no. 2 (1995): 249–286.

26. Anthony Lewis, "The Challenge of Global Justice Now," *Dædalus* 132, no. 1 (2003): 8.

27. See Ruth B. Russell, *A History of the United Nations Charter* (Washington, D.C.: Brookings Institution, 1958); Leland M. Goodrich and Edvard Hambro, *Charter of the United Nations* (Boston: World Peace Foundation, 1946); and Bruno Simma, ed., *The Charter of the United Nations: A Commentary* (Oxford: Oxford University Press, 1995).

28. See, for example, Edward C. Luck, *Mixed Messages: American Politics and International Organization* (Washington, D.C.: Brookings Institution, 1999); and John Gerard Ruggie, *Winning the Peace: America and World Order in the New Era* (New York: Columbia University Press, 1996).

29. See David Mitrany, *A Working Peace System* (London: National Peace Council, 1946). For more theoretical follow-ups, see Ernst B. Haas, *Beyond the Nation-State* (Stanford: Stanford University Press, 1964); and J. S. Nye, *Peace in Parts: Integration and Conflict in Regional Organization* (Boston: Little, Brown & Co., 1971).

30. See Stephen C. Schlesinger, *Act of Creation: The Founding of the United Nations* (New York: Westview Press, 2003).

31. For an overview, see Hall, ed., *The Political Power of Economic Ideas.*

32. Margaret P. Karns and Karen A. Mingst, *International Organizations: The Politics and Processes of Global Governance* (Boulder: Lynne Rienner, 2004), 97. For a selection, see Rorden Wilkinson and Steve Hughes, eds., *Global Governance: Critical Perspectives* (London: Routledge, 2002); Esref Aksu and Joseph A. Camilleri, eds., *Democratizing Global Governance* (New York: Palgrave, 2002); Robert O'Brien, Ann Marie Goetz, Jan Aaart Scholte, and Marc Williams, *Contesting Global Governance: Multilateral Economic Institutions and Global Social Movements* (Cambridge: Cambridge University Press, 2000); Paul Kennedy, Dirk Messner, and Franz Nuscheler, eds., *Global Trends and Global Governance* (London: Pluto, 2002); and Andrew F. Cooper, John English, and Ramesh Thakur, eds., *Enhancing Global Governance: Towards a New Diplomacy* (Tokyo: UN University Press, 2002). The interested reader might also consult the quarterly journal *Global Governance: A Review of Multilateralism and International Organizations,* which began publishing in 1995.

33. See Ernst-Otto Czempiel, "Governance and Democratization," in *Governance without Government: Order and Change in World Politics,* edited by James N. Rosenau and Ernst-Otto Czempiel (Cambridge: Cambridge University Press, 1992), 250–271. Also see Leon Gordenker and Thomas G. Weiss, "Pluralizing Global Governance: Analytical Approaches and Dimensions," in *NGOs, the UN, and Global Governance,* edited by Leon Gordenker and Thomas G. Weiss (London: Lynne Rienner, 1996), 17–47.

34. Commission on Global Governance, *Our Global Neighbourhood* (Oxford: Oxford University Press, 1995), 2.

35. Ramesh Thakur and Thomas G. Weiss, *The UN and Global Governance: A History of an Idea and Its Prospects* (Bloomington: Indiana University Press, forthcoming). This is a book in the United Nations Intellectual History Project series.

36. James N. Rosenau, "Governance, Order and Change in World Politics," in Rosenau and Czempiel, eds. *Governance without Government: Order and Change in World Politics,* 3.

37. See Harold K. Jacobson, "The Changing United Nations," in *Foreign Policy in the Sixties: The Issues and the Instruments,* edited by Roger Hilsman and Robert C. Good (Baltimore: Johns Hopkins University Press, 1965), 67–89.

38. The Universal Declaration of Human Rights, the ILO Declaration on Core Rights at Work, and the Rio Principles on Environment and Development.

39. The North-South Roundtable discussed the proposal in Bretton Woods in 1993. See Mahbub ul Haq, Richard Jolly, Paul Streeten, and Khadija Haq, eds., *The UN and the Bretton Woods Institutions: New Challenges for the 21st Century* (Basingstoke: Macmillan, 1995). See also a fuller paper by Frances Stewart and Sam Daws, *An Economic and Social Security Council at the United Nations,* Queen Elizabeth House Working Paper Series, No. 68, March 2001.

9. A Revolutionary Idea

1. This idea was first spelled out by the League of Nations in 1921 and is known as the Noblemaire principle, named after the chairman of the committee convened to codify the international character of secretariats. This principle was included in the UN Charter in Articles 100–101.

2. Egon Ranshofen-Wertheimer, *The International Secretariat: A Great Experiment in International Administration* (Washington, D.C.: Carnegie Endowment for International Peace, 1945).

3. Hammarskjöld, "The International Civil Servant in Law and in Fact," quotes on pp. 329 and 349.

4. James Barros, *Betrayal from Within* (New Haven: Yale University Press, 1969).

5. Erskine Childers with Brian Urquhart, *Renewing the United Nations System* (Uppsala: Dag Hammarskjöld Foundation, 1994), 26–29.

6. Professional positions in the UN are, in ascending order: five entry and middle management levels, P-1 to P-5; two director levels, D-1 and D-2; assistant secretary-general; under-secretary-general; deputy-secretary-general; secretary-general.

7. Hilkka Pietilä, *Engendering the Global Agenda: The Story of Women and the United Nations* (Geneva: UN Non-Governmental Liaison Service, 2002), v. See also Hilkka Pietilä and Jeanne Vickers, *Making Women Matter: The Role of the United Nations*, 3rd ed. (London: Zed, 1996).

8. Ernst B. Haas, *When Knowledge Is Power: Three Models of Change in International Organization* (Berkeley: University of California Press, 1990).

9. This is a reference to the mythical location in Minnesota of Garrison Keillor's stories, where "all the women are strong, all the men are good-looking, and all the children are above average."

10. Boutros Boutros-Ghali, *Unvanquished: A U.S.-U.N. Saga* (New York: Random House, 1999). See also a short volume that emerged from the project's interview, *Boutros Boutros-Ghali: Entretiens avec Yves Berthelot* (Paris: Editions du Rocher, 2002).

11. Kofi Annan, *Renewing the United Nations: A Programme for Reform* (New York: United Nations, 1997).

12. Kofi Annan, "The Quiet Revolution," *Global Governance* 4, no. 2 (April–June 1998): 123–138.

13. Samantha Power, "Business as Usual at the U.N.," *Foreign Policy* 144 (September/October 2004): 38–39.

14. *A More Secure World: Our Shared Responsibility. Report of the High-level Panel on Threats, Challenges and Change*, GA document A/59/565, 29 November 2004.

15. Gil Loescher, "Foreword," in *The United Nations and Global Security*, edited by Richard M. Price and Mark W. Zacher (New York: Palgrave, 2004), vi.

10. The Power of Ideas and People Inside the UN

1. Brian Urquhart, *Hammarskjöld* (New York: Harper Collins, 1972).

2. Trygve Lie, *In the Cause of Peace: Seven Years with the United Nations* (New York: Macmillan, 1954); and U Thant, *Portfolio for Peace: Excerpts from the Writings and*

Speeches of U Thant, Secretary-General of the United Nations, on Major World Issues 1961–1968 (New York: United Nations, 1968).

3. Seymour Maxwell Finger, *Bending with the Winds: Kurt Waldheim and the United Nations* (New York: Praeger, 1990).

4. Kurt Waldheim, *In the Eye of the Storm: A Memoir* (Bethesda, Md.: Adler & Adler, 1986).

5. Javier Pérez de Cuéllar, *Pilgrimage for Peace: A Secretary-General's Memoirs* (New York: St. Martin's, 1997).

6. See Harold K. Jacobson, *Networks of Interdependence: International Organizations and the Global Political System,* 2nd ed. (New York: Knopf, 1984). See also Christer Jönsson, "Interorganization Theory and International Organization," *International Studies Quarterly* 30, no. 1 (1986): 39–57.

7. Erskine Childers with Brian Urquhart, *Renewing the United Nations System* (Uppsala: Dag Hammarskjöld Foundation, 1994), 32.

8. *A Capacity Study of the United Nations Development System* (Geneva: United Nations, 1969) volume I, document DP/5, iii.

9. See, for example, Arthur Lall, *Multilateral Negotiation and Mediation: Instruments and Methods* (New York: Pergamon, 1985); and Thomas G. Weiss, *Multilateral Development Diplomacy in UNCTAD* (London: Macmillan, 1986).

10. Donald J. Puchala and Roger A. Coate, *The Challenge of Relevance: The United Nations in a Changing World Environment* (Hanover, N.H.: Academic Council on the UN System, 1989), 53.

11. See, for example, John G. Hadwen and Johan Kaufmann, *How United Nations Decisions Are Made,* foreword by Paul G. Hoffman (Leyden: A. W. Sythoff, 1960); Johan Kaufmann, *Conference Diplomacy: An Introductory Analysis* (New York: Oceana Publications, 1968); Johan Kaufmann, *United Nations Decision Making* (Netherlands: Alphen aan den Rijn, 1980); Johan Kaufmann, ed., *Effective Negotiation: Case Studies in Conference Diplomacy* (Dordrecht: Nijhoff, 1989); and Johan Kaufmann, *The Diplomacy of International Relation: Selected Writings* (The Hague: Kluwer Law International, 1998).

12. Nico Schrijver, "Innemende diplomat" [Endearing Diplomat], *NRC-Handelsblad,* 21 December 1999. Translation by Nico Schrijver.

11. Blending Outside Intellectual Energies

1. See Emanuel Adler and Peter M. Haas, "Epistemic Communities, World Order, and the Creation of a Reflective Research Program," *International Organization* 46, no. 1 (Winter 1992): 367–390. See also Peter M. Haas and Ernst B. Haas, "Learning to Learn: Improving International Governance," *Global Governance* 1, no. 3 (September–December 1995): 255–284.

2. See, for example, Leon Gordenker, Roger A. Coate, Christer Jönsson, and Peter Söderholm, *International Cooperation in Response to AIDS* (London: Pinter, 1995); and Peter Söderholm, *Global Governance of AIDS: Partnership with Civil Society* (Lund, Sweden: Lund University Press, 1997).

3. See, for example, Peter M. Haas, Robert O. Keohane, and Marc A. Levy, eds., *Institutions for the Earth: Sources of Effective International Environmental Protection* (Cambridge, Mass.: MIT Press, 1992); Peter M. Haas, *Saving the Mediterranean* (New York: Columbia University Press, 1990); Elinor Ostrom, *Governing the Commons: The Evolution of Institutions for Collective Action* (Cambridge: Cambridge University Press, 1990); Oran R. Young, *International Cooperation: Building Regimes for Natural Resources and the Environment* (Ithaca: Cornell University Press, 1989); and Branislav Gosovic, *The Quest for World Environmental Cooperation* (London: Routledge, 1992).

4. Peter A. Hall, "Introduction," in Hall, ed., *The Political Power of Economic Ideas*, 26. See also Peter Hall, "Policy Paradigms, Social Learning, and the State" *Comparative Politics*, 25 (April 1993): 275–296.

5. Emmerij, Jolly, and Weiss, *Ahead of the Curve?* 26–42.

6. Charles Parltrow Sale, *The Specialist* (St. Louis: Specialist Publishing Company, 1929).

7. John Gerard Ruggie, "International Regimes, Transactions, and Change: Embedded Liberalism in the Post-War Economic Order," *International Organization* 36, no. 2 (Spring 1982), 379–415.

8. Kenneth Waltz, *Theory of International Politics* (Reading, Mass.: Addison-Wesley, 1979).

9. Among other works, Doyle had in mind John Mearscheimer, "The False Promise of International Institutions," *International Security* 19 (Winter 1994–1995): 5–49.

10. W. W. Rostow, *The Stages of Economic Growth: A Non-Communist Manifesto* (Cambridge: Cambridge University Press, 1960).

11. For example, many observers point to *Report of the Panel on United Nations Peace Operations*, UN document A/55/305–S/2000/809, August 21, 2000; and *A More Secure World: Our Shared Responsibility. Report of the High-level Panel on Threats, Challenges and Change*, GA document A/59/565, 29 November 2004.

12. Commission on International Development, *Partners in Development* (New York: Praeger, 1969).

13. Independent Commission on International Development Issues, *North-South: A Programme for Survival* (London: Pan Books, 1980); and *Common Crisis North-South: Co-operation for World Recovery* (Cambridge, Mass.: MIT Press, 1983).

14. Independent Commission on Disarmament and Security Issues, *Common Security: A Blueprint for Survival* (New York: Simon & Schuster, 1982).

15. World Commission on Environment and Development, *Our Common Future* (Oxford: Oxford University Press, 1987).

16. Independent Commission on International Humanitarian Issues, *Winning the Human Race?* (London: Zed Books, 1988).

17. South Commission, *The Challenge to the South* (Oxford: Oxford University Press, 1990).

18. Commission on Global Governance, *Our Global Neighbourhood*.

19. Independent Commission on Intervention and State Sovereignty, *The Responsibility to Protect*.

20. Commission on Human Security, *Human Security Now.*

21. Meadows, Meadows, Randers, and Behrens, *The Limits To Growth.* This was revisited two decades later by D. H. Meadows, D. L. Meadows, and J. Randers, *Beyond the Limits: A Global Collapse or a Sustainable Future* (London: Earthscan, 1992).

22. Carnegie Commission on Preventing Deadly Conflict, *Preventing Deadly Conflict* (New York: Carnegie Corporation of New York, 1997).

23. World Commission on Culture and Development, *Our Creative Diversity* (Paris: UNESCO, 1995). This was a UNESCO commission and is more like the UN panels referred to earlier. See endnote 11 in this chapter.

24. *We the Peoples: Civil Society, the UN and Global Governance, Report of the panel of Eminent Persons on United Nations-Civil Society Relations,* document A/58/817, 11 June 2004.

25. See Steve Charnowitz, "Two Centuries of Participation: NGOs and International Governance," *Michigan Journal of International Law* 18, no. 2 (Winter 1997): 183–286.

26. See Union of International Associations, "International Organizations by Type (Table 1)," in *Yearbook of International Organizations,* 40th ed. (München: K. G. Saur, 2003), available at www.uia.org//uiastats/stbv196.htm.

27. Helmut Anheier, Marlies Glasius, and Mary Kaldor, "Introducing Global Civil Society," in *Global Civil Society 2001,* edited by Anheier, Glasius, and Kaldor (Oxford: Oxford University Press, 2001), 4.

28. Terje Tvedt, "Development NGOs—Actors in a New International Social System," draft paper, 3 November 1997, Centre for Development Studies, University of Bergen. See also Colette Chabbott, "Development INGOs," in *Constructing World Culture: International Non-Governmental Organizations Since 1875,* edited by John Boli and George M. Thomas (Stanford: Stanford University Press, 1999), 222–248.

29. Julie Fisher, *The Road from Rio: Sustainable Development and the Nongovern-mental Movement in the Third World* (Westport, Conn.: Praeger; 1993).

30. Robin Guthrie, *Civic, Civil, or Servile?* (Geneva: International Standing Conference on Philanthropy, 1994), 7.

31. "NGOs: Sins of the Secular Missionaries," *The Economist,* 29 January–4 February 2000, 25–27.

32. Anheier, Glasius, and Kaldor, "Introducing Global Civil Society," 17.

33. Ann M. Florini, ed., *The Third Force: The Rise in Transnational Civil Society* (Washington, D.C.: Carnegie Endowment, 2000), 3.

34. John G. Ruggie, "global_governance.net: The Global Compact as Learning Network," *Global Governance* 7, no. 4 (October–December 2001): 371–378. See also Tagi Sagafi-Nejad, in collaboration with John Dunning, *The UN and Transnationals, from Code to Compact* (Bloomington: Indiana University Press, forthcoming). This is a book in the United Nations Intellectual History Project series.

35. Sen, *Poverty and Famines.*

36. See United Nations, *The World Conferences: Developing Priorities for the 21st Century* (New York: United Nations, 1997); Michael Schechter, ed., *United Nations-Sponsored World Conferences: Focus on Impact and Follow-Up* (Tokyo: UN University

Press, 2001); and Jacques Fomerand, "UN Conferences: Media Events or Genuine Diplomacy?" *Global Governance* 2, no. 3 (September–December 1996): 361–375.

37. "Secretary-General Inaugurates UN Conference on Human Settlements (HABITAT II)," Press Release HAB/IST/3, June 3, 1996, available at http://www.un.org/Conferences/habitat/eng-pres/3/habist3.htm.

12. The Legacy and Future Intellectual Challenges

1. For a longer treatment of this literature and the Project's approach, see Thomas G. Weiss and Tatiana Carayannis, "The UN, Its Economic and Social Ideas, and Their Agents: Toward an Analytical Framework," *Global Social Policy* 1, no. 1 (April 2001): 25–48. See also Bøås and McNeill, *Global Institutions and Development: Framing the World?*

2. United Nations, *Beyond Conventional Wisdom in Development Policy: An Intellectual History of UNCTAD 1964–2004* (New York and Geneva: United Nations, 2004).

3. See Nicholas J. Wheeler and Tim Dunne, "Good International Citizenship: A Third Way for British Foreign Policy," *International Affairs* 74, no. 4 (1998): 847–870.

4. Lloyd Axworthy, "Human Security and Global Governance: Putting People First," *Global Governance* 7, no. 1 (2001): 19–23.

5. See Andrew Linklater, "The Good International Citizen and the Crisis in Kosovo," in *Kosovo and the Challenge of Humanitarian Intervention: Selective Imagination, Collective Action, and International Citizenship*, edited by Ramesh Thakur and Albrecht Schnabel (Tokyo: UN University Press, 2000), 493.

6. For an assessment of the impact of targets, see Jolly, Emmerij, Ghai, and Lapeyre, *UN Contributions to Development Theory and Practice*, 247–275.

7. UNCTAD, *Zimbabwe: Towards a New Order, an Economic and Social Survey* (Geneva: UNCTAD, 1980).

8. Luke Tamborinyoka, "Chidzero Dies," *The Daily News*, 9 August 2002.

9. Walter Marwizi, "Zanu PF Exploits Chidzero," *The Standard*, 4 August 2002.

10. The Arria Formula, named after UN ambassador Diego Arria of Venezuela, refers to the practice of holding informal meetings outside of the Security Council whereby council members are briefed by experts on a particular matter of concern to the council. For further information, see James Paul, "The Arria Formula," *Global Policy Forum*, revised October 2003, available at http://www.globalpolicy.org/security/mtgsetc/arria.htm.

11. See Emmerij, Jolly, and Weiss, *Ahead of the Curve?*, 205–214; and Jolly, Emmerij, Ghai, and Lapeyre, *UN Contributions to Development Thinking and Practice*, 299–316.

12. See, for example, Jane Boulden and Thomas G. Weiss, eds., *Terrorism and the UN: Before and After September 11* (Bloomington: Indiana University Press, 2004); and Thomas G. Weiss, Margaret E. Crahan, and John Goering, eds., *Wars on Terrorism and Iraq: Human Rights, Unilateralism, and U.S. Foreign Policy* (London: Routledge, 2004).

13. Theodore C. Sorensen, "JFK's Strategy of Peace," *World Policy Journal* XX, no. 3 (Fall 2003): 4.

14. See Jane Boulden and Thomas G. Weiss, "Tactical Multilateralism: Coaxing America Back to the UN," *Survival* 46, no. 3 (Autumn 2004): 103–114.

15. See Stewart Patrick and Shepard Forman, eds., *Multilateralism and U.S. Foreign Policy: Ambivalent Engagement* (Boulder: Lynne Rienner, 2002); and Stewart Patrick, "Beyond Coalitions of the Willing: Assessing U.S. Multilateralism," *Ethics & International Affairs* 17, no. 1 (2003): 37–54. A companion volume of non-U.S. reactions is David M. Malone and Yuen Foong Khong, eds., *Unilateralism and U.S. Foreign Policy: International Perspectives* (Boulder: Lynne Rienner, 2003).

16. Andrew Hurrell, "International Law and the Changing Constitution of International Society," in *The Role of Law in International Politics: Essays in International Relations and International Law,* edited by Michael Byers (Oxford: Oxford University Press, 2000), 344.

17. See Mats Berdal, "The UN Security Council: Ineffective but Indispensable," *Survival* 45, no. 2 (Summer 2003): 7–30; Shashi Tharoor, "Why America Still Needs the United Nations," *Foreign Affairs* 82, no. 5 (September/October 2003): 67–80; and Madeleine K. Albright, "Think Again: United Nations," *Foreign Policy,* no. 138 (September/October 2003): 16–24.

18. G. John Ikenberry, "Is American Multilateralism in Decline?" *Perspectives on Politics* 1, no. 3 (September 2003): 545.

19. See Boulden and Weiss, "Tactical Multilateralism."

20. K. J. Holsti, *Taming the Sovereigns: Institutional Change in International Politics* (Cambridge: Cambridge University Press, 2004), 316.

21. United Nations, "The Nobel Peace Prize 2001," *UN Chronicle* 38, no. 4 (December–February 2001–2002): 4.

Appendix 2

1. Grele, *Envelopes of Sound,* 135.

Index of Persons Interviewed

Index of Subjects

About the Authors

Thomas G. Weiss is presidential professor of political science at The CUNY Graduate Center and Director of the Ralph Bunche Institute for International Studies, where he is co-director of the United Nations Intellectual History Project and editor of *Global Governance.* In 2000–2001 he was the research director of the International Commission on Intervention and State Sovereignty. From 1990 to 1998, he was research professor at Brown University's Watson Institute for International Studies, held a number of administrative assignments (director of the Global Security Program, associate dean of the faculty, associate director), served as the executive director of the Academic Council on the UN System, and co-directed the Humanitarianism and War Project. He has also been executive director of the International Peace Academy, a member of the UN Secretariat, and a consultant to several public and private agencies. His most recent books are *Ahead of the Curve? UN Ideas and Global Challenges* (with Louis Emmerij and Richard Jolly; Indiana University Press, 2001); *The Responsibility To Protect: Research, Bibliography, and Background* (2001); *Military-Civilian Interactions: Humanitarian Crises and the Responsibility to Protect* (2nd ed., 2004); *The United Nations and Changing World Politics* (4th ed., 2004); *Terrorism and the UN: Before and After September 11* (co-edited with Jane Boulden; Indiana University Press, 2004); and *Wars on Terrorism and Iraq: Human Rights, Unilateralism, and U.S. Foreign Policy* (co-edited with Margaret E. Crahan and John Goering; 2004).

Tatiana Carayannis is research manager of the United Nations Intellectual History Project. Until 2000 she was an adjunct instructor in Political Science at CUNY and before that a researcher at the Carnegie Corporation of New York. Between 1989 and 1995 she served as program officer for Africa/Special Projects at the Institute for International Education. Some of her recent publications include "The Democratic Republic of Congo: 1996–2002," in *Dealing with Conflict in Africa: The Role of the United Nations and Regional Organizations,* ed. Jane Boulden (2003); "The Network Wars of the Congo: Towards a New Analytic Approach," *Journal of Asian and African Studies* (2003); "The Role of UN Economic and Social Ideas," in *Work in Progress: A Review of*

Research Activities of the United Nations University (2002); and "Whither United Nations Economic and Social Ideas? A Research Agenda," *Journal of Global Social Policy* (2001). She is currently completing a doctoral dissertation in political science on networks, multilateral institutions, and the Congo wars.

Louis Emmerij is senior research fellow at The CUNY Graduate Center's Ralph Bunche Institute for International Studies, where he is co-director of the United Nations Intellectual History Project. Until 1999 he was special advisor to the president of the Inter-American Development Bank. Before that he had a distinguished career as president of the OECD Development Centre, rector of the Institute of Social Studies in The Hague, and director of the ILO's World Employment Programme. His books include *UN Contributions to Development Thinking and Practice* (with Richard Jolly, Dharam Ghai, and Frédéric Lapeyre; Indiana University Press, 2004); *Ahead of the Curve? UN Ideas and Global Challenges; Economic and Social Development into the 21st Century* (1997); *Limits to Competition* (1995); *Nord-Sud: La Grenade Degoupilée* (1992); *Restoring Financial Flows to Latin America* (co-edited; 1991); *Science, Technology and Science Education in the Development of the South* (1989); *One World or Several?* (edited; 1989); and *Development Policies and the Crisis of the 1980s* (1987).

Richard Jolly is senior research fellow at The CUNY Graduate Center's Ralph Bunche Institute for International Studies, where he is co-director of the United Nations Intellectual History Project, and professor emeritus at the University of Sussex. Until mid-2000 he was special adviser to the UNDP administrator and architect of the widely acclaimed *Human Development Report*. Before this, he served for fourteen years as UNICEF's deputy executive director for programs and prior to that a decade as the director of the Institute of Development Studies at the University of Sussex. Publications to which he has contributed include *UN Contributions to Development Thinking and Practice; Ahead of the Curve? UN Ideas and Global Challenges; Development with a Human Face* (1998); *The UN and the Bretton Woods Institutions: New Challenges for the Twenty-First Century* (co-edited; 1995); *Adjustment with a Human Face* (1987); *Disarmament and World Development* (1984); and *Planning Education for African Development* (1969).

About the Project

Ideas and concepts are a main driving force in human progress, and they are arguably the most important contribution of the United Nations. Yet there has been little historical study of the origins and evolution of the history of economic and social ideas cultivated within the world organization and of their impact on wider thinking and international action. The United Nations Intellectual History Project is filling this knowledge gap about the UN by tracing the origins and analyzing the evolution of key ideas and concepts about international economic and social development born or nurtured under UN auspices. The UNIHP began operations in mid-1999 when the secretariat, the hub of a worldwide network of specialists on the UN, was established at the Ralph Bunche Institute for International Studies of The CUNY Graduate Center.

The UNIHP has two main components, oral history interviews and a series of books on specific topics. The seventy-three in-depth oral history interviews with leading contributors to crucial ideas and concepts within the UN system provide the raw material for this volume. Complete and indexed transcripts will be made available to researchers and the general public in 2006.

The project has commissioned fifteen studies about the major economic and social ideas or concepts that are central to UN activity, which are being published by Indiana University Press:

- *Ahead of the Curve? UN Ideas and Global Challenges,* by Louis Emmerij, Richard Jolly, and Thomas G. Weiss (2001)

- *Unity and Diversity in Development Ideas: Perspectives from the UN Regional Commissions,* edited by Yves Berthelot with contributions from Adebayo Adedeji, Yves Berthelot, Leelananda de Silva, Paul Rayment, Gert Rosenthal, and Blandine Destremeau (2003)

- *Quantifying the World: UN Contributions to Statistics,* by Michael Ward (2004)

- *UN Contributions to Development Thinking and Practice,* by Richard Jolly, Louis Emmerij, Dharam Ghai, and Frédéric Lapeyre (2004)

- *The UN and Global Political Economy: Trade, Finance, and Development,* by John Toye and Richard Toye (2004)

- *UN Voices: The Struggle for Development and Social Justice,* by Thomas G. Weiss, Tatiana Carayannis, Louis Emmerij, and Richard Jolly (2005)

Forthcoming titles:

- *Human Security and the UN: A Critical History,* by S. Neil MacFarlane and Yuen Foong Khong (2005)

- *Women Enrich the UN and Development,* by Devaki Jain (2005)

- *The UN and Human Rights Ideas: The Unfinished Revolution,* by Roger Normand and Sarah Zaidi (2005)

- *The UN and Development Cooperation,* by Olav Stokke (2006)

- *The UN and the Global Commons: Development without Destruction,* by Nico Schrijver (2006)

- *The UN and Transnationals: From Code to Compact,* by Tagi Sagafi-nejad, in collaboration with John Dunning (2006)

- *The UN and Global Governance: An Idea and Its Prospects,* by Ramesh Thakur and Thomas G. Weiss (2007)

- *The United Nations: A History of Ideas and Their Future,* by Richard Jolly, Louis Emmerij, and Thomas G. Weiss (2007)

The project is also collaborating on *The Oxford Handbook on the UN,* edited by Thomas G. Weiss and Sam Daws, forthcoming.

For further information, the interested reader should contact:

UN Intellectual History Project
The CUNY Graduate Center
365 Fifth Avenue, Suite 5203
New York, New York 10016-4309
212-817-1920 Tel
212-817-1565 FAX
UNHistory@gc.cuny.edu
www.unhistory.org